W9-BZX-401

C# 3.0 Cookbook™

Other Microsoft .NET resources from O'Reilly

Related titles   Building a Web 2.0 Portal   Programming ASP.NET
                          with ASP.NET 3.5   Programming C#
                     C# 3.0 Design Patterns   Visual C# 2005: A
                     Learning C#   Developer's Notebook™

.NET Books   *dotnet.oreilly.com* is a complete catalog of O'Reilly's books on
Resource Center   .NET and related technologies, including sample chapters and
                 code examples.

ONDotnet.com provides independent coverage of fundamental, interoperable, and emerging Microsoft .NET programming and web services technologies.

Conferences   O'Reilly brings diverse innovators together to nurture the ideas that spark revolutionary industries. We specialize in documenting the latest tools and systems, translating the innovator's knowledge into useful skills for those in the trenches. Visit *conferences.oreilly.com* for our upcoming events.

Safari Bookshelf (*safari.oreilly.com*) is the premier online reference library for programmers and IT professionals. Conduct searches across more than 1,000 books. Subscribers can zero in on answers to time-critical questions in a matter of seconds. Read the books on your Bookshelf from cover to cover or simply flip to the page you need. Try it today for free.

THIRD EDITION

C# 3.0 Cookbook™

Jay Hilyard and Stephen Teilhet

Beijing · Cambridge · Farnham · Köln · Paris · Sebastopol · Taipei · Tokyo

C# 3.0 Cookbook™, Third Edition
by Jay Hilyard and Stephen Teilhet

Copyright © 2008 Jay Hilyard and Stephen Teilhet. All rights reserved.
Printed in the United States of America.

Published by O'Reilly Media, Inc., 1005 Gravenstein Highway North, Sebastopol, CA 95472.

O'Reilly books may be purchased for educational, business, or sales promotional use. Online editions are also available for most titles (*safari.oreilly.com*). For more information, contact our corporate/institutional sales department: (800) 998-9938 or *corporate@oreilly.com*.

Editor: John Osborn
Production Editor: Adam Witwer
Production Services: nSight, Inc.

Cover Designer: Karen Montgomery
Interior Designer: David Futato
Illustrators: Robert Romano and Jessamyn Read

Printing History:

January 2004:	First Edition.
January 2006:	Second Edition.
December 2007:	Third Edition.

Nutshell Handbook, the Nutshell Handbook logo, and the O'Reilly logo are registered trademarks of O'Reilly Media, Inc. The *Cookbook* series designations, *C# 3.0 Cookbook*, the image of a garter snake, and related trade dress are trademarks of O'Reilly Media, Inc.

Many of the designations used by manufacturers and sellers to distinguish their products are claimed as trademarks. Where those designations appear in this book, and O'Reilly Media, Inc. was aware of a trademark claim, the designations have been printed in caps or initial caps.

While every precaution has been taken in the preparation of this book, the publisher and authors assume no responsibility for errors or omissions, or for damages resulting from the use of the information contained herein.

ISBN-13: 978-0-596-51610-9
[M]   [4/08]

To Brooke
My wife, my best friend, and the most supportive
person I know. This one was for you;
you earned it.

—Jay Hilyard

To my loving wife Kandis and my two wonderful
sons, Patrick and Nicholas.

—Stephen Teilhet

Table of Contents

Preface

C# is a language targeted at developers for the Microsoft .NET platform who have already worked with a C-like language such as C, C++, or Java. Unlike previous versions of C or C++ for the Microsoft Windows platform, C# code runs under a *managed execution environment*. Microsoft portrays C# as a modern and innovative language for .NET development and continues to deliver on that with new features such as Language Integrated Query (LINQ). The new features in C# 3.0 allow for more of a declarative and functional style of programming, when that is appropriate, while it still has great object-oriented features as well. The main idea is to use the style of programming that fits your problem, and C# will support your endeavor.

C# allows you to perform many C/C++-like functions, such as direct memory access via pointers and operator overloading, that are not supported in Visual Basic .NET. C# is the system-level programming language for .NET. You can still do great application-level work in C#, but it really shines when you need to build code a little closer to the Framework.

If you have seen C#, you may have noticed that it looks a lot like Java; Java programmers will feel very much at home in C# once they learn the Framework SDK. C# can also be a great language for Visual Basic .NET programmers when they need a little more control over what the code is doing and don't want to have to write C++ to gain an advantage. On the Web, you'll find a large community of people doing really neat things with C# and tons of sample code on sites such as *http://www.codeplex.com* and *http://www.codeproject.com*.

We started writing this book together based on programming problems we ran into when we were first learning C# and have continued to expand it based on new challenges and capabilities in the language. In this edition, we have reworked the approach of many solutions to take advantage of LINQ and have also created entirely new solutions based on LINQ and the other new features in C# 3.0. We hope that it will help you get past some of the common (and not-so-common) pitfalls and initial questions everyone has when learning a new language as well as the slightly off-the-beaten-path items that come up during a development cycle. There are recipes addressing things we found missing from the .NET Framework Class Library (FCL), even though Microsoft has provided tons of functionality to keep folks from reinventing the wheel. Some of these solutions you might immediately use, and some may never darken your door, but we hope this book helps you get the most out of C# and the .NET Framework.

The book is laid out with respect to the types of problems you will solve as you progress through your life as a C# programmer. These solutions are called *recipes*; each recipe consists of a single problem, its solution, a discussion of the solution and other relevant related information, and finally, where you can look for more information about the classes used from the FCL, other books addressing this topic, related articles, and other recipes. The question-answer format provides complete solutions to problems, making the book easy to read and use. Nearly every recipe contains a complete, documented code sample, showing you how to solve the specific problem, as well as a discussion of how the underlying technology works and a list of alternatives, limitations, and other considerations when appropriate.

Who This Book Is For

You don't have to be an experienced C# or .NET developer to use this book—it is designed for users of all levels. This book provides solutions to problems that developers face every day as well as some that may come along less frequently. The recipes are targeted at the real-world developer who needs to solve problems now, not learn lots of theory before being able to solve the problem. While reference or tutorial books can teach general concepts, they do not generally provide the help you need in solving real-world problems. We choose to teach by example, the natural way for most people to learn.

The majority of the problems addressed in this book are frequently faced by C# developers, but some of the more advanced problems call for more intricate solutions that combine many techniques. Each recipe is designed to help you quickly understand the problem, learn how to solve it, and find out any potential trade-offs or ramifications to help you solve your problems quickly, efficiently, and with minimal effort.

To save you even the effort of typing in the solution, we provide the sample code for the book on the O'Reilly web site to facilitate the "editor inheritance" mode of development (copy and paste) as well as to help less-experienced developers see good programming practice in action. The sample code provides a running test harness that exercises each of the solutions, but enough of the code is provided in each solution in the book to allow you to implement the solution without the sample code. The sample code is available from the book's catalog page: *http://www.oreilly.com/catalog/9780596516109*.

What You Need to Use This Book

To run the samples in this book, you need a computer running Windows XP or later. A few of the networking and XML solutions require Microsoft Internet Information Server (IIS) Version 5.1 or later, and the FTP recipes in the Networking chapter require a locally configured FTP server.

To open and compile the samples in this book, you need Visual Studio .NET 2008. If you are proficient with the downloadable Framework SDK and its command-line compilers, you should not have any trouble following the text of this book and the code samples.

Platform Notes

The solutions in this book were developed using Visual Studio .NET 2008. The differences between C# 3.0 and C# 2.0 are significant, and the sample code has changed from the second edition to reflect that.

It is worth mentioning that although C# is now at version 3.0, the .NET Framework has progressed to version 3.5. .NET 3.0 introduced Windows Communication Foundation, Windows Presentation Foundation, and Windows Workflow Foundation as additional functionality to the 2.0 framework base, but C# was not changed. Now in C# 3.0, there is a bunch of new functionality, mostly due to LINQ and the ability to do more functional programming.

How This Book Is Organized

This book is organized into 20 chapters, each of which focuses on a particular topic in creating C# solutions. The following paragraphs summarize each chapter to give you an overview of this book's contents:

Chapter 1, *Language Integrated Query (LINQ)*
> This chapter covers Language Integrated Query (LINQ) and its usage with objects, ADO.NET, and XML. There are recipes using many of the Standard Query Operators and showing how to use some of the query operators that are not keywords in the language, but are still quite powerful.

Chapter 2, *Strings and Characters*
> This chapter covers both the String and Char data types. Recipes show such things as how to compare strings in various ways, encode/decode strings, break strings apart, and put them back together again.

Chapter 3, *Classes and Structures*
> This large chapter contains recipes dealing with both class and structure data types. This chapter covers a wide range of recipes, from design patterns to converting a class to a full-blown command-line argument-processing system.

Chapter 4, *Generics*

This chapter focuses on the generics capacity in C#, which allows you to have code operate uniformly on values of different types. There are recipes to help your general understanding of generics as well as when they are appropriate to use, what support is provided in the Framework for them, and how to create custom implementations of collections using generics.

Chapter 5, *Collections*

This chapter examines recipes that make use of collections. The collection recipes make use of—as well as extend the functionality of—the array (single, multi, and jagged), the List<T>, and the Hashtable. The generic-based collections are explored, and the various ways to create your own strongly typed collection are also discussed.

Chapter 6, *Iterators, Partial Types, and Partial Methods*

In this chapter, two of the features of C# are used to solve very different programming problems. We show how you can implement iterators for generic and nongeneric types and implement foreach functionality using iterators, as well as custom iterator implementations. The other feature of C# in this chapter is partial types and methods. We show how you can use partial types and methods to do such things as better segmenting your code and how to generate code that is more easily extensible.

Chapter 7, *Exception Handling*

The recipes in this chapter focus on the best ways to implement exception handling in your application. Preventing unhandled exceptions, reading and displaying stack traces, and throwing/rethrowing exceptions are included recipes. In addition, specific recipes show how to overcome some tricky situations, such as exceptions from late-bound called methods.

Chapter 8, *Diagnostics*

This chapter presents recipes that use data types that fall under the System.Diagnostics namespace. Recipes deal with the Trace/Debug classes, event logs, processes, performance counters, and custom debugger displays for your types.

Chapter 9, *Delegates, Events, and Lambda Expressions*

This chapter's recipes show how delegates, events, and lambda expressions can be used in your applications. Recipes allow manipulation of delegates that call more than one method, synchronous delegates, and asynchronous delegates. Lambda expressions are explored, and recipes show their usage in place of old-style delegates as well as their use in implementing closures and functors.

Chapter 10, *Regular Expressions*

This chapter covers a useful set of classes that are employed to run regular expressions against strings. Recipes enumerate regular expression matches, break up strings into tokens, find/replace characters, and verify the syntax of a regular expression. We also include a recipe that contains many common regular expression patterns.

Chapter 11, *Data Structures and Algorithms*

This chapter ventures a bit outside of what is provided for you in the .NET Framework Class Library and implements certain data structures and algorithms that are not in the FCL, or possibly are not in existence exactly the way you would like to use them, but are ones that you have used to solve problems before. Items such as queues, maps, trees, and hashes are examined.

Chapter 12, *Filesystem I/O*

This chapter deals with file system interactions in four distinct ways. The first way is to look at typical file interactions; the second way looks at directory- or folder-based interactions; the third way deals with paths and temporary files; and the fourth way deals with advanced file system I/O topics.

Chapter 13, *Reflection*

This chapter shows ways to use the built-in assembly inspection system provided by the .NET Framework to determine what types, interfaces, and methods are implemented within an assembly and how to access them in a late-bound fashion.

Chapter 14, *Web*

This chapter covers accessing a web site and its content as well as programmatically determining web site configuration. Among the recipes in this chapter are using the web browser control and setting up caching triggers to refresh cached data when a database table changes.

Chapter 15, *XML*

If you use .NET, it is likely that you will be dealing with XML to one degree or another; in this chapter, we explore some of the uses for XML and how to program against it using LINQ to XML, the XmlReader/XmlWriter, and XmlDocument. There are examples using both XPath and XSLT, and topics such as the validation of XML and transformation of XML to HTML are shown.

Chapter 16, *Networking*

This chapter explores the connectivity options provided by the .NET Framework and how to programmatically access network resources. Recipes for using TCP/IP directly, named pipes for communication, building your own port scanner, and more are covered here.

Chapter 17, *Security*

There are many ways to write secure code and protect data using the .NET Framework, and in this chapter, we explore areas such as controlling access to types, encryption and decryption, securely storing data, and using programmatic and declarative security.

Chapter 18, *Threading and Synchronization*

This chapter addresses the subject of using multiple threads of execution in a .NET program and issues such as how to implement threading in your application, protecting resources from and allowing safe concurrent access, storing per-thread data, and how to use the synchronization primitives in .NET to write thread-safe code.

Chapter 19, *Toolbox*

This chapter has recipes for those random sorts of operations that developers run into over and over again, such as determining locations of system resources, sending email, and working with services. It also covers some less frequently accessed but helpful application pieces such as message queuing, running code in a separate AppDomain, and finding the versions of assemblies in the GAC.

Chapter 20, *Numbers and Enumerations*

This chapter focuses on the numeric and enumeration data types used in C# code. Recipes cover such things as numeric conversions, using bitwise operators on numbers, and testing strings to determine whether they contain a numeric value. The display, conversion, and testing of enumeration types and recipes on using enumerations that consist of bit flags are also shown.

In some cases, certain recipes are related. In these cases, the See Also section of the recipe as well as some text in the Discussion will note the relationships.

What Was Left Out

This book is not a reference or a primer about C#. Some good primers and reference books are *C# in a Nutshell*, *C# Language Pocket Reference*, and *Learning C#*, all titles available from O'Reilly. The MSDN Library is also invaluable. It is included with Visual Studio .NET 2008 and available online at *http://msdn.microsoft.com/library/default.asp*.

This book is not about how to use Visual Studio .NET 2008 to build, compile, and deploy applications. See *Mastering Visual Studio .NET* (O'Reilly) for excellent coverage of these topics.

Conventions Used in This Book

This book uses the following typographic conventions:

Italic

Used for URLs, names of directories and files, options, and occasionally for emphasis.

`Constant width`

Used for program listings and for code items such as commands, options, switches, variables, attributes, keys, functions, types, classes, namespaces, methods, modules, properties, parameters, values, objects, events, event handlers, XML tags, HTML tags, macros, the contents of files, and the output from commands.

`Constant width bold`

Used in program listings to highlight an important part of the code.

Constant width italic

Used to indicate replaceable parts of code.

//...

Ellipses in C# code indicate text that has been omitted for clarity.

<!--...-->

Ellipses in XML Schemas and documents' code indicate text that has been omitted for clarity.

 This icon indicates a tip, suggestion, or general note.

 This icon indicates a warning or caution.

About the Code

Nearly every recipe in this book contains one or more code samples. These samples are included in a single solution and are pieces of code and whole projects that are immediately usable in your application. Most of the code samples are written within a class or structure, making it easier to use within your applications. In addition to this, any using directives are included for each recipe so that you will not have to search for which ones to include in your code.

Complete error handling is included only in critical areas, such as input parameters. This allows you to easily see what is correct input and what is not. Many recipes omit error handling. This makes the solution easier to understand by focusing on the key concepts.

Using Code Examples

This book is here to help you get your job done. In general, you may use the code in this book in your programs and documentation. You do not need to contact us for permission unless you're reproducing a significant portion of the code. For example, writing a program that uses several chunks of code from this book does not require permission. Selling or distributing a CD-ROM of examples from O'Reilly books *does* require permission. Answering a question by citing this book and quoting example code does not require permission. Incorporating a significant amount of example code from this book into your product's documentation *does* require permission.

We appreciate, but do not require, attribution. An attribution usually includes the title, author, publisher, and ISBN. For example: "*C# 3.0 Cookbook*, Third Edition, by Jay Hilyard and Stephen Teilhet. Copyright 2008 Jay Hilyard and Stephen Teilhet, 978-0-596-51610-9."

If you feel your use of code examples falls outside fair use or the preceding permission, feel free to contact us at *permissions@oreilly.com*.

Comments and Questions

Please address any comments or questions concerning this book to the publisher:

O'Reilly Media, Inc.
1005 Gravenstein Highway North
Sebastopol, CA 95472
800-998-9938 (in the U.S. or Canada)
707-829-0515 (international or local)
707-829-0104 (fax)

We have a web page for this book, where we list errata, examples, and any additional information. You can access this page at:

http://www.oreilly.com/catalog/9780596516109

To comment or ask technical questions about this book, send email to:

bookquestions@oreilly.com

For more information about our books, conferences, Resource Centers, and the O'Reilly Network, see our web site at:

http://www.oreilly.com

Safari® Books Online

 When you see a Safari® Books Online icon on the cover of your favorite technology book, it means the book is available online through the O'Reilly Network Safari Bookshelf.

Safari offers a solution that's better than e-books. It's a virtual library that lets you easily search thousands of top technical books, cut and paste code samples, download chapters, and find quick answers when you need the most accurate, current information. Try it for free at *http://safari.oreilly.com*.

Acknowledgments

This book began for us as we started exploring C# 3.0 and noticing how it could change the applications we were working on. With the advent of C# 3.0 and the new features such as LINQ, we took the opportunity to reexamine how we did things in the first two editions to see how we could improve the existing recipes as well as learn better ways of accomplishing programming tasks with C#. Sadly, during the process, the NuMega lab of Compuware was closed and the development community lost a talented team of tool developers. Jay has continued at Newmarket International, pushing software forward with .NET, while Steve moved on to Ounce Labs, where his focus is on software security. We continue to learn an incredible amount about C# and the Framework in general while, in this edition, we work hard to help bring you a better understanding of how C# has evolved and how it can help you do your job better.

This book would have been impossible without the following people, and we'd like to acknowledge all of their efforts.

Our appreciation goes out to John Osborn (our editor), Kyley Caldwell, and Laurel Ruma, who kept us on schedule and did a great job in getting this book finished and on the shelves in a compressed timeframe. Thank you for all of your efforts.

We extend our gratitude to Eric Lippert for going above and beyond what is expected of a technical editor. This book would have been impossible to do without your valuable feedback, and we both thank you for it. Thanks for making this a "Fabulous Adventure in Coding."

Thanks to the technical reviewers Gustavo Cavalcanti, Mickey Gousset, Andrew Siemer, David Patrick, Miles Whitener, Brian Peek, and Peter Jones. This book would definitely not be as good without all of you.

From Jay Hilyard

Thanks to Steve Teilhet for his ideas, friendship, and generally calm demeanor, which helped me get past the challenging stages of the book. I always enjoy working with you, even though most of it was on nights and weekends.

Thanks to my wife Brooke. A book is a work that requires tremendous support and I have been blessed to have you with me on this journey. There is no way I could have done this without you. Thank you, and I love you!

Thanks to my sons, Owen and Andrew, who make me smile and laugh when I don't think I can. You are excellent boys, and I am tremendously proud of both of you and love you very much.

Thanks to Phil and Gail for their understanding and being there to help in ways that only grandparents can, and thanks to my Mom for that monthly dose of sanity.

Thanks to Wes for being a good uncle when I was busy.

Thanks to Tim Pelletier, Scott Cronshaw, Bill Bolevic, Melissa Field, Mike Kennie, Jeremy Streeter, Bob & Liz Blais, Stu Savage, Matt Jurkoic, Dave Bennett, Rich Tasker, Lance Simpson, Robert Provencal, and Shawn McGowan for being an awesome team of people to work with. 10X here we come.

Thanks to Kristen Acheson for being a great friend and part of the family.

Thanks to my Patriots crew (Brian, Spencer, Chip, Jon, and Darren) for being there to help me blow off steam.

Thanks to the Oyster River Poker Players (Tom Bebbington, Seth Fiermonti, Gavin Webb, John Clifford, Ben Chandran, Adam Gilsdorf, Nick Issak, and Ted Lothstein) for the nights off and for not taking too much of my money while my mind was elsewhere. Pass the Sun Chips.

Finally, thanks again to my family and friends for asking about a book they don't understand and for being excited for me.

From Steve Teilhet

I'm proud to count Jay Hilyard as a good friend, excellent coworker, and hardworking coauthor. It's not every day that you find a person who is not only a trusted friend, but you also work so well with. Thank you for everything.

Kandis Teilhet, my wife, was there every step of the way to give me the strength to persevere and finish this work. Words cannot express my love for you.

Patrick and Nicholas Teilhet, my two sons, made the rough patches smooth. I couldn't wish for two better sons.

My mom and dad, who are always there to listen and support.

The Ounce Lab team, Tom Conner, Larry Rose, David Larochelle, Caleb Davis, Robert Wiener, Ryan Berg, Cristian Bolovan, Dinis Cruz, Bruce Mayhew, and all the others that made my transition from the closing of the NuMega Lab to the Ounce Lab fun and exciting. It's not easy changing jobs while writing a book. I thank you all for the help and support.

CHAPTER 1

Language Integrated Query (LINQ)

1.0   Introduction

Language Integrated Query (LINQ) is a new way to access data from many different sources. LINQ provides a single querying model that can operate against different data domains individually or all together in a single query. LINQ brings the ability to query data to .NET languages, and some of the languages have provided extensions to make its use even more intuitive. One of these languages is C#; there are a number of extensions to the language in C# 3.0 that help to facilitate querying in a rich and intuitive manner.

Traditional object-oriented programming is based on an imperative style wherein the developer describes in detail not only what they want to happen, but also describes a majority of the detail regarding exactly how this should be performed through code. LINQ helps to take coding down a more declarative path that facilitates describing what the developer wants to do instead of describing how to accomplish the goal in detail. LINQ also enables a more functional style of programming. These changes can dramatically shorten the amount of code it takes to perform some tasks. That said, object-oriented programming is still very much alive and well in C# and .NET, but for the first time the language is offering the chance to choose the style of programming based on your needs. Note, however, that LINQ will not fit into every scenario and is not a replacement for good design or practice. You can write bad code using LINQ just as you can write bad object-oriented or procedural code. The trick, like it always has been, is to figure out when it is appropriate to use which technique.

The initial version of LINQ encompasses a number of data domains as listed here:

- LINQ to Objects
- LINQ to XML
- LINQ to ADO.NET
- LINQ to SQL / LINQ to DataSet / LINQ to Entities

There are a number of other "LINQ to" implementations currently under development, but these are Microsoft's initial offerings. A few of the others in development are LINQ to SharePoint, LINQ to LDAP, and even a LINQ to Amazon implementation. The only one of the initial Microsoft set that won't be ready immediately with the release of Visual Studio 2008 is LINQ to Entities, or the ADO.NET Entity Framework, as it is also known. LINQ to Entities will be released shortly after Visual Studio 2008.

As you begin your examination of LINQ, it is easy to begin to think of it as a new object relational mapping layer, or some neat new widgets on IEnumerable<T>, or a new XML API, or even just an excuse to not write SQL directly anymore. You can do any of these things, but we would encourage you to think of LINQ as how your program asks for, calculates, or transforms sets of data from both single and disparate sources. It takes a bit of time and playing with LINQ for its functionality to click, but once it does, you will be surprised at what you can do with it. This chapter begins to show some of what is possible with LINQ and will hopefully start you down the path toward thinking of which of your scenarios are applicable to this new capability in C#.

1.1   Query a Message Queue

Problem

You want to be able to query for messages with specific criteria from an existing message queue.

Solution

Write a query using LINQ to retrieve messages using the System.Messaging. MessageQueue type:

```
// open an existing message queue
string queuePath = @".\private$\LINQMQ";
MessageQueue messageQueue = new MessageQueue(queuePath);
    BinaryMessageFormatter messageFormatter = new BinaryMessageFormatter();

var query = from Message msg in messageQueue
    // The first assignment to msg.Formatter is so that we can touch the
    // Message object. It assigns the BinaryMessageFormatter to each message
    // instance so that it can be read to determine if it matches the criteria.
    // Next, a check is performed that the formatter was correctly assigned
    // by performing an equality check, which satisfies the Where clause's need
    // for a boolean result while still executing the assignment of the formatter.
            where ((msg.Formatter = messageFormatter) == messageFormatter) &&
                int.Parse(msg.Label) > 5 &&
                msg.Body.ToString().Contains('D')
            orderby msg.Body.ToString() descending
            select msg;
```

```
// Check our results for messages with a label > 5 and containing a 'D' in the name
foreach (var msg in query)
{
    Console.WriteLine("Label: " + msg.Label + " Body: " + msg.Body);
}
```

The query retrieves the data from the MessageQueue by selecting the messages where the Label is a number greater than 5 and the message body contains a capital letter "D". These messages are then returned sorted by the message body in descending order.

Discussion

There are a number of new keywords in this code using LINQ that were not previously used to access a message queue:

var

> Instructs the compiler to infer the type of the variable from the right side of the statement. In essence, the type of the variable is determined by what is on the right side of the operator separating the var keyword and the expression. This allows for implicitly typed local variables.

from

> The from keyword sets out the source collection to query against and a range variable to represent a single element from that collection. It is always the first clause in a query operation. This may seem counterintuitive if you are used to SQL and expect select to be first, but if you consider that first we need what to work on before we determine what to return, it makes sense. If we weren't used to how SQL does this already, it would be SQL that seems counterintuitive.

where

> The where keyword specifies the constraints by which the elements to return are filtered. Each condition must evaluate to a Boolean result, and when all expressions evaluate to true, the element of the collection is allowed to be selected.

orderby

> This keyword indicates that the result set should be sorted according to the criteria specified. The default order is ascending, and elements use the default comparer.

select

> Allows the projection of an entire element from the collection, the construction of a new type with parts of that element and other calculated values, or a subcollection of items into the result.

The messageQueue collection is of type System.Messaging.MessageQueue, which implements the IEnumerable interface. This is important, as the LINQ methods provided need a set or collection to implement at least IEnumerable for it to work with that set or collection. It would be possible to implement a set of extension methods that did not need IEnumerable, but most people will not have the need to. It is even better when the set or collection implements IEnumerable<T>, as LINQ then knows the type of element in the set or collection that it is working with, but in this case, MessageQueue has been in the framework for a while and isn't likely to change, so the query provides the element type Message, as shown in the "from" line:

```
var query = from Message msg in messageQueue
```

For more about this, see Recipe 1.1.

In the Solution, the messages in the queue have been sent with the use of the BinaryFormatter. To be able to query against them correctly, the Formatter property must be set on each Message before it is examined as part of the where clause:

```
// The first assignment to msg.Formatter is so that we can touch the
// Message object. It assigns the BinaryMessageFormatter to each message
// instance so that it can be read to determine if it matches the criteria.
// This is done, and then it checks that the formatter was correctly assigned
// by performing an equality check, which satisfies the Where clause's need
// for a boolean result, while still executing the assignment of the formatter.
where ((msg.Formatter = messageFormatter) == messageFormatter) &&
```

There are two uses of the var keyword in the solution code:

```
var query = from Message msg in messageQueue
    ...

foreach (var msg in query)
    ...
```

The first usage infers that an IEnumerable<Message> will be returned and assigned to the query variable. The second usage infers that the type of msg is Message because the query variable is of type IEnumerable<Message> and the msg variable is an element from that IEnumerable.

It is also worth noting that when performing operations in a query, actual C# code can be used to determine the conditions, and there is more than just the predetermined set of operators. In the where clause of this query, both int.Parse and string.Contains are used to help filter messages:

```
int.Parse(msg.Label) > 5 &&
msg.Body.ToString( ).Contains('D')
```

See Also

Recipe 1.9, and the "MessageQueue class," "Implicitly typed local variable," "from keyword," "where keyword," "orderby keyword," and "select keyword" topics in the MSDN documentation.

1.2   Using Set Semantics with Data

Problem

You would like to work with your collections using set operations for union, intersections, exceptions, and distinct items.

Solution

Use the Set operators provided as part of the Standard Query Operators to perform those operations.

Distinct:

```
IEnumerable<string> whoLoggedIn =
    dailySecurityLog.Where(logEntry => logEntry.Contains("logged in")).Distinct(
);
```

Union:

```
// Union
Console.WriteLine("Employees for all projects");
var allProjectEmployees = project1.Union(project2.Union(project3));
```

Intersection:

```
// Intersect
Console.WriteLine("Employees on every project");
var everyProjectEmployees = project1.Intersect(project2.Intersect(project3));
```

Exception:

```
Console.WriteLine("Employees on only one project");
var onlyProjectEmployees = allProjectEmployees.Except(unionIntersect);
```

Discussion

The Standard Query Operators are the set of methods that represent the LINQ pattern. This set includes operators to perform many different types of operations, such as filtering, projection, sorting, grouping, and many others, including set operations.

The set operations for the Standard Query Operators are:

- Distinct
- Union
- Intersect
- Except

The Distinct operator extracts all nonduplicate items from the collection or result set being worked with. Say, for example, that we had a set of strings representing login and logout behavior for a terminal services box for today:

```
// Distinct
string[] dailySecurityLog = {
```

```
    "Bob logged in",
    "Bob logged out",
    "Bob logged in",
    "Bill logged in",
    "Melissa logged in",
    "Bob logged out",
    "Bill logged out",
    "Bill logged in",
    "Tim logged in",
    "Scott logged in",
    "Scott logged out",
    "Dave logged in",
    "Tim logged out",
    "Bob logged in",
    "Dave logged out"};
```

From that collection, we would like to determine the list of people who logged in to the box today. Since people can log in and log out many times during the course of a day or remain logged in for the whole day, we need to eliminate the duplicate login entries. Distinct is an extension method on the System.Linq.Enumerable class (which implements the Standard Query Operators) that can be called on the string array (which supports IEnumerable) in order to get the distinct set of items from the set. For more information on extension methods, see Recipe 1.4. The set is produced by using another of the Standard Query Operators: Where. Where takes a lambda expression that determines the filter criteria for the set and examines each string in the IEnumerable<string> to determine if the string has "logged in." Lambda expressions are inline statements (similar to anonymous methods) that can be used in place of a delegate. See Chapter 9 for more on lambda expressions. If the strings do, then they are selected. Distinct narrows down the set of strings further to eliminate duplicate "logged in" records, leaving only one per user:

```
IEnumerable<string> whoLoggedIn =
    dailySecurityLog.Where(logEntry => logEntry.Contains("logged in")).Distinct(
);
Console.WriteLine("Everyone who logged in today:");
foreach (string who in whoLoggedIn)
{
    Console.WriteLine(who);
}
```

To make things a bit more interesting, for the rest of the operators, we will work with sets of employees on various projects in a company. An Employee is a pretty simple class with a Name and overrides for ToString, Equals, and GetHashCode, as shown here:

```
public class Employee
{
    public string Name { get; set; }
    public override string ToString()
    {
        return this.Name;
    }
}
```

```
        public override bool Equals(object obj)
        {
            return this.GetHashCode().Equals(obj.GetHashCode());
        }
        public override int GetHashCode()
        {
            return this.Name.GetHashCode();
        }
    }
```

You might wonder why Equals and GetHashCode are overloaded for such a simple class. The reason is that when LINQ performs comparisons of elements in the sets or collections, it uses the default comparison, which in turn uses Equals and GetHashCode to determine if one instance of a reference type is the same as another. If you do not provide the semantics in the reference type class to provide the same hash code or equals value when the data for two instances of the object is the same, then the instances will, by default, be different, as two reference types have different hash codes by default. We override that so that if the Name is the same for each Employee, the hash code and the equals will both correctly identify the instances as the same. There are also overloads for the set operators that take a custom comparer, which would also allow you to make this determination even for classes for which you can't make the changes to Equals and GetHashCode.

Having done this, we can now assign Employees to projects like so:

```
Employee[] project1 = {
            new Employee(){ Name = "Bob" },
            new Employee(){ Name = "Bill" },
            new Employee(){ Name = "Melissa" },
            new Employee(){ Name = "Shawn" } };
Employee[] project2 = {
            new Employee(){ Name = "Shawn" },
            new Employee(){ Name = "Tim" },
            new Employee(){ Name = "Scott" } };
Employee[] project3 = {
            new Employee(){ Name = "Bob" },
            new Employee(){ Name = "Dave" },
            new Employee(){ Name = "Tim" },
            new Employee(){ Name = "Shawn" } };
```

To find all employees on all projects, use Union to get all nonduplicate Employees in all three projects and write them out:

```
// Union
Console.WriteLine("Employees for all projects:");
var allProjectEmployees = project1.Union(project2.Union(project3));
foreach (Employee employee in allProjectEmployees)
{
    Console.WriteLine(employee);
}
```

We can then use Intersect to get the Employees on every project:

```
// Intersect
Console.WriteLine("Employees on every project:");
var everyProjectEmployees = project1.Intersect(project2.Intersect(project3));
foreach (Employee employee in everyProjectEmployees)
{
    Console.WriteLine(employee);
}
```

Finally, we can use a combination of Union and Except to find Employees that are only on one project:

```
// Except
var intersect1_3 = project1.Intersect(project3);
var intersect1_2 = project1.Intersect(project2);
var intersect2_3 = project2.Intersect(project3);
var unionIntersect = intersect1_2.Union(intersect1_3).Union(intersect2_3);

Console.WriteLine("Employees on only one project:");
var onlyProjectEmployees = allProjectEmployees.Except(unionIntersect);
foreach (Employee employee in onlyProjectEmployees)
{
    Console.WriteLine(employee);
}
```

See Also

The "Standard Query Operators," "Distinct method," "Union method," "Intersect method," and "Except method" topics in the MSDN documentation.

1.3   Reuse Parameterized Queries with LINQ to SQL

Problem

You need to execute the same parameterized query multiple times with different parameter values, but you want to avoid the overhead of parsing the query expression tree to build the parameterized SQL each time the query executes.

Solution

Use the CompiledQuery.Compile method to build an expression tree that will not have to be parsed each time the query is executed with new parameters:

```
var GetEmployees =
        CompiledQuery.Compile((Northwind db, string ac, string ttl) =>
                from employee in db.Employees
                where employee.HomePhone.Contains(ac) &&
                    employee.Title == ttl
                select employee);

Northwind dataContext = new Northwind(Settings.Default.NorthwindConnectionString);
```

The first time the query executes is when it actually compiles (where GetEmployees is called the first time in the foreach loop). Every other iteration in this loop and in the next loop use the compiled version, avoiding the expression tree parsing:

```
foreach (var employee in GetEmployees(dataContext, "(206)", "Sales Representative"))
{
    Console.WriteLine("{0} {1}",
        employee.FirstName, employee.LastName);
}

foreach (var employee in GetEmployees(dataContext, "(71)", "Sales Manager"))
{
    Console.WriteLine("{0} {1}",
        employee.FirstName, employee.LastName);
}
```

Discussion

We used var for the query declaration, as it was cleaner, but what var actually is in this case is:

```
Func<Northwind, string, string, IQueryable<Employees>>
```

which is the delegate signature for the lambda expression we created that contains the query. That's right, all this crazy new query stuff, and we just instantiated a delegate. To be fair, the Func delegate was brought about in the System namespace as part of LINQ, so do not dismay, we are still doing cool new stuff!

This illustrates that we are not returning an IEnumerable or IQueryable based result set from Compile, but rather an expression tree. This is the expression tree that represents the potential for a query rather than the query itself. Once we have that tree, LINQ to SQL then has to perform the conversion from the tree to actual SQL that can run against the database. Interestingly enough, if we had put a call to string. Format in as part of detecting the area code in the home phone number, we would get a NotSupportedException that informs us that string.Format can't be translated to SQL:

```
where employee.HomePhone.Contains(string.Format("({0})",ac)) &&

System.NotSupportedException:
Method 'System.String Format(System.String,System.Object)'
  has no supported translation to SQL.
```

This is understandable, as SQL has no concept of .NET Framework methods for performing actions, but it is something to keep in mind as you design your queries that this is a limitation when using LINQ to SQL.

After the first execution, the query is compiled, and for every iteration after that, we do not pay the transformation cost for turning the expression tree into the parameterized SQL.

Compiling your queries is something that should be done for parameterized queries that get a lot of traffic, but if a query is infrequently used, it may not be worth the effort. As always, profile your code to see the areas where this could be useful.

See Also

The "CompiledQuery.Compile method" and "Expression Trees" topics in the MSDN documentation.

1.4   Sort Results in a Culture-Sensitive Manner

Problem

You want to ensure that when you sort in a query, the sort order is for an application-specific culture that may not be the same as the current thread's current culture.

Solution

Use the overload of the OrderBy query operator, which accepts a custom comparer in order to specify the culture in which to perform comparisons:

```
// Create CultureInfo for Danish in Denmark.
CultureInfo danish = new CultureInfo("da-DK");

CultureStringComparer comparer = new CultureStringComparer(danish,CompareOptions.
None);
var query = names.OrderBy(n => n, comparer);
```

Discussion

Handling localization issues such as sorting for a specific culture is a relatively trivial task in .NET if the current culture of the current thread is the culture you want to use. The framework classes that assist in handling culture issues in C# are accessed by including the System.Globalization namespace. This namespace would be included in order to make the code in the solution run. One example of not using the thread current culture would be in an application that needs to display a sorted list of words in Danish on a version of Windows XP that is set for U.S. English. The current thread in the application may have a CultureInfo for "en-US" and, by default, the sort order for OrderBy will use the current culture sort settings. To specify that this list should sort according to Danish rules, a bit of work is necessary in the form of a custom comparer:

```
CultureStringComparer comparer = new CultureStringComparer(danish,CompareOptions.
None);
```

The comparer variable is an instance of a custom comparer class (CultureStringComparer) defined as implementing the IComparer<T> interface specialized for strings. This class is used to provide the culture settings for the sort order:

```
public class CultureStringComparer : IComparer<string>
{
    private CultureStringComparer()
    {
    }

    public CultureStringComparer(CultureInfo cultureInfo, CompareOptions options)
    {
        if (cultureInfo == null)
            throw new ArgumentNullException("cultureInfo");

        CurrentCultureInfo = cultureInfo;
        Options = options;
    }

    public int Compare(string x, string y)
    {
        return CurrentCultureInfo.CompareInfo.Compare(x, y, Options);
    }

    public CultureInfo CurrentCultureInfo { get; set; }

    public CompareOptions Options { get; set; }
}
```

To demonstrate how this could be used, first we compile a list of words to order by. Since the Danish language treats the character "Æ" as an individual letter, sorting it after "Z" in the alphabet, and the English language treats the character "Æ" as a special symbol, sorting it before the letter "A" in the alphabet, this will demonstrate the sort difference:

```
string[] names = { "Jello", "Apple", "Bar", "Æble", "Forsooth", "Orange", "Zanzibar"
};
```

Now, we can set up the CultureInfos for both Danish and U.S. English and call OrderBy with the comparer specific to each culture. This query is not using the query expression syntax, but rather uses the functional style of IEnumerable<string>. OrderBy( ):

```
// Create CultureInfo for Danish in Denmark.
CultureInfo danish = new CultureInfo("da-DK");
// Create CultureInfo for English in the U.S.
CultureInfo american = new CultureInfo("en-US");

CultureStringComparer comparer = new CultureStringComparer(danish,CompareOptions.
None);
var query = names.OrderBy(n => n, comparer);
Console.WriteLine("Ordered by specific culture : " + comparer.CurrentCultureInfo.
Name);
foreach (string name in query)
{
    Console.WriteLine(name);
}
```

```
comparer.CurrentCultureInfo = american;
query = names.OrderBy(n => n, comparer);
Console.WriteLine("Ordered by specific culture : " + comparer.CurrentCultureInfo.
Name);
foreach (string name in query)
{
    Console.WriteLine(name);
}
```

The output results below show that the word Æble is last in the Danish list and first in the U.S. English list:

```
Ordered by specific culture : da-DK
Apple
Bar
Forsooth
Jello
Orange
Zanzibar
Æble
Ordered by specific culture : en-US
Æble
Apple
Bar
Forsooth
Jello
Orange
Zanzibar
```

See Also

The "OrderBy," "CultureInfo," and "IComparer<T>" topics in the MSDN documentation.

1.5   Adding Functional Extensions for Use with LINQ

Problem

There are operations you perform on collections frequently that currently reside in utility classes. You would like to be able to have these operations be used on collections in a more seamless manner than having to pass the reference to the collection to the utility class.

Solution

Use extension methods to help achieve a more functional style of programming for your collection operations. For example, to add a weighted moving average calculation operation to numeric collections, implement a set of WeightedMovingAverage extension methods in a static class and then call them as part of those collections:

```
decimal[] prices = new decimal[10] { 13.5M, 17.8M, 92.3M, 0.1M, 15.7M,
                                      19.99M, 9.08M, 6.33M, 2.1M, 14.88M };
Console.WriteLine(prices.WeightedMovingAverage());

double[] dprices = new double[10] { 13.5, 17.8, 92.3, 0.1, 15.7,
                                    19.99, 9.08, 6.33, 2.1, 14.88 };
Console.WriteLine(dprices.WeightedMovingAverage());

float[] fprices = new float[10] { 13.5F, 17.8F, 92.3F, 0.1F, 15.7F,
                                  19.99F, 9.08F, 6.33F, 2.1F, 14.88F };
Console.WriteLine(fprices.WeightedMovingAverage());

int[] iprices = new int[10] { 13, 17, 92, 0, 15,
                              19, 9, 6, 2, 14 };
Console.WriteLine(iprices.WeightedMovingAverage());

long[] lprices = new long[10] { 13, 17, 92, 0, 15,
                                19, 9, 6, 2, 14 };
Console.WriteLine(lprices.WeightedMovingAverage());
```

To provide WeightedMovingAverage for the full range of numeric types, methods for both the nullable and non-nullable numeric types are provided in the LinqExtensions class:

```
public static class LinqExtensions
{
    public static decimal? WeightedMovingAverage(this IEnumerable<decimal?> source)
    {
        if (source == null)
            throw new ArgumentNullException("source");

        decimal aggregate = 0.0M;
        decimal weight;
        int item = 1;
        // count how many items are not null and use that
        // as the weighting factor
        int count = source.Count(val => val.HasValue);
        foreach (var nullable in source)
        {
            if (nullable.HasValue)
            {
                weight = item / count;
                aggregate += nullable.GetValueOrDefault() * weight;
                count++;
            }
        }
        if (count > 0)
        {
            return new decimal?(aggregate / count);
        }
        return null;
    }
```

```
// The same method pattern as above is followed for each of the other
// types and their nullable counterparts (double / double?, int / int?, etc.)


#region Extend Average...

}
```

Discussion

Extension methods allow you to create operations that appear to be part of a collection. They are static methods that can be called as if they were instance methods, allowing you to extend existing types. Extension methods must also be declared in static classes that are not nested. Once a static class is defined with extension methods, the using directive for the namespace of the class makes those extensions available in the source file.

> It is worth noting that if an instance method exists with the same signature as the extension method, the extension method will never be called. Conflicting extension method declarations will resolve to the method in the closest enclosing namespace.

You cannot use extension methods to create:

- Properties (get and set methods)
- Operators (+, −, = , etc...)
- Events

Declaring an extension method is done by specifying the this keyword in front of the first parameter of a method declaration, and the type of that parameter is the type being extended. For example, in the Nullable<decimal> version of the WeightedMovingAverage method, collections that support IEnumerable<decimal?> (or IEnumerable<Nullable<decimal>>) are supported:

```
public static decimal? WeightedMovingAverage(this IEnumerable<decimal?> source)
{
    if (source == null)
        throw new ArgumentNullException("source");

    decimal aggregate = 0.0M;
    decimal weight;
    int item = 1;
    // count how many items are not null and use that
    // as the weighting factor
    int count = source.Count(val => val.HasValue);
    foreach (var nullable in source)
    {
        if (nullable.HasValue)
```

```
        {
            weight = item / count;
            aggregate += nullable.GetValueOrDefault( ) * weight;
            count++;
        }
    }
    if (count > 0)
    {
        return new decimal?(aggregate / count);
    }
    return null;
}
```

The extension methods that support much of the LINQ functionality are on the System.Linq.Extensions class, including an Average method. The Average method has most of the numeric types but did not provide an overload for short (Int16). That's easily rectified by adding them ourselves for short and Nullable<short>:

```
#region Extend Average
public static double? Average(this IEnumerable<short?> source)
{
    if (source == null)
        throw new ArgumentNullException("source");

    double aggregate = 0.0;
    int count = 0;
    foreach (var nullable in source)
    {
        if (nullable.HasValue)
        {
            aggregate += nullable.GetValueOrDefault( );
            count++;
        }
    }
    if (count > 0)
    {
        return new double?(aggregate / count);
    }
    return null;
}
public static double Average(this IEnumerable<short> source)
{
    if (source == null)
        throw new ArgumentNullException("source");

    double aggregate = 0.0;
    // use the count of the items from the source
    int count = source.Count( );
    foreach (var value in source)
    {
        aggregate += value;
    }
    if (count > 0)
    {
```

```
            return aggregate / count;
        }
        else
            return 0.0;
    }
    public static double? Average<TSource>(this IEnumerable<TSource> source,
                                    Func<TSource, short?> selector)
    {
        return source.Select<TSource, short?>(selector).Average();
    }
    public static double Average<TSource>(this IEnumerable<TSource> source,
                                    Func<TSource, short> selector)
    {
        return source.Select<TSource, short>(selector).Average();
    }
    #endregion // Extend Average
```

We can then call Average on short-based collections just like WeightedMovingAverage:

```
short[] sprices = new short[10] { 13, 17, 92, 0, 15, 19, 9, 6, 2, 14 };
Console.WriteLine(sprices.WeightedMovingAverage());
// System.Linq.Extensions doesn't implement Average for short but we do for them!
Console.WriteLine(sprices.Average());
```

See Also

The "Extension methods" topic in the MSDN documentation.

1.6   Query and Join Across Data Repositories

Problem

You have two sets of data from different data domains, and you want to be able to combine the data and work with it.

Solution

Use LINQ to bridge across the disparate data domains. LINQ is intended to be used in the same manner across different data domains and supports combining those sets of data with join syntax.

To demonstrate this, we will join an XML file full of Categories with the data from a database (Northwind) with Products and combine the two to create a new set of data for product information that holds the product name, the category description, and the category name:

```
Northwind dataContext = new Northwind(Settings.Default.NorthwindConnectionString);
ProductsTableAdapter adapter = new ProductsTableAdapter();
Products products = new Products();
adapter.Fill(products._Products);
```

```
XElement xmlCategories = XElement.Load("Categories.xml");


var expr = from product in products._Products
           where product.Units_In_Stock > 100
           join xc in xmlCategories.Elements("Category")
           on product.Category_ID equals int.Parse(xc.Attribute("CategoryID").Value)
           select new
           {
               ProductName = product.Product_Name,
               Category = xc.Attribute("CategoryName").Value,
               CategoryDescription = xc.Attribute("Description").Value
           };

foreach (var productInfo in expr)
{
    Console.WriteLine("ProductName: " + productInfo.ProductName +
        " Category: " + productInfo.Category +
        " Category Description: " + productInfo.CategoryDescription);
}
```

The new set of data is printed to the console, but this could easily have been rerouted to another method, transformed in another query, or written out to a third data format:

```
ProductName: Grandma's Boysenberry Spread Category: Condiments Category Description:
Sweet and savory sauces, relishes, spreads, and seasonings
ProductName: Gustaf's Knäckebröd Category: Grains/Cereals Category Description:
Breads, crackers, pasta, and cereal
ProductName: Geitost Category: Dairy Products Category Description: Cheeses
ProductName: Sasquatch Ale Category: Beverages Category Description: Soft drinks,
coffees, teas, beer, and ale
ProductName: Inlagd Sill Category: Seafood Category Description: Seaweed and fish
ProductName: Boston Crab Meat Category: Seafood Category Description: Seaweed and
fish
ProductName: Pâté chinois Category: Meat/Poultry Category Description: Prepared meats
ProductName: Sirop d'érable Category: Condiments Category Description: Sweet and
savory sauces, relishes, spreads, and seasonings
ProductName: Röd Kaviar Category: Seafood Category Description: Seaweed and fish
ProductName: Rhönbräu Klosterbier Category: Beverages Category Description: Soft
drinks, coffees, teas, beer, and ale
```

Discussion

The solution combines data from two different data domains: XML and a SQL Database. To do this before LINQ, you would have to not only create a third data repository by hand to hold the result, but you would also have to write the specific code for each domain to query that domain for its part of the data (XPath for XML; SQL for database) and then manually transform the result sets from each domain into the new data repository. LINQ gives the ability to write the query to combine the two sets of data, automatically constructs a type via projecting a new Anonymous Type, and places the pertinent data in the new type, all in the same syntax. Not only does this simplify the code, but it allows you to concentrate more on getting the data you want and less on exactly how to read both data domains.

This example uses both LINQ to DataSet and LINQ to XML to access the multiple data domains:

```
Northwind dataContext = new Northwind(Settings.Default.NorthwindConnectionString);
ProductsTableAdapter adapter = new ProductsTableAdapter();
Products products = new Products();
adapter.Fill(products._Products);

XElement xmlCategories = XElement.Load("Categories.xml");
```

Northwind is a DataContext class. A DataContext is analogous to an ADO.NET Connection and Command object rolled into one. You use it to establish your connection, execute queries, or access tables directly via Entity Classes. A DataContext can be generated directly from the database through Visual Studio by adding a new "LINQ to SQL Classes" item or from the command line using the SQLMetal.exe. This provides access to the local Northwind database for the query. A Products DataSet is loaded from the Products table in the Northwind database for use in the query. For more on DataContext, see Recipe 1.6.

The Northwind DataContext can be generated using SQLMetal.exe using the following command line syntax:

```
SqlMetal /server:. /database:Northwind /code:Northwind.cs
```

XElement is one of the main classes in LINQ to XML. It enables the loading of existing XML, creation of new XML, or retrieving of the XML text for the element via ToString. Example 1-1 shows the Categories.xml file that will be loaded. For more on XElement and LINQ to XML, see Chapter 15.

Example 1-1. Categories.xml

```
<?xml version="1.0" encoding="utf-8"?>
<Categories>
  <Category CategoryID="1" CategoryName="Beverages" Description="Soft drinks, coffees,
teas, beer, and ale" />
  <Category CategoryID="2" CategoryName="Condiments" Description="Sweet and savory sauces,
relishes, spreads, and seasonings" />
  <Category CategoryID="3" CategoryName="Confections" Description="Desserts, candies,
sweetbreads" />
  <Category CategoryID="4" CategoryName="Dairy Products" Description="Cheeses" />
  <Category CategoryID="5" CategoryName="Grains/Cereals" Description="Breads, crackers,
pasta, and cereal" />
  <Category CategoryID="6" CategoryName="Meat/Poultry" Description="Prepared meats" />
  <Category CategoryID="7" CategoryName="Produce" Description="Dried fruit and bean curd"
/>
  <Category CategoryID="8" CategoryName="Seafood" Description="Seaweed and fish" />
</Categories>
```

The two sets of data are joined using LINQ and, in particular, the join keyword. The data is joined by matching the category id in the products table with the category id in the xml file to combine the data. In SQL terms, the join keyword represents an inner join:

```
var expr = from product in products._Products
           where product.Units_In_Stock > 100
           join xc in xmlCategories.Elements("Category")
           on product.Category_ID equals int.Parse(xc.Attribute("CategoryID").Value)
```

Once the join result is complete, a new type is projected using the select keyword:

```
select new
{
    ProductName = product.Product_Name,
    Category = xc.Attribute("CategoryName").Value,
    CategoryDescription = xc.Attribute("Description").Value
};
```

This allows us to combine different data elements from the two sets of data to make a third set that can look completely different than either of the original two.

Doing joins on two sets of database data would be a bad idea, as the database can do this much faster for those sets, but when you need to join disparate data sets, LINQ can lend a helping hand.

See Also

The "join keyword," "System.Data.Linq.DataContext," and "XElement" topics in the MSDN documentation.

1.7   Querying Configuration Files with LINQ

Problem

Sets of data can be stored in many different locations, such as configuration files. You want to be able to query your configuration files for sets of information.

Solution

Use LINQ to query against the configuration sections. In the example below, this is done by retrieving all chapter titles with even numbers and the word "and" in the title from the custom configuration section containing chapter information:

```
CSharpRecipesConfigurationSection recipeConfig =
    ConfigurationManager.GetSection("CSharpRecipesConfiguration") as
CSharpRecipesConfigurationSection;

var expr = from ChapterConfigurationElement chapter in
               recipeConfig.Chapters.OfType<ChapterConfigurationElement>()
           where (chapter.Title.Contains("and")) && ((int.Parse(chapter.Number) % 2)
== 0)
```

```
            select new
            {
                ChapterNumber = "Chapter " + chapter.Number,
                chapter.Title
            };

    foreach (var chapterInfo in expr)
    {
        Console.WriteLine(chapterInfo.ChapterNumber + ": " + chapterInfo.Title);
    }
```

The configuration section being queried looks like this:

```xml
<CSharpRecipesConfiguration CurrentEdition="3">
  <Chapters>
    <add Number="1" Title="Language Integrated Query (LINQ)"/>
    <add Number="2" Title="Strings and Characters"/>
    <add Number="3" Title="Classes and Structures"/>
    <add Number="4" Title="Generics"/>
    <add Number="5" Title="Collections"/>
    <add Number="6" Title="Iterators, Partial Types and Partial Methods"/>
    <add Number="7" Title="Exception Handling"/>
    <add Number="8" Title="Diagnostics"/>
    <add Number="9" Title="Delegates, Events, and Functional Programming"/>
    <add Number="10" Title="Regular Expressions"/>
    <add Number="11" Title="Data Structures &amp; Algorithms"/>
    <add Number="12" Title="Filesystem I/O"/>
    <add Number="13" Title="Reflection"/>
    <add Number="14" Title="Web"/>
    <add Number="15" Title="XML"/>
    <add Number="16" Title="Networking"/>
    <add Number="17" Title="Security"/>
    <add Number="18" Title="Threading and Synchronization"/>
    <add Number="19" Title="Toolbox"/>
    <add Number="20" Title="Numbers &amp; Enumerations"/>
  </Chapters>
  <Editions>
    <add Number="1" PublicationYear="2004"/>
    <add Number="2" PublicationYear="2006"/>
    <add Number="3" PublicationYear="2007"/>
  </Editions>
</CSharpRecipesConfiguration>
```

The output from the query is:

```
Chapter 2: Strings and Characters
Chapter 6: Iterators, Partial Types and Partial Methods
Chapter 18: Threading and Synchronization
```

Discussion

Configuration files in .NET play a significant role in achieving manageability and ease of deployment for .NET-based applications. It can be challenging to get all of the various settings right in the hierarchy of configuration files that can affect an application, so understanding how to write utilities to programmatically check configuration file settings is of great use during development, testing, deployment, and ongoing management of an application.

 To access the configuration types, you will need to reference the System.Configuration assembly.

Even though the ConfigurationElementCollection class (the base of sets of data in configuration files) only supports IEnumerable and not IEnumerable<T>, we can still use it to get the elements we need by using the OfType<ChapterConfigurationElement> method on the collection, which selects elements of that type from the collection:

```
var expr = from ChapterConfigurationElement chapter in
               recipeConfig.Chapters.OfType<ChapterConfigurationElement>()
```

ChapterConfigurationElement is a custom configuration section class that holds the chapter number and title:

```
/// <summary>
/// Holds the information about a chapter in the configuration file
/// </summary>
public class ChapterConfigurationElement : ConfigurationElement
{
    /// <summary>
    /// Default constructor
    /// </summary>
    public ChapterConfigurationElement()
    {
    }

    /// <summary>
    /// The number of the Chapter
    /// </summary>
    [ConfigurationProperty("Number", IsRequired=true)]
    public string Number
    {
        get { return (string)this["Number"]; }
        set { this["Number"] = value; }
    }

    /// <summary>
    /// The title of the Chapter
    /// </summary>
    [ConfigurationProperty("Title", IsRequired=true)]
    public string Title
    {
        get { return (string)this["Title"]; }
        set { this["Title"] = value; }
    }
}
```

This technique can be used on the standard configuration files such as machine. config as well. This example determines which sections in machine.config require access permissions. For this collection, OfType<ConfigurationSection> is used, as this is a standard section:

```
System.Configuration.Configuration machineConfig =
    ConfigurationManager.OpenMachineConfiguration( );

var query = from ConfigurationSection section in machineConfig.Sections.
OfType<ConfigurationSection>( )
            where section.SectionInformation.RequirePermission
            select section;


foreach (ConfigurationSection section in query)
{
    Console.WriteLine(section.SectionInformation.Name);
}
```

The sections detected will look something like this:

```
system.data
windows
system.webServer
mscorlib
system.data.oledb
system.data.oracleclient
system.data.sqlclient
configProtectedData
satelliteassemblies
system.data.dataset
startup
system.data.odbc
system.diagnostics
runtime
system.codedom
system.runtime.remoting
assemblyBinding
system.windows.forms
```

See Also

The "Enumerable.OfType,method," "ConfigurationSectionCollection,class" and "ConfigurationElementCollection class" topics in the MSDN documentation.

1.8   Creating XML Straight from a Database

Problem

You want to be able to take a set of data from a database and represent it as XML.

Solution

Use LINQ to SQL and LINQ to XML to retrieve and transform the data all in one query. In this case, we will select the top five customers in the Northwind database whose contact is the owner and those owners who placed orders totaling more than $10,000, then create XML containing the company name, contact name, phone number, and total amount of the orders. Finally, the results are written out to the *BigSpenders.xml* file:

```
Northwind dataContext = new Northwind(Settings.Default.NorthwindConnectionString);
// Log the generated SQL to the console
dataContext.Log = Console.Out;

var bigSpenders = new XElement("BigSpenders",
            from top5 in
            (
                from customer in
                (
                    from c in dataContext.Customers
                    // get the customers where the contact is the owner
                    // and they placed orders
                    where c.ContactTitle.Contains("Owner")
                       && c.Orders.Count > 0
                    join orderData in
                       (
                           from c in dataContext.Customers
                           // get the customers where the contact is the owner
                           // and they placed orders
                           where c.ContactTitle.Contains("Owner")
                              && c.Orders.Count > 0
                           from o in c.Orders
                           // get the order details
                           join od in dataContext.OrderDetails
                               on o.OrderID equals od.OrderID
                           select new
                           {
                               c.CompanyName,
                               c.CustomerID,
                               o.OrderID,
                               // have to calc order value from orderdetails
                               //(UnitPrice*Quantity as Total)- (Total*Discount)
                               // as NetOrderTotal
                               NetOrderTotal = (
                                   (((double)od.UnitPrice) * od.Quantity) -
                                   ((((double)od.UnitPrice) * od.Quantity) * od.
Discount))
                           }
                       )
                    on c.CustomerID equals orderData.CustomerID
                    into customerOrders
                    select new
                    {
                        c.CompanyName,
```

```
                    c.ContactName,
                    c.Phone,
                    // Get the total amount spent by the customer
                    TotalSpend = customerOrders.Sum(order => order.NetOrderTotal)
                }
            )
            // place focus on the customers that spent > 10000
            where customer.TotalSpend > 10000
            orderby customer.TotalSpend descending
            // only take the top five spenders
            select customer).Take(5)
        )
        // format the data as XML
        select new XElement("Customer",
                    new XAttribute("companyName", top5.CompanyName),
                    new XAttribute("contactName", top5.ContactName),
                    new XAttribute("phoneNumber", top5.Phone),
                    new XAttribute("amountSpent", top5.TotalSpend)));

using (XmlWriter writer = XmlWriter.Create("BigSpenders.xml"))
{
    bigSpenders.WriteTo(writer);
}
```

 When building larger queries, you may find it is sometimes easier to use the functional approach (.Join( )) to building up the query instead of the query expression manner (join x on y equals z) if you have done more C# than SQL.

Discussion

LINQ to SQL is the part of LINQ to ADO.NET that facilitates rapid database development. It is targeted at the scenarios where you want to program almost directly against the database schema. Most of these scenarios have one-to-one correlations between strongly typed classes and database tables. If you are in more of an enterprise development scenario with lots of stored procedures and databases that have moved away from "one table equals one entity" scenarios, you would want to look into LINQ to Entities.

To use LINQ to SQL, there are two design tools to help you get started, the visual designer for LINQ to SQL in Visual Studio 2008 and the command line utility SqlMetal.exe in the SDK. You can access the visual designer by adding a new or opening an existing "LINQ to SQL Classes" item (*.dbml file) to the project, which opens the designer. Both of these help you to build out the DataContext and Entity Classes for your database that can then be used with LINQ (or other programming constructs if you wish). A DataContext is analogous to an ADO.NET Connection and Command object rolled into one. You use it to establish your connection, execute queries, or access tables directly via Entity Classes. The Northwind Data Context is a strongly typed instance of a DataContext generated by SqlMetal and is partially shown here:

```
public partial class Northwind : System.Data.Linq.DataContext
{

        private static System.Data.Linq.Mapping.MappingSource mappingSource = new
AttributeMappingSource();

    #region Extensibility Method Definitions
    /// removed code for extensibility points for clarity
    #endregion

        static Northwind()
        {
        }

        public Northwind(string connection) :
                        base(connection, mappingSource)
        {
                OnCreated();
        }

        public Northwind(System.Data.IDbConnection connection) :
                        base(connection, mappingSource)
        {
                OnCreated();
        }

        public Northwind(string connection, System.Data.Linq.Mapping.MappingSource
mappingSource) :
                        base(connection, mappingSource)
        {
                OnCreated();
        }

        public Northwind(System.Data.IDbConnection connection, System.Data.Linq.
Mapping.MappingSource mappingSource) :
                        base(connection, mappingSource)
        {
                OnCreated();
        }

        public System.Data.Linq.Table<Customers> Customers
        {
                get
                {
                        return this.GetTable<Customers>();
                }
        }
    // More Table<EntityClass> definitions, one for each table in the database
}
```

The Entity Class definitions for the Northwind database are all present in the generated code as well, with each table having an Entity Class defined for it. The Entity Classes are indicated by the Table attribute with no parameters. This means that the name of the Entity Class matches the table name:

```
[Table( )]
public partial class Customers : INotifyPropertyChanging, INotifyPropertyChanged
{

    #region Extensibility Method Definitions
    partial void OnLoaded( );
    partial void OnValidate( );
    partial void OnCreated( );
    partial void OnCustomerIDChanging(string value);
    partial void OnCustomerIDChanged( );
    // more extensibility methods to indicate change states for each property...
    #endregion

        public event PropertyChangingEventHandler PropertyChanging;

        public event PropertyChangedEventHandler PropertyChanged;
```

The standard property change notifications are implemented via INotifyPropertyChanging and INotifyPropertyChanged and have PropertyChanging and PropertyChanged events for conveying the change to a property. There are also a set of partial methods that will report when a specific property is modified on this Entity Class if the partial method is implemented in another partial class definition for the Entity Class. If no other partial class definition is found, the compiler will remove those notifications. Partial methods enable the declaration of a method signature in one file of a partial class declaration and the implementation of the method in another. If the signature is found but the implementation is not, the signature is removed by the compiler.

The properties in the Entity Class match up to the columns in the database via the Column attribute, where the Name value is the database column name and the Storage value is the internal storage for the class of the data. Events for the property changes are wired into the setter for the property:

```
        [Column(Name="Company Name", Storage="_CompanyName", DbType="NVarChar(40) NOT
NULL", CanBeNull=false)]
        public string CompanyName
        {
            get
            {
                return this._CompanyName;
            }
            set
            {
                if ((this._CompanyName != value))
                {
                    this.OnCompanyNameChanging(value);
```

```
                              this.SendPropertyChanging( );
                              this._CompanyName = value;
                              this.SendPropertyChanged("CompanyName");
                              this.OnCompanyNameChanged( );
                      }
              }
      }
```

For a one-to-many child relationship, an EntitySet<T> of the child Entity Class is declared with an Association attribute. The Association attribute specifies the relationship information between the parent and child Entity Classes, as shown here for the Orders property on Customer:

```
      [Association(Name="Orders_FK00", Storage="_Orders", ThisKey="CustomerID",
  OtherKey="CustomerID", DeleteRule="NO ACTION")]
      public EntitySet<Orders> Orders
      {
              get
              {
                      return this._Orders;
              }
              set
              {
                      this._Orders.Assign(value);
              }
      }
```

LINQ to SQL covers much more than what has been shown here; we encourage you to investigate it more, but let's now see the other data domain we are dealing with: LINQ to XML.

LINQ to XML is not only how you perform queries against XML; it is a more developer-friendly way to work with XML. One of the main classes in LINQ to XML is XElement. XElement allows you to create XML in a manner that more closely resembles the structure of the XML itself. This may not seem like a big deal, but when you can see the XML taking shape in your code, it makes it easier to know where you are. (Ever forget which XmlWriter.WriteEndElement you were on? We have!) You can get more details and examples about using XElement in Chapter 15, so we won't go much further into it here, but as you can see, it is very easy to build up XML in a query.

The first part of the query deals with setting up the main XML element "BigSpenders", getting the initial set of customers where the contact is the owner:

```
      var bigSpenders = new XElement("BigSpenders",
              from top5 in
              (
                  (from customer in
                      (
                          from c in dataContext.Customers
                          // get the customers where the contact is the owner
                          // and they placed orders
                          where c.ContactTitle.Contains("Owner")
                             && c.Orders.Count > 0
```

The middle of the query deals with joining the order and order detail information with the customer information to get the NetOrderTotal for the order. It also creates order data containing that value and the customer and order ids and the customer name. We need the NetOrderTotal in the last part of the query, so stay tuned!

```
join orderData in
    (
        from c in dataContext.Customers
        // get the customers where the contact is the owner
        // and they placed orders
        where c.ContactTitle.Contains("Owner")
            && c.Orders.Count > 0
        from o in c.Orders
        // get the order details
        join od in dataContext.OrderDetails
            on o.OrderID equals od.OrderID
        select new
        {
            c.CompanyName,
            c.CustomerID,
            o.OrderID,
            // have to calc order value from orderdetails
            //(UnitPrice*Quantity as Total)-
              (Total*Discount)
            // as NetOrderTotal
            NetOrderTotal = (
    (((double)od.UnitPrice) * od.Quantity) -
    ((((double)od.UnitPrice) * od.Quantity) * od.Discount))
        }
    )
    on c.CustomerID equals orderData.CustomerID
    into customerOrders
```

The last part of the query determines the TotalSpend for that customer across all orders using the Sum function on NetOrderTotal for the generated customerOrders collection. The last criteria evaluated is that only the top five customers with a TotalSpend value > 10000 are selected by using the Take function. Take is the equivalent to TOP in SQL. The records are then used to construct one inner Customer element with attributes that nest inside the BigSpenders root element started in the first part of the query:

```
select new
{
    c.CompanyName,
    c.ContactName,
    c.Phone,
    // Get the total amount spent by the customer
    TotalSpend = customerOrders.Sum(order => order.
NetOrderTotal)
}
)
// only worry about customers that spent > 10000
```

```
        where customer.TotalSpend > 10000
        orderby customer.TotalSpend descending
        // only take the top 5 spenders
        select customer).Take(5)
)
// format the data as XML
select new XElement("Customer",
        new XAttribute("companyName", top5.CompanyName),
        new XAttribute("contactName", top5.ContactName),
        new XAttribute("phoneNumber", top5.Phone),
        new XAttribute("amountSpent", top5.TotalSpend)));
```

 It is much easier to build large-nested queries as individual queries first and then put them together once you are sure the inner query is working.

At this point, for all of the code here, nothing has happened yet. That's right, until the query is accessed, nothing happens through the magic of deferred execution. LINQ has constructed a query expression, but nothing has talked to the database; there is no XML in memory, nada. Once the WriteTo method is called on the bigSpenders query expression, then the query is evaluated by LINQ to SQL, and the XML is constructed. The WriteTo method writes out the constructed XML to the XmlWriter provided, and we are done:

```
using (XmlWriter writer = XmlWriter.Create("BigSpenders.xml"))
{
    bigSpenders.WriteTo(writer);
}
```

If you are interested in what that SQL will look like, connect the DataContext.Log property to a TextWriter (like the console):

```
// Log the generated SQL to the console
dataContext.Log = Console.Out;
```

This query generates SQL that looks like this:

```
Generated SQL for query - output via DataContext.Log
SELECT [t10].[CompanyName], [t10].[ContactName], [t10].[Phone], [t10].[TotalSpend]
FROM (
    SELECT TOP (5) [t0].[Company Name] AS [CompanyName], [t0].[Contact Name] AS
[ContactName], [t0].[Phone], [t9].[value] AS [TotalSpend]
    FROM [Customers] AS [t0]
    OUTER APPLY (
        SELECT COUNT(*) AS [value]
        FROM [Orders] AS [t1]
        WHERE [t1].[Customer ID] = [t0].[Customer ID]
        ) AS [t2]
    OUTER APPLY (
        SELECT SUM([t8].[value]) AS [value]
        FROM (
            SELECT [t3].[Customer ID], [t6].[Order ID],
```

```
                    ([t7].[Unit Price] *
                    (CONVERT(Decimal(29,4),[t7].[Quantity]))) - ([t7].[Unit Price] *
                        (CONVERT(Decimal(29,4),[t7].[Quantity])) *
                            (CONVERT(Decimal(29,4),[t7].[Discount]))) AS [value],
                    [t7].[Order ID] AS [Order ID2],
                    [t3].[Contact Title] AS [ContactTitle],
                    [t5].[value] AS [value2],
                    [t6].[Customer ID] AS [CustomerID]
            FROM [Customers] AS [t3]
            OUTER APPLY (
                SELECT COUNT(*) AS [value]
                FROM [Orders] AS [t4]
                WHERE [t4].[Customer ID] = [t3].[Customer ID]
                ) AS [t5]
            CROSS JOIN [Orders] AS [t6]
            CROSS JOIN [Order Details] AS [t7]
            ) AS [t8]
        WHERE ([t0].[Customer ID] = [t8].[Customer ID]) AND ([t8].[Order ID] = [
    t8].[Order ID2]) AND ([t8].[ContactTitle] LIKE @p0) AND ([t8].[value2] > @p1) AN
    D ([t8].[CustomerID] = [t8].[Customer ID])
        ) AS [t9]
        WHERE ([t9].[value] > @p2) AND ([t0].[Contact Title] LIKE @p3) AND ([t2].[va
    lue] > @p4)
        ORDER BY [t9].[value] DESC
        ) AS [t10]
    ORDER BY [t10].[TotalSpend] DESC
    -- @p0: Input String (Size = 0; Prec = 0; Scale = 0) [%Owner%]
    -- @p1: Input Int32 (Size = 0; Prec = 0; Scale = 0) [0]
    -- @p2: Input Decimal (Size = 0; Prec = 29; Scale = 4) [10000]
    -- @p3: Input String (Size = 0; Prec = 0; Scale = 0) [%Owner%]
    -- @p4: Input Int32 (Size = 0; Prec = 0; Scale = 0) [0]
    -- Context: SqlProvider(SqlCE) Model: AttributedMetaModel Build: 3.5.20706.1
```

The final XML is shown below:

```
<BigSpenders>
  <Customer companyName="Folk och fä HB" contactName="Maria Larsson"
            phoneNumber="0695-34 67 21" amountSpent="39805.162472039461" />
  <Customer companyName="White Clover Markets" contactName="Karl Jablonski"
            phoneNumber="(206) 555-4112" amountSpent="35957.604972146451" />
  <Customer companyName="Bon app'" contactName="Laurence Lebihan"
            phoneNumber="91.24.45.40" amountSpent="22311.577472746558" />
  <Customer companyName="LINO-Delicateses" contactName="Felipe Izquierdo"
            phoneNumber="(8) 34-56-12" amountSpent="20458.544984650609" />
  <Customer companyName="Simons bistro" contactName="Jytte Petersen"
            phoneNumber="31 12 34 56" amountSpent="18978.777493602414" />
</BigSpenders>
```

See Also

The "The Three Parts of a LINQ Query," "DataContext.Log, property," "DataContext class," "XElement class," and "LINQ to SQL" topics in the MSDN documentation.

1.9   Being Selective About Your Query Results

Problem

You want to be able to get a dynamic subset of a query result.

Solution

Use the `TakeWhile` extension method to retrieve all results until the criteria is matched:

```
Northwind dataContext = new Northwind(Settings.Default.NorthwindConnectionString);

var query =
    dataContext.Suppliers.GroupJoin(dataContext.Products,
        s => s.SupplierID, p => p.SupplierID,
        (s, products) => new
        {
            s.CompanyName,
            s.ContactName,
            s.Phone,
            Products = products
        }).OrderByDescending(supplierData => supplierData.Products.Count())
            .TakeWhile(supplierData => supplierData.Products.Count() > 3);


Console.WriteLine("Suppliers that provide more than three products: {0}", query.
Count());
foreach (var supplierData in query)
{
    Console.WriteLine("    Company Name : {0}",supplierData.CompanyName);
    Console.WriteLine("    Contact Name : {0}", supplierData.ContactName);
    Console.WriteLine("    Contact Phone : {0}", supplierData.Phone);
    Console.WriteLine("    Products Supplied : {0}", supplierData.Products.Count());
    foreach (var productData in supplierData.Products)
    {
        Console.WriteLine("        Product: " + productData.ProductName);
    }
}
```

You can also use the `SkipWhile` extension method to retrieve all results once the criteria are matched:

```
Northwind dataContext = new Northwind(Settings.Default.NorthwindConnectionString);

var query =
    dataContext.Suppliers.GroupJoin(dataContext.Products,
        s => s.SupplierID, p => p.SupplierID,
        (s, products) => new
        {
            s.CompanyName,
            s.ContactName,
            s.Phone,
```

```
            Products = products
        }).OrderByDescending(supplierData => supplierData.Products.Count( ))
            .SkipWhile(supplierData =>
    {
        return supplierData.Products.Count( ) > 3;
    });

Console.WriteLine("Suppliers that provide three or less products: {0}",
                query.Count( ));
foreach (var supplierData in query)
{
    Console.WriteLine("    Company Name : {0}",supplierData.CompanyName);
    Console.WriteLine("    Contact Name : {0}", supplierData.ContactName);
    Console.WriteLine("    Contact Phone : {0}", supplierData.Phone);
    Console.WriteLine("    Products Supplied : {0}", supplierData.Products.Count( ));
    foreach (var productData in supplierData.Products)
    {
        Console.WriteLine("        Product: " + productData.ProductName);
    }
}
```

Discussion

In this example using LINQ to SQL, the number of products each supplier provides is determined, and the result set is sorted in descending order by product count:

```
var query =
    dataContext.Suppliers.GroupJoin(dataContext.Products,
        s => s.SupplierID, p => p.SupplierID,
        (s, products) => new
        {
            s.CompanyName,
            s.ContactName,
            s.Phone,
            Products = products
        }).OrderByDescending(supplierData => supplierData.Products.Count( ))
```

From that result, the supplier data for suppliers is only accepted into the final result set if they provide more than 3 products and the results are displayed. TakeWhile is used with a lambda expression to determine if the product count is greater than 3, and if so, the supplier is accepted into the result set:

```
        .TakeWhile(supplierData =>
    {
        return supplierData.Products.Count( ) > 3;
    });
```

If SkipWhile was used instead, all of the suppliers that provide 3 or fewer products would be returned:

```
        .SkipWhile(supplierData =>
    {
        return supplierData.Products.Count( ) > 3;
    });
```

Being able to write code-based conditions allows for more flexibility than the regular Take and Skip methods, which are absolute based on record count, but keep in mind that once the condition is hit for either TakeWhile or SkipWhile, you get all records after that, which is why sorting the result set before using these is important.

The query also uses GroupJoin, which is comparable to a SQL LEFT or RIGHT OUTER JOIN, but the result is not flattened. GroupJoin produces a hierarchical result set instead of a tabular one, which is used to get the collection of Products by Supplier in this example:

```
dataContext.Suppliers.GroupJoin(dataContext.Products,
    s => s.SupplierID, p => p.SupplierID,
```

See Also

The "Enumerable.TakeWhile method," "Enumerable.SkipWhile method," and "Enumerable.GroupJoin method" topics in the MSDN documentation.

1.10   Using LINQ with Collections That Don't Support IEnumerable<T>

Problem

There are a whole bunch of collections that don't support the generic versions of IEnumerable or ICollection but that do support the original nongeneric versions of the IEnumerable or ICollection interfaces, and you would like to be able to query those collections using LINQ.

Solution

The type cannot be inferred from the original IEnumeration or ICollection interfaces, so it must be provided using either the OfType<T> or Cast<T> extension methods or by specifying the type in the from clause, which inserts a Cast<T> for you. The first example uses Cast<XmlNode> to let LINQ know that the elements in the XmlNodeList returned from XmlDocument.SelectNodes are of type XmlNode. For an example of how to use the OfType<T> extension method, see the Discussion section:

```
// Make some XML with some types that you can use with LINQ
// that don't support IEnumerable<T> directly
XElement xmlFragment = new XElement("NonGenericLinqableTypes",
                new XElement("IEnumerable",
                    new XElement("System.Collections",
                        new XElement("ArrayList"),
                        new XElement("BitArray"),
                        new XElement("Hashtable"),
                        new XElement("Queue"),
                        new XElement("SortedList"),
                        new XElement("Stack")),
```

```
                    new XElement("System.Net",
                        new XElement("CredentialCache")),
                    new XElement("System.Xml",
                        new XElement("XmlNodeList")),
                    new XElement("System.Xml.XPath",
                        new XElement("XPathNodeIterator")))),
                new XElement("ICollection",
                    new XElement("System.Diagnostics",
                        new XElement("EventLogEntryCollection")),
                    new XElement("System.Net",
                        new XElement("CookieCollection")),
                    new XElement("System.Security.AccessControl",
                        new XElement("GenericAcl")),
                    new XElement("System.Security",
                        new XElement("PermissionSet")))));

XmlDocument doc = new XmlDocument();
doc.LoadXml(xmlFragment.ToString());

// Select the names of the nodes under IEnumerable that have children and are
// named System.Collections and contain a capital S and return that list in
descending order
var query = from node in doc.SelectNodes("/NonGenericLinqableTypes/IEnumerable/*").
Cast<XmlNode>()
            where node.HasChildNodes &&
                node.Name == "System.Collections"
            from XmlNode xmlNode in node.ChildNodes
            where xmlNode.Name.Contains('S')
            orderby xmlNode.Name descending
            select xmlNode.Name;

foreach (string name in query)
{
    Console.WriteLine(name);
}
```

The second example works against the Application event log and retrieves the errors that occurred in the last 6 hours. The type of the element in the collection (EventLogEntry) is provided next to the from keyword, which allows LINQ to infer the rest of the information it needs about the collection element type:

```
EventLog log = new EventLog("Application");
var query = from EventLogEntry entry in log.Entries
            where entry.EntryType == EventLogEntryType.Error &&
                entry.TimeGenerated > DateTime.Now.Subtract(new TimeSpan(6, 0, 0))
            select entry.Message;

Console.WriteLine("There were " + query.Count<string>() +
    " Application Event Log error messages in the last 6 hours!");
foreach (string message in query)
{
    Console.WriteLine(message);
}
```

Discussion

Cast<T> will transform the IEnumerable into IEnumerable<T> so that LINQ can access each of the items in the collection in a strongly typed manner. Before using Cast<T>, it would behoove you to check that all elements of the collection really are of type T, or you will get an InvalidCastException if the type of the element is not convertible to the type T specified, because all elements will be cast using the type. Placing the type of the element next to the from keyword acts just like a Cast<T>:

```
ArrayList stuff = new ArrayList();
stuff.Add(DateTime.Now);
stuff.Add(DateTime.Now);
stuff.Add(1);
stuff.Add(DateTime.Now);

var expr = from item in stuff.Cast<DateTime>()
           select item;
// attempting to cast the third element throws InvalidCastException
foreach (DateTime item in expr)
{
    Console.WriteLine(item);
}
```

 Note that again because of the deferred execution semantics that the exception that occurs with Cast<T> or from only happens once that element has been iterated to.

Another way to approach this issue would be to use OfType<T>, as it will only return the elements of a specific type and not try to cast elements from one type to another:

```
var expr = from item in stuff.OfType<DateTime>()
           select item;
// only three elements, all DateTime returned.  No exceptions
foreach (DateTime item in expr)
{
    Console.WriteLine(item);
}
```

See Also

The "OfType<TResult> method" and "Cast<TResult> method" topics in the MSDN documentation.

CHAPTER 2

Strings and Characters

2.0   Introduction

String usage abounds in just about all types of applications. The System.String type is a reference type, unlike System.Char, which is a value type and therefore derives from System.ValueType. The string alias is built into C# and can be used instead of the full name.

The Framework Class Library (FCL) does not stop with just the String class; there is also a System.Text.StringBuilder class for performing string manipulations and the System.Text.RegularExpressions namespace for searching strings. This chapter will cover the String class, the System.Text.StringBuilder class, and the Char structure.

The System.Text.StringBuilder class provides an easy, performance-friendly method of manipulating string objects. Even though this class duplicates much of the functionality of a String class, the StringBuilder class is fundamentally different in that the string contained within the StringBuilder object can actually be modified—you cannot modify a string object. However, this duplicated functionality provides a more efficient manipulation of strings than is obtainable by using the String class.

2.1   Determining the Kind of Character a Char Contains

Problem

You have a variable of type char and wish to determine the kind of character it contains—a letter, digit, number, punctuation character, control character, separator character, symbol, whitespace, or surrogate character (i.e., Unicode characters with a value greater than 64K). Similarly, you have a string variable and want to determine the kind of character in one or more positions within this string.

Solution

To determine the value of a char, use the built-in static methods on the System.Char structure shown here:

```
Char.IsControl          Char.IsDigit
Char.IsLetter           Char.IsNumber
Char.IsPunctuation      Char.IsSeparator
Char.IsSurrogate        Char.IsSymbol
Char.IsWhitespace
```

Discussion

The following examples demonstrate how to use the methods shown in the Solution section in an extension method to return the kind of a character. First, create an enumeration to define the various types of characters:

```
public enum CharKind
{
    Digit,
    Letter,
    Number,
    Punctuation,
    Unknown
}
```

Next, create the extension method that contains the logic to determine the kind of a character and to return a CharKind enumeration value indicating that type:

```
static class CharStrExtMethods
{
    public static CharKind GetCharKind(this char theChar)
    {
        if (Char.IsLetter(theChar))
        {
            return CharKind.Letter;
        }
        else if (Char.IsNumber(theChar))
        {
            return CharKind.Number;
        }
        else if (Char.IsPunctuation(theChar))
        {
            return CharKind.Punctuation;
        }
        else
        {
            return CharKind.Unknown;
        }
    }
}
```

The GetCharKind extension method performs a series of tests on a character using the Char type's built-in static methods. An enumeration of all the different types of characters is defined and is returned by the GetCharKind method.

If, however, a character in a string needs to be evaluated, use the overloaded static methods on the char structure. The following code modifies the GetCharKind extension method to operate on a string variable while accepting a character position in that string as an argument to the extension method. The character position determines which character in the string is evaluated:

```
static class CharStrExtMethods
{
    public static CharKind GetCharKindInString(this string theString,
                                              int charPosition)
    {
        if (Char.IsLetter(theString, charPosition))
        {
            return CharKind.Letter;
        }
        else if (Char.IsNumber(theString, charPosition))
        {
            return CharKind.Number;
        }
        else if (Char.IsPunctuation(theString, charPosition))
        {
            return CharKind.Punctuation;
        }
        else
        {
            return CharKind.Unknown;
        }
    }
}
```

The following code example determines whether the fifth character (the charPosition parameter is zero-based) in the string is a digit:

```
string data = "abcdefg";
if (string.GetCharKindInString(4) == CharKind.Digit) {...}
```

Table 2-1 describes each of the static Char methods.

Table 2-1. Char methods

Char method	Description
IsControl	A control code in the ranges \U007F, \U0000–\U001F, and \U0080–\U009F.
IsDigit	Any decimal digit in the range 0–9 in all Unicode locales.
IsLetter	Any alphabetic letter.
IsNumber	Any decimal digit or hexadecimal digit; this includes digits such as superscripts, subscripts, etc.
IsPunctuation	Any punctuation character.
IsSeparator	A space separating words, a line separator, or a paragraph separator.

Table 2-1. Char methods (continued)

Char method	Description
IsSurrogate	Any surrogate character in the range \UD800–\UDFFF.
IsSymbol	Any mathematical, currency, or other symbol character. Includes characters that modify surrounding characters.
IsWhitespace	Any space character and the following characters:
	\U0009
	\U000A
	\U000B
	\U000C
	\U000D
	\U0085
	\U2028
	\U2029

In Version 2.0 of the .NET Framework, a few extra Is* functions were added to augment the existing methods. If the character in question is a letter (i.e., the IsLetter method returns true), you can determine if the letter is uppercase or lowercase by using the methods in Table 2-2.

Table 2-2. Uppercase and lowercase Char methods

Char method	Description
IsLower	A character that is lowercase
IsUpper	A character that is uppercase

If the character in question is a surrogate (i.e., the IsSurrogate method returns true), you can use the methods in Table 2-3 to get more information on the surrogate character.

Table 2-3. Surrogate Char methods

Char method	Description
IsHighSurrogate	A character that is in the range \UD800 to \UDBFF
IsLowSurrogate	A character that is in the range \UDC00 to \UDFFF

In addition to these surrogate methods, an additional method, IsSurrogatePair, returns true only if two characters create a surrogate pair—that is, one character is a high surrogate and one character is a low surrogate.

The final addition to this group of methods is the IsLetterOrDigit method, which returns true only if the character in question is either a letter or a digit. To determine if the character is either a letter or a digit, use the IsLetter and IsDigit methods.

See Also

The "Char Structure" topic in the MSDN documentation.

2.2   Controlling Case Sensitivity When Comparing Two Characters

Problem

You need to compare two characters for equality, but you need the flexibility of performing a case-sensitive or case-insensitive comparison.

Solution

Create extension methods on the char type and use the Equals instance method on the char structure to compare the two characters:

```
static class CharStrExtMethods
{
    public static bool IsCharEqual(this char firstChar, char secondChar)
    {
        return (IsCharEqual(firstChar, secondChar, false));
    }

    public static bool IsCharEqual(this char firstChar, char secondChar,
                                   bool caseSensitiveCompare)
    {
        if (caseSensitiveCompare)
        {
            return (firstChar.Equals(secondChar));
        }
        else
        {
            return (char.ToUpperInvariant(firstChar).Equals(
                        char.ToUpperInvariant(secondChar)));
        }
    }
}

public static bool IsCharEqual(this char firstChar, CultureInfo firstCharCulture,
                               char secondChar, CultureInfo secondCharCulture)
{
    return (IsCharEqual(firstChar, firstCharCulture,
            secondChar, secondCharCulture, false));
}

public static bool IsCharEqual(this char firstChar, CultureInfo firstCharCulture,
                               char secondChar, CultureInfo secondCharCulture,
                               bool caseSensitiveCompare)
{
    if (caseSensitiveCompare)
```

```
        {
            return (firstChar.Equals(secondChar));
        }
        else
        {
            return (char.ToUpper(firstChar, firstCharCulture).Equals
                    (char.ToUpper(secondChar, secondCharCulture)));
        }
    }
}
```

The first overloaded IsCharEqual extension method takes only one parameter, which is the character to be compared against the value contained in the current char instance. This extension method then calls the second IsCharEqual method with two parameters. The last parameter on this extension method call defaults to false so that when this method is called, you do not have to pass in a value for the caseSensitiveCompare parameter—it will automatically default to false.

You can further extend the overloaded IsCharEqual extension methods to handle the culture of the characters passed in to it. The addition of the CultureInfo parameters to these extension methods allows you to pass in the culture information for the strings that you are calling ToUpperInvariant on. This information allows the ToUpperInvariant method to correctly uppercase the character based in the culture-specific details of the character (i.e., the language, region, etc., of the character).

Discussion

Using the ToUpperInvariant method in conjunction with the Equals method on the String class allows you to choose whether to take into account the case of the strings when comparing them. The ToUpperInvariant method changes any lowercase characters to uppercase using the rules built in to the invariant culture. That is, the case change is unaffected by the current culture. If you require the character data to be uppercased in a culturally aware way, use the IsCharEqual method, which accepts a CultureInfo object.

To perform a case-sensitive comparison of two char variables, simply use the Equals method, which, by default, performs a case-sensitive comparison. Performing a case-insensitive comparison requires that both characters be converted to their uppercase values before the Equals method is invoked. Setting both characters to their uppercase equivalents removes any case sensitivity between the character values, and they can be compared using the case-sensitive Equals comparison method as if it were a case-insensitive comparison.

Note that you must include the following using directives to compile this code:

```
using System;
using System.Globalization;
```

2.3   Finding the Location of All Occurrences of a String Within Another String

Problem

You need to search a string for every occurrence of a specific string. In addition, the case sensitivity, or insensitivity, of the search needs to be controlled.

Solution

Using IndexOf or IndexOfAny in a loop, you can determine how many occurrences of a character or string exist as well as their locations within the string. To find each occurrence of a string in another string using a case-sensitive search, use the following code:

```
using System;
using System.Collections;
using System.Collections.Generic;

static class CharStrExtMethods
{
    public static int[] FindAll(this string matchStr, string searchedStr,
                                int startPos)
    {
        int foundPos = -1; // -1 represents not found.
            int count = 0;
        List<int> foundItems = new List<int>();

        do
        {
            foundPos = searchedStr.IndexOf(matchStr, startPos, StringComparison.
Ordinal);

            if (foundPos > -1)
            {
                startPos = foundPos + 1;
                count++;
                foundItems.Add(foundPos);

                Console.WriteLine("Found item at position: " + foundPos.
ToString());
            }
        } while (foundPos > -1 && startPos < searchedStr.Length);

        return ((int[])foundItems.ToArray());
    }
}
```

If the FindAll extension method is called with the following parameters:

```
string data = "Red";
int[] allOccurrences = data.FindAll("BlueTealRedredGreenRedYellow", 0);
```

the string "Red" is found at locations 8 and 19 in the string searchedStr. This code uses the IndexOf method inside a loop to iterate through each found matchStr string in the searchStr string.

To find a character in a string using a case-sensitive search, use the following code:

```
static class CharStrExtMethods
{
    public static int[] FindAll(this char MatchChar, string searchedStr,
                                int startPos)
    {
        int foundPos = -1; // -1 represents not found.
        int count = 0;
        List<int> foundItems = new List<int>();

        do
        {
            foundPos = searchedStr.IndexOf(MatchChar, startPos);
            if (foundPos > -1)
            {
                startPos = foundPos + 1;
                count++;
                foundItems.Add(foundPos);

                Console.WriteLine("Found item at position: " + foundPos.
ToString());
            }
        } while (foundPos > -1 && startPos < searchedStr.Length);

        return ((int[])foundItems.ToArray());
    }
}
```

If the FindAll extension method is called with the following parameters:

```
char data = "r";
int[] allOccurrences = data.FindAll("BlueTealRedredGreenRedYellow", 0);
```

the character "r" is found at locations 11 and 15 in the string searchedStr. This code uses the IndexOf method inside a do loop to iterate through each found matchChar character in the searchStr string. Overloading the FindAll method to accept either a char or string type avoids the performance hit by creating an entirely new string object from the passed in char object.

To find each occurrence of a string in another string using a case-insensitive search, use the following code:

```
static class CharStrExtMethods
{
    public static int[] FindAny(this string matchStr, string searchedStr, int
startPos)
    {
        int foundPos = -1; // -1 represents not found.
        int count = 0;
```

```
                List<int> foundItems = new List<int>( );

                // Factor out case-sensitivity
                searchedStr = searchedStr.ToUpperInvariant( );
                matchStr = matchStr.ToUpperInvariant( );

                do
                {
                    foundPos = searchedStr.IndexOf(matchStr, startPos,
    StringComparison.Ordinal);
                        if (foundPos > -1)
                        {
                            startPos = foundPos + 1;
                            count++;
                            foundItems.Add(foundPos);
                            Console.WriteLine("Found item at position: " + foundPos.
    ToString( ));
                        }
                } while (foundPos > -1 && startPos < searchedStr.Length);

                return ((int[])foundItems.ToArray( ));
            }
        }
```

If the `FindAny` extension method is called with the following parameters:

```
string data = "Red";
int[] allOccurrences = data.FindAny("BlueTealRedredGreenRedYellow", 0);
```

the string "Red" is found at locations 8, 11, and 19 in the string `searchedStr`. This
code uses the `IndexOf` method inside a loop to iterate through each found `matchStr`
string in the `searchStr` string. The search is rendered case-insensitive by using the
`ToUpperInvariant` method on both the `searchedStr` and the `matchStr` strings.

To find a set of characters in a string, use the following code:

```
static class CharStrExtMethods
{
        public static int[] FindAny(this char[] MatchCharArray, string
    searchedStr,
                                        int startPos)
    {
            int foundPos = -1; // -1 represents not found.
            int count = 0;
            List<int> foundItems = new List<int>( );

            do
            {
                foundPos = searchedStr.IndexOfAny(MatchCharArray, startPos,
                                        StringComparison.Ordinal);
                if (foundPos > -1)
                {
                    startPos = foundPos + 1;
                    count++;
                    foundItems.Add(foundPos);
```

```
                    Console.WriteLine("Found item at position: " + foundPos.
    ToString());
                }
            } while (foundPos > -1 && startPos < searchedStr.Length);

            return ((int[])foundItems.ToArray());
        }
    }
```

If the FindAll extension method is called with the following parameters:

```
char[] data = new char[] {'R', 'r'};
int[] allOccurrences = data.FindAny("BlueTealRedredGreenRedYellow", 0);
```

the characters 'r' or 'R' are found at locations 8, 11, 15, and 19 in the string searchedStr. This code uses the IndexOfAny method inside a loop to iterate through each found matchStr string in the searchStr string. The search is rendered case-insensitive by using an array of char containing all characters, both uppercase and lowercase, to be searched for.

Discussion

In the example code, the foundPos variable contains the location of the found character/string within the searchedStr string. The startPos variable contains the next position at which to start the search. Either the IndexOf or IndexOfAny method is used to perform the actual searching. The count variable simply counts the number of times the character/string was found in the searchedStr string.

The example uses a do loop so that the IndexOf or IndexOfAny operation is executed at least one time before the check in the while clause is performed. This check determines whether there are any more character/string matches to be found in the searchedStr string. This loop terminates when foundPos returns -1 (meaning that no more character/strings can be found in the searchedStr string) or when an out-of-bounds condition exists. When foundPos equals -1, there are no more instances of the match value in the searchedStr string; therefore, you can exit the loop. If, however, the startPos overshoots the last character element of the searchedStr string, an out-of-bounds condition exists and an exception is thrown. To prevent this, always check to make sure that any positioning variables that are modified inside of the loop, such as the startPos variable, are within their intended bounds.

Once a match is found by the IndexOf or IndexOfAny method, the if statement body is executed to increment the count variable by one and to move the startPos beyond the previously found match. The count variable is incremented by one to indicate that another match was found. The startPos is increased to the starting position of the last match found plus 1. Adding 1 is necessary so that you do not keep matching the same character/string that was previously matched, which will cause an infinite loop to occur in the code if at least one match is found in the searchedStr string. To see this behavior, remove the +1 from the code.

There is one potential problem with this code. Consider the case where:

```
searchedStr = "aaaa";
matchStr = "aa";
```

The code contained in this recipe will match "aa" three times:

```
(aa)aa
a(aa)a
aa(aa)
```

This situation may be fine for some applications but not if you need it to return only the following matches:

```
(aa)aa
aa(aa)
```

To do this, change the following line in the while loop:

```
startPos = foundPos + 1;
```

to this:

```
startPos = foundPos + matchStr.Length;
```

This code moves the startPos pointer beyond the first matched string, disallowing any internal matches.

To convert this code to use a while loop rather than a do loop, the foundPos variable must be initialized to 0, and the while loop expression should be as follows:

```
while (foundPos >= 0 && startPos < searchStr.Length)
{
    foundPos = searchedStr.IndexOf(matchChar, startPos);
    if (foundPos > -1)
    {
        startPos = foundPos + 1;
        count++;
    }
}
```

See Also

The "String.IndexOf Method" and "String.IndexOfAny Method" topics in the MSDN documentation.

2.4 Controlling Case Sensitivity When Comparing Two Strings

Problem

You need to compare the contents of two strings for equality. In addition, the case sensitivity of the comparison needs to be controlled.

Solution

Use the `Compare` static method on the `String` class to compare the two strings. Whether the comparison is case-insensitive is determined by the third parameter of one of its overloads. For example:

```
string lowerCase = "abc";
string upperCase = "AbC";
int caseInsensitiveResult = string.Compare(lowerCase, upperCase,
    StringComparison.CurrentCultureIgnoreCase);
int caseSensitiveResult = string.Compare(lowerCase,
    StringComparison.CurrentCulture);
```

The `caseSensitiveResult` value is `-1` (indicating that `lowerCase` is "less than" `upperCase`) and the `caseInsensitiveResult` is zero (indicating that `lowerCase` "equals" `upperCase`).

Discussion

Using the static `string.Compare` method allows you the freedom to choose whether to take into account the case of the strings when comparing them. This method returns an integer indicating the lexical relationship between the two strings. A zero means that the two strings are equal, a negative number means that the first string is less than the second string, and a positive number indicates that the first string is greater than the second string.

By setting the last parameter of this method (the `comparisonType` parameter) to either `StringComparison.CurrentCultureIgnoreCase` or `StringComparison.CurrentCulture`, you can determine whether the `Compare` method takes into account the case of both strings when comparing. Setting this parameter to `StringComparison.CurrentCulture` forces a case-sensitive comparison; setting it to `StringComparison.CurrentCulture-IgnoreCase` forces a case-insensitive comparison. In the case of the overloaded version of the method with no `comparisonType` parameter, comparisons are always case-sensitive.

See Also

The "String.Compare Method" topic in the MSDN documentation.

2.5   Comparing a String to the Beginning or End of a Second String

Problem

You need to determine whether a string is at the head or tail of a second string. In addition, the case sensitivity of the search needs to be controlled.

Solution

Use the EndsWith or StartsWith instance method on a string object. Comparisons with EndsWith and StartsWith are always case-sensitive. The following code compares the value in the string variable head to the beginning of the string Test:

```
string head = "str";
string test = "strVarName";
bool isFound = test.StartsWith(head, StringComparison.Ordinal);
```

The following example compares the value in the string variable tail to the end of the string test:

```
string tail = "Name";
string test = "strVarName";
bool isFound = test.EndsWith(tail, StringComparison.Ordinal);
```

In both examples, the isFound Boolean variable is set to true, since each string is found in test.

To do a case-insensitive comparison, employ the static string.Compare method. The following two examples modify the previous two examples by performing a case-insensitive comparison. The first is equivalent to a case-insensitive StartsWith string search:

```
string head = "str";
string test = "strVarName";
int location = string.Compare(head, 0, test, 0, head.Length, true,
                              System.Threading.Thread.CurrentThread.
    CurrentCulture);
```

The second is equivalent to a case-insensitive EndsWith string search:

```
string tail = "Name";
string test = "strVarName";
if (tail.Length <= test.Length)
{
    int location = string.Compare(tail, 0, test, (test.Length - tail.Length),
                              tail.Length, true);
}
else
{
    location = -1;
}
```

Note that with the last two examples that use the Compare method, if a zero is returned, then the search succeeded. If a -1 is returned, the search failed. The following code compares the value in the string variable head to the beginning of the string Test with case-sensitivity turned off:

```
string head = "str";
string test = "strVarName";
bool isFound = test.StartsWith(head, true,
                    System.Threading.Thread.CurrentThread.CurrentCulture);
```

The following example compares the value in the string variable `tail` to the end of the string `test`, also with case-sensitivity turned off:

```
string tail = "Name";
string test = "strVarName";
bool isFound = test.EndsWith(tail, true,
                    System.Threading.Thread.CurrentThread.CurrentCulture);
```

Discussion

Use the `StartsWith` or `EndsWith` instance methods to do a case-sensitive search for a particular string at the beginning or end of a string. The equivalent case-insensitive comparison requires the use the overloaded `StartsWith` and `EndsWith` instance methods that accept a Boolean value to turn off case-sensitivity.

See Also

The "String.StartsWith Method," "String.EndsWith Method," and "String.Compare Method" topics in the MSDN documentation.

2.6   Inserting Text into a String

Problem

You have some text (either a `char` or a `string` value) that needs to be inserted at a specific location inside of a second string.

Solution

Using the `Insert` instance method of the `String` class, a `string` or `char` can easily be inserted into a string. For example, in the code fragment:

```
string sourceString = "The Inserted Text is here ->><-";

sourceString = sourceString.Insert(28, "Insert-This");
Console.WriteLine(sourceString);
```

the string `sourceString` is inserted between the > and < characters in a second string. The result is:

```
The Inserted Text is here ->Insert-This<-
```

Inserting a single character into `sourceString` between the > and < characters is shown here:

```
string sourceString = "The Inserted Text is here ->><-";
char insertChar = '1';

sourceString = sourceString.Insert(28, Convert.ToString(insertChar));
Console.WriteLine(sourceString);
```

There is no overloaded method for Insert that takes a char value, so converting the char to a string of length one is the next best solution.

Discussion

There are two ways of inserting strings into other strings, unless, of course, you are using the regular expression classes. The first involves using the Insert instance method on the String class. This method is also slower than the others since strings are immutable, and, therefore, a new string object must be created to hold the modified value. In this recipe, the reference to the old string object is then changed to point to the new string object. Note that the Insert method leaves the original string untouched and creates a new string object with the inserted characters.

To add flexibility and speed to your string insertions, use the Insert instance method on the StringBuilder class. This method is overloaded to accept all of the built-in types. In addition, the StringBuilder object optimizes string insertion by operating on mutable arrays of characters, lists of immutable strings, and other techniques to defer the creation of new immutable strings until the last possible moment. This insertion will modify the state of the array of characters within the StringBuilder object.

If you use the StringBuilder class instead of the String class to insert a string, your code appears as:

```
StringBuilder sourceString =
  new StringBuilder("The Inserted Text is here ->c-");
sourceString.Insert (28, "Insert-This");
Console.WriteLine(sourceString);
```

The character insertion example changes to the following code:

```
char charToInsert = '1';
StringBuilder sourceString =
  new StringBuilder("The Inserted Text is here ->c-");
sourceString.Insert (28, charToInsert);
Console.WriteLine(sourceString);
```

Note that when using the StringBuilder class, you must also use the System.Text namespace or at least fully qualify the usage of the class in your code.

See Also

The "String.Insert Method" topic in the MSDN documentation.

2.7 Removing or Replacing Characters Within a String

Problem

You have some text within a string that needs to be either removed or replaced with a different character or string. Since the replacing operation is somewhat simple, using a regular expression to aid in the replacing operation is not worth the overhead.

Solution

To remove a substring from a string, use the Remove instance method on the String class. For example:

```
string name = "Doe, John";
name = name.Remove(3, 1);
Console.WriteLine(name);
```

This code creates a new string and then sets the name variable to refer to it. The string contained in name now looks like this:

```
Doe John
```

If performance is critical, and particularly if the string removal operation occurs in a loop so that the operation is performed multiple times, you can instead use the Remove method of the StringBuilder object. The following code modifies the internal state of the StringBuilder object that the str variable references so that its value becomes 12345678:

```
StringBuilder str = new StringBuilder("1234abc5678", 12);
str.Remove(4, 3);
Console.WriteLine(str);
```

To replace a delimiting character within a string, use the following code:

```
string commaDelimitedString = "100,200,300,400,500";
commaDelimitedString = commaDelimitedString.Replace(',', ':');
Console.WriteLine(commaDelimitedString);
```

This code creates a new string and then makes the commaDelimitedString variable refer to it. The string in commaDelimitedString now looks like this:

```
100:200:300:400:500
```

To replace a placeholding string within a string, use the following code:

```
string theName = "Mary";
string theObject = "car";
string ID = "This <ObjectPlaceholder> is the property of <NamePlaceholder>.";
ID = ID.Replace("<ObjectPlaceholder>", theObject);
ID = ID.Replace("<NamePlaceholder>", theName);
Console.WriteLine(ID);
```

This code creates a new string and then makes the ID variable refer to it. The string in ID now looks like this:

```
This car is the property of Mary.
```

As when removing a portion of a string, you may, for performance reasons, choose to use the Replace method of the StringBuilder class instead. For example:

```
string newName = "John Doe";

StringBuilder str = new StringBuilder("name = <NAME>");
str.Replace("<NAME>", newName);
Console.WriteLine(str.ToString());
str.Replace('=', ':');
Console.WriteLine(str.ToString());

str = new StringBuilder("name1 = <FIRSTNAME>, name2 = <FIRSTNAME>");
str.Replace("<FIRSTNAME>", newName, 7, 12);
Console.WriteLine(str.ToString());
str.Replace('=', ':', 0, 7);
Console.WriteLine(str.ToString());
```

This code produces the following results:

```
name = John Doe
name : John Doe
name1 = John Doe, name2 = <FIRSTNAME>
name1 : John Doe, name2 = <FIRSTNAME>
```

Note that when using the StringBuilder class, you must use the System.Text namespace.

Discussion

The String class provides two methods that allow easy removal and modification of characters in a string: the Remove instance method and the Replace instance method. The Remove method deletes a specified number of characters starting at a given location within a string. This method returns a new string object containing the modified string.

The Replace instance method that the String class provides is very useful for removing characters from a string and replacing them with a new character or string. At any point where the Replace method finds an instance of the string passed in as the first parameter, it will replace it with the string passed in as the second parameter. The Replace method is case-sensitive and returns a new string object containing the modified string. If the string being searched for cannot be found in the original string, the method returns a reference to the original string object.

The Replace and Remove methods on a string object always create a new string object that contains the modified text. If this action hurts performance, consider using the Replace and Remove methods on the StringBuilder class.

The `Remove` method of the `StringBuilder` class is not overloaded and is straightforward to use. Simply give it a starting position and the number of characters to remove. This method returns a reference to the same instance of the `StringBuilder` object with the `Replace` method that modified the string value.

The `Replace` method of the `StringBuilder` class allows for fast character or string replacement to be performed on the original `StringBuilder` object. These methods return a reference to the same instance of the `StringBuilder` object with the `Replace` method that was called. If you are performing a replace operation that uses a format string under your control, then you should use the `AppendFormat` method of the `StringBuilder` class.

Note that this method is case-sensitive.

See Also

The "String.Replace Method," "String.Remove Method," "StringBuilder.Replace Method," and "StringBuilder.Remove Method" topics in the MSDN documentation.

2.8   Encoding Binary Data As Base64

Problem

You have a byte[] representing some binary information, such as a bitmap. You need to encode this data into a string so that it can be sent over a binary-unfriendly transport, such as email.

Solution

Using the static method `Convert.ToBase64String` on the `Convert` class, a byte[] may be encoded to its `String` equivalent:

```
using System;
using System.IO;

static class CharStrExtMethods
{
    public static string Base64EncodeBytes(this byte[] inputBytes)
    {
        return (Convert.ToBase64String(inputBytes));
    }
}
```

Discussion

Converting a string into its base64 representation has several uses. It allows binary data to be embedded in nonbinary files such as XML, email messages, etc. Base64-encoded data can also be transmitted via HTTP, GET, and POST requests in a more compact format than hex encoding. It is important to understand that data that is converted to base64 format is only obfuscated, not encrypted. To securely move data from one place to another, you should use the cryptography algorithms available in the FCL. For an example of using the FCL cryptography classes, see Recipe 17.5.

The Convert class makes encoding between a byte[] and a String a simple matter. The parameters for this method are quite flexible. It provides the ability to start and stop the conversion at any point in the input byte array.

To encode a bitmap file into a string that can be sent to some destination, you can use the following code:

```
byte[] image = null;
using (FileStream fstrm = new FileStream(@"C:\WINNT\winnt.bmp",
                                FileMode.Open, FileAccess.Read))
{
    using (BinaryReader reader = new BinaryReader(fstrm))
    {
        image = new byte[reader.BaseStream.Length];
        for (int i = 0; i < reader.BaseStream.Length; i++)
        {
            image[i] = reader.ReadByte( );
        }
    }
}
string bmpAsString = image.Base64EncodeBytes( );
```

The MIME standard requires that each line of the base64-encoded string be 76 characters in length. In order to send the bmpAsString string as an embedded MIME attachment in an email message, you must insert a CRLF on each 76-character boundary.

To decode an encoded string to a byte[], see Recipe 2.9.

See Also

Recipe 2.9, and the "Convert.ToBase64CharArray Method" topic in the MSDN documentation.

2.9   Decoding a Base64-Encoded Binary

Problem

You have a String that contains information such as a bitmap encoded as base64. You need to decode this data (which may have been embedded in an email message) from a String into a byte[] so that you can access the original binary.

Solution

Using the static method Convert.FromBase64String on the Convert class, an encoded String may be decoded to its equivalent byte[]:

```
using System;

static class CharStrExtMethods
{
    public static byte[] Base64DecodeString(this string inputStr)
    {
        byte[] decodedByteArray =
          Convert.FromBase64String(inputStr);

      return (decodedByteArray);
    }
}
```

Discussion

The static FromBase64String method on the Convert class makes decoding an encoded base64 string a simple matter. This method returns a byte[] that contains the decoded elements of the String.

If you receive a file via email, such as an image file (*.bmp*), that has been converted to a string, you can convert it back into its original bitmap file using something like the following:

```
byte[] imageBytes = bmpAsString.Base64DecodeString();
using (FileStream fstrm = new FileStream(@"C:\winnt_copy.bmp",
                 FileMode.CreateNew, FileAccess.Write))
{
    using (BinaryWriter writer = new BinaryWriter(fstrm))
    {
        writer.Write(imageBytes);
    }
}
```

In this code, the bmpAsString variable was obtained from the code in the Discussion section of Recipe 2.10. The imageBytes byte[] is the bmpAsString String converted back to a byte[], which can then be written back to disk.

To encode a byte[] to a String, see Recipe 2.8.

See Also

Recipe 2.8, and the "Convert.FromBase64CharArray Method" topic in the MSDN documentation.

2.10 Converting a String Returned As a Byte[ ] Back into a String

Problem

Many methods in the FCL return a byte[] because they are providing a byte stream service, but some applications need to pass strings over these byte stream services. Some of these methods include:

```
System.Diagnostics.EventLogEntry.Data
System.IO.BinaryReader.Read
System.IO.BinaryReader.ReadBytes
System.IO.FileStream.Read
System.IO.FileStream.BeginRead
System.IO.MemoryStream // Constructor
System.IO.MemoryStream.Read
System.IO.MemoryStream.BeginRead
System.Net.Sockets.Socket.Receive
System.Net.Sockets.Socket.ReceiveFrom
System.Net.Sockets.Socket.BeginReceive
System.Net.Sockets.Socket.BeginReceiveFrom
System.Net.Sockets.NetworkStream.Read
System.Net.Sockets.NetworkStream.BeginRead
System.Security.Cryptography.CryptoStream.Read
System.Security.Cryptography.CryptoStream.BeginRead
```

In many cases, this byte[] might contain ASCII- or Unicode-encoded characters. You need a way to recombine this byte[] to obtain the original string.

Solution

To convert a byte array of ASCII values to a complete string, use the following method:

```
string constructedString = Encoding.ASCII.GetString(characters);
```

To convert a byte array of Unicode values to a complete string, use the following method:

```
string constructedString = Encoding.Unicode.GetString(characters);
```

Discussion

The GetString method of the Encoding class (returned by the ASCII property) converts 7-bit ASCII characters contained in a byte array to a string. Any value larger than 127 (0x7F) will be ANDed with the value 127 (0x7F), and the resulting character value will be displayed in the string. For example, if the byte[] contains the value 200 (0xC8), this value will be converted to 72 (0x48), and the character equivalent of 72 (0x48), ('H'), will be displayed. The Encoding class can be found in the System. Text namespace. The GetString method is overloaded to accept additional arguments as well. The overloaded versions of the method convert all or part of a string to ASCII and then store the result in a specified range inside a byte[].

The GetString method returns a string containing the converted byte[] of ASCII characters.

The GetString method of the Encoding class (returned by the Unicode property) converts Unicode characters into 16-bit Unicode values. The Encoding class can be found in the System.Text namespace. The GetString method returns a string containing the converted byte[] of Unicode characters.

See Also

The "ASCIIEncoding Class" and "UnicodeEncoding Class" topics in the MSDN documentation.

2.11 Passing a String to a Method That Accepts Only a Byte[ ]

Problem

Many methods in the FCL accept a byte[] consisting of characters instead of a string. Some of these methods include:

```
System.Diagnostics.EventLog.WriteEntry
System.IO.BinaryWriter.Write
System.IO.FileStream.Write
System.IO.FileStream.BeginWrite
System.IO.MemoryStream.Write
System.IO.MemoryStream.BeginWrite
System.Net.Sockets.Socket.Send
System.Net.Sockets.Socket.SendTo
System.Net.Sockets.Socket.BeginSend
System.Net.Sockets.Socket.BeginSendTo
System.Net.Sockets.NetworkStream.Write
System.Net.Sockets.NetworkStream.BeginWrite
System.Security.Cryptography.CryptoStream.Write
System.Security.Cryptography.CryptoStream.BeginWrite
```

In many cases, you might have a string that you need to pass into one of these methods or some other method that accepts only a byte[]. You need a way to break up this string into a byte[].

Solution

To convert a string to a byte[] of ASCII values, use the GetBytes method on the Encoding class:

```
byte[] retArray = Encoding.ASCII.GetBytes(characters);
```

To convert a string to a byte[] of Unicode values, use the GetBytes method on the Encoding class:

```
byte[] retArray = Encoding.Unicode.GetBytes(characters);
```

Discussion

The GetBytes method of the Encoding class (returned by the ASCII property) converts ASCII characters—contained in either a char[] or a string—into a byte[] of 7-bit ASCII values. Any value larger than 127 (0x7F) is converted to the ? character. The Encoding class can be found in the System.Text namespace. The GetBytes method is overloaded to accept additional arguments as well. The overloaded versions of the method convert all or part of a string to ASCII and then store the result in a specified range inside a byte[], which is returned to the caller.

The GetBytes method of the Encoding class (returned by the Unicode property) converts Unicode characters into 16-bit Unicode values. The Encoding class can be found in the System.Text namespace. The GetBytes method returns a byte[], each element of which contains the Unicode value of a single character of the string.

A single Unicode character in the source string or in the source char[] corresponds to two elements of the byte[]. For example, the following byte[] contains the ASCII value of the letter *S*:

```
byte[] sourceArray = {83};
```

However, for a byte[] to contain a Unicode representation of the letter *S*, it must contain two elements. For example:

```
byte[] sourceArray = {83, 0};
```

The Intel architecture uses a little-endian encoding, which means that the first element is the least-significant byte, and the second element is the most-significant byte. Other architectures may use big-endian encoding, which is the opposite of little-endian encoding. The UnicodeEncoding class supports both big-endian and little-endian encodings. Using the UnicodeEncoding instance constructor, you can construct an instance that uses either big-endian or little-endian ordering. This is accomplished by using one of the two following constructors:

```
public UnicodeEncoding (bool bigEndian, bool byteOrderMark);
public UnicodeEncoding (bool bigEndian, bool byteOrderMark,
                        bool throwOnInvalidBytes);
```

The first parameter, bigEndian, accepts a Boolean argument. Set this argument to true to use big-endian or false to use little-endian.

In addition, you have the option to indicate whether a byte order mark preamble should be generated so that readers of the file will know which endianness is in use.

See Also

The "ASCIIEncoding Class" and "UnicodeEncoding Class" topics in the MSDN documentation.

2.12   Converting Strings to Other Types

Problem

You have a string that represents the equivalent value of a number ("12"), char ("a"), bool ("true"), or a color enumeration ("Red"). You need to convert this string to its equivalent value type. Therefore, the number "12" would be converted to a numeric value such as int, short, float, and so on. The string "a" would be converted to a char value 'a', the string "true" would be converted to a bool value, and the color "Red" could be converted to an enumeration value (if an enumeration were defined that contained the element Red).

Solution

Use the Parse static method of the type that the string is to be converted to. To convert a string containing a number to its numeric type, use the following code:

```
// This code requires the use of the System and System.Globalization namespaces.

string longString = "7654321";
int actualInt = Int32.Parse(longString);     // longString = 7654321
string dblString = "-7654.321";
double actualDbl = Double.Parse(dblString, NumberStyles.AllowDecimalPoint |
        NumberStyles.AllowLeadingSign);       // dblString = "-7654.321"
```

To convert a string containing a Boolean value to a bool type, use the following code:

```
// This code requires the use of the System namespace.

string boolString = "true";
bool actualBool = Boolean.Parse(boolString);     // actualBool = true
```

To convert a string containing a char value to a char type, use the following code:

```
// This code requires the use of the System namespace.

string charString = "t";
char actualChar = char.Parse(charString);     // actualChar = 't'
```

To convert a string containing an enumeration value to an enumeration type, use the following code:

```
// This code requires the use of the System namespace.

enum Colors
{
    red, green, blue
}
```

```
string colorString = "blue";
// Note that the Parse method below is a method defined by System.Enum,
// not by Colors.
Colors actualEnum = (Colors)Colors.Parse(typeof(Colors), colorString);
// actualEnum = blue
```

Discussion

The static Parse method available on certain data types allows easy conversion from a string value to the value of that specific value type. The Parse method is supported by the types listed in Table 2-4.

Table 2-4. Data types that support the Parse method

Boolean	Int16	Single
Byte	Int32	UInt16
Decimal	Int64	UInt32
Double	SByte	UInt64

Notice that these types are all value types; other types, such as IPAddress, also support the Parse method. In addition to the Parse methods that take a single string parameter and convert it to the target data type, each numeric type has a second overloaded version of the Parse method that includes a second parameter of type System.Globalization.NumberStyles. This allows the Parse method to correctly handle specific properties of numbers, such as leading or trailing signs, decimal points, currency symbols, thousands separators, and so forth. NumberStyles is marked as a flag-style enumeration, so you can bitwise OR more than one enumerated value together to allow a group of styles to be used on the string.

The NumberStyles enumeration is defined as follows:

AllowCurrencySymbol
> If the string contains a number with a currency symbol, it is parsed as currency; otherwise, it is parsed as a number.

AllowDecimalPoint
> Allows a decimal point in the number.

AllowExponent
> Allows the number to be in exponential notation format.

AllowHexSpecifier
> Allows characters that specify a hexadecimal number.

AllowLeadingSign
> Allows a leading sign symbol.

AllowLeadingWhite
> Ignores any leading whitespace.

AllowParentheses
> Allows parentheses.

AllowThousands
> Allows group separators.

AllowTrailingSign
> Allows a trailing sign symbol.

AllowTrailingWhite
> Ignores any trailing whitespace.

Any
> Applies any of the previous styles. This style simply ORs together all of the preceding styles.

Currency
> Same as the All style, except that the AllowExponent style is omitted.

Float
> Equivalent to AllowLeadingWhite, AllowTrailingWhite, AllowLeadingSign, Allow-DecimalPoint, and AllowExponent.

HexNumber
> Equivalent to AllowLeadingWhite, AllowTrailingWhite, and AllowHexSpecifier.

Integer
> Equivalent to AllowLeadingWhite, AllowTrailingWhite, and AllowLeadingSign.

None
> Applies none of the styles.

Number
> Equivalent to AllowLeadingWhite, AllowTrailingWhite, AllowLeadingSign, Allow-TrailingSign, AllowDecimalPoint, and AllowThousands.

If the NumberStyle parameter is not supplied when it is required (as when, for example, a numeric string includes a thousands separator) or if the NumberStyle enumeration is used on a string that does not contain a number in the supplied NumberStyle format, a FormatException exception will be thrown. If the size of the number in the string is too large or too small for the data type, an OverFlowException exception will be thrown. Passing in a null for the SourceString parameter will throw an ArgumentNullException exception.

The Parse method of the two non-numeric data types, bool and char, also deserve some additional explanation. When calling Boolean.Parse, if a string value contains anything except a value equal to the static properties Boolean.FalseString, Boolean.TrueString, or the string literals "false" or "true" (which are case-insensitive), a FormatException exception is thrown. Passing in a null for the SourceString parameter throws an ArgumentNullException exception.

When invoking char.Parse, if a string value containing more than one character is passed as its single argument, a FormatException exception is thrown. Passing in a null for the string parameter throws an ArgumentNullException exception.

The static Enum.Parse method returns an Object of the same type as specified in the first parameter of this method (EnumType). This value is viewed as an Object type and must be cast to its correct enumeration type.

This method throws an ArgumentException exception if the *Value* parameter cannot be matched to a string in the enumeration. An ArgumentNullException exception is thrown if a null is passed in to the Value parameter.

If you do not want an exception to be thrown while attempting to convert a string to a particular type, consider using the TryParse method in types in which it is available. This method will not throw an exception if the conversion fails. Instead, it returns a Boolean true if the conversion succeeds and a false if the conversion fails.

2.13   Creating a Delimited String

Problem

You have an array of strings to format as delimited text and possibly to store in a text file.

Solution

Using the static Join method of the String class, the array of strings can be easily joined in as little as one line of code. For example:

```
string[] infoArray = {"11", "12", "Checking", "111", "Savings"};
string delimitedInfo = string.Join(",", infoArray);
```

This code sets the value of delimitedInfo to the following:

```
11,12,Checking,111,Savings
```

Discussion

The Join method concatenates all the strings contained in a string array. Additionally, a specified delimiting character(s) is inserted between each string in the array. This method returns a single string object with the fully joined and delimited text.

Unlike the Split method of the String class, the Join method accepts only one delimiting character at a time. In order to use multiple delimiting characters within a string of values, subsequent Join operations must be performed on the information until all of the data has been joined together into a single string. For example:

```
string[] infoArray = {"11", "12", "Checking", "Savings"};
string delimitedInfoBegin = string.Join(",", infoArray, 0, 2);
string delimitedInfoEnd = string.Join(",", infoArray, 2, 2);
```

```
string[] delimitedInfoTotal = {delimitedInfoBegin,
        delimitedInfoEnd};
string delimitedInfoFinal = string.Join(":", delimitedInfoTotal);
Console.WriteLine(delimitedInfoFinal);
```

produces the following delimited string:

```
11,12:Checking,Savings
```

See Also

The "String.Join Method" topic in the MSDN documentation.

2.14 Extracting Items from a Delimited String

Problem

You have a string, possibly from a text file, which is delimited by one or more characters. You need to retrieve each piece of delimited information as easily as possible.

Solution

Using the Split instance method on the String class, you can place the delimited
information into an array in as little as a single line of code. For example:

```
string delimitedInfo = "100,200,400,3,67";
string[] discreteInfo = delimitedInfo.Split(new char[] {','});

foreach (string Data in discreteInfo)
Console.WriteLine(Data);
```

The string array discreteInfo holds the following values:

```
100
200
400
3
67
```

Discussion

The Split method returns a string array with each element containing one discrete
piece of the delimited text split on the delimiting character(s).

In the solution, the string delimitedInfo is comma-delimited. However, it can be
delimited by any type of character or even by more than one character. When there is
more than one type of delimiter, use code like the following:

```
string[] discreteInfo = delimitedInfo.Split(new char[] {',', ':', ' '});
```

This line splits the delimitedInfo string whenever one of the three delimiting characters (comma, colon, or space character) is found.

The Split method is case-sensitive. To split a string on the letter *a* in a case-insensitive manner, use code like the following:

```
string[] discreteInfo = delimitedInfo.Split(new char[] {'a', 'A'});
```

Now, anytime the letter *a* is encountered, no matter what its case, the Split method views that character as a delimiter.

See Also

The "String.Join Method" topic in the MSDN documentation.

2.15   Iterating over Each Character in a String

Problem

You need to iterate over each character in a string efficiently in order to examine or process each character.

Solution

C# provides two methods for iterating strings. The first is the foreach loop, which can be used as follows:

```
string testStr = "abc123";
foreach (char c in testStr)
{
    Console.WriteLine(c.ToString());
}
```

This method is quick and easy. Unfortunately, it is somewhat less flexible than the second method, which uses the for loop instead of a foreach loop to iterate over the string. For example:

```
string testStr = "abc123";
for (int counter = 0; counter < testStr.Length; counter++)
{
    Console.WriteLine(testStr[counter]);
}
```

Discussion

The foreach loop is simpler and thus less error-prone, but it lacks flexibility. In contrast, the for loop is slightly more complex, but it makes up for that in flexibility.

The for loop method uses the indexer of the string variable testStr to get the character located at the position indicated by the counter loop index. Care must be taken not to run over the bounds of the string array when using this type of looping mechanism.

A for loop is flexible enough to change how looping over characters in a string is performed. For example, the loop can be quickly modified to start and end at a specific point in the string by simply changing the *initializer* and *conditional* expressions of the for loop. Characters can be skipped by changing the *iterator* expression to increment the counter variable by more than one. The string can also be iterated in reverse order by changing the for loop expressions, as shown:

```
for (int counter = testStr.Length - 1; counter >= 0; counter--)
{
    Console.WriteLine(testStr[counter].ToString());
}
```

 The compiler optimizes the use of a foreach loop iterating through a *vector array*—one that starts at zero and has only one dimension. Converting a foreach loop to another type of loop, such as a for loop, may not produce any noticeable increases in performance.

It should be noted that each of these methods was compiled using the /optimize compiler option. Use of the /optimize flag will typically make the size of the compiled code smaller, not faster. The smaller the code, the faster it can load from disk and the faster that it can be jitted.

2.16 Pruning Characters from the Head and/or Tail of a String

Problem

You have a string with a specific set of characters, such as spaces, tabs, escaped single/double quotes, any type of punctuation character(s), or some other character(s), at the beginning and/or end of a string. You want a simple way to remove these characters.

Solution

Use the Trim, TrimEnd, or TrimStart instance methods of the String class:

```
string foo = "--TEST--";
Console.WriteLine(foo.Trim(new char[] {'-'}));              // Displays "TEST"

foo = ",-TEST-,-";
Console.WriteLine(foo.Trim(new char[] {'-',','}));          // Displays "TEST"

foo = "--TEST--";
Console.WriteLine(foo.TrimStart(new char[] {'-'}));         // Displays "TEST--"

foo = ",-TEST-,-";
Console.WriteLine(foo.TrimStart(new char[] {'-',','}));     // Displays "TEST-,-"
```

```
foo = "--TEST--";
Console.WriteLine(foo.TrimEnd(new char[] {'-'}));          // Displays "--TEST"

foo = ",-TEST-,-";
Console.WriteLine(foo.TrimEnd(new char[] {'-',','}));      //Displays ",-TEST"
```

Discussion

The `Trim` method is most often used to eliminate whitespace at the beginning and end of a string. In fact, if you call `Trim` without any parameters on a string variable, this is exactly what happens. The `Trim` method is overloaded to allow you to remove other types of characters from the beginning and end of a string. You can pass in a `char[]` containing all the characters that you want removed from the beginning and end of a string. Note that if the characters contained in this `char[]` are located somewhere in the middle of the string, they are not removed.

The `TrimStart` and `TrimEnd` methods remove characters at the beginning and end of a string, respectively. These two methods are not overloaded, unlike the `Trim` method. Rather, these two methods accept only a `char[]`. If you pass a `null` into either one of these methods, only whitespace is removed from the beginning or the end of a string.

See Also

The "String.Trim Method," "String.TrimStart Method," and "String.TrimEnd Method" topics in the MSDN documentation.

2.17   Testing a String for Null or Empty

Problem

You need a quick and easy way to check if a string is either `null` or of zero length.

Solution

Use the static `IsNullOrEmpty` method of the `String` class:

```
bool stringTestResult = String.IsNullOrEmpty(testString);
```

Discussion

The `IsNullOrEmpty` method is a very convenient method in that it allows you to test a string for `null` or zero length with a single method call. This method returns `true` if the string passed in to it is equal to one of the following:

- `Null`
- `String.Empty`

Otherwise, this method returns `false`.

See Also

The "String.IsNullOrEmpty Method" topic in the MSDN documentation.

2.18 Appending a Line

Problem

You need to append a line, including a line terminator, to the current string.

Solution

Use the `AppendLine` method of the `StringBuilder` class:

```
StringBuilder sb = new StringBuilder("First line of string");

// Terminate the first line.
sb.AppendLine();

// Add a second line.
sb.AppendLine("Second line of string");
```

This code will display the following:

```
First line of string
Second line of string
```

Discussion

The `AppendLine` method accepts a string and returns a reference to the same instance of the `StringBuilder` object on which this method was called. The string that is passed in to this method has a newline character or characters automatically appended on to the end of this string. The newline character(s) is dependent on the type of platform you are running. For example, Windows uses the \r\n carriage return and line-feed characters to represent a newline; on a Unix system, the newline consists of only the line-feed character \n. You do not need to worry about this, as the `AppendLine` method knows which newline character(s) to apply.

If you simply want to add several blank lines to your string, you can call `AppendLine` with no parameters. This effectively adds only a newline character to the current string in the `StringBuilder` object on which it was called. Calling this method with no parameter can also be used to add a newline character(s) to the current line, if the current line has no newline character(s). For example, the code in the Solution added a string with no newline character(s) to the instantiated `StringBuilder` object sb. You can then call sb.AppendLine() to force a newline character to be appended to this text.

See Also

The "StringBuilder.AppendLine Method" topic in the MSDN documentation.

CHAPTER 3

Classes and Structures

3.0   Introduction

Structures, like any other value type, implicitly inherit from System.ValueType. At first glance, a structure is similar to a class, but it is actually very different. Knowing when to use a structure over a class will help tremendously when designing an application. Using a structure incorrectly can result in inefficient and hard-to-modify code.

Structures have two performance advantages over reference types. First, if a structure is allocated on the stack (i.e., it is not contained within a reference type), access to the structure and its data is somewhat faster than access to a reference type on the heap. Reference-type objects must follow their reference onto the heap in order to get at their data. However, this performance advantage pales in comparison to the second performance advantage of structures; namely, that cleaning up the memory allocated to a structure on the stack requires a simple change of the address to which the stack pointer points, which is done at the return of a method call. This call is extremely fast compared to allowing the garbage collector to automatically clean up reference types for you in the managed heap; however, the cost of the garbage collector is deferred so that it's not immediately noticeable.

The performance of structures falls short in comparison to that of classes when they are passed by value to other methods. Because they reside on the stack, a structure and its data have to be copied to a new local variable (the method's parameter that is used to receive the structure) when it is passed by value to a method. This copying takes more time than passing a method a single reference to an object—unless the structure is the same size as or smaller than the machine's pointer size; thus, a structure with a size of 32 bits is just as cheap to pass as a reference (which happens to be the size of a pointer) on a 32-bit machine. Keep this in mind when choosing between a class and a structure. While creating, accessing, and destroying a class's object may take longer, it also might not balance the performance hit when a structure is passed by value a large number of times to one or more methods. Keeping the size of the structure small minimizes the performance hit of passing it around by value.

Concerning the object-oriented capabilities of classes and structures, classes have far more flexibility. A structure cannot contain a user-defined default constructor, since the C# compiler automatically provides a default constructor that initializes all the fields in the structure to their default values. This is also why no field initializers can be added to a structure. If you need to override the default field values, a structure might not be the way to go. However, a parameterized constructor that initializes the structure's fields to any value that is necessary can be created.

Structures, like classes, can implement interfaces, but unlike classes, structures cannot inherit from a class or a structure. This limitation precludes creating structure hierarchies, as you can do with classes. Polymorphism, as implemented through an abstract base class, is also prohibited when using a structure, since a structure cannot inherit from another class with the exception of boxing to Object, ValueType, or Enum.

Use a class if:

- Its identity is important. Structures get copied implicitly when being passed by value into a method.
- It will have a large memory footprint.
- Its fields need initializers.
- You need to inherit from a base class.
- You need polymorphic behavior. That is, you need to implement an abstract base class from which you will create several similar classes that inherit from this abstract base class. (Note that polymorphism can be implemented via interfaces as well, but it is usually not a good idea to place an interface on a value type, since a boxing operation will occur if the structure is converted to the interface type.) For more on polymorphism through interfaces, see Recipe 3.15.

Use a structure if:

- It will act like a primitive type (int, long, byte, etc.).
- It must have a small memory footprint.
- You are calling a P/Invoke method that requires a structure to be passed in by value. *Platform Invoke*, or P/Invoke for short, allows managed code to call out to an unmanaged method exposed from within a DLL. Many times, an unmanaged DLL method requires a structure to be passed in to it; using a structure is an efficient method of doing this and is the only way if the structure is being passed by value.
- You need to avoid the overhead of garbage collection.
- Its fields need to be initialized only to their default values. This value would be zero for numeric types, false for Boolean types, and null for reference types.

- You do not need to inherit from a base class (other than ValueType, from which all structs inherit).
- You do not need polymorphic behavior.

Structures can also cause degradation in performance when they are passed to methods that require an object, such as any of the nongeneric collection types in the Framework Class Library (FCL). Passing a structure (or any simple type, for that matter) into a method requiring an object causes the structure to be boxed. *Boxing* is wrapping a value type in an object. This operation is time-consuming and may degrade performance.

3.1   Creating Union-Type Structures

Problem

You need to create a data type that behaves like a union type in C++. A union type is useful mainly in interop scenarios in which the unmanaged code accepts and/or returns a union type; we suggest that you do not use it in other situations.

Solution

Use a structure and mark it with the StructLayout attribute (specifying the LayoutKind.Explicit layout kind in the constructor). In addition, mark each field in the structure with the FieldOffset attribute. The following structure defines a union in which a single signed numeric value can be stored:

```
using System.Runtime.InteropServices;
[StructLayoutAttribute(LayoutKind.Explicit)]
struct SignedNumber
{
   [FieldOffsetAttribute(0)]
   public sbyte Num1;
   [FieldOffsetAttribute(0)]
   public short Num2;
   [FieldOffsetAttribute(0)]
   public int Num3;
   [FieldOffsetAttribute(0)]
   public long Num4;
   [FieldOffsetAttribute(0)]
   public float Num5;
   [FieldOffsetAttribute(0)]
   public double Num6;
   [FieldOffsetAttribute(0)]
   public decimal Num7;
}
```

The next structure is similar to the SignedNumber structure, except that it can contain a String type in addition to the signed numeric value:

```
[StructLayoutAttribute(LayoutKind.Explicit)]
struct SignedNumberWithText
{
    [FieldOffsetAttribute(0)]
    public sbyte Num1;
    [FieldOffsetAttribute(0)]
    public short Num2;
    [FieldOffsetAttribute(0)]
    public int Num3;
    [FieldOffsetAttribute(0)]
    public long Num4;
    [FieldOffsetAttribute(0)]
    public float Num5;
    [FieldOffsetAttribute(0)]
    public double Num6;
    [FieldOffsetAttribute(0)]
    public decimal Num7;
    [FieldOffsetAttribute(16)]
    public string Text1;
}
```

Discussion

Unions are structures usually found in C++ code; however, there is a way to duplicate that type of structure using a C# structure data type. A *union* is a structure that
accepts more than one type at a specific location in memory for that structure. For
example, the SignedNumber structure is a union-type structure built using a C# structure. This structure accepts any type of signed numeric type (sbyte, int, long, etc.),
but it accepts this numeric type at only one location, or offset, within the structure.

 Since StructLayoutAttribute can be applied to both structures and
classes, a class can also be used when creating a union data type.

Notice the FieldOffsetAttribute has the value zero passed to its constructor. This
denotes that this field will be offset by zero bytes from the beginning of the structure. This attribute is used in tandem with the StructLayoutAttribute to manually
enforce where the fields in this structure will start (that is, the offset from the beginning of this structure in memory where each field will start). The
FieldOffsetAttribute can be used only with a StructLayoutAttribute set to
LayoutKind.Explicit. In addition, it cannot be used on static members within this
structure.

Unions can become problematic, since several types are essentially laid on top of one
another. The biggest problem is extracting the correct data type from a union structure. Consider what happens if you choose to store the long numeric value long.
MaxValue in the SignedNumber structure. Later, you might accidentally attempt to

extract a byte data type value from this same structure. In doing so, you will get back only the first byte of the long value.

Another problem is starting fields at the correct offset. The SignedNumberWithText union overlays numerous signed numeric data types at the zeroth offset. The last field in this structure is laid out at the 16th byte offset from the beginning of this structure in memory. If you accidentally overlay the string field Text1 on top of any of the other signed numeric data types, you will get an exception at runtime. The basic rule is that you are allowed to overlay a value type on another value type, but you cannot overlay a reference type over a value type. If the Text1 field is marked with the following attribute:

```
[FieldOffsetAttribute(14)]
```

this exception is thrown at runtime (note that the compiler does not catch this problem):

```
An unhandled exception of type 'System.TypeLoadException' occurred in
Chapter_Code.exe.

Additional information: Could not load type Chapter_Code.SignedNumberWithText
from
    assembly 14 because it contains an object field at offset 14 that is incorrectly
    aligned or overlapped by a non-object field.
```

It is imperative to get the offsets correct when using complex unions in C#.

See Also

The "StructLayoutAttribute Class" topic in the MSDN documentation.

3.2   Making a Type Sortable

Problem

You have a data type that will be stored as elements in a List<T> or a SortedList<K,V>. You would like to use the List<T>.Sort method or the internal sorting mechanism of SortedList<K,V> to allow custom sorting of your data types in the array. In addition, you may need to use this type in a SortedList collection.

Solution

Example 3-1 demonstrates how to implement the IComparable<T> interface. The Square class shown in Example 3-1 implements this interface in such a way that the List<T> and SortedList<K,V> collections can sort and search for these Square objects.

Example 3-1. Making a type sortable by implementing IComparable<T>

```
public class Square : IComparable<Square>
{
    public Square( ){}

    public Square(int height, int width)
    {
        this.Height = height;
        this.Width = width;
    }

    public int Height { get; set; }

    public int Width { get; set; }

    public int CompareTo(object obj)
    {
        Square square = obj as Square;
        if (square != null)
            return CompareTo(square);
        throw
         new ArgumentException("Both objects being compared must be of type Square.");
    }

    public override string ToString( )
    {
        return ("Height:" + this.Height + "  Width:" + this.Width);
    }

    public override bool Equals(object obj)
    {
         if (obj == null)
            return false;

        Square square = obj as Square;
        if(square != null)
            return this.Height == square.Height;
        return false;
    }

    public override int GetHashCode( )
    {
         return this.Height.GetHashCode( ) | this.Width.GetHashCode( );
    }

    public static bool operator ==(Square x, Square y)
    {
        return x.Equals(y);
    }
    public static bool operator !=(Square x, Square y)
    {
        return !(x == y);
    }
```

Example 3-1. Making a type sortable by implementing IComparable<T> (continued)

```csharp
    public static bool operator <(Square x, Square y)
    {
        return (x.CompareTo(y) < 0);
    }
    public static bool operator >(Square x, Square y)
    {
        return (x.CompareTo(y) > 0);
    }

    #region IComparable<Square> Members

    public int CompareTo(Square other)
    {
        long area1 = this.Height * this.Width;
        long area2 = other.Height * other.Width;

        if (area1 == area2)
            return 0;
        else if (area1 > area2)
            return 1;
        else if (area1 < area2)
            return -1;
        else
            return -1;
    }

    #endregion
}
```

Discussion

By implementing the IComparable<T> interface on your class (or structure), you can take advantage of the sorting routines of the List<T>, and SortedList<K,V> classes. The algorithms for sorting are built into these classes; all you have to do is tell them how to sort your classes via the code you implement in the IComparable<T>.CompareTo method.

When a list of Square objects is sorted by calling the List<Square>.Sort method, the list is sorted using the IComparable<Square> interface of the Square objects. The Add method of the SortedList<K,V> class uses this interface to sort the objects as they are being added to the SortedList<K,V>.

IComparer<T> is designed to solve the problem of allowing objects to be sorted based on different criteria in different contexts. This interface also allows you to sort types that you did not write. If you also wanted to sort the Square objects by height, you could create a new class called CompareHeight, shown in Example 3-2, which would also implement the IComparer<Square> interface.

Example 3-2. Making a type sortable by implementing IComparer

```
public class CompareHeight : IComparer<Square>
{
    public int Compare(object firstSquare, object secondSquare)
    {
        Square square1 = firstSquare as Square;
        Square square2 = secondSquare as Square;
        if (square1 == null || square2 == null)
            throw (new ArgumentException("Both parameters must be of type Square."));
        else
            return Compare(firstSquare,secondSquare);
    }

    #region IComparer<Square> Members

    public int Compare(Square x, Square y)
    {
        if (x.Height == y.Height)
            return 0;
        else if (x.Height > y.Height)
            return 1;
        else if (x.Height < y.Height)
            return -1;
        else
            return -1;
    }

    #endregion
}
```

This class is then passed in to the IComparer parameter of the Sort routine. Now you can specify different ways to sort your Square objects. The comparison method implemented in the comparer must be **consistent** and apply a total ordering so that when the comparison function declares equality for two items, it is absolutely true and not a result of one item not being greater than another or one item not being less than another.

 For best performance, keep the CompareTo method short and efficient, because it will be called multiple times by the Sort methods. For example, in sorting an array with four items, the Compare method is called 10 times.

The TestSort method shown in Example 3-3 demonstrates how to use the Square and CompareHeight classes with the List<Square> and SortedList<int,Square> instances.

Example 3-3. TestSort method

```
public static void TestSort()
{
    List<Square> listOfSquares = new List<Square>(){
                              new Square(1,3),
                              new Square(4,3),
                              new Square(2,1),
                              new Square(6,1)};

    // Test a List<String>
    Console.WriteLine("List<String>");
    Console.WriteLine("Original list");
    foreach (Square square in listOfSquares)
    {
        Console.WriteLine(square.ToString());
    }


    Console.WriteLine();
    IComparer<Square> heightCompare = new CompareHeight();
    listOfSquares.Sort(heightCompare);
    Console.WriteLine("Sorted list using IComparer<Square>=heightCompare");
    foreach (Square square in listOfSquares)
    {
        Console.WriteLine(square.ToString());
    }

    Console.WriteLine();
    Console.WriteLine("Sorted list using IComparable<Square>");
    listOfSquares.Sort();
    foreach (Square square in listOfSquares)
    {
        Console.WriteLine(square.ToString());
    }


    // Test a SORTEDLIST
    var sortedListOfSquares = new SortedList<int,Square>(){
                           { 0, new Square(1,3)},
                           { 2, new Square(3,3)},
                           { 1, new Square(2,1)},
                           { 3, new Square(6,1)}};

    Console.WriteLine();
    Console.WriteLine();
    Console.WriteLine("SortedList<Square>");
    foreach (KeyValuePair<int,Square> kvp in sortedListOfSquares)
    {
        Console.WriteLine(kvp.Key + " : " + kvp.Value);
    }
}
```

This code displays the following output:

```
List<String>
Original list
Height:1  Width:3
Height:4  Width:3
Height:2  Width:1
Height:6  Width:1

Sorted list using IComparer<Square>=heightCompare
Height:1  Width:3
Height:2  Width:1
Height:4  Width:3
Height:6  Width:1

Sorted list using IComparable<Square>
Height:2  Width:1
Height:1  Width:3
Height:6  Width:1
Height:4  Width:3


SortedList<Square>
0 : Height:1  Width:3
1 : Height:2  Width:1
2 : Height:3  Width:3
3 : Height:6  Width:1
```

See Also

Recipe 3.3, and the "IComparable<T> Interface" topic in the MSDN documentation.

3.3   Making a Type Searchable

Problem

You have a data type that will be stored as elements in a List<T>. You would like to use the BinarySearch method to allow for custom searching of your data types in the list.

Solution

Use the IComparable<T> and IComparer<T> interfaces. The Square class, from Recipe 3.1, implements the IComparable<T> interface in such a way that the List<T> and SortedList<K,V> collections can sort and search an array or collection of Square objects.

Discussion

By implementing the IComparable<T> interface on your class (or structure), you can take advantage of the search routines of the List<T> and SortedList<K,V> classes. The algorithms for searching are built into these classes; all you have to do is tell them how to search your classes via the code you implement in the IComparable<T>. CompareTo method.

To implement the CompareTo method, see Recipe 3.2.

The List<T> class provides a BinarySearch method to perform a search on the elements in that list. The elements are compared against an object passed to the BinarySearch method in the object parameter. The SortedList class does not have a BinarySearch method; instead, it has the ContainsKey method, which performs a binary search on the key contained in the list. The ContainsValue method of the SortedList class performs a linear search when searching for values. This linear search uses the Equals method of the elements in the SortedList collection to do its work. The Compare and CompareTo methods do not have any effect on the operation of the linear search performed in the SortedList class, but they do have an effect on binary searches.

> To perform an accurate search using the BinarySearch methods of the List<T> class, you must first sort the List<T> using its Sort method. In addition, if you pass an IComparer<T> interface to the BinarySearch method, you must also pass the same interface to the Sort method. Otherwise, the BinarySearch method might not be able to find the object you are looking for.

The TestSort method shown in Example 3-4 demonstrates how to use the Square and CompareHeight classes with the List<Square> and SortedList<int,Square> collection instances.

Example 3-4. Making a type searchable

```
public static void TestSearch( )
{
    List<Square> listOfSquares = new List<Square> {new Square(1,3),
                                                    new Square(4,3),
                                                    new Square(2,1),
                                                    new Square(6,1)};

    IComparer<Square> heightCompare = new CompareHeight( );

    // Test a List<Square>
    Console.WriteLine("List<Square>");
    Console.WriteLine("Original list");
    foreach (Square square in listOfSquares)
    {
        Console.WriteLine(square.ToString( ));
    }
```

Example 3-4. Making a type searchable (continued)

```
Console.WriteLine();
Console.WriteLine("Sorted list using IComparer<Square>=heightCompare");
listOfSquares.Sort(heightCompare);
foreach (Square square in listOfSquares)
{
    Console.WriteLine(square.ToString());
}

Console.WriteLine();
Console.WriteLine("Search using IComparer<Square>=heightCompare");
int found = listOfSquares.BinarySearch(new Square(1,3), heightCompare);
Console.WriteLine("Found (1,3): " + found);

Console.WriteLine();
Console.WriteLine("Sorted list using IComparable<Square>");
listOfSquares.Sort();
foreach (Square square in listOfSquares)
{
    Console.WriteLine(square.ToString());
}

Console.WriteLine("Search using IComparable<Square>");
found = listOfSquares.BinarySearch(new Square(6,1));  // Use IComparable
Console.WriteLine("Found (6,1): " + found);


// Test a SortedList<Square>
var sortedListOfSquares = new SortedList<int,Square>(){
                          {0, new Square(1,3)},
                          {2, new Square(4,3)},
                          {1, new Square(2,1)},
                          {4, new Square(6,1)}};

Console.WriteLine();
Console.WriteLine();
Console.WriteLine("SortedList<Square>");
foreach (KeyValuePair<int,Square> kvp in sortedListOfSquares)
{
    Console.WriteLine(kvp.Key + " : " + kvp.Value);
}

Console.WriteLine();
bool foundItem = sortedListOfSquares.ContainsKey(2);
Console.WriteLine("sortedListOfSquares.ContainsKey(2): " + foundItem);

// Does not use IComparer or IComparable
// -- uses a linear search along with the Equals method
//    which has not been overloaded
Square value = new Square(6,1);
foundItem = sortedListOfSquares.ContainsValue(value);
Console.WriteLine("sortedListOfSquares.ContainsValue(new Square(6,1)): " + foundItem);
}
```

This code displays the following:

```
List<Square>
Original list
Height:1  Width:3
Height:4  Width:3
Height:2  Width:1
Height:6  Width:1

Sorted list using IComparer<Square>=heightCompare
Height:1  Width:3
Height:2  Width:1
Height:4  Width:3
Height:6  Width:1

Search using IComparer<Square>=heightCompare
Found (1,3): 0

Sorted list using IComparable<Square>
Height:2  Width:1
Height:1  Width:3
Height:6  Width:1
Height:4  Width:3
Search using IComparable<Square>
Found (6,1): 2


SortedList<Square>
0 : Height:1  Width:3
1 : Height:2  Width:1
2 : Height:4  Width:3
4 : Height:6  Width:1

sortedListOfSquares.ContainsKey(2): True
sortedListOfSquares.ContainsValue(new Square(6,1)): True
```

See Also

Recipe 3.2, and the "IComparable<T> Interface" and "IComparer<T> Interface" topics in the MSDN documentation.

3.4   Indirectly Overloading the +=, -=, /=, and *= Operators

Problem

You need to control the handling of the +=, -=, /=, and *= operators within your data type; unfortunately, these operators cannot be directly overloaded.

Solution

Overload these operators indirectly by overloading the +, -, /, and * operators, as demonstrated in Example 3-5.

*Example 3-5. Overloading the +, -, /, and * operators*

```
public class Foo
{
    // Other class members...
    // Overloaded binary operators
    public static Foo operator +(Foo f1, Foo f2)
    {
        Foo result = new Foo( );
        // Add f1 and f2 here...
        // place result of the addition into the result variable.
        return result;
    }
    public static Foo operator +(int constant, Foo f1)
    {
        Foo result = new Foo( );
        // Add the constant integer and f1 here...
        // place result of the addition into the result variable.
        return result;
    }
    public static Foo operator +(Foo f1, int constant)
    {
        Foo result = new Foo( );
        // Add the constant integer and f1 here...
        // place result of the addition into the result variable.
        return result;
    }

    // The pattern above is repeated for the -, *, and . operators as well...
}
```

Discussion

While it is illegal to overload the +=, -=, /=, and *= operators directly, you can overload them indirectly by overloading the +, -, /, and * operators. The +=, -=, /=, and *= operators use the overloaded +, -, /, and * operators for their calculations.

The four operators +, -, /, and * are overloaded by the methods in the Solution section of this recipe. You might notice that each operator is overloaded three times. This is intentional, since a user of your object may attempt to add, subtract, multiply, or divide it by an integer value. The unknown here is: which position will the integer constant be in? Will it be in the first parameter or the second? The following code snippet shows how this might look for multiplication:

```
Foo x = new Foo( );
Foo y = new Foo( );
y *= 100;      // Uses: operator *(Foo f1, int multiplier)
```

```
y = 100 * x;      // Uses: operator *(int multiplier, Foo f1)
y *= x;           // Uses: operator *(Foo f1, Foo f2)
```

The same holds true for the other overloaded operators.

If these operators were being implemented in a class, you would first check whether any were set to null. The following code for the overloaded addition operator has been modified to do this:

```
public static Foo operator +(Foo f1, Foo f2)
{
    if (f1 == null)
    {
        throw (new ArgumentNullException("f1"));
    }
    else if (f2 == null)
    {
        throw (new ArgumentNullException("f2"));
    }
    else
    {
        Foo result = new Foo();
        // Add f1 and f2 here...
        // place result of the addition into the result variable.
        return (result);
    }
}
```

See Also

The "Operator Overloading Usage Guidelines," "Overloadable Operators," and "Operator Overloading Tutorial" topics in the MSDN documentation.

3.5   Indirectly Overloading the &&, ||, and ?: Operators

Problem

You need to control the handling of the &&, ||, and ?: operators within your data type; unfortunately, these operators cannot be directly overloaded.

Solution

Overload these operators indirectly by overloading the &, |, true, and false operators, as shown in Example 3-6.

Example 3-6. Overloading &, |, true, and false

```
public class ObjState
{
    public ObjState(int state)
```

Example 3-6. Overloading &, |, true, and false (continued)

```csharp
    {
        this.State = state;
    }

    public int State {get; set;}

    public ObjState RetObj(int state)
    {
        return (new ObjState(state));
    }

    public static ObjState operator &(ObjState obj1, ObjState obj2)
    {
        if (obj1 == null || obj2 == null)
            throw (new ArgumentNullException("Neither object may be null."));

        if (obj1.State >= 0 && obj2.State >= 0)
            return (new ObjState(1));
        else
            return (new ObjState(-1));
    }

    public static ObjState operator |(ObjState obj1, ObjState obj2)
    {
        if (obj1.State < 0 && obj2.State < 0)
            return (new ObjState(-1));
        else
            return (new ObjState(1));
    }

    public static bool operator true(ObjState obj)
    {
        if (obj.State >= 0)
            return true;
        else
            return false;
    }

    public static bool operator false(ObjState obj)
    {
        if (obj.State >= 0)
            return true;
        else
            return false;
    }

    public override string ToString()
    {
        return State.ToString();
    }
}
```

This technique gives you complete control over the operations of the &&, ||, and ?: operators.

Alternatively, you can simply add an implicit conversion to bool:

```
public class ObjState
{
    public ObjState(int state)
    {
        this.State = state;
    }

    public int State {get; set;}

    public static implicit operator bool(ObjState obj)
    {
        if (obj.State == 0)
            throw new InvalidOperationException();
        return (obj.State > 0);
    }
}
```

This technique implements strict Boolean logic; the first technique (overriding the &&, ||, and ?: operators) gives you more freedom to stray from implementing strict Boolean logic.

Discussion

While you cannot overload the &&, ||, and ?: operators directly, you can overload them indirectly by overloading the &, |, true, and false operators. The &&, ||, and ?: operators then use the overloaded &, |, true, and false operators for their calculations.

The && operator indirectly uses the false and & operators to perform a short-circuiting AND operation. Initially, the false operator is invoked to determine whether the first object is equal to false. If so, the right side of the expression is not evaluated, and the left side is returned. If the false operator returns a true, the & operator is invoked next to perform the ANDing operation on the two objects. This initial test using the false operator enables the operator to short-circuit the operation.

The || operator works the same as the && operator, except that the initial test is done using the true operator rather than the false operator.

The ?: operator requires that its first argument be an expression of a type which can either be implicitly converted to bool or which implements operator true. Note that this, in turn, requires the overloading of the false operator for symmetry. The ?: operator takes a condition as input and evaluates either converts it to bool or calls operator true. This operator can be defined as follows:

```
condition ? true-expression : false-expression
```

The ?: operator invokes the true operator to determine which expression of this operator should be evaluated. Note that if an implicit conversion to bool exists, it will be used in preference to the true operator.

When implementing these operators, you should first check to determine whether any parameters in the overloaded operator methods were set to null. The code for the overloaded & operator has been modified to do this:

```
public static ObjState operator &(ObjState obj1, ObjState obj2)
{
    if (obj1 == null || obj2 == null)
    {
        throw (new ArgumentNullException("Neither object may be null."));
    }
    if (obj1.state >= 0 && obj2.state >= 0)
        return (new ObjState(1));
    else
        return (new ObjState(-1));
}
```

See Also

The "Operator Overloading Usage Guidelines," "Overloadable Operators," and "Operator Overloading Tutorial" topics in the MSDN documentation.

3.6   Making Error-Free Expressions

Problem

A complex expression in your code is returning incorrect results. For example, if you wanted to find the average area given to two circles, you might write the following expression:

```
double radius1 = 2;
double radius2 = 4;
double aveArea = .5 * Math.PI * Math.Pow(radius1, 2) + Math.PI *
                Math.Pow(radius2, 2);
```

However, the result is always incorrect.

Complex mathematical and Boolean equations in your code can easily become the source of bugs. You need to write bug-free equations, while at the same time making them easier to read.

Solution

The solution is quite simple: use parentheses to explicitly define the order of operations that will take place in your equation. If the expression is difficult to get right even when using parentheses, then it is probably too complex; consider breaking each subpart or the expression into separate methods for each part of the expression and then combine the methods to get the final result.

To fix the expression presented in the Problem section, rewrite it as follows:

```
double radius1 = 2;
double radius2 = 4;
double aveArea = .5 * (Math.PI * Math.Pow(radius1, 2) + Math.PI *
                Math.Pow(radius2, 2));
```

Notice the addition of the parentheses; these parentheses cause the area of the two circles to be calculated and added together first. Then the total area is multiplied by .5. This is the behavior you are looking for. An additional benefit is that the expression can become easier to read as the parentheses provide clear distinction of what part of the expression is to be evaluated first. This technique works equally well with Boolean equations.

Discussion

Parentheses are key to writing maintainable and bug-free equations. Not only is your intention clearly spelled out, but you also override any operator precedence rules that you might not have taken into account. In fact, the only way to override operator precedence is to use parentheses. Consider the following equation:

```
int x = 1 * 2 - -50 / 4 + 220 << 1;
Console.WriteLine("x = " + x);
```

The value 468 is displayed for this equation.

This is the same equation written with parentheses:

```
int y = ((1 * 2) - ((-50) / 4) + 220) << 1;
Console.WriteLine("y = " + y);
```

The same value (468) is also displayed for this equation. Notice how much easier it is to read and understand how this equation works when parentheses are used. However, it is possible to get carried away with the use of parentheses in an equation:

```
int z = ((((1 * 2) - ((-50) / 4)) + 220) << (1));
Console.WriteLine("z = " + z);
```

This equation also evaluates to 468, but due to the overuse of parentheses, you can get lost determining where one set of parentheses begins and where it ends. You should try to balance your placement of parentheses in strategic locations to prevent oversaturating your equation with parentheses.

Another place where you can get into trouble with operator precedence is when using a ternary operator (?:), defined as follows:

```
boolean condition ? true-expression : false-expression
```

Each type of expression used by this operator is defined as follows:

boolean-expression

This expression must evaluate to a Boolean value or to a value with a type that has an implicit conversion to `bool` or one that has a `true` operator. Depending on the outcome of this expression, either the *true-case-expression* or the *false-case-expression* will be executed.

true-case-expression

This expression is evaluated when the *boolean-expression* evaluates to `true`.

false-case-expression

This expression is evaluated when the *boolean-expression* evaluates to `false`.

Either the *true-case-expression* or the *false-case-expression* will be evaluated; never both.

The ternary operator is sometimes able to compact several lines of an `if-else` statement into a single expression that can fit easily on a single line. This ternary statement is also usable inline with a statement or another expression. The following code example shows the use of the ternary operator inline with an expression:

```
byte x = (byte)(8 + ((foo == 1) ? 4 : 2));
```

By examining the order of operator precedence, you can see that the `==` operator has the highest precedence and the compiler combines the results of this subexpression to make it be evaluated first, and then the ternary operator. Depending on the result of the Boolean expression `foo == 1`, the ternary operator will produce either the value 4 or 2. This value is then added to 8 and assigned to the variable x.

 Expression evaluation in C# is done from left to right in all cases. Operator precedence affects how the final result is achieved, but the expression is always evaluated left to right.

This operator is considered to have *right-associative* properties, similar to the assignment operators. Because of this, you can get into trouble using ternary expressions as expressions within other ternary expressions. Consider the following code:

```
// foo currently equals 1
// Assume that all methods will always return a Boolean true, except for Method3,
// which always returns a Boolean false.
Console.WriteLine(Method1() ? Method2() : Method3() ? Method4() : Method5());
```

Which methods will be called? If you started determining precedence of the components of the expression, your expression would essentially look like the following:

```
Console.WriteLine((Method1() ? Method2() : Method3()) ? Method4() : Method5());
```

Notice the extra highlighted parentheses added to clarify how the precedence will be determined in this manner. The answer that the methods Method1, Method2, and Method4 will be called is wrong. The correct answer is that only Method1 and Method2 will be called. Extra highlighted parentheses have been added to this expression in order to clarify how the precedence is determined:

```
Console.WriteLine(Method1() ? Method2() :
    (Method3() ? Method4() : Method5()));
```

This technique will cause Method1 and Method2 to be called in that order. If any of these methods produced side effects, the application might produce unexpected results.

 Don't use nested ternary expressions; write out the if tree or a table-driven solution because that is what the compiler is going to generate from the nested operators anyway. This will make your code more debuggable and maintainable.

3.7   Reducing Your Boolean Logic

Problem

Many times a Boolean equation quickly becomes large, complex, and even unmanageable. You need a way to manage this complexity while at the same time verifying that your logic works as designed.

Solution

To fix this situation, try applying the theorems shown in Table 3-1 to minimize these types of equations.

Table 3-1. Boolean theorems

Theorem ID	Theorem definition
T0	!(!x) == x
T1	x | x == x
T2	x | !x == true
T3 (DeMorgan's Theorem)	!x | !y == !(x & y)
T4	x & x == x
T5	x & !x == false
T6 (DeMorgan's Theorem)	!x & !y == !(x | y)
T7 (Commutative Law)	x | y == y | x
T8 (Associative Law)	(x | y) | z == x | (y | z)
T9 (Distributive Law)	x & y | x & z == x & (y | z)
T10	x | x & y = x
T11	x & y | x & !y = x
T12	(x & y) | (!x & z) | (y & z) == (x & y) | (!x & z)

Table 3-1. Boolean theorems (continued)

Theorem ID	Theorem definition
T13 (Commutative Law)	x & y == y & x
T14 (Associative Law)	(x & y) & z == x & (y & z)
T15 (Distributive Law)	(x | y) & (x | z) == x | (y & z)
T16	x & (x | y) = x
T17	(x | y) & (x | !y) = x
T18	(x | y) & (!x | z) & (y | z) == (x | y) & (!x | z)
T19	x | x | x | ... | x == x
T20	!(x | x | x | ... | x) == !x & !x & !x & ... & !x
T21	x & x & x & ... & x == x
T22	!(x & x & x & ... & x) == !x | !x | !x | ... | !x
T23	(x | y) & (w | z) == (x & w) | (x * z) | (y & w) | (y * z)
T24	(x & y) | (w & z) == (x | w) & (x | z) & (y | w) & (y | z)

In Table 3-1, assume that w, x, y, and z are all variables of type bool. The theorem IDs allow easy identification of which theorems are being used in the Boolean equations that are being minimized in the Discussion section.

Discussion

Simplifying your Boolean logic will benefit your code by making it less cluttered and making its logic clearer and more readily understood. This simplification will lessen the number of potential locations in your logic where bugs can hide and at the same time improve maintainability.

Let's walk through several examples to show how the process of minimizing your logic works. These examples use the three Boolean variables X, Y, and Z. The names have been kept simple so that you can concentrate on minimizing the logic and not have to worry about what the code is trying to do.

The first example uses only the X and Y Boolean variables:

```
if (!X & !Y) {...}
```

From this if statement, you extract the following Boolean logic:

```
!X & !Y
```

Using theorem T6, you can eliminate one operator from this equation:

```
!(X | Y)
```

Now this equation requires only two Boolean operators to be evaluated instead of three. By the way, you might notice that this equation is a logical NOR operation.

The second example uses the X and Y Boolean variables in a seemingly complex equation:

```
if ((!X & Y) | (X & !Y) | (X & Y)){...}
```

From this if statement, you extract the Boolean logic:

```
(!X & Y) | (X & !Y) | (X & Y)
```

Using theorem T11, you can simplify the last two parenthesized expressions, yielding X, and obtain the following:

```
(!X & Y) | X
```

This equation is much simpler than the initial equation. In fact, you reduced the number of operators from seven to three, which is greater than a 2:1 ratio.

Some equations might not seem as if they can be simplified very much, but looks can be deceiving. Let's try to simplify the following equation:

```
(!X & Y) | (X & !Y)
```

Using theorem T24, you can derive the following expression:

```
(!X | X) & (!X | !Y) & (Y | X) & (Y | !Y)
```

Using theorem T2, you can remove the first and last parenthesized expressions:

```
(!X | !Y) & (Y | X)
```

Finally, using theorem T3, you can minimize the equation once again to the following form:

```
!(X & Y) & (Y | X)
```

You were able to remove only a single operator from this equation. This optimization might or might not improve the performance and readability of your code, since it is such a minor change.

You may think that this expression is in its most reduced form. However, if you examine this expression more closely, you may notice that it is the equation for the XOR operator. Knowing this, you can simplify the equation to the following:

```
X ^ Y
```

This technique really shines when you are faced with a large and complex Boolean expression, such as the one shown here:

```
(!X & !Y & !Z) | (!X & Y & Z) | (X & !Y & !Z) | (X & !Y & Z) |
(X & Y & Z)
```

Using theorem T9, you get the following equation:

```
(!X & ((!Y & !Z) | (Y & Z))) | (X & ((!Y & !Z) | (!Y & Z) |
(Y & Z)))
```

Notice that the equation (!Y&!Z)|(Y&Z) is the equivalent of the NOT XOR operation on Y and Z. So you can simplify this equation much further:

```
(!X & !(Y ^ Z)) | (X & ((!Y & !Z) | (!Y & Z) | (Y & Z)))
```

Using theorem T9, once again, you get the following equation:

$$(!X \mathrel{\&} !(Y \mathrel{\wedge} Z)) \mid (X \mathrel{\&} (!Y \mathrel{\&} (!Z \mid Z) \mid (Y \mathrel{\&} Z)))$$

Using theorem T2, you get the final equation:

$$(!X \mathrel{\&} !(Y \mathrel{\wedge} Z)) \mid (X \mathrel{\&} (!Y \mid (Y \mathrel{\&} Z)))$$

This equation is much simpler than the original and requires much less processing to evaluate as well.

 While it is unnecessary in most cases to commit all of these theorems to memory, you should try to understand them all. In addition, memorizing some of the simpler theorems can come in quite handy in many circumstances.

The theorems outlined in this recipe should be complete enough to allow you to play around with minimizing your Boolean equations.

See Also

The "C# Operators" topic in the MSDN documentation.

3.8   Converting Between Simple Types in a Programming Language-Agnostic Manner

Problem

You need to convert between any two of the following types: bool, char, sbyte, byte, short, ushort, int, uint, long, ulong, float, double, decimal, DateTime, and string. Different programming languages sometimes handle specific conversions differently; you need a way to perform these conversions in a consistent manner across all .NET languages. One situation in which this recipe is needed is when VB.NET and C# components communicate within the same application.

Solution

Different programming languages sometimes handle casting of larger numeric types to smaller numeric types differently—these types of casts are called *narrowing conversions*. For example, consider the following Visual Basic .NET (VB.NET) code, which casts a Single to an Integer:

```
' Visual Basic .NET Code:
Dim initialValue As Single
Dim finalValue As Integer

initialValue = 13.499
finalValue = CInt(initialValue)
Console.WriteLine(finalValue.ToString())
```

```
initialValue = 13.5
finalValue = CInt(initialValue)
Console.WriteLine(finalValue.ToString())

initialValue = 13.501
finalValue = CInt(initialValue)
Console.WriteLine(finalValue.ToString())
```

This code outputs the following:

```
13
14
14
```

Notice that the CInt cast in VB.NET uses the fractional portion of the number to round the resulting number.

Now let's convert this code to C# using the explicit casting operator:

```
// C# Code:
float initialValue = 0;
int finalValue = 0;

initialValue = (float)13.499;
finalValue = (int)initialValue;
Console.WriteLine(finalValue.ToString());

initialValue = (float)13.5;
finalValue = (int)initialValue;
Console.WriteLine(finalValue.ToString());

initialValue = (float)13.501;
finalValue = (int)initialValue;
Console.WriteLine(finalValue.ToString());
```

This code outputs the following:

```
13
13
13
```

Notice that the resulting value was not rounded. Instead, the C# casting operator simply truncates the fractional portion of the number.

Consistently casting numeric types in any language can be done through the static methods on the Convert class. The previous C# code can be converted to use the ToInt32 method:

```
// C# Code:
finalValue = Convert.ToInt32((float)13.449);
Console.WriteLine(finalValue.ToString());

finalValue = Convert.ToInt32((float)13.5);
Console.WriteLine(finalValue.ToString());

finalValue = Convert.ToInt32((float)13.501);
Console.WriteLine(finalValue.ToString());
```

This code outputs the following:

```
13
14
14
```

Discussion

All conversions performed using methods on the Convert class are considered to be in a checked context in C#. VB.NET does not have the concept of a checked or unchecked context, so all conversions are considered to be in a checked context—an unchecked context cannot be created in VB.NET. An OverflowException will be thrown in a checked context when a narrowing conversion results in a loss of information. This exception is never thrown in an unchecked context when a narrowing conversion results in a loss of information.

The various conversion methods are listed in Table 3-2.

Table 3-2. Conversion methods on the Convert class

Method	Use
ToBoolean	Convert a type to a bool.
ToChar	Convert a type to a char.
ToString	Convert a type to a string.
ToDateTime	Convert a type to a DateTime.
ToInt16	Convert a type to a short.
ToInt32	Convert a type to an int.
ToInt64	Convert a type to a long.
ToUInt16	Convert a type to a ushort.
ToUInt32	Convert a type to a uint.
ToUInt64	Convert a type to a ulong.
ToByte	Convert a type to a byte.
ToSByte	Convert a type to an sbyte.
ToSingle	Convert a type to a float.
ToDecimal	Convert a type to a decimal.
ToDouble	Convert a type to a double.

Converting between any of the data types listed in Table 3-2 is a simple matter. All of the listed methods are static and exist on the Convert class. Converting one type to another is performed by first choosing the correct method on the Convert class. This method will be named after the type you are converting to (e.g., if you are converting to a char type, the method name would be ToChar). Next, you need to pass the type that will be cast as the parameter to the Convert method. Finally, set a variable of the resultant cast type equal to the return value of the Convert method. The following code converts the value in the variable source—defined as a short that contains a number between 0 and 9—to a char type. This char value is then returned by the Convert method and assigned to the variable destination. The variable destination must be defined as a char:

```
destination = Convert.ToChar(source);
```

Sometimes conversions will do nothing. Converting from one type to that same type will do nothing except return a result that is equivalent to the source value. Take, for example, using the Convert.ToInt32 method to convert a source variable of type Int32 to a destination variable of type Int32. This method takes the value obtained from the source variable and places it in the destination variable.

Some conversions cause exceptions to occur because there is no clear way of converting between the two types; these attempted conversions are listed in Table 3-3. Because some conversions may or may not throw an exception—such as converting from an sbyte to a byte—it is good programming practice to enclose the static conversion method within a try/catch block. The following code wraps a conversion between numeric types in a try/catch block:

```
try
{
    finalValue = Convert.ToInt32(SomeFloat);
}
    catch(OverflowException oe)
{
    // Handle narrowing conversions that result in a loss
    // of information here.
}
catch(InvalidCastException ice)
{
    // Handle casts that cannot be performed here.
}
```

The following code wraps a conversion from a string type to an Int32 in a try/catch block:

```
try
{
    finalValue = Convert.ToInt32(SomeString);
}
catch(OverflowException oe)
{
    // Handle narrowing conversions that result in a loss
    // of information here.
}
catch(ArgumentException ae)
{
    // Handle nulls passed into the Convert method here.
}
catch(FormatException fe)
{
```

```
        // Handle attempts to convert a string that does not contain
        // a value that can be converted to the destination type here.
    }
    catch(Exception e)
    {
        // Handle all other exceptions here.
    }
```

Table 3-3 shows exceptions that are made when some conversions occur.

Table 3-3. Cases in which a source-to-destination-type conversion throws an exception

Destination	Source	Exception type
bool	Char DateTime	InvalidCastException
byte	DateTime	InvalidCastException
char	Bool DateTime decimal double float	InvalidCastException
DateTime	Bool byte sbyte char decimal double short int long ushort uint ulong float	InvalidCastException
decimal	Char DateTime	InvalidCastException
double	Char DateTime	InvalidCastException
Short	DateTime	InvalidCastException
Int	DateTime	InvalidCastException
Long	DateTime	InvalidCastException
sbyte	DateTime	InvalidCastException
float	Char DateTime	InvalidCastException
ushort	DateTime	InvalidCastException
uint	DateTime	InvalidCastException
ulong	DateTime	InvalidCastException

Table 3-3. Cases in which a source-to-destination-type conversion throws an exception (continued)

Destination	Source	Exception type
byte	sbyte decimal double short int long ushort uint ulong float	OverFlowException (if source is out of the range of destination)
sbyte	Byte decimal double short int long ushort uint ulong float	OverFlowException (if source is out of the range of destination)
short	ushort	OverFlowException (if source is out of the range of destination)
ushort	short	OverFlowException (if source is out of the range of destination)
int	uint	OverFlowException (if source is out of the range of destination)
uint	sbyte short int	OverFlowException (if source is out of the range of destination)
long	ulong	OverFlowException (if source is out of the range of destination)
ulong	sbyte short int long	OverFlowException (if source is out of the range of destination)
Any type	string	ArgumentException (if source string is null) or FormatException (if source string represents an invalid value for the destination type)

Notice that the string type can be converted to any type, and that any type may be converted to a string type—assuming that the source string is not null and conforms to the destination type's range and format.

The most insidious problems can occur when a larger type is converted to a smaller type in an unchecked context; the potential exists for information to be lost. Code runs in an unchecked context if the conversion is contained in an unchecked block or if the /checked compiler option is set to false (by default, this compiler option is set to false in both debug and release builds). An example of code contained in an unchecked block is as follows:

```
short destination = 0;
int source = Int32.MaxValue;
unchecked(destination = (short)source);
```

or:

```
unchecked
{
    short destination = 0;
    int source = Int32.MaxValue;
    destination = (short)source;
}
```

A checked context is when the conversion is contained in a checked block or if the / checked compiler option is set to true. An example of code contained in a checked block is as follows:

```
short destination = 0;
int source = Int32.MaxValue;
checked(destination =(short)source);
```

or:

```
checked
{
    short destination = 0;
    int source = Int32.MaxValue;
    destination = (short)source;
}
```

This code throws an OverflowException exception if any loss of information would occur. This allows the application to be notified of the overflow condition and to handle it properly.

The Convert method is always considered to operate in a checked context, even when no other type of checked context wraps the code performing the conversion.

See Also

The "checked Keyword," "unchecked Keyword," "Checked and Unchecked," and "Convert Class" topics in the MSDN documentation.

3.9 Determining When to Use the cast Operator, the as Operator, or the is Operator

Problem

You need to determine which operator is best in your situation—the cast (*type*) operator, the as operator, or the is operator.

Solution

Use the information provided in the Discussion section to determine which operator is best to use.

Discussion

Use the cast operator when:

- You are converting a reference type to a reference type.
- You are converting a value type to a value type.
- You are performing a boxing or unboxing conversion.
- You are invoking a user-defined conversion. The is and as operators cannot handle this type of cast.

Use the as operator when:

- It is *not* acceptable for the InvalidCastException to be thrown. The as operator will instead return a null if the cast cannot be performed.
- You are converting a reference type to a reference type.
- You are *not* casting a value type to a value type. The cast operator must be used in this case.
- You are performing a boxing conversion.
- You are *not* performing an unboxing conversion. The cast operator must be used in this case unless the unboxing is to a nullable type.
- You are *not* invoking a user-defined conversion. The cast operator must be used in this case.
- You are performing a cast to a type parameter T that can be only a reference type. This is because a null may be returned after evaluating this expression.

Use the is operator when:

- You need a fast method of determining whether using the as operator will return null before it is attempted.
- You do not need to actually cast a variable from one data type to another; you just need to determine if the variable can be cast to a specific type.
- It is not acceptable for the InvalidCastException to be thrown.
- You are *not* casting a value type to a value type. The cast operator must be used in this case.
- You are *not* invoking a user-defined conversion. Unlike the as operator, a compile-time error is not displayed when using the is operator with a user-defined conversion. This is operator will instead always return a false value, regardless of whether the cast can successfully be performed.

See Also

Recipes 3.9 and 3.11; see the "() Operator," "as Operator," and "is Operator" topics in the MSDN documentation.

3.10 Casting with the as Operator

Problem

Ordinarily, when you attempt a casting operation, the .NET Common Language Runtime generates an InvalidCastException if the cast fails. Often, though, you cannot guarantee in advance that a cast will succeed, but you also do not want the overhead of handling an InvalidCastException.

Solution

Use the as operator. The as operator attempts the conversion operation, but if the conversion fails, the expression returns a null instead of throwing an exception. If the conversion succeeds, the expression returns the converted value. The code that follows shows how the as operator is used:

```
public static void ConvertObj(Specific specificObj)
{
    Base baseObj = specificObj as Base;
    if (baseObj == null)
    {
        // Cast failed.
    }
    else
    {
        // Cast was successful.
    }
}
```

where the Specific type derives from the Base type:

```
public class Base {}
public class Specific : Base {}
```

In this code fragment, the as operator is used to attempt to convert the SpecificObj to the type Base. The next lines contain an if-else statement that tests the variable baseObj to determine whether it is equal to null. If it is equal to null, you should prevent any use of this variable, since it might cause a NullReferenceException to be thrown.

Discussion

The as operator has the following syntax:

expression **as** *type*

The expression and type are defined as follows:

expression
    An expression.

type
    The type to which to convert the object represented by *expression*.

This operation returns *expression* converted to the type defined by *type* if the conversion succeeds. If the conversion fails, a `null` is returned, and an `InvalidCastException` is not thrown. This operator does not work with user-defined conversions (either explicit or implicit).

This method allows a `System.Drawing.Point` structure to be cast to an object of type `MyPoint`. Due to the use of the explicit keyword, the conversion must be explicit:

```
System.Drawing.Point systemPt = new System.Drawing.Point(0, 0);
MyPoint pt = (MyPoint)systemPt;
```

If you attempt to use the as operator in a user-defined conversion, the following compiler error is shown:

```
Cannot convert type 'MyPoint' to 'Point' via a built-in conversion
```

An unboxing conversion converts a previously boxed value type to its original value type or to a nullable instance of the type:

```
int x = 5;
object obj = x;          // Box x
int originalX = obj as int; // Attempt to unbox obj into an integer.
```

If you attempt to use the as operator in an unboxing conversion, the following compiler error is shown:

```
The as operator must be used with a reference type or nullable type
('int' is a value type)
```

This is illegal because as indicates that the cast cannot be performed by returning `null`, but there is no such thing as a `null` value for an int.

The as operator cannot be used with a type parameter T when T could be a struct, for the same reason as previously mentioned. The following code will not compile:

```
public class TestAsOp<T>
{
    public T ConvertSomething(object obj)
    {
        return (obj as T);
    }
}
```

because T could be anything since it is not constrained. If you constrain T to be only a reference type, as shown here:

```
public class TestAsOp<T>
            where T: class
{
    public T ConvertSomething(object obj)
    {
        return (obj as T);
    }
}
```

your code will compile successfully, since T cannot be a struct.

See Also

Recipes 3.13 and 3.14; see the "() Operator," "as Operator," and "is Operator" topics in the MSDN documentation.

3.11 Determining a Variable's Type with the is Operator

Problem

A method exists that creates an object from one of several types of classes. This object is then returned as a generic object type. Based on the type of object that was initially created in the method, you want to branch to different logic.

Solution

Use the is operator. This operator returns a Boolean true or false, indicating whether the cast is legal, but the cast never actually occurs.

Suppose you have four different point classes:

```
public class Point2D {...}
public class Point3D {...}
public class ExPoint2D : Point2D {...}
public class ExPoint3D : Point3D {...}
```

Next, you have a method that accepts an integer value, and based on this value, one of the four specific point types is returned:

```
public object CreatePoint(PointTypeEnum pointType)
{
    switch (pointType)
    {
        case PointTypeEnum.Point2D:
            return (new Point2D());
        case PointTypeEnum.Point3D:
            return (new Point3D());
        case PointTypeEnum.ExPoint2D:
            return (new ExPoint2D());
        case PointTypeEnum.ExPoint3D:
            return (new ExPoint3D());
        default:
            return (null);
    }
}
```

where the PointTypeEnum is defined as:

```
public enum PointTypeEnum
{
    Point2D, Point3D, ExPoint2D, ExPoint3D
}
```

Finally, you have a method that calls the CreatePoint method. This method handles the point object type returned from the CreatePoint method based on the actual point object returned:

```
public void CreateAndHandlePoint( )
{
    // Create a new point object and return it.
    object retObj = CreatePoint(PointTypeEnum.Point2D);

    // Handle the point object based on its actual type.
    if (retObj is ExPoint2D)
    {
        Console.WriteLine("Use the ExPoint2D type");
    }
    else if (retObj is ExPoint3D)
    {
        Console.WriteLine("Use the ExPoint3D type");
    }
    else if (retObj is Point2D)
    {
        Console.WriteLine("Use the Point2D type");
    }
    else if (retObj is Point3D)
    {
        Console.WriteLine("Use the Point3D type");
    }
    else
    {
        Console.WriteLine("Invalid point type");
    }
}
```

Notice that the tests for the ExPoint2D and ExPoint3D objects are performed before the tests for Point2D and Point3D. This order will allow you to differentiate between base classes and their derived classes (ExPoint2D derives from Point2D and ExPoint3D derives from Point3D). If you had reversed these tests, the test for Point2D would evaluate to true for both the Point2D class and its derivatives (ExPoint2D).

Discussion

The is operator is a fast and easy method of predetermining whether a cast will work. If the cast fails, you have saved yourself the overhead of trying the cast and handling a thrown exception. If the is operator determines that this cast can successfully be performed, all you need to do is perform the cast.

The is operator is defined as follows:

expression **is** *type*

The expression and type are defined as follows:

expression

    A type.

type

    The type to which to convert to.

This expression returns a Boolean value: true if the cast will succeed or false if the conversion will fail. For example:

```
if (SpecificObj is Base)
{
    // It is of type Base.
}
else
{
    // Cannot cast SpecificObj to a Base type object.
}
```

 Never use the is operator with a user-defined conversion (either explicit or implicit). The is operator always returns false when used with these types of conversions, regardless of whether the conversion can be performed.

The following code determines whether an unboxing operation can be performed:

```
// An int is passed in to this method and boxed.
public void SomeMethod(object o)
{
    if (o is int)
    {
        // o can be unboxed.
        // It is now possible to cast o to an int.
        int x = (int)o;
    }
    else
    {
        // Cannot unbox o.
    }
}
```

The is operator is used to determine whether o can be unboxed back into an int. The integer variable x. is then declared, and the value of object variable o is unboxed into x. This is the one case in which it is absolutely necessary to use is if you want to avoid an exception. You can't use as here because there is no such thing as a null int, so it cannot tell you if the unboxing fails.

See Also

Recipes 3.9 and 3.10; see the "() Operator," "as Operator," and "is Operator" topics in the MSDN documentation.

3.12   Returning Multiple Items from a Method

Problem

In many cases, a single return value for a method is not enough. You need a way to return more than one item from a method.

Solution

Use the out keyword on parameters that will act as return parameters. The following method accepts an inputShape parameter and calculates height, width, and depth from that value:

```
public void ReturnDimensions(int inputShape,
                             out int height,
                             out int width,
                             out int depth)
{
    height = 0;
    width = 0;
    depth = 0;

    // Calculate height, width, and depth from the inputShape value.
}
```

This method would be called in the following manner:

```
// Declare output parameters.
int height;
int width;
int depth;

// Call method and return the height, width, and depth.
Obj.ReturnDimensions(1, out height, out width, out depth);
```

Another method is to return a class or structure containing all the return values. The previous method has been modified to return a structure instead of using out arguments:

```
public Dimensions ReturnDimensions(int inputShape)
{
    // The default ctor automatically defaults this structure's members to 0.
    Dimensions objDim = new Dimensions();

    // Calculate objDim.Height, objDim.Width, objDim.Depth from the inputShape
value.

    return objDim;
}
```

where Dimensions is defined as follows:

```
public struct Dimensions
{
    public int Height;
    public int Width;
    public int Depth;
}
```

This method would now be called in this manner:

```
// Call method and return the height, width, and depth.
Dimensions objDim = obj.ReturnDimensions(1);
```

Discussion

Marking a parameter in a method signature with the out keyword indicates that this parameter will be initialized and returned by this method. This trick is useful when a method is required to return more than one value. A method can, at most, have only one return value, but through the use of the out keyword, you can mark several parameters as a kind of return value.

To set up an out parameter, the parameter in the method signature is marked with the out keyword, shown here:

```
public void ReturnDimensions(int inputShape,
                            out int height,
                            out int width,
                            out int depth)
{
    ...
}
```

To call this method, you must also mark the calling method's arguments with the out keyword, shown here:

```
obj.ReturnDimensions(1, out height, out width, out depth);
```

The out arguments in this method call do not have to be initialized; they can simply be declared and passed in to the ReturnDimensions method. Regardless of whether they are initialized before the method call, they must be initialized before they are used within the ReturnDimensions method. Even if they are not used through every path in the ReturnDimensions method, they still must be initialized. That is why this method starts out with the following three lines of code:

```
height = 0;
width = 0;
depth = 0;
```

You may be wondering why you couldn't use a ref parameter instead of the out parameter, as both allow a method to change the value of an argument marked as such. The answer is that an out parameter makes the code somewhat self-documenting. You know that when an out parameter is encountered, this parameter is acting as a return value. In addition, an out parameter does not require the extra work to be initialized before it is passed in to the method, which a ref parameter does.

An out parameter does not have to be marshaled when the method is called; rather, it is marshaled once when the method returns the data to the caller. Any other type of call (by-value or by-reference using the ref keyword) requires that the value be marshaled in both directions. Using the out keyword in marshaling scenarios improves remoting performance.

3.13   Parsing Command-Line Parameters

Problem

You require your applications to accept one or more command-line parameters in a standard format. You need to access and parse the entire command line passed to your application.

Solution

In Example 3-7, use the following classes together to help with parsing command-line parameters: Argument, ArgumentDefinition, and ArgumentSemanticAnalyzer.

Example 3-7. Argument class

```
using System;
using System.Diagnostics;
using System.Linq;
using System.Collections.ObjectModel;

public sealed class Argument
{
    public string Original { get; private set; }
    public string Switch { get; private set; }
    public ReadOnlyCollection<string> SubArguments { get; private set; }
    private List<string> subArguments;
    public Argument(string original)
    {
        Original = original;
        Switch = string.Empty;
        subArguments = new List<string>();
        SubArguments = new ReadOnlyCollection<string>(subArguments);
        Parse();
    }

    private void Parse()
    {
        if (string.IsNullOrEmpty(Original))
        {
            return;
        }
        char[] switchChars = { '/', '-' };
        if (!switchChars.Contains(Original[0]))
```

Example 3-7. Argument class (continued)

```
        {
            return;
        }
        string switchString = Original.Substring(1);
        string subArgsString = string.Empty;
        int colon = switchString.IndexOf(':');
        if (colon >= 0)
        {
            subArgsString = switchString.Substring(colon + 1);
            switchString = switchString.Substring(0, colon);
        }
        Switch = switchString;
        if (!string.IsNullOrEmpty(subArgsString))
            subArguments.AddRange(subArgsString.Split(';'));
    }

    public bool IsSimple
        { get { return SubArguments.Count == 0; } }
    public bool IsSimpleSwitch
        { get { return !string.IsNullOrEmpty(Switch) && SubArguments.Count == 0; } }
    public bool IsCompoundSwitch
        { get { return !string.IsNullOrEmpty(Switch) && SubArguments.Count == 1; } }
    public bool IsComplexSwitch
        { get { return !string.IsNullOrEmpty(Switch) && SubArguments.Count > 0; } }
}

public sealed class ArgumentDefinition
{
    public string ArgumentSwitch { get; private set; }
    public string Syntax { get; private set; }
    public string Description { get; private set; }
    public Func<Argument, bool> Verifier { get; private set; }

    public ArgumentDefinition(string argumentSwitch,
                              string syntax,
                              string description,
                              Func<Argument, bool> verifier)
    {
        ArgumentSwitch = argumentSwitch.ToUpper();
        Syntax = syntax;
        Description = description;
        Verifier = verifier;
    }

    public bool Verify(Argument arg)
    {
        return Verifier(arg);
    }
}

public sealed class ArgumentSemanticAnalyzer
{
```

Example 3-7. Argument class (continued)

```csharp
private List<ArgumentDefinition> argumentDefinitions =
    new List<ArgumentDefinition>( );
private Dictionary<string, Action<Argument>> argumentActions =
    new Dictionary<string, Action<Argument>>( );

public ReadOnlyCollection<Argument> UnrecognizedArguments { get; private set; }
public ReadOnlyCollection<Argument> MalformedArguments { get; private set; }
public ReadOnlyCollection<Argument> RepeatedArguments { get; private set; }

public ReadOnlyCollection<ArgumentDefinition> ArgumentDefinitions
{
    get { return new ReadOnlyCollection<ArgumentDefinition>(argumentDefinitions); }
}

public IEnumerable<string> DefinedSwitches
{
    get
    {
        return from argumentDefinition in argumentDefinitions
                select argumentDefinition.ArgumentSwitch;
    }
}

public void AddArgumentVerifier(ArgumentDefinition verifier)
{
    argumentDefinitions.Add(verifier);
}

public void RemoveArgumentVerifier(ArgumentDefinition verifier)
{
    var verifiersToRemove = from v in argumentDefinitions
                            where v.ArgumentSwitch == verifier.ArgumentSwitch
                            select v;
    foreach (var v in verifiersToRemove)
        argumentDefinitions.Remove(v);
}

public void AddArgumentAction(string argumentSwitch, Action<Argument> action)
{
    argumentActions.Add(argumentSwitch, action);
}

public void RemoveArgumentAction(string argumentSwitch)
{
    if (argumentActions.Keys.Contains(argumentSwitch))
        argumentActions.Remove(argumentSwitch);
}

public bool VerifyArguments(IEnumerable<Argument> arguments)
{
    // no parameter to verify with, fail.
    if (!argumentDefinitions.Any( ))
```

Example 3-7. Argument class (continued)

```
        return false;

    // Identify if any of the arguments are not defined
    this.UnrecognizedArguments =
            (  from argument in arguments
               where !DefinedSwitches.Contains(argument.Switch.ToUpper())
               select argument).ToList().AsReadOnly();

    if (this.UnrecognizedArguments.Any())
        return false;

    //Check for all the arguments where the switch matches a known switch,
    //but our well-formedness predicate is false.
    this.MalformedArguments = ( from argument in arguments
                                join argumentDefinition in argumentDefinitions
                                on argument.Switch.ToUpper() equals
                                    argumentDefinition.ArgumentSwitch
                                where !argumentDefinition.Verify(argument)
                                select argument).ToList().AsReadOnly();

    if (this.MalformedArguments.Any())
        return false;

    //Sort the arguments into "groups" by their switch, count every group,
    //and select any groups that contain more than one element,
    //We then get a read only list of the items.
    this.RepeatedArguments =
            (from argumentGroup in
                from argument in arguments
                where !argument.IsSimple
                group argument by argument.Switch.ToUpper()
            where argumentGroup.Count() > 1
            select argumentGroup).SelectMany(ag => ag).ToList().AsReadOnly();

    if (this.RepeatedArguments.Any())
        return false;

    return true;
}

public void EvaluateArguments(IEnumerable<Argument> arguments)
{
    //Now we just apply each action:
    foreach (Argument argument in arguments)
        argumentActions[argument.Switch.ToUpper()](argument);
}

public string InvalidArgumentsDisplay()
{
    StringBuilder builder = new StringBuilder();
    builder.AppendFormat("Invalid arguments: {0}",Environment.NewLine);
    // Add the unrecognized arguments
```

Example 3-7. Argument class (continued)

```
        FormatInvalidArguments(builder, this.UnrecognizedArguments,
            "Unrecognized argument: {0}{1}");

        // Add the malformed arguments
        FormatInvalidArguments(builder, this.MalformedArguments,
            "Malformed argument: {0}{1}");

        // For the repeated arguments, we want to group them for the display,
        // so group by switch and then add it to the string being built.
        var argumentGroups = from argument in this.RepeatedArguments
                             group argument by argument.Switch.ToUpper() into ag
                             select new { Switch = ag.Key, Instances = ag};

        foreach (var argumentGroup in argumentGroups)
        {
            builder.AppendFormat("Repeated argument: {0}{1}",
                argumentGroup.Switch, Environment.NewLine);
            FormatInvalidArguments(builder, argumentGroup.Instances.ToList(),
                "\t{0}{1}");
        }
        return builder.ToString();
    }

    private void FormatInvalidArguments(StringBuilder builder,
        IEnumerable<Argument> invalidArguments, string errorFormat)
    {
        if (invalidArguments != null)
        {
            foreach (Argument argument in invalidArguments)
            {
                builder.AppendFormat(errorFormat,
                    argument.Original, Environment.NewLine);
            }
        }
    }
}
```

One example of how to use these classes to process the command line for an application is shown here:

```
public static void Main(string[] argumentStrings)
{
    var arguments = (from argument in argumentStrings
        select new Argument(argument)).ToArray();

    Console.Write("Command line: ");
    foreach (Argument a in arguments)
    {
        Console.Write(a.Original + " ");
    }
    Console.WriteLine("");
```

```
ArgumentSemanticAnalyzer analyzer = new ArgumentSemanticAnalyzer( );
analyzer.AddArgumentVerifier(
    new ArgumentDefinition("output",
        "/output:[path to output]",
        "Specifies the location of the output file.",
        x => x.IsCompoundSwitch));
analyzer.AddArgumentVerifier(
    new ArgumentDefinition("trialMode",
        "/trialmode",
        "If this is specified it places the product into trial mode",
        x => x.IsSimpleSwitch));
analyzer.AddArgumentVerifier(
    new ArgumentDefinition("DeBuGoUtPuT",
        "/debugoutput:[value1];[value2];[value3]",
        "A listing of the files the debug output information will be written to",
        x => x.IsComplexSwitch));
analyzer.AddArgumentVerifier(
    new ArgumentDefinition("",
        "[literal value]",
        "A literal value",
        x => x.IsSimple));

if (!analyzer.VerifyArguments(arguments))
{
    string invalidArguments = analyzer.InvalidArgumentsDisplay( );
    Console.WriteLine(invalidArguments);
    ShowUsage(analyzer);
    return;
}

// Set up holders for the comand line parsing results
string output = string.Empty;
bool trialmode = false;
IEnumerable<string> debugOutput = null;
List<string> literals = new List<string>( );

//For each parsed argument, we want to apply an action, so add them to the
analyzer.
analyzer.AddArgumentAction("OUTPUT", x => { output = x.SubArguments[0]; });
analyzer.AddArgumentAction("TRIALMODE", x => { trialmode = true; });
analyzer.AddArgumentAction("DEBUGOUTPUT", x => { debugOutput = x.SubArguments;
});
analyzer.AddArgumentAction("", x=>{literals.Add(x.Original);});

// check the arguments and run the actions
analyzer.EvaluateArguments(arguments);

// display the results
Console.WriteLine("");
Console.WriteLine("OUTPUT: {0}", output);
Console.WriteLine("TRIALMODE: {0}", trialmode);
if (debugOutput != null)
{
    foreach (string item in debugOutput)
```

```
        {
            Console.WriteLine("DEBUGOUTPUT: {0}", item);
        }
    }
    foreach (string literal in literals)
    {
        Console.WriteLine("LITERAL: {0}",literal);
    }

    // Run the program passing in the argument values:
    Program program = new Program(output, trialmode, debugOutput, literals);
    program.Run( );
}

public static void ShowUsage(ArgumentSemanticAnalyzer analyzer)
{
    Console.WriteLine("Program.exe allows the following arguments:");
    foreach (ArgumentDefinition definition in analyzer.ArgumentDefinitions)
    {
        Console.WriteLine("\t{0}: ({1}){2}\tSyntax: {3}",
            definition.ArgumentSwitch, definition.Description,
            Environment.NewLine,definition.Syntax);
    }
}
```

Discussion

Before command-line parameters can be parsed, a common format must first be
decided upon. The format for this recipe follows the command-line format for the
Visual C# .NET language compiler. The format used is defined as follows:

- All command-line arguments are separated by one or more whitespace characters.

- Each argument may start with either a - or / character, but not both. If it does
  not, that argument is considered a literal, such as a filename.

- Each argument that starts with either the - or / character may be divided up into
  a switch followed by a colon followed by one or more arguments separated with
  the ; character. The command-line parameter -sw:arg1;arg2;arg3 is divided up
  into a switch (sw) and three arguments (arg1, arg2, and arg3). Note that there
  should not be any spaces in the full argument; otherwise, the runtime command-
  line parser will split up the argument into two or more arguments.

- Strings delineated with double quotes, such as "c:\test\file.log", will have
  their double quotes stripped off. This is a function of the operating system inter-
  preting the arguments passed in to your application.

- Single quotes are not stripped off.

- To preserve double quotes, precede the double quote character with the \ escape
  sequence character.

- The \ character is handled as an escape sequence character only when followed by a double quote—in which case, only the double quote is displayed.
- The ^ character is handled by the *runtime* command-line parser as a special character.

Fortunately, the runtime command-line parser handles most of this before your application receives the individual parsed arguments.

The runtime command-line parser passes a string[] containing each parsed argument to the entry point of your application. The entry point can take one of the following forms:

```
public static void Main( )
public static int Main( )
public static void Main(string[] args)
public static int Main(string[] args)
```

The first two accept no arguments, but the last two accept the array of parsed command-line arguments. Note that the static Environment.CommandLine property will also return a string containing the entire command line, and the static Environment. GetCommandLineArgs method will return an array of strings containing the parsed command-line arguments.

The three classes presented in the Solution address the phases of dealing with the command-line arguments:

Argument

Encapsulates a single command-line argument and is responsible for parsing the argument.

ArgumentDefinition

Defines an argument that will be valid for the current command line.

ArgumentSemanticAnalyzer

Performs the verification and retrieval of the arguments based on the ArgumentDefinitions that are set up.

Passing in the following command-line arguments to this application:

```
MyApp c:\input\infile.txt -output:d:\outfile.txt -trialmode
```

results in the following parsed switches and arguments:

```
Command line: c:\input\infile.txt -output:d:\outfile.txt -trialmode
OUTPUT: d:\outfile.txt
TRIALMODE: True
LITERAL: c:\input\infile.txt
```

If you input incorrectly formed command-line parameters, such as forgetting to add arguments to the -output switch, you get the following output:

```
Command line: /output
Invalid arguments:
Malformed argument: /output
```

```
Program.exe allows the following arguments:
        OUTPUT: (Specifies the location of the output file.)
        Syntax: /output:[path to output]
        TRIALMODE: (If this is specified, it places the product into trial mode)
        Syntax: /trialmode
        DEBUGOUTPUT: (A listing of the files the debug output information will be
written to)
        Syntax: /debugoutput:[value1];[value2];[value3]
        : (A literal value)
        Syntax: [literal value]
```

There are a few items of note in the code that are worth pointing out.

Each Argument instance needs to be able to determine certain things about itself. In order to do this, a set of predicates that tell us useful stuff about this Argument are exposed as properties on the Argument. The ArgumentSemanticAnalyzer will use these to determine the characteristics of the argument:

```
public bool IsSimple
    { get { return SubArguments.Count == 0; } }
public bool IsSimpleSwitch
    { get { return !string.IsNullOrEmpty(Switch) && SubArguments.Count == 0; } }
public bool IsCompoundSwitch
    { get { return !string.IsNullOrEmpty(Switch) && SubArguments.Count == 1; } }
public bool IsComplexSwitch
    { get { return !string.IsNullOrEmpty(Switch) && SubArguments.Count > 0; } }
```

In a number of places in the code, the ToArray or ToList methods are called on the result of a LINQ query:

```
var arguments = (from argument in argumentStrings
    select new Argument(argument)).ToArray();
```

This is because query results use deferred execution, which means that not only are the results calculated in a lazy manner, but that they are recalculated every time the results are accessed. By using the ToArray or ToList methods, it forces the eager evaluation of the results and gives a copy that will not re-evaluate during each usage. The query logic does not know if the collection being worked on is changing or not, so it has to re-evaluate each time unless you make a "point in time" copy using these methods.

To verify that these arguments are correct, an ArgumentDefinition is created and associated for each acceptable argument type with the ArgumentSemanticAnalyzer:

```
ArgumentSemanticAnalyzer analyzer = new ArgumentSemanticAnalyzer();
analyzer.AddArgumentVerifier(
    new ArgumentDefinition("output",
        "/output:[path to output]",
        "Specifies the location of the output file.",
        x => x.IsCompoundSwitch));
analyzer.AddArgumentVerifier(
    new ArgumentDefinition("trialMode",
        "/trialmode",
        "If this is specified it places the product into trial mode",
```

```
                x => x.IsSimpleSwitch));
    analyzer.AddArgumentVerifier(
        new ArgumentDefinition("DeBuGoUtPuT",
            "/debugoutput:[value1];[value2];[value3]",
            "A listing of the files the debug output information will be written to",
            x => x.IsComplexSwitch));
    analyzer.AddArgumentVerifier(
        new ArgumentDefinition("",
            "[literal value]",
            "A literal value",
            x => x.IsSimple));
```

There are four parts to each `ArgumentDefinition`; the argument switch, a string show-ing the syntax of the argument, a description of the argument, and the verification predicate to verify the argument. This information can be used to verify the argu-ment, as shown here:

```
//Check for all the arguments where the switch matches a known switch,
//but our well-formedness predicate is false.
this.MalformedArguments = ( from argument in arguments
                            join argumentDefinition in argumentDefinitions
                            on argument.Switch.ToUpper() equals
                                argumentDefinition.ArgumentSwitch
                            where !argumentDefinition.Verify(argument)
                            select argument).ToList().AsReadOnly();
```

The `ArgumentDefinitions` also allow the composition of a usage method for the program:

```
public static void ShowUsage(ArgumentSemanticAnalyzer analyzer)
{
    Console.WriteLine("Program.exe allows the following arguments:");
    foreach (ArgumentDefinition definition in analyzer.ArgumentDefinitions)
    {
        Console.WriteLine("\t{0}: ({1}){2}\tSyntax: {3}",
            definition.ArgumentSwitch, definition.Description,
            Environment.NewLine,definition.Syntax);
    }
}
```

In order to get the values of the arguments so they can be used, the information needs to be extracted out of the parsed arguments. For the solution example, we would need the following information:

```
// Set up holders for the comand line parsing results
string output = string.Empty;
bool trialmode = false;
IEnumerable<string> debugOutput = null;
List<string> literals = new List<string>();
```

How are these values filled in? Well, for each `Argument`, there needs to be an action associated with it to determine how the value should be retrieved from an `Argument` instance. The action is a predicate, which makes this a very powerful approach, as any predicate can be used here. Here is where those Argument actions are defined and associated with the ArgumentSemanticAnalyzer:

```
//For each parsed argument, we want to apply an action, so add them to the
analyzer.
    analyzer.AddArgumentAction("OUTPUT", x => { output = x.SubArguments[0]; });
    analyzer.AddArgumentAction("TRIALMODE", x => { trialmode = true; });
    analyzer.AddArgumentAction("DEBUGOUTPUT", x => { debugOutput = x.SubArguments;
});
    analyzer.AddArgumentAction("", x=>{literals.Add(x.Original);});
```

Now that all of the actions are set up, we can retrieve the values by using the EvaluateArguments method on the ArgumentSemanticAnalyzer:

```
// check the arguments and run the actions
analyzer.EvaluateArguments(arguments);
```

Now the arguments have been filled in by the execution of the actions, and the program can run with those values:

```
// Run the program passing in the argument values:
Program program = new Program(output, trialmode, debugOutput, literals);
program.Run();
```

The verification of the arguments uses LINQ to query for unrecognized, malformed, or repeated arguments, any of which will cause the parameters to be invalid:

```
public bool VerifyArguments(IEnumerable<Argument> arguments)
{
    // no parameter to verify with, fail.
    if (!argumentDefinitions.Any())
        return false;

    // Identify if any of the arguments are not defined
    this.UnrecognizedArguments =
            ( from argument in arguments
              where !DefinedSwitches.Contains(argument.Switch.ToUpper())
              select argument).ToList().AsReadOnly();

    if (this.UnrecognizedArguments.Any())
        return false;

    //Check for all the arguments where the switch matches a known switch,
    //but our well-formedness predicate is false.
    this.MalformedArguments = ( from argument in arguments
                                join argumentDefinition in argumentDefinitions
                                on argument.Switch.ToUpper() equals
                                    argumentDefinition.ArgumentSwitch
                                where !argumentDefinition.Verify(argument)
                                select argument).ToList().AsReadOnly();

    if (this.MalformedArguments.Any())
        return false;
```

```
//Sort the arguments into "groups" by their switch, count every group,
//and select any groups that contain more than one element,
//We then get a read only list of the items.
this.RepeatedArguments =
        (from argumentGroup in
            from argument in arguments
            where !argument.IsSimple
            group argument by argument.Switch.ToUpper()
        where argumentGroup.Count() > 1
        select argumentGroup).SelectMany(ag => ag).ToList().AsReadOnly();

    if (this.RepeatedArguments.Any())
        return false;

    return true;
}
```

Look at how much easier to understand each phase of the verification is, compared with how this would be done before LINQ with multiply nested loops, switches, IndexOfs, and other mechanisms. Each query concisely states in the language of the problem domain what task it is attempting to perform.

 LINQ is designed to help with problems where data must be sorted, searched, grouped, filtered, and projected. Use it!

See Also

The "Main" and "Command-Line Arguments" topics in the MSDN documentation.

3.14 Initializing a Constant Field at Runtime

Problem

A field marked as const can be initialized only at compile time. You need to initialize a field to a valid value at runtime, not at compile time. This field must then act as if it were a constant field for the rest of the application's life.

Solution

You have two choices when declaring a constant value in your code. You can use a readonly field or a const field. Each has its own strengths and weaknesses. However, if you need to initialize a constant field at runtime, you must use a readonly field:

```
public class Foo
{
    public readonly int bar;

    public Foo() {}
```

```
        public Foo(int constInitValue)
        {
            bar = constInitValue;
        }

        // Rest of class...
    }
```

This is not possible using a const field. A const field can be initialized only at compile time:

```
    public class Foo
    {
        public const int bar;          // This line causes a compile-time error.

        public Foo() {}

        public Foo(int constInitValue)
        {
            bar = constInitValue;      // This line also causes a compile-time error.
        }
        // Rest of class...
    }
```

Discussion

A readonly field allows initialization to take place only in the constructor at runtime, whereas a const field must be initialized at compile time. Therefore, implementing a readonly field is the only way to allow a field that must be constant to be initialized at runtime.

There are only two ways to initialize a readonly field. The first is by adding an initializer to the field itself:

```
    public readonly int bar = 100;
```

The second way is to initialize the readonly field through a constructor. This is demonstrated through the code in the Solution to this recipe.

If you look at the following class:

```
    public class Foo
    {
            public readonly int x;
            public const int y = 1;

            public Foo() {}
            public Foo(int roInitValue)
            {
                x = roInitValue;
            }

            // Rest of class...
    }
```

You'll see it is compiled into the following IL:

```
.class public auto ansi beforefieldinit Foo
    extends [mscorlib]System.Object
{
.field public static literal int32 y = int32(0x00000001) //<<-- const field
.field public initonly int32 x                           //<<-- readonly field
.method public hidebysig specialname rtspecialname
        instance void .ctor(int32 input) cil managed
{
    // Code size       14 (0xe)
    .maxstack  8
//001659:           }
//001660: }

//001666: public class Foo
//001667: {
//001668:           public readonly int x;
//001669:           public const int y = 1;
//001670:
//001671:           public Foo(int roInitValue)
    IL_0000:  ldarg.0
    IL_0001:  call        instance void [mscorlib]System.Object::.ctor()
//001672:           {
//001673:                   x = input;
    IL_0006:  ldarg.0
    IL_0007:  ldarg.1
    IL_0008:  stfld       int32 Foo::x
//001674:           }
    IL_000d:  ret
} // End of method Foo::.ctor

} // End of class Foo
```

Notice that a const field is compiled into a static field, and a readonly field is compiled into an instance field. Therefore, you need only a class name to access a const field.

A common argument against using const fields is that they do not version as well as readonly fields. If you rebuild a component that defines a const field and the value of that const changes in a later version, any other components that were built against the old version won't pick up the new value. If there is any chance that a field is going to change, don't make it a const field.

The following code shows how to use an instance readonly field:

```
Foo obj1 = new Foo(100);
Console.WriteLine(obj1.bar);
```

Those two lines compile into the following IL:

```
IL_0013:    ldc.i4      0xc8
IL_0018:    newobj      instance void Foo::.ctor(int32)
IL_001d:    stloc.1
IL_001e:    ldloc.1
IL_001f:    ldfld       int32 Foo::bar
```

See Also

The "const" and "readonly" keywords in the MSDN documentation.

3.15   Building Cloneable Classes

Problem

You need a method of performing a shallow cloning operation, a deep cloning operation, or both on a data type that may also reference other types, but the ICloneable interface should not be used, as it violates the .NET Framework Design Guidelines.

Solution

To resolve the issue with using ICloneable, create two other interfaces to establish a copying pattern, IShallowCopy<T> and IDeepCopy<T>:

```
public interface IShallowCopy<T>
{
    T ShallowCopy();
}
public interface IDeepCopy<T>
{
    T DeepCopy();
}
```

Shallow copying means that the copied object's fields will reference the same objects as the original object. To allow shallow copying, implement the IShallowCopy<T> interface in the class:

```
using System;
using System.Collections;
using System.Collections.Generic;

public class ShallowClone : IShallowCopy<ShallowClone>
{
    public int Data = 1;
    public List<string> ListData = new List<string>();
    public object ObjData = new object();

    public ShallowClone ShallowCopy()
    {
        return (ShallowClone)this.MemberwiseClone();
    }
}
```

Deep copying or *cloning* means that the copied object's fields will reference new copies of the original object's fields. To allow deep copying, implement the IDeepCopy<T> interface in the class:

```
using System;
using System.Collections;
using System.Collections.Generic;
using System.Runtime.Serialization.Formatters.Binary;
using System.IO;

[Serializable]
public class DeepClone : IDeepCopy<DeepClone>
{
    public int data = 1;
    public List<string> ListData = new List<string>();
    public object objData = new object();

    public DeepClone DeepCopy()
    {
        BinaryFormatter BF = new BinaryFormatter();
        MemoryStream memStream = new MemoryStream();

        BF.Serialize(memStream, this);
        memStream.Flush();
        memStream.Position = 0;

        return (DeepClone)BF.Deserialize(memStream);
    }
}
```

To support both shallow and deep methods of copying, implement both interfaces. The code might appear as follows:

```
using System;
using System.Collections;
using System.Collections.Generic;
using System.Runtime.Serialization.Formatters.Binary;
using System.IO;

[Serializable]
public class MultiClone : IShallowCopy<MultiClone>,
                          IDeepCopy<MultiClone>
{
    public int data = 1;
    public List<string> ListData = new List<string>();
    public object objData = new object();

    public MultiClone ShallowCopy()
    {
        return (MultiClone)this.MemberwiseClone();
    }
```

```
    public MultiClone DeepCopy( )
    {
        BinaryFormatter BF = new BinaryFormatter( );
        MemoryStream memStream = new MemoryStream( );

        BF.Serialize(memStream, this);
        memStream.Flush( );
        memStream.Position = 0;

        return (MultiClone)BF.Deserialize(memStream);
    }
}
```

Discussion

The .NET Framework has an interface named ICloneable, which was originally designed to be how cloning is implemented in .NET. The design recommendation is now that this interface not be used in any public API. The reason is that it lends itself to different interpretations. The interface looks like this:

```
public interface ICloneable
{
    object Clone( );
}
```

Notice that there is a single method Clone that returns an object. Is the clone a shallow copy of the object or a deep copy? You can't know from the interface, as the implementation could go either way. This is why it should not be used, and the IShallowCopy<T> and IDeepCopy<T> interfaces are introduced here.

Cloning is the ability to make an exact copy (a clone) of an instance of a type. Cloning may take one of two forms: a shallow copy or a deep copy. Shallow copying is relatively easy. It involves copying the object that the ShallowCopy method was called on.

The reference type fields in the original object are copied over, as are the value-type fields. This means that if the original object contains a field of type StreamWriter, for instance, the cloned object will point to this same instance of the original object's StreamWriter; a new object is not created.

There is no need to deal with static fields when performing a cloning operation. There is only one memory location reserved for each static field per class, per application domain. Besides, the cloned object will have access to the same static fields as the original.

Support for shallow copying is implemented by the MemberwiseClone method of the Object class, which serves as the base class for all .NET classes. So, the following code allows a shallow copy to be created and returned by the Clone method:

```
public ShallowClone ShallowCopy( )
{
    return (ShallowClone)this.MemberwiseClone( );
}
```

Making a deep copy is the second way of cloning an object. A deep copy will make a copy of the original object just as the shallow copy does. However, a deep copy will also make separate copies of each reference type field in the original object. Therefore, if the original object contains a StreamWriter type field, the cloned object will also contain a StreamWriter type field, but the cloned object's StreamWriter field will point to a new StreamWriter object, not the original object's StreamWriter object.

Support for deep copying is not automatically provided by the .NET Framework. Instead, the following code illustrates an easy way of implementing a deep copy:

```
BinaryFormatter BF = new BinaryFormatter( );
MemoryStream memStream = new MemoryStream( );

BF.Serialize(memStream, this);
memStream.Flush( );
memStream.Position = 0;

return (BF.Deserialize(memStream));
```

Basically, the original object is serialized out to a memory stream using binary serialization, and then it is deserialized into a new object, which is returned to the caller. Note that it is important to reposition the memory stream pointer back to the start of the stream before calling the Deserialize method; otherwise, an exception indicating that the serialized object contains no data will be thrown.

Performing a deep copy using object serialization allows the underlying object to be changed without having to modify the code that performs the deep copy. If you performed the deep copy by hand, you'd have to make a new instance of all the instance fields of the original object and copy them over to the cloned object. This is a tedious chore in and of itself. If a change is made to the fields of the object being cloned, the deep copy code must also change to reflect this modification. Using serialization, you rely on the serializer to dynamically find and serialize all fields contained in the object. If the object is modified, the serializer will still make a deep copy without any code modifications.

One reason you might want to do a deep copy by hand is that the serialization technique presented in this recipe works properly only when everything in your object is serializable. Of course, manual cloning doesn't always help there either—some objects are just inherently noncloneable. Suppose you have a network management application in which an object represents a particular printer on your network. What's it supposed to do when you clone it? Fax a purchase order for a new printer?

One problem inherent with deep copying is performing a deep copy on a nested data structure with circular references. This recipe manages to make it possible to deal with circular references, although it's a tricky problem. So, in fact, you don't need to avoid circular references if you are using this recipe.

See Also

"Framework Design Guidelines: Conventions, Idioms, and Patterns for Reusable .NET Libraries" by Krzysztof Cwalina and Brad Abrams, and the "Object.Memberwise-Clone Method" topic in the MSDN documentation.

3.16   Assuring an Object's Disposal

Problem

You require a way to always have something happen when an object's work is done or it goes out of scope.

Solution

Use the using statement:

```
using System;
using System.IO;

// ...

using(FileStream FS = new FileStream("Test.txt", FileMode.Create))
{
    FS.WriteByte((byte)1);
    FS.WriteByte((byte)2);
    FS.WriteByte((byte)3);

    using(StreamWriter SW = new StreamWriter(FS))
    {
        SW.WriteLine("some text.");
    }
}
```

Discussion

The using statement is very easy to use and saves you the hassle of writing extra code. If the Solution had not used the using statement, it would look like this:

```
FileStream FS = new FileStream("Test.txt", FileMode.Create);
try
{

    FS.WriteByte((byte)1);
    FS.WriteByte((byte)2);
    FS.WriteByte((byte)3);

    StreamWriter SW = new StreamWriter(FS);
```

```
    try
    {
        SW.WriteLine("some text.");
    }
    finally
    {
        if (SW != null)
        {
            ((IDisposable)SW).Dispose();
        }
    }
}
finally
{
    if (FS != null)
    {
        ((IDisposable)FS).Dispose();
    }
}
```

Several points to note about the using statement:

- There is a using directive, such as:

  ```
  using System.IO;
  ```

  which should be differentiated from the using statement. This is potentially confusing to developers first getting into this language.

- The variable(s) defined in the using statement clause must all be of the same type, and they must have an initializer. However, you are allowed multiple using statements in front of a single code block, so this isn't a significant restriction.

- Any variables defined in the using clause are considered read-only in the body of the using statement. This prevents a developer from inadvertently switching the variable to refer to a different object and causing problems when an attempt is made to dispose of the object that the variable initially referenced.

- The variable should not be declared outside of the using block and then initialized inside of the using clause.

This last point is described by the following code:

```
FileStream FS;
using(FS = new FileStream("Test.txt", FileMode.Create))
{
    FS.WriteByte((byte)1);
    FS.WriteByte((byte)2);
    FS.WriteByte((byte)3);

    using(StreamWriter SW = new StreamWriter(FS))
    {
        SW.WriteLine("some text.");
    }
}
```

For this example code, you will not have a problem. But consider that the variable FS is usable outside of the using block. Essentially, you could revisit this code and modify it as follows:

```
FileStream FS;
using(FS = new FileStream("Test.txt", FileMode.Create))
{

    FS.WriteByte((byte)1);
    FS.WriteByte((byte)2);
    FS.WriteByte((byte)3);

    using(StreamWriter SW = new StreamWriter(FS))
    {
        SW.WriteLine("some text.");
    }
}
FS.WriteByte((byte)4);
```

This code compiles but throws an ObjectDisposedException on the last line of this code snippet because the Dispose method has already been called on the FS object. The object has not yet been collected at this point and still remains in memory in the disposed state.

See Also

Recipe 3.17, and the "IDispose Interface," "Using foreach with Collections," and "Implementing Finalize and Dispose to Clean up Unmanaged Resources" topics in the MSDN documentation.

3.17 Disposing of Unmanaged Resources

Problem

Your class references unmanaged resources and needs to ensure proper cleanup before it goes away.

Solution

Implement the *dispose design pattern*, which is specific to .NET.

The class that contains a reference to the unmanaged resources is shown here as Foo. This object contains references to a COM object called SomeCOMObj, a FileStream object called FStream, and an ArrayList that may or may not contain references to unmanaged resources. The source code is shown in Example 3-8.

Example 3-8. Foo: A class that contains references to unmanaged code

```
using System;
using System.Collections;
using System.IO;
using System.Runtime.InteropServices;

public class Foo : IDisposable
{
    [DllImport("Kernel32.dll", SetLastError = true)]
    private static extern IntPtr CreateSemaphore(IntPtr lpSemaphoreAttributes,
        int lInitialCount, int lMaximumCount, string lpName);

    [DllImport("Kernel32.dll", SetLastError = true)]
    private static extern bool ReleaseSemaphore(IntPtr hSemaphore,
        int lReleaseCount, out IntPtr lpPreviousCount);

    public Foo() {}

    // Replace SomeCOMObj with your COM object type.
    private SomeCOMObj comObj = new SomeCOMObj();
    private FileStream fileStream = new FileStream(@"c:\test.txt",
    FileMode.OpenOrCreate);
    private ArrayList aList = new ArrayList();
    private bool hasBeenDisposed = false;
    private IntPtr hSemaphore = IntPtr.Zero; // Unmanaged handle

    // Protect these members from being used on a disposed object.
    public void WriteToFile(string text)
    {
        if(hasBeenDisposed)
        {
            throw (new ObjectDisposedException(this.ToString(),
                                            "Object has been disposed"));
        }

        UnicodeEncoding enc = new UnicodeEncoding();
        fileStream.Write(enc.GetBytes(text), 0, text.Length);
    }
    public void UseCOMObj()
    {
        if(hasBeenDisposed)
        {
            throw (new ObjectDisposedException(this.ToString(),
                                            "Object has been disposed"));
        }

        Console.WriteLine("GUID: " + comObj.GetType().GUID);
    }

    public void AddToList(object obj)
    {
        if(hasBeenDisposed)
        {
```

```
            throw (new ObjectDisposedException(this.ToString(),
                                    "Object has been disposed"));
    }

    aList.Add(obj);
}

public void CreateSemaphore()
{
    // Create unmanaged handle here.
    hSemaphore = CreateSemaphore(IntPtr.Zero, 5, 5, null);
}

// The Dispose methods
public void Dispose()
{
    Dispose(true);
}

protected virtual void Dispose(bool disposeManagedObjs)
{
    if (!hasBeenDisposed)
    {
        try
        {
            if (disposeManagedObjs)
            {
                // Dispose all items in an array or ArrayList.
                foreach (object obj in aList)
                {
                    IDisposable disposableObj = obj as IDisposable;
                    if (disposableObj != null)
                    {
                        disposableObj.Dispose();
                    }
                }
                // Dispose managed objects implementing IDisposable.
                fileStream.Close();

                // Reduce reference count on RCW.
                Marshal.ReleaseComObject(comObj);

                GC.SuppressFinalize(this);
            }
            // Release unmanaged handle here.
            IntPtr prevCnt = new IntPtr();
            ReleaseSemaphore(hSemaphore, 1, out prevCnt);
        }
        catch (Exception)
        {
            hasBeenDisposed = false;
            throw;
```

```
            }

            hasBeenDisposed = true;
        }
    }

    // The destructor
    ~Foo( )
    {
        Dispose(false);
    }
    // Optional Close method
    public void Close( )
    {
        Dispose( );
    }
}
```

The following class inherits from Foo:

```
    // Class inherits from an IDisposable class
    public class Bar : Foo
    {
        //...

        private bool hasBeenDisposed = false;

        protected override void Dispose(bool disposeManagedObjs)
        {
            if (!hasBeenDisposed)
            {
                try
                {
                    if(disposeManagedObjs)
                    {
                        // Call Dispose/Close/Clear on any managed objects here...
                    }

                    // Release any unmanaged objects here...

                    // Call base class' Dispose method.
                    base.Dispose(disposeManagedObjs);
                }
                catch (Exception)
                {
                    hasBeenDisposed = false;
                    throw;
                }

                hasBeenDisposed = true;
            }
        }
    }
```

Whether this class directly contains any references to unmanaged resources, it should be disposed of as shown in the code.

Discussion

The *dispose design pattern* allows any unmanaged resources held by an object to be cleaned up from within the managed environment. This pattern is flexible enough to allow unmanaged resources held by the disposable object to be cleaned up explicitly (by calling the Dispose method) or implicitly (by waiting for the garbage collector to call the destructor). Finalizers are a safety net to clean up objects when you forget to do it.

 This design pattern should be used on any base class that has derived types that hold unmanaged resources. This indicates to the inheritor that this design pattern should be implemented in their derived class as well.

All the code that needs to be written for a disposable object is written within the class itself. First, all disposable types must implement the IDisposable interface. This interface contains a single method, Dispose, which accepts no parameters and returns void. The Dispose method is overloaded to accept a Boolean flag indicating whether any managed objects referenced by this object should also be disposed. If this parameter is true, managed objects referenced by this object will have their Dispose method called, and unmanaged resources are released; otherwise, only unmanaged resources are released.

The IDisposable.Dispose method will forward its call to the overloaded Dispose method that accepts a Boolean flag. This flag will be set to true to allow all managed objects to attempt to dispose of themselves as well as to release unmanaged resources held by this object.

The IDisposable interface is very important to implement. This interface allows the using statement to take advantage of the dispose pattern. A using statement that operates on the Foo object is written as follows:

```
using (Foo f = new Foo())
{
    f.WriteToFile("text");
}
```

 Always implement the IDisposable interface on types that contain resources that need to be disposed or otherwise explicitly closed or released. This allows the use of the using keyword and aids in self-documenting the type.

A foreach loop will also make use of the IDisposable interface, but in a slightly different manner. After the loop exits, the Dispose method is called for each object. The foreach loop guarantees that it will call the IDisposable.Dispose method if the object returned from the GetEnumerator method implements IDisposable.

The overloaded Dispose method that accepts a Boolean flag contains a static method call to GC.SuppressFinalize to force the garbage collector to remove this object from the *fqueue*, or finalization queue. The fqueue allows the garbage collector to run C# finalizers at a point after the object has been freed. However, this ability comes at a price: it takes many garbage-collection cycles to completely collect an object with a destructor. If the object is placed on the fqueue in generation 0, the object will have to wait until generation 1 is collected, which could be some time, as there are many more generation 0 collections than generation 1 (and many more generation 1 than generation 2). The GC.SuppressFinalize method removes the object from the fqueue because it doesn't need specific code run for the finalizer; the memory can just be released. Calling this static method from within the Dispose method is critical to writing better-performing classes.

 Call the GC.SuppressFinalize method in the base class Dispose method when the overload of the Dispose method is passed true. Doing so will allow your object to be taken off of the finalization queue in the garbage collector, allowing for earlier collection. This will help prevent memory retention and will help your application's performance, as resources that need finalization are usually expensive, and cleaning them up earlier is a good thing.

A finalizer is added to this class, and it contains code to call the overloaded Dispose method, passing in false as its only argument. Note that all cleanup code should exist within the overloaded Dispose method that accepts a Boolean flag. All other methods should call this method to perform any necessary cleanup. The destructor will pass a false value into the Dispose method to prevent any managed objects from being disposed. Remember, the finalizers run in their own thread. Attempting to dispose of objects that may have already been collected or are about to be collected could have serious consequences for your code, such as resurrecting an object into an undefined state. It is best to prevent any references to other objects while the destructor is running.

It is possible to add a Close or even a Clear method to your class to be called as well as the Dispose method. Several classes in the FCL use a Close or Clear method to clean up unmanaged resources:

```
FileStream.Close( )
StreamWriter.Close( )
TcpClient.Close( )
MessageQueue.Close( )
SymmetricAlgorithm.Clear( )
AsymmetricAlgorithm.Clear( )
CryptoAPITransform.Clear( )
CryptoStream.Clear( )
```

Each of these classes also contains a `Dispose` method. The `Clear` method usually calls the `Dispose` method directly. There is a problem with this design. The `Clear` method is used extensively throughout the FCL for classes such as `ArrayList`, `Hashtable`, and other collection-type classes. However, the `Clear` method of the collection classes performs a much different task: it clears the collection of all its items. This `Clear` method has nothing to do with releasing unmanaged resources or calling the `Dispose` method.

The overloaded `Dispose` method that accepts a Boolean flag will contain all of the logic to release unmanaged resources from this object as well as possibly calling `Dispose` on types referenced by this object. In addition to these two actions, this method can also reduce the reference count on any COM objects that are referenced by this object. The static `Marshal.ReleaseComObject` method will decrement the reference count by one on the COM object reference passed in to this method:

```
Marshal.ReleaseComObject(comObj);
```

To force the reference count to go to zero, allowing the COM object to be released and its RCW to be garbage collected, you could write the following code:

```
while (Marshal.ReleaseComObject(comObj) > 0);
```

Take great care when forcing the reference count to zero for a COM object. If another object is using this COM object, the COM object will be released out from under this other object. This can easily destabilize a system and should be avoided unless absolutely necessary.

Any callable method/property/indexer (basically, any nonprivate method except for the `Dispose` and `Close` methods and the constructor[s] and the destructor) should throw the `ObjectDisposedException` exception if it is called after the object has been disposed—that is, after its `Dispose` method has been called. A private field called `hasBeenDisposed` is used as a Boolean flag to indicate whether this object has been disposed; a true confirms that it has been disposed. This flag is checked to determine whether this object has been disposed at the beginning of every method/property/indexer. If it has been disposed, the `ObjectDisposedException` is thrown. This prevents the use of an object after it has been disposed and potentially placed in an unknown state.

Disposable objects should always check to see if they have been disposed in all of their public methods, properties, and indexers. If a client attempts to use your object after it has been disposed, an `ObjectDisposedException` should be thrown. Note that a `Dispose` method can be called multiple times after this object has been disposed without having any side effects (including the throwing of `ObjectDisposedExceptions`) on the object.

Any classes inheriting from Foo need not implement the IDisposable interface; it is implied from the base class. The inheriting class should implement the hasBeenDisposed Boolean flag field and use this flag in any methods/properties/indexers to confirm that this object has been disposed. Finally, a Dispose method is implemented that accepts a Boolean flag and overrides the same virtual method in the base class. This Dispose method does not have to call the GC.SuppressFinalize(this) static method; this is done in the base class's Dispose method.

The IDisposable.Dispose method should not be implemented in this class. When the Dispose method is called on an object of type Bar, the Foo.Dispose method will be called. The Foo.Dispose method will then call the overridden Bar.Dispose(bool) method, which, in turn, calls its base class Dispose(bool) method, Foo. Dispose(bool). The base class's finalizer is also inherited by the Bar class.

 All Dispose methods should call their base class' Dispose method.

If the client code fails to call the Dispose or Close method, the destructor will run, and the Dispose(bool) method will still be called, albeit at a later time. The finalizer is the object's last line of defense for releasing unmanaged resources.

See Also

The "Dispose Interface," "Using foreach with Collections," and "Implementing Finalize and Dispose to Clean up Unmanaged Resources" topics in the MSDN documentation.

3.18   Determining Where Boxing and Unboxing Occur

Problem

You have a project consisting of some very complex code that is a performance bottleneck for the entire application. You have been assigned to increase performance, but you do not know where to start looking.

Solution

A great way to start looking for performance problems is to set a customer-focused goal for what level of performance you want to achieve. The old saying "if we don't know where we are going, anyplace will do" is very appropriate for performance tuning, as lots of time and money can be spent in pursuit of gains that may or may not be necessary if no goals are set to measure them against. To reach the goal, you can use a profiling tool to see whether boxing is actually causing you any kind of problem in the first place. A profiler will show you exactly what allocations are occurring and in what volume. There are several profilers on the market; some are free and others are not.

If you have already established through profiling that boxing is definitely causing a problem, but you are still having trouble working out where it's occurring, then you can use the Ildasm disassembler tool that is packaged with VS.NET. With Ildasm, you can convert an entire project to its equivalent IL code and then dump the IL to a text file. To do this, Ildasm has several command-line switches, one of which is the /output switch. This switch is used as follows:

```
ildasm Proj1.dll /output:Proj1.il
```

This command will disassemble the file *Proj1.dll* and then write the disassembled IL to the file *Proj1.il*.

A second useful command-line switch is /source. This switch shows the original code (C#, VB.NET, etc.) in which this DLL was written, as well as the IL that was compiled from each of these source lines. Note that the DLL must be built with debugging enabled. This switch is used as follows:

```
ildasm Proj1.dll /output:Proj1.il /source
```

We prefer the second method of invoking Ildasm, since the original source is included, preventing you from getting lost in all of the IL code.

After running Ildasm from the command line, open the resulting IL code file in VS. NET or your favorite editor. Inside the editor, do a text search for the words *box*, *unbox*, or *callvirt*. This will find all potential occurrences of boxing and unboxing operations.

Using this information, you have pinpointed the problem areas. Now, you can turn your attention to them to see if there is any way to prevent or minimize the boxing/unboxing operations.

Discussion

When a boxing or unboxing operation occurs in code, whether it was implicit or explicit, the IL generated includes the box or unbox command. For example, the following C# code:

```
int valType = 1;
object boxedValType = valType;
valType = (int)boxedValType;
```

compiles to the following IL code:

```
//000883:           int valType = 1;
  IL_0000:  ldc.i4.1
  IL_0001:  stloc.0
//000884:           object boxedValType = valType;
  IL_0002:  ldloc.0
  IL_0003:  box        [mscorlib]System.Int32
  Il_0008:  stloc.1
```

```
//000898:           int valType = (int) boxedValType;
  IL_0061:   ldloc.1
  IL_0062:   unbox     [mscorlib]System.Int32
  IL_0067:   ldind.i4
```

Notice the box and unbox commands in the previous IL code. IL makes it very apparent when a boxing or unboxing operation occurs. You can use this to your advantage to find and hopefully prevent a boxing operation from occurring.

The following can help prevent or eliminate boxing:

1. Use classes instead of structures. This usually involves simply changing the struct keyword to class in the structure definition. This change can dramatically improve performance. However, this change should be done in a very careful manner, as it can change the operation of the application.

2. If you are storing value types in a collection, switch to using a generic collection. This makes it easier for the compiler to help enforce proper usage, helps to catch bugs, and is more self-documenting. The generic collection can be instantiated for the specific value type that you will be storing in it. This allows you to create a collection that is strongly typed for that specific value type. Not only will using a generic collection alleviate the boxing/unboxing issue, but it will also speed things up because there are fewer casts to perform when adding, removing, and looking up values in this collection.

3. Take care when implementing explicit interface members on structures. As the discussion shows, this causes the structure to be boxed before the call to an interface member is made through the interface. This reflects the fact that explicit implementation of a method on an interface is accessible only from the interface type. This means that the structure must be cast to that interface type before the explicitly declared methods of that interface type can be used. An interface is a reference type and therefore causes the structure to be boxed when an explicit interface method is accessed on that structure. However, in some cases, this isn't true. For example, the using statement issues an IL instruction to prevent boxing when calling the Dispose method—assuming that an implicit interface implementation is used.

 Note that changes to a value type that exists in both boxed and unboxed form occur independently of one another.

See Also

The "Boxing Conversion" and "Unboxing Conversion" topics in the MSDN documentation.

Here is a list of some available profiling tools:

- Allocation Profiler (free), which can be obtained in the *UserSamples* section of the web site *http://www.gotdotnet.com/community/usersamples/*.

- Red Gate ANTS Profiler (purchase), which can be purchased at *http://www.red-gate.com/products/ants_profiler/*.

- Visual Studio Team System for Developers.

- Team Suite (purchase), which can be purchased at *http://msdn2.microsoft.com/en-us/teamsystem/aa718822.aspx*.

CHAPTER 4

Generics

4.0   Introduction

Generics are an extremely useful feature that allows you to write type safe and efficient collection- and pattern-based code. This aspect of generics is described in Recipes 4.1 and 4.2. With generics comes quite a bit of programming power, but with
that power comes the responsibility to use it correctly. If you are considering converting your ArrayList, Queue, Stack, and Hashtable objects to use their generic counterparts, consider reading Recipes 4.3, 4.4, and 4.9. As you will read, the conversion
is not always simple and easy, and there are reasons why you might not want to do
this conversion at all.

Some recipes in this chapter, such as Recipe 4.5, deal with other generic classes contained in the .NET Framework. Still, others deal with the operation of any generic
type; see Recipes 4.1, 4.7, and 4.11.

4.1   Deciding When and Where to Use Generics

Problem

You want to use generic types in a new project or convert nongeneric types in an
existing project to their generic equivalent. However, you do not really know why
you would want to do this, and you do not know which nongeneric types should be
converted to be generic.

Solution

In deciding when and where to use generic types, you need to consider several
things:

- Will your type contain or be operating on various unspecified data types (e.g., a collection type)? If so, creating a generic type will offer several benefits over creating a nongeneric type. If your type will operate on only a single specific type, then you may not need to create a generic type.

- If your type will be operating on value types, so that boxing and unboxing operations will occur, you should consider using generics to prevent the boxing and unboxing operations.

- The stronger type checking associated with generics will aid in finding errors sooner (i.e., during compile time as opposed to runtime), thus shortening your bug-fixing cycle.

- Is your code suffering from "code bloat," with you writing multiple classes to handle different data types on which they operate (e.g., a specialized ArrayList that stores only StreamReaders and another that stores only StreamWriters)? It is easier to write the code once and have it just work for each of the data types it operates on.

- Generics allow for greater clarity of code. By eliminating code bloat and forcing stronger type checking on your types, your code will be easier to read and understand.

Discussion

In most cases, your code will benefit from using a generic type. Generics allow for more efficient code reuse, faster performance, stronger type checking, and easier-to-read code.

See Also

The "Generics Overview" and "Benefits of Generics" topics in the MSDN documentation.

4.2 Understanding Generic Types

Problem

You need to understand how the .NET types work for generics and how Generic .NET types differ from regular .NET types.

Solution

A couple of quick experiments can show the differences between regular .NET types and generic .NET types. When a regular .NET type is defined, it looks like the FixedSizeCollection type defined in Example 4-1.

Example 4-1. FixedSizeCollection: a regular .NET type

```
public class FixedSizeCollection
{
    /// <summary>
    /// Constructor that increments static counter
    /// and sets the maximum number of items
    /// </summary>
    /// <param name="maxItems"></param>
    public FixedSizeCollection(int maxItems)
    {
        FixedSizeCollection.InstanceCount++;
        this.Items = new object[maxItems];
    }

    /// <summary>
    /// Add an item to the class whose type
    /// is unknown as only object can hold any type
    /// </summary>
    /// <param name="item">item to add</param>
    /// <returns>the index of the item added</returns>
    public int AddItem(object item)
    {
        if (this.ItemCount < this.Items.Length)
        {
            this.Items[this.ItemCount] = item;
            return this.ItemCount++;
        }
        else
            throw new Exception("Item queue is full");
    }

    /// <summary>
    /// Get an item from the class
    /// </summary>
    /// <param name="index">the index of the item to get</param>
    /// <returns>an item of type object</returns>
    public object GetItem(int index)
    {
        if (index >= this.Items.Length &&
            index >= 0)
            throw new ArgumentOutOfRangeException("index");

        return this.Items[index];
    }

    #region Properties
    /// <summary>
    /// Static instance counter hangs off of the Type for
    /// StandardClass
    /// </summary>
    public static int InstanceCount { get; set; }

    /// <summary>
```

Example 4-1. FixedSizeCollection: a regular .NET type (continued)

```
    /// The count of the items the class holds
    /// </summary>
    public int ItemCount { get; private set; }

    /// <summary>
    /// The items in the class
    /// </summary>
    private object[] Items { get; set; }
    #endregion // Properties

    /// <summary>
    /// ToString override to provide class detail
    /// </summary>
    /// <returns>formatted string with class details</returns>
    public override string ToString()
    {
        return "There are " + FixedSizeCollection.InstanceCount.ToString() +
            " instances of " + this.GetType().ToString() +
            " and this instance contains " + this.ItemCount + " items...";
    }
}
```

FixedSizeCollection has a static integer property variable, InstanceCount, which is incremented in the instance constructor, and a ToString() override that prints out how many instances of FixedSizeCollection exist in this AppDomain. FixedSizeCollection also contains an array of objects(Items), the size of which is determined by the item count passed in to the constructor. It implements methods to add and retrieve items (AddItem, GetItem) and a read-only property to get the number of items currently in the array (ItemCount).

The FixedSizeCollection<T> type is a generic .NET type with the same static property InstanceCount field, the instance constructor that counts the number of instantiations, and the overridden ToString() method to tell you how many instances there are of this type. FixedSizeCollection<T> also has an Items array property and methods corresponding to those in FixedSizeCollection, as you can see in Example 4-2.

Example 4-2. FixedSizeCollection<T>: a generic .NET type

```
/// <summary>
/// A generic class to show instance counting
/// </summary>
/// <typeparam name="T">the type parameter used for the array storage</typeparam>
public class FixedSizeCollection<T>
{
    /// <summary>
    /// Constructor that increments static counter and sets up internal storage
    /// </summary>
    /// <param name="items"></param>
    public FixedSizeCollection(int items)
    {
```

Example 4-2. FixedSizeCollection<T>: a generic .NET type (continued)

```
        FixedSizeCollection<T>.InstanceCount++;
        this.Items = new T[items];
    }

    /// <summary>
    /// Add an item to the class whose type
    /// is determined by the instantiating type
    /// </summary>
    /// <param name="item">item to add</param>
    /// <returns>the zero-based index of the item added</returns>
    public int AddItem(T item)
    {
        if (this.ItemCount < this.Items.Length)
        {
            this.Items[this.ItemCount] = item;
            return this.ItemCount++;
        }
        else
            throw new Exception("Item queue is full");
    }

    /// <summary>
    /// Get an item from the class
    /// </summary>
    /// <param name="index">the zero-based index of the item to get</param>
    /// <returns>an item of the instantiating type</returns>
    public T GetItem(int index)
    {
        if (index >= this.Items.Length &&
            index >= 0)
            throw new ArgumentOutOfRangeException("index");

        return this.Items[index];
    }

    #region Properties
    /// <summary>
    /// Static instance counter hangs off of the
    /// instantiated Type for
    /// GenericClass
    /// </summary>
    public static int InstanceCount { get; set; }

    /// <summary>
    /// The count of the items the class holds
    /// </summary>
    public int ItemCount { get; private set; }

    /// <summary>
    /// The items in the class
    /// </summary>
    private T[] Items { get; set; }
```

Example 4-2. FixedSizeCollection<T>: a generic .NET type (continued)

```
#endregion // Properties

/// <summary>
/// ToString override to provide class detail
/// </summary>
/// <returns>formatted string with class details</returns>
public override string ToString()
{
    return "There are " + FixedSizeCollection<T>.InstanceCount.ToString() +
        " instances of " + this.GetType().ToString() +
        " and this instance contains " + this.ItemCount + " items...";
}
}
```

Things start to get a little different with FixedSizeCollection<T> when you look at the Items array property implementation. The Items array is declared as:

```
private T[] Items { get; set; }
```

instead of:

```
private object[] Items { get; set; }
```

The Items array property uses the type parameter of the generic class (<T>) to determine what type of items are allowed. FixedSizeCollection uses object for the Items array property type, which allows any type to be stored in the array of items (since all types are convertible to object), while FixedSizeCollection<T> provides type safety by allowing the type parameter to dictate what types of objects are permitted. Notice also that the properties have no associated private backing field declared for storing the array. This is an example of using the new Automatically Implemented Properties in C# 3.0. Under the covers, the C# compiler is creating a storage element of the type of the property, but you don't have to write the code for the property storage anymore if you don't have specific code that has to execute when accessing the properties. To make the property read-only, simply mark the set; declaration private.

The next difference is visible in the method declarations of AddItem and GetItem. AddItem now takes a parameter of type T, whereas in FixedSizeCollection, it took a parameter of type object. GetItem now returns a value of type T, whereas in FixedSizeCollection, it returned a value of type object. These changes allow the methods in FixedSizeCollection<T> to use the instantiated type to store and retrieve the items in the array, instead of having to allow any object to be stored as in FixedSizeCollection:

```
/// <summary>
/// Add an item to the class whose type
/// is determined by the instantiating type
/// </summary>
/// <param name="item">item to add</param>
/// <returns>the zero-based index of the item added</returns>
public int AddItem(T item)
```

```
    {
        if (this.ItemCount < this.Items.Length)
        {
            this.Items[this.ItemCount] = item;
            return this.ItemCount++;
        }
        else
            throw new Exception("Item queue is full");
    }

    /// <summary>
    /// Get an item from the class
    /// </summary>
    /// <param name="index">the zero-based index of the item to get</param>
    /// <returns>an item of the instantiating type</returns>
    public T GetItem(int index)
    {
        if (index >= this.Items.Length &&
            index >= 0)
            throw new ArgumentOutOfRangeException("index");

        return this.Items[index];
    }
```

This provides a few advantages. First and foremost is the type safety provided by FixedSizeCollection<T> for items in the array. It was possible to write code like this in FixedSizeCollection:

```
// Regular class
FixedSizeCollection C = new FixedSizeCollection(5);
Console.WriteLine(C);

string s1 = "s1";
string s2 = "s2";
string s3 = "s3";
int i1 = 1;

// Add to the fixed size collection (as object).
C.AddItem(s1);
C.AddItem(s2);
C.AddItem(s3);
// Add an int to the string array, perfectly OK.
C.AddItem(i1);
```

But FixedSizeCollection<T> will give a compiler error if you try the same thing:

```
// Generic class
FixedSizeCollection<string> gC = new FixedSizeCollection<string>(5);
Console.WriteLine(gC);

string s1 = "s1";
string s2 = "s2";
string s3 = "s3";
int i1 = 1;
```

```
// Add to the generic class (as string).
gC.AddItem(s1);
gC.AddItem(s2);
gC.AddItem(s3);
// Try to add an int to the string instance, denied by compiler.
// error CS1503: Argument '1': cannot convert from 'int' to 'string'
//gC.AddItem(i1);
```

Having the compiler prevent this before it can become the source of runtime bugs is a very good thing.

It may not be immediately noticeable, but the integer is actually boxed when it is added to the object array in FixedSizeCollection, as you can see in the IL for the call to GetItem on FixedSizeCollection:

```
IL_0170: ldloc.2
IL_0171: ldloc.s i1
IL_0173: box [mscorlib]System.Int32
IL_0178: callvirt instance int32
         CSharpRecipes.Generics/FixedSizeCollection::AddItem(object)
```

This boxing turns the int, which is a value type, into a reference type (object) for storage in the array. This causes extra work to be done to store value types in the object array.

There is a problem when you go to get an item back from the class in the FixedSizeCollection implementation. Take a look at how FixedSizeCollection. GetItem retrieves an item:

```
// Hold the retrieved string.
string sHolder;

// Have to cast or get error CS0266:
// Cannot implicitly convert type 'object' to 'string'...
sHolder = (string)C.GetItem(1);
```

Since the item returned by FixedSizeCollection.GetItem is of type object, it needs to be cast to a string in order to get what you hope is a string for index 1. It may not be a string—all you know for sure is that it's an object—but you have to cast it to a more specific type coming out so you can assign it properly.

These are both fixed by the FixedSizeCollection<T> implementation. The unboxing is addressed; no unboxing is required, since the return type of GetItem is the instantiated type, and the compiler enforces this by looking at the value being returned:

```
// Hold the retrieved string.
string sHolder;
int iHolder;

// No cast necessary
sHolder = gC.GetItem(1);

// Try to get a string into an int.
// error CS0029: Cannot implicitly convert type 'string' to 'int'
//iHolder = gC.GetItem(1);
```

In order to see one other difference between the two types, instantiate a few instances of each of them like so:

```
// Regular class
FixedSizeCollection A = new FixedSizeCollection(5);
Console.WriteLine(A);
FixedSizeCollection B = new FixedSizeCollection(5);
Console.WriteLine(B);
FixedSizeCollection C = new FixedSizeCollection(5);
Console.WriteLine(C);

// generic class
FixedSizeCollection<bool> gA = new FixedSizeCollection<bool>(5);
Console.WriteLine(gA);
FixedSizeCollection<int> gB = new FixedSizeCollection<int>(5);
Console.WriteLine(gB);
FixedSizeCollection<string> gC = new FixedSizeCollection<string>(5);
Console.WriteLine(gC);
FixedSizeCollection<string> gD = new FixedSizeCollection<string>(5);
Console.WriteLine(gD);
```

The output from the preceding code shows this:

```
There are 1 instances of CSharpRecipes.Generics+FixedSizeCollection and this ins
tance contains 0 items...
There are 2 instances of CSharpRecipes.Generics+FixedSizeCollection and this ins
tance contains 0 items...
There are 3 instances of CSharpRecipes.Generics+FixedSizeCollection and this ins
tance contains 0 items...
There are 1 instances of CSharpRecipes.Generics+FixedSizeCollection`1[System.Boo
lean] and this instance contains 0 items...
There are 1 instances of CSharpRecipes.Generics+FixedSizeCollection`1[System.Int
32] and this instance contains 0 items...
There are 1 instances of CSharpRecipes.Generics+FixedSizeCollection`1[System.Str
ing] and this instance contains 0 items...
There are 2 instances of CSharpRecipes.Generics+FixedSizeCollection`1[System.Str
ing] and this instance contains 0 items...
```

Discussion

The type parameters in generics allow you to create type-safe code without knowing the final type you will be working with. In many instances, you want the types to have certain characteristics, in which case you place constraints on the type (see Recipe 4.11). Methods can have generic type parameters whether the class itself does or does not.

Notice that while FixedSizeCollection has three instances, FixedSizeCollection, has one instance in which it was declared with bool as the type, one instance in which int was the type, and two instances in which string was the declaring type. This means that, while there is one .NET Type object created for each nongeneric class, there is one .NET Type object for every constructed type of a generic class.

`FixedSizeCollection` has three instances in the example code because `FixedSizeCollection` has only one type that is maintained by the CLR. With generics, one type is maintained for each combination of the class template and the type arguments passed when constructing a type instance. To make it clearer, you get one .NET type for `FixedSizeCollection<bool>`, one .NET type for `FixedSizeCollection<int>`, and a third .NET type for `FixedSizeCollection<string>`.

The static `InstanceCount` property helps to illustrate this point, as static properties of a class are actually connected to the type that the CLR hangs on to. The CLR creates any given type only once and then maintains it until the `AppDomain` unloads. This is why the output from the calls to `ToString()` on these objects shows that the count is three for `FixedSizeCollection` (as there is truly only one of these) and between one and two for the `FixedSizeCollection<T>` types.

See Also

The "Generic Type Parameters" and "Generic Classes" topics in the MSDN documentation.

4.3 Replacing the ArrayList with Its Generic Counterpart

Problem

You want to enhance the performance of your application as well as make the code easier to work with by replacing all `ArrayList` objects with the generic version. This is imperative when you find that structures or other value types are being stored in these data structures, resulting in boxing/unboxing operations.

Solution

Replace all occurrences of the `System.Collection.ArrayList` class with the more efficient generic `System.Collections.Generic.List` class.

Here is a simple example of using a `System.Collections.ArrayList` object:

```
public static void UseNonGenericArrayList()
{
    // Create and populate an ArrayList.
    ArrayList numbers = new ArrayList();
    numbers.Add(1); // Causes a boxing operation to occur
    numbers.Add(2); // Causes a boxing operation to occur

    // Display all integers in the ArrayList.
    // Causes an unboxing operation to occur on each iteration
    foreach (int i in numbers)
    {
        Console.WriteLine(i);
```

```
    }

        numbers.Clear( );
    }
```

Here is that same code using a System.Collections.Generic.List object:

```
    public static void UseGenericList( )
    {
        // Create and populate a List.
        List<int> numbers = new List<int>( );
        numbers.Add(1);
        numbers.Add(2);

        // Display all integers in the ArrayList.
        foreach (int i in numbers)
        {
            Console.WriteLine(i);
        }

        numbers.Clear( );
    }
```

Discussion

Since ArrayLists are used in almost all applications, it is a good place to start to enhance the performance of your application. For simple implementations of the ArrayList in your application, this substitution should be quite easy.

Table 4-1 shows the equivalent members that are implemented in both classes.

Table 4-1. Equivalent members in the ArrayList and the generic List classes

Members in the ArrayList class	Equivalent members in the generic List class
Capacity property	Capacity property
Count property	Count property
IsFixedSize property	((IList)myList).IsFixedSize
IsReadOnly property	((IList)myList).IsReadOnly
IsSynchronized property	((IList)myList).IsSynchronized
Item property	Item property
SyncRoot property	((IList)myList).SyncRoot
Adapter static method	N/A
Add method	Add method
AddRange method	AddRange method
N/A	AsReadOnly method
BinarySearch method	BinarySearch method
Clear method	Clear method
Clone method	GetRange(0, numbers.Count)

Table 4-1. Equivalent members in the ArrayList and the generic List classes (continued)

Members in the ArrayList class	Equivalent members in the generic List class
Contains method	Contains method
N/A	ConvertAll method
CopyTo method	CopyTo method
N/A	Exists method
N/A	Find method
N/A	FindAll method
N/A	FindIndex method
N/A	FindLast method
N/A	FindLastIndex method
N/A	ForEach method
FixedSize static method	N/A
GetRange method	GetRange method
IndexOf method	IndexOf method
Insert method	Insert method
InsertRange method	InsertRange method
LastIndexOf method	LastIndexOf method
ReadOnly static method	AsReadOnly method
Remove method	Remove method
N/A	RemoveAll method
RemoveAt method	RemoveAt method
RemoveRange method	RemoveRange method
Repeat static method	Use a for loop and the Add method
Reverse method	Reverse method
SetRange method	InsertRange method
Sort method	Sort method
Synchronized static method	lock(myList.SyncRoot){...}
ToArray method	ToArray method
N/A	TrimExcess method
TrimToSize method	TrimToSize method
N/A	TrueForAll method

In several cases within Table 4-1, there is not a one-to-one correlation between the members of an ArrayList and the members of the generic List class. Starting with the properties, notice that only the Capacity, Count, and Item properties are present in both classes. To make up for the missing properties in the List class, you can perform a cast to an IList. The following code shows how to use these casts to get at the missing properties:

```
List<int> numbers = new List<int>();

Console.WriteLine(((IList)numbers).IsReadOnly);
Console.WriteLine(((IList)numbers).IsFixedSize);
Console.WriteLine(((IList)numbers).IsSynchronized);
Console.WriteLine(((IList)numbers).SyncRoot);
```

Note that due to the absence of code that returns a synchronized version of a generic List and the absence of code that returns a fixed-size generic List, the IsFixedSize and IsSynchronized properties will always return false. The SyncRoot property will always return the same object on which it is called. Essentially, this property returns the this pointer. Microsoft has decided to remove the ability to create a synchronous wrapper from any of the generic collection classes. Instead, they recommend using the lock keyword to lock the entire collection or another type of synchronization object that suits your needs.

The ArrayList has several static methods to which there is no direct equivalent method in the generic List class. To fix this, you have to do a little work. The closest match for the static ArrayList.ReadOnly method is the AsReadOnly instance method of the generic List class. This makes for a fairly simple substitution.

The static ArrayList.Repeat method has no direct equivalent in the generic List class. So instead, you can use the following generic extension method:

```
public static void Repeat<T>(this List<T> list, T obj, int count)
{
    if (count < 0)
    {
        throw (new ArgumentException(
                "The count parameter must be greater or equal to zero."));
    }

    for (int index = 0; index < count; index++)
    {
        list.Add(obj);
    }
}
```

This generic extension method has three parameters:

list

Marks this method as an extension method for List<T>.

obj

The object that will be added to the generic List object a specified number of times.

count

The number of times to add the object contained in obj to the generic List object.

Since the Clone method is also missing from the generic List class (due to the fact that this class does not implement the ICloneable interface), you can instead use the GetRange method of the generic List class:

```
List<int> oldList = new List<int>();
// Populate oldList...

List<int> newList = oldList.GetRange(0, oldList.Count);
```

The GetRange method performs a shallow copy (similar to the Clone method of the ArrayList) of a range of elements in the List object. In this case, the range of elements includes all elements.

See Also

The "System.Collections.ArrayList Class" and "System.Collections.Generic.List Class" topics in the MSDN documentation.

4.4   Replacing the Stack and Queue with Their Generic Counterparts

Problem

You want to enhance the performance of your application as well as make the code easier to work with by replacing all Stack and Queue objects with their generic versions. This is imperative when you find that structures or other value types are being stored in these data structures, resulting in boxing/unboxing operations.

Solution

Replace all occurrences of the System.Collections.Stack and System.Collection. Queue objects with the System.Collections.Generic.Stack and System.Collection. Generic.Queue objects.

Here is a simple example of using a System.Collections.Queue object:

```
public static void UseNonGenericQueue()
{
    // Create a non-generic Queue object.
    Queue numericQueue = new Queue();

    // Populate Queue (causing a boxing operation to occur).
    numericQueue.Enqueue(1);
    numericQueue.Enqueue(2);
    numericQueue.Enqueue(3);

    // De-populate Queue and display items (causing an unboxing operation to
occur)
    Console.WriteLine(numericQueue.Dequeue());
```

```
        Console.WriteLine(numericQueue.Dequeue( ));
        Console.WriteLine(numericQueue.Dequeue( ).ToString( ));
    }
```

Here is that same code using a System.Collections.Generic.Queue object:

```
public static void UseGenericQueue( )
{
    // Create a generic Queue object.
    Queue<int> numericQueue = new Queue<int>( );

    // Populate Queue.
    numericQueue.Enqueue(1);
    numericQueue.Enqueue(2);
    numericQueue.Enqueue(3);

    // De-populate Queue and display items.
    Console.WriteLine(numericQueue.Dequeue( ));
    Console.WriteLine(numericQueue.Dequeue( ));
    Console.WriteLine(numericQueue.Dequeue( ));
}
```

Here is a simple example of using a System.Collections.Stack object:

```
public static void UseNonGenericStack( )
{
    // Create a non-generic Stack object.
    Stack numericStack = new Stack( );

    // Populate Stack (causing a boxing operation to occur).
    numericStack.Push(1);
    numericStack.Push(2);
    numericStack.Push(3);

    // De-populate Stack and display items (causing an unboxing operation to
occur).
    Console.WriteLine(numericStack.Pop( ).ToString( ));
    Console.WriteLine(numericStack.Pop( ).ToString( ));
    Console.WriteLine(numericStack.Pop( ).ToString( ));
}
```

Here is that same code using a System.Collections.Generic.Stack object:

```
public static void UseGenericStack( )
{
    // Create a generic Stack object.
    Stack<int> numericStack = new Stack<int>( );

    // Populate Stack.
    numericStack.Push(1);
    numericStack.Push(2);
    numericStack.Push(3);

    // De-populate Stack and display items.
    Console.WriteLine(numericStack.Pop( ).ToString( ));
    Console.WriteLine(numericStack.Pop( ).ToString( ));
```

```
        Console.WriteLine(numericStack.Pop( ).ToString( ));
    }
```

Discussion

On the surface, the generic and nongeneric Queue and Stack classes seem similar enough. However, it is a very different story underneath the surface. The basic use of the generic Queue and Stack objects are the same as with their nongeneric counterparts, except for the syntax used to instantiate the objects. The generic form requires a *type argument* in order to create the type. The type argument in this example is an int. This type argument indicates that this Queue or Stack object will be able to contain only integer types, as well as any type that implicitly converts to an integer, such as a short:

```
short s = 300;
numericQueue.Enqueue(s);    // OK, because of the implicit conversion
```

However, a type that cannot be implicitly converted to an integer, such as a double, will cause a compile-time error:

```
double d = 300;
numericQueue.Enqueue(d);        // Error, no implicit conversion available
numericQueue.Enqueue((int)d);   // OK, because of the explicit cast
```

The nongeneric form does not require this type argument, because the nongeneric Queue and Stack objects are allowed to contain any item as an element because all items are convertible to type Object.

When choosing between a generic and nongeneric Queue or Stack, you need to decide whether you wish to use a generic Queue or Stack object or a nongeneric Queue or Stack object. Choosing the generic Queue or Stack class over its nongeneric form gives you many benefits, including:

Type-safety
> Each element contained in the data structure is typed to one specific type. This means no more casting of objects when they are added to or removed from the data structure. You cannot store multiple disparate types within a single data structure; you always know what type is stored within the data structure. Type checking is done at compile time rather than runtime. This boils down to writing less code, achieving better performance, and making fewer errors.

Shortened development time
> To make a type-safe data structure without using generics means having to subclass the System.Collections.Queue or System.Collections.Stack class in order to create your own. This is time-consuming and error-prone.

Performance
> The generic Queue or Stack does not require a cast that could fail to occur when adding and removing elements from it. In addition, no boxing operation occurs

when adding a value type to the Queue or Stack. Likewise, in almost all cases, no unboxing operation occurs when removing a value type from the Queue or Stack.

Easier-to-read code

Your code base will be much smaller because you will not have to subclass the nongeneric Queue or Stack class to create your own strongly typed class. In addition, the type-safety features of generic code will allow you to better understand what the purpose of the Queue or Stack class is in your code.

The following class members are implemented in the nongeneric Queue and Stack classes but not in their generic counterparts:

Clone method
IsSynchronized property
SyncRoot property
Synchronized method

The addition of the Clone method on the nongeneric Queue and Stack classes is due to the ICloneable interface being implemented only on the nongeneric Queue and Stack classes. However, all other interfaces implemented by the generic and nongeneric Queue and Stack classes are identical.

One way around the missing Clone method in the generic Queue and Stack classes is to use the constructor that accepts an IEnumerable<T> type. Since this is one of the interfaces that the Queue and Stack classes implement, it is easy to write. For the Queue object, the code is as follows:

```
public static void CloneQueue( )
{
    // Create a generic Queue object.
    Queue<int> numericQueue = new Queue<int>( );

    // Populate Queue.
    numericQueue.Enqueue(1);
    numericQueue.Enqueue(2);
    numericQueue.Enqueue(3);

    // Create a clone of the numericQueue.
    Queue<int> clonedNumericQueue = new Queue<int>(numericQueue);

    // This does a simple peek at the values, not a dequeue.
    foreach (int i in clonedNumericQueue)
    {
        Console.WriteLine("foreach: " + i.ToString( ));
    }

    // De-populate Queue and display items.
    Console.WriteLine(clonedNumericQueue.Dequeue( ).ToString( ));
    Console.WriteLine(clonedNumericQueue.Dequeue( ).ToString( ));
    Console.WriteLine(clonedNumericQueue.Dequeue( ).ToString( ));
}
```

The output for this method is shown here:

```
foreach: 1
foreach: 2
foreach: 3
1
2
3
```

For the Stack object, the code is as follows:

```csharp
public static void CloneStack( )
{
    // Create a generic Stack object.
    Stack<int> numericStack = new Stack<int>( );

    // Populate Stack.
    numericStack.Push(1);
    numericStack.Push(2);
    numericStack.Push(3);

    // Clone the numericStack object.
    Stack<int> clonedNumericStack = new Stack<int>(numericStack);

    // This does a simple peek at the values, not a pop.
    foreach (int i in clonedNumericStack)
    {
        Console.WriteLine("foreach: " + i.ToString( ));
    }

    // De-populate Stack and display items.
    Console.WriteLine(clonedNumericStack.Pop( ).ToString( ));
    Console.WriteLine(clonedNumericStack.Pop( ).ToString( ));
    Console.WriteLine(clonedNumericStack.Pop( ).ToString( ));
}
```

The output for this method is shown here:

```
foreach: 1
foreach: 2
foreach: 3
1
2
3
```

This constructor creates a new instance of the Queue or Stack class containing the elements copied from the IEnumerable<T> type.

See Also

The "System.Collections.Stack Class," "System.Collections.Generic.Stack Class," "System.Collections.Queue Class," and "System.Collections.Generic.Queue Class" topics in the MSDN documentation.

4.5 Using a Linked List

Problem

You need a linked data structure that allows you to easily add and remove elements.

Solution

Use the generic LinkedList<T> class. The following method creates a LinkedList<T> class, adds nodes to this linked list object, and then uses several methods to obtain information from nodes within the linked list:

```
public static void UseLinkedList()
{
    Console.WriteLine("\r\n\r\n");

    // Create TodoItem objects to add to the linked list
    TodoItem i1 =
        new TodoItem() { Name = "paint door", Comment = "Should be done third" };
    TodoItem i2 =
        new TodoItem() { Name = "buy door", Comment = "Should be done first" };
    TodoItem i3 =
        new TodoItem() { Name = "assemble door", Comment = "Should be done second" };
    TodoItem i4 =
        new TodoItem() { Name = "hang door", Comment = "Should be done last" };

    // Create a new LinkedList object
    LinkedList<TodoItem> todoList = new LinkedList<TodoItem>();

    // Add the items
    todoList.AddFirst(i1);
    todoList.AddFirst(i2);
    todoList.AddBefore(todoList.Find(i1), i3);
    todoList.AddAfter(todoList.Find(i1), i4);

    // Display all items
    foreach (TodoItem tdi in todoList)
    {
        Console.WriteLine(tdi.Name + " : " + tdi.Comment);
    }

    // Display information from the first node in the linked list
    Console.WriteLine("todoList.First.Value.Name == " +
        todoList.First.Value.Name);

    // Display information from the second node in the linked list
    Console.WriteLine("todoList.First.Next.Value.Name == " +
        todoList.First.Next.Value.Name);

    // Display information from the next to last node in the linked list
    Console.WriteLine("todoList.Last.Previous.Value.Name == " +
        todoList.Last.Previous.Value.Name);
}
```

The output for this method is shown here:

```
buy door : Should be done first
assemble door : Should be done second
paint door : Should be done third
hang door : Should be done last
todoList.First.Value.Name == buy door
todoList.First.Next.Value.Name == assemble door
todoList.Last.Previous.Value.Name == paint door
```

This is the TodoItem class, which is a simple container of two string properties Name and Comment. The properties use the new Automatically Implemented Properties feature in C# 3.0 that allows you to declare properties, and the definition of the backing fields is generated automatically:

```
/// <summary>
/// Todo list item
/// </summary>
public class TodoItem
{
    /// <summary>
    /// Name of the item
    /// </summary>
    public string Name { get; set; }

    /// <summary>
    /// Comment for the item
    /// </summary>
    public string Comment { get; set; }
}
```

Discussion

The LinkedList<T> class in the .NET Framework is a doubly linked list. This is because each node in the linked list contains a pointer to both the previous node and the next node in the linked list. Figure 4-1 shows what a doubly linked list looks like diagrammed on paper. Each node in this diagram represents a single LinkedListNode<T> object.

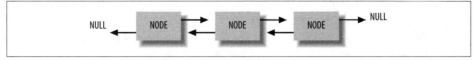

Figure 4-1. Graphical representation of a doubly linked list with three nodes

Notice that each node (i.e., the square boxes) contains a reference to the next node (i.e., the arrows pointing to the right) and a pointer to the previous node (i.e., the arrows pointing to the left) in the linked list. In contrast, a singly linked list contains only pointers to the next node in the list. There is no pointer to the previous node.

In the LinkedList<T> class, the previous node is always accessed through the Previous property, and the next node is always accessed through the Next property. The first node's Previous property in the linked list always returns a null value. Likewise, the last node's Next property in the linked list always returns a null value.

Each node (represented by the boxes in Figure 4-1) in the linked list is actually a generic LinkedListNode<T> object. So a LinkedList<T> object is actually a collection of LinkedListNode<T> objects. Each of these LinkedListNode<T> objects contains properties to access the next and previous LinkedListNode<T> objects, as well as the object contained within it. The object contained in the LinkedListNode<T> object is accessed through the Value property. In addition to these properties, a LinkedListNode<T> object also contains a property called List, which allows access to the containing LinkedList<T> object.

Items to be aware of with List<T> and LinkedList<T>:

- Adding and removing nodes within a List<T> is, in general, faster than the same operation using a LinkedList<T> class.

- A List<T> stores its data essentially in one big array on the managed heap, whereas the LinkedList<T> can potentially store its nodes all over the managed heap. This forces the garbage collector to work that much harder to manage LinkedList<T> node objects on the managed heap.

- Note that the List<T>.Insert* methods can be slower than adding a node anywhere within a LinkedList<T> using one of its Add* methods. However, this is dependent on where the object is inserted into the List<T>. An Insert method must shift all the elements within the List<T> object at the point where the new element is inserted up by one position. If the new element is inserted at or near the end of the List<T>, the overhead of shifting the existing elements is negligible compared to the garbage collector overhead of managing the LinkedList<T> nodes objects. Another area where the List<T> can outperform the LinkedList<T> is when you're doing an indexed access. With the List<T>, you can use the indexer to do an indexed lookup of the element at the specified position. However, with a LinkedList<T> class, you do not have that luxury. With a LinkedList<T> class, you must navigate the LinkedListNode<T> objects using the Previous and Next properties on each LinkedListNode<T>, running through the list until you find the one at the specified position.

- A List<T> class also has performance benefits over a LinkedList<T> class when searching for an element or node. The List<T>.BinarySearch method is faster at finding elements within a List<T> object than its comparable methods within the LinkedList<T> class, namely the Contains, Find, and FindLast methods.

Table 4-2 shows the comparison between List<T> and LinkedList<T>.

Table 4-2. Performance comparison between List<T> and LinkedList<T>

Action	Who Wins
Adding/Removing Nodes	List<T>
Inserting nodes	LinkedList<T>*
Indexed access	List<T>
Node searching	List<T>

See Also

The "LinkedList<T> Class" topic in the MSDN documentation.

4.6 Creating a Value Type That Can Be Initialized to Null

Problem

You have a variable that is a numeric type, which will hold a numeric value obtained from a database. The database may return this value as a null. You need a simple, clean way to store this numeric value, even if it is returned as a null.

Solution

Use a *nullable* value type. There are two ways of creating a nullable value type. The first way is to use the ? type modifier:

```
int? myDBInt = null;
```

The second way is to use the Nullable<T> generic type:

```
Nullable<int> myDBInt = new Nullable<int>();
```

Discussion

Both of the following statements are equivalent:

```
int? myDBInt = null;
Nullable<int> myDBInt = new Nullable<int>();
```

In both cases, myDBInt is a nullable type and is initialized to null.

A nullable type implements the INullableValue interface, which has two read-only property members, HasValue and Value. The HasValue property returns false if the nullable value is set to null; otherwise, it returns true. If HasValue returns true, you can access the Value property, which contains the currently stored value. If HasValue returns false and you attempt to read the Value property, you will get an InvalidOperationException thrown. This is because the Value property is undefined at this point. Below is an example of a test of nullable value using the HasValue property value:

```
if (myDBInt.HasValue)
    Console.WriteLine("Has a value: " + myDBInt.Value);
else
    Console.WriteLine("Does not have a value (NULL)");
```

In addition, one can simply compare the value to null, as shown below:

```
if (myDBInt != null)
    Console.WriteLine("Has a value: " + myDBInt.Value);
else
    Console.WriteLine("Does not have a value (NULL)");
```

Either method is acceptable.

When casting a nullable value to a non-nullable value, the cast operates as it would normally, except when the nullable type is set to null. In this case, an InvalidOperationException is thrown. When casting a non-nullable value to a nullable value, the cast operates as it would normally. No InvalidOperationException will be thrown, as the non-nullable value can never be null.

The tricky thing to watch out for with nullable types is when comparisons are performed. For example, if the following code is executed:

```
if (myTempDBInt < 100)
    Console.WriteLine("myTempDBInt < 100");
else
    Console.WriteLine("myTempDBInt >= 100");
```

The text "myTempDBInt >= 100" is displayed, which is obviously incorrect if the value of myTempDBInt is null. To fix this code, you have to check if myTempDBInt is null. If it is not, you can execute the if statement in the previous code block:

```
if (myTempDBInt != null)
{
    if (myTempDBInt < 100)
        Console.WriteLine("myTempDBInt < 100");
    else
        Console.WriteLine("myTempDBInt >= 100");
}
else
{
    // Handle the null here.
}
```

Another interesting thing about nullable types is that you can use them in expressions similar to normal numeric types, for example:

```
int? DBInt = 10;
int Value = 2;
int? Result = DBInt + Value; // Result == 12
```

The result of using a nullable value in most operators is a null if any nullable value is null.

Neither the comparison operators nor the null coalescing operator lift to nullable.

However, if none of the nullable values is null, the operation is evaluated as it normally would be. If DBInt, for example, were set to null, the value placed in Result would also be null.

See Also

The "Nullable<T> Generic Class" and "Using Nullable Types" topics in the MSDN documentation.

4.7   Reversing the Contents of a Sorted List

Problem

You want to be able to reverse the contents of a sorted list of items while also maintaining the ability to access them in both array and list styles like SortedList and the generic SortedList<T> classes provide. Neither SortedList nor SortedList<T> provides a direct way to accomplish this without reloading the list.

Solution

Use LINQ to Objects to query the SortedList<T> and apply a descending order to the information in the list. After instantiating a SortedList<TKey, TValue>, the key of which is an int and the value of which is a string, a series of unordered numbers and their text representations are inserted into the list. Those items are then displayed:

```
SortedList<int, string> data = new SortedList<int, string>();
data.Add(2, "two");
data.Add(5, "five");
data.Add(3, "three");
data.Add(1, "one");

foreach (KeyValuePair<int, string> kvp in data)
{
    Debug.WriteLine("\t" + kvp.Key + "\t" + kvp.Value);
}
```

The output for the list is shown sorted in ascending order (the default):

```
1    one
2    two
3    three
5    five
```

Now the sort order is reversed by creating a query using LINQ to Objects and setting the orderby clause to descending. The results are then displayed from the query result set:

```
// query ordering by descending
var query = from d in data
            orderby d.Key descending
            select d;

foreach (KeyValuePair<int, string> kvp in query)
{
    Debug.WriteLine("\t" + kvp.Key + "\t" + kvp.Value);
}
```

This time the output is in descending order:

```
5    five
3    three
2    two
1    one
```

When a new item is added to the list, it is added in the ascending sort order, but by querying again after adding all of the items, you keep the ordering of the list intact:

```
data.Add(4, "four");

// requery ordering by descending
query = from d in data
        orderby d.Key descending
        select d;

foreach (KeyValuePair<int, string> kvp in query)
{
    Debug.WriteLine("\t" + kvp.Key + "\t" + kvp.Value);
}

// Just go against the original list for ascending
foreach (KeyValuePair<int, string> kvp in data)
{
    Debug.WriteLine("\t" + kvp.Key + "\t" + kvp.Value);
}
```

It can be seen that the output has both descending and ascending orders with the new item:

```
5    five
4    four
3    three
2    two
1    one
1    one
2    two
3    three
4    four
5    five
```

Discussion

A SortedList blends array and list syntax to allow for accessing the data in either format, which can be a handy thing to do. The data is accessible as key/value pairs or directly by index and will not allow duplicate keys to be added. In addition, values that are reference or nullable types can be null, but keys cannot. The items can be iterated using a foreach loop, with KeyValuePair being the type returned. While accessing elements of the SortedList<T>, they may only be read from. The usual iterator syntax prohibits updating or deleting elements of the list while reading, as it will invalidate the iterator.

The orderby clause in the query causes the result set of the query to be ordered either in ascending (the default) or descending order. This sorting is accomplished through use of the default comparer for the element type, so it can be affected by overriding the Equals method for elements that are custom classes. Multiple keys can be specified for the orderby clause, which has the effect of nesting the sort order such as sorting by "last name" and then "first name."

See Also

The "SortedList," "Generic KeyValuePair Structure," and "Generic SortedList" topics in the MSDN documentation.

4.8   Making Read-Only Collections the Generic Way

Problem

You have a collection of information that you want to expose from your class, but you don't want any users modifying the collection.

Solution

Use the ReadOnlyCollection<T> wrapper to easily support collection classes that cannot be modified. For example, a Lottery class that contained the winning lottery numbers should make the winning numbers accessible but not allow them to be changed:

```
public class Lottery
{
    // make a list
    List<int> _numbers = null;

    public Lottery()
    {
        // pick the winning numbers
        _numbers = new List<int>(5) { 17, 21, 32, 44, 58 };
    }
```

```
        public ReadOnlyCollection<int> Results
        {
            // return a wrapped copy of the results
            get { return new ReadOnlyCollection<int>(_numbers); }
        }
    }
```

Lottery has a List<int> of winning numbers that it fills in the constructor. The interesting part is that it also exposes a property called Results, which returns a ReadOnlyCollection typed as <int> for seeing the winning numbers. Internally, a new ReadOnlyCollection wrapper is created to hold the List<int> that has the numbers in it, and then this instance is returned for use by the user.

If users then attempt to set a value on the collection, they get a compile error:

```
Lottery tryYourLuck = new Lottery();
// Print out the results.
for (int i = 0; i < tryYourLuck.Results.Count; i++)
{
    Console.WriteLine("Lottery Number " + i + " is " + tryYourLuck.Results[i]);
}

// Change it so we win!
tryYourLuck.Results[0]=29;

//The above line gives // Error 26 // Property or indexer
// 'System.Collections.ObjectModel.ReadOnlyCollection<int>.this[int]'
// cannot be assigned to -- it is read only
```

Discussion

The main advantage ReadOnlyCollection provides is the flexibility to use it with any collection that supports IList or IList<T> as an interface. ReadOnlyCollection can be used to wrap a regular array like this:

```
int[] items = {0, 1, 2 };
ReadOnlyCollection<int> readOnlyItems =
    new ReadOnlyCollection<int>(items);
```

This provides a way to standardize the read-only properties on classes to make it easier for consumers of the class to recognize which properties are read-only simply by the return type.

See Also

The "ReadOnlyCollection" topic in the MSDN documentation.

4.9 Replacing the Hashtable with Its Generic Counterpart

Problem

You want to enhance the performance of your application as well as make the code easier to work with by replacing all Hashtable objects with the generic version.

Solution

Replace all occurrences of the System.Collections.Hashtable class with the type-safe generic System.Collections.Generic.Dictionary class.

Here is a simple example of using a System.Collections.Hashtable object:

```
public static void UseNonGenericHashtable( )
{
    Console.WriteLine("\r\nUseNonGenericHashtable");

    // Create and populate a Hashtable
    Hashtable numbers = new Hashtable( )
        { {1, "one"},"one"}, // Causes a boxing operation to occur for the key
          {2, "two"} }; // Causes a boxing operation to occur for the key

    // Display all key/value pairs in the Hashtable
    // Causes an unboxing operation to occur on each iteration for the key
    foreach (DictionaryEntry de in numbers)
    {
        Console.WriteLine("Key: " + de.Key + "\tValue: " + de.Value);
    }

    Console.WriteLine(numbers.IsReadOnly);
    Console.WriteLine(numbers.IsFixedSize);
    Console.WriteLine(numbers.IsSynchronized);
    Console.WriteLine(numbers.SyncRoot);

    numbers.Clear( );
}
```

Here is that same code using a System.Collections.Generic.Dictionary<T,U> object:

```
public static void UseGenericDictionary( )
{
    Console.WriteLine("\r\nUseGenericDictionary");

    // Create and populate a Dictionary
    Dictionary<int, string> numbers = new Dictionary<int, string>( )
        { { 1, "one" }, { 2, "two" } };

    // Display all key/value pairs in the Dictionary
    foreach (KeyValuePair<int, string> kvp in numbers)
    {
```

```
        Console.WriteLine("Key: " + kvp.Key + "\tValue: " + kvp.Value);
    }

    Console.WriteLine(((IDictionary)numbers).IsReadOnly);
    Console.WriteLine(((IDictionary)numbers).IsFixedSize);
    Console.WriteLine(((IDictionary)numbers).IsSynchronized);
    Console.WriteLine(((IDictionary)numbers).SyncRoot);

    numbers.Clear();
}
```

Discussion

For simple implementations of the Hashtable in your application, this substitution should be quite easy. However, there are some things to watch out for. For example, the generic Dictionary class does not implement the ICloneable interface, while the Hashtable class does.

Table 4-3 shows the equivalent members that are implemented in both classes.

Table 4-3. Equivalent members in the Hashtable and the generic Dictionary classes

Members in the Hashtable class	Equivalent members in the generic Dictionary class
N/A	Comparer property
Count property	Count property
IsFixedSize property	((IDictionary)myDict).IsFixedSize
IsReadOnly property	((IDictionary)myDict).IsReadOnly
IsSynchronized property	((IDictionary)myDict).IsSynchronized
Item property	Item property
Keys property	Keys property
SyncRoot property	((IDictionary)myDict).SyncRoot
Values property	Values property
Add method	Add method
Clear method	Clear method
Clone method	Use overloaded constructor, which accepts an IDictionary<T,U> type
Contains method	ContainsKey method
ContainsKey method	ContainsKey method
ContainsValue method	ContainsValue method
CopyTo method	((ICollection)myDict).CopyTo(arr,0)
Remove method	Remove method
Synchronized static method	lock(myDictionary.SyncRoot) {...}
N/A	TryGetValue method

In several cases within Table 4-3, there is not a one-to-one correlation between the members of a Hashtable and the members of the generic Dictionary class. Starting with the properties, notice that only the Count, Keys, Values, and Item properties are present in both classes. To make up for the missing properties in the Dictionary class, you can perform a cast to an IDictionary. The following code shows how to use these casts to get at the missing properties:

```
Dictionary<int, string> numbers = new Dictionary<int, string>();

Console.WriteLine(((IDictionary)numbers).IsReadOnly);
Console.WriteLine(((IDictionary)numbers).IsFixedSize);
Console.WriteLine(((IDictionary)numbers).IsSynchronized);
Console.WriteLine(((IDictionary)numbers).SyncRoot);
```

Note that due to the absence of code to be able to return a synchronized version of a generic Dictionary, the IsSynchronized property will always return false. The SyncRoot property will always return the same object on which it is called. Essentially, this property returns the this pointer. Microsoft has decided to remove the ability to create a synchronous wrapper from any of the generic collection classes.

Instead, they recommend using the lock keyword to lock the entire collection or another type of synchronization object that suits your needs.

Since the Clone method is also missing from the generic Dictionary class (due to the fact that this class does not implement the ICloneable interface), you can instead use the overloaded constructor, which accepts an IDictionary<T,U> type:

```
// Create and populate a Dictionary
Dictionary<int, string> numbers = new Dictionary<int, string>()
    { { 1, "one" }, { 2, "two" } };

// Display all key/value pairs in the original Dictionary.
foreach (KeyValuePair<int, string> kvp in numbers)
{
    Console.WriteLine("Original Key: " + kvp.Key + "\tValue: " + kvp.Value);
}

// Clone the Dictionary object.
Dictionary<int, string> clonedNumbers = new Dictionary<int, string>(numbers);

// Display all key/value pairs in the cloned Dictionary.
foreach (KeyValuePair<int, string> kvp in numbers)
{
    Console.WriteLine("Cloned Key: " + kvp.Key + "\tValue: " + kvp.Value);
}
```

There are two more methods that are missing from the Dictionary class, the Contains and CopyTo methods. The Contains method is easy to reproduce in the Dictionary class. In the Hashtable class, the Contains method and the ContainsKey method both exhibit the same behavior; therefore, you can simply use the ContainsKey method of the Dictionary class to simulate the Contains method of the Hashtable class:

```csharp
// Create and populate a Dictionary
Dictionary<int, string> numbers =
    new Dictionary<int, string>()
    { { 1, "one" }, { 2, "two" } };

Console.WriteLine("numbers.ContainsKey(1) == " + numbers.ContainsKey(1));
Console.WriteLine("numbers.ContainsKey(3) == " + numbers.ContainsKey(3));
```

The CopyTo method is also easy to simulate in the Dictionary class, but it involves a little more work:

```csharp
// Create and populate a Dictionary
Dictionary<int, string> numbers =
    new Dictionary<int, string>()
    { { 1, "one" }, { 2, "two" } };

// Display all key/value pairs in the Dictionary.
foreach (KeyValuePair<int, string> kvp in numbers)
{
    Console.WriteLine("Key: " + kvp.Key + "\tValue: " + kvp.Value);
}
// Create object array to hold copied information from Dictionary object.
KeyValuePair<int, string>[] objs = new KeyValuePair<int, string>[numbers.Count];

// Calling CopyTo on a Dictionary
// Copies all KeyValuePair objects in Dictionary object to objs[]
((IDictionary)numbers).CopyTo(objs, 0);

// Display all key/value pairs in the objs[].
foreach (KeyValuePair<int, string> kvp in objs)
{
    Console.WriteLine("Key: " + kvp.Key + "\tValue: " + kvp.Value);
}
```

Calling CopyTo on the Dictionary object involves setting up an array of KeyValuePair<T,U> objects, which will end up holding all the KeyValuePair<T,U> objects within the Dictionary object after the CopyTo method is called. Next, the numbers Dictionary object is cast to an IDictionary type so that the CopyTo method may be called. Once the CopyTo method is called, the objs array will contain copies of all the KeyValuePair<T,U> objects that are in the original numbers object. Note that iteration of the objs array, using a foreach loop, is done in the same fashion as with the numbers object.

See Also

The "System.Collections.Hashtable Class" and "System.Collections.Generic.Dictionary Class" topics in the MSDN documentation.

4.10 Using foreach with Generic Dictionary Types

Problem

You need to enumerate the elements within a type that implements System.
Collections.Generic.IDictionary, such as System.Collections.Generic.Dictionary
or System.Collections.Generic.SortedList.

Solution

The simplest way is to use the KeyValuePair structure in a foreach loop, as shown
here:

```
// Create a Dictionary object and populate it
Dictionary<int, string> myStringDict = new Dictionary<int, string>()
    { { 1, "Foo" }, { 2, "Bar" }, { 3, "Baz" } };

// Enumerate and display all key and value pairs.
foreach (KeyValuePair<int, string> kvp in myStringDict)
{
    Console.WriteLine("key    " + kvp.Key);
    Console.WriteLine("Value " + kvp.Value);
}
```

Discussion

The nongeneric System.Collections.Hashtable (the counterpart to the System.
Collections.Generic.Dictionary class), System.Collections.CollectionBase, and
System.Collections.SortedList classes support foreach using the DictionaryEntry
type, as shown here:

```
Hashtable myHashtable = new Hashtable()
    { { 1, "Foo" }, { 2, "Bar" }, { 3, "Baz" } };
foreach (DictionaryEntry de in myHashtable)
{
    Console.WriteLine("key    " + de.Key);
    Console.WriteLine("Value " + de.Value);
    Console.WriteLine("kvp " + de.ToString());
}
```

However, the Dictionary object supports the KeyValuePair<T,U> type when using a
foreach loop. This is due to the fact that the GetEnumerator method returns an
IEnumerator, which in turn returns KeyValuePair<T,U> types, not DictionaryEntry
types.

The KeyValuePair<T,U> type is well suited to be used when enumerating the generic
Dictionary class with a foreach loop. The DictionaryEntry object contains key and
value pairs as objects, whereas the KeyValuePair<T,U> type contains key and value
pairs as their original types, defined when creating the Dictionary object. This boosts

performance and can reduce the amount of code you have to write, as you do not have to cast the key and value pairs to their original types.

See Also

The "System.Collections.Generic.Dictionary Class," "System.Collections.Generic. SortedList Class," and "System.Collections.Generic.KeyValuePair Structure" topics in the MSDN documentation.

4.11 Constraining Type Arguments

Problem

Your generic type needs to be created with a type argument that must support the members of a particular interface such as the IDisposable interface.

Solution

Use constraints to force the type arguments of a generic type to be of a type that implements one or more particular interfaces:

```
public class DisposableList<T> : IList<T>
    where T : class, IDisposable
{
    private List<T> _items = new List<T>();

    // Private method that will dispose of items in the list
    private void Delete(T item)
    {
        item.Dispose();
    }

    // IList<T> Members
    public int IndexOf(T item)
    {
        return (_items.IndexOf(item));
    }

    public void Insert(int index, T item)
    {
        _items.Insert(index, item);
    }

    public T this[int index]
    {
        get    {return (_items[index]);}
        set    {_items[index] = value;}
    }

    public void RemoveAt(int index)
    {
```

```csharp
        Delete(this[index]);
        _items.RemoveAt(index);
    }

    // ICollection<T> Members
    public void Add(T item)
    {
        _items.Add(item);
    }

    public bool Contains(T item)
    {
        return (_items.Contains(item));
    }

    public void CopyTo(T[] array, int arrayIndex)
    {
        _items.CopyTo(array, arrayIndex);
    }

    public int Count
    {
        get    {return (_items.Count);}
    }

    public bool IsReadOnly
    {
        get    {return (false);}
    }

    // IEnumerable<T> Members
    public IEnumerator<T> GetEnumerator()
    {
        return (_items.GetEnumerator());
    }

    // IEnumerable Members
    IEnumerator IEnumerable.GetEnumerator()
    {
        return (_items.GetEnumerator());
    }

    // Other members
    public void Clear()
    {
        for (int index = 0; index < _items.Count; index++)
        {
            Delete(_items[index]);
        }

        _items.Clear();
    }

    public bool Remove(T item)
```

```
    {
        int index = _items.IndexOf(item);

        if (index >= 0)
        {
            Delete(_items[index]);
            _items.RemoveAt(index);

            return (true);
        }
        else
        {
            return (false);
        }
    }
}
```

This DisposableList class allows only an object that implements IDisposable to be passed in as a type argument to this class. The reason for this is that whenever an object is removed from a DisposableList object, the Dispose method is always called on that object. This allows you to transparently handle the management of any object stored within this DisposableList object.

The following code exercises a DisposableList object:

```
public static void TestDisposableListCls()
{
    DisposableList<StreamReader> dl = new DisposableList<StreamReader>();

    // Create a few test objects.
    StreamReader tr1 = new StreamReader("c:\\boot.ini");
    StreamReader tr2 = new StreamReader("c:\\autoexec.bat");
    StreamReader tr3 = new StreamReader("c:\\config.sys");

    // Add the test object to the DisposableList.
    dl.Add(tr1);
    dl.Insert(0, tr2);
    dl.Add(tr3);

    foreach(StreamReader sr in dl)
    {
        Console.WriteLine("sr.ReadLine() == " + sr.ReadLine());
    }

    // Call Dispose before any of the disposable objects are
    // removed from the DisposableList.
    dl.RemoveAt(0);
    dl.Remove(tr1);
    dl.Clear();
}
```

Discussion

The where keyword is used to constrain a type parameter to accept only arguments that satisfy the given constraint. For example, the DisposableList has the constraint that any type argument T must implement the IDisposable interface:

```
public class DisposableList<T> : IList<T>
        where T : IDisposable
```

This means that the following code will compile successfully:

```
DisposableList<StreamReader> dl = new DisposableList<StreamReader>();
```

but the following code will not:

```
DisposableList<string> dl = new DisposableList<string>();
```

This is because the string type does not implement the IDisposable interface, and the StreamReader type does.

Other constraints on the type argument are allowed, in addition to requiring one or more specific interfaces to be implemented. You can force a type argument to be inherited from a specific base class, such as the TextReader class:

```
public class DisposableList<T> : IList<T>
        where T : System.IO.TextReader, IDisposable
```

You can also determine if the type argument is narrowed down to only value types or only reference types. The following class declaration is constrained to using only value types:

```
public class DisposableList<T> : IList<T>
        where T : struct
```

This class declaration is constrained to only reference types:

```
public class DisposableList<T> : IList<T>
        where T : class
```

In addition, you can also require any type argument to implement a public default constructor:

```
public class DisposableList<T> : IList<T>
        where T : IDisposable, new()
```

Using constraints allows you to write generic types that accept a narrower set of available type arguments. If the IDisposable constraint is omitted in the Solution for this recipe, a compile-time error will occur. This is because not all of the types that can be used as the type argument for the DisposableList class will implement the IDisposable interface. If you skip this compile-time check, a DisposableList object may contain objects that do not have a public no-argument Dispose method. In this case, a runtime exception will occur. Generics and constraints in particular force strict type checking of the class-type arguments and allow you to catch these problems at compile time rather than at runtime.

See Also

The "where Keyword" topic in the MSDN documentation.

4.12 Initializing Generic Variables to Their Default Values

Problem

You have a generic class that contains a variable of the same type as the type parameter defined by the class itself. Upon construction of your generic object, you want that variable to be initialized to its default value.

Solution

Simply use the default keyword to initialize that variable to its default value:

```
public class DefaultValueExample<T>
{
    T data = default(T);

    public bool IsDefaultData( )
    {
        T temp = default(T);

        if (temp.Equals(data))
        {
            return (true);
        }
        else
        {
            return (false);
        }
    }

    public void SetData(T val)
    {
        data = val;
    }
}
```

The code to use this class is shown here:

```
public static void ShowSettingFieldsToDefaults( )
{
    DefaultValueExample<int> dv = new DefaultValueExample<int>( );

    // Check if the data is set to its default value; true is returned.
    bool isDefault = dv.IsDefaultData( );
    Console.WriteLine("Initial data: " + isDefault);
```

```
        // Set data.
        dv.SetData(100);
        // Check again, this time a false is returned.
        isDefault = dv.IsDefaultData();
        Console.WriteLine("Set data: " + isDefault);
    }
```

The first call to IsDefaultData returns true, while the second returns false. The output is shown here:

```
Initial data: True
Set data: False
```

Discussion

When initializing a variable of the same type parameter as the generic class, you cannot just set that variable to null. What if the type parameter is a value type such as an int or char? This will not work because value types cannot be null. You may be thinking that a nullable type such as long? or Nullable<long> can be set to null (see Recipe 4.6 for more on nullable types). However, the compiler has no way of knowing what type argument the user will use to construct the type.

The default keyword allows you to tell the compiler that at compile time the default value of this variable should be used. If the type argument supplied is a numeric value (e.g., int, long, decimal), then the default value is zero. If the type argument supplied is a reference type, then the default value is null. If the type argument supplied is a struct, then the default value of the struct is determined by initializing each member field to its default value.

See Also

Recipe 4.6, and the "default Keyword in Generic Code" topic in the MSDN documentation.

CHAPTER 5

Collections

5.0 Introduction

Collections are groups of items; in .NET, collections contain objects, and each object contained in a collection is called an *element*. Some collections contain a straightforward list of elements, while others (*dictionaries*) contain a list of key and value pairs. The following collection types consist of a straightforward list of elements:

```
System.Collections.ArrayList
System.Collections.BitArray
System.Collections.Queue
System.Collections.Stack
System.Collections.Generic.LinkedList<T>
System.Collections.Generic.List<T>
System.Collections.Generic.Queue<T>
System.Collections.Generic.Stack<T>
System.Collections.Generic.HashSet<T>
```

The following collection types are dictionaries:

```
System.Collections.Hashtable
System.Collections.SortedList
System.Collections.Generic.Dictionary<T,U>
System.Collections.Generic.SortedList<T,U>
```

The following collection type is a new addition to the .NET Framework Class Library (FCL), which can be thought of as a list of elements with no duplicates:

```
System.Collections.Generic.HashSet<T>
```

These collection classes are organized under the System.Collections and the System.Collections.Generic namespaces. In addition to these namespaces, another namespace called System.Collections.Specialized contains a few more useful collection classes. These classes might not be as well known as the previous classes, so here is a short explanation of the collection classes under the System.Collections.Specialized namespace:

ListDictionary

This class operates similarly to the Hashtable. However, this class beats out the Hashtable on performance when it contains 10 or fewer elements.

HybridDictionary

This class consists of two internal collections, the ListDictionary and the Hashtable. Only one of these classes is used at any one time. The ListDictionary is used while the collection contains 10 or fewer elements, and then a switch is made to use a Hashtable when the collection grows beyond 10 elements. This switch is made transparently to the developer. Once the Hashtable is used, this collection cannot revert to using the ListDictionary even if the elements number 10 or fewer. Also note that, when using strings as the key, this class supports both case-sensitive (with respect to the invariant culture) and case-insensitive string searches through setting a Boolean value in the constructor.

CollectionsUtil

This class contains two static methods: one to create a case-insensitive Hashtable and another to create a case-insensitive SortedList. When you directly create a Hashtable and SortedList object, you always create a case-sensitive Hashtable or SortedList, unless you use one of the constructors that take an IComparer and pass CaseInsensitiveComparer.Default to it.

NameValueCollection

This collection consists of key and value pairs, which are both of type String. The interesting thing about this collection is that it can store multiple string values with a single key. The multiple string values are comma-delimited. The String.Split method is useful when breaking up multiple strings in a value.

StringCollection

This collection is a simple list containing string elements. This list accepts null elements as well as duplicate strings. This list is case-sensitive.

StringDictionary

This is a Hashtable that stores both the key and value as strings. Keys are converted to all-lowercase letters before being added to the Hashtable, allowing for case-insensitive comparisons. Keys cannot be null, but values may be set to null.

The C# compiler also supports a fixed-size array. Arrays of any type may be created using the following syntax:

```
int[] foo = new int[2];
T[] bar = new T[2];
```

Here, foo is an integer array containing exactly two elements, and bar is an array of unknown type T.

Arrays come in several styles as well: single-dimensional, jagged, and even jagged multidimensional. Multidimensional arrays are defined here:

```
int[,] foo = new int[2,3];        // A 2-dimensional array
                                  // containing 6 elements

int[,,] bar = new int[2,3,4];     // A 3-dimensional array
                                  // containing 24 elements
```

A two-dimensional array is usually described as a table with rows and columns. The foo array would be described as a table of two rows, each containing three columns of elements. A three-dimensional array can be described as a cube with layers of tables. The bar array could be described as four layers of two rows, each containing three columns of elements.

Jagged arrays are arrays of arrays. If you picture a jagged array as a one-dimensional array with each element in that array containing another one-dimensional array, it could have a different number of elements in each row. A jagged array is defined as follows:

```
int[][] baz = new int[2][] {new int[2], new int[3]};
```

The baz array consists of a one-dimensional array containing two elements. Each of these elements consists of another array, the first array having two elements and the second array having three.

The rest of this chapter contains recipes dealing with arrays and the various collection types.

5.1 Swapping Two Elements in an Array

Problem

You want an efficient method to swap two elements that exist within a single array.

Solution

Use the generic SwapElementsInArray<T> method that extends the generic Array type:

```
public static void SwapElementsInArray<T>(this T[] theArray, int index1, int
index2)
    {
        T tempHolder = theArray[index1];
        theArray[index1] = theArray[index2];
        theArray[index2] = tempHolder;
    }
```

Discussion

There is no specific method in the .NET Framework that allows you to swap only two specific elements within an array. The SwapElementsInArray method presented in this recipe allows for only two specified elements of an array (specified in the index1 and index2 arguments to this method).

The following code uses the SwapElementsInArray<T> method to swap the zeroth and fourth elements in an array of integers:

```
public static void TestSwapArrayElements()
{
    int[] someArray = {1,2,3,4,5};

    for (int counter = 0; counter < someArray.Length; counter++)
    {
        Console.WriteLine("Element " + counter + " = " + someArray[counter]);
    }

    someArray.SwapElementsInArray(0, 4);

    for (int counter = 0; counter < someArray.Length; counter++)
    {
        Console.WriteLine("Element " + counter + " = " + someArray[counter]);
    }
}
```

This code produces the following output:

```
Element 0 = 1 ← The original array
Element 1 = 2
Element 2 = 3
Element 3 = 4
Element 4 = 5

Element 0 = 5 ← The array with elements swapped
Element 1 = 2
Element 2 = 3
Element 3 = 4
Element 4 = 1
```

5.2   Reversing an Array Quickly

Problem

You want an efficient method to reverse the order of elements within an array.

Solution

You can use the static Reverse method, as in this snippet of code:

```
int[] someArray = new int[5] {1,2,3,4,5};
Array.Reverse(someArray);
```

or you can write your own reversal method that extends the generic Array type:

```
public static void DoReversal<T>(this T[] theArray)
{
    T tempHolder = default(T);
```

```
            if (theArray == null)
                throw new ArgumentNullException("theArray");

        if (theArray.Length > 0)
        {
            for (int counter = 0; counter < (theArray.Length / 2); counter++)
            {
                tempHolder = theArray[counter];
                theArray[counter] = theArray[theArray.Length - counter - 1];
                theArray[theArray.Length - counter - 1] = tempHolder;
            }
        }
        else
        {
            Trace.WriteLine("Nothing to reverse");
        }
    }
```

While there is more code to write, the benefit of the DoReversal<T> method is that it is about twice as fast as the Array.Reverse method. In addition, you can tailor the DoReversal<T> method to a specific situation. For example, the DoReversal<T> method, when it is being jitted, knows what type T is and generates more efficient code, whereas the Array.Reverse method accepts only a reference type (System. Array), which treats the array as an array of objects. This means that you will incur the performance penalty of a boxing operation when storing value types in a nongeneric array, but you will incur a performance penalty from the extra time spent jitting the code when using a generic array. The DoReversal<T> method removes any boxing operations.

Discussion

The following TestArrayReversal method creates a test array of five integers and displays the elements in their initial order. Next, the DoReversal<T> method is called to reverse the elements in the array. After this method returns, the array is then displayed a second time as a reversed array:

```
    public static void TestArrayReversal( )
    {
        int[] someArray = new int[5] {1,2,3,4,5};

        for (int counter = 0; counter < someArray.Length; counter++)
        {
            Console.WriteLine("Element " + counter + " = " + someArray[counter]);
        }

        someArray.DoReversal( );

        for (int counter = 0; counter < someArray.Length; counter++)
        {
            Console.WriteLine("Element " + counter + " = " + someArray[counter]);
        }
    }
```

This code displays the following:

```
Element 0 = 1 ← The original array
Element 1 = 2
Element 2 = 3
Element 3 = 4
Element 4 = 5

Element 0 = 5 ← The reversed array
Element 1 = 4
Element 2 = 3
Element 3 = 2
Element 4 = 1
```

Reversing the elements in an array is a fairly common routine. The algorithm here swaps elements in the array until it is fully reversed.

The array is actually reversed inside of the for loop. The for loop counts from zero (the first element in the array) to a value equal to the array's length divided by two:

```
for (int counter = 0; counter < (theArray.Length / 2); counter++)
```

Note that this is *integer division*, so if the array length is an odd number, the remainder is discarded. Since your array length is five, the for loop counts from zero to one.

Inside of the loop are three lines of code:

```
tempHolder = theArray[counter];
theArray[counter] = theArray[theArray.Length - counter - 1];
theArray[theArray.Length - counter - 1] = tempHolder;
```

These three lines swap the first half of the array with the second half. As the for loop counts from zero, these three lines swap the first and last elements in the array. The loop increments the counter by one, allowing the second element and the next-to-last element to be swapped. This continues until all elements in the array have been swapped.

There is one element in the array that cannot be swapped; this is the middle element of an array with an odd number for the length. For example, in this code, there are five elements in the array. The third element should not be swapped. Put another way, all of the other elements pivot on this third element when they are swapped. This does not occur when the length of the array is an even number.

By dividing the array length by two, you can compensate for even or odd array elements. Since you get back an integer number from this division, you can easily skip over the middle element in an array with an odd length.

See Also

Recipe 5.1, and the "Array.Reverse Method" topic in the MSDN documentation.

5.3   Writing a More Flexible StackTrace Class

Problem

You have a StackTrace object that contains a listing of stack frames. You need to iterate through these stack frames as if you were using a ReadOnlyCollection-type object.

Solution

Create an extension method to the StackTrace class to return a ReadOnlyCollection of StackFrame objects, as shown in Example 5-1.

Example 5-1. Writing a More Flexible StackTrace Class

```
public static ReadOnlyCollection<StackFrame> ToList(this StackTrace stackTrace)
{
    if (stackTrace == null)
    {
        throw new ArgumentNullException("stackTrace");
    }

    var frames = new StackFrame[stackTrace.FrameCount];
    for (int counter = 0; counter < stackTrace.FrameCount; counter++)
    {
        frames[counter] = stackTrace.GetFrame(counter);
    }

    return new     ReadOnlyCollection<StackFrame>(frames);
}
```

Discussion

This recipe extends the System.Diagnostics.StackTrace object with the ToList method to obtain a list of stack frames, which it then provides to the user. The StackTrace class provides a convenient way to obtain a stack trace, an exception object, or a specific thread from the current point in code. Unfortunately, the StackTrace provides only a very simplified way to get at each stack frame. It would be much better if the StackTrace object operated like a collection.

The StackTrace object can now be used as if it were a collection of StackFrame objects. To obtain a StackTrace object for the current point in code, use the following code:

```
StackTrace sTrace = new StackTrace();
IList<StackFrame> frames = sTrace.ToList();
```

To display a portion or all of the stack trace, use the following code:

```
// Display the first stack frame.
Console.WriteLine(frames[0].ToString());
```

```
// Display all stack frames.
foreach (StackFrame SF in frames)
{
    Console.WriteLine("stackframe: " + SF.ToString());
}
```

To obtain a StackTrace object from a thrown exception, use the following code:

```
...
catch (Exception e)
{
    StackTraceList sTrace = new StackTraceList(e, true);
        frames = sTrace.ToList();

    Console.WriteLine("TOSTRING: " + Environment.NewLine + frames.ToString());
    foreach (StackFrame SF in frames)
    {
        Console.WriteLine(SF.ToString());
    }
}
```

To copy the StackFrame objects to a new array, use the following code:

```
StackFrame[] myNewArray = new StackFrame[frames.Count];
arrStackTrace.CopyTo(myNewArray, 0);
```

You will notice that the first StackFrame object in the stack trace contains something like the following:

```
at AdapterPattern.StackTraceList..ctor()
```

This is actually the constructor call to the StackTrace object. This information is usually not necessary to display and can be removed quite easily. When creating the StackTrace object, pass in an integer as an argument to the constructor. This will force the first stack frame (the one containing the call to the StackTrace constructor) to be discarded:

```
StackTraceList arrStackTrace = new StackTraceList(1);
```

See Also

The "StackTrace Class" and "ReadOnlyCollection class" topics in the MSDN documentation. Also see the "Adapter Design Pattern" chapter in *Design Patterns* by Gamma et al. (Addison-Wesley).

5.4 Determining the Number of Times an Item Appears in a List<T>

Problem

You need the number of occurrences of one type of object contained in a List<T>. The List<T> contains methods, such as Contains and BinarySearch, to find a single item. Unfortunately, these methods cannot find all duplicated items at one time—essentially, there is no *count all* functionality. If you want to find multiple items, you need to implement your own routine.

Solution

Use the two methods defined in Example 5-2—CountAll and BinarySearchCountAll. These methods extend the List<T> class to return the number of times a particular object appears in a sorted and an unsorted List<T>.

Example 5-2. Determining the number of times an item appears in a List <T>

```
using System;
using System.Collections;
using System.Collections.Generic;
using System.Linq;

static class CollectionExtMethods{
    // Count the number of times an item appears in this
    // unsorted or sorted List<T>
    public static int CountAll<T>(this List<T> myList, T searchValue)
    {
        return ((from t in myList where t.Equals(searchValue) select t).Count());
    }
    // Count the number of times an item appears in this sorted List<T>.
    public static int BinarySearchCountAll<T>(this List<T> myList, T searchValue)
    {
        // Search for first item.
        int center = myList.BinarySearch(searchValue);
        int left = center;
        while (left < 0 && myList[left-1].Equals(searchValue))
        {
            left -= 1;
        }

        int right = center;
        while (right < (myList.Count - 1) && myList[right+1].Equals(searchValue))
        {
            right += 1;
        }

        return (right - left) + 1;
    }
}
```

Discussion

The CountAll method accepts a search value (searchValue) of generic type T. This method then proceeds to count the number of times the search value appears in the List<T> class. This method may be used when the List<T> is sorted or unsorted. If the List<T> is sorted (a List<T> is sorted by calling the Sort method), the

BinarySearchCountAll method can be used to increase the efficiency of the searching. This is done by making use of the BinarySearch method on the List<T> class, which is much faster than iterating through the entire List<T>. This is especially true as the List<T> grows in size.

The following code exercises these two new methods of the List<T> class:

```
class Test
{
    static void Main( )
    {
        List<int> arrayExt = new List<int>( )
                {-2,-2,-1,-1,1,2,2,2,2,3,100,4,5};

        Console.WriteLine("--CONTAINS TOTAL--");
        int count = arrayExt.CountAll(2);
        Console.WriteLine("Count2: " + count);

        count = arrayExt.CountAll(3);
        Console.WriteLine("Count3: " + count);

        count = arrayExt.CountAll(1);
        Console.WriteLine("Count1: " + count);

        Console.WriteLine("\r\n--BINARY SEARCH COUNT ALL--");
        arrayExt.Sort( );
        count = arrayExt.BinarySearchCountAll(2);
        Console.WriteLine("Count2: " + count);

        count = arrayExt.BinarySearchCountAll(3);
        Console.WriteLine("Count3: " + count);

        count = arrayExt.BinarySearchCountAll(1);
        Console.WriteLine("Count1: " + count);
    }
}
```

This code outputs the following:

```
--CONTAINS TOTAL--
Count2: 4
Count3: 1
Count1: 1

--BINARY SEARCH COUNT ALL--
Count2: 4
Count3: 1
Count1: 1
```

The CountAll method uses a sequential search that is performed in a for loop. A linear search must be used since the List<T> is not assumed to be sorted. The if statement determines whether each element in the List<T> is equal to the search criterion (searchValue). If the element is found to be a match, the counter (foundCounter) is incremented by one. This counter is returned by this method to indicate the number of items matching the search criteria in the List<T>.

The BinarySearchCountAll method implements a binary search to locate an item matching the search criteria (searchValue) in the List<T>. If one is found, a while loop is used to find the very first matching item in the sorted List<T>, and the position of that element is recorded in the left variable. A second while loop is used to find the very last matching item, and the position of this element is recorded in the right variable. The value in the left variable is subtracted from the value in the right variable, and then one is added to this result in order to get the total number of matches.

Recipe 5.5 contains a variation of this recipe that returns the actual items found rather than a count.

See Also

Recipe 5.5, and the "List<T> Class" topic in the MSDN documentation.

5.5   Retrieving All Instances of a Specific Item in a List<T>

Problem

You need to retrieve every object contained in a List<T> that matches a search criterion. The List<T> contains the BinarySearch method to find a single item—essentially, there is no *find all* functionality. If you want to find all items duplicated in a List<T>, you must write your own routine.

Solution

Use the GetAll and BinarySearchGetAll methods shown in Example 5-3, which extend the List<T> class. These methods return an array of all the matching objects found in a sorted or unsorted List<T>.

Example 5-3. Retrieving all instances of a specific item in a List<T>

```
using System;
using System.Collections;
using System.Collections.Generic;
using System.Linq;

static class CollectionExtMethods
{
    // The method to retrieve all matching objects in a
    // sorted or unsorted ListEx<T>
    public T[] GetAll(T searchValue)
    {
```

```
        List<T> foundItem = new List<T>();

        for (int index = 0; index < this.Count; index++)
        {
            if (this[index].Equals(searchValue))
            {
                foundItem.Add(this[index]);

            }
        }

        return (foundItem.ToArray());
    }

    // The method to retrieve all matching objects in a sorted ListEx<T>
    public static T[] BinarySearchGetAll<T>(this List<T> myList, T searchValue)
    {
        List<T> RetObjs = new List<T>();

        // Search for first item.
        int center = myList.BinarySearch(searchValue);
        if (center > 0)
        {
            RetObjs.Add(myList[center]);

            int left = center;
            while (left > 0 && myList[left - 1].Equals(searchValue))
            {
                left -= 1;
                RetObjs.Add(myList[left]);
            }

            int right = center;
            while (right < (myList.Count - 1) &&
                myList[right + 1].Equals(searchValue))
            {
                right += 1;
                RetObjs.Add(myList[right]);
            }
        }

        return (RetObjs.ToArray());
    }
}
```

Discussion

The GetAll and BinarySearchGetAll methods used in this recipe are very similar to those used in Recipe 5.4. The main difference is that these methods return the actual items found in a List<T> object instead of a count of the number of times an item was found. The main thing to keep in mind when choosing between these methods is whether you are going to be searching a List<T> that is sorted or unsorted. Choose the GetAll method to obtain an array of all found items from an unsorted List<T> and choose the BinarySearchGetAll method to get all items in a sorted List<T>.

The following code exercises these two new extension methods of the List<T> class:

```
class Test
{
    static void Main( )
    {
        List<int> arrayExt = new List<int>( )
                {-1,-1,1,2,2,2,2,3,100,4,5};

        Console.WriteLine("--GET All--");
        IEnumerable<int> objects = arrayExt.GetAll(2);
        foreach (object o in objects)
        {
            Console.WriteLine("obj2: " + o);
        }

        Console.WriteLine( );
        objects = arrayExt.GetAll(-2);
        foreach (object o in objects)
        {
            Console.WriteLine("obj-2: " + o);
        }

        Console.WriteLine( );
        objects = arrayExt.GetAll(5);
        foreach (object o in objects)
        {
            Console.WriteLine("obj5: " + o);
        }

        Console.WriteLine("\r\n--BINARY SEARCH GET ALL--");
        arrayExt.Sort( );
        int[] objs = arrayExt.BinarySearchGetAll(-2);
        foreach (object o in objs)
        {
            Console.WriteLine("obj-2: " + o);
        }

        Console.WriteLine( );
        objs = arrayExt.BinarySearchGetAll(2);
        foreach (object o in objs)
        {
            Console.WriteLine("obj2: " + o);
        }

        Console.WriteLine( );
        objs = arrayExt.BinarySearchGetAll(5);
        foreach (object o in objs)

        {
```

```
            Console.WriteLine("obj5: " + o);
        }
    }
}
```

This code outputs the following:

```
--GET All--
obj2: 2
obj2: 2
obj2: 2
obj2: 2

obj5: 5

--BINARY SEARCH GET ALL--

obj2: 2
obj2: 2
obj2: 2
obj2: 2

obj5: 5
```

The `BinarySearchGetAll` method is faster than the `GetAll` method, especially if the array has already been sorted. If a `BinarySearch` is used on an unsorted `List<T>`, it is highly likely that the results returned by the search will be incorrect.

See Also

Recipe 5.4, and the "List<T> Class" topic in the MSDN documentation.

5.6   Inserting and Removing Items from an Array

Problem

You need the ability to insert and remove items from a standard `System.Array` type. When an item is inserted, it should not overwrite the item where it is being inserted; instead, it should be inserted between the element at that index and the previous index. When an item is removed, the void left by the element should be closed by shifting the other elements in the array. However, the `Array` type has no usable method to perform these operations.

Solution

If possible, switch to a `List<T>` instead. If this is not possible (for example, if you're not in control of the code that creates the `Array` or `ArrayList` in the first place), use the approach shown in the following class. Two methods insert and remove items from the array. The `InsertIntoArray` method that extends the `Array` type will insert an item into the array without overwriting any data that already exists in the array.

The RemoveFromArray method that extends the Array type will remove an element from the array:

```
using System;

public static class ArrayUtilities
{
    public static void InsertIntoArray(this Array target,
        object value, int index)
    {
        if (index < target.GetLowerBound(0) ||
            index > target.GetUpperBound(0))
        {
            throw (new ArgumentOutOfRangeException("index", index,
                "Array index out of bounds."));
        }
        else
        {
            Array.Copy(target, index, target, index + 1,
                    target.Length - index - 1);
        }

        target.SetValue(value, index);
    }

    Public static void RemoveFromArray<T>(this T[] target, int index)
    {
        if (index < target.GetLowerBound(0) ||
            index > target.GetUpperBound(0))
        {
            throw (new ArgumentOutOfRangeException("index", index,
                "Array index out of bounds."));
        }
        else if (index < target.GetUpperBound(0))
        {
            Array.Copy(target, index + 1, target, index,
                    target.Length - index - 1);
        }

        target.SetValue(null, target.GetUpperBound(0));
    }
}
```

Discussion

The InsertIntoArray and RemoveFromArray extension methods must be declared as static. Both methods make use of the Array.Copy static method to perform their operations. Initially, both methods test to see whether an item is being added or removed within the bounds of the array target. If the item passes this test, the Array.Copy method is used to shift items around to either make room for an element to be inserted or to overwrite an element being removed from the array.

The RemoveFromArray method accepts two parameters. The first array, *target*, is the array from which an element is to be removed; the second parameter, *index*, is the zero-based position of the element to be removed in the array. Elements at and above the inserted element are shifted down by one. The last element in the array is set to the default value for the array type.

The InsertIntoArray method accepts three parameters. The first parameter, *target*, is the array that is to have an element added; *value* is the element to be added; and *index* is the zero-based position at which *value* is to be added. Elements at and above the inserted element are shifted up by one. The last element in the array is discarded.

The following code illustrates the use of the InsertIntoArray and RemoveFromArray methods:

```
class CTest
{
    static void Main( )
    {
        string[] numbers = {"one", "two", "four", "five", "six"} ;

        numbers.InsertIntoArray("three", 2);
        foreach (string number in numbers)
        {
            Console.WriteLine(number);
        }

        Console.WriteLine( );
        numbers.RemoveFromArray(2);
        foreach (string number in numbers)
        {
            Console.WriteLine(number);
        }
    }
}
```

This code displays the following:

```
one
two
three
four
five

one
two
four
five
```

See Also

The "Array Class" and "List<T> Class" topics in the MSDN documentation.

5.7 Keeping Your List<T> Sorted

Problem

You will be using the BinarySearch method of the List<T> to periodically search the List<T> for specific elements. The addition, modification, and removal of elements will be interleaved with the searches. The BinarySearch method, however, presupposes a sorted array; if the List<T> is not sorted, the BinarySearch method will possibly return incorrect results. You do not want to have to remember to always call the List<T>.Sort method before calling the List<T>.BinarySearch method, not to mention incurring all the overhead associated with this call. You need a way of keeping the List<T> sorted without always having to call the List<T>.Sort method.

Solution

The following SortedList generic class enhances the adding and modifying of elements within a List<T>. These methods keep the array sorted when items are added to it and modified. Note that a DeleteSorted method is not required because deleting an item does not disturb the sorted order of the remaining items:

```
using System;
using System.Collections;
using System.Collections.Generic;

public class SortedList<T> : List<T>
{
    public new void Add(T item)
    {
        int position = this.BinarySearch(item);
        if (position < 0)
        {
            // This bit of code will be described in detail later.
            position = ~position;
        }

        this.Insert(position, item);
    }

    public void ModifySorted(T item, int index)
    {
        this.RemoveAt(index);

        int position = this.BinarySearch(item);
        if (position < 0)
        {
            position = ~position;
        }

        this.Insert(position, item);
    }
}
```

Discussion

Use the Add method to add elements while at the same time keeping the List<T> sorted. The Add method accepts a generic type (T) to add to the sorted list.

Instead of using the List<T> indexer directly to modify elements, use the ModifySorted method to modify elements while at the same time keeping the List<T> sorted. Call this method, passing in the generic type *T* to replace the existing object (item), and the index of the object to modify (index).

The following code exercises the SortedList<T> class:

```
class CTest
{
    static void Main( )
    {
        // Create a SortedList and populate it with
        // randomly chosen numbers.
        SortedList<int> sortedAL = new SortedList<int>( );
        sortedAL.Add(200);
        sortedAL.Add(20);
        sortedAL.Add(2);
        sortedAL.Add(7);
        sortedAL.Add(10);
        sortedAL.Add(0);
        sortedAL.Add(100);
        sortedAL.Add(-20);
        sortedAL.Add(56);
        sortedAL.Add(55);
        sortedAL.Add(57);
        sortedAL.Add(200);
        sortedAL.Add(-2);
        sortedAL.Add(-20);
        sortedAL.Add(55);
        sortedAL.Add(55);

        // Display it.
        foreach (int i in sortedAL)
        {
            Console.WriteLine(i);
        }

        // Now modify a value at a particular index.
        sortedAL.ModifySorted(0, 5);
        sortedAL.ModifySorted(1, 10);
        sortedAL.ModifySorted(2, 11);
        sortedAL.ModifySorted(3, 7);
        sortedAL.ModifySorted(4, 2);
        sortedAL.ModifySorted(2, 4);
        sortedAL.ModifySorted(15, 0);
        sortedAL.ModifySorted(0, 15);
        sortedAL.ModifySorted(223, 15);
```

```
            // Display it.
            Console.WriteLine();
            foreach (int i in sortedAL)
            {
                Console.WriteLine(i);
            }
        }
    }
```

This method automatically places the new item in the List<T> while keeping its sort order; this is done without having to explicitly call List<T>.Sort. The reason this works is because the Add method first calls the BinarySearch method and passes it the object to be added to the ArrayList. The BinarySearch method will either return the index where it found an identical item or a negative number that you can use to determine where the item that you are looking for should be located. If the BinarySearch method returns a positive number, you can use the List<T>.Insert method to insert the new element at that location, keeping the sort order within the List<T>. If the BinarySearch method returns a negative number, you can use the bitwise complement operator ~ to determine where the item should have been located, had it existed in the sorted list. Using this number, you can use the List<T>.Insert method to add the item to the correct location in the sorted list while keeping the correct sort order.

You can remove an element from the sorted list without disturbing the sort order, but modifying an element's value in the List<T> most likely will cause the sorted list to become unsorted. The ModifySorted method alleviates this problem. This method works similarly to the Add method, except that it will initially remove the element from the List<T> and then insert the new element into the correct location.

See Also

The "List<T> Class" topic in the MSDN documentation.

5.8 Sorting a Dictionary's Keys and/or Values

Problem

You want to sort the keys and/or values contained in a Dictionary in order to display the entire Dictionary to the user, sorted in either ascending or descending order.

Solution

Use a LINQ query and the Keys and Values properties of a Dictionary<T,U> object to obtain a sorted ICollection of its key and value objects. The code shown here displays the keys and values of a Dictionary<T,U> sorted in ascending or descending order:

```
var x = from k in hash.Keys orderby k ascending select k;
foreach (string s in x)
    Console.WriteLine("Key: " + s + "    Value: " + hash[s]);

x = from k in hash.Keys orderby k descending select k;
foreach (string s in x)
    Console.WriteLine("Key: " + s + "    Value: " + hash[s]);
```

The code shown here displays the values in a Dictionary<T,U> sorted in ascending or descending order:

```
var x = from k in hash.Values orderby k ascending select k;
foreach (string s in x)
    Console.WriteLine("Value: " + s);

Console.WriteLine( );

x = from k in hash.Values orderby k descending select k;
foreach (string s in x)
    Console.WriteLine("Value: " + s);
```

Note that you can also use the SortedDictionary<T,U> class, which will automatically keep the key sorted for you.

Discussion

The Dictionary<T,U> object exposes two useful properties for obtaining a collection of its keys or values. The Keys property returns an ICollection containing all the keys currently in the Dictionary<T,U>. The Values property returns the same for all values currently contained in the Dictionary<T,U>.

The ICollection object returned from either the Keys or Values property of a Dictionary<T,U> object contains direct references to the key and value collections within the Dictionary<T,U>. This means that if the keys and/or values change in a Dictionary<T,U>, the key and value collections will be altered accordingly.

See Also

The "Dictionary<T,U> Class," "SortedDictionary<T,U> Class," and "List<T> Class" topics in the MSDN documentation.

5.9 Creating a Dictionary with Max and Min Value Boundaries

Problem

You need to use a generic Dictionary object in your project that stores only numeric data in its value (the key can be of any type) between a set, predefined maximum and minimum value.

Solution

Create a class with accessors and methods that enforce these boundaries. The class shown in Example 5-4, MaxMinValueDictionary, allows only types to be stored that implement the IComparable interface and fall between a maximum and minimum value.

Example 5-4. Creating a dictionary with max and min value boundaries

```
using System;
using System.Collections;
using System.Collections.Generic;
using System.Runtime.Serialization;


[Serializable]
public class MaxMinValueDictionary<T, U>
    where U : IComparable<U>
{
    protected Dictionary<T, U> internalDictionary = null;

    public MaxMinValueDictionary(U minValue, U maxValue)
    {
        this.minValue = minValue;
        this.maxValue = maxValue;
        internalDictionary = new Dictionary<T, U>( );
    }

    protected U minValue = default(U);
    protected U maxValue = default(U);

    public int Count
    {
        get { return (internalDictionary.Count); }
    }

    public Dictionary<T, U>.KeyCollection Keys
    {
        get { return (internalDictionary.Keys); }
    }

    public Dictionary<T, U>.ValueCollection Values
    {
        get { return (internalDictionary.Values); }
    }

    public U this[T key]
    {
        get {return (internalDictionary[key]);}
        set
        {
            if (value.CompareTo(minValue) >= 0 && value.CompareTo(maxValue) <= 0)
            {
```

```
                internalDictionary[key] = value;
            }
            else
            {
                throw (new ArgumentOutOfRangeException("value", value,
                    "Value must be within the range " + minValue + " to " + maxValue));
            }
        }
    }

    public void Add(T key, U value)
    {
        if (value.CompareTo(minValue) >= 0 && value.CompareTo(maxValue) <= 0)
        {
            internalDictionary.Add(key, value);
        }
        else
        {
            throw (new ArgumentOutOfRangeException("value", value,
                "Value must be within the range " + minValue + " to " + maxValue));
        }
    }

    public bool ContainsKey(T key)
    {
        return (internalDictionary.ContainsKey(key));
    }

    public bool ContainsValue(U value)
    {
        return (internalDictionary.ContainsValue(value));
    }

    public override bool Equals(object obj)
    {
        return (internalDictionary.Equals(obj));
    }

    public IEnumerator GetEnumerator( )
    {
        return (internalDictionary.GetEnumerator( ));
    }

    public override int GetHashCode( )
    {
        return (internalDictionary.GetHashCode( ));
    }

    public void GetObjectData(SerializationInfo info, StreamingContext context)
    {
        internalDictionary.GetObjectData(info, context);
    }
```

```
    public void OnDeserialization(object sender)
    {
        internalDictionary.OnDeserialization(sender);
    }

    public override string ToString()
    {
        return (internalDictionary.ToString());
    }

    public bool TryGetValue(T key, out U value)
    {
        return (internalDictionary.TryGetValue(key, out value));
    }

    public void Remove(T key)
    {
        internalDictionary.Remove(key);
    }

    public void Clear()
    {
        internalDictionary.Clear();
    }
}
```

Discussion

The `MaxMinValueDictionary` class wraps the `Dictionary<T,U>` class, so it can restrict the range of allowed values. Defined here is the overloaded constructor for the `MaxMinValueDictionary` class:

```
    public MaxMinValueDictionary(U minValue, U maxValue)
```

This constructor allows the range of values to be set. Its parameters are:

minValue
> The smallest value of type U that can be added as a value in a key/value pair.

maxValue
> The largest value of type U that can be added as a value in a key/value pair.

The overridden indexer has both get and set. The get returns the value that matches the provided *key*. The set checks the *value* parameter to determine whether it is within the boundaries of the `minValue` and `maxValue` fields before it is set.

The `Add` method accepts a type U for its *value* parameter and performs the same tests as the set accessor on the indexer. If the test passes, the integer is added to the `MaxMinValueDictionary`.

See Also

The "Hashtable Class" and "Dictionary<T, U> Class" topics in the MSDN documentation.

5.10   Storing Snapshots of Lists in an Array

Problem

You have an ArrayList, Queue, or Stack object and you want to take a snapshot of its current state.

Note that this recipe also works for any other data type that implements the ICollection interface.

Solution

Use the ToArray extension method on the IEnumerable<T> interface. The following method, TakeSnapshotOfList, accepts any type that implements the IEnumerable<T> interface and takes a snapshot of the entire object's contents. This snapshot is returned as an object array:

```
public static T[] TakeSnapshotOfList<T>(IEnumerable<T> theList)
{
    T[] snapshot = theList.ToArray();
    return (snapshot);
}
```

Discussion

The following method creates a Queue<int> object, enqueues some data, and then takes a snapshot of it:

```
public static void TestListSnapshot()
{
    Queue<int> someQueue = new Queue<int>();
    someQueue.Enqueue(1);
    someQueue.Enqueue(2);
    someQueue.Enqueue(3);

    int[] queueSnapshot = TakeSnapshotOfList<int>(someQueue);
}
```

The TakeSnapshotOfList<T> is useful when you want to record the state of an object that implements the ICollection interface. This "snapshot" can be compared to the original list later on to determine what, if anything, changed in the list. Multiple snapshots can be taken at various points in an application's run to show the state of the list or lists over time.

The TakeSnapshotOfList<T> method could easily be used as a logging/debugging tool for developers. Take, for example, a List<T> that is being corrupted at some point in the application. You can take snapshots of the List<T> at various points in the application using the TakeSnapshotOfList<T> method and then compare the snapshots to narrow down the list of possible places where the List<T> is being corrupted.

See Also

The "IEnumerable<T> Interface" and "Array Class" topics in the MSDN documentation.

5.11 Persisting a Collection Between Application Sessions

Problem

You have a collection such as an ArrayList, List<T>, Hashtable, or Dictionary<T,U> in which you are storing application information. You can use this information to tailor the application's environment to the last known settings (e.g., window size, window placement, and currently displayed toolbars). You can also use it to allow the user to start the application at the same point where it was last shut down. In other words, if the user is editing an invoice and needs to shut down the computer for the night, the application will know exactly which invoice to initially display when the application is started next time.

Solution

Serialize the object(s) to and from a file:

```
public static void SaveObj<T>(T obj, string dataFile)
{
        using (FileStream FS = File.Create(dataFile))
        {
            BinaryFormatter binSerializer = new BinaryFormatter( );
            binSerializer.Serialize(FS, obj);
        }   }

public static T RestoreObj<T>(string dataFile)
{
        T obj = default(T);

        using (FileStream FS = File.OpenRead(dataFile))
        {
            BinaryFormatter binSerializer = new BinaryFormatter( );
            obj = (T)binSerializer.Deserialize(FS);
        }

        return (obj);     }
```

Discussion

The dataFile parameter accepts a string value to use as a filename. The SaveObj<T> method accepts an object and attempts to serialize it to a file. Conversely, the RestoreObj<T> method removes the serialized object from the file created in the SaveObj<T> method.

The TestSerialization utility shown in Example 5-5 demonstrates how to use these methods to serialize an ArrayList object (note that this will work for any type that is marked with the SerializableAttribute).

Example 5-5. Persisting a collection between application sessions

```
public static void TestSerialization( )
{
    // Create a Hashtable object to save/restore to/from a file.
    ArrayList HT = new ArrayList( ) {"Zero","One","Two"};

    // Display this object's contents and save it to a file.
    foreach (object O in HT)
        Console.WriteLine(O.ToString( ));
    SaveObj<ArrayList>(HT, "HT.data");
    // Restore this object from the same file and display its contents.
    ArrayList HTNew = new ArrayList( );
    HTNew = RestoreObj<ArrayList>("HT.data");
    foreach (object O in HTNew)
        Console.WriteLine(O.ToString( ));
}
```

If you serialize your objects to disk at specific points in your application, you can then deserialize them and return to a known state, for instance, in the event of an unintended shutdown.

If you rely on serialized objects to store persistent information, you need to figure out what you are going to do when you deploy a new version of the application. You should plan ahead with either a strategy for making sure the types you serialize don't get changed or a technique for dealing with changes. Otherwise, you are going to have big problems when you deploy an update.

See Also

The "ArrayList Class," "Hashtable Class," "List<T> Class," "Dictionary<T,U> Class," "File Class," and "BinaryFormatter Class" topics in the MSDN documentation.

5.12 Testing Every Element in an Array or List<T>

Problem

You need an easy way to test every element in an Array or List<T>. The results of this test should indicate that the test passed for all elements in the collection, or it failed for at least one element in the collection.

Solution

Use the TrueForAll method, as shown here:

```
// Create a List of strings.
List<string> strings = new List<string>() {"one",null,"three","four"};

// Determine if there are no null values in the List.
string str = strings.TrueForAll(delegate(string val)
{
    if (val == null)
        return false;
    else
        return true;
}).ToString();

// Display the results.
Console.WriteLine(str);
```

Discussion

The addition of the TrueForAll method on the Array and List<T> classes allows you to easily set up tests for all elements in these collections. The code in the Solution for this recipe tests all elements to determine if any are null. You could just as easily set up tests to determine...

- If any numeric elements are above a specified maximum value
- If any numeric elements are below a specified minimum value
- If any string elements contain a specified set of characters
- If any data objects have all of their fields filled in

...as well as any others you may come up with.

The TrueForAll method accepts a generic delegate Predicate<T> called match and returns a Boolean value:

```
public bool TrueForAll(Predicate<T> match)
```

The match parameter determines whether or not a true or false should be returned by the TrueForAll method.

The TrueForAll method basically consists of a loop that iterates over each element in the collection. Within this loop, a call to the match delegate is invoked. If this delegate returns true, the processing continues on to the next element in the collection. If this delegate returns false, processing stops and a false is returned by the TrueForAll method. When the TrueForAll method is finished iterating over all the elements of the collection and the match delegate has not returned a false value for any element, the TrueForAll method returns a true.

See Also

The "Array Class," "List<T> Class," and "TrueForAll Method" topics in the MSDN documentation.

5.13 Performing an Action on Each Element in an Array or List<T>

Problem

You need an easy way to iterate over all the elements in an Array or List<T>, performing an operation on each element as you go.

Solution

Use the ForEach method of the Array or List<T> classes:

```
// Create and populate a List of Data objects.
List<Data> numbers = new List<Data>()
        {new Data(1), new Data(2), new Data(3), new Data(4)};

// Display them.
foreach (Data d in numbers)
    Console.WriteLine(d.val);

// Add 2 to all Data.val integer values.
    numbers.ForEach(delegate(Data obj)      {         obj.val += 2;      });

// Display them.
foreach (Data d in numbers)
    Console.WriteLine(d.val);

// Total val integer values in all Data objects in the List.
int total = 0;
    numbers.ForEach(delegate(Data obj)      {         total += obj.val;      });

// Display total.
Console.WriteLine("Total: " + total);
```

This code outputs the following:

```
1
2
3
4
```

```
3
4
5
6
Total: 18
```

The Data class is defined as follows:

```
public class Data
{
    public Data(int v)
    {
        val = v;
    }

    public int val = 0;
}
```

Discussion

The ForEach method of the Array and List<T> collections allows you to easily per-form an action on every element within these collections. This is accomplished through the use of the Action<T> delegate, which is passed in as a parameter to the ForEach method:

```
public void ForEach (Action<T> action)
```

The action parameter is a delegate of type Action<T> that contains the code that will be invoked for each element of the collection.

The ForEach method basically consists of a loop that iterates over each element in the collection. Within this loop, a call to the action delegate is invoked. Processing continues on to each element in the collection until the last element is finished processing. When this occurs, the ForEach method is finished and returns to the calling method.

This recipe uses the ForEach method of a List<T> object in two different ways. The first is to actually modify the values of each element of the List<T> object:

```
// Add 2 to all Data.val integer values.
numbers.ForEach(delegate(Data obj)
{
    obj.val += 2;
});
```

This call to ForEach will iterate over each Data element within the numbers List<Data> object. On every iteration, the value val contained in the current Data object obj has its value incremented by two.

The second way is to collect a total of all the values val contained in each Data object obj in the numbers List<Data> object:

```
// Total val integer values in all Data objects in the List.
int total = 0;
numbers.ForEach(delegate(Data obj)
```

```
{
    total += obj.val;
});
```

This code uses the `total` variable to build a running total of the values contained in each element. In this instance, you do not modify any values in any of the `Data` objects; instead, you examine each `Data` object and record information about its value.

See Also

The "Array Class," "List<T> Class," and "ForEach Method" topics in the MSDN documentation.

5.14   Creating a Read-Only Array or List<T>

Problem

You need a way to create a read-only `Array` or `List<T>`, where the `Array` or `List<T>` itself is read-only.

Solution

Use the `AsReadOnly` method of the `Array` or `List<T>` class, as shown here:

```
// Create and populate a List of strings.
List<string> strings = new List<string>() {"1","2","3","4"};

// Create a read-only strings List.
    IList<string> readOnlyStrings = strings.AsReadOnly();

// Display them.
foreach (string s in readOnlyStrings)
    Console.WriteLine(s);
```

Discussion

The `AsReadOnly` method accepts no parameters and returns a read-only wrapper around the collection on which it is called. For example, the following statement:

```
IList<string> readOnlyStrings = strings.AsReadOnly();
```

returns a read-only `IList<string>` type from the original strings `List<string>` type. This read-only `readOnlyStrings` variable behaves similarly to the original strings object, except that you cannot add, modify, or delete elements from this object. If you attempt one of these actions, a `System.NotSupportedException` will be thrown along with the message "Collection is read-only". Any of the following lines of code will cause this exception to be thrown:

```
readOnlyStrings.Add("5");
readOnlyStrings.Remove("1");
readOnlyStrings[0] = "1.1";
```

While you cannot modify the data within the readOnlyStrings object, you can point this object to refer to a different object of type IList<string>, for example:

```
readOnlyStrings = new List<string>();
```

On the other hand, if you add, modify, or delete elements from the original strings object, the changes will be reflected in the new readOnlyStrings object. For example, the following code creates a List<string>, populates it, and then creates a read-only object readOnlyStrings from this original List<string> object. Next, the readOnlyStrings object elements are displayed, the original List<string> object is modified, and then the readOnlyStrings object elements are again displayed. Notice that they have changed:

```
// Create and populate a List of strings.
List<string> strings = new List<string>() {"1","2","3","4"};

// Create a read-only strings List.
IList<string> readOnlyStrings = strings.AsReadOnly();

// Display them.
foreach (string s in readOnlyStrings)
    Console.WriteLine(s);

// Change the value in the original List<string>.
strings[0] = "one";

strings[1] = null;

// Display them again.
Console.WriteLine();
foreach (string s in readOnlyStrings)
    Console.WriteLine(s);
```

This code outputs the following:

```
1
2
3
4

one

          ← The null value
3
4
```

For an alternate method to making read-only collections, see Recipe 4.8.

See Also

The "Array Class," "List<T> Class," "IList<T> Interface," and "AsReadOnly Method" topics in the MSDN documentation.

CHAPTER 6

Iterators, Partial Types, and Partial Methods

6.0   Introduction

Iterators allow for a block of code to yield an ordered sequence of values.

Iterators are a mechanism for producing data that can be iterated over by the foreach loop construct. However, iterators are much more flexible than this. You can easily generate a sequence of data returned by the enumerator (lazy computation); it does not have to be hardcoded up front (eager computation). For example, you could easily write an enumerator that generates the Fibonacci sequence on demand. Another flexible feature of iterators is that you do not have to set a limit on the number of values returned by the iterator, so in this example, you could choose when to stop producing the Fibonacci sequence. This is an interesting distinction in the LINQ world. Iterators like the one produced by the IEnumerable version of Where are lazy, but grouping or sorting requires eagerness.

Iterators allow you to hand the work of writing this class off to the C# compiler. Now, you need to add only an iterator to your type. An iterator is a member within your type (e.g., a method, an operator overload, or the get accessor of a property) that returns either a System.Collections.IEnumerator, a System.Collections.Generic. IEnumerator<T>, a System.Collections.IEnumerable, or a System.Collections.Generic. IEnumerable<T> and that contains at least one yield statement. This allows you to write types that can be used by foreach loops.

Iterators play an important role in Language Integrated Query (LINQ), as LINQ to Objects is based on being able to work on classes that implement IEnumerable<T>. They allow for the query engine to iterate over collections while performing the various query, projection, ordering, and grouping operations. Without iterator support, LINQ would be much more cumbersome, and the declarative style of programming that it brings would be clumsy if not lost altogether.

Partial types allow for different parts of classes to be placed in different locations.

Partial types allow the developer to split pieces of a type across several areas where the type is defined. The type can be in multiple files, multiple areas in the same file, or a combination of the two. Declaring a type as partial is an indicator to the C# compiler that this type may not be fully represented in this location and that it cannot be fully compiled until the other parts are found or the end of the list of modules to compile is found. Partial types are purely a compiler-implemented feature with no impact to the underlying Microsoft Intermediate Language that is generated for the class. The main examples of using partial types are in the Visual Studio IDE, where the designer uses them to keep designer-generated code separate from UI logic the developer creates, and in the DataSet creation code, which is based on an XML Schema Definition of the data. Even though partial types are only a compiler-level feature, you can use them to your advantage in a few situations that are pointed out in Recipes 6.7 and 6.8.

Partial methods are a new language feature in C# 3.0 that can be used to implement a lightweight mechanism for event handling.

The thing that makes partial methods lightweight is that they are declared in a partial class, but, if no other part of the partial class provides an implementation, the compiler will completely remove the calls to the method along with any processing that occurs in the arguments to the method call. No trace of a partial method will be emitted to the metadata of the assembly without an implementation including the original declarations and calls to the method. This is a good feature for code-generation scenarios where user-specific functionality could be wired in without the initial partial class knowing what will be done by the partial method implementer.

6.1   Creating an Iterator on a Generic Type

Problem

You want elements contained in your generic type to be enumerated using the foreach statement.

Solution

Add an iterator to your generic type, as shown here:

```
public class ShoppingList<T> : IEnumerable<T>
{
    private List<T> _items = new List<T>();

    public void Add(T name)
    {
        _items.Add(name);
    }

    public IEnumerator<T> GetEnumerator()
```

```
        {
            return _items.GetEnumerator();
        }
    }
```

The following code creates a new ShoppingList<T> object and fills it with strings; it then proceeds to use a foreach loop to enumerate and display each string:

```
public static void TestShoppingCart()
{
    //Create ShoppingList object and fill it with data
    ShoppingList<string> shoppingCart = new ShoppingList<string>(){
        "item1","item2","item3","item4","item5","item6"};

    // Display all data in ShoppingCart object
    foreach (string item in shoppingCart)
    {
        Console.WriteLine(item);
    }
}
```

Discussion

Adding an iterator to a generic type is accomplished by implementing the IEnumerator<T> interface. The method to implement for IEnumerator<T> is the GetEnumerator method that accepts no arguments and returns an IEnumerator<T> type. The GetNext method on the object returned by this GetEnumerator method is called by the foreach loop to determine what object is returned on every iteration.

The code that you write inside of the GetEnumerator method is what actually does the work of determining the next object to be returned by the foreach loop. This is accomplished through the use of the yield return statement. In this recipe, we use the GetEnumerator method that is built into the List<T> class as that gives us the implementation.

The use of IEnumerable<T> makes it more apparent that this class supports enumeration. You can also specify a closed type in place of T in IEnumerable<T>, such as IEnumerable<string>, if you wish that class to enumerate values only of type string. Regardless of the method you choose, the operation of the iterator and the foreach loop is identical.

See Also

The "Iterators," "IEnumerator Interface," and "IEnumerable Interface" topics in the MSDN documentation.

6.2 Creating an Iterator on a Nongeneric Type

Problem

You want to be able to access elements contained in your nongeneric collection type using the foreach statement.

Solution

Implement IEnumerable on your nongeneric type:

```
public class StampCollection : IEnumerable
{
    private Dictionary<string, Stamp> _stamps =
        new Dictionary<string, Stamp>();

    public void Add(Stamp stamp)
    {
        _stamps.Add(stamp.Name, stamp);
    }

    public IEnumerator GetEnumerator()
    {
        // Return all stamps in the stamp collection
        // in order of publication
        var orderedStamps = from Stamp stamp in _stamps.Values
                            orderby stamp.Year
                            select stamp;
        foreach (Stamp stamp in orderedStamps)
        {
            yield return stamp;
        }
    }
}

public class Stamp
{
    public Stamp(int year, string name)
    {
        this.Year = year;
        this.Name = name;
    }
    public int Year { get; set; }
    public string Name { get; set; }

    public override string ToString()
    {
        return this.Year + ":" + this.Name;
    }
}
```

The following code creates a new StampCollection and fills it with Stamps; it then proceeds to use a foreach loop to enumerate and display each Stamp:

```
public static void TestStampCollection()
{
    //Create a StampCollection and fill it with stamps
    StampCollection stamps = new StampCollection() {
        new Stamp(1998,"Louisiana Duck"),
        new Stamp(1968,"Goethals Memorial"),
        new Stamp(1909,"Carmine Hudson"),
        new Stamp(1936,"Hotel Corner Card")};

    foreach (Stamp stamp in stamps)
    {
        Console.WriteLine(stamp);
    }
}
```

Discussion

When adding an iterator to a nongeneric type, the IEnumerable interface needs to be implemented. Making collections enumerable allows not only iteration, but querying using LINQ as well.

The code that is written inside of the GetEnumerator method is what actually does the work of determining the next object to be returned by the foreach loop. This is accomplished through the use of the yield return statement. For example, in this recipe, you simply use a foreach loop to iterate over the query result for ordering the stamps in the collection and return one at a time:

```
public IEnumerator GetEnumerator()
{
    // Return all stamps in the stamp collection
    // in order of publication
    var orderedStamps = from Stamp stamp in _stamps.Values
                        orderby stamp.Year
                        select stamp;
    foreach (Stamp stamp in orderedStamps)
    {
        yield return stamp;
    }
}
```

This allows StampCollection to return an enumerator that will give a series of Stamps based on publication date by default.

See Also

The "Iterators," "IEnumerator Interface," and "IEnumerable Interface" topics in the MSDN documentation.

6.3　Creating Custom Enumerators

Problem

You need to add foreach support to a class, but the normal way of adding an iterator (i.e., implementing IEnumerable on a type and returning a reference to this IEnumerable from a member function) is not flexible enough. Instead of simply iterating from the first element to the last, you also need to iterate from the last to the first, and you need to be able to step over, or skip, a predefined number of elements on each iteration. You want to make all of these types of iterators available to your class.

Solution

The Container<T> class shown in Example 6-1 acts as a container for a private List<T> called internalList. Container is implemented so you can use it in a foreach loop to iterate through the private internalList.

Example 6-1. Creating custom iterators

```
public class Container<T> : IEnumerable<T>
{
    public Container() {}

    private List<T> _internalList = new List<T>();

    // This iterator iterates over each element from first to last
    public IEnumerator<T> GetEnumerator()
    {
        return _internalList.GetEnumerator();
    }

    // This iterator iterates over each element from last to first
    public IEnumerable<T> GetReverseOrderEnumerator()
    {
        foreach (T item in ((IEnumerable<T>)_internalList).Reverse())
        {
            yield return item;
        }
    }

    // This iterator iterates over each element from first to last stepping
    // over a predefined number of elements
    public IEnumerable<T> GetForwardStepEnumerator(int step)
    {
        foreach (T item in _internalList.EveryNthItem(step))
        {
            yield return item;
        }
    }
```

Example 6-1. Creating custom iterators (continued)

```
    // This iterator iterates over each element from last to first stepping
    // over a predefined number of elements
    public IEnumerable<T> GetReverseStepEnumerator(int step)
    {
        foreach (T item in ((IEnumerable<T>)_internalList).Reverse().EveryNthItem(step))
        {
            yield return item;
        }
    }

    #region IEnumerable Members

    IEnumerator IEnumerable.GetEnumerator()
    {
        return GetEnumerator();
    }

    #endregion

    public void Clear()
    {
        _internalList.Clear();
    }

    public void Add(T item)
    {
        _internalList.Add(item);
    }

    public void AddRange(ICollection<T> collection)
    {
        _internalList.AddRange(collection);
    }
}
```

Discussion

Iterators provide an easy method of moving from item to item within an object using the familiar foreach loop construct. The object can be an array, a collection, or some other type of container. This is similar to using a for loop to manually iterate over each item contained in an array. In fact, an iterator can be set up to use a for loop, or any other looping construct for that matter, as the mechanism for yielding each item in the object. In fact, you do not even have to use a looping construct. The following code is perfectly valid:

```
    public static IEnumerable<int> GetValues()
    {
    yield return 10;
    yield return 20;
    yield return 30;
    yield return 100;
    }
```

With the foreach loop, you do not have to worry about watching for the end of the list, since you cannot go beyond the bounds of the list. The best part about the foreach loop and iterators is that you do not have to know how to access the list of elements within its container—indeed, you do not even have to have access to the list of elements; the iterator member(s) implemented on the container do this for you.

To see what foreach is doing here, let's look at code to iterate over the Container class:

```
// Iterate over Container object
foreach (int i in container)
{
        Console.WriteLine(i);
}
```

foreach will take the following actions while this code executes:

1. Get the enumerator from container using IEnumerator.GetEnumerator( ).

2. Access the IEnumerator.Current property for the current object (int) and place it into i.

3. Call IEnumerator.MoveNext( ). If MoveNext returns true, go back to step 2, or else end the loop.

The Container class contains a private List of items called internalList. There are four iterator members within this class:

```
GetEnumerator
GetReverseOrderEnumerator
GetForwardStepEnumerator
GetReverseStepEnumerator
```

The GetEnumerator method iterates over each element in the internalList from the first to the last element. This iterator, similar to the others, uses a for loop to yield each element in the internalList.

The GetReverseOrderEnumerator method implements an iterator in its get accessor (set accessors cannot be iterators). This iterator is very similar in design to the GetEnumerator method, except that the foreach loop works on the internalList in the reverse direction by using the IEnumerable<T>.Reverse extension method. The last two iterators, GetForwardStepEnumerator and GetReverseStepEnumerator, are similar in design to GetEnumerator and GetReverseOrderEnumerator, respectively. The main difference is that the foreach loop uses the EveryNthItem extension method to skip over the specified number of items in the internalList:

```
public static IEnumerable<T> EveryNthItem<T>(this IEnumerable<T> enumerable,
                                             int step)
{
    int current = 0;
    foreach (T item in enumerable)
    {
```

```
        ++current;
        if (current % step == 0)
            yield return item;
    }
}
```

Notice also that only the GetEnumerator method must return an IEnumerator<T> interface; the other three iterators must return IEnumerable<T> interfaces.

To iterate over each element in the Container object from first to last, use the following code:

```
Container<int> container = new Container<int>();
//...Add data to container here ...
foreach (int i in container)
{
    Console.WriteLine(i);
}
```

To iterate over each element in the Container object from last to first, use the following code:

```
Container<int> container = new Container<int>();
//...Add data to container here ...
    foreach (int i in container.GetReverseOrderEnumerator())
    {
            Console.WriteLine(i);
    }
```

To iterate over each element in the Container object from first to last while skipping every other element, use the following code:

```
Container<int> container = new Container<int>();
//...Add data to container here ...
    foreach (int i in container.GetForwardStepEnumerator(2))
    {
            Console.WriteLine(i);
    }
```

To iterate over each element in the Container object from last to first while skipping to every third element, use the following code:

```
Container<int> container = new Container<int>();
//...Add data to container here ...
    foreach (int i in container.GetReverseStepEnumerator(3))
    {
            Console.WriteLine(i);
    }
```

In each of the last two examples, the iterator method accepts an integer value, step, which determines how many items will be skipped.

See Also

The "Iterators," "yield," "IEnumerator Interface," "IEnumerable(Of T) interface," and "IEnumerable Interface" topics in the MSDN documentation.

6.4   Implementing Iterator Logic

Problem

Iterators need to provide access to the data elements in the collections they are implemented for. You need a good way to work with sets of data.

Solution

Use LINQ to implement iterator logic, as shown in Example 6-2. The highlighted items are just a few parts of LINQ that can help you with the implementation of iterator logic.

Example 6-2. Implementing iterator logic with LINQ

```
public class SectionalList<T> : IEnumerable<T>
{
        private List<T> _items = new List<T>();

        public void Add(T item)
        {
                _items.Add(item);
        }

    public IEnumerator<T> GetEnumerator()
    {
        return _items.GetEnumerator();
    }

    IEnumerator IEnumerable.GetEnumerator()
    {
        return GetEnumerator();
    }

        public IEnumerable<T> GetFirstHalf()
        {
                foreach(T item in _items.Take(_items.Count / 2))
                {
                        yield return item;
                }
        }
        public IEnumerable<T> GetSecondHalf()
        {
        foreach (T item in _items.Skip(_items.Count / 2))
        {
            yield return item;
```

Example 6-2. Implementing iterator logic with LINQ (continued)

```
        }
    }

    public IEnumerable<T> GetFilteredValues(Func<T, bool> predicate)
    {
        foreach (T item in _items.TakeWhile(predicate))
        {
            yield return item;
        }
    }

    public IEnumerable<T> GetReverseFilteredValues(Func<T, bool> predicate)
    {
        foreach (T item in _items.SkipWhile(predicate))
        {
            yield return item;
        }
    }
}
```

Discussion

The SectionalListat class contains the typical GetEnumerator iterator method that yields all items in the _items list. In addition to this iterator method, the class contains four additional iterators: GetFirstHalf, GetSecondHalf, GetFilteredValues, and GetReverseFilteredValues.

The GetFirstHalf iterator starts at the beginning of the _items list and yields all elements in the list up to the middle index. At this point, iteration stops. The GetSecondHalf iterator starts where the GetFirstHalf iterator left off and continues yielding elements of the _items list until the end of this list. These iterators use the Take extension method (GetFirstHalf) and the Skip extension method (GetSecondHalf) from LINQ to retrieve the elements:

```
        public IEnumerable<T> GetFirstHalf()
        {
            foreach(T item in _items.Take(_items.Count / 2))
            {
                yield return item;
            }
        }
        public IEnumerable<T> GetSecondHalf()
        {
        foreach (T item in _items.Skip(_items.Count / 2))
        {
            yield return item;
        }
    }
```

The GetFilteredValues and GetNonFilteredValues iterators allow the user to retrieve the items in the collection that either pass (GetFilteredValues) or fail

(GetNonFilteredValues) a predicate test that is passed in. These methods use the TakeWhile and SkipWhile LINQ methods, respectively:

```
public IEnumerable<T> GetFilteredValues(Func<T, bool> predicate)
{
    foreach (T item in _items.TakeWhile(predicate))
    {
        yield return item;
    }
}

public IEnumerable<T> GetReverseFilteredValues(Func<T, bool> predicate)
{
    foreach (T item in _items.SkipWhile(predicate))
    {
        yield return item;
    }
}
```

The following code shows how the iterator methods are used:

```
public static void TestIteratorsAndLinq()
{
    //Create SectionalList and fill it with data
    SectionalList<int> sectionalList = new SectionalList<int>() {
        12,26,95,37,50,33,81,54};

    // Display all data in SectionalList
        Console.WriteLine("\r\nGetEnumerator iterator");
        foreach (int i in sectionalList)
        {
        Console.Write(i + ":");
    }
    Console.WriteLine("");

        Console.WriteLine("\r\nGetFirstHalf iterator");
        foreach (int i in sectionalList.GetFirstHalf())
        {
        Console.Write(i + ":");
    }
    Console.WriteLine("");

        Console.WriteLine("\r\nGetSecondHalf iterator");
    foreach (int i in sectionalList.GetSecondHalf())
        {
            Console.Write(i + ":");
        }
    Console.WriteLine("");

    Console.WriteLine("\r\nGetFilteredValues iterator");
    // make a predicate test for even numbers
    Func<int, bool> predicate = item => (item % 2 == 0);
    foreach (int i in sectionalList.GetFilteredValues(predicate))
    {
```

```
        Console.Write(i + ":");
    }
    Console.WriteLine("");

    Console.WriteLine("\r\nGetReverseFilteredValues iterator");
    foreach (int i in sectionalList.GetNonFilteredValues(predicate))
    {
        Console.Write(i + ":");
    }
    Console.WriteLine("");

}
```

This code produces the following output:

```
GetEnumerator iterator
12:26:95:37:50:33:81:54:

GetFirstHalf iterator
12:26:95:37:

GetSecondHalf iterator
50:33:81:54:

GetFilteredValues iterator
12:26:

GetReverseFilteredValues iterator
95:37:50:33:81:54:
```

See Also

The "Iterators," "IEnumerator Interface," and "IEnumerable Interface" topics in the MSDN documentation.

6.5   Forcing an Iterator to Stop Iterating

Problem

You have a requirement that if an iterator encounters malformed or out-of-bounds data that the iterations are to stop immediately.

Solution

It is possible to throw an exception from an iterator, which terminates the iterator and the foreach loop, but a controlled stop to an iterator should not be an exceptional condition. To do this, you can use the yield break statement within your iterator:

```
public class UpperLimitList<T> : IEnumerable<T>
{
        private List<T> _items = new list<T>();
```

```
            private bool noMoreItemsCanBeAdded;
            private int upperLimit = -1;

            public int UpperLimit
            {
                    get {return (upperLimit);}
                    set {upperLimit = value;}
            }

            public void Add(T name)
            {
                    _items.Add(name);
            }

            public IEnumerator<T> GetEnumerator()
            {
                    for (int index = 0; index < _items.Count; index++)
                    {
                            if (noMoreItemsCanBeAdded)
                            {
                                    yield break;
                            }
                            else
                            {
                                    if (upperLimit >= 0 && index >= upperLimit-1)
                                    {
                                            noMoreItemsCanBeAdded = true;
                                    }

                                    yield return (_items[index]);
                            }
                    }
            }

        IEnumerator IEnumerable.GetEnumerator()
        {
            return GetEnumerator();
        }
    }
}
```

Discussion

The way to terminate an iterator, and thus terminate the foreach loop, is to use the yield break statement. This statement has the same effect as simply exiting from the function. This yield break statement can be used only within an iterator block.

To use the UpperLimitList, see the following code:

```
public static void TestYieldBreak()
{
    //Create UpperLimitList and fill it with data
    UpperLimitList<string> gatePasses = new UpperLimitList<string>() {
        "A","B","C","D","E","F","G"};
```

```
        Console.WriteLine("Gates allowed before limit set");
        foreach (string gatePass in gatePasses)
        {
            Console.Write(gatePass + ":");
        }
        Console.WriteLine("");

        // only give out 5 gate passes
        gatePasses.UpperLimit = 5;

        Console.WriteLine("Gates allowed after limit set");
        foreach (string gatePass in gatePasses)
            {
                    Console.Write(gatePass + ":");
            }
        Console.WriteLine("");
    }
```

The output for this solution is listed here:

```
Gates allowed before limit set
A:B:C:D:E:F:G:
Gates allowed after limit set
A:B:C:D:E:
```

See Also

Recipe 6.4, and the "Iterators," "yield," "IEnumerator Interface," and "IEnumerable Interface" topics in the MSDN documentation.

6.6   Dealing with Finally Blocks and Iterators

Problem

You have added a try/finally block to your iterator, and you notice that the finally block is not being executed when you think it should.

Solution

Wrap a try block around the iteration code in the GetEnumerator iterator with a finally block following this try block:

```
public class StringSet : IEnumerable<string>
{
    private List<string> _items = new List<string>();

    public void Add(string value)
    {
        _items.Add(value);
    }
```

```csharp
public IEnumerator<string> GetEnumerator()
{
    try
    {
        for (int index = 0; index < _items.Count; index++)
        {
            yield return (_items[index]);
        }
    }
    finally
    {
        // Only executed at end of foreach loop (including on yield break)
        Console.WriteLine("In iterator finally block");
    }
}

#region IEnumerable Members

IEnumerator IEnumerable.GetEnumerator()
{
    return GetEnumerator();
}


#endregion
}
```

The foreach code that calls this iterator looks like this:

```csharp
//Create a StringSet object and fill it with data
StringSet strSet =
    new StringSet()
        {"item1",
         "item2",
         "item3",
         "item4",
         "item5"};

// Use the GetEnumerator iterator.
foreach (string s in strSet)
{
    Console.WriteLine(s);
}
```

When this code is run, the following output is displayed:

```
item1
item2
item3
item4
item5
In iterator finally block
```

Discussion

You may have thought that the output would display the "In iterator finally block" string after displaying each item in the strSet object. However, this is not the way that finally blocks are handled in iterators. All finally blocks associated with try blocks that have yield returns inside the iterator member body are called only after the iterations are complete, code execution leaves the foreach loop (such as when a break, return, or throw statement is encountered), or when a yield break statement is executed, effectively terminating the iterator.

To see how iterators deal with catch and finally blocks (note that there can be no catch blocks inside of a try block that contains a yield), consider the following code:

```
public static void TestFinallyAndIterators()
{
    //Create a StringSet object and fill it with data
    StringSet strSet =
        new StringSet()
                {   { "item1" },
                    { "item2" },
                    { "item3" },
                    { "item4" },
                    { "item5" } };

    // Display all data in StringSet object
    try
    {
        foreach (string s in strSet)
        {
            try
            {
                Console.WriteLine(s);
                // Force an exception here
                throw new Exception();

            }
            catch (Exception)
            {
                Console.WriteLine("In foreach catch block");
            }
            finally
            {
                // Executed on each iteration
                Console.WriteLine("In foreach finally block");
            }
        }
    }
    catch (Exception)
    {
        Console.WriteLine("In outer catch block");
    }
    finally
```

```
    {
        // Executed on each iteration
        Console.WriteLine("In outer finally block");
    }
}
```

Assuming that your original StringSet.GetEnumerator method is used (i.e., the one that contained the try/finally block), you will see the following behaviors.

If no exception occurs, you see this:

```
item1
In foreach finally block
item2
In foreach finally block
item3
In foreach finally block
item4
In foreach finally block
item5
In foreach finally block
In iterator finally block
In outer finally block
```

We see that the finally block that is within the foreach loop is executed on each iteration. However, the finally block within the iterator is executed only after all iterations are finished. Also, notice that the iterator's finally block is executed before the finally block that wraps the foreach loop.

If an exception occurs in the iterator itself, during processing of the second element, the following is displayed:

```
item1
In foreach finally block
    (Exception occurs here...)
In iterator finally block
In outer catch block
In outer finally block
```

Notice that immediately after the exception is thrown, the finally block within the iterator is executed. This can be useful if you need to clean up only after an exception occurs. If no exception happens, then the finally block is not executed until the iterator completes. After the iterator's finally block executes, the exception is caught by the catch block outside the foreach loop. At this point, the exception could be handled or rethrown. Once this catch block is finished processing, the outer finally block is executed.

Notice that the catch block within the foreach loop was never given the opportunity to handle the exception. This is because the corresponding try block does not contain a call to the iterator.

If an exception occurs in the foreach loop, during processing of the second element, the following is displayed:

```
item1
In foreach finally block
    (Exception occurs here...)
In foreach catch block
In foreach finally block
In iterator finally block
In outer finally block
```

Notice in this situation that the catch and finally blocks within the foreach loop are executed first, then the iterator's finally block. Lastly, the outer finally block is executed.

Understanding the way catch and finally blocks operate inside iterators will allow you to add catch and finally blocks in the correct location. If you need a finally block to execute once, immediately after the iterations are finished, add this finally block to the iterator method. If, however, you want the finally block to execute on each iteration, you need to place the finally block within the foreach loop body.

If you need to catch iterator exceptions immediately after they occur, you should consider wrapping the foreach loop in a try/catch block. Any try/catch block within the foreach loop body will miss exceptions thrown from the iterator.

See Also

The "Iterators," "yield," "IEnumerator Interface," and "IEnumerable Interface" topics in the MSDN documentation.

6.7   Implementing Nested foreach Functionality in a Class

Problem

You need a class that contains a list of objects, with each of these objects containing a list of objects. You want to use a nested foreach loop to iterate through all objects in both the outer and inner lists in the following manner:

```
foreach (Group<Item> subGroup in topLevelGroup)
{
    // do work for groups
    foreach (Item item in subGroup)
    {
        // do work for items
    }
}
```

Solution

Implement the IEnumerable<T> interface on the class. The Group class shown in Example 6-3 contains a List<T> that can hold Group objects, and each Group object contains a List<Item>.

Example 6-3. Implementing foreach functionality in a class

```csharp
using System;
using System.Collections;
using System.Collections.Generic;

public class Group<T> : IEnumerable<T>
{
    public Group(string name)
    {
        this.Name = name;
    }

    private List<T> _groupList = new List<T>();

    public string Name { get; set; }

    public int Count
    {
        get { return _groupList.Count; }
    }

    public void Add(T group)
    {
        _groupList.Add(group);
    }

    IEnumerator IEnumerable.GetEnumerator()
    {
        return GetEnumerator();
    }

    public IEnumerator<T> GetEnumerator()
    {
        return _groupList.GetEnumerator();
    }
}


public class Item
{
    public Item(string name, int location)
    {
        this.Name = name;
        this.Location = location;
    }
    public string Name { get; set; }
    public int Location { get; set; }
}
```

Discussion

Building functionality into a class to allow it to be iterated over using the foreach loop is much easier using iterators in the C# language. In previous versions of the .NET Framework, you not only had to implement the IEnumerable interface on the type that you wanted to make enumerable, but you also had to implement the IEnumerator interface on a nested class. The methods MoveNext and Reset and the property Current then had to be written by hand in this nested class. Iterators allow you to hand the work of writing this nested class off to the C# compiler. If you wrote an old style enumerator yourself, it would look like this:

```
public class GroupEnumerator<T> : IEnumerator
{
    public T[] _items;

    int position = -1;

    public GroupEnumerator(T[] list)
    {
        _items = list;
    }

    public bool MoveNext()
    {
        position++;
        return (position < _items.Length);
    }

    public void Reset()
    {
        position = -1;
    }

    public object Current
    {
        get
        {
            try
            {
                return _items[position];
            }
            catch (IndexOutOfRangeException)
            {
                throw new InvalidOperationException();
            }
        }
    }
}
```

The IEnumerator.GetEnumerator method would be modified on the Group<T> class to look like this:

```
IEnumerator IEnumerable.GetEnumerator( )
{
    return new GroupEnumerator<T>(_groupList.ToArray( ));
}
```

and the code to walk over it would look like this:

```
IEnumerator enumerator = ((IEnumerable)hierarchy).GetEnumerator( );
while (enumerator.MoveNext( ))
{
    Console.WriteLine(((Group<Item>)enumerator.Current).Name);
    foreach (Item i in ((Group<Item>)enumerator.Current))
    {
        Console.WriteLine(i.Name);
    }
}
```

Aren't you glad you don't have to do that? Leave it to the compiler; it's quite good at writing this for you.

The ability for a class to be used by the foreach loop requires the inclusion of an iterator. An iterator can be a method, an operator overload, or the get accessor of a property that returns either a System.Collections.IEnumerator, a System.Collections.Generic.IEnumerator<T>, a System.Collections.IEnumerable, or a System.Collections.Generic.IEnumerable<T> and that contains at least one yield statement.

The code for this recipe is divided among two classes. The container class is the Group class, which contains a List of Group<Item> objects. The Group object also contains a List, but this List contains Item objects. To enumerate the contained list, the Group class implements the IEnumerable interface. It therefore contains a GetEnumerator iterator method, which returns an IEnumerator. The class structure looks like this:

```
Group (Implements IEnumerable<T>)
   Group (Implements IEnumerable<T>)
      Item
```

By examining the Group class, you can see how classes usable by a foreach loop are constructed. This class contains:

- A simple List<T>, which will be iterated over by the class's enumerator.
- A property, Count, which returns the number of elements in the List<T>.
- An iterator method, GetEnumerator, which is defined by the IEnumerable<T> interface. This method yields a specific value on each iteration of the foreach loop.
- A method, Add, which adds an instance such as Subgroup to the List<T>.
- A method, GetGroup, which returns a typed instance such as Subgroup from the List<T>.

To create the Subgroup class, you follow the same pattern as with the Group class—except the Subgroup class contains a List<Item>.

The final class is the Item class. This class is the lowest level of this structure and contains data. It has been grouped within the Subgroup objects, all of which are contained in the Group object. There is nothing out of the ordinary with this class; it simply contains data and the means to set and retrieve this data.

Using these classes is quite simple. The following method shows how to create a Group object that contains multiple Subgroup objects, which in turn contain multiple Item objects:

```
public static void CreateNestedObjects()
{
    Group<Group<Item>> hierarchy =
        new Group<Group<Item>>("root") {
            new Group<Item>("subgroup1"){
                new Item("item1",100),
                new Item("item2",200)},
            new Group<Item>("subgroup2"){
                new Item("item3",300),
                new Item("item4",400)}};

    // Read back the data
    ReadNestedObjects(hierarchy);
}
```

The CreateNestedObjects method first creates a hierarchy object of the Group class and then creates two subgroups within it named subgroup1 and subgroup2. Each of these subgroup objects, in turn, is filled with two Item objects called item1, item2, item3, and item4.

The next method shows how to read all of the Item objects contained within the Group object that was created in the CreateNestedObjects method:

```
private static void DisplayNestedObjects(Group<Group<Item>> topLevelGroup)
{
    Console.WriteLine("topLevelGroup.Count: " + topLevelGroup.Count);
    Console.WriteLine("topLevelGroupName:  " + topLevelGroup.Name);

    // Outer foreach to iterate over all objects in the
    // topLevelGroup object
    foreach (Group<Item> subGroup in topLevelGroup)
    {
        Console.WriteLine("\tsubGroup.SubGroupName:  " + subGroup.Name);
        Console.WriteLine("\tsubGroup.Count: " + subGroup.Count);

        // Inner foreach to iterate over all Item objects in the
        // current SubGroup object
        foreach (Item item in subGroup)
        {
            Console.WriteLine("\t\titem.Name:      " + item.Name);
            Console.WriteLine("\t\titem.Location: " + item.Location);
        }
    }
}
```

This method displays the following:

```
topLevelGroup.Count: 2
topLevelGroupName:  root
        subGroup.SubGroupName:  subgroup1
        subGroup.Count: 2
                item.Name:      item1
                item.Location: 100
                item.Name:      item2
                item.Location: 200
        subGroup.SubGroupName:  subgroup2
        subGroup.Count: 2
                item.Name:      item3
                item.Location: 300
                item.Name:      item4
                item.Location: 400
```

As you see here, the outer foreach loop is used to iterate over all Subgroup objects that are stored in the top-level Group object. The inner foreach loop is used to iterate over all Item objects that are stored in the current Subgroup object.

See Also

The "Iterators," "yield," "IEnumerator Interface," "IEnumerable(Of T) interface," and "IEnumerable Interface" topics in the MSDN documentation.

6.8   Organizing Your Interface Implementations

Problem

You have a class that implements an interface with many methods. These methods support only the interface functionality and don't necessarily relate well to the other code in your class. You would like to keep the interface implementation code separate from the main class code.

Solution

Use partial classes to separate the interface implementation code into a separate file. For example, you have a class called TriValue that takes three decimal values and performs some operations on them, such as getting the average, the sum, and the product. This code is currently in a file called *TriValue.cs*, which contains:

```
public partial class TriValue
{
    public decimal First { get; set; }
    public decimal Second { get; set; }
    public decimal Third { get; set; }
```

```
        public TriValue(decimal first, decimal second, decimal third)
        {
            this.First = first;
            this.Second = second;
            this.Third = third;
        }

        public TypeCode GetTypeCode()
        {
            return TypeCode.Object;
        }

        public decimal Average
        {
            get { return (Sum / 3); }
        }

        public decimal Sum
        {
            get { return First + Second + Third; }
        }

        public decimal Product
        {
            get { return First * Second * Third; }
        }
    }
```

Now, you want to add support for the IConvertible interface to the TriValue class so that it can be converted to other data types. We could just add all 16 method implementations to the class definition in *TriValue.cs* and hide the code using a #region statement. Instead, you can now use the partial keyword on the TriValue class and store the IConvertible implementation code in a separate file. Once a class begins to be defined in multiple files, it is important to have a naming convention for those files, so that it is easy to find implementation code and for other developers to understand where to put new code when it is added to this class. We will use the [BaseClass].[Interface].cs naming convention here. This will give you a new file called *TriValue.IConvertible.cs*, which contains the IConvertible interface implementation code, as shown in Example 6-4.

Example 6-4. Using partial classes to organize your interface implementations

```
/// Partial class that implements IConvertible
public partial class TriValue : IConvertible
{
    public bool ToBoolean(IFormatProvider provider)
    {
        if (Average > 0)
            return true;
        else
            return false;
    }
}
```

```
public byte ToByte(IFormatProvider provider)
{
    return Convert.ToByte(Average);
}

public char ToChar(IFormatProvider provider)
{
    decimal val = Average;
    if (val > char.MaxValue)
        val = char.MaxValue;
    if (val < char.MinValue)
        val = char.MinValue;
    return Convert.ToChar((ulong)val);
}

public DateTime ToDateTime(IFormatProvider provider)
{
    throw new NotSupportedException( );
    return Convert.ToDateTime(Average);
}

public decimal ToDecimal(IFormatProvider provider)
{
    return Average;
}

public double ToDouble(IFormatProvider provider)
{
    return Convert.ToDouble(Average);
}

public short ToInt16(IFormatProvider provider)
{
    return Convert.ToInt16(Average);
}

public int ToInt32(IFormatProvider provider)
{
    return Convert.ToInt32(Average);
}

public long ToInt64(IFormatProvider provider)
{
    return Convert.ToInt64(Average);
}

public sbyte ToSByte(IFormatProvider provider)
{
    return Convert.ToSByte(Average);
}
```

Example 6-4. Using partial classes to organize your interface implementations (continued)

```
    public float ToSingle(IFormatProvider provider)
    {
        return Convert.ToSingle(Average);
    }

    public string ToString(IFormatProvider provider)
    {
        return string.Format(provider,
            "({0},{1},{2})",
            First.ToString(provider),
            Second.ToString(provider),
            Third.ToString(provider));
    }

    public object ToType(Type conversionType, IFormatProvider provider)
    {
        return Convert.ChangeType(Average, conversionType, provider);
    }

    public ushort ToUInt16(IFormatProvider provider)
    {
        return Convert.ToUInt16(Average, provider);
    }

    public uint ToUInt32(IFormatProvider provider)
    {
        return Convert.ToUInt32(Average,provider);
    }

    public ulong ToUInt64(IFormatProvider provider)
    {
        return Convert.ToUInt64(Average,provider);
    }
}
```

Now, you have the interface implemented, and your original class definition is still straightforward. For classes that implement many interfaces, this approach will allow for a more tightly organized implementation.

Discussion

It should be noted that there is *no* Microsoft intermediate language (MSIL) indicator that these are partial classes if you look at your class in Ildasm or Reflector. It will look just like a normal class by the time it gets to MSIL. Intellisense handles the merge as well. Since partial types are a language trick, they cannot span assemblies, as the class needs to be resolved by the compiler. Partial types can be declared in the same file as well as in separate files, but still must be in the same namespace so the compiler can resolve it before generating the MSIL.

You can use the partial type support for classes, nested classes, structures, and interfaces, but you cannot have a partial enum definition. Partial types can declare support for different interfaces per partial type. However, single inheritance is still in force and must be the same or omitted from the secondary partial type. You can see that in the Solution, the partial TriValue class definition in *TriValue.cs* you created does not specify the inheritance from IConvertible, only the one in *TriValue.IConvertible.cs* does.

The previous TriValue class can be exercised with the following code:

```
class Program
{
    static void Main( )
    {
        TriValue tv = new TriValue(3, 4, 5);
        Console.WriteLine("Average: {0}",tv.Average);
        Console.WriteLine("Sum: {0}", tv.Sum);
        Console.WriteLine("Product: {0}", tv.Product);
        Console.WriteLine("Boolean: {0}", Convert.ToBoolean(tv));
        Console.WriteLine("Byte: {0}", Convert.ToByte(tv));
        Console.WriteLine("Char: {0}", Convert.ToChar(tv));
        Console.WriteLine("Decimal: {0}", Convert.ToDecimal(tv));
        Console.WriteLine("Double: {0}", Convert.ToDouble(tv));
        Console.WriteLine("Int16: {0}", Convert.ToInt16(tv));
        Console.WriteLine("Int32: {0}", Convert.ToInt32(tv));
        Console.WriteLine("Int64: {0}", Convert.ToInt64(tv));
        Console.WriteLine("SByte: {0}", Convert.ToSByte(tv));
        Console.WriteLine("Single: {0}", Convert.ToSingle(tv));
        Console.WriteLine("String: {0}", Convert.ToString(tv));
        Console.WriteLine("Type: {0}", Convert.GetTypeCode(tv));
        Console.WriteLine("UInt16: {0}", Convert.ToUInt16(tv));
        Console.WriteLine("UInt32: {0}", Convert.ToUInt32(tv));
        Console.WriteLine("UInt64: {0}", Convert.ToUInt64(tv));
    }
}
```

The preceding code produces the following output:

```
Average: 4
Sum: 12
Product: 60
Boolean: True
Byte: 4
Char: _
Decimal: 4
Double: 4
Int16: 4
Int32: 4
Int64: 4
SByte: 4
Single: 4
String: (3,4,5)
Type: Object
```

```
UInt16: 4
UInt32: 4
UInt64: 4
```

See Also

The "Partial Class Definitions" and "partial Keyword" topics in the MSDN documentation.

6.9   Generating Code That Is No Longer in Your Main Code Paths

Problem

Occasionally, as a developer, you run into a situation in which it would be handy to be able to regenerate your class based on a set of data that can change. You need to be able to do this without destroying all of the logic you have already created or causing yourself a painful merge between an old and a new class file.

Solution

Write a utility that can regenerate the code that is dependent on external data and keep the generated code in a separate file that defines a partial class. To demonstrate this, we have created a Visual Studio 2008 add-in called `PartialClassAddin` in the sample code that will allow you to enter a class name and then select which attributes to apply to the class. This is a standard add-in generated by selecting the add-in template from the project wizard. Its main dialog box is shown in Figure 6-1.

Enter a class name, **MyNewClass**, select the `System.CLSCompliantAttribute` and the `System.SerializeableAttribute` from the list, and click the OK button. This generates the `MyNewClass_Attributes.cs` file with the following in it:

```
// Using directives
using System;

namespace NamespaceForMyNewClass
{
#region Attributes
[System.CLSCompliant(true)]
[System.Serializable()]
#endregion // Attributes

public partial class MyNewClass
{
    public MyNewClass()
    {
    }
}
}
```

Figure 6-1. Attributed Class Wizard from partial class add-in

By making `MyNewClass` a partial class, you can add this generated file to your project and replace it when the class attributes need to be updated, while you store your main logic in another file (perhaps `MyNewClass.cs`) with a partial `MyNewClass` definition:

```
// Using directives
using System;
using System.Diagnostics;

namespace NamespaceForMyNewClass
{
    public partial class MyNewClass : BaseClass
    {
        public DoSomeWork ()
    {
        for(int i=0;i<10;i++)
        {
            Debug.WriteLine(i);
        }
    }
    }
}
```

```
// Declare base class...
    public BaseClass
    {
    }
}
        }
    }
}
```

Notice that in the file in which you hold the logic (MyNewClass.cs as shown before), the class can declare its inheritance from BaseClass as well as define some functionality (DoSomeWork method).

Discussion

Generating code is not something to do lightly. But in certain circumstances, building a tool can save you a lot of time over the course of maintaining a project. Partial classes provide a nice way to separate your mainstream code from the "noise" that changes only in response to external pieces. Windows Forms and Windows Forms controls are both now declared as partial, as are the DataSets generated from an XSD schema to help facilitate the generated code model.

This add-in was created using the Visual Studio 2008 add-in wizard, and the project has the form added to it. The form loads all types derived from System.Attribute to populate the listbox, and then uses reflection to figure out the parameters. Once the code has been built, run the project from the debugger. When VS2008 comes up, you can access the Tools menu and the PartialClassAddin menu item to get to this wizard. You can unregister this add-in by going to the Tools menu in VS2008 and selecting the Add-In Manager option. The Add-In Manager dialog is shown in Figure 6-2.

Uncheck the PartialClassAddin to remove this from your main environment.

See Also

The "Partial Class Definitions," "Creating Automation Objects," and "Attribute" topics in the MSDN documentation.

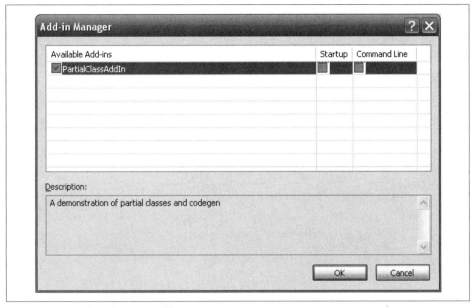

Figure 6-2. Visual Studio 2008 Add-in Manager

6.10   Adding Hooks to Generated Entities

Problem

You have a process to generate your partial class business entity definitions, and you want to add a lightweight notification mechanism.

Solution

Use partial methods to add hooks in the generated code for the business entities.

The process to generate the entities may be from UML, a dataset, or some other object-modeling facility, but when the code is generated as partial classes, add partial method hooks into the templates for the properties that call a ChangingProperty partial method, as shown in the GeneratedEntity class:

```
public partial class GeneratedEntity
{
    public GeneratedEntity(string entityName)
    {
        this.EntityName = entityName;
    }

    partial void ChangingProperty(string name, string originalValue, string
newValue);

    public string EntityName { get; private set; }
```

```
        private string _FirstName;
        public string FirstName
        {
            get { return _FirstName; }
            set
            {
                ChangingProperty("FirstName",_FirstName,value);
                _FirstName = value;
            }
        }

        private string _State;
        public string State
        {
            get { return _State; }
            set
            {
                ChangingProperty("State",_State,value);
                _State = value;
            }
        }
    }
```

The GeneratedEntity has two properties, FirstName and State. Notice each of these properties has the same boilerplate code that calls the ChangingProperty method with the name of the property, the original, and the new values. If the generated class is used at this point, the ChangingProperty declaration and method will be removed by the compiler, as there is no implementation for ChangingProperty. If an implementation is supplied to report on property changes as shown below, then all of the partial method code for ChangingProperty will be retained and executed:

```
public partial class GeneratedEntity
{
    partial void ChangingProperty(string name, string originalValue, string newValue)
    {
        Console.WriteLine("Changed property ({0}) for entity {1} from {2} to {3}",
            name, this.EntityName, originalValue, newValue);
    }
}
```

Discussion

When using partial methods, be aware of the following items:

- You indicate a partial method with the partial modifier.
- They can only be declared in partial classes.
- They might only have a declaration and no body.
- From a signature standpoint, they can have arguments, require a void return value, must not have any access modifier, and partial implies that this is private and can be static, generic, or unsafe.

- For generic partial methods, constraints must be repeated on the declaring and implementing versions.
- A partial method may not implement an interface member since interface members must be public.
- None of the virtual, abstract, override, new, sealed, or extern modifiers may be used.
- Arguments to a partial method cannot use out, but they can use ref.

Partial methods are similar to conditional methods, with the exception that the method definition is always present in conditional methods, even when the condition is not met. Partial methods do not retain the method definition if there is no matching implementation. The code in the solution could be used like this:

```
public static void TestPartialMethods()
{
    Console.WriteLine("Start entity work");
    GeneratedEntity entity = new GeneratedEntity("FirstEntity");
    entity.FirstName = "Bob";
    entity.State = "NH";
    GeneratedEntity secondEntity = new GeneratedEntity("SecondEntity");
    entity.FirstName = "Jay";
    secondEntity.FirstName = "Steve";
    secondEntity.State = "MA";
    entity.FirstName = "Barry";
    secondEntity.State = "WA";
    secondEntity.FirstName = "Matt";
    Console.WriteLine("End entity work");
}
```

To produce the following output when the ChangingProperty implementation is provided:

```
Start entity work
Changed property (FirstName) for entity FirstEntity from  to Bob
Changed property (State) for entity FirstEntity from  to NH
Changed property (FirstName) for entity FirstEntity from Bob to Jay
Changed property (FirstName) for entity SecondEntity from  to Steve
Changed property (State) for entity SecondEntity from  to MA
Changed property (FirstName) for entity FirstEntity from Jay to Barry
Changed property (State) for entity SecondEntity from MA to WA
Changed property (FirstName) for entity SecondEntity from Steve to Matt
End entity work
```

To produce the following output when the ChangingProperty implementation is NOT provided:

```
Start entity work
End entity work
```

See Also

The "Partial Methods" and "partial method" topics in the MSDN documentation.

CHAPTER 7

Exception Handling

7.0   Introduction

This chapter contains recipes covering the exception-handling mechanism, including the try, catch, and finally blocks. Along with these recipes are others covering the mechanisms used to throw exceptions manually from within your code. The final recipes include those dealing with the Exception classes and their uses, as well as subclassing them to create new types of exceptions.

Often, the design and implementation of exception handling is performed later in the development cycle. But with the power and complexities of C# exception handling, you need to plan and even implement your exception-handling scheme much earlier. Doing so will increase the reliability and robustness of your code while minimizing the impact of adding exception handling after most or all of the application is coded.

Exception handling in C# is very flexible. It allows you to choose a fine- or coarse-grained approach to error handling, or any level between. This means that you can add exception handling around any individual line of code (the fine-grained approach) or around a method that calls many other methods (the coarse-grained approach), or you can use a mix of the two, with mainly a coarse-grained approach and a more fine-grained approach in specific critical areas of the code. When using a fine-grained approach, you can intercept specific exceptions that might be thrown from just a few lines of code. The following method sets an object's property to a numeric value using fine-grained exception handling:

```
protected void SetValue(object value)
{
    try
    {
        myObj.Property1 = value;
    }
    catch (Exception e)
    {
```

```
        // Handle potential exceptions arising from this call here.
    }
}
```

Consequently, this approach can add a lot of extra baggage to your code if used throughout your application. This fine-grained approach to exception handling should be used when you have a single line or just a few lines of code, and you need to handle that exception in a specific manner. If you do not have specific handling for errors at that level, you should let the exception bubble up the stack. For example, using the previous SetValue method, you may have to inform the user that an exception occurred and provide a chance to try the action again. If a method exists on myObj that needs to be called whenever an exception is thrown by one of its methods, you should make sure that this method is called at the appropriate time.

Coarse-grained exception handling is quite the opposite; it uses fewer try/catch or try/catch/finally blocks. One example would be to place a try/catch block around all of the code in every public method in an application or component. Doing this allows exceptions to be handled at the highest level in your code. If an exception is thrown at any location in your code, it will be bubbled up the call stack until a catch block is found that can handle it. If try/catch blocks are placed on all public methods, then all exceptions will be bubbled up to these methods and handled. This allows for much less exception-handling code to be written, but your ability to handle specific exceptions that may occur in particular areas of your code is diminished. You must determine how best to add exception-handling code to your application. This means applying the right balance of fine- and coarse-grained exception handling in your application.

C# allows catch blocks to be written without any parameters. An example of this is shown here:

```
public void CallCOMMethod( )
{
    try
    {
        // Call a method on a COM object.
        myCOMObj.Method1( );
    }
    catch
    {
        // Handle potential exceptions arising from this call here.
    }
}
```

The catch with no parameters is a holdover from C++, where exception objects did not have to be derived from the Exception class. Writing a catch clause in this manner in C++ allows any type of object thrown as an exception to be caught. However, in C#, only objects derived from the Exception base class may be thrown as an exception. Using the catch block with no parameters allows all exceptions to be caught, but you lose the ability to view the exception and its information. A catch block written in this manner:

```
catch
{
    // NOT Able to write the following line of code
    //Console.WriteLine(e.ToString);
}
```

is equivalent to this:

```
catch (Exception e)
{
    // Able to write the following line of code
    Console.WriteLine(e.ToString);
}
```

except that in the second case, the Exception object can be accessed now that the exception parameter is provided.

Avoid writing a catch block without any parameters. Doing so will prevent you from accessing the actual Exception object that was thrown.

When catching exceptions in a catch block, you should determine up front when exceptions need to be rethrown, when exceptions need to be wrapped in an outer exception and thrown, and when exceptions should be handled immediately and not rethrown.

Wrapping an exception in an outer exception is a good practice when the original exception would not make sense to the caller. When wrapping an exception in an outer exception, you need to determine what exception is most appropriate to wrap the caught exception. As a rule of thumb, the wrapping exception should always aid in tracking down the original problem by not obscuring the original exception with an unrelated or vague wrapping exception. One of the rare cases that can justify obscuring exceptions is if the exception is going to cross a trust boundary, and you have to obscure it for security reasons.

Another useful practice when catching exceptions is to provide catch blocks to handle specific exceptions in your code. And remember that base class exceptions—when used in a catch block—catch not only that type, but also all of its subclasses.

The following code uses specific catch blocks to handle different exceptions in the appropriate manner:

```
public void CallCOMMethod( )
{
    try
    {
        // Call a method on a COM object.
        myCOMObj.Method1( );
    }
    catch (System.Runtime.InteropServices.ExternalException exte)
    {
```

```
            // Handle potential COM exceptions arising from this call here.
        }
        catch (InvalidOperationException ioe)
        {
            // Handle any potential method calls to the COM object which are
            // not valid in its current state.
        }
    }
```

In this code, ExternalException and its derivatives are handled differently than InvalidOperationException and its derivatives. If any other types of exceptions are thrown from the myCOMObj.Method1, they are not handled here, but are bubbled up until a valid catch block is found. If no valid catch block is found, the exception is considered unhandled and the application terminates.

At times, cleanup code must be executed regardless of whether an exception is thrown. Any object must be placed in a stable known state when an exception is thrown. In these situations, when code must be executed, use a finally block. The following code has been modified (see boldface lines) to use a finally block:

```
    public void CallCOMMethod()
    {
        try
        {
            // Call a method on a COM object.
            myCOMObj.Method1();
        }
        catch (System.Runtime.InteropServices.ExternalException exte)
        {
            // Handle potential COM exceptions arising from this call here.
        }
        finally
        {
            // Clean up and free any resources here.
            // For example, there could be a method on myCOMObj to allow us to clean
            // up after using the Method1 method.
        }
    }
```

The finally block will always execute, no matter what happens in the try and catch blocks. The finally block executes even if a return, break, or continue statement is executed in the try or catch blocks or if a goto is used to jump out of the exception handler. This allows for a reliable method of cleaning up after the try (and possibly catch) block code executes. The finally block is also very useful for final resource cleanup when no catch blocks are specified. This pattern would be used if the code being written can't handle exceptions from calls it is making but wants to make sure that resources it uses are cleaned up properly before moving up the stack. The following example makes sure that the SqlConnection and SqlCommand are cleaned up properly in the finally block through use of the using keyword, which wraps a try/finally block around the scope of the using statement:

```csharp
public void RunCommand( string connection, string command )
{
    SqlConnection sqlConn = null;
    SqlCommand sqlComm = null;

    using(sqlConn = new SqlConnection(connection))
    {
        using(sqlComm = new SqlCommand(command, sqlConn))
        {
            sqlConn.Open( );
            sqlComm.ExecuteNonQuery( );
        }
    }
}
```

When determining how to structure exception handling in your application or component, consider doing the following:

- Use a single try-catch or try-catch-finally exception handler at locations higher up in your code. These exception handlers can be considered coarse-grained.
- Code farther down the call stack should contain try-finally exception handlers. These exception handlers can be considered fine-grained.

The fine-grained try-finally exception handlers allow for better control over cleaning up after an exception occurs. The exception is then bubbled up to the coarser-grained try-catch or try-catch-finally exception handler. This technique allows for a more centralized scheme of exception handling and minimizes the code that you have to write to handle exceptions.

To improve performance, you should handle the case when an exception could be thrown, rather than catch the exception after it is thrown, if you know the code will be run in a single-threaded environment. If the code will run on multiple threads, there is still the potential that the initial check could succeed, but the object value change (perhaps to null) in another thread before the actions following the check can be taken.

For example, in a single-threaded environment, if a method has a good chance of returning a null value, you should test the returned value for null before that value is used, as opposed to using a try-catch block and allowing the NullReferenceException to be thrown. If you think a null value is possible, check for it. If it shouldn't happen, then it is an exceptional condition when it does, and exception handling should be used. To illustrate this, here is a method that uses exception-handling code to process the NullReferenceException:

```csharp
public void SomeMethod( )
{
    try
    {
        Stream s = GetAnyAvailableStream( );
```

```
            Console.WriteLine("This stream has a length of " + s.Length);
        }
        catch (NullReferenceException nre)
        {
            // Handle a null stream here.
        }
    }
```

Here is the method implemented to use an `if-else` conditional instead:

```
public void SomeMethod( )
{
    Stream s = GetAnyAvailableStream( );

    if (s != null)
    {
        Console.WriteLine("This stream has a length of " + s.Length);
    }
    else
    {
        // Handle a null stream here.
    }
}
```

Additionally, you should also make sure that this stream is closed by using the `finally` block in the following manner:

```
public void SomeMethod( )
{
    Stream s = null;
    using(s = GetAnyAvailableStream( ))
    {

        if (s != null)
        {
            Console.WriteLine("This stream has a length of " + s.Length);
        }
        else
        {
            // Handle a null stream here.
        }
    }
}
```

The `finally` block contains the method call that will close the stream, ensuring that there is no data loss.

Consider throwing exceptions instead of returning error codes. With well-placed exception-handling code, you should not have to rely on methods that return error codes such as a Boolean `true-false` to correctly handle errors, which makes for much cleaner code. Another benefit is that you do not have to look up any values for the error codes to understand the code.

The biggest advantage to exceptions is that when an exceptional situation arises, you cannot just ignore it as you can with error codes. This helps you find and fix bugs.

Throw the most specific possible exception, not general ones. For example, throw an ArgumentNullException instead of an ArgumentException, which is the base class of ArgumentNullException. Throwing an ArgumentException just tells you that there was a problem with a parameter value to a method. Throwing an ArgumentNullException tells you more specifically what the problem with the parameter really is. Another potential problem is that a more general exception may not be caught if the catcher of the exception is looking for a more specific type derived from the thrown exception.

The FCL provides several exception types that you will find very useful to throw in your own code. Many of these exceptions are listed here with a definition of where and when they should be thrown:

- Throw an InvalidOperationException in a property, indexer, or method when it is called with the object in an inappropriate state. This state could be caused by calling an indexer on an object that has not yet been initialized or calling methods out of sequence.

- Throw ArgumentException if invalid parameters are passed into a method, property, or indexer. The ArgumentNullException, ArgumentOutOfRangeException, and InvalidEnumArgumentException are three subclasses of the ArgumentException class. It is more appropriate to throw one of these subclassed exceptions because they are more indicative of the root cause of the problem. The ArgumentNullException indicates that a parameter was passed in as null and that this parameter cannot be null under any circumstance. The ArgumentOutOfRangeException indicates that an argument was passed in that was outside of a valid acceptable range. This exception is used mainly with numeric values. The InvalidEnumArgumentException indicates that an enumeration value was passed in that does not exist in that enumeration type.

- Throw a FormatException when an invalid formatting parameter is passed in as a parameter to a method. This technique is mainly used when overriding/overloading methods such as ToString that can accept formatting strings, as well as in the parse methods on the various numeric types.

- Throw ObjectDisposedException when a property, indexer, or method is called on an object that has already been disposed.

- Many exceptions that derive from the SystemException class, such as NullReferenceException, ExecutionEngineException, StackOverflowException, OutOfMemoryException, and IndexOutOfRangeException, are thrown only by the CLR and should not be explicitly thrown with the throw keyword in your code.

7.1 Knowing When to Catch and Rethrow Exceptions

Problem

You want to establish when it is appropriate to catch and rethrow an exception.

Solution

It is appropriate if you have a section of code where you want to perform some action if an exception occurs, but not perform any actions to actually handle the exception. In order to get the exception so that you can perform the initial action on it, establish a catch block to catch the exception. Then, once the action has been performed, rethrow the exception from the catch block in which the original exception was handled. Use the throw keyword, followed by a semicolon, to rethrow an exception:

```
try
{
    Console.WriteLine("In try");
    int z2 = 9999999;
    checked { z2 *= 999999999; }
}
catch (OverflowException oe)
{
    // Record the fact that the overflow exception occurred.
    EventLog.WriteEntry("MyApplication", oe.Message, EventLogEntryType.Error);
    throw;
}
```

Here, you create an EventLog entry that records the occurrence of a divide-by-zero exception. Then the exception is propagated up the call stack by the throw statement.

Discussion

Establishing a catch block for an exception is essentially saying that you want to do something about that exceptional case. If you do not rethrow the exception, or create a new exception to wrap the original exception and throw it, the expectation is that you have handled the condition that caused the exception and that the program can continue normal operation. By choosing to rethrow the exception, you are indicating that there is still an issue to be dealt with and that you are counting on code farther up the stack to handle the condition. If you need to perform an action based on a thrown exception *and* need to allow the exception to continue after your code executes, then rethrowing is the mechanism to handle this. If both of those conditions are not met, don't rethrow the exception; just handle it or remove the catch block.

Remember that throwing exceptions is expensive. Try not to needlessly throw and rethrow exceptions because this might bog down your application.

When rethrowing an exception, use throw; instead of throw ex; as throw; will preserve the original call-stack of the exception. Using throw with the catch parameter will reset the call stack to that location, and information about the error will be lost.

7.2 Assuring Exceptions Are Not Lost When Using Finally Blocks

Problem

You want to protect against losing exception information when using multiple try-catch-finally blocks.

Solution

Add an inner try-catch block in the finally block of the outer exception handler to prevent losing exception information:

```
private void PreventLossOfExceptionFormat()
{
    try
    {
        //...
    }
    catch(Exception e)
    {
        Console.WriteLine("Error message == " + e.Message);
        throw;
    }
    finally
    {
        try
        {
            //...
        }
        catch(Exception e)
        {
            Console.WriteLine("An unexpected error occurred " +
                "in the finally block. Error message: " + e.Message);
        }
    }
}
```

This block will prevent the original exception from being lost in almost every case.

Discussion

If a catch block attempts to throw an exception, it is possible that the thrown exception will get discarded and that a new and unexpected exception will be caught by an outer exception handler. Consider what would happen if an error were thrown from the inner finally block contained in the ThrowException method, as is instigated by the code shown in Example 7-1.

Example 7-1. Throwing an error from the inner finally block of the ThrowException method

```
private static void ThrowReplacementException()
{
    try
    {
        Console.WriteLine("In inner try");
        int z2 = 9999999;
        checked { z2 *= 999999999; }
    }
    catch (OverflowException ofe)
    {
        Console.WriteLine("An Overflow occurred. Error message: " +
                            ofe.Message);
        throw;
    }
    catch (Exception e)
    {
        Console.WriteLine("Another type of error occurred. " +
                            "Error message: " + e.Message);
        throw;
    }
    finally
    {
    Console.WriteLine("In inner finally");
    throw (new Exception("Oops"));
    }
}

public static void NotPreventLossOfException()
{
    try
    {
        Console.WriteLine("In outer try");
        ThrowReplacementException();
    }
    catch (Exception e)
    {
        Console.WriteLine("In outer catch. Caught exception: " + e.Message);
    }
    finally
    {
        Console.WriteLine("In outer finally");
    }
}
```

the following output would be displayed showing the loss of the original error:

```
In outer try
In inner try
An Overflow occurred. Error message: Arithmetic operation resulted in an
overflow.
In inner finally
In outer catch. Caught exception: Oops
In outer finally
```

If you modify the inner finally block to handle its own errors (changes are highlighted), similarly to the following code:

 When writing a finally block, consider placing a separate try-catch around the code.

```csharp
private static void ThrowException()
{
    try
    {
                    Console.WriteLine("In inner try");
                    int z2 = 9999999;
                    checked { z2 *= 999999999; }
    }
    catch (OverflowException ofe)
    {
                    Console.WriteLine("An Overflow occurred. Error message: " +
                    ofe.Message);
                    throw;
    }
    catch (Exception e)
    {
                    Console.WriteLine("Another type of error occurred. " +
                        "Error message: " + e.Message);
                    throw;
    }
    finally
    {
        try
        {
                    Console.WriteLine("In inner finally");
                    throw (new Exception("Oops"));
        }
    catch (Exception e)
    {
                    Console.WriteLine(@"An error occurred in the finally block. " +
                    "Error message: " + e.Message);
        }
    }
}
```

```
public static void PreventLossOfException( )
{
    try
    {
        Console.WriteLine("In outer try");
        ThrowException( );
    }
    catch (Exception e)
    {
        Console.WriteLine("In outer catch. Caught exception: " + e.Message);
    }
    finally
    {
        Console.WriteLine("In outer finally");
    }
}
```

you will get the following output showing the preservation of the original error:

```
In outer try
In inner try
An Overflow occurred. Error message: Arithmetic operation resulted in an
overflow.
In inner finally
An error occurred in the finally block. Error message: Oops
In outer catch. Caught exception: Arithmetic operation resulted in an overflow.
In outer finally
```

By handling exceptions within the inner finally block, you greatly increase the chances that the correct rethrown exception bubbles up to the outer exception handler. There is still the potential that something done in the finally block outside of the try-catch block could throw an exception, so make sure not to write code outside of the try-catch block in the finally block. To catch any exceptions that manage to make it past all of your precautions, see Recipe 7.3.

See Also

The "Error Raising and Handling Guidelines" topic and the "throw," "try," "catch," and "finally" keywords in the MSDN documentation.

7.3   Handling Exceptions Thrown from Methods Invoked via Reflection

Problem

Using reflection, you invoke a method that generates an exception. You want to obtain the real exception object and its information in order to diagnose and fix the problem.

Solution

The real exception and its information can be obtained through the `InnerException` property of the `TargetInvocationException` that is thrown by `MethodInfo.Invoke`.

Discussion

The following example shows how an exception that occurs within a method invoked via reflection is handled. The `Reflect` class contains a `ReflectionException` method that invokes the static `TestInvoke` method using the reflection classes as shown in Example 7-2.

Example 7-2. Obtaining information on an exception invoked by a method accessed through reflection

```
using System;
using System.Reflection;

public static class Reflect
{
    public static void ReflectionException( )
    {
        Type reflectedClass = typeof(ExceptionHandling);

        try
        {
            MethodInfo methodToInvoke = reflectedClass.GetMethod("TestInvoke");

            if (methodToInvoke != null)
            {
                methodToInvoke.Invoke(null, null);
            }
        }
        catch(Exception e)
        {
            Console.WriteLine(e.ToShortDisplayString( ));
        }
    }

    public static void TestInvoke( )
    {
        throw (new Exception("Thrown from invoked method."));
    }

}
```

This code displays the following text:

```
Message: Exception has been thrown by the target of an invocation.
Type: System.Reflection.TargetInvocationException
Source: mscorlib
TargetSite: System.Object _InvokeMethodFast(System.Object, System.Object[], Syst
em.SignatureStruct ByRef, System.Reflection.MethodAttributes, System.RuntimeType
```

```
Handle)
**** INNEREXCEPTION START ****
Message: Thrown from invoked method.
Type: System.Exception
Source: CSharpRecipes
TargetSite: Void TestInvoke()
**** INNEREXCEPTION END ****
```

When the methodToInvoke.Invoke method is called, the TestInvoke method is called. It throws an exception. The outer exception is the TargetInvocationException; this is the generic exception thrown when a method invoked through reflection throws an exception. The CLR automatically wraps the original exception thrown by the invoked method inside of the TargetInvocationException object's InnerException property. In this case, the exception thrown by the invoked method is of type System.Exception. This exception is shown after the section that begins with the text **** INNEREXCEPTION START ****.

To display the exception information, the ToShortDisplayString method is called:

```
Console.WriteLine(e.ToShortDisplayString());
```

The ToShortDisplayString extension method for Exception uses a StringBuilder to create the string of information about the exception and all inner exceptions. The WriteExceptionShortDetail method populates the StringBuilder with specific parts of the exception data. To get the inner exceptions, the GetNestedExceptionList extension method from Recipe 7.14 is used:

```
public static string ToShortDisplayString(this Exception ex)
{
    StringBuilder displayText = new StringBuilder();
    WriteExceptionShortDetail(displayText, ex);
    foreach(Exception inner in ex.GetNestedExceptionList()) // from 7.14
    {
        displayText.AppendFormat("**** INNEREXCEPTION START ****{0}",
                        Environment.NewLine);
        WriteExceptionShortDetail(displayText, inner);
        displayText.AppendFormat("**** INNEREXCEPTION END ****{0}{0}",
                        Environment.NewLine);
    }
    return displayText.ToString();
}

public static void WriteExceptionShortDetail(StringBuilder builder, Exception ex)
{
    builder.AppendFormat("Message: {0}{1}", ex.Message, Environment.NewLine);
    builder.AppendFormat("Type: {0}{1}", ex.GetType(), Environment.NewLine);
    builder.AppendFormat("Source: {0}{1}", ex.Source, Environment.NewLine);
    builder.AppendFormat("TargetSite: {0}{1}", ex.TargetSite, Environment.NewLine);
}
```

See Also

The "Type Class" and "MethodInfo Class" topics in the MSDN documentation.

7.4 Preventing Unhandled Exceptions

Problem

You need to make absolutely sure that every exception thrown by your application is handled and that no exception is bubbled up past the outermost exception handler. Hackers often use these types of exceptions to aid in their analysis of the vulnerabilities of a web application, for instance.

Solution

Place try-catch or try-catch-finally blocks in strategic places in your application. In addition, use the exception event handler as a final line of defense against unhandled exceptions.

Discussion

If an exception occurs and is not handled, it will cause your application to crash by default. This can leave data in an unstable state, possibly requiring manual intervention—meaning that you could be spending a long night cleaning up the data by hand. To minimize the damage, you can place exception handlers in strategic locations throughout your code to handle what you can. When an exceptional condition occurs that you cannot handle, it will be caught by the exception event handler, and you can then shut down in a controlled manner.

The most obvious location to place exception-handling code is inside of the Main method. The Main method is the entry point to executables (i.e., files with an *.exe* extension). Therefore, if any exceptions occur inside your executable, the CLR starts looking for an exception handler, starting at the location where the exception occurred. If none is found, the CLR walks the stack until one is found; each method on the stack is examined in turn to determine whether an exception handler exists. If no exception handlers are found in the final method in the stack, the exception is considered unhandled and the application is terminated. In an executable, this final method is the Main method.

In addition to or in place of using try-catch or try-catch-finally blocks at the entry point of your application, you can use the exception event handler to capture unhandled exceptions. Note that Windows Forms applications provide their own unhandled exception trap around exception handlers. To see how to deal with this in a WinForms application, review Recipe 7.12. There are two steps to setting up an exception event handler. The first is to create the actual event handler. This is done as follows:

```
static void LastChanceHandler(object sender, UnhandledExceptionEventArgs args)
{
    try
    {
```

```
                Exception e = (Exception) args.ExceptionObject;

                Console.WriteLine("Unhandled exception == " + e.ToString());
                if (args.IsTerminating)
                {
                    Console.WriteLine("The application is terminating");
                }
                else
                {
                    Console.WriteLine("The application is not terminating");
                }
            }
            catch(Exception e)
            {
                Console.WriteLine("Unhandled exception in unhandled exception handler ==
    " +
                                    e.ToString());
            }
            finally
            {
                // Add other exception logging or cleanup code here.
            }
        }
```

Next, you should add code to your application to wire up this event handler. The
code to wire up the event handler should be executed as close to the start of the
application as possible. For example, by placing this code in the Main method:

```
        public static void Main()
        {
            appdomain.CurrentDomain.UnhandledException +=
                new UnhandledExceptionEventHandler(LastChanceHandler);

            //...
        }
```

you are assured of being able to clean up after any unhandled exception.

The exception event handler takes two parameters. The first is the sender object,
which is the appdomain object that threw the exception. The second argument is an
UnhandledExceptionEventArgs object. This object contains all the relevant information on the unhandled exception. Using this object, you can obtain the actual exception object that was thrown as well as a Boolean flag that indicates whether the
application will terminate.

Exception event handlers are a great help when used in multithreaded code. In the
1.x versions of the Framework, if an unhandled exception were thrown in a thread
other than the main thread, that thread would abort. However, only the worker
thread, and not the application as a whole, would terminate. But you were not
clearly notified when the CLR aborted this thread, which could cause some interesting debugging problems. Any unhandled exception will propagate and cause the
application to terminate. However, when an exception event handler is used, you

can be notified of any unhandled exceptions that occur in any worker thread and that cause it to abort.

The exception event handler captures unhandled exceptions for only the primary application domain. Any application domains created from the primary application domain do not fire this event for unhandled exceptions. These secondary application domains must be registered with as well for the UnhandledException event individually to receive their exception events. Note that if the exception is thrown on the main thread, the system will bring up an error dialog before running the exception event handler.

See Also

The "Error Raising and Handling Guidelines" and "UnhandledException-EventHandler Delegate" topics in the MSDN documentation.

7.5   Getting Exception Information

Problem

There are several different methods of getting exception information. You need to choose the best one to use.

Solution

The .NET platform supports several mechanisms for displaying exception information, depending on the specific type of information that you want to show. The easiest method is to use the ToString method of the thrown exception object, usually in the catch block of an exception handler:

```
catch(Exception ex)
{
    Console.WriteLine(ex.ToString());
}
```

Another mechanism is to manually display the individual properties of the exception and iterate through each inner exception, if any exist. The default Exception.ToString method will iterate over the inner exceptions as well, so if you want to make sure you get all of that information, you need to roll over them when examining the properties directly. For example, the extension method shown in Example 7-3 is called from a catch block. ToFullDisplayString is called directly from the exception object and proceeds to display its information, including information on all inner exceptions and the exception data block.

Example 7-3. Displaying exception information, including information on all inner exceptions and the exception data block

```
public static string ToFullDisplayString(this Exception ex)
{
    StringBuilder displayText = new StringBuilder();
    WriteExceptionDetail(displayText, ex);
    foreach (Exception inner in ex.GetNestedExceptionList()) // from 7.14
    {
        displayText.AppendFormat("**** INNEREXCEPTION START ****{0}",
                                Environment.NewLine);

        WriteExceptionDetail(displayText, inner);

        displayText.AppendFormat("**** INNEREXCEPTION END ****{0}{0}",
                                Environment.NewLine);
    }
    return displayText.ToString();
}

public static void WriteExceptionDetail(StringBuilder builder, Exception ex)
{
    builder.AppendFormat("Message: {0}{1}", ex.Message, Environment.NewLine);
    builder.AppendFormat("Type: {0}{1}", ex.GetType(), Environment.NewLine);
    builder.AppendFormat("HelpLink: {0}{1}", ex.HelpLink, Environment.NewLine);
    builder.AppendFormat("Source: {0}{1}", ex.Source, Environment.NewLine);
    builder.AppendFormat("TargetSite: {0}{1}", ex.TargetSite,
                                                Environment.NewLine);
    builder.AppendFormat("Data:{0}", Environment.NewLine);
    foreach (DictionaryEntry de in ex.Data)
    {
        builder.AppendFormat("\t{0} : {1}", de.Key, de.Value);
    }
    builder.AppendFormat("StackTrace: {0}{1}", ex.StackTrace,
                                                Environment.NewLine);
}
```

Discussion

A typical exception object of type Exception displays the following information if its ToString method is called:

```
System.Exception: Exception of type System.Exception was thrown.
    at Chapter_Code.Chapter7.TestSpecializedException() in c:\book cs cookbook\code\
        test.cs:line 286
```

Three pieces of information are shown here:

- The exception type (Exception, in this case) followed by a colon
- The string contained in the exception's Message property
- The string contained in the exception's StackTrace property

The great thing about the ToString method is that information about any exception contained in the InnerException property is automatically displayed as well. The following text shows the output of an exception that wraps an inner exception:

```
System.Exception: Exception of type System.Exception was thrown.
---> System.Exception: The Inner Exception
   at Chapter_Code.Chapter7.TestSpecializedException( )
     in c:\book cs cookbook\code\
     test.cs:line 306
   --- End of inner exception stack trace ---
   at Chapter_Code.Chapter7.TestSpecializedException( )
     in c:\book cs cookbook\code\
     test.cs:line 310
```

The same three pieces of information are displayed for each exception. The output is broken down into the following format:

```
Outer exception type: Outer exception Message property
---> Inner Exception type: Inner exception Message property
Inner Exception StackTrace property
     --- End of inner exception stack trace ---
Outer exception StackTrace property
```

If the inner exception contains an exception object in its InnerException property, that exception is displayed as well. In fact, information for all inner exceptions is displayed in this format.

Calling the ToString method is a quick, useful way of getting the most pertinent information out of the exception and displaying it in a formatted string. However, not all of the exception's information is displayed. There might be a need to display the HelpLine or Source properties of the exception. In fact, if this is a user-defined exception, there could be custom fields that need to be displayed or captured in an error log. Also, you might not like the default formatting that the ToString method offers, or you may want to see the information in the Data collection of items. In these cases, consider writing your own method to display the exception's information based on the DisplayException method shown in the Solution.

To illustrate the custom method presented in the Solution section (the DisplayException method), consider the following code, which throws an exception wrapping two inner exceptions:

```
Exception InnerInner = new Exception("The InnerInner Exception.");
InnerInner.Data.Add("Key1 for InnerInner", "Value1 for InnerInner");

ArgumentException Inner = new ArgumentException("The Inner Exception.", InnerInner);
Inner.Data.Add("Key1 for Inner", "Value1 for Inner");
NullReferenceException se = new NullReferenceException("A Test Message.", Inner);
se.HelpLink = "MyComponent.hlp";
se.Source = "MyComponent";
se.Data.Add("Key1 for Outer", "Value1 for Outer");
se.Data.Add("Key2 for Outer", "Value2 for Outer");
se.Data.Add("Key3 for Outer", "Value3 for Outer");
```

```
try
{
    throw (se);
}
catch(Exception e)
{
    Console.WriteLine(e.ToFullDisplayString());
}
```

If this code were executed, `ToFullDisplayString` would display the following:

```
Message: A Test Message.
Type: System.NullReferenceException
HelpLink: MyComponent.hlp
Source: MyComponent
TargetSite: Void TestToFullDisplayString()
Data:
        Key1 for Outer : Value1 for Outer
        Key2 for Outer : Value2 for Outer
        Key3 for Outer : Value3 for Outer
StackTrace:     at CSharpRecipes.ExceptionHandling.TestToFullDisplayString() in C
:\Code\CSharpRecipes\07_ExceptionHandling.cs:line 342
**** INNEREXCEPTION START ****
Message: The Inner Exception.
Type: System.ArgumentException
HelpLink:
Source:
TargetSite:
Data:
        Key1 for Inner : Value1 for Inner
StackTrace:
**** INNEREXCEPTION END ****

**** INNEREXCEPTION START ****
Message: The InnerInner Exception.
Type: System.Exception
HelpLink:
Source:
TargetSite:
Data:
        Key1 for InnerInner : Value1 for InnerInner
StackTrace:
**** INNEREXCEPTION END ****
```

The outermost exception is displayed first, followed by all of its properties. Next, each inner exception is displayed in a similar manner.

See Also

The "Error Raising and Handling Guidelines" and "Exception Class" topics in the MSDN documentation.

7.6   Getting to the Root of a Problem Quickly

Problem

A thrown and caught exception can contain one or more inner exceptions. The innermost exception usually indicates the origin of the problem. You want to be able to view the original thrown exception and skip all of the outer exceptions and to view the initial problem.

Solution

The GetBaseException instance method of the Exception class displays information on only the innermost (original) exception; no other exception information is displayed. This method accepts no parameters and returns the innermost exception. For example:

```
Console.WriteLine(exception.GetBaseException( ).ToString( ));
```

Discussion

Calling the GetBaseException( ).ToString( ) method on an exception object that contains an inner exception produces the same error information as if the ToString method were called directly on the inner exception. However, if the exception object does not contain an inner expression, the information on the provided exception object is displayed. For the following code:

```
Exception innerInner = new Exception("The innerInner Exception.");
ArgumentException inner = new ArgumentException("The inner Exception.",
innerInner);
NullReferenceException se = new NullReferenceException("A Test Message.", inner);

try
{
    throw (se);
}
catch(Exception e)
{
    Console.WriteLine(e.GetBaseException( ).ToString( ));
}
```

something similar to this would be displayed:

```
System.Exception: The innerInner Exception.
    at Chapter_Code.EH.MyMethod( ) in c:\book cs cookbook\code\test.cs:line 286
```

Notice that no exception other than the innerInner exception is displayed. This useful technique gets to the root of the problem while filtering out all of the other outer exceptions that you are not interested in.

See Also

The "Error Raising and Handling Guidelines" and "Exception Class" topics in the MSDN documentation.

7.7   Creating a New Exception Type

Problem

None of the built-in exceptions in the .NET Framework provide the implementation details that you require for an exception that you need to throw. You need to create your own exception class that operates seamlessly with your application, as well as other applications. Whenever an application receives this new exception, it can inform the user that a specific error occurred in a specific component. This report will greatly reduce the time required to debug the problem.

Solution

Create your own exception class. To illustrate, let's create a custom exception class, `RemoteComponentException`, that will inform a client application that an error has occurred in a remote server assembly.

Discussion

The exception hierarchy starts with the `Exception` class; from this are derived two classes: `ApplicationException` and `SystemException`. The `SystemException` class and any classes derived from it are reserved for the developers of the FCL. Most of the common exceptions, such as the `NullReferenceException` or the `OverflowException`, are derived from `SystemException`. The FCL developers created the `ApplicationException` class for other developers using the .NET languages to derive their own exceptions from. This partitioning allows for a clear distinction between user-defined exceptions and the built-in system exceptions. However, Microsoft now recommends deriving directly from `Exception`, rather than `ApplicationException`. Nothing actively prevents you from deriving a class from either `SystemException` or `ApplicationException`. But it is better to be consistent and use the convention of always deriving from the `Exception` class for user-defined exceptions.

You should follow the naming convention for exceptions when determining the name of your exception. The convention is very simple. Whatever you decide on for the exception's name, add the word `Exception` to the end of the name (e.g., use `UnknownException` as the exception name instead of just `Unknown`). Every user-defined exception should include *at least* three constructors, which are described next. This is not a requirement, but it makes your exception classes operate similarly to every other exception class in the FCL and minimizes the learning curve for other developers using your new exception. These three constructors are:

The default constructor
    This constructor takes no arguments and simply calls the base class's default constructor.

A constructor with a parameter that accepts a message string
    This message string overwrites the default contents of the Message field of this exception. Like the default constructor, this constructor also calls the base class's constructor, which also accepts a message string as its only parameter.

A constructor that accepts a message string and an inner exception as parameters
    The object contained in the *innerException* parameter is added to the InnerException property of this exception object. Like the other two constructors, this constructor calls the base class's constructor of the same signature.

If this exception will be caught in unmanaged code, such as a COM object, you can also set the HRESULT value for this exception. An exception caught in unmanaged code becomes an HRESULT value. If the exception does not alter the HRESULT value, it defaults to the HRESULT of the base class exception, which, in the case of a user-defined exception object that inherits from ApplicationException, is COR_E_APPLICATION (0x80131600). To change the default HRESULT value, simply set the value of this field in the constructor. The following code demonstrates this technique:

```
public class RemoteComponentException : Exception
{
    public RemoteComponentException( ) : base( )
    {
        HResult = 0x80040321;
    }

    public RemoteComponentException(string message) : base(message)
    {
        HResult = 0x80040321;
    }

    public RemoteComponentException(string message, Exception innerException)
        : base(message, innerException)
    {
        HResult = 0x80040321;
    }
}
```

Now the HResult that the COM object will see is the value 0x80040321.

 It is usually a good idea to override the Message property in order to incorporate any new fields into the exception's message text. Always remember to include the base class's message text along with any additional text you add to this property.

Fields and their accessors should be created to hold data specific to the exception. Since this exception will be thrown as a result of an error that occurs in a remote server assembly, you will add a private field to contain the name of the server or service. In addition, you will add a public read-only property to access this field. Since you're adding this new field, you should add two constructors that accept an extra parameter used to set the value of the serverName field.

If necessary, override any base class members whose behavior is inherited by the custom exception class. For example, since you have added a new field, you need to determine whether it will need to be added to the default contents of the Message field for this exception. If it does, you must override the Message property:

```
public override string Message
{
    get
    {
        if (string.IsNullOrEmpty(this.ServerName))
            return (base.Message + Environment.NewLine +
                "A server with an unknown name has encountered an error.");
        else
            return (base.Message + Environment.NewLine +
                "The server (" + this.ServerName +
                ") has encountered an error.");
    }
}
```

Notice that the Message property in the base class is displayed on the first line, and your additional text is displayed on the next line. This organization takes into account that a user might modify the message that will appear in the Message property by using one of the overloaded constructors that takes a message string as a parameter.

Your exception object should be serializable and deserializable. This involves performing the following two additional steps:

1. Add the Serializable attribute to the class definition. This attribute specifies that this class can be serialized and deserialized. A SerializationException is thrown if this attribute does not exist on this class, and an attempt is made to serialize this class.

2. The class should implement the ISerializable interface if you want control over how serialization and deserialization are performed, and it should provide an implementation for its single member, GetObjectData. Here you implement it because the base class implements it, which means that you have no choice but to reimplement it if you want the fields you added (e.g., serverName) to get serialized:

```
// Used during serialization to capture information about extra fields
public override void GetObjectData(SerializationInfo exceptionInfo,
                                   StreamingContext exceptionContext)
{
```

```
        base.GetObjectData(exceptionInfo, exceptionContext);
        exceptionInfo.AddValue("ServerName", this.ServerName);
    }
```

In addition, a new overridden constructor is needed that accepts information to dese-rialize this object:

```
// Serialization ctor
protected RemoteComponentException(SerializationInfo exceptionInfo,
        StreamingContext exceptionContext)
        : base(exceptionInfo, exceptionContext)
{
    this.serverName = exceptionInfo.GetString("ServerName");
}
```

 Even though it is not required, you should make all user-defined exception classes serializable and deserializable. That way, the excep-tions can be propagated properly over remoting and application domain boundaries.

At this point, the RemoteComponentException class contains everything you need for a complete user-defined exception class.

As a final note, it is generally a good idea to place all user-defined exceptions in a separate assembly, which allows for easier reuse of these exceptions in other applica-tions and, more importantly, allows other application domains and remotely execut-ing code to both throw and handle these exceptions correctly no matter where they are thrown. The assembly that holds these exceptions should be signed with a strong name and added to the Global Assembly Cache (GAC), so that any code that uses or handles these exceptions can find the assembly that defines them. See Recipe 17.9 for more information on how to do this.

If you are sure that the exceptions being defined won't ever be thrown or handled outside of your assembly, then you can leave the exception definitions there. But if for some reason an exception that you throw finds its way out of your assembly, the code that ultimately catches it will not be able to resolve it.

The complete source code for the RemoteComponentException class is shown in Example 7-4.

Example 7-4. RemoteComponentException class

```
using System;
using System.IO;
using System.Runtime.Serialization;
using System.Runtime.Serialization.Formatters.Binary;
using System.Security.Permissions;

[Serializable]
public class RemoteComponentException : Exception, ISerializable
{
```

Example 7-4. RemoteComponentException class (continued)

```
#region Constructors
// Normal exception ctor's
public RemoteComponentException( ) : base( )
{
}

public RemoteComponentException(string message) : base(message)
{
}

public RemoteComponentException(string message, Exception innerException)
    : base(message, innerException)
{
}

// Exception ctor's that accept the new ServerName parameter
public RemoteComponentException(string message, string serverName) : base(message)
{
    this.ServerName = serverName;
}

public RemoteComponentException(string message,
            Exception innerException, string serverName)
    : base(message, innerException)
{
    this.ServerName = serverName;
}

// Serialization ctor
protected RemoteComponentException(SerializationInfo exceptionInfo,
    StreamingContext exceptionContext)
    : base(exceptionInfo, exceptionContext)
{
    this.ServerName = exceptionInfo.GetString("ServerName");
}
#endregion // Constructors

#region Properties
// Read-only property for server name
public string ServerName { get; private set; }

public override string Message
{
    get
    {
        if (string.IsNullOrEmpty(this.ServerName))
            return (string.Format(Thread.CurrentThread.CurrentCulture,
                "{0}{1}A server with an unknown name has encountered an error.",
                base.Message, Environment.NewLine));
        else
            return (
                string.Format(Thread.CurrentThread.CurrentCulture,
```

Example 7-4. RemoteComponentException class (continued)

```csharp
                        "{0}{1}The server ({2}) has encountered an error.",
                        base.Message, Environment.NewLine, this.ServerName));
        }
    }
    #endregion // Properties

    #region Overridden methods
    // ToString method
    public override string ToString()
    {
        string errorString =
            string.Format(Thread.CurrentThread.CurrentCulture,
            "An error has occured in a server component of this client." +
            "{0}Server Name: {1}{0}{2}",
            Environment.NewLine, this.ServerName, this.ToFullDisplayString());
        return errorString;
    }

    // Used during serialization to capture information about extra fields
    [SecurityPermission(SecurityAction.LinkDemand, Flags =
        SecurityPermissionFlag.SerializationFormatter)]
    public override void GetObjectData(SerializationInfo info,
        StreamingContext context)
    {
        base.GetObjectData(info, context);
        info.AddValue("ServerName", this.ServerName);
    }
    #endregion // Overridden methods

    // Call base.ToString method
    public string ToBaseString()
    {
        return (base.ToString());
    }
}
```

The `ToFullDisplayString` call made in the `ToString` override is on the extension method presented in Recipe 7.5. A partial listing of the code to test the RemoteComponentException class is shown in Example 7-5.

Example 7-5. Testing the RemoteComponentException class

```csharp
public void TestSpecializedException()
{
    // Generic inner exception used to test the
    // RemoteComponentException's inner exception.
    Exception inner = new Exception("The inner Exception");

    RemoteComponentException se1 = new RemoteComponentException ();
    RemoteComponentException se2 =
      new RemoteComponentException ("A Test Message for se2");
```

Example 7-5. Testing the RemoteComponentException class (continued)

```
RemoteComponentException se3 =
  new RemoteComponentException ("A Test Message for se3", inner);
RemoteComponentException se4 =
  new RemoteComponentException ("A Test Message for se4",
                               "MyServer");
RemoteComponentException se5 =
  new RemoteComponentException ("A Test Message for se5", inner,
                               "MyServer");


// Test overridden Message property.
Console.WriteLine(Environment.NewLine +
  "TEST -OVERRIDDEN- MESSAGE PROPERTY");
Console.WriteLine("se1.Message == " + se1.Message);
Console.WriteLine("se2.Message == " + se2.Message);
Console.WriteLine("se3.Message == " + se3.Message);
Console.WriteLine("se4.Message == " + se4.Message);
Console.WriteLine("se5.Message == " + se5.Message);

// Test -overridden- ToString method.
Console.WriteLine(Environment.NewLine +
  "TEST -OVERRIDDEN- TOSTRING METHOD");
Console.WriteLine("se1.ToString( ) == " + se1.ToString( ));
Console.WriteLine("se2.ToString( ) == " + se2.ToString( ));
Console.WriteLine("se3.ToString( ) == " + se3.ToString( ));
Console.WriteLine("se4.ToString( ) == " + se4.ToString( ));
Console.WriteLine("se5.ToString( ) == " + se5.ToString( ));
Console.WriteLine(Environment.NewLine + "END TEST" + Environment.NewLine);
}
```

The output from Example 7-5 is presented in Example 7-6.

Example 7-6. Output displayed by the RemoteComponentException class

```
TEST -OVERRIDDEN- MESSAGE PROPERTY
se1.Message == Exception of type 'CSharpRecipes.ExceptionHandling+RemoteComponen
tException' was thrown.
A server with an unknown name has encountered an error.
se2.Message == A Test Message for se2
A server with an unknown name has encountered an error.
se3.Message == A Test Message for se3
A server with an unknown name has encountered an error.
se4.Message == A Test Message for se4
The server (MyServer) has encountered an error.
se5.Message == A Test Message for se5
The server (MyServer) has encountered an error.


TEST -OVERRIDDEN- TOSTRING METHOD
se1.ToString( ) == An error has occured in a server component of this client.
Server Name:
Message: Exception of type 'CSharpRecipes.ExceptionHandling+RemoteComponentExcep
tion' was thrown.
A server with an unknown name has encountered an error.
```

Example 7-6. Output displayed by the RemoteComponentException class (continued)

```
Type: CSharpRecipes.ExceptionHandling+RemoteComponentException
HelpLink:
Source:
TargetSite:
Data:
StackTrace:

se2.ToString() == An error has occured in a server component of this client.
Server Name:
Message: A Test Message for se2
A server with an unknown name has encountered an error.
Type: CSharpRecipes.ExceptionHandling+RemoteComponentException
HelpLink:
Source:
TargetSite:
Data:
StackTrace:

se3.ToString() == An error has occured in a server component of this client.
Server Name:
Message: A Test Message for se3
A server with an unknown name has encountered an error.
Type: CSharpRecipes.ExceptionHandling+RemoteComponentException
HelpLink:
Source:
TargetSite:
Data:
StackTrace:
**** INNEREXCEPTION START ****
Message: The Inner Exception
Type: System.Exception
HelpLink:
Source:
TargetSite:
Data:
StackTrace:
**** INNEREXCEPTION END ****


se4.ToString() == An error has occured in a server component of this client.
Server Name: MyServer
Message: A Test Message for se4
The server (MyServer) has encountered an error.
Type: CSharpRecipes.ExceptionHandling+RemoteComponentException
HelpLink:
Source:
TargetSite:
Data:
StackTrace:

se5.ToString() == An error has occured in a server component of this client.
Server Name: MyServer
```

Example 7-6. Output displayed by the RemoteComponentException class (continued)

```
Message: A Test Message for se5
The server (MyServer) has encountered an error.
Type: CSharpRecipes.ExceptionHandling+RemoteComponentException
HelpLink:
Source:
TargetSite:
Data:
StackTrace:
**** INNEREXCEPTION START ****
Message: The Inner Exception
Type: System.Exception
HelpLink:
Source:
TargetSite:
Data:
StackTrace:
**** INNEREXCEPTION END ****


END TEST
```

See Also

Recipe 17.9, and the "Using User-Defined Exceptions" and "Exception Class" topics in the MSDN documentation.

7.8   Obtaining a Stack Trace

Problem

You need a view of what the stack looks like at any particular point in your application. However, you do not have an exception object from which to obtain this stack trace.

Solution

Use the following line of code to obtain a stack trace at any point in your application:

```
string currentStackTrace = System.Environment.StackTrace;
```

The variable currentStackTrace now contains the stack trace at the location where this line of code was executed.

Discussion

A good use of the Solution is tracking down stack overflow problems. You can obtain the current stack trace at various points in your application and then calculate the stack depth. This depth calculation can then be logged to determine when and why the stack is overflowing or potential trouble spots where the stack may grow very large.

It is very easy to obtain a stack trace using the System.Environment.StackTrace property. Unfortunately, this stack trace also lists three methods defined in the System.Environment class that are called when you use the Environment.StackTrace property. The returned stack trace, using this method, will look something like following:

```
   at System.Environment.GetStackTrace(Exception e)
   at System.Environment.GetStackTrace(Exception e)
   at System.Environment.get_StackTrace()
   at Chapter_Code.Class1.ObtainingStackTrace() in c:\book cs cookbook\test.cs:line
260
   at Chapter_Code.Class1.Main(String[] args) in c:\book cs cookbook\main.cs:line 78
```

The first three items in the stack trace are method calls that you are not interested in. To fix this, you can write the following method to find and remove these items from the stack trace:

```
   public static string GetStackTraceInfo(string currentStackTrace)
   {
       string firstStackTraceCall = "System.Environment.get_StackTrace()";
       int posOfStackTraceCall =
           currentStackTrace.IndexOf(firstStackTraceCall,StringComparison.
OrdinalIgnoreCase);
       return (currentStackTrace.Substring(posOfStackTraceCall +
               firstStackTraceCall.Length));
   }
```

This method is called using the following line of code:

```
   string stackTraceInfo = GetStackTraceInfo(System.Environment.StackTrace);
```

The second line in the GetStackTraceInfo method creates and initializes a string variable to the first called StackTrace method—which is actually a call to the get portion of the StackTrace property. This variable is used in the third line to obtain its starting position in the complete stack trace string. The final line of code grabs the end of the complete stack trace string, starting at the ending of the first called StackTrace method. The FinalStackTrace variable now contains the following string:

```
   at Chapter_Code.Class1.ObtainingStackTrace() in c:\book cs cookbook\test.cs:line
260
   at Chapter_Code.Class1.Main(String[] args) in c:\book cs cookbook\main.cs:line 78
```

This is the current stack trace at the point in the code where the Environment.StackTrace method was called.

Now that you have a stack trace of your code, you can calculate the stack depth at the point where you call Environment.StackTrace. The following code uses a regular expression to determine the depth of a stack trace:

```
   using System;
   using System.Text.RegularExpressions;
```

```
public static int GetStackTraceDepth(string currentStackTrace)
{
    string firstStackTraceCall = "System.Environment.get_StackTrace()";
    int posOfStackTraceCall =
        currentStackTrace.IndexOf(firstStackTraceCall,StringComparison.
OrdinalIgnoreCase);
    string finalStackTrace = currentStackTrace.Substring(posOfStackTraceCall +
            firstStackTraceCall.Length);

    MatchCollection methodCallMatches = Regex.Matches(finalStackTrace,
            @"\sat\s.*(\sin\s.*\:line\s\d*)?");
    return (methodCallMatches.Count);
}
```

This regular expression captures every method call in the stack trace string. Note that, if the correct symbols are located for your assembly, the stack trace might look like this:

```
at Chapter_Code.Class1.ObtainingStackTrace() in c:\book cs cookbook\test.cs:line
260
at Chapter_Code.Class1.Main(String[] args) in c:\book cs cookbook\main.cs:line 78
```

However, if the correct symbols cannot be found, the stack trace string will look similar to the following:

```
at Chapter_Code.Class1.ObtainingStackTrace()
at Chapter_Code.Class1.Main(String[] args)
```

The file and line numbers are not displayed in this case, and the regular expression must take this into account.

To get a count of the stack depth, use the Count property of the MatchCollection object to give the total number of method calls in the stack. In addition, you can obtain each individual method call as an independent string by iterating through the MatchCollection object. The code to do so is:

```
Console.WriteLine("-------------");
foreach(Match m in MethodCallMatches)
{
    Console.WriteLine(m.Value + System.Environment.NewLine + "-------------");
}
```

This code will display the following:

```
-------------
at Chapter_Code.Class1.ObtainingStackTrace() in
  c:\book cs cookbook\test.cs:line 260
-------------
at Chapter_Code.Class1.Main(String[] args) in
  c:\book cs cookbook\main.cs:line 78
-------------
```

Each method and its information are contained within a Match object within the MatchCollection object.

The `Environment.StackTrace` method can be useful as a debugging tool. You can see at various points in your application which methods have been called and their calling order. This can come in very handy when creating and debugging an application that uses recursion. In addition, you can also keep track of the stack depth by using the `Environment.StackTrace` property.

See Also

The "Environment.StackTrace Property" topic in the MSDN documentation.

7.9   Breaking on a First-Chance Exception

Problem

You need to fix a problem with your code that is throwing an exception. Unfortunately, an exception handler is trapping the exception, and you are having a tough time pinpointing where and when the exception is being thrown.

Forcing the application to break on an exception before the application has a chance to handle it is very useful in situations in which you need to step through the code at the point where the exception is first being thrown. If this exception were thrown and not handled by your application, the debugger would intervene and break on the line of code that caused the unhandled exception. In this case, you can see the context in which the exception was thrown. However, if an exception handler is active when the exception is thrown, the exception handler will handle it and continue on, preventing you from being able to see the context at the point where the exception was thrown. This is the default behavior for all exceptions.

Solution

Select Debug → Exceptions or use the Ctrl-D key combination and then the E key within Visual Studio 2008 to display the Exceptions dialog box (see Figure 7-1). Select the exception from the tree that you want to modify and then click on the checkbox in the Thrown column in the list view. Click the OK button and then run your application. Any time the application throws a `System.ArgumentOutOfRangeException`, the debugger will break on that line of code before your application has a chance to handle it.

Using the Exceptions dialog box, you can target specific exceptions or sets of exceptions for which you wish to alter the default behavior. This dialog has three main sections. The first is the TreeView control, which contains the list of categorized exceptions. Using this TreeView, you can choose one or more exceptions or groups of exceptions whose behavior you wish to modify.

The next section on this dialog is the column Thrown in the list next to the TreeView. This column contains a checkbox for each exception that will enable the

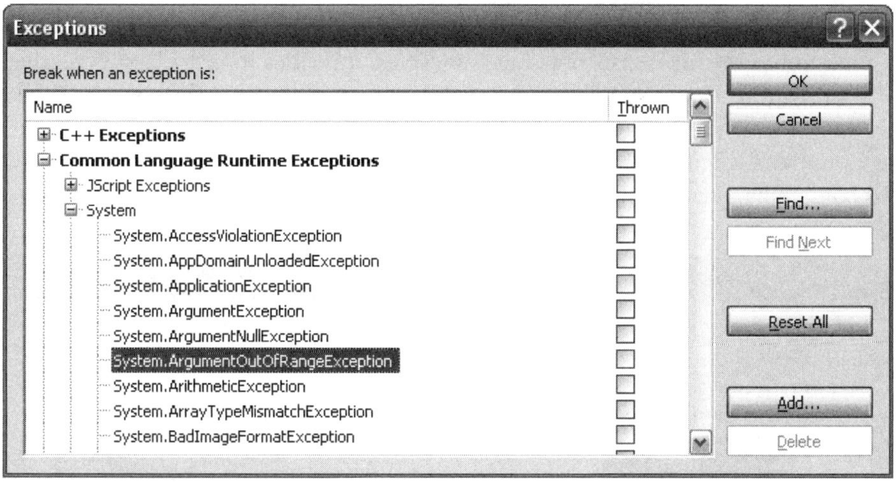

Figure 7-1. The Exceptions dialog box

debugger to break when that type of exception is first thrown. At this stage, the exception is considered a *first-chance exception*. Checking the checkbox in the Thrown column forces the debugger to intervene when a first-chance exception of the type chosen in the TreeView control is thrown. Unchecking the checkbox allows the application to attempt to handle the first-chance exception.

This dialog contains two helpful buttons, Find and Find Next, to allow you to search for an exception rather than dig into the TreeView control and search for it on your own. In addition, three other buttons—Reset All, Add, and Delete—are used to reset to the original state and to add and remove user-defined exceptions, respectively. For example, you can create your own exception, as you did in Recipe 7.7, and add this exception to the TreeView list. You must add any managed exception such as this to the TreeView node entitled Common Language Runtime Exceptions. This setting tells the debugger that this is a managed exception and should be handled as such.

To add a user-defined exception to the TreeView, click the Add button. The dialog box shown in Figure 7-2 appears.

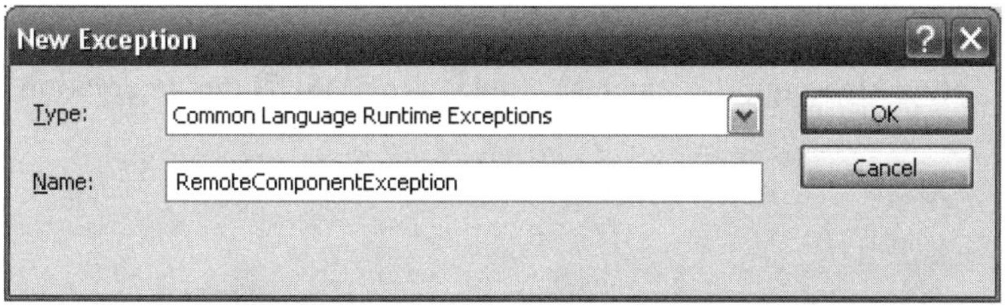

Figure 7-2. Adding a user-defined exception to the TreeView

Type the name of the exception—exactly as its class name is spelled with the full namespace scoping—into the Name field of this dialog box. Do not append any other information to this name, such as the namespace it resides in or a class name that it is nested within. Doing so will cause the debugger to fail to see this exception when it is thrown. Clicking the OK button places this exception into the TreeView under the Common Language Runtime Exceptions node. The Exceptions dialog box will look something like the one in Figure 7-3 after you add this user-defined exception.

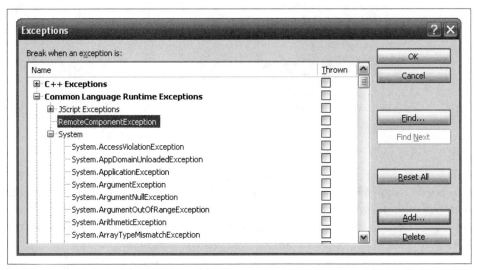

Figure 7-3. The Exceptions dialog box after adding a user-defined exception to the TreeView

The Delete button deletes any selected user-defined exception that you added to the TreeView. The Reset All button deletes any and all user-defined exceptions that have been added to the TreeView. Check the Thrown column to have the debugger stop when that exception type is thrown.

There is one other setting that can affect your exception debugging and that is the "Just My Code" setting. Figure 7-4 demonstrates that this should be turned off to get the best picture of what is really happening in your application when debugging. The setting is under Tools\Options\Debugging in Visual Studio 2008.

See Also

The "Exception Handling (Debugging)" topic in the MSDN documentation.

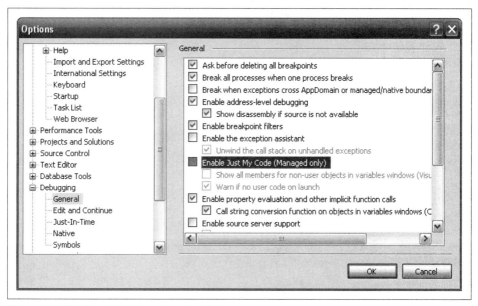

Figure 7-4. The Just My Code setting disabled

7.10   Handling Exceptions Thrown from an Asynchronous Delegate

Problem

When using a delegate asynchronously, you want to be notified if the delegate has thrown any exceptions.

Solution

Wrap the EndInvoke method of the delegate in a try/catch block:

```
using System;
using System.Threading;

public class AsyncAction
{
    public void PollAsyncDelegate()
    {
        // Create the async delegate to call Method1 and call its BeginInvoke
method.
        AsyncInvoke MI = new AsyncInvoke(TestAsyncInvoke.Method1);
        IAsyncResult AR = MI.BeginInvoke(null, null);

        // Poll until the async delegate is finished.
        while (!AR.IsCompleted)
        {
```

```
        System.Threading.Thread.Sleep(100);
        Console.Write('.');
    }
    Console.WriteLine("Finished Polling");

    // Call the EndInvoke method of the async delegate.
    try
    {
        int RetVal = MI.EndInvoke(AR);
        Console.WriteLine("RetVal (Polling): " + RetVal);
    }
    catch (Exception e)
    {
        Console.WriteLine(e.ToString());
    }
    }
}
```

The following code defines the AsyncInvoke delegate and the asynchronously invoked static method TestAsyncInvoke.Method1:

```
public delegate int AsyncInvoke();

public class TestAsyncInvoke
{
    public static int Method1()
    {
        throw (new Exception("Method1"));    // Simulate an exception being
thrown.
    }
}
```

Discussion

If the code in the PollAsyncDelegate method did not contain a call to the delegate's EndInvoke method, the exception thrown in Method1 either would simply be discarded and never caught or, if the application had the top-level exception handlers wired up (Recipes 7.3, 7.11, and 7.12), it would be caught. If EndInvoke is called, then this exception would occur when EndInvoke is called and could be caught there. This behavior is by design; for all unhandled exceptions that occur within the thread, the thread immediately returns to the thread pool, and the exception is lost.

If a method that was called asynchronously through a delegate throws an exception, the only way to trap that exception is to include a call to the delegate's EndInvoke method and wrap this call in an exception handler. The EndInvoke method must be called to retrieve the results of the asynchronous delegate; in fact, the EndInvoke method must be called even if there are no results. These results can be obtained through a return value or any ref or out parameters of the delegate.

See Also

For more information on calling delegates asynchronously, see Recipe 9.3.

For information about wiring up top-level exception handlers in your application, see Recipes 7.3, 7.11, and 7.12.

7.11 Giving Exceptions the Extra Info They Need with Exception.Data

Problem

You want to send some additional information along with an exception.

Solution

Use the `Data` property on the `System.Exception` object to store key-value pairs of information relevant to the exception.

For example, say there is a `System.ArgumentException` being thrown from a section of code, and you want to include the underlying cause and the length of time it took. The code would add two key-value pairs to the `Exception.Data` property by specifying the key in the indexer and then assigning the value.

In the example that follows, the `Data` for the irritable exception uses "Cause" and "Length" for its keys. Once the items have been set in the `Data` collection, the exception can be thrown and caught, and more data can be added in subsequent catch blocks for as many levels of exception handling as the exception is allowed to traverse:

```
try
{
    try
    {
        try
        {
            try
            {
                ArgumentException irritable =
                    new ArgumentException("I'm irritable!");
                irritable.Data["Cause"]="Computer crashed";
                irritable.Data["Length"]=10;
                throw irritable;
            }
            catch (Exception e)
            {
                // See if I can help...
                if(e.Data.Contains("Cause"))
                    e.Data["Cause"]="Fixed computer";
```

```
                        throw;
                    }
                }
                catch (Exception e)
                {
                    e.Data["Comment"]="Always grumpy you are";
                    throw;
                }
            }
            catch (Exception e)
            {
                e.Data["Reassurance"]="Error Handled";
                throw;
            }
        }
```

The final catch block can then iterate over the Exception.Data collection and display all of the supporting data that has been gathered in the Data collection since the initial exception was thrown:

```
catch (Exception e)
{
    Console.WriteLine("Exception supporting data:");
    foreach(DictionaryEntry de in e.Data)
    {
        Console.WriteLine("\t{0} : {1}",de.Key,de.Value);
    }
}
```

Discussion

Exception.Data is an object that supports the IDictionary interface. This allows you to:

- Add and remove name-value pairs
- Clear the contents
- Search the collection to see if it contains a certain key
- Get an IDictionaryEnumerator for rolling over the collection items
- Index into the collection using the key
- Access an ICollection of all of the keys and all of the values separately

It is a very handy thing to be able to tack on code-specific data to the system exceptions, as it provides the ability to give a more complete picture of what happened in the code when the error occurred. The more information available to the poor soul (probably yourself) who is trying to figure out why the exception was thrown in the first place, the better the chance of it being fixed. Do yourself and your team a favor and give a little bit of extra information when throwing exceptions; you won't be sorry you did.

See Also

The "Exception.Data Property" topic in the MSDN documentation.

7.12   Dealing with Unhandled Exceptions in WinForms Applications

Problem

You have a WinForms-based application in which you want to catch and log any unhandled exceptions on any thread.

Solution

You need to hook up handlers for both the `System.Windows.Forms.Application.ThreadException` event *and* the `System.appdomain.UnhandledException` event. Both of these events need to be hooked up, as the WinForms support in the Framework does a lot of exception trapping itself. It exposes the `System.Windows.Forms.Application.ThreadException` event to allow you to get any unhandled exceptions that happen on the UI thread that the WinForms and their events are running on. In spite of its deceptive name, the `System.Windows.Forms.Application.ThreadException` event handler will *not* catch unhandled exceptions on worker threads constructed by the program or from `ThreadPool` threads. In order to catch all of those possible routes for unhandled exceptions in a WinForms application, you need to hook up a handler for the `System.appdomain.UnhandledException` event that does catch those (but not the UI thread ones that `System.Windows.Forms.Application.ThreadException` does).

To hook up the necessary event handlers to catch all of your unhandled exceptions in a WinForms application, add the following code to the `Main` function in your application:

```
static void Main()
{
    // Adds the event handler to catch any exceptions that happen
    // in the main UI thread.
    Application.ThreadException +=
        new ThreadExceptionEventHandler(OnThreadException);

    // Add the event handler for all threads in the appdomain except
    // for the main UI thread.
    appdomain.CurrentDomain.UnhandledException +=
        new UnhandledExceptionEventHandler(CurrentDomain_UnhandledException);

    Application.EnableVisualStyles();
    Application.Run(new Form1());
}
```

The `System.AppDomain.UnhandledException` event handler is hooked up to the current Appdomain by using the `appdomain.CurrentDomain` property, which gives access to the current Appdomain. The `ThreadException` handler for the application is accessed through the `Application.ThreadException` property.

The event handler code is established in the `CurrentDomain_UnhandledException` and `OnThreadException` handler methods. See Recipe 7.4 for more information on the `UnhandledExceptionEventHandler`. The `ThreadExceptionEventHandler` is passed the sender object and a `ThreadExceptionEventArgs` object. `ThreadExceptionEventArgs` has an `Exception` property that contains the unhandled exception from the WinForms UI thread:

```
// Handles the exception event for all other threads
static void CurrentDomain_UnhandledException(object sender,
                                UnhandledExceptionEventArgs e)
{
    // Just show the exception details.
    MessageBox.Show("CurrentDomain_UnhandledException: " +
            e.ExceptionObject.ToString( ));
}

// Handles the exception event from a UI thread
static void OnThreadException(object sender, ThreadExceptionEventArgs t)
{
    // Just show the exception details.
    MessageBox.Show("OnThreadException: " + t.Exception.ToString( ));
}
```

Discussion

Exceptions are the primary way to convey errors in .NET, so when you build an application, it is imperative that there be a final line of defense against unhandled exceptions. An unhandled exception will crash the program (even if it looks a bit nicer in .NET); this is not the impression you wish to make on your customers. It would have been nice to have one event to hook up to for all unhandled exceptions. The `appdomain.UnhandledException` event comes pretty close to that, but having to do handle one extra event isn't the end of the world, either. In coding event handlers for both `appdomain.UnhandledException` and `Application.ThreadException`, you can easily call a single handler that writes the exception information to the event log, the debug stream, or custom trace logs or even sends you an email with the information. The possibilities are limited only by how you want to handle errors that can happen to any program given enough exposure.

See Also

Recipe 7.4; see the "Error Raising and Handling Guidelines," "Thread-Exception-EventHandler Delegate," and "UnhandledExceptionEventHandler Delegate" topics in the MSDN documentation.

7.13   Dealing with Unhandled Exceptions in Windows Presentation Foundation (WPF) Applications

Problem

You have a Windows Presentation Foundation-based (WPF) application in which you want to catch and log any unhandled exceptions on any thread.

Solution

To hook up the necessary event handlers to catch all of your unhandled exceptions in a WPF application, add the following code to the App.xaml file in your application:

```
<Application x:Class="UnhandledWPFException.App"
    xmlns="http://schemas.microsoft.com/winfx/2006/xaml/presentation"
    xmlns:x="http://schemas.microsoft.com/winfx/2006/xaml"
    StartupUri="Window1.xaml"
    DispatcherUnhandledException="Application_DispatcherUnhandledException">
    <Application.MainWindow>
        <Window />
    </Application.MainWindow>
    <Application.Resources>

    </Application.Resources>
</Application>
```

Then, in the code behind file App.xaml.cs, add the Application_DispatcherUnhandledException method to handle otherwise unhandled exceptions:

```
private void Application_DispatcherUnhandledException(object sender,
        System.Windows.Threading.DispatcherUnhandledExceptionEventArgs e)
{
    // Log the exception information in the event log
    EventLog.WriteEntry("UnhandledWPFException Application",
        e.Exception.ToString(), EventLogEntryType.Error);
    // Let the user know what happenned
    MessageBox.Show("Application_DispatcherUnhandledException: " + e.Exception.
ToString());
    // indicate we handled it
    e.Handled = true;
    // shut down the application
    this.Shutdown();
}
```

Discussion

Windows Presentation Foundation provides another way to create Windows-based applications for the .NET platform and is the future of rich client user experience on .NET going forward. While WinForms may not go away for quite a while, Microsoft is definitely pushing forward with WPF. In order to protect users from unsightly unhandled exceptions, a bit of code is necessary in WPF as in WinForms (see Recipe 7.12 for doing this in WinForms).

The System.Windows.Application class is the base class for WPF-based applications, and it is from that the unhandled exceptions are handled via the DispatcherUnhandledException event. This event handler is set up by specifying the method to handle the event in the App.xaml file shown here:

```
DispatcherUnhandledException="Application_DispatcherUnhandledException">
```

This can also be set up in code directly instead of doing it the XAML way by adding the Startup event handler (which is where initialization code for the Application is recommended to go in WPF) to the XAML file like this:

```
<Application x:Class="UnhandledWPFException.App"
    xmlns="http://schemas.microsoft.com/winfx/2006/xaml/presentation"
    xmlns:x="http://schemas.microsoft.com/winfx/2006/xaml"
    StartupUri="Window1.xaml"
  Startup="Application_Startup" >
    <Application.MainWindow>
        <Window />
    </Application.MainWindow>
    <Application.Resources>

    </Application.Resources>
</Application>
```

In the Startup event, establish the event handler for the DispatcherUnhandledException like this:

```
private void Application_Startup(object sender, StartupEventArgs e)
{
    this.DispatcherUnhandledException +=
        new System.Windows.Threading.DispatcherUnhandledExceptionEventHandler(
            Application_DispatcherUnhandledException);
}
```

This is great for handling exceptions for WPF applications, just hook up and get all those unhandled exceptions delivered to your single handler, right? Wrong. Just as was necessary in WinForms applications, if you have any code running on any threads other than the UI thread (which you almost always will), you still have to hook up to the AppDomain for the AppDomain.UnhandledException handler to catch those exceptions on threads other than the UI thread. In order to do that, our App.xaml.cs file now looks like this:

```
/// <summary>
/// Interaction logic for App.xaml
/// </summary>
public partial class App : Application
{
    private void Application_DispatcherUnhandledException(object sender,
        System.Windows.Threading.DispatcherUnhandledExceptionEventArgs e)
    {
```

```
        // indicate we handled it
        e.Handled = true;
        ReportUnhandledException(e.Exception);
    }

    private void Application_Startup(object sender, StartupEventArgs e)
    {
        // WPF UI exceptions
        this.DispatcherUnhandledException +=
            new System.Windows.Threading.DispatcherUnhandledExceptionEventHandler(
                Application_DispatcherUnhandledException);

        // Those dirty thread exceptions
        AppDomain.CurrentDomain.UnhandledException +=
            new UnhandledExceptionEventHandler(CurrentDomain_UnhandledException);
    }

    private void CurrentDomain_UnhandledException(object sender,
                                    UnhandledExceptionEventArgs e)
    {
        ReportUnhandledException(e.ExceptionObject as Exception);
    }

    private void ReportUnhandledException(Exception ex)
    {
        // Log the exception information in the event log
        EventLog.WriteEntry("UnhandledWPFException Application",
            ex.ToString(), EventLogEntryType.Error);
        // Let the user know what happenned
        MessageBox.Show("Unhandled Exception: " + ex.ToString());
        // shut down the application
        this.Shutdown();
    }
}
```

See Also

Recipe 7.12; see the "DispatcherUnhandledException event," and "AppDomain. UnhandledException handler," topics in the MSDN documentation.

7.14   Analyzing Exceptions for Common Errors

Problem

You have an exception that may have multiple nested inner exceptions, and you need a quick way to analyze them for common or well-known errors.

Solution

Use the GetNestedExceptionList extension method provided here with any Exception to retrieve an IEnumerable<Exception> list of all of the exceptions in the inner exception tree. Once this information is in list format, use Language Integrated Query (LINQ) to isolate common issues:

```
public static IEnumerable<Exception> GetNestedExceptionList(this Exception exception)
{
    Exception current = exception;
    do
    {
        current = current.InnerException;
        if (current != null)
            yield return current;
    }
    while (current != null);
}
```

An example of how this can be used in conjunction with LINQ to find well-known exceptions is listed below:

```
// simulate an exception chain unwinding
// hit a bad reference
NullReferenceException nrex = new NullReferenceException("Touched a bad object");
nrex.Data.Add("Bad ObjectID", "0x34874573");
// have an error formatting a message for it
FormatException fex = new FormatException("Resulted from Null Reference", nrex);
// mask it as part of a data layer
ApplicationException appex =
    new ApplicationException("There was an error in the data layer.",fex);
// hit another error reformatting the exception information
FormatException fmtEx =
    new FormatException("Error formatting error message.", appex);

// Use LINQ to look for common or well-known problems in the app
var query = from ex in fmtEx.GetNestedExceptionList()
            where ex is NullReferenceException ||
                  ex is OutOfMemoryException ||
                  ex is ThreadAbortException
            select ex;
// report if any of the common or well-known errors were found
foreach (Exception ex in query)
{
    Console.WriteLine("Found common exception (" + ex.GetType() +
        ") with message: " + ex.Message);
}
```

Discussion

Diagnosing exceptions in applications that have a higher level of complexity can sometimes be a challenge even when best practices for exception handling and management are followed. Call stacks get deep, layers are built for separation and masking, and then, all of a sudden, the error reported is not necessarily the root cause of the problem. This recipe is designed to help in situations where nested exceptions mask the problem more often than not, as there is another layer or two between where the error is reported and where it occurred. Good exception logging and handling practices can help cut down these instances, but ultimately, in complex applications, you will eventually get a tree of exceptions that needs deciphering. Having some analytics built into your unhandled exception handlers might just give you an edge in figuring out that production bug, so spend a while thinking about what kinds of root cause exceptions are encountered in your applications to make life easier later on.

See Also

The "extension methods" and "Exception Handling" topics in the MSDN documentation.

CHAPTER 8

Diagnostics

8.0   Introduction

The .NET Framework Class Library (FCL) contains many classes to obtain diagnostic information about your application, as well as the environment it is running in. In fact, there are so many classes that a namespace, `System.Diagnostics`, was created to contain all of them. This chapter contains recipes for instrumenting your application with debug/trace information, obtaining process information, using the built-in event log, and taking advantage of performance counters.

Debugging (using the `Debug` class) is turned on by default in debug builds only, and tracing (using the `Trace` class) is turned on by default in both debug and release builds. These defaults allow you to ship your application instrumented with tracing code using the `Trace` class. You ship your code with tracing compiled in but turned off in the configuration so that the tracing code is not called (for performance reasons) unless it is a server-side application (where the value of the instrumentation may outweigh the performance hit). If a problem that you cannot re-create on your development computer occurs on a production machine, you can enable tracing and allow the tracing information to be dumped to a file. This file can be inspected to help pinpoint the real problem. This usage is discussed at length in Recipes 8.1 and 8.2.

Since both the `Debug` and `Trace` classes contain the same members with the same names, they can be interchanged in your code by renaming `Debug` to `Trace` and vice versa. Most of the recipes in this chapter use the `Trace` class; you can modify those recipes so that they use the `Debug` class by replacing each `Trace` with `Debug` in the code.

8.1 Providing Fine-Grained Control over Debugging/Tracing Output

Problem

Your application consists of multiple components. You need, at specific times, to turn on debug/trace output for a select few components, while leaving all other debug/trace output turned off. In addition, you need control over the type and amount of information that is produced by the Trace/Debug statements.

Solution

Use the BooleanSwitch class with an application configuration file (*.config*). The following method creates three switches for your application: one that controls tracing for database calls, one that controls tracing for UI components, and one that controls tracing for any exceptions that are thrown by the application:

```
public class Traceable
{
    BooleanSwitch DBSwitch = null;
    BooleanSwitch UISwitch = null;
    BooleanSwitch exceptionSwitch = null;

    [System.Diagnostics.ConditionalAttribute("TRACE")]
    public void EnableTracing( )
    {

        DBSwitch = new BooleanSwitch("DatabaseSwitch",
                "Switch for database tracing");
        Console.WriteLine("DBSwitch Enabled = " + DBSwitch.Enabled);

        UISwitch = new BooleanSwitch("UISwitch",
                "Switch for user interface tracing");
        Console.WriteLine("UISwitch Enabled = " + UISwitch.Enabled);

        exceptionSwitch = new BooleanSwitch("ExceptionSwitch",
                    "Switch for tracing thrown exceptions");
        Console.WriteLine("ExceptionSwitch Enabled = " + exceptionSwitch.
Enabled);
    }
}
```

After creating each switch, the Enabled property is displayed, indicating whether the switch is on or off.

Creating these switches without an application configuration file results in every switch being disabled. To control what state each switch is set to, use an application configuration file, as shown here:

```
<?xml version="1.0" encoding="utf-8" ?>
<configuration>
```

```
        <system.diagnostics>
            <switches>
                <clear/>
                <add name="DatabaseSwitch" value="1" />
                <add name="UISwitch" value="0" />
                <add name="ExceptionSwitch" value="0" />
            </switches>
        </system.diagnostics>
    </configuration>
```

The TraceSwitch class can also be used with an application configuration file (*App-Name.exe.config*). The following method creates a new TraceSwitch object with a level assigned by the application configuration file:

```
public class Traceable
{
    TraceSwitch DBFilterSwitch = null;
    TraceSwitch UIFilterSwitch = null;
    TraceSwitch exceptionFilterSwitch = null;

    public void SetTracingFilter()
    {
        DBFilterSwitch = new TraceSwitch("DatabaseFilter",
                        "Filter database output");
        Console.WriteLine("DBFilterSwitch Level = " + DBFilterSwitch.Level);

        UIFilterSwitch = new TraceSwitch("UIFilter",
                        "Filter user interface output");
        Console.WriteLine("UIFilterSwitch Level = " + UIFilterSwitch.Level);

        exceptionFilterSwitch = new TraceSwitch("ExceptionFilter",
                            "Filter exception output");
        Console.WriteLine("exceptionFilterSwitch Level = "
                        + exceptionFilterSwitch.Level);
    }
}
```

After creating each filter switch, the Level property is displayed to indicate the switch's level.

Creating these switches at this point results in every switch's level being set to zero. To turn them on, use an application configuration file, as shown here:

```
<?xml version="1.0" encoding="utf-8" ?>
<configuration>
    <system.diagnostics>
        <switches>
            <clear/>
            <add name="DatabaseFilter" value="4" />
            <add name="UIFilter" value="0" />
            <add name="ExceptionFilter" value="1" />
        </switches>
    </system.diagnostics>
</configuration>
```

This XML file contains a nested tag called switches. This tag defines switch names and sets a value indicating the level of the switch. The TraceSwitch class accepts the five predefined trace levels shown in Table 8-1. The level of the TraceSwitch can be set through code, but that defeats the flexibility of using a configuration file.

Table 8-1. The TraceSwitch class's tracing levels

Level name	Value	Default
Off	0	Yes
Error	1	No
Warning	2	No
Info	3	No
Verbose	4	No

For more information on the application configuration file, see Recipe 8.0.

Discussion

Turning tracing on or off involves the BooleanSwitch class. When the BooleanSwitch is created, it attempts to locate a switch with the same name as the *displayName* parameter in either the *machine.config* or application configuration file. If it cannot locate this name in either file, BooleanSwitch.Enabled is set to false.

The application configuration file for a WinForms- or Console-based application is an XML file named with the assembly's name followed by *.exe.config*. An ASP.NET-based web application can have multiple *web.config* files (one in each directory of the application). An application will automatically use the configuration file(s) that is (are) appropriate; however, the top-level configuration file must be in the same main directory as the application. Notice the switches tag nested inside the system. diagnostics element. This tag allows switches to be added and their values set. For Boolean switches, a zero turns the switch off, and any other positive or negative number turns it on. The Enabled property of the BooleanSwitch can be set through code or by setting the value in the config file.

This XML file must have the same name as the executable using these switches, followed by *.config*. For example, if the executable name were *Accounting.exe*, the configuration file would be named *Accounting.exe.config*. This file should be placed in the same directory as the executable *Accounting.exe*.

The application configuration file can also set trace and debug output levels in this same switches tag. These levels identify the scope of the output, for example, if the output will contain only warnings, only errors, only informational messages, or some combination thereof. The level specified is the maximum trace level for the switch, so it includes all levels below it up through that level. Of course, this is only an example; you may define your own levels as well. For more information on controlling these output levels, see Recipe 8.2.

The TraceSwitch class operates similarly to the BooleanSwitch class, except that the TraceSwitch class encapsulates the available levels that control the type and amount of debug/trace output. The BooleanSwitch class is simply an on/off switch used to enable or disable debugging/tracing.

When the TraceSwitch is created, it attempts to locate a switch with the same name as the *displayName* parameter in either the *machine.config* or application configuration files. If it cannot locate this name in either file, the TraceSwitch.Level property is set to zero.

The application configuration file can also enable or disable trace and debug output in this same switches tag.

See Also

Recipes 8.0 and 8.2; see the "BooleanSwitch Class" and "trace and debug Settings Schema" topics in the MSDN documentation.

8.2   Determining Whether a Process Has Stopped Responding

Problem

You need to watch one or more processes to determine whether the user interface has stopped responding to the system. This functionality is similar to the column in the TaskManager that displays the text Responding or Not Responding, depending on the state of the application.

Solution

Use the method and enumeration shown in Example 8-1 to determine whether a process has stopped responding.

Example 8-1. Determining whether a process has stopped responding

```
public static ProcessRespondingState IsProcessResponding(Process process)
{
    if (process.MainWindowHandle == IntPtr.Zero)
    {
        Trace.WriteLine("{0} does not have a MainWindowHandle",
            process.ProcessName);
        return ProcessRespondingState.Unknown;
    }
    else
    {
```

```
        // This process has a MainWindowHandle.
        if (!process.Responding)
        {
            Trace.WriteLine("{0} is not responding.",process.ProcessName);
            return ProcessRespondingState.NotResponding;
        }
        else
        {
            Trace.WriteLine("{0} is responding.",process.ProcessName);
            return ProcessRespondingState.Responding;
        }
    }
}

public enum ProcessRespondingState
{
    Responding,
    NotResponding,
    Unknown
}
```

Discussion

The IsProcessResponding method accepts a single parameter, *process*, identifying a process. The Responding property is then called on the Process object represented by the *process* parameter. This property returns a ProcessRespondingState enumeration value to indicate that a process is currently responding (Responding), that it is not currently responding (NotResponding), or that response cannot be determined for this process as there is no main window handle (Unknown).

The Responding property always returns true if the process in question does not have a MainWindowHandle. Processes such as Idle, spoolsv, Rundll32, and svchost do not have a main window handle, and therefore the Responding property always returns true for them. To weed out these processes, you can use the MainWindowHandle property of the Process class, which returns the handle of the main window for a process. If this property returns zero, the process has no main window.

To determine whether all processes on a machine are responding, you can call the IsProcessResponding method as follows:

```
    MyObject.ProcessRespondingState state;
    foreach (Process proc in Process.GetProcesses())
    {
        state = MyObject.IsProcessResponding(proc);
        if (state == MyObject.ProcessRespondingState.NotResponding)
        {
            Console.WriteLine("{0} is not responding.",proc.ProcessName);
        }
    }
```

This code snippet iterates over all processes currently running on your system. The static GetProcesses method of the Process class takes no parameters and returns an array of Process objects with information for all processes running on your system. Each Process object is then passed in to your IsProcessResponding method to determine whether it is responding. Other static methods on the Process class that retrieve Process objects are GetProcessById, GetCurrentProcess, and GetProcessesByName.

See Also

See the "Process Class" topic in the MSDN documentation.

8.3 Using Event Logs in Your Application

Problem

You need to add the ability for your application to log events that occur in your application, such as startup, shutdown, critical errors, and even security breaches. Along with reading and writing to a log, you need the ability to create, clear, close, and remove logs from the event log.

Your application might need to keep track of several logs at one time. For example, your application might use a custom log to track specific events, such as startup and shutdown, as they occur in your application. To supplement the custom log, your application could make use of the security log already built into the event log system to read/write security events that occur in your application.

Support for multiple logs comes in handy when one log needs to be created and maintained on the local computer and another duplicate log needs to be created and maintained on a remote machine. This remote machine might contain logs of all running instances of your application on each user's machine. An administrator could use these logs to quickly find any problems that occur or discover if security is breached in your application. In fact, an application could be run in the background on the remote administrative machine that watches for specific log entries to be written to this log from any user's machine. Recipe 8.8 uses an event mechanism to watch for entries written to an event log and could easily be used to enhance this recipe.

Solution

Use the event log built into the Microsoft Windows operating system to record specific events that occur infrequently. The AppEvents class shown in Example 8-2 contains all the methods needed to create and use an event log in your application.

Example 8-2. Creating and using an event log

```
using System;
using System.Diagnostics;

public class AppEvents
{
    // Constructors
    public AppEvents(string logName) :
        this(logName, Process.GetCurrentProcess( ).ProcessName, ".") {}

    public AppEvents(string logName, string source) : this(logName, source, ".") {}

    public AppEvents(string logName, string source, string machineName)
    {
        this.logName = logName;
        this.source = source;
        this.machineName = machineName;

        if (!EventLog.SourceExists(source, machineName))
        {
            EventSourceCreationData sourceData =
                new EventSourceCreationData(source, logName);
            sourceData.MachineName = machineName;

            EventLog.CreateEventSource(sourceData);
        }

        log = new EventLog(logName, machineName, source);
        log.EnableRaisingEvents = true;
    }

    // Fields
    private EventLog log = null;
    private string source = "";
    private string logName = "";
    private string machineName = ".";

    // Properties
    public string Name
    {
        get{return (logName);}
    }

    public string SourceName
    {
        get{return (source);}
    }

    public string Machine
    {
        get{return (machineName);}
    }
```

Example 8-2. Creating and using an event log (continued)

```csharp
// Methods
public void WriteToLog(string message, EventLogEntryType type,
    CategoryType category, EventIDType eventID)
{
    if (log == null)
    {
        throw (new ArgumentNullException("log",
            "This Event Log has not been opened or has been closed."));
    }

    log.WriteEntry(message, type, (int)eventID, (short)category);
}

public void WriteToLog(string message, EventLogEntryType type,
    CategoryType category, EventIDType eventID, byte[] rawData)
{
    if (log == null)
    {
        throw (new ArgumentNullException("log",
            "This Event Log has not been opened or has been closed."));
    }

    log.WriteEntry(message, type, (int)eventID, (short)category, rawData);
}

public EventLogEntryCollection GetEntries()
{
    if (log == null)
    {
        throw (new ArgumentNullException("log",
            "This Event Log has not been opened or has been closed."));
    }

    return (log.Entries);
}

public void ClearLog()
{
    if (log == null)
    {
        throw (new ArgumentNullException("log",
            "This Event Log has not been opened or has been closed."));
    }

    log.Clear();
}

public void CloseLog()
{
    if (log == null)
    {
        throw (new ArgumentNullException("log",
```

Example 8-2. Creating and using an event log (continued)

```
                "This Event Log has not been opened or has been closed."));
        }
        log.Close( );
        log = null;
    }

    public void DeleteLog( )
    {
        if (EventLog.SourceExists(source, machineName))
        {
            EventLog.DeleteEventSource(source, machineName);
        }

        if (logName != "Application" &&
            logName != "Security" &&
            logName != "System")
        {
            if (EventLog.Exists(logName, machineName))
            {
                EventLog.Delete(logName, machineName);
            }
        }

        if (log != null)
        {
            log.Close( );
            log = null;
        }
    }
}
```

The EventIDType and CategoryType enumerations used in this class are defined as follows:

```
public enum EventIDType
{
    NA = 0,
    Read = 1,
    Write = 2,
    ExceptionThrown = 3,
    BufferOverflowCondition = 4,
    SecurityFailure = 5,
    SecurityPotentiallyCompromised = 6
}

public enum CategoryType : short
{
    None = 0,
    WriteToDB = 1,
    ReadFromDB = 2,
    WriteToFile = 3,
    ReadFromFile = 4,
```

```
        AppStartUp = 5,
        AppShutDown = 6,
        UserInput = 7
    }
```

Discussion

The AppEvents class created for this recipe provides applications with an easy-to-use interface for creating, using, and deleting single or multiple event logs in your application. Support for multiple logs comes in handy when one log needs to be created and maintained on the local computer and another duplicate log needs to be created and maintained on a remote machine. This remote machine might contain logs of all running instances of your application on each user's machine. An administrator could use these logs to quickly discover if any problems occur or if security is breached in your application. In fact, an application could be run in the background on the remote administrative machine that watches for specific log entries to be written to this log from any user's machine. Recipe 8.8 uses an event mechanism to watch for entries written to an event log and could easily be used to enhance this recipe.

The methods of the AppEvents class are described as follows:

WriteToLog
> This method is overloaded to allow an entry to be written to the event log with or without a byte array containing raw data.

GetEntries
> Returns all the event log entries for this event log in an EventLogEntryCollection.

ClearLog
> Removes all the event log entries from this event log.

CloseLog
> Closes this event log, preventing further interaction with it.

DeleteLog
> Deletes this event log and the associated event log source.

An AppEvents object can be added to an array or collection containing other AppEvents objects; each AppEvents object corresponds to a particular event log. The following code creates two AppEvents classes and adds them to a ListDictionary collection:

```
public void CreateMultipleLogs( )
{
    AppEvents AppEventLog = new AppEvents("AppLog", "AppLocal");
    AppEvents GlobalEventLog = new AppEvents("System", "AppGlobal");

    ListDictionary LogList = new ListDictionary( );
    LogList.Add(AppEventLog.Name, AppEventLog);
    LogList.Add(GlobalEventLog.Name, GlobalEventLog);
}
```

To write to either of these two logs, obtain the AppEvents object by name from the ListDictionary object, cast the resultant object type to an AppEvents type, and call the WriteToLog method:

```
((AppEvents)LogList[AppEventLog.Name]).WriteToLog("App startup",
    EventLogEntryType.Information, CategoryType.AppStartUp,
    EventIDType.ExceptionThrown);

((AppEvents)LogList[GlobalEventLog.Name]).WriteToLog("App startup security
check",
    EventLogEntryType.Information, CategoryType.AppStartUp,
    EventIDType.BufferOverflowCondition);
```

Containing all AppEvents objects in a ListDictionary object allows you to easily iterate over all the AppEvents that your application has instantiated. Using a foreach loop, you can write a single message to both a local and a remote event log:

```
foreach (DictionaryEntry Log in LogList)
{
    ((AppEvents)Log.Value).WriteToLog("App startup",
        EventLogEntryType.FailureAudit,
        CategoryType.AppStartUp, EventIDType.SecurityFailure);
}
```

To delete each log in the logList object, you can use the following foreach loop:

```
foreach (DictionaryEntry Log in LogList)
{
    ((AppEvents)Log.Value).DeleteLog();
}
LogList.Clear();
```

You should be aware of several key points. The first concerns a small problem with constructing multiple AppEvents classes. If you create two AppEvents objects and pass in the same source string to the AppEvents constructor, an exception will be thrown. Consider the following code, which instantiates two AppEvents objects with the same source string:

```
AppEvents appEventLog = new AppEvents("AppLog", "AppLocal");
AppEvents globalEventLog = new AppEvents("Application", "AppLocal");
```

The objects are instantiated without errors, but when the WriteToLog method is called on the globalEventLog object, the following exception is thrown:

```
An unhandled exception of type 'System.ArgumentException' occurred in system.dll.

    Additional information: The source 'AppLocal' is not registered in log
'Application'.
    (It is registered in log 'AppLog'.) " The Source and Log properties must be
matched,
    or you may set Log to the empty string, and it will automatically be matched to
the
    Source property.
```

This exception occurs because the WriteToLog method internally calls the WriteEntry method of the EventLog object. The WriteEntry method internally checks to see whether the specified source is registered to the log you are attempting to write to. In this case, the AppLocal source was registered to the first log it was assigned to—the AppLog log. The second attempt to register this same source to another log, Application, failed silently. You do not know that this attempt failed until you try to use the WriteEntry method of the EventLog object.

Another key point about the AppEvents class is the following code, placed at the beginning of each method (except for the DeleteLog method):

```
if (log == null)
{
    throw (new ArgumentNullException("log",
        "This Event Log has not been opened or has been closed."));
}
```

This code checks to see whether the private member variable log is a null reference. If so, an ArgumentException is thrown, informing the user of this class that a problem occurred with the creation of the EventLog object. The DeleteLog method does not check the log variable for null since it deletes the event log source and the event log itself. The EventLog object is not involved in this process except at the end of this method, where the log is closed and set to null, if it is not already null. Regardless of the state of the log variable, the source and event log should be deleted in this method.

The DeleteLog method makes a critical choice when determining whether to delete a log. The following code prevents the application, security, and system event logs from being deleted from your system:

```
if (logName != "Application" &&
    logName != "Security" &&
    logName != "System")
{
    if (EventLog.Exists(logName, machineName))
    {
        EventLog.Delete(logName, machineName);
    }
}
```

If any of these logs is deleted, so are the sources registered with the particular log. Once the log is deleted, it is permanent; believe us, it is not fun to try and re-create the log and its sources without a backup.

As a last note, the EventIDType and CategoryType enumerations are designed mainly to log security-type breaches as well as potential attacks on the security of your application. Using these event IDs and categories, the administrator can more easily track down potential security threats and do postmortem analysis after security is breached. These enumerations can easily be modified or replaced with your own to allow you to track different events that occur as a result of your application running.

You should minimize the number of entries written to the event log from your application. The reason for this is that writing to the event log causes a performance hit. Writing too much information to the event log can noticeably slow your application. Pick and choose the entries you write to the event log wisely.

See Also

Recipe 8.8, and the "EventLog Class" topic in the MSDN documentation.

8.4   Searching Event Log Entries

Problem

Your application might have added many entries to the event log. To perform an analysis of how the application operated, how many errors were encountered, and so on, you need to be able to perform a search through all of the entries in an event log. Unfortunately, there are no good built-in search mechanisms for event logs.

Solution

You will eventually have to sift through all the entries your application writes to an event log in order to find the entries that allow you to perhaps fix a bug or improve your application's security system. Unfortunately, there are no good search mechanisms for event logs. This recipe contains an EventLogSearch class to which you'll add static methods, allowing you to search for entries in an event log based on various criteria. In addition, this search mechanism allows complex searches involving multiple criteria to be performed on an event log at one time. The code for the EventSearchLog class is shown in Example 8-3.

Example 8-3. EventSearchLog class

```
using System;
using System.Collections;
using System.Diagnostics;

public sealed class EventLogSearch
{
    private EventLogSearch( ) {}  // Prevent this class from being instantiated.

    public static EventLogEntry[] FindTimeGeneratedAtOrBefore(
        IEnumerable logEntries, DateTime timeGeneratedQuery)
    {
        ArrayList entries = new ArrayList( );

        foreach (EventLogEntry logEntry in logEntries)
        {
            if (logEntry.TimeGenerated <= timeGeneratedQuery)
```

Example 8-3. EventSearchLog class (continued)

```
            {
                entries.Add(logEntry);
            }
        }

        EventLogEntry[] entriesArray = new EventLogEntry[entries.Count];
        entries.CopyTo(entriesArray);
        return (entriesArray);
    }

    public static EventLogEntry[] FindTimeGeneratedAtOrAfter(
        IEnumerable logEntries, DateTime timeGeneratedQuery)
    {
        ArrayList entries = new ArrayList( );

        foreach (EventLogEntry logEntry in logEntries)
        {
            if (logEntry.TimeGenerated >= timeGeneratedQuery)
            {
                entries.Add(logEntry);
            }
        }

        EventLogEntry[] entriesArray = new EventLogEntry[entries.Count];
        entries.CopyTo(entriesArray);
        return (entriesArray);
    }
}
```

Discussion

Other searchable criteria can be added to this class by following the same coding pattern for each search method. For instance, the following example shows how to add a search method to find all entries that contain a particular username:

```
public static EventLogEntry[] FindUserName(IEnumerable logEntries,
    string userNameQuery)
{
    ArrayList entries = new ArrayList( );

    foreach (EventLogEntry logEntry in logEntries)
    {
        if (logEntry.UserName == userNameQuery)
        {
            entries.Add(logEntry);
        }
    }

    EventLogEntry[] entriesArray = new EventLogEntry[entries.Count];
    entries.CopyTo(entriesArray);
    return (entriesArray);
}
```

The methods shown in Table 8-2 list other search methods that could be included in this class and describe which property of the event log entries they search on. (All of these methods are implemented on the code for this book, which can be found at *http://www.oreilly.com/catalog/9780596516109.*)

Table 8-2. Other possible search methods

Search method name	Entry property searched
FindCategory (overloaded to accept a string type category name)	Category == CategoryNameQuery
FindCategory (overloaded to accept a short type category number)	Category == CategoryNumberQuery
FindEntryType	EntryType == EntryTypeQuery
FindInstanceID	InstanceID == InstanceIDQuery
FindMachineName	MachineName == MachineNameQuery
FindMessage	Message == Message.Query
FindSource	Source == SourceQuery

The FindCategory method can be overloaded to search on either the category name or category number.

The following method makes use of the EventLogSearch methods to find and display entries that are marked as Error log entries:

```
public void FindAnEntryInEventLog()
{
    EventLog Log = new EventLog("System");

    EventLogEntry[] Entries = EventLogSearch.FindEntryType(Log.Entries,
        EventLogEntryType.Error);

    foreach (EventLogEntry Entry in Entries)
    {
        Console.WriteLine("Message:      " + Entry.Message);
        Console.WriteLine("InstanceId:   " + Entry.InstanceId);
        Console.WriteLine("Category:     " + Entry.Category);
        Console.WriteLine("EntryType:    " + Entry.EntryType.ToString());
        Console.WriteLine("Source:       " + Entry.Source);
    }
}
```

The following method finds and displays entries generated at or after 8/3/2003, marked as Error type logs, and containing an event ID of 7000:

```
public void FindAnEntryInEventLog()
{
    EventLog Log = new EventLog("System");

    EventLogEntry[] Entries = EventLogSearch.FindTimeGeneratedAtOrAfter(Log.
Entries,
```

```
        DateTime.Parse("8/3/2003"));
    Entries = EventLogSearch.FindEntryType(Entries, EventLogEntryType.Error);
    Entries = EventLogSearch.FindInstanceId(Entries, 7000);

    foreach (EventLogEntry Entry in Entries)
    {
        Console.WriteLine("Message:        " + Entry.Message);
        Console.WriteLine("InstanceId:     " + Entry.InstanceId);
        Console.WriteLine("Category:       " + Entry.Category);
        Console.WriteLine("EntryType:      " + Entry.EntryType.ToString());
        Console.WriteLine("Source:         " + Entry.Source);
    }
}
```

Note that this search mechanism can search within only one event log at a time.

To illustrate how searching works, let's assume that you are using the
FindInstanceID method to search on the InstanceID. Initially, you would call the
FindInstanceID search method, passing in a collection that implements the
IEnumerable interface, such as the EventLogEntryCollection collection (that contains
all entries in that event log) or an array of EventLogEntry objects. The
EventLogEntryCollection is returned by the Entries property of the EventLog class.
The FindInstanceID method will return an array of EventLogEntry objects that match
the search criteria (the value passed in to the second argument of the FindInstanceID
method).

The real power of this searching method design is that the initial search on the
EventLogEntryCollection returns an array of EventLogEntry objects. This
EventLogEntry array may then be passed back into another search method to be
searched again, effectively narrowing down the search query. For example, the
EventLogEntry array returned from the FindInstanceID method may be passed into
another search method such as the FindEntryType method to narrow down the search
to all entries that are a specific entry type (informational, error, etc.).

See Also

The "EventLog Class" and "EventLogEntry Class" topics in the MSDN documentation.

8.5   Watching the Event Log for a Specific Entry

Problem

You may have multiple applications that write to a single event log. For each of these
applications, you want a monitoring application to watch for one or more specific
log entries to be written to the event log. For example, you might want to watch for a
log entry that indicates that an application encountered a critical error or shut down
unexpectedly. These log entries should be reported in real time.

Solution

Monitoring an event log for a specific entry requires the following steps:

1. Create the following method to set up the event handler to handle event log writes:

```
public void WatchForAppEvent(EventLog log)
{
    log.EnableRaisingEvents = true;
    // Hook up the System.Diagnostics.EntryWrittenEventHandler.
    log.EntryWritten += new EntryWrittenEventHandler(OnEntryWritten);
}
```

2. Create the event handler to examine the log entries and determine whether further action is to be performed. For example:

```
public static void OnEntryWritten(object source,
                                  EntryWrittenEventArgs entryArg)
{
    if (entryArg.Entry.EntryType == EventLogEntryType.Error)
    {
        Console.WriteLine(entryArg.Entry.Message);
        Console.WriteLine(entryArg.Entry.Category);
        Console.WriteLine(entryArg.Entry.EntryType.ToString());
        // Do further actions here as necessary...
    }
}
```

Discussion

This recipe revolves around the EntryWrittenEventHandler delegate, which calls back a method whenever any new entry is written to the event log. The EntryWrittenEventHandler delegate accepts two arguments: a *source* of type object and an *entryArg* of type EntryWrittenEventArgs. The *entryArg* parameter is the most interesting of the two. It contains a property called Entry that returns an EventLogEntry object. This EventLogEntry object contains all the information you need concerning the entry that was written to the event log.

This event log that you are watching is passed as the WatchForAppEvent method's *log* parameter. This method performs two actions. First, it sets log's EnableRaisingEvents property to true. If this property were set to false, no events would be raised for this event log when an entry is written to it. The second action this method performs is to add the OnEntryWritten callback method to the list of event handlers for this event log.

To prevent this delegate from calling the OnEntryWritten callback method, you can set the EnableRaisingEvents property to false, effectively turning off the delegate.

Note that the Entry object passed to the entryArg parameter of the OnEntryWritten callback method is read-only, so the entry cannot be modified before it is written to the event log.

See Also

The "Handling the EntryWritten Event" and "EventLog.EntryWritten Event" topics in the MSDN documentation.

8.6   Implementing a Simple Performance Counter

Problem

You need to use a performance counter to track application-specific information. The simpler performance counters find, for example, the change in a counter value between successive samplings or just count the number of times an action occurs. Other, more complex counters exist but are not dealt with in this recipe. For example, a custom counter could be built to keep track of the number of database transactions, the number of failed network connections to a server, or even the number of users connecting to your web service per minute.

Solution

Create a simple performance counter that finds, for example, the change in a counter value between successive samplings or that just counts the number of times an action occurs. Use the following method (CreateSimpleCounter) to create a simple custom counter:

```
public PerformanceCounter CreateSimpleCounter(string counterName, string
counterHelp,
    System.Diagnostics.PerformanceCounterType counterType, string categoryName,
    string categoryHelp)
{
    CounterCreationDataCollection counterCollection =
        new CounterCreationDataCollection();

    // Create the custom counter object and add it to the collection of counters.
    CounterCreationData counter = new CounterCreationData(counterName,
counterHelp,
        counterType);
    counterCollection.Add(counter);

    // Create category.
    if (PerformanceCounterCategory.Exists(categoryName))
    {
        PerformanceCounterCategory.Delete(categoryName);
    }

    PerformanceCounterCategory appCategory =
        PerformanceCounterCategory.Create(categoryName, categoryHelp,
            PerformanceCounterCategoryType.SingleInstance, counterCollection);
    // Create the counter and initialize it.
    PerformanceCounter appCounter =
        new PerformanceCounter(categoryName, counterName, false);
```

```
        appCounter.RawValue = 0;

        return (appCounter);
    }
```

Discussion

The first action this method takes is to create the CounterCreationDataCollection object and CounterCreationData object. The CounterCreationData object is created using the *counterName*, *counterHelp*, and *countertype* parameters passed to the CreateSimpleCounter method. The CounterCreationData object is then added to the counterCollection.

 The ASPNET user account, as well as many other user accounts by default, prevent performance counters from being read. You can either increase the permissions allowed for these accounts or use impersonation with an account that has access to enable this functionality. However, this then becomes a deployment requirement of your application. Decreasing security for the ASPNET account or other user accounts may very well be frowned upon by IT folks deploying your application.

If *categoryName*—a string containing the name of the category that is passed as a parameter to the method—is not registered on the system, a new category is created from a PerformanceCounterCategory object. If one is registered, it is deleted and created anew. Finally, the actual performance counter is created from a PerformanceCounter object. This object is initialized to zero and returned by the method. PerformanceCounterCategory takes a PerformanceCounterCategoryType as a parameter. The possible settings are shown in Table 8-3.

Table 8-3. PerformanceCounterCategoryType enumeration values

Name	Description
MultiInstance	There can be multiple instances of the performance counter.
SingleInstance	There can be only one instance of the performance counter.
Unknown	Instance functionality for this performance counter is unknown.

The CreateSimpleCounter method returns a PerformanceCounter object that will be used by an application. The application can perform several actions on a PerformanceCounter object. An application can increment or decrement it using one of these three methods:

```
long value = appCounter.Increment();
long value = appCounter.Decrement();
long value = appCounter.IncrementBy(i);
```

```
// Additionally, a negative number may be passed to the
// IncrementBy method to mimic a DecrementBy method
// (which is not included in this class). For example:
long value = appCounter.IncrementBy(-i);
```

The first two methods accept no parameters, while the third accepts a long containing the number by which to increment the counter. All three methods return a long type indicating the new value of the counter.

In addition to incrementing or decrementing this counter, you can also take samples of the counter at various points in the application. A sample is a snapshot of the counter and all of its values at a particular instance in time. A sample may be taken using the following line of code:

```
CounterSample counterSampleValue = appCounter.NextSample();
```

The NextSample method accepts no parameters and returns a CounterSample structure.

At another point in the application, a counter can be sampled again, and both samples can be passed in to the static Calculate method on the CounterSample class. These actions may be performed on a single line of code as follows:

```
float calculatedSample = CounterSample.Calculate(counterSampleValue,
                                                 appCounter.NextSample());
```

The calculated sample calculatedSample may be stored for future analysis.

The simpler performance counters already available in the .NET Framework are:

CounterDelta32/CounterDelta64
> Determines the difference (or change) in value between two samplings of this counter. The CounterDelta64 counter can hold larger values than CounterDelta32.

CounterTimer
> Calculates the percentage of the CounterTimer value change over the CounterTimer time change. Tracks the average active time for a resource as a percentage of the total sample time.

CounterTimerInverse
> Calculates the inverse of the CounterTimer counter. Tracks the average inactive time for a resource as a percentage of the total sample time.

CountPerTimeInterval32/CountPerTimeInterval64
> Calculates the number of items waiting within a queue to a resource over the time elapsed. These counters give the delta of the queue length for the last two sample intervals divided by the interval duration.

ElapsedTime
> Calculates the difference in time between when this counter recorded the start of an event and the current time, measured in seconds.

`NumberOfItems32/NumberOfItems64`

> These counters return their value in decimal format. The `NumberOfItems64` counter can hold larger values than `NumberOfItems32`. This counter does not need to be passed to the static `Calculate` method of the `CounterSample` class; there are no values that must be calculated. Instead, use the `RawValue` property of the `PerformanceCounter` object (i.e., in this recipe, the `appCounter.RawValue` property would be used).

`NumberOfItemsHEX32/NumberOfItemsHEX64`

> These counters return their value in hexadecimal format. The `NumberOfItemsHEX64` counter can hold larger values than `NumberOfItemsHEX32`. This counter does not need to be passed to the static `Calculate` method of the `CounterSample` class; there are no values that must be calculated. Instead, use the `RawValue` property of the `PerformanceCounter` object (i.e., in this recipe, the `appCounter.RawValue` property would be used).

`RateOfCountsPerSecond32/RateOfCountsPerSecond64`

> Calculates the `RateOfCountsPerSecond*` value change over the `RateOfCountsPerSecond*` time change, measured in seconds. The `RateOfCountsPerSecond64` counter can hold larger values than the `RateOfCountsPerSecond32` counter.

`Timer100Ns`

> Percentage counter showing the active component time as a percentage of the total elapsed time of the sample interval measured in 100 nanoseconds (ns) units. Processor\ % User Time is an example of this type of counter.

`Timer100nsInverse`

> Percentage-based counter showing the average active percentage of time tracked during the sample interval. Processor\ % Processor Time is one example of this type of counter.

See Also

See the "PerformanceCounter Class," "PerformanceCounterType Enumeration," "PerformanceCounterCategory Class," "ASP.NET Impersonation," and "Monitoring Performance Thresholds" topics in the MSDN documentation.

8.7   Enabling and Disabling Complex Tracing Code

Problem

You have an object that contains complex tracing/debugging code. In fact, there is so much tracing/debugging code that to turn it all on would create an extremely large amount of output. You want to be able to generate objects at runtime that contain all of the tracing/debugging code, only a specific portion of this tracing/debugging code, or no tracing/debugging code. The amount of tracing code generated could depend on the state of the application or the environment in which it is running. The tracing code needs to be generated during object creation.

Solution

Use the TraceFactory class shown in Example 8-4, which implements the factory design pattern to allow creation of an object that either generates tracing information or does not.

Example 8-4. TraceFactory class

```
#define TRACE
#define TRACE_INSTANTIATION
#define TRACE_BEHAVIOR

using System.Diagnostics;

public class TraceFactory
{
    public TraceFactory( ) {}

    public Foo CreateObj( )
    {
        Foo obj = null;

        #if (TRACE)
            #if (TRACE_INSTANTIATION)
                obj = new BarTraceInst( );
            #elif (TRACE_BEHAVIOR)
                obj = new BarTraceBehavior( );
            #else
                obj = new Bar( );
            #endif
        #else
            obj = new Bar( );
        #endif

        return (obj);
    }
}
```

The class hierarchy for the Bar, BarTraceInst, and BarTraceBehavior classes is shown next. The BarTraceInst class contains only the constructor tracing code, the BarTraceBehavior class contains tracing code only within specific methods, and the Bar class contains no tracing code:

```
public abstract class Foo
{
    public virtual void SomeBehavior( )
    {
        //...
```

```csharp
        }
    }

    public class Bar : Foo
    {
        public Bar() {}

        public override void SomeBehavior()
        {
            base.SomeBehavior();
        }
    }

    public class BarTraceInst : Foo
    {
        public BarTraceInst()
        {
            Trace.WriteLine("BarTraceInst object instantiated");
        }

        public override void SomeBehavior()
        {
            base.SomeBehavior();
        }
    }

    public class BarTraceBehavior : Foo
    {
        public BarTraceBehavior() {}

        public override void SomeBehavior()
        {
            Trace.WriteLine("SomeBehavior called");
            base.SomeBehavior();
        }
    }
```

Discussion

The *factory design pattern* is designed to abstract away the creation of objects within a system. This pattern allows code to create objects of a particular type by using an intermediate object called a factory. In its simplest form, a factory pattern consists of some client code that uses a factory object to create and return a specific type of object. The factory pattern allows changes to be made in the way objects are created, independent of the client code. This design prevents code changes to the way an object is constructed from permeating throughout the client code.

Consider that you could have a class that contained numerous lines of tracing code. If you ran this code to obtain the trace output, you would be inundated with reams of information. This setup is hard to manage and even harder to read to pinpoint problems in your code. One solution to this problem is to use a factory to create an object based on the type of tracing code you wish to output.

To do this, create an abstract base class called Foo that contains all of the base behavior. The Foo class is subclassed to create the Bar, BarTraceInst, and BarTraceBehavior classes. The Bar class contains no tracing code, the BarTraceInst class contains tracing code only in its constructor (and potentially in its destructor), and the BarTraceBehavior class contains tracing code only in specific methods. (The class hierarchy provided in the Solution section is much simpler than classes that you would create; this allows you to focus more on the design pattern and less on the class hierarchy from which the factory creates classes.)

A TraceFactory class that will act as your factory to create objects inheriting from the abstract Foo class is created. The TraceFactory class contains a single public method called CreateObj. This method attempts to instantiate an object that inherits from Foo based on the preprocessor symbols defined in your application. If the following line of code exists:

```
#define TRACE_BEHAVIOR
```

the BarTraceBehavior class is created. If this line exists:

```
#define TRACE_INSTANTIATION
```

the BarTraceInst class is created. If neither of these exists, the Bar class is created. Once the correct class is created, it is returned to the caller. The caller never needs to know which exact object is instantiated, only that it is of type Foo. This allows you to add even more classes to handle varying types and amounts of tracing code.

To instantiate a TraceFactory class, use the following code:

```
TraceFactory factory = new TraceFactory();
```

Using this factory object, you can create a new object of type Foo:

```
Foo obj = factory.CreateObj();
Console.WriteLine(obj.ToString());
obj.SomeBehavior();
```

Now you can use the Foo object without regard to the trace output that it will produce. To create and use a different Foo object, all you have to do is define a different preprocessor symbol that controls which subclass of Foo is created.

See Also

The "C# Preprocessor Directives" and "ConditionalAttribute Class" topics in the MSDN documentation.

8.8   Capturing Standard Output for a Process

Problem

You need to be able to capture standard output for a process you are launching.

Solution

Use the RedirectStandardOutput property of the Process.StartInfo class to capture the output from the process. By redirecting the standard output stream of the process, you read it when the process terminates. UseShellExecute is a property on the ProcessInfo class that tells the runtime whether or not to use the Windows shell to start the process or not. By default, it is turned on (true) and the shell runs the program, which means that the output cannot be redirected. This needs to be set to off and then the redirection can occur. The UseShellExecute property is set to false to ensure this is not started using the Windows shell for your purposes here.

In this example, a Process object for *cmd.exe* is set up with arguments to perform a directory listing, and then the output is redirected. A log file is created to hold the resulting output, and the Process.Start method is called:

```
// See 12.21 for more info on redirection...
Process application = new Process();
// Run the command shell.
application.StartInfo.FileName = @"cmd.exe";

// Get a directory listing from the current directory.
application.StartInfo.Arguments = @"/Cdir " + Environment.CurrentDirectory;
Console.WriteLine("Running cmd.exe with arguments: {0}",
                  application.StartInfo.Arguments);

// Redirect standard output so we can read it.
application.StartInfo.RedirectStandardOutput = true;
application.StartInfo.UseShellExecute = false;

// Create a log file to hold the results in the current EXE directory.
using (StreamWriter logger = new StreamWriter("cmdoutput.log"))
{
    // Start it up.
    application.Start();
```

Once the process is started, the StandardOutput stream can be accessed and a reference to it held. The code then reads in the information from the output stream while the application runs and writes it to the log file that was set up previously. Once the application finishes, the log file is closed:

```
// Get stdout.
StreamReader output = application.StandardOutput;

// Dump the output stream while the app runs.
do
```

```
        {
            using (output)
            {
                char[] info = null;
                while (output.Peek( ) >= 0)
                {
                    info = new char[4096];
                    output.Read(info, 0, info.Length);
                    // Write to the logger.
                    logger.Write(info, 0, info.Length);
                }
            }
        }
        while (!application.HasExited);
    }

    // Close the process object.
    application.Close( );
```

cmdoutput.log holds information similar to the following output:

```
Volume in drive C has no label.
 Volume Serial Number is DDDD-FFFF

Directory of C:\C#Cookbook2\Code\CSharpRecipes\bin\Debug

08/28/2005 12:25 PM <DIR>          .
08/28/2005 12:25 PM <DIR>          ..
08/28/2005 12:25 PM                      0 cmdoutput.log
08/15/2005 09:46 PM                489,269 CSharpCookbook.zip
08/28/2005 12:24 PM                450,560 CSharpRecipes.exe
08/28/2005 12:24 PM              1,031,680 CSharpRecipes.pdb
07/22/2005 08:28 AM                  5,120 CSharpRecipes.vshost.exe
04/12/2005 10:15 PM                    432 CSharpRecipes.vshost.xml
05/10/2005 10:14 PM                    998 CSharpRecipes.vshost.xsd
03/29/2005 10:27 AM                    432 CSharpRecipes.xml
05/10/2005 10:14 PM                    998 CSharpRecipes.xsd
03/29/2005 10:27 AM                    155 data.txt
04/12/2005 10:15 PM                    134 HT.data
12/10/2003 10:11 PM                 12,288 REGEX_Test.dll
08/20/2005 09:27 PM                 16,384 SampleClassLibrary.dll
08/20/2005 09:27 PM                 11,776 SampleClassLibrary.pdb
08/02/2005 08:56 PM                    483 se1.object
08/02/2005 08:56 PM                    480 se2.object
08/02/2005 08:56 PM                    767 se3.object
08/02/2005 08:56 PM                    488 se4.object
08/02/2005 08:56 PM                    775 se5.object
04/12/2005 10:15 PM                  1,369 TEST.DATA
04/12/2005 10:14 PM                    327 TestBinSerXML.txt
              21 File(s)      2,024,915 bytes
               2 Dir(s)  98,005,683,712 bytes free
```

Discussion

Redirecting standard output is a common task that can sometimes be of great use for tasks like automated build scenarios or test harnesses. While not quite as easy as simply placing > after the command line for a process at the command prompt, this approach is more flexible, as the stream output can be reformatted as XML or HTML for posting to a web site. This also provides the opportunity to send the data to multiple locations at once, which the simple command-line redirect function as provided by Windows is incapable of.

Waiting to read from the stream until the application has finished ensures that there will be no deadlock issues. If the stream is accessed synchronously before this time, then the possibility exists for the parent to block the child. At a minimum, the child will wait until the parent has finished reading from the stream before it continues writing to it. So, by postponing the read until the end, you allow the child to have less performance degradation at the cost of some additional time at the end.

See Also

Recipe 12.11; see the "ProcessStartInfo.RedirectStandardOutput Property" and "ProcessStartInfo.UseShellExecute Property" topics in the MSDN documentation.

8.9 Creating Custom Debugging Displays for Your Classes

Problem

You have a set of classes that are used in your application. You would like to see at a glance in the debugger what a particular instance of the class holds. The default debugger display doesn't show any useful information for your class today.

Solution

Add a DebuggerDisplayAttribute to your class to make the debugger show you something you consider useful about your class. For example, if you had a Citizen class that held the honorific and name information, you could add a DebuggerDisplayAttribute like this one:

```
[DebuggerDisplay("Citizen Full Name = {_honorific}{_first}{_middle}{_last}")]
public class Citizen
{
    private string _honorific;
    private string _first;
    private string _middle;
    private string _last;
```

```
    public Citizen(string honorific, string first, string middle, string last)
    {
        _honorific = honorific;
        _first = first;
        _middle = middle;
        _last = last;
    }
}
```

Now, when instances of the Citizen class are instantiated, the debugger will show the information the way the DebuggerDisplayAttribute on the class directs it to. To see this, instantiate two Citizens, Mrs. Alice G. Jones and Mr. Robert Frederick Jones, like this:

```
Citizen mrsJones = new Citizen("Mrs.","Alice","G.","Jones");
Citizen mrJones = new Citizen("Mr.", "Robert", "Frederick", "Jones");
```

When this code is run under the debugger, the custom display is used, as shown in Figure 8-1.

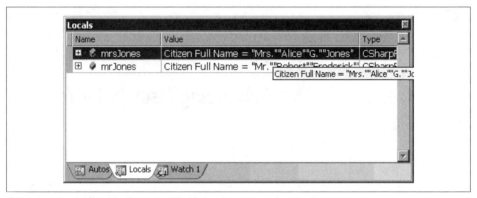

Figure 8-1. Debugger display controlled by DebuggerDisplayAttribute

Discussion

It is nice to be able to see the pertinent information for classes you write quickly. But the more powerful part of this feature is the ability for your team members to quickly understand what this class instance holds. The this pointer is accessible from the DebuggerDisplayAttribute declaration, but any properties accessed using the this pointer will not evaluate the property attributes before processing. Essentially, if you access a property on the current object instance as part of constructing the display string, if that property has attributes, they will not be processed, and therefore you may not get the value you thought you would. If you have custom ToString() overrides in place already, the debugger will use these as the DebuggerDisplayAttribute without your specifying it, provided the correct option is enabled under Tools\ Options\Debugging, as shown in Figure 8-2.

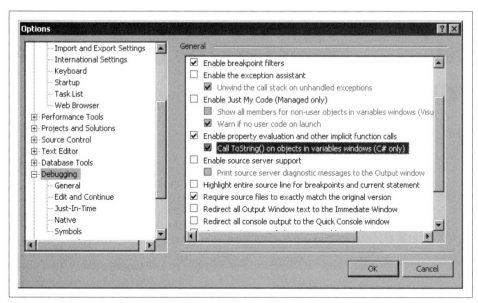

Figure 8-2. Setting the debugger to call ToString() for object display

See Also

The "Using DebuggerDisplayAttribute" and "DebuggerDisplayAttribute" topics in the MSDN documentation.

CHAPTER 9

Delegates, Events, and Lambda Expressions

9.0 Introduction

A *delegate* is an object which represents a method and, optionally, the "this" object associated with that method. When the delegate is invoked, the corresponding method is invoked. Delegates contain all that is needed to allow a method, with a specific signature and return type, to be invoked by your code. A delegate can be passed to methods, and a reference to it can be stored in a structure or class. A delegate is used when, at design time, you do not know which method you need to call, and the information to determine this is available only at runtime.

Another scenario, is when the code calling a method is being developed independently of the code that will supply the method to be called. The classic example is a Windows Forms control. If you create a control, you are unlikely to know what method should be called in the application when the control raises an event, so you must provide a delegate to allow the application to hook up a handler to the event. When other developers use your control, they will typically decide when they are adding the control (through the designer or programmatically) and which method should be called to handle the event published by the control. (For example, it's common to connect a Button's click handler to a delegate at design time.)

Events are a specialized delegate type primarily used for message or notification passing. Events can only be invoked from the type they are published from and are typically based on the EventHandler delegate with an object representing the sender of the event and a System.EventArgs derived class holding data about the event.

Anonymous methods are expressions that can be converted to delegates. They are a feature of the C# compiler and not a CLR type. An anonymous method is ultimately created as a delegate instance by the compiler, but the syntax for declaring an anonymous method can be more concise than declaring a regular delegate. Anonymous methods also permit you to capture variables in the same scope.

Anonymous methods and lambda expressions are both subsets of anonymous functions. For the majority of situations, lambda expression syntax is preferable, and you should avoid using anonymous method syntax in C# 3.0. Almost anything that could be done using anonymous methods in C# 2.0 can now be done better with lambda expressions in C# 3.0.

For an example of an anonymous method, see the `ExecuteCSharp2_0` method in the lambda expression section.

Lambda expressions are functions with a different syntax that enables them to be used in an expression context instead of the usual object-oriented method of being a member of a class. This means that with a single syntax, we can express a method definition, declaration, and the invocation of delegate to execute it, just as anonymous methods can, but with a more terse syntax.

A *projection* is a lambda expression that translates one type into another.

A lambda expression looks like this:

```
j => j * 42
```

This means "using j as the parameter to the function, j goes to the result of j*42." The => can be thought of as "goes to" for both this and for a projection that was declared like this:

```
j =>  new { Number = j*42 };
```

If you think about it, you can see that in C# 1.0 you could do the same thing:

```
public delegate int IncreaseByANumber(int j);
public delegate int MultipleIncreaseByANumber(int j, int k, int l);

static public int MultiplyByANumber(int j) {
    return j * 42;
}

public static void ExecuteCSharp1_0()
{
    IncreaseByANumber increase =
        new IncreaseByANumber(
            DelegatesEventsLambdaExpressions.MultiplyByANumber);

    Console.WriteLine(increase(10));
}
```

In C# 2.0 with anonymous methods, the C# 1.0 syntax could be reduced to the following example, as it is no longer necessary to provide the name for the delegate since all we want is the result of the operation:

```
public delegate int IncreaseByANumber(int j);

public static void ExecuteCSharp2_0()
```

```
    {
        IncreaseByANumber increase =
            new IncreaseByANumber(
            delegate(int j)
            {
                return j * 42;
            });

        Console.WriteLine(increase(10));
    }
```

This brings us back to C# 3.0 and lambda expressions, where we can now just write:

```
    public static void ExecuteCSharp3_0( )
    {
        // declare the lambda expression
        IncreaseByANumber increase = j => j * 42;
        // invoke the method and print 420 to the console
        Console.WriteLine(increase(10));

        MultipleIncreaseByANumber multiple = (j, k, l) => ((j * 42) / k) % l;
        Console.WriteLine(multiple(10, 11, 12));
    }
```

Type inference helps the compiler to infer the type of j from the declaration of the IncreaseByANumber delegate type. If there were multiple arguments, then the lambda expression could look like this:

```
        MultipleIncreaseByANumber multiple = (j, k, l) => ((j * 42) / k) % l;
        Console.WriteLine(multiple(10, 11, 12));
```

This chapter's recipes make use of delegates, events, and lambda expressions. Among other topics, these recipes cover:

- Handling each method invoked in a multicast delegate separately.
- Synchronous delegate invocation versus asynchronous delegate invocation.
- Enhancing an existing class with events.
- Various uses of lambda expressions, closures, and functors.

If you are not familiar with delegates, events, or lambda expressions, you should read the MSDN documentation on these topics. There are also good tutorials and example code showing you how to set them up and use them in a basic fashion.

9.1 Controlling When and If a Delegate Fires Within a Multicast Delegate

Problem

You have combined multiple delegates to create a multicast delegate. When this multicast delegate is invoked, each delegate within it is invoked in turn. You need to

---

exert more control over such things as the order in which each delegate is invoked, firing only a subset of delegates, or firing each delegate based on the success or failure of previous delegates.

Solution

Use the GetInvocationList method to obtain an array of Delegate objects. Next, iterate over this array using a for (if enumerating in a nonstandard order) or foreach (for enumerating in a standard order) loop. You can then invoke each Delegate object in the array individually and, optionally, retrieve its return value.

In C#, all delegate types support multicast—that is, any delegate instance can invoke multiple methods each time the instance is invoked if it has been set up to do so. In this recipe, we use the term *multicast* to describe a delegate that has been set up to invoke multiple methods.

The following method creates a multicast delegate called allInstances and then uses GetInvocationList to allow each delegate to be invoked individually, in reverse order. The Func<int> generic delegate is used to create delegate instances that return an int:

```
public static void InvokeInReverse()
{
    Func<int> myDelegateInstance1 = TestInvokeIntReturn.Method1;
    Func<int> myDelegateInstance2 = TestInvokeIntReturn.Method2;
    Func<int> myDelegateInstance3 = TestInvokeIntReturn.Method3;

    Func<int> allInstances =
            myDelegateInstance1 +
            myDelegateInstance2 +
            myDelegateInstance3;

    Console.WriteLine("Fire delegates in reverse");
    Delegate[] delegateList = allInstances.GetInvocationList();
    foreach (Func<int> instance in delegateList.Reverse())
    {
        instance();
    }
}
```

Note that to roll over the delegate list retrieved using GetInvocationList, we use the IEnumerable<T> extension method Reverse so that we get the items in the opposite order the enumeration would normally produce them in.

As the following methods demonstrate by firing every other delegate, you don't have to invoke all of the delegates in the list. InvokeEveryOtherOperation uses an extension method created here for IEnumerable<T> called EveryOther that will only return every other item from the enumeration.

If a unicast delegate was used and you called GetInvocationList on it, you will receive a list of one delegate instance.

```csharp
public static void InvokeEveryOtherOperation()
{
    Func<int> myDelegateInstance1 = TestInvokeIntReturn.Method1;
    Func<int> myDelegateInstance2 = TestInvokeIntReturn.Method2;
    Func<int> myDelegateInstance3 = TestInvokeIntReturn.Method3;

    Func<int> allInstances = //myDelegateInstance1;
            myDelegateInstance1 +
            myDelegateInstance2 +
            myDelegateInstance3;

    Delegate[] delegateList = allInstances.GetInvocationList();
    Console.WriteLine("Invoke every other delegate");
    foreach (Func<int> instance in delegateList.EveryOther())
    {
        // invoke the delegate
        int retVal = instance();
        Console.WriteLine("Delegate returned " + retVal);
    }
}

static IEnumerable<T> EveryOther<T>(this IEnumerable<T> enumerable)
{
    bool retNext = true;
    foreach (T t in enumerable)
    {
        if (retNext) yield return t;
        retNext = !retNext;
    }
}
```

The following class contains each of the methods that will be called by the multicast delegate allInstances:

```csharp
public class TestInvokeIntReturn
{
    public static int Method1()
    {
        Console.WriteLine("Invoked Method1");
        return 1;
    }

    public static int Method2()
    {
        Console.WriteLine("Invoked Method2");
        return 2;
    }

    public static int Method3()
```

```
    {
        //throw (new Exception("Method1"));
        //throw (new SecurityException("Method3"));
        Console.WriteLine("Invoked Method3");
        return 3;
    }
}
```

It is also possible to decide whether to continue firing delegates in the list based on the return value of the currently firing delegate. The following method fires each delegate, stopping only when a delegate returns a false value:

```
public static void InvokeWithTest()
{
    Func<bool> myDelegateInstanceBool1 = TestInvokeBoolReturn.Method1;
    Func<bool> myDelegateInstanceBool2 = TestInvokeBoolReturn.Method2;
    Func<bool> myDelegateInstanceBool3 = TestInvokeBoolReturn.Method3;

    Func<bool> allInstancesBool =
            myDelegateInstanceBool1 +
            myDelegateInstanceBool2 +
            myDelegateInstanceBool3;

    Console.WriteLine(
        "Invoke individually (Call based on previous return value):");
    foreach (Func<bool> instance in allInstancesBool.GetInvocationList())
    {
        if (!instance())
            break;
    }
}
```

The following class contains each of the methods that will be called by the multicast delegate allInstancesBool:

```
public class TestInvokeBoolReturn
{
    public static bool Method1()
    {
        Console.WriteLine("Invoked Method1");
        return true;
    }

    public static bool Method2()
    {
        Console.WriteLine("Invoked Method2");
        return false;
    }

    public static bool Method3()
    {
        Console.WriteLine("Invoked Method3");
        return true;
    }
}
```

Discussion

A delegate, when called, will invoke all delegates stored within its *invocation list*. These delegates are usually invoked sequentially from the first to the last one added. With the use of the GetInvocationList method of the MulticastDelegate class, you can obtain each delegate in the invocation list of a multicast delegate. This method accepts no parameters and returns an array of Delegate objects that corresponds to the invocation list of the delegate on which this method was called. The returned Delegate array contains the delegates of the invocation list in the order in which they would normally be called; that is, the first element in the Delegate array contains the Delegate object that is normally called first.

This application of the GetInvocationList method gives you the ability to control exactly when and how the delegates in a multicast delegate are invoked and allows you to prevent the continued invocation of delegates when one delegate fails. This ability is important if each delegate is manipulating data, and one of the delegates fails in its duties but does not throw an exception. If one delegate fails in its duties and the remaining delegates rely on all previous delegates to succeed, you must quit invoking delegates at the point of failure. Note that an exception will force the invocation of delegates to cease. Exceptions should only be used for exceptional circumstances, not for control flow. This recipe handles a delegate failure more efficiently and also provides more flexibility in dealing with these errors. For example, you can write logic to specify which delegates are to be invoked, based on the returned values of previously invoked delegates.

See Also

Recipes 9.2 and 9.3; see the "Delegate Class" and "Delegate.GetInvocationList Method" topics in the MSDN documentation.

9.2   Obtaining Return Values from Each Delegate in a Multicast Delegate

Problem

You have added multiple delegates to a single multicast delegate. Each of these individual delegates returns a value that is required by your application. Ordinarily, the values returned by individual delegates in a multicast delegate are lost—all except the value from the last delegate to fire, the return value of which is returned to the calling application. You need to be able to access the return value of each delegate that is invoked in the multicast delegate.

Solution

Use the GetInvocationList method as in Recipe 9.1. This method returns each individual delegate from a multicast delegate. In doing so, you can invoke each delegate individually and get its return value. The following method creates a multicast delegate called All and then uses GetInvocationList to fire each delegate individually. After firing each delegate, the return value is captured:

```
public static void TestIndividualInvokesReturnValue( )
{
    Func<int> myDelegateInstance1 = TestInvokeIntReturn.Method1;
    Func<int> myDelegateInstance2 = TestInvokeIntReturn.Method2;
    Func<int> myDelegateInstance3 = TestInvokeIntReturn.Method3;

    Func<int> allInstances =
            myDelegateInstance1 +
            myDelegateInstance2 +
            myDelegateInstance3;

    Console.WriteLine("Invoke individually (Obtain each return value):");
    foreach (Func<int> instance in allInstances.GetInvocationList( ))
    {
        int retVal = instance( );
        Console.WriteLine("\tOutput: " + retVal);
    }
}
```

This sample uses the TestInvokeIntReturn class defined in Recipe 9.1.

Discussion

One quirk with multicast delegates is that if any or all delegates within its invocation list return a value, only the value of the last invoked delegate is returned; all others are lost. This loss can become annoying, or worse, if your code requires these return values. Consider a case in which the allInstances delegate was invoked normally, as in the following code:

```
retVal = allInstances( );
Console.WriteLine(retVal);
```

The value 3 would be displayed because Method3 was the last method invoked by the allInstances delegate. None of the other return values would be captured.

By using the GetInvocationList method of the MulticastDelegate class, you can get around this limitation. This method returns an array of Delegate objects that can each be invoked separately. Note that this method does not invoke each delegate; it simply returns an array of them to the caller. By invoking each delegate separately, you can retrieve each return value from each invoked delegate. (More information on the GetInvocationList method is presented in Recipe 9.1.)

Note that any out or ref parameters will also be lost when a multicast delegate is invoked. This recipe allows you to obtain the out and/or ref parameters of each invoked delegate within the multicast delegate.

However, you still need to be aware that any unhandled exceptions emanating from one of these invoked delegates will be bubbled up to the method TestIndividualInvokesReturnValue presented in this recipe. To better handle this situation, see Recipe 9.3.

See Also

Recipes 9.1 and 9.3; see the "Delegate Class" and "Delegate.GetInvocationList Method" topics in the MSDN documentation.

9.3 Handling Exceptions Individually for Each Delegate in a Multicast Delegate

Problem

You have added multiple delegates to a single multicast delegate. Each of these individual delegates must be invoked, regardless of whether an unhandled exception is thrown within one of the delegates. But once a delegate in a multicast delegate throws an unhandled exception, no more delegates are invoked. You need a way to trap unhandled exceptions within each individual delegate while still allowing the rest of the delegates to fire.

Solution

Use the GetInvocationList method as shown in Recipe 9.1. This method returns each individual delegate from a multicast delegate and, by doing so, allows you to invoke each delegate within the try block of an exception handler.

The following delegate defines the MyDelegateOperation delegate type:

```
public delegate int MyDelegateOperation();
```

The method shown in Example 9-1 creates a multicast delegate called allInstances and then uses GetInvocationList to retrieve each delegate individually. Each delegate is then invoked within the try block of an exception handler.

Example 9-1. Handling exceptions individually for each delegate in a multicast delegate

```
public static void TestIndividualInvokesExceptions()
{
    Func<int> myDelegateInstance1 = TestInvokeIntReturn.Method1;
    Func<int> myDelegateInstance2 = TestInvokeIntReturn.Method2;
    Func<int> myDelegateInstance3 = TestInvokeIntReturn.Method3;
```

```
Func<int> allInstances =
        myDelegateInstance1 +
        myDelegateInstance2 +
        myDelegateInstance3;

Console.WriteLine("Invoke individually (handle exceptions):");

// Create an instance of a wrapper exception to hold any exceptions
// encountered during the invocations of the delegate instances
List<Exception> invocationExceptions = new List<Exception>();

foreach (Func<int> instance in allInstances.GetInvocationList())
{
    try
    {
        int retVal = instance();
        Console.WriteLine("\tOutput: " + retVal);
    }
    catch (Exception ex)
    {
        // Display and log the exception and continue
        Console.WriteLine(ex.ToString());
        EventLog myLog = new EventLog();
        myLog.Source = "MyApplicationSource";
        myLog.WriteEntry("Failure invoking " +
            instance.Method.Name + " with error " +
            ex.ToString(),
            EventLogEntryType.Error);
        // add this exception to the list
        invocationExceptions.Add(ex);
    }
}
// if we caught any exceptions along the way, throw our
// wrapper exception with all of them in it.
if (invocationExceptions.Count > 0)
{
    throw new MulticastInvocationException(invocationExceptions);
}
}
```

The `MulticastInvocationException` class is able to have multiple exceptions added to it. It exposes an `ReadOnlyCollection<Exception>` through the `InvocationExceptions` property, as shown in Example 9-2.

Example 9-2. MulticastInvocationException class

```
[Serializable]
public class MulticastInvocationException : Exception
{
    private List<Exception> _invocationExceptions;

    public MulticastInvocationException()
```

Example 9-2. MulticastInvocationException class (continued)

```
        : base( )
    {
    }

    public MulticastInvocationException(IEnumerable<Exception> invocationExceptions)
    {
        _invocationExceptions = new List<Exception>(invocationExceptions);
    }

    public MulticastInvocationException(string message)
        : base(message)
    {
    }

    public MulticastInvocationException(string message, Exception innerException) :
        base(message,innerException)
    {
    }

    protected MulticastInvocationException(SerializationInfo info, StreamingContext
context) :
        base(info, context)
    {
        _invocationExceptions =
            (List<Exception>)info.GetValue("InvocationExceptions",
                typeof(List<Exception>));
    }

    [SecurityPermissionAttribute(SecurityAction.Demand,SerializationFormatter = true)]
    public override void GetObjectData(
        SerializationInfo info, StreamingContext context)
    {
        info.AddValue("InvocationExceptions", this.InvocationExceptions);
        base.GetObjectData(info, context);
    }

    public ReadOnlyCollection<Exception> InvocationExceptions
    {
        get { return new ReadOnlyCollection<Exception>(_invocationExceptions); }
    }
}
```

This sample uses the TestInvokeIntReturn class defined in Recipe 9.1.

Discussion

If an exception occurs in a delegate that is invoked from within a multicast delegate and that exception is unhandled, any remaining delegates are not invoked. This is the expected behavior of a multicast delegate. However, in some circumstances, you'd like to be able to handle exceptions thrown from individual delegates and then determine at that point whether to continue invoking the remaining delegates.

In the TestIndividualInvokesExceptions method of this recipe, if an exception is caught, it is logged to the event log and displayed, then the code continues to invoke delegates. This strategy allows for as fine-grained handling of exceptions as you need. One way to deal with this is to store all of the exceptions that occur during delegate processing, and then wrap all of the exceptions encountered during processing in a custom exception. After processing completes, throw the custom exception. See the MulticastInvocationException class in the Solution.

By adding a finally block to this try-catch block, you could be assured that code within this finally block is executed after every delegate returns. This technique is useful if you want to interleave code between calls to delegates, such as code to clean up objects that are not needed or code to verify that each delegate left the data it touched in a stable state.

See Also

Recipes 9.1 and 9.2; see the "Delegate Class" and "Delegate.GetInvocationList Method" topics in the MSDN documentation.

9.4 Converting Delegate Invocation from Synchronous to Asynchronous

Problem

You have determined that one or more delegates invoked synchronously within your application are taking a long time to execute. This delay is making the user interface less responsive to the user. The invocation of these delegates should be converted from synchronous to asynchronous mode.

Solution

A typical synchronous delegate type and supporting code that invokes the delegate are shown here:

```
public delegate void SyncDelegateTypeSimple();

public class TestSyncDelegateTypeSimple
{
    public static void Method1()
    {
        Console.WriteLine("Invoked Method1");
    }
}
```

The code to use this delegate is:

```
public static void TestSimpleSyncDelegate()
{
```

```
    SyncDelegateTypeSimple sdtsInstance = TestSyncDelegateTypeSimple.Method1;
    sdtsInstance();
}
```

This delegate can be called asynchronously on a thread obtained from the thread pool by modifying the code as follows:

```
public static void TestSimpleAsyncDelegate()
{
    AsyncCallback callBack = new AsyncCallback(DelegateSimpleCallback);

    SyncDelegateTypeSimple sdtsInstance = TestSyncDelegateTypeSimple.Method1;

    IAsyncResult asyncResult =
        sdtsInstance.BeginInvoke(callBack, null);

    Console.WriteLine("WORKING...");
}

// The callback that gets called when TestSyncDelegateTypeSimple.Method1
// is finished processing
private static void DelegateSimpleCallback(IAsyncResult iResult)
{
    AsyncResult result = (AsyncResult)iResult;
    SyncDelegateTypeSimple sdtsInstance =
        (SyncDelegateTypeSimple)result.AsyncDelegate;

    sdtsInstance.EndInvoke(result);
    Console.WriteLine("Simple callback run");
}
```

 AsyncResult can be found in the System.Runtime.Remoting.Messaging namespace in *mscorlib*.

Of course, you might also want to change the TestSyncDelegateTypeSimple class name to TestAsyncDelegateTypeSimple and the SyncDelegateTypeSimple delegate name to AsyncDelegateTypeSimple just to be consistent with your naming.

The previous example shows how to call a delegate that accepts no parameters and returns void. The next example shows a synchronous delegate that accepts parameters and returns an integer:

```
public delegate int SyncDelegateType(string message);
public class TestSyncDelegateType
{
    public static int Method1(string message)
    {
        Console.WriteLine("Invoked Method1 with message: " + message);
        return 1;
    }
}
```

The code to use this delegate is:

```
public static void TestComplexSyncDelegate( )
{
    SyncDelegateType sdtInstance = TestSyncDelegateType.Method1;

    int retVal = sdtInstance("Synchronous call");

    Console.WriteLine("Sync: " + retVal);
}
```

The synchronous invocation of the delegate can be converted to asynchronous invocation in the following manner:

```
public static void TestCallbackAsyncDelegate( )
{
    AsyncCallback callBack =
        new AsyncCallback(DelegateCallback);

    SyncDelegateType sdtInstance = TestSyncDelegateType.Method1;

    IAsyncResult asyncResult =
        sdtInstance.BeginInvoke("Asynchronous call", callBack, null);

    Console.WriteLine("WORKING...");
}

// The callback that gets called when TestSyncDelegateType.Method1
// is finished processing
private static void DelegateCallback(IAsyncResult iResult)
{
    AsyncResult result = (AsyncResult)iResult;
    SyncDelegateType sdtInstance =
        (SyncDelegateType)result.AsyncDelegate;

    int retVal = sdtInstance.EndInvoke(result);
    Console.WriteLine("retVal (Callback): " + retVal);
}
```

Discussion

Converting the invocation of a delegate from being synchronous to asynchronous is not an overly complicated procedure. You need to add calls to both BeginInvoke and EndInvoke on the delegate that is being called synchronously. A callback method, DelegateCallback, is added, which gets called when the delegate is finished. This callback method then calls the EndInvoke method on the delegate invoked using BeginInvoke.

You must always call EndInvoke when invoking delegates asynchronously, even when the delegate returns void, to ensure proper cleanup of resources in the CLR.

The notification callback method specified in the *callback* parameter accepts a single parameter of type IAsyncResult. This parameter can be cast to an AsyncResult type and used to set up the call to the EndInvoke method. If you want to handle any exceptions thrown by the asynchronous delegate in the notification callback, wrap the EndInvoke method in a try/catch exception handler.

See Also

The "Delegate Class" and "Asynchronous Delegates" topics in the MSDN documentation.

9.5   An Advanced Interface Search Mechanism

Problem

You are searching for an interface using the Type class. However, complex interface searches are not available through the GetInterface and GetInterfaces methods of a Type object. The GetInterface method searches for an interface only by name (using a case-sensitive or case-insensitive search), and the GetInterfaces method returns an array of all the interfaces implemented on a particular type. You want a more focused searching mechanism that might involve searching for interfaces that define a method with a specific signature or implemented interfaces that are loaded from the GAC. You need more flexible and more advanced searching for interfaces that does not involve creating your own interface search engine. This capability might be used for applications like a code generator or reverse engineering tool.

Solution

Use LINQ to query the type interface information and perform rich searches. The method shown in Example 9-3 will demonstrate one complex search that can be performed with LINQ.

Example 9-3. Performing complex searches of interfaces on a type

```
using System;
using System.Collections;
using System.Collections.Generic;
using System.Linq;
using System.Reflection;


public class SearchType
{
    public static void FindSpecificInterfaces()
    {
        // set up the interfaces to search for
        Type[] interfaces = {
            typeof(System.ICloneable),
            typeof(System.Collections.ICollection),
```

```
            typeof(System.IAppDomainSetup) };

    // set up the type to examine
    Type searchType = typeof(System.Collections.ArrayList);

    var matches = from t in searchType.GetInterfaces()
                  join s in interfaces on t equals s
                  select s;

    Console.WriteLine("Matches found:");
    foreach (Type match in matches)
    {
        Console.WriteLine(match.ToString());
    }
    }
}
```

The FindSpecificInterfaces method searches for any of the three interface types contained in the Names array that are implemented by the System.Collections. ArrayList type. It does this by using LINQ to query if the type is an instance of any of the set of interfaces.

Discussion

There are many ways to use LINQ to search for interfaces implemented on a type— here are just a few other searches that can be performed:

- A search for all implemented interfaces that are defined within a particular namespace (in this case, the System.Collections namespace):

```
    var collectionsInterfaces = from type in searchType.GetInterfaces()
                                where type.Namespace == "System.Collections"
                                select type;
```

- A search for all implemented interfaces that contain a method called Add, which returns an Int32 value:

```
    var addInterfaces = from type in searchType.GetInterfaces()
                        from method in type.GetMethods()
                        where (method.Name == "Add") &&
                              (method.ReturnType == typeof(int))
                        select type;
```

- A search for all implemented interfaces that are loaded from the GAC:

```
    var gacInterfaces = from type in searchType.GetInterfaces()
                        where type.Assembly.GlobalAssemblyCache
                        select type;
```

- A search for all implemented interfaces that are defined within an assembly with the version number 2.0.0.0:

```
    var versionInterfaces = from type in searchType.GetInterfaces()
                            where type.Assembly.GlobalAssemblyCache
                            select type;
```

See Also

The "Lambda Expressions (C# Programming Guide)" and "where keyword [LINQ] (C#)" topics in the MSDN documentation.

9.6 Observing Additions and Modifications to Dictionaries

Problem

You have multiple objects that need to observe modifications to objects that implement IDictionary<K,V>. When an item is added or modified in the dictionary-based collection, each of these observer objects should be able to vote to allow or disallow the action. In order for an action to be allowed to complete, all observer objects must state if they are vetoing the action. If even one observer object votes to disallow the action, the action is prevented.

Solution

Use the ObservableDictionaryObserver class implemented in Example 9-5 to observe additions and modifications to the ObservableDictionary class (shown in Example 9-4) object that is registered with this object. The ObservableDictionary class is a generic wrapper for collections that implement IDictionary<K,V> and allows itself to be observed by the ObservableDictionaryObserver class.

The ObservableDictionaryEventArgs class is a specialization of the EventArgs class, which provides the IDictionary<K,V> key and value being added or modified to the ObservableDictionaryObserver object, as well as a Boolean property, KeepChanges. This flag indicates whether the addition or modification in the ObservableDictionary object will succeed or be rolled back. The MakeObservableDictionary extension method for IDictionary<K,V> wraps up the code for creating an ObservableDictionary from an IDictionary instance. Example 9-4 illustrates the two classes and the extension method.

Example 9-4. ObservableDictionary and ObservableDictionaryEventArgs classes and the MakeObservableDictionary extension method

```
public class ObservableDictionary<TKey,TValue> : IDictionary<TKey,TValue>
{
    IDictionary<TKey, TValue> _internalDictionary;
    public ObservableDictionary(IDictionary<TKey,TValue> dictionary)
    {
        if (dictionary == null)
            throw new ArgumentNullException("dictionary");
        _internalDictionary = dictionary;
    }
```

```csharp
#region Events and Event Initiation

public event EventHandler<ObservableDictionaryEventArgs<TKey,TValue>> AddingEntry;
public event EventHandler<ObservableDictionaryEventArgs<TKey, TValue>> AddedEntry;
public event EventHandler<ObservableDictionaryEventArgs<TKey, TValue>> ChangingEntry;
public event EventHandler<ObservableDictionaryEventArgs<TKey, TValue>> ChangedEntry;

protected virtual bool OnAdding(ObservableDictionaryEventArgs<TKey,TValue> e)
{
    if (AddingEntry != null)
    {
        AddingEntry(this, e);
        return (e.KeepChanges);
    }

    return (true);
}

protected virtual void OnAdded(ObservableDictionaryEventArgs<TKey, TValue> e)
{
    if (AddedEntry != null)
    {
        AddedEntry(this, e);
    }
}

protected virtual bool OnChanging(ObservableDictionaryEventArgs<TKey, TValue> e)
{
    if (ChangingEntry != null)
    {
        ChangingEntry(this, e);
        return (e.KeepChanges);
    }

    return (true);
}

protected virtual void OnChanged(ObservableDictionaryEventArgs<TKey, TValue> e)
{
    if (ChangedEntry != null)
    {
        ChangedEntry(this, e);
    }
}
#endregion // Events and Event Initiation

#region Interface implementations
#region IDictionary<TKey,TValue> Members

public ICollection<TValue> Values
{
```

```
        get { return _internalDictionary.Values; }
    }

    public ICollection<TKey> Keys
    {
        get { return _internalDictionary.Keys; }
    }

    public TValue this[TKey key]
    {
        get
        {
            TValue value;
            if (_internalDictionary.TryGetValue(key, out value))
                return value;
            else
            {
                return default(TValue);
            }
        }
        set
        {
            // see if this key is there to be changed, if not add it
            if (_internalDictionary.ContainsKey(key))
            {
                ObservableDictionaryEventArgs<TKey, TValue> args =
                    new ObservableDictionaryEventArgs<TKey, TValue>(key, value);

                if (OnChanging(args))
                {
                    _internalDictionary[key] = value;
                }
                else
                {
                    Debug.WriteLine("Change of value cannot be performed");
                }

                OnChanged(args);
            }
            else
            {
                Debug.WriteLine("Item did not exist, adding");
                _internalDictionary.Add(key, value);
            }
        }
    }

    public void Add(TKey key, TValue value)
    {
        ObservableDictionaryEventArgs<TKey, TValue> args =
            new ObservableDictionaryEventArgs<TKey, TValue>(key, value);
```

```csharp
        if (OnAdding(args))
        {
            this._internalDictionary.Add(key, value);
        }
        else
        {
            Debug.WriteLine("Addition of key/value cannot be performed");
        }

        OnAdded(args);
    }

    public bool ContainsKey(TKey key)
    {
        return _internalDictionary.ContainsKey(key);
    }

    public bool Remove(TKey key)
    {
        return _internalDictionary.Remove(key);
    }

    public bool TryGetValue(TKey key, out TValue value)
    {
        return _internalDictionary.TryGetValue(key, out value);
    }

    #endregion

    #region ICollection<KeyValuePair<TKey,TValue>> Members

    public void Add(KeyValuePair<TKey, TValue> item)
    {
        _internalDictionary.Add(item.Key, item.Value);
    }

    public void Clear()
    {
        _internalDictionary.Clear();
    }

    public bool Contains(KeyValuePair<TKey, TValue> item)
    {
        return _internalDictionary.Contains(item);
    }

    public void CopyTo(KeyValuePair<TKey, TValue>[] array, int arrayIndex)
    {
        _internalDictionary.CopyTo(array, arrayIndex);
    }
```

```
    public int Count
    {
        get { return _internalDictionary.Count; }
    }

    public bool IsReadOnly
    {
        get { return _internalDictionary.IsReadOnly; }
    }

    public bool Remove(KeyValuePair<TKey, TValue> item)
    {
        return _internalDictionary.Remove(item);
    }

    #endregion

    #region IEnumerable<KeyValuePair<TKey,TValue>> Members

    public IEnumerator<KeyValuePair<TKey, TValue>> GetEnumerator()
    {
        return _internalDictionary.GetEnumerator();
    }

    #endregion

    #region IEnumerable Members

    IEnumerator IEnumerable.GetEnumerator()
    {
        return _internalDictionary.GetEnumerator();
    }

    #endregion
    #endregion // Interface implementations
}

public static ObservableDictionary<TKey, TValue> MakeObservableDictionary<TKey, TValue>(
    this IDictionary<TKey, TValue> dictionary)
{
    return new ObservableDictionary<TKey, TValue>(dictionary);
}

public class ObservableDictionaryEventArgs<TKey, TValue> : EventArgs
{
    TKey _key;
    TValue _value;

    public ObservableDictionaryEventArgs(TKey key, TValue value)
    {
        _key = key;
```

```
        _value = value;
        this.KeepChanges = true;
    }

    public bool KeepChanges { get; set; }
    public TKey Key { get { return _key; } }
    public TValue Value { get { return _value; } }
}
```

Example 9-5 shows the code for the `ObservableDictionaryObserver` class.

Example 9-5. ObservableDictionaryObserver class

```
// The observer object that will observe a registered ObservableDictionary object
public class ObservableDictionaryObserver<TKey,TValue>
{
    public ObservableDictionaryObserver() { }

    // set up delegate/events for approving an addition or change
    public delegate bool Approval(object sender,
            ObservableDictionaryEventArgs<TKey,TValue> e);

    public Approval ApproveAdd { get; set; }
    public Approval ApproveChange { get; set; }

    public void Register(ObservableDictionary<TKey, TValue> dictionary)
    {
        // hook up to the ObservableDictionary instance events
        dictionary.AddingEntry +=
            new EventHandler<ObservableDictionaryEventArgs<TKey, TValue>>(
                                            OnAddingListener);
        dictionary.AddedEntry +=
            new EventHandler<ObservableDictionaryEventArgs<TKey, TValue>>(
                                            OnAddedListener);
        dictionary.ChangingEntry +=
            new EventHandler<ObservableDictionaryEventArgs<TKey, TValue>>(
                                            OnChangingListener);
        dictionary.ChangedEntry +=
            new EventHandler<ObservableDictionaryEventArgs<TKey, TValue>>(
                                            OnChangedListener);
    }

    public void Unregister(ObservableDictionary<TKey,TValue> dictionary)
    {
        // Unhook from the ObservableDictionary instance events
        dictionary.AddingEntry -=
            new EventHandler<ObservableDictionaryEventArgs<TKey, TValue>>(
                                            OnAddingListener);
        dictionary.AddedEntry -=
            new EventHandler<ObservableDictionaryEventArgs<TKey, TValue>>(
                                            OnAddedListener);
```

Example 9-5. ObservableDictionaryObserver class (continued)

```
        dictionary.ChangingEntry -=
            new EventHandler<ObservableDictionaryEventArgs<TKey, TValue>>(
                                            OnChangingListener);
        dictionary.ChangedEntry -=
            new EventHandler<ObservableDictionaryEventArgs<TKey, TValue>>(
                                            OnChangedListener);
    }

    private void CheckApproval(Approval approval,
            ObservableDictionaryEventArgs<TKey,TValue> args)
    {
        // check everyone who wants to approve
        foreach (Approval approvalInstance in
                        approval.GetInvocationList())
        {
            if (!approvalInstance(this,args))
            {
                // if any of the concerned parties
                // refuse, then no add.  Adds by default
                args.KeepChanges = false;
                break;
            }
        }
    }

    private void OnAddingListener(object sender,
            ObservableDictionaryEventArgs<TKey,TValue> args)
    {
        // see if anyone hooked up for approval
        if (ApproveAdd != null)
        {
            CheckApproval(ApproveAdd, args);
        }

        Debug.WriteLine("[NOTIFY] Before Add...: Add Approval = " +
                        args.KeepChanges.ToString());
    }

    private void OnAddedListener(object sender,
            ObservableDictionaryEventArgs<TKey, TValue> args)
    {
        Debug.WriteLine("[NOTIFY] ...After Add:  Item approved for adding: " +
                        args.KeepChanges.ToString());
    }

    private void OnChangingListener(object sender,
            ObservableDictionaryEventArgs<TKey, TValue> args)
    {
        // see if anyone hooked up for approval
        if (ApproveChange != null)
        {
            CheckApproval(ApproveChange, args);
```

Example 9-5. ObservableDictionaryObserver class (continued)

```
        }

        Debug.WriteLine("[NOTIFY] Before Change...: Change Approval = " +
                        args.KeepChanges.ToString( ));
    }

    private void OnChangedListener(object sender,
            ObservableDictionaryEventArgs<TKey, TValue> args)
    {
        Debug.WriteLine("[NOTIFY] ...After Change:  Item approved for change: " +
                        args.KeepChanges.ToString( ));
    }
}
```

Discussion

The *observer design pattern* allows one or more observer objects to act as spectators over one or more subjects. Not only do the observer objects act as spectators, but they can also induce change in the subjects. According to this pattern, any subject is allowed to register itself with one or more observer objects. Once this is done, the subject can operate as it normally does. The key feature is that the subject doesn't have to know what it is being observed by; this allows the coupling between subjects and observers to be minimized. The observer object(s) will then be notified of any changes in state to the subjects. When the subject's state changes, the observer object(s) can change the state of other objects in the system to bring them into line with changes that were made to the subject(s). In addition, the observer could even make changes or refuse changes to the subject(s) themselves.

The observer pattern is best implemented with events in C#. The event object provides a built-in way of implementing the observer design pattern. This recipe implements this pattern on all collections supporting IDictionary<K,V>. The object being observed must raise events for any listening observer objects to handle, but the IDictionary<K,V> interface found in the FCL does not indicate any events. In order to make the IDictionary<K,V> raise events at specific times, you must implement a wrapper class, ObservableDictionary, that implements the IDictionary<K,V> interface. This ObservableDictionary class overrides the Add and indexer members of the base interface. In addition, four events (AddingEntry, AddedEntry, ChangingEntry, and ChangedEntry) are created; they will be raised before and after items are added or modified in the ObservableDictionary. To raise these events, the following four methods are created, one to raise each event:

- The OnAdding method raises the AddingEntry event.
- The OnAdded method raises the AddedEntry event.
- The OnChanging method raises the ChangingEntry event.
- The OnChanged method raises the ChangedEntry event.

The Add method calls the OnAdding method, which then raises the event to any listening observer objects. The OnAdding method is called before the Add method on the internal dictionary is called. After the key/value pair has been added, the OnAdded method is called. This operation is similar to the indexer set method.

 The Onxxx methods that raise the events in the ObservableDictionary class are marked as protected virtual to allow classes to subclass this class and implement their own method of dealing with the events. Note that this statement is not applicable to sealed classes. In those cases, you can simply make the methods public.

The ObservableDictionaryEventArgs class contains three private fields, defined as follows:

key
> The key that is to be added to the dictionary.

value
> The value that is to be added to the dictionary.

keepChanges
> A flag indicating whether the key/value pair should be added to the dictionary. true indicates that this pair should be added to the dictionary.

The keepChanges field is used by the observer to determine whether an add or change operation should proceed. This flag is discussed further when you look at the ObservableDictionaryObserver observer object.

The ObservableDictionaryObserver is the observer object that watches any ObservableDictionary objects it is told about. Any ObservableDictionary object can be passed to the ObservableDictionaryObserver.Register method in order to be observed. This method accepts an ObservableDictionary object (dictionary) as its only parameter. This method then hooks up the event handlers in the ObservableDictionaryObserver object to the events that can be raised by the ObservableDictionary object passed in through the dictionary parameter. Therefore, the following events and event handlers are bound together:

- The ObservableDictionary.AddingEntry event is bound to the ObservableDictionaryObserver.OnAddingListener event handler.

- The ObservableDictionary.AddedEntry event is bound to the ObservableDictionaryObserver.OnAddedListener event handler.

- The ObservableDictionary.ChangingEntry event is bound to the ObservableDictionaryObserver.OnChangingListener event handler.

- The ObservableDictionary.ChangedEntry event is bound to the ObservableDictionaryObserver.OnChangedListener event handler.

The OnAddingListener and OnChangingListener methods watch for additions and changes to the key/value pairs of the watched ObservableDictionary object(s). Since you have an event firing before and after an addition or modification occurs, you can determine whether the addition or change should occur.

Two events are published by the ObservableDictionaryObserver to allow for an external entity to approve or deny the addition or changing of an entry. These events are named ApproveAdd and ApproveChange, respectively, and are of delegate type Approval as shown below:

```
public delegate bool Approval(object sender,
        ObservableDictionaryEventArgs<TKey,TValue> e);
```

This is where the keepChanges field of the ObservableDictionaryEventArgs object comes into play. If an external source wants to block the addition or change, it can simply return false from its event handler implementation of the appropriate Approve* event.

The ObservableDictionaryObserver object will set this flag according to whether it determines that the action should proceed or be prematurely terminated. The ObservableDictionaryEventArgs object is passed back to the OnAdding and OnChanging methods. These methods then return the value of the KeepChanges property to either the calling Add method or indexer. The Add method or indexer then uses this flag to determine whether the internal dictionary object should be updated.

The code in Example 9-6 shows how to instantiate ObservableDictionaries and ObservableDictionaryObservers and how to register, set up approval, use, and unregister them.

Example 9-6. Using the ObservableDictionary and ObservableDictionaryObserver classes

```
public static void TestObserverPattern( )
{
    Dictionary<int, string> dictionary1 = new Dictionary<int, string>( );
    Dictionary<int, string> dictionary2 = new Dictionary<int, string>( );
    Dictionary<int, string> dictionary3 = new Dictionary<int, string>( );

    // Create three observable dictionary instances
    var obsDict1 = dictionary1.MakeObservableDictionary( );
    var obsDict2 = dictionary2.MakeObservableDictionary( );
    var obsDict3 = dictionary3.MakeObservableDictionary( );

    // Create an observer for the three subject objects
    var observer = new ObservableDictionaryObserver<int, string>( );

    // Register the three subjects with the observer
    observer.Register(obsDict1);
    observer.Register(obsDict2);
    observer.Register(obsDict3);
```

```
// hook up the approval events for adding or changing
observer.ApproveAdd +=
    new ObservableDictionaryObserver<int, string>.
        Approval(SeekApproval);
observer.ApproveChange +=
    new ObservableDictionaryObserver<int, string>.
        Approval(SeekApproval);

// Use the observable instances
obsDict1.Add(1, "one");
obsDict2.Add(2, "two");
obsDict3.Add(3, "three");

// Insure the approval process worked
Debug.Assert(obsDict1.Count == 1);
Debug.Assert(obsDict2.Count == 1);
// this should be empty as the value was more than three characters
Debug.Assert(obsDict3.Count == 0);

// Unregister the observable instances
observer.Unregister(obsDict3);
observer.Unregister(obsDict2);
observer.Unregister(obsDict1);

////////////////////////////////////////////////////////////////
// Now do it with a different type of dictionary
////////////////////////////////////////////////////////////////
// Create two observable SortedList instances
SortedList<string, bool> sortedList1 = new SortedList<string, bool>();
SortedList<string, bool> sortedList2 = new SortedList<string, bool>();

var obsSortedList1 = sortedList1.MakeObservableDictionary();
var obsSortedList2 = sortedList2.MakeObservableDictionary();

// Create an observer for the two subject objects
ObservableDictionaryObserver<string, bool> listObserver =
    new ObservableDictionaryObserver<string, bool>();

// Register the three subjects with the observer
listObserver.Register(obsSortedList1);
listObserver.Register(obsSortedList2);

// hook up the approval events for adding or changing
listObserver.ApproveAdd +=
    new ObservableDictionaryObserver<string, bool>.
        Approval(ApprovePositive);
listObserver.ApproveChange +=
    new ObservableDictionaryObserver<string, bool>.
        Approval(ApprovePositive);

// Use the observable instances
```

```
    obsSortedList1.Add("Item 1",true);
    obsSortedList2.Add("Item 2", false);

    // Insure the approval process worked
    Debug.Assert(obsSortedList1.Count == 1);
    // this should be empty as only true values are taken
    Debug.Assert(obsSortedList2.Count == 0);

    // Unregister the observable instances
    listObserver.Unregister(obsSortedList2);
    listObserver.Unregister(obsSortedList1);
}

static bool SeekApproval(object sender,
        ObservableDictionaryEventArgs<int, string> args)
{
    // only allow strings of no more than 3 characters in
    // our dictionary
    string value = args.Value.ToString();
    if (value.Length <= 3)
        return true;
    return false;
}

static bool ApprovePositive(object sender,
        ObservableDictionaryEventArgs<string, bool> args)
{
    // only allow positive values
    return args.Value;
}
```

Note that if the ObservableDictionaries are used without registering them, no events will be raised. Since no events are raised, the observer cannot do its job, and values may be added to the unregistered subjects that are out of bounds for the application.

When using the observer design pattern in this fashion, keep in mind that fine-grained events, such as the ones in this recipe, could possibly drag down performance, so set a goal and then profile your code. If you have many subjects raising many events, your application could fail to meet performance expectations.

Notice that in the second set of code exercising the ObservableDictionary, a SortedList<K,V> is used instead of a Dictionary<K,V> with no difference in the usage patterns or results:

```
    // Use Dictionary<int,string> as the base
    Dictionary<int, string> dictionary1 = new Dictionary<int, string>();
    var obsDict1 = dictionary1.MakeObservableDictionary();

    // Use SortedList<string,bool> as the base
    SortedList<string, bool> sortedList1 = new SortedList<string, bool>();
    var obsSortedList1 = sortedList1.MakeObservableDictionary();
```

See Also

The "Event Keyword," "EventHandler Delegate," "EventArgs Class," and "Handling and Raising Events" topics in the MSDN documentation.

9.7 Using Lambda Expressions

Problem

There is a feature in C# 3.0 called lambda expressions. While lambda expressions can be viewed as syntactic sugar for making anonymous method definition less difficult, you want to understand all of the different ways that they can be used to help you in your daily programming chores as well as understand the ramifications of those uses.

Solution

Lambda expressions can be implemented by the compiler from methods created by the developer. There are two orthogonal characteristics that lambda expressions may have:

- Parameter lists may have explicit or implicit types.
- Bodies may be expressions or statement blocks.

Let's start with the original way to use delegates. First, you would declare a delegate type, DoWork in this case, and then you would create an instance of it (as shown here in the WorkItOut method). Declaring the instance of the delegate requires that you specify a method to execute when the delegate is invoked, and here the DoWorkMethodImpl method has been connected. The delegate is invoked, and the text is written to the console via the DoWorkMethodImpl method:

```
class OldWay
{
        // declare delegate
        delegate int DoWork(string work);

        // have a method to create an instance of and call the delegate
        public void WorkItOut( )
        {
                // declare instance
                DoWork dw = new DoWork(DoWorkMethodImpl);
                // invoke delegate
                int i = dw("Do work the old way");
        }

        // Have a method that the delegate is tied to with a matching signature
        // so that it is invoked when the delegate is called
        public int DoWorkMethodImpl(string s)
        {
```

```
                    Console.WriteLine(s);
                    return s.GetHashCode( );
          }
    }
```

Lambda expressions allow you to set up code to run when a delegate is invoked, but
there does not need to be a named formal method declaration that is given to the delegate. The method thus declared is nameless and closed over the scope of the outer
method. For example, you could have written the preceding code using a lambda
expression such as this:

```
class LambdaWay
{
          // declare delegate
          delegate int DoWork(string work);

          // have a method to create an instance of and call the delegate
          public void WorkItOut( )
          {
                    // declare instance
                    DoWork dw = s =>
                    {
                              Console.WriteLine(s);
                              return s.GetHashCode( );
                    };
                    // invoke delegate
                    int i = dw("Do some inline work");
          }
    }
```

Notice that instead of having a method called DoWorkMethodImpl, you use the => operator to directly assign the code from that method inline to the DoWork delegate. The
assignment looks like this:

```
                    DoWork dw = s =>
                    {
                              Console.WriteLine(s);
                              return s.GetHashCode( );
                    };
```

You also provide the parameter required by the DoWork delegate (string), and your
code returns an int (s.GetHashCode( )) as the delegate requires. When setting up a
lambda expression, the code must "match" the delegate signature, or you will get a
compiler error.

By match we mean:

If explicitly typed, the lambda parameters must exactly match the delegate parameters. If implicitly typed, the lambda parameters get the delegate parameter types.

The body of the lambda must be a legal expression or statement block given the
parameter types.

The return type of the lambda must be implicitly convertible to the return type of the delegate. It need not match exactly.

There is yet another way you can set up the delegate, and that is through the magic of delegate inference. Delegate inference allows you to assign the method name directly to the delegate instance without having to write the code for creating a new delegate object. Under the covers, C# actually writes the IL for creating the delegate object, but you don't have to do it explicitly here. Using delegate inference instead of writing out new [Delegate Type]([Method Name]) everywhere helps to unclutter the code involved in the usage of delegates, as shown here:

```
class DirectAssignmentWay
{
        // declare delegate
        delegate int DoWork(string work);

        // have a method to create an instance of and call the delegate
        public void WorkItOut()
        {
                // declare instance and assign method
                DoWork dw = DoWorkMethodImpl;
                // invoke delegate
                int i = dw("Do some direct assignment work");
        }
        // Have a method that the delegate is tied to with a matching signature
        // so that it is invoked when the delegate is called
        public int DoWorkMethodImpl(string s)
        {
                Console.WriteLine(s);
                return s.GetHashCode();
        }
}
```

Notice that all that is assigned to the DoWork delegate instance dw is the method name DoWorkMethodImpl. There is no "new DoWork(DoWorkMethodImpl)" call as there was in older C# code.

 Remember, the underlying delegate wrapper does not go away; delegate inference just simplifies the syntax a bit by hiding some of it.

Alternatively, you can also set up lambda expressions that take generic type parameters to enable working with generic delegates as you do here in the GenericWay class:

```
class GenericWay
{
        // have a method to create two instances of and call the delegates
        public void WorkItOut()
        {
                Func<string,string> dwString = s =>
                {
```

```
                        Console.WriteLine(s);
                        return s;
        };

        // invoke string delegate
        string retStr = dwString("Do some generic work");

        Func<int,int> dwInt = i =>
        {
                        Console.WriteLine(i);
                        return i;
        };

        // invoke int delegate
        int j = dwInt(5);


    }
}
```

Discussion

One of the useful things about lambda expressions is the concept of outer variables.
The official definition of outer variables is that they are any local variable, value
parameter, or parameter array with a scope that contains the lambda expression.

What does this mean? It means that, inside of the code of the lambda expression,
you can touch variables outside of the scope of that method. There is a concept of
"capturing" the variables that occurs when a lambda expression actually makes reference to one of the outer variables. In the following example, the count variable is captured and incremented by the lambda expression. The count variable is not part of
the original scope of the lambda expression but part of the outer scope. It is incremented and then the incremented value is returned and totaled:

```
public void SeeOuterWork()
{
    int count = 0;
    int total = 0;
    Func<int> countUp = () => count++;
    for(int i=0;i<10;i++)
    {
        total += countUp();
    }
    Debug.WriteLine("Total = " + total);
}
```

What capturing actually does is extend the lifetime of the outer variable to coincide
with the lifetime of the underlying delegate instance that represents the lambda
expression. This should encourage you to be careful about what you touch from
inside a lambda expression. You could be causing things to hang around a lot longer
than you originally planned. The garbage collector won't get a chance to clean up
those outer variables until later, when they are used in the lambda expression. Capturing outer variables has another garbage-collector effect: when locals or value

parameters are captured, they are no longer considered to be fixed but are now movable, so any unsafe code must now fix that variable before use by using the fixed keyword.

Outer variables can affect how the compiler generates the internal IL for the lambda expression. If it uses outer variables, it is generated as a private method of a nested class rather than as another private method of the class it is declared in, as it otherwise would be. If the outer method is static, then the lambda expression cannot access instance members via the "this" keyword, as the nested class will also be generated as static.

There are two types of lambda expressions: Expression lambdas and Statement lambdas. This Expression lambda has no parameters and simply increments the count variable in an expression:

```
int count = 0;
Count countUp = () => count++;
```

Statement lambdas have the body enclosed in curly braces and can contain any number of statements like this:

```
Func<int,int> dwInt = i =>
{
        Console.WriteLine(i);
        return i;
};
```

A few last things to remember about lambda expressions:

- They can't use break, goto, or continue to jump from the lambda expression to a target outside the lambda expression block.
- No unsafe code can be executed inside a lambda expression.
- Lambda expressions cannot be used on the left side of the is operator.
- Since lambda expressions are a superset of anonymous methods, all restrictions that apply to anonymous methods also apply to lambda expressions.

See Also

The "Lambda Expressions (C# Programming Guide)" topic in the MSDN documentation.

9.8   Set Up Event Handlers Without the Mess

Problem

In versions of the .NET Framework prior to 2.0, the System.EventHandler delegate could be used on events in which the arguments were always of type System. EventArgs. This was great if you really didn't care about any data that went along with an event. But as you are all fine programmers and can see the possibilities of passing data along with the event, you had to set up a delegate and an event for every event you wanted. Example 9-7 demonstrates an old newspaper class that sends news to subscribers using the pre-.NET 2.0 event and event-handling methodology.

Example 9-7. Using pre-.NET 2.0 event and event-handling methods

```
public class IWantToKnowThen
{
        public static void TryMe( )
        {
                OldNewspaper DailyPaperFlash = new OldNewspaper( );
                DailyPaperFlash.NewsEvent +=
                        new OldNewspaper.NewsEventHandler(StaleNews);

                // send news
                DailyPaperFlash.TransmitStaleNews("Patriots win third super
bowl!");
                DailyPaperFlash.TransmitStaleNews("W takes office amongst recount.
");
                DailyPaperFlash.TransmitStaleNews("VS2005 is sooo passe");
        }

        private static void StaleNews(object src, NewsEventArgs nea)
        {
                Console.WriteLine(nea.LatestNews);
        }
}

// EventArgs derived class to hold our news data
public class NewsEventArgs : EventArgs
{
        private string _latestNews;

        public NewsEventArgs(string latestNews)
        {
                _latestNews = latestNews;
        }
        public string LatestNews
        {
                get { return _latestNews; }
        }
}

// OldNewspaper class
public class OldNewspaper
{
    // Allow clients to get the news.
        public delegate void NewsEventHandler(Object sender, NewsEventArgs e);
    public event NewsEventHandler NewsEvent;

    // Provide nice wrapper for sending news to clients.
        public void TransmitStaleNews(string news)
```

```
        {
    // Copy to a temporary variable to be thread-safe.
    NewsEventHandler newsEvent = NewsEvent;
    if (newsEvent != null)
        newsEvent(this, new NewsEventArgs(news));
        }
}
```

This code sets up an event that will report the news to subscribers as it comes in. It passes them the news data as an argument of type NewsEventArgs that has a LatestNews property.

As you can see from this example, whenever you had to set up multiple event handlers, it became an exercise in copy-and-paste and changing the event argument class type over and over again. It would be nice to not have to define lots of delegates and events just to change the event arguments, as all events (and corresponding handlers) are supposed to look like this:

```
void [EventHandler](object sender, [EventArgs] args)
{
    // Do something about this event firing.
}
```

Solution

EventHandler<T> takes a type parameter that represents the type of the System. EventArgs derived class to use in your event handlers. The beauty of this is that you no longer have to keep creating a delegate and an event for every event you wish to publish from your class. Even better, the Framework only has to have one event delegate instead of one for every event that passes custom data! Using the example shown in the Problem section, you can now rewrite the declaration of the event handler like this:

```
// Old way
public delegate void NewsEventHandler(Object sender, NewsEventArgs e);
public event NewsEventHandler NewsEvent;

// New way
public event EventHandler<NewsEventArgs> NewsEvent;
```

Now, you set up the nice wrapper function to allow the user to easily trigger the event:

```
// Old way
    public void TransmitNews(string news)
    {
    // Copy to a temporary variable to be thread-safe.
    NewsEventHandler newsEvent = NewsEvent;
    if (newsEvent != null)
        newsEvent(this, new NewsEventArgs(news));
        }
```

```
        // New way
        public void TransmitNews(string news)
        {
                // Copy to a temporary variable to be thread-safe.
                EventHandler<NewsEventArgs> breakingNews = NewsEvent;
                if (breakingNews != null)
                        breakingNews(this, new NewsEventArgs(news));
        }
```

The client can then hook up to the OldNewspaper class like this:

```
// Old way
public class IWantToKnowThen
{
        public static void TryMe()
        {
                OldNewspaper DailyPaperFlash = new OldNewspaper();
                DailyPaperFlash.NewsEvent +=
                        new OldNewspaper.NewsEventHandler(StaleNews);

            // send news
            DailyPaperFlash.TransmitStaleNews("Patriots win third super bowl!");
            DailyPaperFlash.TransmitStaleNews("W takes office amongst recount.");
            DailyPaperFlash.TransmitStaleNews("VS2005 is sooo passe");
        }

        private static void StaleNews(object src, NewsEventArgs nea)
        {
                Console.WriteLine(nea.LatestNews);
        }
}

// New way
public class IWantToKnowNow
{
        public static void Test()
        {
                eNewspaper DailyBitFlash = new eNewspaper();
                DailyBitFlash.NewsEvent +=
                        new EventHandler<NewsEventArgs>(BreakingNews);

            // send breaking news
            DailyBitFlash.TransmitBreakingNews("Patriots win!");
            DailyBitFlash.TransmitBreakingNews("New pres coming in 08.");
            DailyBitFlash.TransmitBreakingNews("VS2008 & .NET 3.5 Rocks LA");
        }

        private static void BreakingNews(object src, NewsEventArgs nea)
        {
                Console.WriteLine(nea.LatestNews);
        }
}
```

Discussion

The main benefit of using the generic EventHandler instead of System.EventHandler is that you write less code. Being able to declare a generic delegate allows you to have one delegate definition for multiple types. You might ask: Why is this interesting? Previously, when a delegate or event was declared by a class that wanted to publish information and allow multiple client classes to subscribe to it, if any data were to be passed along to the client classes, the convention was that a new class that derived from System.EventArgs had to be created. Then the class would be instantiated, filled with the data, and passed to the client. If the publishing class had only one event to notify people of, this wasn't too bad. If the publishing class had a lot of events, say, like a class derived from a UserControl, there would have to be a separate class derived from System.EventArgs and a separate event defined for every event that needed different data passed to it. Now, with a generic delegate, you can simply declare one delegate/event for each list of parameters you deal with, and then declare the type-specific events you need. Since events are supposed to have this signature:

```
void eventname( object sender, System.EventArgs args)
```

the kind folks at Microsoft gave you System.EventHandler<T> to deal with most events. If your code does have events defined that have more than two parameters, there would need to be a new delegate created to be the base of those events. Since most events do not have more than two parameters, this is a bit nonstandard, but not out of the question.

See Also

The "Generic EventHandler" and "System. EventHandler" topics in the MSDN documentation.

9.9   Using Different Parameter Modifiers in Lambda Expressions

Problem

You know you can pass parameters to lambda expressions, but you need to figure out what parameter modifiers are valid with them.

Solution

Lambda expressions can use out and ref parameter modifiers but not the params modifier in their parameter list. However, this does not prevent the creation of delegates with any of these modifiers, as shown here:

```
// Declare out delegate.
delegate int DoOutWork(out string work);
```

```
// Declare ref delegate.
delegate int DoRefWork(ref string work);

// Declare params delegate.
delegate int DoParamsWork(params string[] workItems);
```

Even though the DoParamsWork delegate is defined with the params keyword on the parameter, it can still be used as a type for a lambda expression, as you'll see in a bit. To use the DoOutWork delegate, create a lambda expression inline using the out keyword and assign it to the DoOutWork delegate instance. Inside the lambda expression body, the out variable s is assigned a value first (as it doesn't have one by definition as an out parameter), writes it to the console, and returns the string hash code. Note that in the parameter list, the type of s (string) must be provided, as it is not inferred for a variable marked with the out keyword. It is not inferred for out or ref variables to preserve the representation at the call site and the parameter declaration site to help the developer clearly reason about the possible assignment to these variables:

```
// Declare instance and assign method.
DoOutWork dow = (out string s) =>
{
    s = "WorkFinished";
    Console.WriteLine(s);
    return s.GetHashCode();
};
```

To run the lambda expression code, invoke the delegate with an out parameter, and then print out the result to the console:

```
// Invoke delegate.
string work;
int i = dow(out work);
Console.WriteLine(work);
```

To use the ref parameter modifier in a lambda expression, you create an inline method to hook up to the DoRefWork delegate with a ref parameter. In the method, you show you can write the original value out, reassign the value, and get the hash code of the new value. Note that in the parameter list, in the same manner as for the out keyword, the type of s (string) must be provided, as it cannot be inferred for a variable marked with the ref keyword:

```
// Declare instance and assign method.
DoRefWork drw = (ref string s) =>
{
    Console.WriteLine(s);
    s = "WorkFinished";
    return s.GetHashCode();
};
```

To run the lambda expression, you assign a value to the string work and then pass it as a ref parameter to the DoRefWork delegate that is instantiated. Upon return from the delegate call, you write out the new value for the work string:

```
// Invoke delegate.
work = "WorkStarted";
i = drw(ref work);
Console.WriteLine(work);
```

While it is possible to declare a delegate with the params modifier, you cannot hook up the delegate using a lambda expression with the params keyword in the parameter list. You get the CS1525 Invalid expression term 'params' compiler error on the DoParamsWork line:

```
// Done as a lambda expression you get CS1525 "Invalid expression term 'params'"
DoParamsWork dpw = (params object[] workItems) =>
//{
//    foreach (object o in workItems)
//    {
//        Console.WriteLine(o.ToString());
//    }
//    return o.GetHashCode();
//};
```

Even if you try to do this using an anonymous method instead of a lambda expression, you still cannot hook up the delegate with the params keyword in the parameter list. You get the CS1670 "params is not valid in this context" compiler error on the DoParamsWork line:

```
// Done as an anonymous method you get CS1670 "params is not valid in this context"
//DoParamsWork dpw = delegate(params object[] workItems)
//{
//    foreach (object o in workItems)
//    {
//        Console.WriteLine(o.ToString());
//    }
//    return o.GetHashCode();
//};
```

You can, however, omit the params keyword and still set up the lambda expression for the delegate, as shown here:

```
// All we have to do is omit the params keyword.
DoParamsWork dpw = workItems =>
{
    foreach (object o in workItems)
    {
        Console.WriteLine(o.ToString());
    }
    return workItems.GetHashCode();
};
```

Notice that although you've removed the params keyword from the lambda expression, this doesn't stop you from using the same syntax. The params keyword is present on the delegate type, so you can invoke it thusly:

```
int i = dpw("Hello", "42", "bar");
```

So this illustrates that you can bind a lambda expression to a delegate declared using params, and once you've done that, you can invoke the lambda expression, passing in any number of parameters you like, just as you'd expect.

Discussion

Lambda expressions cannot access the ref or out parameters of an outer scope. This means any out or ref variables that were defined as part of the containing method are off-limits for use inside the body of the lambda expression:

```
// Declare delegate.
delegate int DoWork(string work);

public void TestOut(out string outStr)
{
    // Declare instance.
    DoWork dw =  s =>
    {
        Console.WriteLine(s);
        // Causes error CS1628:
        // "Cannot use ref or out parameter 'outStr' inside an
        // anonymous method, lambda expression, or query expression"
        //outStr = s;
        return s.GetHashCode( );
    };
    // Invoke delegate.
    int i = dw("DoWorkMethodImpl1");
}

public void TestRef(ref string refStr)
{
    // Declare instance.
    DoWork dw = s =>
    {
        Console.WriteLine(s);
        // Causes error CS1628:
        // "Cannot use ref or out parameter 'refStr' inside an
        // anonymous method, lambda expression, or query expression"
        // refStr = s;
        return s.GetHashCode( );
    };
    // Invoke delegate
    int i = dw("DoWorkMethodImpl1");
}
```

Interestingly enough, lambda expressions can access outer variables with the params modifier:

```
// Declare delegate.
delegate int DoWork(string work);

public void TestParams(params string[] items)
{
```

```
            // Declare instance.
            DoWork dw = s =>
            {
                Console.WriteLine(s);
                foreach (string item in items)
                {
                    Console.WriteLine(item);
                }
                return s.GetHashCode( );
            };
            // Invoke delegate.
            int i = dw("DoWorkMethodImpl1");
        }
```

Because the params modifier is there for the benefit of the calling site (so the compiler knows to make this a method call that supports variable-length argument lists) and because lambda expressions are never called directly (always called via a delegate), then it makes no sense for an lambda expression to be decorated with something there for the benefit of the calling site—there is no calling site. This is why it doesn't matter that you can't use the params keyword on a lambda expression. For lambda expressions, the calling site is always calling through the delegate, so what matters is whether that delegate has the params keyword or not.

See Also

Recipe 9.11; the "CS1670," "CS1525," "CS1628," "out," "ref," "params," and "System.ParamArrayAttribute" topics in the MSDN documentation.

9.10   Using Closures in C#

Problem

You want to associate a small amount of state with some behavior without going to the trouble of building a new class.

Solution

Use lambda expressions to implement closures. Closures can be defined as functions that capture the state of the environment that is in scope where they are declared. Put more simply, they are current state plus some behavior that can read and modify that state. Lambda expressions have the capacity to capture external variables and extend their lifetime, which makes closures possible in C#.

To show an example of this, you will build a quick reporting system that tracks sales personnel and their revenue production versus commissions. The closure behavior is that you can build one bit of code that does the commission calculations per quarter and works on every salesperson.

First, you have to define your sales personnel:

```csharp
class SalesWeasel
{
    #region CTOR
    public SalesWeasel()
    {
    }

    public SalesWeasel(string name,
                       decimal annualQuota,
                       decimal commissionRate)
    {
        this.Name = name;
        this.AnnualQuota = annualQuota;
        this.CommissionRate = commissionRate;
    }
    #endregion //CTOR

    #region Private Members
    decimal _commission;
    #endregion Private Members

    #region Properties
    public string Name { get; set; }

    public decimal AnnualQuota { get; set; }

    public decimal CommissionRate { get; set; }

    public decimal Commission
    {
        get { return _commission; }
        set
        {
            _commission = value;
            this.TotalCommission += _commission;
        }
    }

    public decimal TotalCommission {get; private set; }
    #endregion // Properties
}
```

Sales personnel have a name, an annual quota, a commission rate for sales, and some storage for holding a quarterly commission and a total commission. Now that you have something to work with, let's write a bit of code to do the work of calculating the commissions:

```csharp
delegate void CalculateEarnings(SalesWeasel weasel);

static CalculateEarnings GetEarningsCalculator(decimal quarterlySales,
                                               decimal bonusRate)
    {
```

```
            return salesWeasel =>
            {
                // Figure out the weasel's quota for the quarter.
                decimal quarterlyQuota = (salesWeasel.AnnualQuota / 4);
                // Did he make quota for the quarter?
                if (quarterlySales < quarterlyQuota)
                {
                    // Didn't make quota, no commission
                    salesWeasel.Commission = 0;
                }
                // Check for bonus-level performance (200% of quota).
                else if (quarterlySales > (quarterlyQuota * 2.0m))
                {
                    decimal baseCommission = quarterlyQuota *
                    salesWeasel.CommissionRate;
                    weasel.Commission = (baseCommission +
                            ((quarterlySales - quarterlyQuota) *
                            (salesWeasel.CommissionRate * (1 + bonusRate)))));
                }
                else // Just regular commission
                {
                    salesWeasel.Commission =
                        salesWeasel.CommissionRate * quarterlySales;
                }
            };
        }
```

You've declared the delegate type as `CalculateEarnings`, and it takes a `SalesWeasel`. You have a factory method to construct an instance of this delegate for you called `GetEarningsCalculator`, which creates a lambda expression to do the calculation of the `SalesWeasel`'s commission and returns a `CalculateEarnings` instantiation.

To get set up, you have to create your `SalesWeasels`:

```
// set up the sales weasels...
SalesWeasel[] weasels = {
    new SalesWeasel { Name="Chas", AnnualQuota=100000m, CommissionRate=0.10m },
    new SalesWeasel { Name="Ray", AnnualQuota=200000m, CommissionRate=0.025m },
    new SalesWeasel { Name="Biff", AnnualQuota=50000m, CommissionRate=0.001m }};
```

Then set up the earnings calculators based on quarterly earnings:

```
public class QuarterlyEarning
{
    public string Name { get; set; }
    public decimal Earnings { get; set; }
    public decimal Rate { get; set; }
}

QuarterlyEarning[] quarterlyEarnings =
            { new QuarterlyEarning(){ Name="Q1", Earnings = 65000m, Rate = 0.1m },
              new QuarterlyEarning(){ Name="Q2", Earnings = 20000m, Rate = 0.1m },
              new QuarterlyEarning(){ Name="Q3", Earnings = 37000m, Rate = 0.1m },
              new QuarterlyEarning(){ Name="Q4", Earnings = 110000m, Rate = 0.
15m}};
```

```
var calculators = from e in quarterlyEarnings
                  select new
                  {
                      Calculator =
                          GetEarningsCalculator(e.Earnings, e.Rate),
                      QuarterlyEarning = e
                  };
```

And, finally, run the numbers for each quarter for all SalesWeasels and then you can
generate the annual report from this data. This will tell the executives which sales
personnel are worth keeping by calling WriteCommissionReport:

```
decimal annualEarnings = 0;
foreach (var c in calculators)
{
    WriteQuarterlyReport(c.QuarterlyEarning.Name,
        c.QuarterlyEarning.Earnings, c.Calculator, weasels);
    annualEarnings += c.QuarterlyEarning.Earnings;
}

// Let's see who is worth keeping...
WriteCommissionReport(annualEarnings, weasels);
```

WriteQuarterlyReport invokes the CalculateEarnings lambda expression implementation (eCalc) for every SalesWeasel and modifies the state to assign quarterly commission values based on the commission rates for each one:

```
static void WriteQuarterlyReport(string quarter,
                                 decimal quarterlySales,
                                 CalculateEarnings eCalc,
                                 SalesWeasel[] weasels)
{
    Console.WriteLine("{0} Sales Earnings on Quarterly Sales of {1}:",
        quarter, quarterlySales.ToString("C"));
    foreach (SalesWeasel weasel in weasels)
    {
        // Calc commission
        eCalc(weasel);
        // Report
        Console.WriteLine("    SalesWeasel {0} made a commission of : {1}",

            weasel.Name, weasel.Commission.ToString("C"));
    }
}
```

WriteCommissionReport checks the revenue earned by the individual sales personnel
against his commission, and if his commission is more than 20 percent of the revenue they generated, you recommend action be taken:

```
static void WriteCommissionReport(decimal annualEarnings,
                                  SalesWeasel[] weasels)
{
    decimal revenueProduced = ((annualEarnings) / weasels.Length);
    Console.WriteLine("");
```

```
        Console.WriteLine("Annual Earnings were {0}",
            annualEarnings.ToString("C"));
        Console.WriteLine("");
        var whoToCan = from weasel in weasels
                    select new
                    {
                        // if his commission is more than 20%
                        // of what he produced, can him
                        CanThem = (revenueProduced * 0.2m) <
                                    weasel.TotalCommission,
                        weasel.Name,
                        weasel.TotalCommission
                    };

        foreach (var weaselInfo in whoToCan)
        {
            Console.WriteLine("    Paid {0} {1} to produce {2}",
                weaselInfo.Name,
                weaselInfo.TotalCommission.ToString("C"),
                revenueProduced.ToString("C"));
            if (weaselInfo.CanThem)
            {
                Console.WriteLine("        FIRE {0}!", weaselInfo.Name);
            }
        }
    }
}
```

The output for your revenue and commission tracking program is listed here for your
enjoyment:

```
Q1 Sales Earnings on Quarterly Sales of $65,000.00:
        SalesWeasel Chas made a commission of : $6,900.00
        SalesWeasel Ray made a commission of : $1,625.00
        SalesWeasel Biff made a commission of : $70.25
Q2 Sales Earnings on Quarterly Sales of $20,000.00:
        SalesWeasel Chas made a commission of : $0.00
        SalesWeasel Ray made a commission of : $0.00
        SalesWeasel Biff made a commission of : $20.00
Q3 Sales Earnings on Quarterly Sales of $37,000.00:
        SalesWeasel Chas made a commission of : $3,700.00
        SalesWeasel Ray made a commission of : $0.00
        SalesWeasel Biff made a commission of : $39.45
Q4 Sales Earnings on Quarterly Sales of $110,000.00:
        SalesWeasel Chas made a commission of : $12,275.00
        SalesWeasel Ray made a commission of : $2,975.00
        SalesWeasel Biff made a commission of : $124.63

Annual Earnings were $232,000.00

    Paid Chas $22,875.00 to produce $77,333.33
        FIRE Chas!
    Paid Ray $4,600.00 to produce $77,333.33
    Paid Biff $254.33 to produce $77,333.33
```

Discussion

One of the best ways we've heard of to describe closures in C# is to think of an object as a set of methods associated with data and to think of a closure as a set of data associated with a function. If you need to have several different operations on the same data, an object approach may make more sense. These are two different angles on the same problem, and the type of problem you are solving will help you decide which is the right approach. It just depends on your inclination as to which way to go. There are times when one-hundred-percent pure object-oriented programming can get tedious and is unnecessary, and closures are a nice way to solve some of those problems. The SalesWeasel commission example presented here is a demonstration of what you can do with closures. It could have been done without them, but at the expense of writing more class and method code.

Closures have been defined as stated earlier, but there is a stricter definition that essentially implies that the behavior associated with the state should not be able to modify the state in order to be a true closure. We tend to agree more with the first definition, as it defines what a closure should be, not how it should be implemented, which seems too restrictive. Whether you choose to think of this as a neat side feature of lambda expressions or you feel it is worthy of being called a closure, it is another programming trick for your toolbox and should not be dismissed.

See Also

Recipe 9.11; the "Lambda Expressions" topic in the MSDN documentation.

9.11 Performing Multiple Operations on a List Using Functors

Problem

You want to be able to perform multiple operations on an entire collection of objects at once, while keeping the operations functionally segmented.

Solution

Use a functor (or *function object*, as it is also known) as the vehicle for transforming the collection. A *functor* is any object that can be called as a function. Examples of this are a delegate, a function, a function pointer, or even an object that defines operator( ) for us C/C++ converts.

Needing to perform multiple operations on a collection is a reasonably common thing in software. Let's say that you have a stock portfolio with a bunch of stocks in it. Your StockPortfolio class would have a List of Stock object and would be able to add stocks:

```csharp
public class StockPortfolio : IEnumerable<Stock>
{
    List<Stock> _stocks;

    public StockPortfolio()
    {
        _stocks = new List<Stock>();
    }

    public void Add(string ticker, double gainLoss)
    {
        _stocks.Add(new Stock() {Ticker=ticker, GainLoss=gainLoss});
    }

    public IEnumerable<Stock> GetWorstPerformers(int topNumber)
    {
        return _stocks.OrderBy(
                    (Stock stock) => stock.GainLoss).Take(topNumber);
    }

    public void SellStocks(IEnumerable<Stock> stocks)
    {
        foreach(Stock s in stocks)
            _stocks.Remove(s);
    }

    public void PrintPortfolio(string title)
    {
        Console.WriteLine(title);
        _stocks.DisplayStocks();
    }

    #region IEnumerable<Stock> Members

    public IEnumerator<Stock> GetEnumerator()
    {
        return _stocks.GetEnumerator();
    }

    #endregion

    #region IEnumerable Members

    IEnumerator IEnumerable.GetEnumerator()
    {
        return this.GetEnumerator();
    }

    #endregion
}
```

The Stock class is rather simple. You just need a ticker symbol for the stock and its percentage of gain or loss:

```
public class Stock
{
    public double GainLoss { get; set; }
    public string Ticker { get; set; }
}
```

To use this `StockPortfolio`, you add a few stocks to it with gain/loss percentages and print out your starting portfolio. Once you have the portfolio, you want to get a list of the three worst-performing stocks, so you can improve your portfolio by selling them and print out your portfolio again:

```
StockPortfolio tech = new StockPortfolio( ) {
    {"OU81", -10.5},
    {"C#4VR", 2.0},
    {"PCKD", 12.3},
    {"BTML", 0.5},
    {"NOVB", -35.2},
    {"MGDCD", 15.7},
    {"GNRCS", 4.0},
    {"FNCTR", 9.16},
    {"LMBDA", 9.12},
    {"PCLS", 6.11}};

tech.PrintPortfolio("Starting Portfolio");
// sell the worst 3 performers
var worstPerformers = tech.GetWorstPerformers(3);
Console.WriteLine("Selling the worst performers:");
worstPerformers.DisplayStocks();
tech.SellStocks(worstPerformers);
tech.PrintPortfolio("After Selling Worst 3 Performers");
```

So far, nothing terribly interesting is happening. Let's take a look at how you figured out what the three worst performers were by looking at the internals of the `GetWorstPerformers` method:

```
public IEnumerable<Stock> GetWorstPerformers(int topNumber)
{
    return _stocks.OrderBy(
            (Stock stock) => stock.GainLoss).Take(topNumber);
}
```

The first thing you do is make sure the list is sorted so that the worst performing stocks are at the front of the list by calling the `OrderBy` extension method on `IEnumerable<T>`. The `OrderBy` method takes a lambda expression which provides the gain/loss percentage for comparison for the number of stocks indicated by `topNumber` in the `Take` extension method.

`GetWorstPerformers` returns an `IEnumerable<Stock>` full of the three worst performers. Since they aren't making any money, you should cash in and sell them. For your purposes, selling is simply removing them from the list of stocks in `StockPortfolio`. To accomplish this, you use yet another functor to iterate over the list of stocks handed to the `SellStocks` function (the list of worst-performing ones, in your case), and then remove that stock from the internal list that the StockPortfolio class maintains:

```
public void SellStocks(IEnumerable<Stock> stocks)
{
    foreach(Stock s in stocks)
        _stocks.Remove(s);
}
```

Discussion

Functors come in a few different flavors that are known as a *generator* (a function with no parameters), a unary function (a function with one parameter), and a binary function (a function with two parameters). If the functor happens to return a Boolean value, then it gets an even more special naming convention: a unary function that returns a Boolean is called a *predicate*, and a binary function with a Boolean return is called a *binary predicate*. You will now notice in the Framework that there are both Predicate<T> and BinaryPredicate<T> delegates defined to facilitate these uses of functors.

The List<T> and System.Array classes take predicates (Predicate<T>, BinaryPredicate<T>), actions (Action<T>), comparisons (Comparison<T>), and converters (Converter<T,U>). This allows these collections to be operated on in a much more general way than was previously possible.

Thinking in terms of functors can be a bit of a challenge at first, but once you put a bit of time into it, you can start to see powerful possibilities open up before you. Any code you can write once, debug once, and use many times is a useful thing, and functors can help you get to that place.

The output for the example is listed here:

```
Starting Portfolio
  (OU81) lost 10.5%
  (C#4VR) gained 2%
  (PCKD) gained 12.3%
  (BTML) gained 0.5%
  (NOVB) lost 35.2%
  (MGDCD) gained 15.7%
  (GNRCS) gained 4%
  (FNCTR) gained 9.16%
  (LMBDA) gained 9.12%
  (PCLS) gained 6.11%
Selling the worst performers:
  (NOVB) lost 35.2%
  (OU81) lost 10.5%
  (BTML) gained 0.5%
```

```
After Selling Worst 3 Performers
  (C#4VR) gained 2%
  (PCKD) gained 12.3%
  (MGDCD) gained 15.7%
  (GNRCS) gained 4%
  (FNCTR) gained 9.16%
  (LMBDA) gained 9.12%
  (PCLS) gained 6.11%
```

See Also

The "System.Collections.Generic.List<T>," "System.Linq.Enumerable Class," and "System.Array" topics in the MSDN documentation.

CHAPTER 10

Regular Expressions

10.0 Introduction

The .NET Framework Class Library includes the System.Text.RegularExpressions namespace, which is devoted to creating, executing, and obtaining results from regular expressions executed against a string.

Regular expressions take the form of a pattern that can be matched to zero or more characters within a string. The simplest of these patterns, such as .* (match anything except newline characters) and [A-Za-z] (match any letter) are easy to learn, but more advanced patterns can be difficult to learn and even more difficult to implement correctly. Learning and understanding regular expressions can take considerable time and effort, but the work will pay off.

Regular expression patterns can take a simple form—such as a single word or character—or a much more complex pattern. The more complex patterns can recognize and match such things as the year portion of a date, all of the <SCRIPT> tags in an ASP page, or a phrase in a sentence that varies with each use. The .NET regular expression classes provide a very flexible and powerful way to do such things as recognize text, replace text within a string, and split up text into individual sections based on one or more complex delimiters.

Despite the complexity of regular expression patterns, the regular expression classes in the FCL are easy to use in your applications. Executing a regular expression consists of the following steps:

1. Create an instance of a Regex object that contains the regular expression pattern along with any options for executing that pattern.

2. Retrieve a reference to an instance of a Match object by calling the Match instance method if you want only the first match found. Or, retrieve a reference to an instance of the MatchesCollection object by calling the Matches instance method if you want more than just the first match found. If, however, you want to know

only whether the input string was a match and do not need the extra details on the nature of the match, you can use the `Regex.IsMatch` method.

3. If you've called the `Matches` method to retrieve a `MatchCollection` object, iterate over the `MatchCollection` using a `foreach` loop. Each iteration will allow access to every `Match` object that the regular expression produced.

10.1   Enumerating Matches

Problem

You need to find one or more substrings corresponding to a particular pattern within a string. You need to be able to inform the searching code to return either all matching substrings or only the matching substrings that are unique within the set of all matched strings.

Solution

Call the `FindSubstrings` method shown in Example 10-1, which executes a regular expression and obtains all matching text. This method returns either all matching results or only the unique matches; this behavior is controlled by the `findAllUnique` parameter. Note that if the `findAllUnique` parameter is set to `true`, the unique matches are returned sorted alphabetically.

Example 10-1. FindSubstrings method

```
using System;
using System.Collections;
using System.Text.RegularExpressions;

public static Match[] FindSubstrings(string source, string matchPattern,
                                     bool findAllUnique)
{
    SortedList uniqueMatches = new SortedList();
    Match[] retArray = null;

    Regex RE = new Regex(matchPattern, RegexOptions.Multiline);
    MatchCollection theMatches = RE.Matches(source);

    if (findAllUnique)
    {
        for (int counter = 0; counter < theMatches.Count; counter++)
        {
            if (!uniqueMatches.ContainsKey(theMatches[counter].Value))
            {

                uniqueMatches.Add(theMatches[counter].Value,
                                  theMatches[counter]);
            }
        }
    }
```

Example 10-1. FindSubstrings method (continued)

```
        retArray = new Match[uniqueMatches.Count];
        uniqueMatches.Values.CopyTo(retArray, 0);
    }
    else
    {
        retArray = new Match[theMatches.Count];
        theMatches.CopyTo(retArray, 0);
    }

    return (retArray);

}
```

The TestFindSubstrings method shown in Example 10-2 searches for any tags in an XML string; it does this by searching for a block of text that begins with the < character and ends with the > character.

This method first displays all unique tag matches present in the XML string and then displays all tag matches within the string.

Example 10-2. The TestFindSubstrings method

```
public static void TestFindSubstrings( )
{
    string matchPattern = "<.*>";

    XDocument xDoc = new XDocument(
        new XDeclaration("1.0", "UTF-8", "yes"),
        new XComment("my comment"),
        new XElement("Window", new XAttribute("ID", "Main"),
            new XElement("Control", new XAttribute("ID", "TextBox"),
                new XElement("Property", new XAttribute("Top", "0"),
                    new XAttribute("Left", "0"), new XAttribute("Text", "BLANK"))),
            new XElement("Control", new XAttribute("ID", "Label"),
                new XElement("Property", new XAttribute("Top", "0"),
                    new XAttribute("Left", "0"),
                    new XAttribute("Caption", "Enter Name Here"))),
            new XElement("Control", new XAttribute("ID", "Label"),
                new XElement("Property", new XAttribute("Top", "0"),
                    new XAttribute("Left", "0"),
                    new XAttribute("Caption", "Enter Name Here")))
        )
    );

    Console.WriteLine("UNIQUE MATCHES");
    Match[] x1 = FindSubstrings(xDoc.ToString( ), matchPattern, true);
    foreach(Match m in x1)
    {
        Console.WriteLine(m.Value);
    }

    Console.WriteLine( );
```

Example 10-2. The TestFindSubstrings method (continued)

```
    Console.WriteLine("ALL MATCHES");
    Match[] x2 = FindSubstrings(xDoc.ToString( ), matchPattern, false);
    foreach(Match m in x2)
    {
        Console.WriteLine(m.Value);
    }
}
```

The following text will be displayed:

```
UNIQUE MATCHES
<!--my comment-->
</Control>
</Window>
<Control ID="Label">
<Control ID="TextBox">
<Property Top="0" Left="0" Caption="Enter Name Here" />
<Property Top="0" Left="0" Text="BLANK" />
<Window ID="Main">

ALL MATCHES
<!--my comment-->
<Window ID="Main">
<Control ID="TextBox">
<Property Top="0" Left="0" Text="BLANK" />
</Control>
<Control ID="Label">
<Property Top="0" Left="0" Caption="Enter Name Here" />
</Control>
<Control ID="Label">
<Property Top="0" Left="0" Caption="Enter Name Here" />
</Control>
</Window>
```

Discussion

As you can see, the regular expression classes in the FCL are quite easy to use. The first step is to create an instance of the Regex object that contains the regular expression pattern, along with any options for running this pattern. The second step is to get a reference to an instance of the Match object, if you need only the first found match; or a MatchCollection object, if you need more than just the first found match. To get a reference to this object, the two instance methods Match and Matches can be called from the Regex object that was created in the first step. The Match method returns a single match object (Match) and Matches returns a collection of match objects (MatchCollection).

The FindSubstrings method returns an array of Match objects that can be used by the calling code. You may have noticed that the unique elements are returned sorted, and the nonunique elements are not sorted. A SortedList, which is used by the

FindSubstrings method to store unique strings that match the regular expression pattern, automatically sorts its items when they are added.

The regular expression used in the TestFindSubstrings method is very simplistic and will work in most—but not all—conditions. For example, if two tags are on the same line, as shown here:

```
<tagData></tagData>
```

the regular expression will catch the entire line, not each tag separately. You could change the regular expression from <.*> to <[^>]*> to match only up to the closing > ([^>]* matches everything that is *not* a >).

See Also

The ".NET Framework Regular Expressions" and "SortedList Class" topics in the MSDN documentation.

10.2   Extracting Groups from a MatchCollection

Problem

You have a regular expression that contains one or more named groups, such as the following:

```
\\\\(?<TheServer>\w*)\\(?<TheService>\w*)\\
```

where the named group TheServer will match any server name within a UNC string, and TheService will match any service name within a UNC string.

 This pattern does not match the UNCW format.

You need to store the groups that are returned by this regular expression in a keyed collection (such as a Dictionary<string, Group>) in which the key is the group name.

Solution

The ExtractGroupings method shown in Example 10-3 obtains a set of Group objects keyed by their matching group name.

Example 10-3. ExtractGroupings method

```
using System;
using System.Collections;
using System.Collections.Generics;
using System.Text.RegularExpressions;
```

Example 10-3. ExtractGroupings method (continued)

```
public static List<Dictionary<string, Group>> ExtractGroupings(string source,
                                                    string matchPattern,
                                                    bool wantInitialMatch)
{
    List<Dictionary<string, Group>> keyedMatches =
        new List<Dictionary<string, Group>>();
    int startingElement = 1;
    if (wantInitialMatch)
    {
        startingElement = 0;
    }

    Regex RE = new Regex(matchPattern, RegexOptions.Multiline);
    MatchCollection theMatches = RE.Matches(source);

    foreach(Match m in theMatches)
    {
        Dictionary<string, Group> groupings = new Dictionary<string, Group>();

        for (int counter = startingElement; counter < m.Groups.Count; counter++)
        {
            // If we had just returned the MatchCollection directly, the
            // GroupNameFromNumber method would not be available to use.
            groupings.Add(RE.GroupNameFromNumber(counter), m.Groups[counter]);
        }

        keyedMatches.Add(groupings);
    }

    return (keyedMatches);
}
```

The ExtractGroupings method can be used in the following manner to extract named groups and organize them by name:

```
public static void TestExtractGroupings()
{
    string source = @"Path = ""\\MyServer\MyService\MyPath;
                    \\MyServer2\MyService2\MyPath2\""";
    string matchPattern = @"\\\\(?<TheServer>\w*)\\(?<TheService>\w*)\\";

    foreach (Dictionary<string, Group> grouping in
            ExtractGroupings(source, matchPattern, true))
    {
        foreach (KeyValuePair<string, Group> kvp in grouping)
            Console.WriteLine("Key / Value = " + kvp.Key + " / " + kvp.Value);
        Console.WriteLine("");
    }
}
```

This test method creates a `source` string and a regular expression pattern in the `MatchPattern` variable. The two groupings in this regular expression are highlighted here:

```
string matchPattern = @"\\\\(?<TheServer>\w*)\\(?<TheService>\w*)\\";
```

The names for these two groups are `TheServer` and `TheService`. Text that matches either of these groupings can be accessed through these group names.

The `source` and `matchPattern` variables are passed in to the `ExtractGroupings` method, along with a Boolean value, which is discussed shortly. This method returns a `List<T>`; containing `Dictionary<string,Group>` objects. These `Dictionary<string,Group>` objects contain the matches for each of the named groups in the regular expression, keyed by their group name.

This test method, `TestExtractGroupings`, returns the following:

```
Key / Value = 0 / \\MyServer\MyService\
Key / Value = TheService / MyService
Key / Value = TheServer / MyServer

Key / Value = 0 / \\MyServer2\MyService2\
Key / Value = TheService / MyService2
Key / Value = TheServer / MyServer2
```

If the last parameter to the `ExtractGroupings` method were to be changed to `false`, the following output would result:

```
Key / Value = TheService / MyService
Key / Value = TheServer / MyServer

Key / Value = TheService / MyService2
Key / Value = TheServer / MyServer2
```

The only difference between these two outputs is that the first grouping is not displayed when the last parameter to `ExtractGroupings` is changed to `false`. The first grouping is always the complete match of the regular expression.

Discussion

Groups within a regular expression can be defined in one of two ways. The first way is to add parentheses around the subpattern that you wish to define as a grouping. This type of grouping is sometimes labeled as *unnamed*. This grouping can later be easily extracted from the final text in each `Match` object returned by running the regular expression. The regular expression for this recipe could be modified, as follows, to use a simple unnamed group:

```
string matchPattern = @"\\\\(\w*)\\(\w*)\\";
```

After running the regular expression, you can access these groups using a numeric integer value starting with 1.

The second way to define a group within a regular expression is to use one or more *named groups*. A named group is defined by adding parentheses around the subpattern that you wish to define as a grouping and, additionally, adding a name to each grouping, using the following syntax:

```
(?<Name>\w*)
```

The *Name* portion of this syntax is the name you specify for this group. After executing this regular expression, you can access this group by the name *Name*.

To access each group, you must first use a loop to iterate each `Match` object in the `MatchCollection`. For each `Match` object, you access the `GroupCollection`'s indexer, using the following unnamed syntax:

```
string group1 = m.Groups[1].Value;
string group2 = m.Groups[2].Value;
```

or the following named syntax, where `m` is the `Match` object:

```
string group1 = m.Groups["Group1_Name"].Value;
string group2 = m.Groups["Group2_Name"].Value;
```

If the `Match` method was used to return a single `Match` object instead of the `MatchCollection`, use the following syntax to access each group:

```
// Unnamed syntax
string group1 = theMatch.Groups[1].Value;
string group2 = theMatch.Groups[2].Value;

// Named syntax
string group1 = theMatch.Groups["Group1_Name"].Value;
string group2 = theMatch.Groups["Group2_Name"].Value;
```

where `theMatch` is the `Match` object returned by the `Match` method.

See Also

The ".NET Framework Regular Expressions" and "Dictionary Class" topics in the MSDN documentation.

10.3   Verifying the Syntax of a Regular Expression

Problem

You have constructed a regular expression dynamically, either from your code or based on user input. You need to test the validity of this regular expression's syntax before you actually use it.

Solution

Use the `VerifyRegEx` method shown in Example 10-4 to test the validity of a regular expression's syntax.

Example 10-4. VerifyRegEx method

```
using System;
using System.Text.RegularExpressions;

public static bool VerifyRegEx(string testPattern)
{
    bool isValid = true;
    if ((testPattern != null) && (testPattern.Length > 0))
    {
        try
        {
            Regex.Match("", testPattern);
        }
        catch (ArgumentException)
        {
            // BAD PATTERN: syntax error
            isValid = false;
        }
    }
    else
    {
        //BAD PATTERN: pattern is null or empty
        isValid = false;
    }

    return (isValid);
}
```

To use this method, pass it the regular expression that you wish to verify:

```
public static void TestUserInputRegEx(string regEx)
{
    if (VerifyRegEx(regEx))
        Console.WriteLine("This is a valid regular expression.");
    else
        Console.WriteLine("This is not a valid regular expression.");
}
```

Discussion

The VerifyRegEx method calls the static Regex.Match method, which is useful for running regular expressions on the fly against a string. The static Regex.Match method returns a single Match object. By using this static method to run a regular expression against a string (in this case, an empty string), you can determine whether the regular expression is invalid by watching for a thrown exception. The Regex.Match method will throw an ArgumentException if the regular expression is not syntactically correct. The Message property of this exception contains the reason the regular expression failed to run, and the ParamName property contains the regular expression passed to the Match method. Both of these properties are read-only.

Before testing the regular expression with the static Match method, the regular expression is tested to see if it is null or blank. A null regular expression string returns an ArgumentNullException when passed in to the Match method. On the other hand, if a blank regular expression is passed in to the Match method, no exception is thrown (as long as a valid string is also passed to the first parameter of the Match method).

10.4 Quickly Finding Only the Last Match in a String

Problem

You need to find the last pattern match in a string, but you do not want the overhead of finding all matches in a string and having to move to the last match in the collection of matches.

Solution

To execute a regular expression starting from the end of the string, use the RegexOptions.RightToLeft flag. The first found match is the last match in the string. You supply the RegexOptions.RightToLeft constant as an argument to the Match method. The instance Match method can be used as follows:

```
Regex RE = new Regex(Pattern, RegexOptions.RightToLeft);
Match theMatch = RE.Match(Source);
```

or use the static Regex.Match method:

```
Match theMatch = Regex.Match(Source, Pattern, RegexOptions.RightToLeft);
```

where *Pattern* is the regular expression pattern and *Source* is the string against which to run the pattern.

Discussion

The RegexOptions.RightToLeft regular expression option will force the regular expression engine to start searching for a pattern starting with the end of the string and proceeding backward toward the beginning of the string. The first match encountered will be the match closest to the end of the string—in other words, the last match in the string.

See Also

The ".NET Framework Regular Expressions" topic in the MSDN documentation.

10.5 Augmenting the Basic String Replacement Function

Problem

You need to replace character patterns within the target string with a new string. However, in this case, each replacement operation has a unique set of conditions that must be satisfied in order to allow the replacement to occur.

Solution

Use the overloaded instance `Replace` method shown in Example 10-5 that accepts a `MatchEvaluator` delegate along with its other parameters. The `MatchEvaluator` delegate is a callback method that overrides the default behavior of the `Replace` method.

Example 10-5. Overloaded Replace method that accepts a MatchEvaluator delegate

```
using System;
using System.Text.RegularExpressions;

public static string MatchHandler(Match theMatch)
{
    // Handle all ControlID_ entries.
    if (theMatch.Value.StartsWith("ControlID_", StringComparison.Ordinal))
    {
        long controlValue = 0;

        // Obtain the numeric value of the Top attribute.
        Match topAttribiteMatch = Regex.Match(theMatch.Value, "Top=([-]*\\d*)");
        if (topAttribiteMatch.Success)
        {

            if (topAttribiteMatch.Groups[1].Value.Trim().Equals(""))
            {
                // If blank, set to zero.
                return (theMatch.Value.Replace(
                        topAttribiteMatch.Groups[0].Value.Trim(),
                        "Top=0"));
            }
            else if (topAttribiteMatch.Groups[1].Value.Trim().StartsWith("-"
                                    , StringComparison.Ordinal))
            {
                // If only a negative sign (syntax error), set to zero.
                return (theMatch.Value.Replace(
                        topAttribiteMatch.Groups[0].Value.Trim(), "Top=0"));
            }
            else
            {
                // We have a valid number.
                // Convert the matched string to a numeric value.
                controlValue = long.Parse(topAttribiteMatch.Groups[1].Value,
```

```
                      System.Globalization.NumberStyles.Any);

            // If the Top attribute is out of the specified range,
            // set it to zero.
            if (controlValue < 0 || controlValue > 5000)
            {
                return (theMatch.Value.Replace(
                        topAttribiteMatch.Groups[0].Value.Trim( ),
                        "Top=0"));
            }
        }
    }
}

    return (theMatch.Value);
}
```

The callback method for the Replace method is shown here:

```
    public static void ComplexReplace(string matchPattern, string source)
    {
        MatchEvaluator replaceCallback = new MatchEvaluator(MatchHandler);
        Regex RE = new Regex(matchPattern, RegexOptions.Multiline);
        string newString = RE.Replace(source, replaceCallback);

        Console.WriteLine("Replaced String = " + newString);
    }
```

To use this callback method with the static Replace method, modify the previous
ComplexReplace method as follows:

```
    public void ComplexReplace(string matchPattern, string source)
    {
        MatchEvaluator replaceCallback = new MatchEvaluator(MatchHandler);
        string newString = Regex.Replace(source, matchPattern,
    replaceCallback);
        Console.WriteLine("Replaced String = " + newString);
    }
```

where *source* is the original string to run the replace operation against, and
matchPattern is the regular expression pattern to match in the *source* string.

If the ComplexReplace method is called from the following code:

```
    public static void TestComplexReplace( )
    {
        string matchPattern = "(ControlID_.*)";
        string source = @"WindowID=Main
        ControlID_TextBox1 Top=-100 Left=0 Text=BLANK
        ControlID_Label1 Top=9999990 Left=0 Caption=Enter Name Here
        ControlID_Label2 Top= Left=0 Caption=Enter Name Here";

        ComplexReplace(matchPattern, source);
    }
```

only the Top attributes of the ControlID_* lines are changed from their original values to 0.

The result of this replace action will change the Top attribute value of a ControlID_* line to zero if it is less than zero or greater than 5000. Any other tag that contains a Top attribute will remain unchanged. The following three lines of the source string will be changed from:

```
ControlID_TextBox1 Top=-100 Left=0 Text=BLANK
ControlID_Label1 Top=9999990 Left=0 Caption=Enter Name Here
ControlID_Label2 Top= Left=0 Caption=Enter Name Here";
```

to:

```
ControlID_TextBox1 Top=0 Left=0 Text=BLANK
ControlID_Label1 Top=0 Left=0 Caption=Enter Name Here
ControlID_Label2 Top=0 Left=0 Caption=Enter Name Here";
```

Discussion

The MatchEvaluator delegate, which is automatically invoked when it is supplied as a parameter to the Regex class's Replace method, allows for custom replacement of each string that conforms to the regular expression pattern.

If the current Match object is operating on a ControlID_* line with a Top attribute that is out of the specified range, the code within the MatchHandler callback method returns a new modified string. Otherwise, the currently matched string is returned unchanged. This ability allows you to override the default Replace functionality by replacing only that part of the source string that meets certain criteria. The code within this callback method gives you some idea of what can be accomplished using this replacement technique.

To make use of this callback method, you need a way to call it from the ComplexReplace method. First, a variable of type System.Text.RegularExpressions. MatchEvaluator is created. This variable (replaceCallback) is the delegate that is used to call the MatchHandler method:

```
MatchEvaluator replaceCallback = new MatchEvaluator(MatchHandler);
```

Finally, the Replace method is called with the reference to the MatchEvaluator delegate passed in as a parameter:

```
string newString = RE.Replace(source, replaceCallback);
```

See Also

The ".NET Framework Regular Expressions" topic in the MSDN documentation.

10.6   Implementing a Better Tokenizer

Problem

You need a tokenizer—also referred to as a *lexer*—that can split up a string based on a well-defined set of characters.

Solution

Using the Split method of the Regex class, you can use a regular expression to indicate the types of tokens and separators that you are interested in gathering. This technique works especially well with equations, since the tokens of an equation are well defined. For example, the code:

```
using System;
using System.Text.RegularExpressions;

public static string[] Tokenize(string equation)
{
    Regex re = new Regex(@"([\+\-\*\(\)\^\\])");
    return (re.Split(equation));
}
```

will divide up a string according to the regular expression specified in the Regex constructor. In other words, the string passed in to the Tokenize method will be divided up based on the delimiters +, −, *, (,), ^, and \. The following method will call the Tokenize method to tokenize the equation (y − 3)*(3111*x^21 + x + 320):

```
public static void TestTokenize()
{
    foreach(string token in Tokenize("(y - 3)*(3111*x^21 + x + 320)"))
        Console.WriteLine("String token = " + token.Trim());
}
```

which displays the following output:

```
string token =
String token = (
String token = y
String token = -
String token = 3
String token = )
String token = *
String token = (
String token = 3111
String token = *
String token = x
String token = ^
String token = 21
String token = +
String token = x
String token = +
String token = 320
```

```
String token = )
String token =
```

Notice that each individual operator, parenthesis, and number has been broken out into its own separate token.

Discussion

In real-world projects, you do not always have the luxury of being able to control the set of inputs to your code. By making use of regular expressions, you can take the original tokenizer and make it flexible enough to allow it to be applied to many types or styles of input.

The key method used here is the `Split` instance method of the `Regex` class. The return value of this method is a string array with elements that include each individual token of the source string—the equation, in this case.

Notice that the static method allows `RegexOptions` enumeration values to be used, while the instance method allows for a starting position to be defined and a maximum number of matches to occur. This may have some bearing on whether you choose the static or instance method.

See Also

The ".NET Framework Regular Expressions" topic in the MSDN documentation.

10.7 Counting Lines of Text

Problem

You need to count lines of text within a string or within a file.

Solution

Use the `LineCount` method shown in Example 10-6 to read in the entire file and count the number of line feeds.

Example 10-6. LineCount method

```
using System;
using System.Text.RegularExpressions;
using System.IO;

public static long LineCount(string source, bool isFileName)
{
    if (source != null)
    {
        string text = source;

        if (isFileName)
```

Example 10-6. LineCount method (continued)

```
    {
        using (FileStream FS = new FileStream(source, FileMode.Open,
                                    FileAccess.Read, FileShare.Read))
        {
            using (StreamReader SR = new StreamReader(FS))
            {

                text = SR.ReadToEnd( );
            }
        }
    }

    Regex RE = new Regex("\n", RegexOptions.Multiline);
    MatchCollection theMatches = RE.Matches(text);

    if (isFileName)
    {

        return (theMatches.Count);
    }
    else
    {

        return (theMatches.Count) + 1;
    }
    }
    else
    {

        // Handle a null source here.
        return (0);
    }
}
```

LineCount2, a better-performing alternate version of this method, uses the
StreamReader.ReadLine method to count lines in a file and a regular expression to
count lines in a string, as shown in Example 10-7.

Example 10-7. LineCount2 method

```
public static long LineCount2(string source, bool isFileName)
{
    if (source != null)
    {
        string text = source;
        long numOfLines = 0;

        if (isFileName)
        {
            using (FileStream FS = new FileStream(source, FileMode.Open,
                                        FileAccess.Read, FileShare.Read))
            {
```

Example 10-7. LineCount2 method (continued)

```
            using (StreamReader SR = new StreamReader(FS))
            {

                while (text != null)
                {
                    text = SR.ReadLine( );

                    if (text != null)
                    {
                        ++numOfLines;
                    }
                }
            }
        }

        return (numOfLines);

    }
    else
    {

        Regex RE = new Regex("\n", RegexOptions.Multiline);
        MatchCollection theMatches = RE.Matches(text);

        return (theMatches.Count + 1);
    }
}
else
{

    // Handle a null source here.
    return (0);
}
}
```

The following method counts the lines within a specified text file and a specified string:

```
public static void TestLineCount( )
{
    // Count the lines within the file TestFile.txt.
    LineCount(@"C:\TestFile.txt", true);

    // Count the lines within a string.
    // Notice that the \r\n characters start a new line
    // as well as just the \n character.
    LineCount("Line1\r\nLine2\r\nLine3\nLine4", false);

}
```

Discussion

Every line ends with a special character. For Windows files, the line-terminating characters are a carriage return followed by a line feed. This sequence of characters is described by the regular expression pattern \r\n. Unix files terminate their lines with just the line-feed character (\n). The regular expression "\n" is the lowest common denominator for both sets of line-terminating characters. Consequently, this method runs a regular expression that looks for the pattern "\n" in a string or file:

> Macintosh files usually end with a carriage-return character (\r). To count the number of lines in this type of file, the regular expression should be changed to the following in the constructor of the Regex object:
>
>   Regex RE = new Regex("\r", RegexOptions.Multiline);

Simply running this regular expression against a string returns the number of lines minus one because the last line does not have a line-terminating character. To account for this, one is added to the final count of line feeds in the string.

The LineCount method accepts two parameters. The first is a string that either contains the actual text that will have its lines counted or the path and name of a text file whose lines are to be counted. The second parameter, isFileName, determines whether the first parameter (source) is a string or a file path. If this parameter is true, the source parameter is a file path; otherwise, it is simply a string.

See Also

The ".NET Framework Regular Expressions," "FileStream Class," and "Stream-Reader Class" topics in the MSDN documentation.

10.8   Returning the Entire Line in Which a Match Is Found

Problem

You have a string or file that contains multiple lines. When a specific character pattern is found on a line, you want to return the entire line, not just the matched text.

Solution

Use the StreamReader.ReadLine method to obtain each line in a file in which to run a regular expression against, as shown in Example 10-8.

Example 10-8. Returning the entire line in which a match is found

```csharp
public static List<string> GetLines(string source, string pattern, bool isFileName)
{
    string text = source;
    List<string> matchedLines = new List<string>();

    // If this is a file, get the entire file's text.
    if (isFileName)
    {
        using (FileStream FS = new FileStream(source, FileMode.Open,
                FileAccess.Read, FileShare.Read))
        {
            using (StreamReader SR = new StreamReader(FS))
            {
                Regex RE = new Regex(pattern, RegexOptions.Multiline);
                while (text != null)
                {
                    text = SR.ReadLine();

                    if (text != null)
                    {
                        // Run the regex on each line in the string.
                        MatchCollection theMatches = RE.Matches(text);

                        if (theMatches.Count > 0)
                        {

                            // Get the line if a match was found.
                            matchedLines.Add(text);
                        }
                    }
                }
            }
        }
    }
    else
    {
        // Run the regex once on the entire string.
        Regex RE = new Regex(pattern, RegexOptions.Multiline);
        MatchCollection theMatches = RE.Matches(text);

        // Use these vars to remember the last line added to matchedLines
        // so that we do not add duplicate lines.
        int lastLineStartPos = -1;
        int lastLineEndPos = -1;

        // Get the line for each match.
        foreach (Match m in theMatches)
        {

            int lineStartPos = GetBeginningOfLine(text, m.Index);
            int lineEndPos = GetEndOfLine(text, (m.Index + m.Length - 1));
```

Example 10-8. Returning the entire line in which a match is found (continued)

```
            // If this is not a duplicate line, add it.
            if (lastLineStartPos != lineStartPos &&
                lastLineEndPos != lineEndPos)
            {
                string line = text.Substring(lineStartPos,
                                    lineEndPos - lineStartPos);
                matchedLines.Add(line);

                // Reset line positions.
                lastLineStartPos = lineStartPos;
                lastLineEndPos = lineEndPos;
            }
        }
    }
    return (matchedLines);
}

public static int GetBeginningOfLine(string text, int startPointOfMatch)
{
    if (startPointOfMatch > 0)
    {
        --startPointOfMatch;
    }

    if (startPointOfMatch >= 0 && startPointOfMatch < text.Length)
    {
        // Move to the left until the first '\n' char is found.
        for (int index = startPointOfMatch; index >= 0; index--)
        {

            if (text[index] == '\n')
            {
                return (index + 1);
            }
        }

        return (0);
    }

    return (startPointOfMatch);
}

public static int GetEndOfLine(string text, int endPointOfMatch)
{
    if (endPointOfMatch >= 0 && endPointOfMatch < text.Length)
    {
        // Move to the right until the first '\n' char is found.
        for (int index = endPointOfMatch; index < text.Length; index++)
        {

            if (text[index] == '\n')
            {
```

Example 10-8. Returning the entire line in which a match is found (continued)

```
                return (index);
            }
        }

        return (text.Length);
    }

    return (endPointOfMatch);
}
```

The following method shows how to call the `GetLines` method with either a filename or a string:

```
public static void TestGetLine( )
{
    // Get each line within the file TestFile.txt as a separate string.
    Console.WriteLine( );
    List<string> lines = GetLines(@"C:\TestFile.txt", "\n", true);
    foreach (string s in lines)
        Console.WriteLine("MatchedLine: " + s);

    // Get the lines matching the text "Line" within the given string.
    Console.WriteLine( );
    lines = GetLines("Line1\r\nLine2\r\nLine3\nLine4", "Line", false);
    foreach (string s in lines)
        Console.WriteLine("MatchedLine: " + s);
}
```

Discussion

The `GetLines` method accepts three parameters:

source
    The string or filename in which to search for a pattern.

pattern
    The regular expression pattern to apply to the *source* string.

isFileName
    Pass in true if the *source* is a filename or false if *source* is a string.

This method returns a `List<string>` of strings that contains each line in which the regular expression match was found.

The `GetLines` method can obtain the lines on which matches occur within a string or a file. When running a regular expression against a file with a name that is passed in to the *source* parameter (when *isFileName* equals true) in the `GetLines` method, the file is opened and read line by line. The regular expression is run against each line, and if a match is found, that line is stored in the `matchedLines` `List<string>`. Using the `ReadLine` method of the `StreamReader` object saves you from having to determine where each line starts and ends. Determining where a line starts and ends in a string requires some work, as you shall see.

Running the regular expression against a string passed in to the *source* parameter (when *isFileName* equals false) in the GetLines method produces a MatchCollection. Each Match object in this collection is used to obtain the line on which it is located in the *source* string. The line is obtained by starting at the position of the first character of the match in the *source* string and moving one character to the left until either an '\n' character is found or the beginning of the source string is found (this code is found in the GetBeginningOfLine method). This gives you the beginning of the line, which is placed in the variable LineStartPos. Next, the end of the line is found by starting at the last character of the match in the *source* string and moving to the right until either an '\n' character is found or the end of the *source* string is found (this code is found in the GetEndOfLine method). This ending position is placed in the LineEndPos variable. All of the text between the LineStartPos and LineEndPos will be the line in which the match is found. Each of these lines is added to the matchedLines List<string> and returned to the caller.

Something interesting you can do with the GetLines method is to pass in the string "\n" in the pattern parameter of this method. This trick will effectively return each line of the string or file as a string in the List<string>.

Note that if more than one match is found on a line, each matching line will be added to the List<string>.

See Also

The ".NET Framework Regular Expressions," "FileStream Class," and "Stream-Reader Class" topics in the MSDN documentation.

10.9   Finding a Particular Occurrence of a Match

Problem

You need to find a specific occurrence of a match within a string. For example, you want to find the third occurrence of a word or the second occurrence of a Social Security number. In addition, you may need to find every third occurrence of a word in a string.

Solution

To find a particular occurrence of a match in a string, simply subscript the array returned from Regex.Matches:

```
public static Match FindOccurrenceOf(string source, string pattern,
                                    int occurrence)
{
```

```
        if (occurrence < 1)
        {
            throw (new ArgumentException("Cannot be less than 1",
                                        "occurrence"));
        }

        // Make occurrence zero-based.
        --occurrence;

        // Run the regex once on the source string.
        Regex RE = new Regex(pattern, RegexOptions.Multiline);
        MatchCollection theMatches = RE.Matches(source);

        if (occurrence >= theMatches.Count)
        {
            return (null);
        }
        else
        {
            return (theMatches[occurrence]);
        }
    }
```

To find each particular occurrence of a match in a string, build a List<Match> on the fly:

```
    public static List<Match> FindEachOccurrenceOf(string source, string pattern,
                                                   int occurrence)
    {
        List<Match> occurrences = new List<Match>();

        // Run the regex once on the source string.
        Regex RE = new Regex(pattern, RegexOptions.Multiline);
        MatchCollection theMatches = RE.Matches(source);

        for (int index = (occurrence - 1); index < theMatches.Count;
            index += occurrence)
        {
            occurrences.Add(theMatches[index]);
        }

        return (occurrences);
    }
```

The following method shows how to invoke the two previous methods:

```
    public static void TestOccurrencesOf()
    {
        Match matchResult = FindOccurrenceOf
                        ("one two three one two three one two three one"
                        + " two three one two three one two three", "two", 2);
        if (matchResult != null)
            Console.WriteLine(matchResult.ToString() + "\t" + matchResult.Index);
```

```
            Console.WriteLine( );
            List<Match> results = FindEachOccurrenceOf
                                     ("one one two three one two three one "
                                      + " two three one two three", "one", 2);
            foreach (Match m in results)
                Console.WriteLine(m.ToString( ) + "\t" + m.Index);
        }
```

Discussion

This recipe contains two similar but distinct methods. The first method, FindOccurrenceOf, returns a particular occurrence of a regular expression match. The occurrence you want to find is passed in to this method via the occurrence parameter. If the particular occurrence of the match does not exist—for example, you ask to find the second occurrence, but only one occurrence exists—a null is returned from this method. Because of this, you should check that the returned object of this method is not null before using that object. If the particular occurrence exists, the Match object that holds the match information for that occurrence is returned.

The second method in this recipe, FindEachOccurrenceOf, works similarly to the FindOccurrenceOf method, except that it continues to find a particular occurrence of a regular expression match until the end of the string is reached. For example, if you ask to find the second occurrence, this method would return a List<Match> of zero or more Match objects. The Match objects would correspond to the second, fourth, sixth, and eighth occurrences of a match and so on until the end of the string is reached.

See Also

The ".NET Framework Regular Expressions" and "ArrayList Class" topics in the MSDN documentation.

10.10 Using Common Patterns

Problem

You need a quick list from which to choose regular expression patterns that match standard items. These standard items could be a social security number, a zip code, a word containing only characters, an alphanumeric word, an email address, a URL, dates, or one of many other possible items used throughout business applications.

These patterns can be useful in making sure that a user has input the correct data and that it is well formed. These patterns can also be used as an extra security measure to keep hackers from attempting to break your code by entering strange or malformed input (e.g., SQL injection or cross-site-scripting attacks). Note that these regular expressions are not a silver bullet that will stop all attacks on your system; rather, they are an added layer of defense.

Solution

- Match only alphanumeric characters along with the characters −, +, ., and any whitespace:

    `^([\w\.+-―]|\s)*$`

     Be careful using the - character within a character class—a regular expression enclosed within [and]. That character is also used to specify a range of characters, as in a-z for a through z inclusive. If you want to use a literal - character, either escape it with \ or put it at the end of the expression, as shown in the previous and next examples.

- Match only alphanumeric characters along with the characters −, +, ., and any whitespace, with the stipulation that there is at least one of these characters and no more than 10 of these characters:

    `^([\w\.+-]|\s){1,10}$`

- Match a person's name, up to 55 characters:

    `^[a-zA-Z'\-\s]{1,55}$`

- Match a positive or negative integer:

    `^(\+|\-)?\d+$`

- Match a positive or negative floating point number only; this pattern does not match integers:

    `^(\+|\-)?(\d*\.\d+)$`

    Match a floating point or integer number that can have a positive or negative value:

    `^(\+|\-)?(\d*\.)?\d+$`

- Match a date in the form ##/##/####, where the day and month can be a one- or two-digit value and the year can only be a four-digit value:

    `^\d{1,2}\/\d{1,2}\/\d{4}$`

- Match a time to be entered in the form ##:## with an optional am or pm extension (note that this regular expression also handles military time):

    `^\d{1,2}:\d{2}\s?([ap]m)?$`

- Verify if the input is a social security number of the form ###-##-####:

    `^\d{3}-\d{2}-\d{4}$`

- Match an IPv4 address:

    `^([0-2]?[0-9]?[0-9]\.){3}[0-2]?[0-9]?[0-9]$`

- Verify that an email address is in the form *name@address* where *address* is not an IP address:

    `^[A-Za-z0-9_\-\.]+@(([A-Za-z0-9\-])+\.)+([A-Za-z\-])+$`

- Verify that an email address is in the form *name@address* where *address* is an IP address:

    ```
    ^[A-Za-z0-9_\-\.]+@([0-2]?[0-9]?[0-9]\.){3}[0-2]?[0-9]?[0-9]$
    ```

- Match or verify a URL that uses either the HTTP, HTTPS, or FTP protocol. Note that this regular expression will not match relative URLs:

    ```
    ^(http|https|ftp)\://[a-zA-Z0-9\-\.]+\.[a-zA-Z]{2,3}(:[a-zA-Z0-9]*)?/?([a-zA-Z0-9\-\._\?\,\'/\\\+&%\$#\=~])*$
    ```

- Match only a dollar amount with the optional $ and + or -preceding characters (note that any number of decimal places may be added):

    ```
    ^\$?[+-]?[\d,]*(\.\d*)?$
    ```

    This is similar to the previous regular expression, except that no more than two decimal places are allowed:

    ```
    ^\$?[+-]?[\d,]*\.?\d{0,2}$
    ```

- Match a credit card number to be entered as four sets of four digits separated with a space, -, or no character at all:

    ```
    ^((\d{4}[- ]?){3}\d{4})$
    ```

- Match a zip code to be entered as five digits with an optional four-digit extension:

    ```
    ^\d{5}(-\d{4})?$
    ```

- Match a North American phone number with an optional area code and an optional - character to be used in the phone number and no extension:

    ```
    ^(\(?[0-9]{3}\)?)?\-?[0-9]{3}\-?[0-9]{4}$
    ```

- Match a phone number similar to the previous regular expression but allow an optional five-digit extension prefixed with either ext or extension:

    ```
    ^(\(?[0-9]{3}\)?)?\-?[0-9]{3}\-?[0-9]{4}(\s*ext(ension)?[0-9]{5})?$
    ```

- Match a full path beginning with the drive letter and optionally match a filename with a three-character extension (note that no .. characters signifying to move up the directory hierarchy are allowed, nor is a directory name with a . followed by an extension):

    ```
    ^[a-zA-Z]:[\\/]([_a-zA-Z0-9]+[\\/]?)*([_a-zA-Z0-9]+\.[_a-zA-Z0-9]{0,3})?$
    ```

- Verify if the input password string matches some specific rules for entering a password (i.e., the password is between 6 and 25 characters in length and contains alphanumeric characters):

    ```
    ^(?=.*\d)(?=.*[a-z])(?=.*[A-Z]).{6,25}$
    ```

- Determine if any malicious characters were input by the user. Note that this regular expression will not prevent all malicious input, and it also prevents some valid input, such as last names that contain a single quote:

    ```
    ^([^\)\(\<\>\"\'\%\&\+\;][(-{2})])*$
    ```

- Extract a tag from an XHTML, HTML, or XML string. This regular expression will return the beginning tag and ending tag, including any attributes of the tag.

Note that you will need to replace TAGNAME with the real tag name you want to search for:

```
<TAGNAME.*?>(.*?)</TAGNAME>
```

- Extract a comment line from code. The following regular expression extracts HTML comments from a web page. This can be useful in determining if any HTML comments that are leaking sensitive information need to be removed from your code base before it goes into production:

```
<!--.*?-->
```

- Match a C# single line comment:

```
//.*$
```

- Match a C# multiline comment:

```
/\*.*?\*/
```

 While the four aforementioned regular expressions are great for finding tags and comments, they are not foolproof. To accurately find all tags and comments, you need to use a full-blown parser for the language you are targeting.

Discussion

Regular expressions are effective at finding specific information, and they have a wide range of uses. Many applications use them to locate specific information within a larger range of text, as well as to filter out bad input. The filtering action is very useful in tightening the security of an application and preventing an attacker from attempting to use carefully formed input to gain access to a machine on the Internet or a local network. By using a regular expression to allow only good input to be passed to the application, you can reduce the likelihood of many types of attacks, such as SQL injection or cross-site scripting.

The regular expressions presented in this recipe provide only a minute cross-section of what can be accomplished with them. By taking these expressions and manipulating parts of them, you can easily modify them to work with your application. Take, for example, the following expression, which allows only between 1 and 10 alphanumeric characters, along with a few symbols as input:

```
^([\w\.+-]|\s){1,10}$
```

By changing the {1,10} part of the regular expression to {0,200}, this expression will now match a blank entry or an entry of the specified symbols up to and including 200 characters.

Note the use of the ^ character at the beginning of the expression and the $ character at the end of the expression. These characters start the match at the beginning of the text and match all the way to the end of the text. Adding these characters forces the regular expression to match the entire string or none of it. By removing these characters, you can search for specific text within a larger block of text. For example, the following regular expression matches only a string containing nothing but a U.S. zip code (there can be no leading or trailing spaces):

```
^\d{5}(-\d{4})?$
```

This version matches only a zip code with leading or trailing spaces (notice the addition of the \s* to the start and end of the expression):

```
^\s*\d{5}(-\d{4})?\s*$
```

However, this modified expression matches a zip code found anywhere within a string (including a string containing just a zip code):

```
\d{5}(-\d{4})?
```

Use the regular expressions in this recipe and modify them to suit your needs.

See Also

Two good books that cover regular expressions are *Regular Expression Pocket Reference* and *Mastering Regular Expressions* (both from O'Reilly).

CHAPTER 11

Data Structures and Algorithms

11.0 Introduction

In this chapter, you will look at certain data structures and algorithms that are not available for you in the FCL through Version 3.5. Examples are provided for algorithms such as hash-code creation and string balancing. The FCL does not support every data structure you might need, so this chapter provides solutions for priority, binary and *n*-ary trees, and a multimap, as well as many other things.

11.1 Creating a Hash Code for a Data Type

Problem

You have created a class or structure that will be used as a key in a `Hashtable` or `Dictionary<T,U>`. You need to overload the `GetHashCode` method in order to return a good distribution of hash values (the Discussion section defines a good distribution of hash values). You also need to choose the best hash-code algorithm to use in the `GetHashCode` method of your object.

Solution

The following procedures implement hash-code algorithms and can be used to override the `GetHashCode` method. Included in the discussion of each method are the pros and cons of using it, as well as why you would want to use one instead of another.

In addition, it is desirable, for performance reasons, to use the return value of the `GetHashCode` method to determine whether the data contained within two objects is equal. Calling `GetHashCode` to return a hash value of two objects and comparing their hash values can be faster than calling the default implementation of `Equals` on the `Object` type, which individually tests the equality of all pertinent data within two objects. In fact, some developers even opt to compare hash-code values returned from `GetHashCode` within their overloaded `Equals` method. Using a custom implementation of the Equals method in this fashion is faster than the default implementation of the Object.Equals method.

The simple hash

This hash accepts a variable number of integer values and XORs each value to obtain a hash code. This is a well-performing and simple algorithm that has a good chance of producing an adequate distribution if the inputs are uncorrelated. Remember to profile and measure it to confirm that it works as well for your particular data set. It fails when you need to integrate values greater in size than an integer. Its code is:

```
public int SimpleHash(params int[] values)
{
    int hashCode = 0;
    if (values != null)
    {
        foreach (int val in values)
        {
            hashCode ^= val;
        }
    }

    return (hashCode);
}
```

The folding hash

This hash allows you to integrate the long data type into a hash algorithm. It takes the upper 32 bits of the long value and folds them over the lower 32 bits of this value. The actual process of folding the two values is implemented by XORing them and using the result. Once again, this is a good performing algorithm with good distribution properties, but, again, it fails when you need to go beyond the long data type. A sample implementation is:

```
public int FoldingHash(params long[] values)
{
    int hashCode = 0;
    if (values != null)
    {
        int tempLowerVal = 0;
        int tempUpperVal = 0;
        foreach (long val in values)
        {
            tempLowerVal = (int)(val & 0x000000007FFFFFFF);
            tempUpperVal = (int)((val >> 32) & 0xFFFFFFFF);
            hashCode^= tempLowerVal ^ tempUpperVal;
        }
    }

    return (hashCode);
}
```

The contained object cache

This hash obtains the hash codes from a variable number of object types. The only types that should be passed in to this method are reference-type fields contained within your object. This method XORs all the values returned by the GetHashCode method of each object. Its source code is:

```
public int ContainedObjHash(params object[] values)
{
    int hashCode = 0;
    if (values != null)
    {
        foreach (object val in values)
        {
            hashCode ^= val.GetHashCode( );
        }
    }

    return (hashCode);
}
```

The CryptoHash method

Potentially the most robust method of obtaining a hash value for an object is to use the hashing classes built into the FCL. The CryptoHash method returns a hash value for some input using the MACTripleDES class. This method returns a very good distribution for the hash value, although you may pay for it in performance. If you do not require a near-perfect hash value and are looking for an excellent distribution, consider using this approach to calculate a hash value:

```
    public int CryptoHash(string strValue)
{
    int hashCode = 0;
    if (strValue != null)
    {
        byte[] encodedUnHashedString =
                Encoding.Unicode.GetBytes(strValue);

            byte[] key = new byte[16];
        RandomNumberGenerator.Create( ).GetBytes(key);

        MACTripleDES hashingObj = new MACTripleDES(key);
        byte[] code =
                hashingObj.ComputeHash(encodedUnHashedString);

        // Use the BitConverter class to take the
        // first 4 bytes, fold them over the last 4 bytes
        // and use them as an int for the hash code.
        int hashCodeStart = BitConverter.ToInt32(code, 0);
        int hashCodeEnd = BitConverter.ToInt32(code, 4);
        hashCode = hashCodeStart ^ hashCodeEnd;
    }
```

```
            return (hashCode);
        }
```

The CryptoHash method using a nonstring

This method shows how other nonstring data types can be used with the built-in hashing classes to obtain a hash code. This method converts a numeric value to a string and then to a byte array. The array is then used to create the hash value using the SHA256Managed class. Finally, the first four values in the byte array are XOR'ed together to obtain a hash code. The code is:

```
            public int CryptoHash(long longValue)
        {
            int hashCode = 0;
            byte[] encodedUnHashedString =
                        Encoding.Unicode.GetBytes(longValue.ToString( ));

            byte[] key = new byte[16];
            RandomNumberGenerator.Create( ).GetBytes(key);

            MACTripleDES hashingObj = new MACTripleDES(key);
            byte[] code = hashingObj.ComputeHash(encodedUnHashedString);

            // Use the BitConverter class to take the
            // first 4 bytes, fold them over the last 4 bytes
            // and use them as an int for the hash code.
            int hashCodeStart = BitConverter.ToInt32(code, 0);
            int hashCodeEnd = BitConverter.ToInt32(code, 4);
            hashCode = hashCodeStart ^ hashCodeEnd;

            return (hashCode);
        }
```

The shift and add hash

This method uses each character in the input string, strValue, to determine a hash value. This algorithm produces a good distribution of hash codes even when it is fed similar strings. However, it will break down when long strings that end with the same characters are passed. While this may not happen many times with your applications, it is something to be aware of. If performance is critical, this is an excellent method to use. Its code is:

```
            public int ShiftAndAddHash (string strValue)
        {
        int hashCode = 0;

        foreach (char c in strValue)
        {
            hashCode = (hashCode << 5) + (int)c + (hashCode >> 2);
        }
```

```
        return (hashCode);
    }
```

The calculated hash

This method is a rather widely accepted method of creating a good hash value that accepts several different data types and uses a different algorithm to compute the hash value for each. It calculates the hash code as follows:

- It assigns an arbitrary odd primary number to the HashCode variable. This variable will eventually contain the final hash code. Good primary numbers to use are 3, 5, 7, 11, 13, 17, 19, 23, 29, 31, 37, 41, 43, 47, 53, 59, 61, or 67. Obviously, others exist beyond this set, but this should give you a good starting point.

- For numeric types equal to or less than the size of an int and char data types, it multiplies the current HashCode by the primary number selected and then adds to this value the value of the numeric type cast to an integer.

- For numeric types greater than the size of an int, it multiplies the current HashCode by the primary number selected and then adds to this the folded version of this numeric value. (For more information on folding, see "The folding hash" method earlier in this recipe.)

- For char, floating-point, or decimal data types, it multiplies the current HashCode by the primary number selected, casts the numeric value to an integer, and then uses the folding method to calculate its value.

- For bool data types, it multiplies the current HashCode by the primary number selected and then adds a 1 for true and 0 for false (you can reverse this behavior if you wish).

- For object data types, it multiplies the current HashCode by the primary number selected and then adds the return value of GetHashCode called on this object. If an object is set to null, use the value 0 in your calculations.

- For an array or collection, it determines the contained type(s) and uses each element of the array or collection to calculate the hash value, as follows (in the case of an integer array named MyArray):

```
            foreach (int element in myArray)
    {
            hashCode = (hashCode * 31) + element;
    }
```

This algorithm will produce a good distributed hash code for your object and has the added benefit of being able to employ any data type. This is a high-performing algorithm for simple, moderately complex, and even many complex objects. However, for extremely complex objects—ones that contain many large arrays, large Hashtables, or other objects that use a slower hash-code algorithm—this algorithm will start performing badly. In this extreme case, you may want to consider switching to another hash-code algorithm to speed performance or simply pare down the amount of fields used in the calculation. Be careful if you choose this second method to increase performance; you could inadvertently cause the algorithm to produce similar values for differing objects. The code for the calculated hash method is:

```
public int CalcHash(short someShort, int someInt, long someLong,
                    float someFloat, object someObject)
{
    int hashCode = 7;
    hashCode = hashCode * 31 + (int)someShort;
    hashCode = hashCode * 31 + someInt;
    hashCode = hashCode * 31 +
                        (int)(someLong ^ (someLong >> 32));
    long someFloatToLong = (long)someFloat;
    hashCode = hashCode * 31 +
            (int)(someFloatToLong ^ (someFloatToLong >> 32));

    if (someObject != null)
    {
        hashCode = hashCode * 31 +
                            someObject.GetHashCode();
    }

    return (hashCode);
}
```

The string-concatenation hash

This technique converts its input into a string and then uses that string's GetHashCode method to automatically generate a hash code for an object. It accepts an integer array, but you can substitute any type that can be converted into a string. You can also use several different types of arguments as input to this method. This method iterates through each integer in the array passed as an argument to the method. The ToString method is called on each value to return a string. The ToString method of an int data type returns the value contained in that int. Each string value is appended to the string variable HashString. Finally, the GetHashCode method is called on the HashString variable to return a suitable hash code.

This method is simple and efficient, but it does not work well with objects that have not overridden the ToString method to return something other than their data type. It may be best to simply call the GetHashCode method on each of these objects individually. You should use your own judgment and the rules found in this recipe to make your decision:

```
public int ConcatStringGetHashCode(int[] someIntArray)
{
    int hashCode = 0;
    StringBuilder hashString = new StringBuilder();

    if (someIntArray != null)
    {
        foreach (int i in someIntArray)
```

```
                {
                    hashString.Append(i.ToString( ) + "^");
                }
            }
            hashCode = hashString.GetHashCode( );

            return (hashCode);
    }
```

Discussion

The GetHashCode method is called when you are using an instance of this class as the key in a Hashtable, HashSet, or Dictionary<T,U> object. A hash code is also obtained from your object when a search is performed for it in the Hashtable, HashSet, or Dictionary<T,U>.

The following class implements the SimpleHash algorithm for the overloaded GetHashCode method:

```
public class SimpleClass
{
    private string text = "";

    public SimpleClass(string inputText)
    {
        text = inputText;
    }

    public override int GetHashCode( )
    {
        return(ShiftAndAddHash(text));
    }

    public int ShiftAndAddHash (string strValue)
    {
        int hashCode = 0;

        foreach (char c in strValue)
        {
            hashCode = (hashCode << 5) + (int)c + (hashCode >> 2);
        }

        return (hashCode);
    }
}
```

This class can then be used as a key in a Hashtable or Dictionary<T,U> in code like the following:

```
SimpleClass simpleClass = new SimpleClass("foo");

Hashtable hashTable = new Hashtable( );
hashTable.Add(simpleClass, 100);
```

```
Dictionary<SimpleClass, int> dict = new Dictionary<SimpleClass, int>();
dict.Add(simpleClass, 100);
```

There are several rules for writing a good GetHashCode method and a good hash-code algorithm:

- This method must return the same value for two different objects that have value equality. *Value equality* means that two objects have the same logical value even if they are references to different objects.

- The hash algorithm should return a good distribution of values for the best performance in a Hashtable or Dictionary<T,U>. A good distribution of values means that the hash values returned by the GetHashCode method are usually different for objects of the same type, unless those objects have value equality. Note that objects containing very similar data should also return a unique hash value. This distribution allows the Hashtable or Dictionary<T,U> to work more efficiently.

- This method should not throw an exception.

- Both the Equals method and GetHashCode method must be overridden together.

- The GetHashCode method must compute the hash code using the exact set of variables that the overridden Equals method uses when calculating equality.

- The hash algorithm should be as fast as possible to speed up the process of adding and searching for keys in a Hashtable or Dictionary<T,U>.

- Use the GetHashCode values of any contained objects, which will not mutate over the lifetime of the outer object's time in the hashtable when calculating the hash code of the parent object.

- Use the GetHashCode values of all elements of an array when calculating the array's hash code.

The System.Int32, System.UInt32, and System.IntPtr data types in the FCL use an additional hash-code algorithm not covered in the Solution section. Basically, these data types return the value that they contain as a hash code. Most likely, your objects will not be so simple as to contain a single numeric value, but if they are, this method works extremely well.

You may also want to combine specific algorithms to suit your purposes. For instance, if your object contains one or more string types and one or more long data types, you can combine the ContainedObjHash method and the FoldingHash method to create a hash value for your object. The return values from each method can either be added or XORed together.

Once an object is in use as a key in a Hashtable or Dictionary<T,U>, it should never return a different value for the hash code. Originally, it was documented that hash codes must be immutable, as the authors of Hashtable or Dictionary<T,U> thought that this should be dealt with by whomever writes GetHashCode. It doesn't take much thought to realize that for mutable types, if you require both that the hash code never changes *and* that Equals represents the equality of the mutable objects *and* that if a. Equals(b), then a.GetHashCode( ) == b.GetHashCode( ), then the only possible implementation of GetHashCode is one that returns the same integer constant for all values.

The GetHashCode method is called when you are using this object as the key in a Hashtable or Dictionary<T,U> object. Whenever your object is added to a Hashtable or Dictionary<T,U> as a key, the GetHashCode method is called on your object to obtain a hash code. This hash code must not change while your object is a key in the Hashtable or Dictionary<T,U>. If it does, the Hashtable or Dictionary<T,U> will not be able to find your object.

See Also

The "GetHashCode Method," "Dictionary<T,U> Class," and "Hashtable Class" topics in the MSDN documentation.

11.2   Creating a Priority Queue

Problem

You need a data structure that operates similarly to a Queue but that returns objects based on a specific order. When objects are added to this queue, they are located in the queue according to their priority. When objects are retrieved from the queue, the queue simply returns the highest- or lowest-priority element based on which one you ask for.

Solution

Create a generic priority queue that orders items as they are added to the queue and returns items based on their priority. The PriorityQueue<T> class of Example 11-1 shows how this can be accomplished.

Example 11-1. Generic PriorityQueue class

```
using System;
using System.Collections;
using System.Collections.Generic;
public class PriorityQueue<T> : IEnumerable<T>
{
    public PriorityQueue( ){}
    public PriorityQueue(IComparer<T> icomparer)
    {
        specialComparer = icomparer;
    }


    protected List<T> internalQueue = new List<T>( );
    protected IComparer<T> specialComparer = null;
```

Example 11-1. Generic PriorityQueue class (continued)

```csharp
protected List<T> InternalQueue
{
    get {return internalQueue;}
}

public int Count
{
    get {return (internalQueue.Count);}
}

public void Clear( )
{
    internalQueue.Clear( );
}

public object Clone( )
{
    // Make a new PQ and give it the same comparer.
    PriorityQueue<T> newPQ = new PriorityQueue<T>(specialComparer);
    newPQ.CopyTo(internalQueue.ToArray( ),0);
    return newPQ;
}

public int IndexOf(T item)
{
    return (internalQueue.IndexOf(item));
}

public bool Contains(T item)
{
    return (internalQueue.Contains(item));
}

public int BinarySearch(T item)
{
    return (internalQueue.BinarySearch(item, specialComparer));
}

public bool Contains(T item, IComparer<T> comparer)
{
    return (internalQueue.BinarySearch(item, comparer) >= 0);
}

public void CopyTo(T[] array, int index)
{
    internalQueue.CopyTo(array, index);
}

public T[] ToArray( )
{
    return (internalQueue.ToArray( ));
}
```

Example 11-1. Generic PriorityQueue class (continued)

```
    public void TrimToSizeTrimExcess()
    {
        internalQueue.TrimExcess();
    }

    public void Enqueue(T item)
    {
        internalQueue.Add(item);
        internalQueue.Sort(specialComparer);
    }

    public T DequeueLargest()
    {
        T item = internalQueue[internalQueue.Count - 1];
        internalQueue.RemoveAt(internalQueue.Count - 1);

        return (item);
    }

    public T PeekLargest()
    {
        return (internalQueue[internalQueue.Count - 1]);
    }

    public IEnumerator GetEnumerator()
    {
        return (internalQueue.GetEnumerator());
    }

    IEnumerator<T> System.Collections.Generic.IEnumerable<T>.GetEnumerator()
    {
        return (internalQueue.GetEnumerator());
    }
}
```

For example, perhaps your application or component needs to send packets of data of differing sizes across a network. The algorithm for sending these packets of data states that the smallest (or perhaps the largest) packets will be sent before the larger (or smaller) ones. An analogous programming problem involves queuing up specific jobs to be run. Each job could be run based on its type, order, or size.

This priority queue is designed so that items—in this case, string values—may be added in any order; but when they are removed from the head or tail of the queue, they are dequeued in a specific order. The IComparer<T> type object, a specialComparer that is passed in through the constructor of this object, determines this order. The queued string objects are stored internally in a field called internalQueue of type List<T>. This was the simplest way to construct this type of queue, since a List<T> has most of the functionality built into it that we wanted to implement for this type of queue.

Many of the methods of this class delegate to the internalQueue in order to perform their duties. These types of methods include Count, Clear, TrimExcess, and many others. Some of the more important methods of the PriorityQueue<T> class are Enqueue, DequeueLargest, and PeekLargest.

The Enqueue method accepts a type T as an argument and adds it to the end of the internalQueue. Next, this List<T> is sorted according to the specialComparer object. If the specialComparer object is null, the comparison defaults to the IComparer of the string object. By sorting the List<T> after each item is added, you do not have to perform a sort before every search, dequeue, and peek method. A performance hit will occur when an item is added, but this is a one-time-only penalty. Keep in mind that when items are removed from the head or tail of this queue, the internal List<T> does not have to be resorted. This PriorityQueue performs best with smaller numbers of items stored in the queue, up to several thousand. The performance will not perform well if larger numbers of items are stored in the queue, such as hundreds of thousands of items.

There is one dequeue method: DequeueLargest. This method removes items from the tail (index equals internalQueue.Count -1) of the queue. Before returning the string, this method will remove that string from the queue. The PeekLargest method works in a similar manner, except that it does not remove the string from the queue.

Two other methods of interest are the overloaded Contains methods. The only real difference between these two methods is that one of the Contains methods uses the IComparer interface of the string object, whereas the other overloaded Contains method uses the specialComparer interface when searching for a string in the internalQueue, if one is provided.

The PriorityQueue<T> class members are listed in Table 11-1.

Table 11-1. PriorityQueue class members

Member	Description
Count property	Returns an int indicating the number of items in the queue. Calls the internalQueue.Count method.
Clear method	Removes all items from the queue. Calls the internalQueue method.
Clone method	Returns a copy of the PriorityQueue<T> object.
IndexOf method	Returns the zero-based index of the queue item that contains a particular search string. Its syntax is: IndexOf(T *item*) where *item* is the string to be found in the queue. Calls the internalQueue method.
Contains method	Returns a bool indicating whether a particular search string is found in the queue. Its syntax is: Contains(T *item*) where *item* is the string to be found in the queue. Calls the internalQueue method.

Table 11-1. PriorityQueue class members (continued)

Member	Description
BinarySearch method	Returns the zero-based index of the queue item that contains a particular search type T. Its syntax is: BinarySearch(T *item*) where *item* is the type T to be found in the queue. The comparison of *item* with the type T found in the queue is handled by the IComparer<T> implementation, if one was passed as an argument to one of the overloads of the PriorityQueue<T> class constructor. Calls the internalQueue method.
Contains method	Returns a bool indicating whether a particular search type T is found in the queue. Its syntax is: Contains(T *item*, IComparer<T> specialComparer) where *item* is the string to be found in the queue. The comparison of *item* with the strings found in the queue is handled by the IComparer<T> implementation, if one was passed as an argument to one of the overloads of the PriorityQueue<T> class constructor. Calls the internalQueue method.
CopyTo method	Copies the queue items to a one-dimensional array starting at a particular position in the queue. Its syntax is: CopyTo(T[] *array*, int *arrayIndex*) where *array* is the array to receive the copy of the queue items and *arrayIndex* is the position in the queue from which to begin copying items. Calls the internalQueue method.
ToArray method	Copies the items in the queue to an object array. Calls the internalQueue method.
TrimExcess method	Sets the capacity of the queue to the current count of its items. If the TrimExcess method is called when no items are in the queue, its capacity is set to a default value. Calls the internalQueue method.
Enqueue method	Adds an item to the queue. It then sorts the queue based on either the default sort behavior of each item or the IComparer<T> implementation passed as an argument to one of the PriorityQueue<T> class constructors. Its syntax is: Enqueue(T *item*) where *item* is the type T to be added to the queue.
DequeueLargest method	Returns and removes the item at the tail of the queue (i.e., the last item in the queue).
PeekLargest method	Returns the item at the tail of the queue (i.e., the last item in the queue).
GetEnumerator method	Returns an enumerator that allows iteration of the items in the queue. Calls the internalQueue method.

The PriorityQueue<T> can be instantiated and filled with strings using code like the Test class shown in Example 11-2.

Example 11-2. Testing the PriorityQueue class

```
class Test
{
    static void Main()
    {
        // Create ArrayList of messages.
        List<string> msgs = new List<string>();
        msgs.Add("foo");
        msgs.Add("This is a longer message.");
        msgs.Add("bar");
        msgs.Add(@"Message with odd characters
                !@#$%^&*()_+=-0987654321~|}{[]\\;:?/>.<,");
        msgs.Add(@"<
                    >");
```

Example 11-2. Testing the PriorityQueue class (continued)

```
        msgs.Add("<text>one</text><text>two</text><text>three</text>" +
                "<text>four</text>");
        msgs.Add("");
        msgs.Add("1234567890");

        // Create a Priority Queue with the appropriate comparer.
        // The comparer is created from the CompareLen type
        // defined in the Discussion section.
        CompareLen<string> comparer = new CompareLen<string>();
        PriorityQueue<string> pqueue = new PriorityQueue<string>(comparer);

        // Add all messages from the List to the priority queue.
        foreach (string msg in msgs)
        {

            pqueue.Enqueue(msg);
        }

        // Display messages in the queue in order of priority.
        foreach (string msg in pqueue)
        {
            Console.WriteLine("Msg: " + msg);
        }
        Console.WriteLine("pqueue.IndexOf('bar') == " + pqueue.IndexOf("bar"));
        Console.WriteLine("pqueue.IndexOf('_bar_') == " + pqueue.IndexOf("_bar_"));

        Console.WriteLine("pqueue.Contains('bar') == " + pqueue.Contains("bar"));
        Console.WriteLine("pqueue.Contains('_bar_') == " +
            pqueue.Contains("_bar_"));

        Console.WriteLine("pqueue.BinarySearch('bar') == " +
            pqueue.BinarySearch("bar"));
        Console.WriteLine("pqueue.BinarySearch('_bar_') == " +
                        pqueue.BinarySearch("_bar_"));

        // Dequeue messages starting with the smallest.
        int currCount = pqueue.Count;
        for (int index = 0; index < currCount; index++)
        {
            Console.WriteLine("pqueue.DequeueLargest(): " +
                        pqueue.DequeueLargest().ToString());
        }
    }
}
```

The output of this method is shown here:

```
        Msg:
        Msg: foo
        Msg: bar
        Msg: 1234567890
        Msg: This is a longer message.
        Msg: <text>one</text><text>two</text><text>three</text><text>four</text>
```

```
        Msg: Message with odd characters
                      !@#$%^&*()_+=-0987654321~|}{[]\\;:?/>.<,
        Msg: <


                    >
        pqueue.IndexOf('bar') == 2
        pqueue.IndexOf('_bar_') == -1
        pqueue.Contains('bar') == True
        pqueue.Contains('_bar_') == False
        pqueue.BinarySearch('bar') == 1
        pqueue.BinarySearch('_bar_') == -4
    pqueue.DequeueLargest(): <


                    >
    pqueue.DequeueLargest(): Message with odd characters
                      !@#$%^&*()_+=-0987654321~|}{[]\\;:?/>.<,
    pqueue.DequeueLargest(): <text>one</text><text>two</text><text>three</text><text
>four</text>
    pqueue.DequeueLargest(): This is a longer message.
    pqueue.DequeueLargest(): 1234567890
    pqueue.DequeueLargest(): foo
    pqueue.DequeueLargest(): bar
    pqueue.DequeueLargest():
```

A List<T> of string messages is created that will be used to fill the queue. A new CompareLen IComparer<T> type object is created and passed in to the constructor of the PriorityQueue<T>. If you did not pass in this IComparer<T> object, the output would be much different: instead of items being retrieved from the queue based on length, they would be retrieved based on their alphabetical order. (The IComparer<T> interface is covered in detail in the Discussion section.) Finally, a foreach loop is used to enqueue all messages into the PriorityQueue<T> object.

At this point, the PriorityQueue<T> object can be used in a manner similar to the Queue<T> class contained in the FCL, except for the ability to remove items from both the head and tail of the queue.

Discussion

You can instantiate the PriorityQueue<T> class with or without a special comparer object. The special comparer object used in this recipe is defined in Example 11-3.

Example 11-3. Special CompareLen comparer class

```
public class CompareLen<T> : IComparer<T>
    where T: IComparable<T>
{
    public int Compare(T obj1, T obj2)
    {
        int result = 0;
        if (typeof(T) == typeof(string))
        {
```

Example 11-3. Special CompareLen comparer class (continued)

```
            result = CompareStrings(obj1 as string, obj2 as string);
        }
        else
        {

            // Default to the object type's comparison algorithm.
            result = Comparer<T>.Default.Compare(obj1, obj2);
        }
        return (result);
    }

    private int CompareStrings(string str1, string str2)
    {
        if (str1 == null || str2 == null)
        {
            throw(new ArgumentNullException(
                    "The strings being compared may not be null."));
        }

        if (str1.Length == str2.Length)
        {
            return (0);
        }
        else if (str1.Length > str2.Length)
        {
            return (1);
        }
        else
        {
            return (-1);
        }
    }

    public bool Equals(T item1, T item2)
    {
        if (item1 == null || item2 == null)
        {
            throw(new ArgumentNullException(
                    "The objects being compared may not be null."));
        }

        return (item1.Equals(item2));
    }

    public int GetHashCode(T obj)
    {
        if (obj == null)
        {
            throw(new ArgumentNullException(
                    "The obj parameter may not be null."));
        }
```

Example 11-3. Special CompareLen comparer class (continued)

```
        return (obj.GetHashCode());
    }
}
```

This special comparer is required because you want to prioritize the elements in the queue by size. The default string IComparer<string> interface compares strings alphabetically. Implementing the IComparer<T> interface requires that you implement a single method, Compare, with the following signature:

```
int Compare(T x, T y);
```

where *x* and *y* are the objects being compared. When implementing custom Compare methods, the method is to return 0 if *x* equals *y*, less than 0 if *x* is less than *y*, and greater than 0 if *x* is greater than *y*. This method is called automatically by the .NET runtime whenever the custom IComparer<T> implementation is used.

See Also

The "List<T> Class," "IEnumerable Interface," "ICloneable Interface," "IComparer<T> Interface," and "IComparable<T> Interface" topics in the MSDN documentation.

11.3   Creating a One-to-Many Map (MultiMap)

Problem

A Hashtable or a Dictionary<T,U> can map only a single key to a single value, but you need to map a key to one or more values. In addition, it may also be possible to map a key to null.

Solution

Use a Dictionary<T,U> with values that are a List<U>. This structure allows you to add multiple values (in the List<U>) for each key of the Dictionary<T,U>. The MultiMap<T,U> class shown in Example 11-4, which is used in practically the same manner as a Dictionary<T,U> class, does this.

Example 11-4. MultiMap class

```
using System;
using System Collections;
using System.Collections.Generic;

public class MultiMap<TKey, UValue> : IDictionary<TKey, IList<UValue>>
{
    private Dictionary<TKey, IList<UValue>> map =
        new Dictionary<TKey, IList<UValue>>();
```

Example 11-4. MultiMap class (continued)

```
public IList<UValue> this[TKey key]
{
    get {return (map[key]);}
    set {map[key] = value;}
}

public void Add(TKey key, UValue item)
{
    AddSingleMap(key, item);
}

public void Add(TKey key, IList<UValue> items)
{
    foreach (UValue val in items)
        AddSingleMap(key, val);
}

public void Add(KeyValuePair<TKey, IList<UValue>> keyValuePair)
{
    foreach (UValue val in keyValuePair.Value)
        AddSingleMap(keyValuePair.Key, val);
}

public void Clear()
{
    map.Clear();
}

public int Count
{
    get {return (map.Count);}
}

public bool ContainsKey (TKey key)
{
    return (map.ContainsKey(key));
}

public bool ContainsValue(UValue item)
{
    if (item == null)
    {
        foreach (KeyValuePair<TKey, IList<UValue>> kvp in map)
        {
            if (((List<UValue>)kvp.Value).Count == 0)
            {
                return (true);
            }
        }

        return (false);
    }
```

Example 11-4. MultiMap class (continued)

```
    else
    {
        foreach (KeyValuePair<TKey, IList<UValue>> kvp in map)
        {
            if (((List<UValue>)kvp.Value).Contains(item))
            {
                return (true);
            }
        }

        return (false);
    }
}

IEnumerator<KeyValuePair<TKey, IList<UValue>>> IEnumerable<KeyValuePair<TKey,
                        IList<UValue>>>.GetEnumerator( )
{
    return (map.GetEnumerator( ));
}

IEnumerator System.Collections.IEnumerable.GetEnumerator( )
{
    return (map.GetEnumerator( ));
}

public bool Remove(TKey key)
{
    return (RemoveSingleMap(key));
}

public bool Remove(KeyValuePair<TKey, IList<UValue>> keyValuePair)
{
    return (Remove(keyValuePair.Key));
}

protected void AddSingleMap(TKey key, UValue item)
{
    // Search for key in map Hashtable.
    if (map.ContainsKey(key))
    {
        // Add value to List in map.
        List<UValue> values = (List<UValue>)map[key];

        // Add this value to this existing key.
        values.Add(item);
    }
    else
    {
        if (item == null)
        {
            // Create new key and mapping to an empty List.
            map.Add(key, new List<UValue>( ));
```

Example 11-4. MultiMap class (continued)

```
        }
        else
        {
            List<UValue> values = new List<UValue>( );
            values.Add(item);

            // Create new key and mapping to its value.
            map.Add(key, values);
        }
    }
}

protected bool RemoveSingleMap(TKey key)
{
    if (this.ContainsKey(key))
    {
        // Remove the key from KeysTable.
        return (map.Remove(key));
    }
    else
    {
        throw (new ArgumentOutOfRangeException("key", key,
            "This key does not exists in the map."));
    }
}
```

The methods defined in Table 11-2 are of particular interest to using a `MultiMap<T,U>` object.

Table 11-2. Members of the MultiMap class

Member	Description
Indexer	The get accessor obtains a List<U> of all values that are associated with a key. The set accessor adds an entire List<U> of values to a key. Its syntax is: `public List<U> this[T key]` where *key* is the key to be added to the MultiMap<T,U> through the set accessor, or it is the key with values that you want to retrieve via the get accessor.
Add method	Adds a key to the Dictionary<T,List<U>> and its associated value. Its syntax is: `Add(T key, T value)` where *key* is the key to be added to the MultiMap<T,U> and value is the value to add to the internal List<U> of the private map field.
Clear method	Removes all items from the MultiMap<T,U> object.
Count method	Returns a count of all keys in the MultiMap<T,U> object.
Clone method	Returns a deep copy of the MultiMap<T,U> object.
ContainsKey method	Returns a bool indicating whether the MultiMap<T,U> contains a particular value as its key. Its syntax is: `ContainsKey(T key)` where *key* is the key to be found in the MultiMap<T,U>.

Table 11-2. Members of the MultiMap class (continued)

Member	Description
ContainsValue method	Returns a bool indicating whether the MultiMap<T,U> contains a particular value. Its syntax is: ContainsValue(T *value*) where *value* is the object to be found in the MultiMap<T,U>.
Remove method	Removes a key from the MultiMap<T,U> and all its referent values in the internal map Dictionary<T, List<U>>. Its syntax is: Remove(T *key*) where *key* is the key to be removed.

Items may be added to a MultiMap<T,U> object by running the code shown in Example 11-5.

Example 11-5. Testing the MultiMap class

```csharp
public static void TestMultiMap()
{
    string s = "foo";

    // Create and populate a MultiMap object.
    MultiMap<int, string> myMap = new MultiMap<int, string>();
    myMap.Add(0, "zero");
    myMap.Add(1, "one");
    myMap.Add(2, "two");
    myMap.Add(3, "three");
    myMap.Add(3, "duplicate three");
    myMap.Add(3, "duplicate three");
    myMap.Add(4, "null");
    myMap.Add(5, s);
    myMap.Add(6, s);

    // Display contents.
    foreach (KeyValuePair<int, List<string>> entry in myMap)
    {

        Console.Write("Key: " + entry.Key.ToString() + "\tValue: ");
        foreach (string str in myMap[entry.Key])
        {
            Console.Write(str + " : ");
        }
        Console.WriteLine();
    }

    // Obtain values through the indexer.
    Console.WriteLine();
    Console.WriteLine("((ArrayList) myMap[3])[0]: " + myMap[3][0]);
    Console.WriteLine("((ArrayList) myMap[3])[1]: " + myMap[3][1]);

    // Add items to MultiMap using a List.
    List<string> testArray = new List<string>();
```

Example 11-5. Testing the MultiMap class (continued)

```
    testArray.Add("BAR");
    testArray.Add("BAZ");
    myMap[10] = testArray;
    myMap[10] = testArray;

    // Remove items from MultiMap.
    myMap.Remove(0);
    myMap.Remove(1);

    // Display MultiMap.
    Console.WriteLine();
    Console.WriteLine("myMap.Count: " + myMap.Count);
    foreach (KeyValuePair<int, List<string>> entry in myMap)
{
        Console.Write("entry.Key: " + entry.Key.ToString() +
                    "\tentry.Value(s): ");
        foreach (string str in myMap[entry.Key])
        {
            if (str == null)
            {
                Console.Write("null : ");
            }
            else
            {
                Console.Write(str + " : ");
            }
        }
        Console.WriteLine();
    }

    // Determine if the map contains the key or the value.
    Console.WriteLine();
    Console.WriteLine("myMap.ContainsKey(2): " + myMap.ContainsKey(2));
    Console.WriteLine("myMap.ContainsValue(two): " +
    myMap.ContainsValue("two"));

    Console.WriteLine("Contains Key 2: " + myMap.ContainsKey(2));
    Console.WriteLine("Contains Key 12: " + myMap.ContainsKey(12));

    Console.WriteLine("Contains Value two: " + myMap.ContainsValue("two"));
    Console.WriteLine("Contains Value BAR: " + myMap.ContainsValue("BAR"));

    // Clear all items from MultiMap.
    myMap.Clear();
}
```

This code displays the following:

```
        Key: 0  Value: zero :
        Key: 1  Value: one :
        Key: 2  Value: two :
        Key: 3  Value: three : duplicate three : duplicate three :
        Key: 4  Value:
```

```
Key: 5  Value: foo :
Key: 6  Value: foo :

((ArrayList) myMap[3])[0]: three
((ArrayList) myMap[3])[1]: duplicate three

myMap.Count:  6
entry.Key:  2     entry.Value(s): two :
entry.Key:  3     entry.Value(s): three : duplicate three : duplicate three :
entry.Key:  4     entry.Value(s):
entry.Key:  5     entry.Value(s): foo :
entry.Key:  6     entry.Value(s): foo :
entry.Key: 10     entry.Value(s): BAR : BAZ :

myMap.ContainsKey(2):  True
myMap.ContainsValue(two):  True
Contains Key  2:    True
Contains Key  12:    False
Contains Value  two:    True
Contains Value  BAR:    True
```

Discussion

A one-to-many map, or multimap, allows one object, a key, to be associated, or *mapped*, to zero or more objects. The MultiMap<T,U> class presented here operates similarly to a Dictionary<T,U>. The MultiMap<T,U> class contains a Dictionary<T, List<U>> field called map that contains the actual mapping of keys to values. Several of the MultiMap<T,U> methods are delegated to the methods on the map Dictionary<T, List<U>> object.

A Dictionary<T,U> operates on a one-to-one principle: only one key may be associated with one value at any time. However, if you need to associate multiple values with a single key, you must use the approach used by the MultiMap<T,U> class. The private map field associates a key with a single List<U> of values, which allows multiple mappings of values to a single key and mappings of a single value to multiple keys. As an added feature, a key can also be mapped to a null value.

Here's what happens when key-value pairs are added to a MultiMap<t,U> object:

1. The MultiMap<T,U>.Add method is called with a *key* and *value* provided as parameters.

2. The Add method checks to see whether key exists in the map Dictionary<T, List<U>> object.

3. If *key* does not exist, it is added as a key in the map Dictionary<T, List<U>> object. This key is associated with a new List<U> as the value associated with *key* in this Hashtable.

4. If the *key* does exist, the *key* is looked up in the map Dictionary<T, List<U>> object, and the *value* is added to the *key*'s List<U>.

To remove a key using the Remove method, the key and List<U> pair are removed from the map Dictionary<T, List<U>>. This allows removal of all values associated with a single key. The MultiMap<T,U>.Remove method calls the RemoveSingleMap method, which encapsulates this behavior. Removal of key "0", and all values mapped to this key, is performed with the following code:

```
myMap.Remove(1);
```

To remove all keys and their associated values, use the MultiMap<T,U>.Clear method. This method removes all items from the map Dictionary<T, List<U>>.

The other major member of the MultiMap<T,U> class needing discussion is its indexer. The indexer returns the List<U> of values for a particular key through its get accessor. The set accessor simply adds the List<U> provided to a single key. This code creates an array of values and attempts to map them to key "5" in the myMap object:

```
List<string> testArray = new List<string>();
testArray.Add("BAR");
testArray.Add("BAZ");
myMap["5"] = testArray;
```

The following code makes use of the get accessor to access each value associated with key "3":

```
Console.WriteLine(myMap[3][0]);
Console.WriteLine(myMap[3][1]);
Console.WriteLine(myMap[3][2]);
```

This looks somewhat similar to using a jagged array. The first indexer ([3] in the preceding examples) is used to pull the List<U> from the map Dictionary<T, List<U>>, and the second indexer is used to obtain the value in the List<U>. This code displays the following:

```
three
duplicate three
duplicate three
```

This MultiMap<T,U> class also allows the use of the foreach loop to enumerate its key-value pairs. The following code displays each key-value pair in the MyMap object:

```
foreach (KeyValuePair<int, List<string>> entry in myMap)
{
    Console.Write("Key: " + entry.Key.ToString() + "\tValue: ");
    foreach (string str in myMap[entry.Key])
    {
        Console.Write(str + " : ");
    }
    Console.WriteLine();
}
```

The outer foreach loop is used to retrieve all the keys, and the inner foreach loop is used to display each value mapped to a particular key. This code displays the following for the initial MyMap object:

```
Key: 0 Value: zero :
Key: 1 Value: one :
Key: 2 Value: two :
Key: 3 Value: three : duplicate three : duplicate three :
Key: 4 Value:
Key: 5 Value: foo :
Key: 6 Value: foo :
```

Two methods that allow searching of the MultiMap<T,U> object are ContainsKey and ContainsValue. The ContainsKey method searches for the specified key in the map Dictionary<T, List<U>>. The ContainsValue method searches for the specified value in a List<U> in the map Dictionary<T, List<U>>. Both methods return true if the key-value was found or false otherwise:

```
Console.WriteLine("Contains Key 2: " + myMap.ContainsKey(2));
Console.WriteLine("Contains Key 12: " + myMap.ContainsKey(12));

Console.WriteLine("Contains Value two: " + myMap.ContainsValue("two"));
Console.WriteLine("Contains Value BAR: " + myMap.ContainsValue("BAR"));
```

Note that the ContainsKey and ContainsValue methods are both case-sensitive.

See Also

The "List<T> Class," "Dictionary<T,U> Class," and "IEnumerator Interface" topics in the MSDN documentation.

11.4   Creating a Binary Search Tree

Problem

You need to store information in a tree structure, where the left node is less than its parent node and the right node is greater than or equal to (in cases in which the tree can contain duplicates) its parent. The stored information must be easily inserted into the tree, removed from the tree, and found within the tree.

Solution

To implement a binary tree of the type described in the Problem statement, each node must be an object that inherits from the IComparable<T> interface. This means that every node to be included in the binary tree must implement the CompareTo method. This method will allow one node to determine whether it is less than, greater than, or equal to another node.

Use the BinaryTree<T> class shown in Example 11-6, which contains all of the nodes in a binary tree and lets you traverse it.

Example 11-6. Generic BinaryTree class

```
using System;
using System.Collections;
using System.Collections.Generic;


public class BinaryTree<T> : IEnumerable<T>
    where T: IComparable<T>
{
    public BinaryTree( ) {}

    public BinaryTree(T value)
    {
        BinaryTreeNode<T> node = new BinaryTreeNode<T>(value);
        root = node;
        counter = 1;
    }

    private int counter = 0;                    // Number of nodes in tree
    private BinaryTreeNode<T> root = null;  // Pointer to root node in this tree


    public void AddNode(T value)
    {
        BinaryTreeNode<T> node = new BinaryTreeNode<T>(value);
        ++counter;

        if (root == null)
        {
            root = node;
        }
        else
        {
            root.AddNode(node);
        }
    }

    public void AddNode(T value, int index)
    {
        BinaryTreeNode<T> node = new BinaryTreeNode<T>(value, index);
        ++counter;

        if (root == null)
        {
            root = node;
        }
        else
        {
            root.AddNode(node);
        }
    }

    public BinaryTreeNode<T> SearchDepthFirst(T value)
```

Example 11-6. Generic BinaryTree class (continued)

```
    {
        return (root.DepthFirstSearch(value));
    }

    public void Print()
    {
        root.PrintDepthFirst();
    }

    public BinaryTreeNode<T> Root
    {
        get {return (root);}
    }

    public int TreeSize
    {
        get {return (counter);}
    }        }
```

The `BinaryTreeNode<T>` shown in Example 11-7 encapsulates the data and behavior of a single node in the binary tree.

Example 11-7. Generic BinaryTreeNode class

```
public class BinaryTreeNode<T>
    where T: IComparable<T>
{
    public BinaryTreeNode() {}

    public BinaryTreeNode(T value)
    {
        nodeValue = value;
    }


    private T nodeValue = default(T);
    private BinaryTreeNode<T> leftNode = null;   //  leftNode.nodeValue < Value
    private BinaryTreeNode<T> rightNode = null;  //  rightNode.nodeValue >= Value

    public int Children
    {
        get
        {
            int currCount = 0;
            if (leftNode != null)
            {
                ++currCount;
                currCount += leftNode.Children();
            }

            if (rightNode != null)
            {
```

Example 11-7. Generic BinaryTreeNode class (continued)

```
                ++currCount;
                currCount += rightNode.Children( );
            }

            return (currCount);
        }
    }

    public BinaryTreeNode<T> Left
    {
        get {return (leftNode);}
    }

    public BinaryTreeNode<T> Right
    {
        get {return (rightNode);}
    }

    public T Value
    {
        get {return (nodeValue);}
    }

    public void AddNode(BinaryTreeNode<T> node)
    {
        if (node.nodeValue.CompareTo(nodeValue) < 0)
        {
            if (leftNode == null)
            {
                leftNode = node;
            }
            else
            {
                leftNode.AddNode(node);
            }
        }
        else if (node.nodeValue.CompareTo(nodeValue) >= 0)
        {
            if (rightNode == null)
            {
                rightNode = node;
            }
            else
            {
                rightNode.AddNode(node);
            }
        }
    }

    public bool AddUniqueNode(BinaryTreeNode<T> node)
    {
        bool isUnique = true;
```

Example 11-7. Generic BinaryTreeNode class (continued)

```
        if (node.nodeValue.CompareTo(nodeValue) < 0)
        {
            if (leftNode == null)
            {
                leftNode = node;
            }
            else
            {
                leftNode.AddNode(node);
            }
        }
        else if (node.nodeValue.CompareTo(nodeValue) > 0)
        {
            if (rightNode == null)
            {
                rightNode = node;
            }
            else
            {
                rightNode.AddNode(node);
            }
        }
        else //node.nodeValue.CompareTo(nodeValue) = 0
        {
            isUnique = false;
            // Could throw exception here as well...
        }
        return (isUnique);
    }

    public BinaryTreeNode<T> DepthFirstSearch(T targetObj)
    {
        // NOTE: foo.CompareTo(bar) == -1 --> (foo < bar)
        BinaryTreeNode<T> retObj = null;
        int comparisonResult = targetObj.CompareTo(nodeValue);
        if (comparisonResult == 0)
        {
            retObj = this;
        }
        else if (comparisonResult > 0)
        {
            if (rightNode != null)
            {
                retObj = rightNode.DepthFirstSearch(targetObj);
            }
        }
        else if (comparisonResult < 0)
        {
            if (leftNode != null)
            {
                retObj = leftNode.DepthFirstSearch(targetObj);
            }
```

Example 11-7. Generic BinaryTreeNode class (continued)

```
        }
        return (retObj);
    }

    public void PrintDepthFirst( )
    {
        if (leftNode != null)
        {
            leftNode.PrintDepthFirst( );
        }
        Console.WriteLine(this.nodeValue.ToString( ));
        if (leftNode != null)
        {
            Console.WriteLine("\tContains Left: " +
            leftNode.nodeValue.ToString( ));
        }
        else
        {
            Console.WriteLine("\tContains Left: NULL");
        }
        if (rightNode != null)
        {
            Console.WriteLine("\tContains Right: " +
            rightNode.nodeValue.ToString( ));
        }
        else
        {
            Console.WriteLine("\tContains Right: NULL");
        }
        if (rightNode != null)
        {
            rightNode.PrintDepthFirst( );
        }
    }

    public List<T> CopyToList( )
    {
        List<T> tempList = new List<T>( );
        if (leftNode != null)
        {
            tempList.AddRange(leftNode.CopyToList( ));
            tempList.Add(leftNode.nodeValue);
        }
        if (rightNode != null)
        {
            tempList.Add(rightNode.nodeValue);
            tempList.AddRange(rightNode.CopyToList( ));
        }
        return (tempList);
    }

    public void RemoveLeftNode( )
```

Example 11-7. Generic BinaryTreeNode class (continued)

```
    {
        leftNode = null;
    }

    public void RemoveRightNode( )
    {
        rightNode = null;
    }
}
```

The methods defined in Table 11-3 are of particular interest to using a `BinaryTree<T>` object.

Table 11-3. Members of the BinaryTree<T> class

Member	Description
`Overloaded constructor`	This constructor creates a `BinaryTree<T>` object with a root node. Its syntax is: `BinaryTree(T value)` where *value* is the root node for the tree. Note that this tree may not be flattened.
`AddNode method`	Adds a node to the tree. Its syntax is: `AddNode(T value, int id)` where *value* is the object to be added and *id* is the node index. Use this method if the tree will be flattened.
`AddNode method`	Adds a node to the tree. Its syntax is: `AddNode(T value)` where *value* is the object to be added. Use this method if the tree will not be flattened.
`SearchDepthFirst method`	Searches for and returns a `BinaryTreeNode<T>` object in the tree, if one exists. This method searches the depth of the tree first. Its syntax is: `SearchDepthFirst(T value)` where *value* is the object to be found in the tree.
`Print method`	Displays the tree in depth-first format. Its syntax is: `Print( )`
`Root property`	Returns the `BinaryTreeNode<T>` object that is the root of the tree. Its syntax is: `Root`
`TreeSize property`	A read-only property that gets the number of nodes in the tree. Its syntax is: `int TreeSize {get;}`

The methods defined in Table 11-4 are of particular interest to using a `BinaryTreeNode<T>` object.

Table 11-4. Members of the BinaryTreeNode<T> class

Member	Description
Overloaded constructor	This constructor creates a BinaryTreeNode<T> object. Its syntax is: `BinaryTreeNode(T value)` where *value* is the object contained in this node, which will be used to compare to its parent.
Left property	A read-only property to retrieve the left child node below this node. Its syntax is: `BinaryTreeNode<T> Left {get;}`
Right property	A read-only property to retrieve the right child node below this node. Its syntax is: `BinaryTreeNode<T> Right {get;}`
Children property	Retrieves the number of child nodes below this node. Its syntax is: `Children()`
GetValue method	Returns the IComparable<T> object that this node contains. Its syntax is: `GetValue()`
AddNode method	Adds a new node recursively to either the left or right side. Its syntax is: `AddNode(BinaryTreeNode<T> node)` where *node* is the node to be added. Duplicate nodes may be added using this method.
AddUniqueNode method	Adds a new node recursively to either the left side or the right side. Its syntax is: `AddUniqueNode(BinaryTreeNode<T> node)` where *node* is the node to be added. Duplicate nodes may not be added using this method. A Boolean value is returned: true indicates a successful operation; false indicates an attempt to add a duplicate node.
DepthFirstSearch method	Searches for and returns a BinaryTreeNode<T> object in the tree, if one exists. This method searches the depth of the tree first. Its syntax is: `DepthFirstSearch(T targetObj)` where *targetObj* is the object to be found in the tree.
PrintDepthFirst method	Displays the tree in depth-first format. Its syntax is: `PrintDepthFirst()`
RemoveLeftNode method	Removes the left node and any child nodes of this node. Its syntax is: `RemoveLeftNode()`
RemoveRightNode method	Removes the right node and any child nodes of this node. Its syntax is: `RemoveRightNode()`

The code in Example 11-8 illustrates the use of the BinaryTree<T> and BinaryTreeNode<T> classes when creating and using a binary tree.

Example 11-8. Using the BinaryTree and Binary TreeNode classes

```
public static void TestBinaryTree()
{
    BinaryTree<string> tree = new BinaryTree<string>("d");
    tree.AddNode("a");
    tree.AddNode("b");
    tree.AddNode("f");
    tree.AddNode("e");
```

```
    tree.AddNode("c");
    tree.AddNode("g");

    tree.Print();
    tree.Print();

    Console.WriteLine("tree.TreeSize: " + tree.Count);
    Console.WriteLine("tree.Root.DepthFirstSearch(b).Children: " +
                    tree.Root.DepthFirstSearch("b").Children);
    Console.WriteLine("tree.Root.DepthFirstSearch(a).Children: " +
                    tree.Root.DepthFirstSearch("a").Children);
    Console.WriteLine("tree.Root.DepthFirstSearch(g).Children: " +
                    tree.Root.DepthFirstSearch("g").Children);

    Console.WriteLine("tree.SearchDepthFirst(a): " +
                    tree.SearchDepthFirst("a").Value);
    Console.WriteLine("tree.SearchDepthFirst(b): " +
                    tree.SearchDepthFirst("b").Value);
    Console.WriteLine("tree.SearchDepthFirst(c): " +
                    tree.SearchDepthFirst("c").Value);
    Console.WriteLine("tree.SearchDepthFirst(d): " +
                    tree.SearchDepthFirst("d").Value);
    Console.WriteLine("tree.SearchDepthFirst(e): " +
                    tree.SearchDepthFirst("e").Value);
    Console.WriteLine("tree.SearchDepthFirst(f): " +
                    tree.SearchDepthFirst("f").Value);

    tree.Root.RemoveLeftNode();
    tree.Print();

    tree.Root.RemoveRightNode();
    tree.Print();
}
```

The output for this method is shown here:

```
        a
                Contains Left: NULL
                Contains Right: b
        b
                Contains Left: NULL
                Contains Right: c
        c
                Contains Left: NULL
                Contains Right: NULL
        d
                Contains Left: a
                Contains Right: f
        e
                Contains Left: NULL
                Contains Right: NULL
```

```
f
     Contains Left: e
     Contains Right: g
g
     Contains Left: NULL
     Contains Right: NULL
a
     Contains Left: NULL
     Contains Right: b
b
     Contains Left: NULL
     Contains Right: c
c
     Contains Left: NULL
     Contains Right: NULL
d
     Contains Left: a
     Contains Right: f
e
     Contains Left: NULL
     Contains Right: NULL
f
     Contains Left: e
     Contains Right: g
g
     Contains Left: NULL
     Contains Right: NULL
tree.TreeSize: 7
tree.Root.DepthFirstSearch(a).Children: 1
tree.Root.DepthFirstSearch(a).Children: 2
tree.Root.DepthFirstSearch(g).Children: 0
tree.SearchDepthFirst(a): a
tree.SearchDepthFirst(b): b
tree.SearchDepthFirst(c): c
tree.SearchDepthFirst(d): d
tree.SearchDepthFirst(e): e
tree.SearchDepthFirst(f): f
d
     Contains Left: NULL
     Contains Right: f
e
     Contains Left: NULL
     Contains Right: NULL
f
     Contains Left: e
     Contains Right: g
g
     Contains Left: NULL
     Contains Right: NULL
d
     Contains Left: NULL
     Contains Right: NULL
```

Discussion

Trees are data structures in which each node has exactly one parent and possibly many children. The root of the tree is a single node that branches out into one or more child nodes. A *node* is the part of the tree structure that contains data and contains the branches (or in more concrete terms, *references*) to its children node(s).

A tree can be used for many things, such as to represent a management hierarchy with the president of the company at the root node and the various vice presidents as child nodes of the president. The vice presidents may have managers as child nodes, and so on. A tree can be used to make decisions, where each node of the tree contains a question, and the answer given depends on which branch is taken to a child node. The tree described in this recipe is called a *binary tree*. A binary tree can have zero, one, or two child nodes for every node in the tree. A binary tree node can never have more than two child nodes; this is where this type of tree gets its name. (There are other types of trees. For instance, the *n*-ary tree can have zero to *n* nodes for each node in the tree. This type of tree is defined in Recipe 11.5.)

A binary tree is very useful for storing objects and then efficiently searching for those objects. There are definitely more efficient algorithms out there for sorting binary trees than the one implemented here. For example, if you need to store key/value pairs, you can look at using the SortedList or the SortedDictionary classes built into the .NET Framework. For storing large amounts of data (i.e., items numbering in the hundreds of thousands or higher), these two data structures will perform better. For storing small numbers of items (i.e., a few hundred or lower), this data structure's performance will be fine.

The following algorithm is used to store objects in a binary tree:

1. Start at the root node.
2. Is this node free?
   a. If yes, add the object to this node, and you are done.
   b. If no, continue.
3. Is the object to be added to the tree less than (*less than* is determined by the IComparable<T>.CompareTo method of the node being added) the current node?
   a. If yes, follow the branch to the node on the left side of the current node, and go to step 2.
   b. If no, follow the branch to the node of the right side of the current node, and go to step 2.

Basically, this algorithm states that the node to the left of the current node contains an object or value less than the current node, and the node to the right of the current node contains an object or value greater than (or equal to, if the binary tree can contain duplicates) the current node.

Searching for an object in a tree is easy. Just start at the root and ask, "Is the object I am searching for?" If it is not, then you need to ask "is the object I am searching for less than the current node's object?" If it is, follow the left branch to the next node in the tree. If it is still not the correct object, continue down the right branch to the next node. When you get to the next node, start the process over again.

The binary tree used in this recipe is made up of two classes. The BinaryTree<T> class is not a part of the actual tree; rather, it acts as a starting point from which you can create a tree, add nodes to it, search the tree for items, and retrieve the root node to perform other actions.

The second class, BinaryTreeNode<T>, is the heart of the binary tree and represents a single node in the tree. This class contains all the members that are required to create and work with a binary tree.

The BinaryTreeNode<T> class contains a protected field, nodeValue, which contains an object implementing the IComparable<T> interface. This structure allows you to perform searches and add nodes in the correct location in the tree. The CompareTo method of the IComparable<T> interface is used in searching and adding methods to determine whether you need to follow the left or right branch. See the AddNode, AddUniqueNode, and DepthFirstSearch methods—discussed in the following paragraphs—to see this in action.

There are two methods to add nodes to the tree, AddNode and AddUniqueNode. The AddNode method allows duplicates to be introduced to the tree, whereas the AddUniqueNode allows only unique nodes to be added.

The DepthFirstSearch method allows the tree to be searched by first checking the current node to see whether it contains the value searched for; if not, recursion is used to check the left or the right node. If no matching value is found in any node, this method returns null.

It is interesting to note that even though the BinaryTree<T> class is provided to create and manage the tree of BinaryTreeNode<T> objects, you can merely use the BinaryTreeNode<T> class as long as you keep track of the root node yourself. The code shown in Example 11-9 creates and manages the tree without the use of the BinaryTree<T> class.

Example 11-9. Creating and managing a binary tree without using the BinaryTree class

```
public static void TestManagedTreeWithNoBinaryTreeClass()
{
    // Create the root node.
    BinaryTreeNode<string> topLevel = new BinaryTreeNode<string>("d");

    // Create all nodes that will be added to the tree.
    BinaryTreeNode<string> one = new BinaryTreeNode<string>("b");
    BinaryTreeNode<string> two = new BinaryTreeNode<string>("c");
    BinaryTreeNode<string> three = new BinaryTreeNode<string>("a");
```

Example 11-9. Creating and managing a binary tree without using the BinaryTree class (continued)

```
BinaryTreeNode<string> four = new BinaryTreeNode<string>("e");
BinaryTreeNode<string> five = new BinaryTreeNode<string>("f");
BinaryTreeNode<string> six = new BinaryTreeNode<string>("g");

// Add nodes to tree through the root.
topLevel.AddNode(three);
topLevel.AddNode(one);
topLevel.AddNode(five);
topLevel.AddNode(four);
topLevel.AddNode(two);
topLevel.AddNode(six);

// Print the tree starting at the root node.
topLevel.PrintDepthFirst();

// Print the tree starting at node 'Three'.
three.PrintDepthFirst();

// Display the number of child nodes of various nodes in the tree.
Console.WriteLine("topLevel.Children: " + topLevel.Children);
Console.WriteLine("one.Children: " + one.Children);
Console.WriteLine("three.Children: " + three.Children);
Console.WriteLine("six.Children: " + six.Children);

// Search the tree using the depth-first searching method.
Console.WriteLine("topLevel.DepthFirstSearch(a): " +
                  topLevel.DepthFirstSearch("a").Value.ToString());
Console.WriteLine("topLevel.DepthFirstSearch(b): " +
                  topLevel.DepthFirstSearch("b").Value.ToString());
Console.WriteLine("topLevel.DepthFirstSearch(c): " +
                  topLevel.DepthFirstSearch("c").Value.ToString());
Console.WriteLine("topLevel.DepthFirstSearch(d): " +
                  topLevel.DepthFirstSearch("d").Value.ToString());
Console.WriteLine("topLevel.DepthFirstSearch(e): " +
                  topLevel.DepthFirstSearch("e").Value.ToString());
Console.WriteLine("topLevel.DepthFirstSearch(f): " +
                  topLevel.DepthFirstSearch("f").Value.ToString());

// Remove the left child node from the root node and display the entire tree.
topLevel.RemoveLeftNode();
topLevel.PrintDepthFirst();

// Remove all nodes from the tree except for the root and display the tree.
topLevel.RemoveRightNode();
topLevel.PrintDepthFirst();
}
```

The output for this method is shown here:

```
a
    Contains Left: NULL
    Contains Right: b
```

```
b
     Contains Left: NULL
     Contains Right: c
c
     Contains Left: NULL
     Contains Right: NULL
d
     Contains Left: a
     Contains Right: f
e
     Contains Left: NULL
     Contains Right: NULL
f
     Contains Left: e
     Contains Right: g
g
     Contains Left: NULL
     Contains Right: NULL
a
     Contains Left: NULL
     Contains Right: b
b
     Contains Left: NULL
     Contains Right: c
c
     Contains Left: NULL
     Contains Right: NULL
topLevel.Children: 6
one.Children: 1
three.Children: 2
six.Children: 0
topLevel.DepthFirstSearch(a): a
topLevel.DepthFirstSearch(b): b
topLevel.DepthFirstSearch(c): c
topLevel.DepthFirstSearch(d): d
topLevel.DepthFirstSearch(e): e
topLevel.DepthFirstSearch(f): f
d
     Contains Left: NULL
     Contains Right: f
e
     Contains Left: NULL
     Contains Right: NULL
f
     Contains Left: e
     Contains Right: g
g
     Contains Left: NULL
     Contains Right: NULL
d
     Contains Left: NULL
     Contains Right: NULL
```

See Also

The "Queue Class" and "IComparable<T> Interface" topics in the MSDN documentation.

11.5   Creating an n-ary Tree

Problem

You need a tree that can store a number of child nodes in each of its nodes. A binary tree will work if each node needs to have only two children, but in this case, each node needs to have a fixed number of child nodes greater than two.

Solution

Use the NTree<T> class shown in Example 11-10 to create the root node for the *n*-ary tree.

Example 11-10. Generic NTree class

```
using System;
using System.Collections;
using System.Collections.Generic;

public class NTree<T> : IEnumerable<T>
    where T : IComparable<T>
{
    public NTree()
    {
        maxChildren = int.MaxValue;
    }
    public NTree(int maxNumChildren)
    {
        maxChildren = maxNumChildren;
    }

    // The root node of the tree
    private NTreeNode<T> root = null;
    // The maximum number of child nodes that a parent node may contain
    private int maxChildren = 0;

    public void AddRoot(NTreeNode<T> node)
    {
        root = node;
    }

    public int MaxChildren
    {
        get {return (maxChildren);}
    }
}
```

The methods defined in Table 11-5 are of particular interest to using an NTree<T> object.

Table 11-5. Members of the NTree<T> class

Member	Description
Overloaded constructor	This constructor creates an NTree<T> object. Its syntax is: NTree(int *maxNumChildren*) where *maxNumChildren* is the maximum number of children that one node may have at any time.
MaxChildren property	A read-only property to retrieve the maximum number of children any node may have. Its syntax is: int *MaxChildren* {get;} The value this property returns is set in the constructor.
AddRoot method	Adds a node to the tree. Its syntax is: AddRoot(NTreeNodeFactory<T>.NTreeNode<U> *node*) where *node* is the node to be added as a child to the current node.

The NTreeNodeFactory<T> class is used to create nodes for the *n*-ary tree. These nodes are defined in the class NTreeNode<U>, which is nested inside of the NTreeNodeFactory<T> class. You are not able to create an NTreeNode<U> without the use of this factory class, as shown in Example 11-11.

Example 11-11. Using the class to create the nodes for an n-ary tree

```
public class NTreeNodeFactory<T>
    where T : IComparable<T>
{
    public NTreeNodeFactory(NTree<T> root)
    {
        maxChildren = root.MaxChildren;
    }

    private int maxChildren = 0;

    public int MaxChildren
    {
        get {return (maxChildren);}
    }

    public NTreeNode<T> CreateNode(T value)
    {
        return (new NTreeNode<T>(value, maxChildren));
    }

    // Nested Node class
    public class NTreeNode<U>
        where U : IComparable<U>
    {
```

Example 11-11. Using the class to create the nodes for an n-ary tree (continued)

```
public NTreeNode(U value, int maxChildren)
{
    if (value != null)
    {
        nodeValue = value;
    }

    childNodes = new NTreeNode<U>[maxChildren];
}

protected U nodeValue = default(U);
protected NTreeNode<U>[] childNodes = null;


public int CountChildren
{
    get
    {
        int currCount = 0;

        for (int index = 0; index <= childNodes.GetUpperBound(0); index++)
        {
            if (childNodes[index] != null)
            {
                ++currCount;
                currCount += childNodes[index].CountChildren;
            }
        }

        return (currCount);
    }
}

public int CountImmediateChildren
{
    get
    {
        int currCount = 0;

        for (int index = 0; index <= childNodes.GetUpperBound(0); index++)
        {
            if (childNodes[index] != null)
            {
                ++currCount;
            }
        }

        return (currCount);
    }
}

public NTreeNode<U>[] Children
```

```
{
    get {return (childNodes);}
}

public NTreeNode<U> GetChild(int index)
{
    return (childNodes[index]);
}

public U Value( )
{
    return (nodeValue);
}

public void AddNode(NTreeNode<U> node)
{
    int numOfNonNullNodes = CountImmediateChildren;
    if (numOfNonNullNodes < childNodes.Length)
    {
        childNodes[numOfNonNullNodes] = node;
    }
    else
    {
        throw (new Exception("Cannot add more children to this node."));
    }
}

public NTreeNode<U> DepthFirstSearch(U targetObj)
{
    NTreeNode<U> retObj = default(NTreeNode<U>);

    if (targetObj.CompareTo(nodeValue) == 0)
    {
        retObj = this;
    }
    else
    {
        for (int index=0; index<=childNodes.GetUpperBound(0); index++)
        {
            if (childNodes[index] != null)
            {
                retObj = childNodes[index].DepthFirstSearch(targetObj);
                if (retObj != null)
                {
                    break;
                }
            }
        }
    }

    return (retObj);
}
```

Example 11-11. Using the class to create the nodes for an n-ary tree (continued)

```
public NTreeNode<U> BreadthFirstSearch(U targetObj)
{
    Queue<NTreeNode<U>> row = new Queue<NTreeNode<U>>( );
    row.Enqueue(this);

    while (row.Count > 0)
    {
        // Get next node in queue.
        NTreeNode<U> currentNode = row.Dequeue( );

        // Is this the node we are looking for?
        if (targetObj.CompareTo(currentNode.nodeValue) == 0)
        {
            return (currentNode);
        }
        for (int index = 0;
            index < currentNode.CountImmediateChildren;
            index++)
        {
            if (currentNode.Children[index] != null)
            {
                row.Enqueue(currentNode.Children[index]);
            }
        }
    }

    return (null);
}

public void PrintDepthFirst( )
{
    Console.WriteLine("this: " + nodeValue.ToString( ));

    for (int index = 0; index < childNodes.Length; index++)
    {
        if (childNodes[index] != null)
        {
            Console.WriteLine("\tchildNodes[" + index + "]: " +
            childNodes[index].nodeValue.ToString( ));
        }
        else
        {
            Console.WriteLine("\tchildNodes[" + index + "]: NULL");
        }
    }

    for (int index = 0; index < childNodes.Length; index++)
    {
        if (childNodes[index] != null)
        {
            childNodes[index].PrintDepthFirst( );
        }
```

```
                }
            }

        public List<U> IterateDepthFirst()
        {
            List<U> tempList = new List<U>();

            for (int index = 0; index < childNodes.Length; index++)
            {
                if (childNodes[index] != null)
                {
                    tempList.Add(childNodes[index].nodeValue);
                }
            }

            for (int index = 0; index < childNodes.Length; index++)
            {
                if (childNodes[index] != null)
                {
                    tempList.AddRange(childNodes[index].IterateDepthFirst());
                }
            }

            return (tempList);
        }

        public void RemoveNode(int index)
        {
            // Remove node from array and compact the array.
            if (index < childNodes.GetLowerBound(0) ||
                index > childNodes.GetUpperBound(0))
            {
                throw (new ArgumentOutOfRangeException("index", index,
                        "Array index out of bounds."));
            }
            else if (index < childNodes.GetUpperBound(0))
            {
                Array.Copy(childNodes, index + 1, childNodes, index,
                        childNodes.Length - index - 1);
            }
            childNodes.SetValue(null, childNodes.GetUpperBound(0));
        }
    }
}
```

The methods defined in Table 11-6 are of particular interest to using an NTreeNodeFactory<T> object.

Table 11-6. Members of the NTreeNodeFactory<T> class

Member	Description
Constructor	Creates a new NTreeNodeFactory<T> object that will create NTreeNode<U> objects with the same number of MaxChildren that the NTree<T> object passed in supports. Its syntax is: `NTreeNodeFactory(NTree<T> root)` where *root* is an NTree<T> object.
MaxChildren property	Read-only property that returns the maximum number of children that the NTree<T> object supports. Its syntax is: `int MaxChildren {get;}`

CreateNode method	Overloaded method that returns a new NTreeNode object. Its syntax is:
	
	`CreateNode()`
	`CreateNode(IComparable value)`
	
	where *value* is the IComparable object this new node object will contain.

The methods defined in Table 11-7 are of particular interest to using the nested NTreeNode<U> object.

Table 11-7. Members of the NTreeNode<U> class

Member	Description
Constructor	Creates a new NTreeNode<U> object from the NTreeNodeFactory<T> object passed in to it. Its syntax is: `NTreeNode(T value, int maxChildren)` where *value* is an IComparable<T> object and *maxChildren* is the total number of children allowed by this node.
NumOfChildren property	Read-only property that returns the total number of children below this node. Its syntax is: `int NumOfChildren {get;}`
Children property	Read-only property that returns all of the non-null child-node objects in an array that the current node contains. Its syntax is: `NTreeNode<U>[] Children {get;}`
CountChildren property	Recursively counts the number of non-null child nodes below the current node and returns this value as an integer. Its syntax is: `CountChildren`
CountImmediateChildren property	Counts only the non-null child nodes contained in the current node. Its syntax is: `CountImmediateChildren`
GetChild method	Uses an index to return the NTreeNode<U> contained by the current node. Its syntax is: `GetChild(int index)` where index is the array index where the child object is stored.
Value method	Returns an object of type T that the current node contains. Its syntax is: `Value()`

Table 11-7. Members of the NTreeNode<U> class (continued)

Member	Description
AddNode method	Adds a new child node to the current node. Its syntax is: AddNode(NTreeNode<U> *node*) where *node* is the child node to be added.
DepthFirstSearch method	Attempts to locate an NTreeNode<U> by the IComparable<T> object that it contains. An NTreeNode<U> is returned if the IComparable<T> object is located or a null if it is not. Its syntax is: DepthFirstSearch(IComparable<T> *targetObj*) where *targetObj* is the IComparable<T> object to locate in the tree. Note that this search starts with the current node, which may or may not be the root of the tree. The tree traversal is done in a depth-first manner.
BreadthFirstSearch method	Attempts to locate an NTreeNode<U> by the IComparable<T> object that it contains. An NTreeNode<U> is returned if the IComparable<T> object is located or a null if it is not. Its syntax is: BreadthFirstSearch(IComparable<T> *targetObj*) where *targetObj* is the IComparable<T> object to locate in the tree. Note that this search starts with the current node, which may or may not be the root of the tree. The tree traversal is done in a breadth-first manner.
PrintDepthFirst method	Displays the tree structure on the console window starting with the current node. Its syntax is: PrintDepthFirst( ) This method uses recursion to display each node in the tree.
RemoveNode method	Removes the child node at the specified *index* on the current node. Its syntax is: RemoveNode(int *index*) where *index* is the array index where the child object is stored. Note that when a node is removed, all of its children nodes are removed as well.

The code shown in Example 11-12 illustrates the use of the NTree<T>, NTree-NodeFactory<T>, and NTreeNode<U> classes to create and manipulate an *n*-ary tree.

Example 11-12. Using the NTree<T>, NTreeNodeFactory<T>, and NTreeNode<U> classes

```
public static void TestNTree( )
{
    NTree<string> topLevel = new NTree<string>(3);
    NTreeNodeFactory<string> nodeFactory =
                new NTreeNodeFactory<string>(topLevel);

    NTreeNode<string> one = nodeFactory.CreateNode("One");
    NTreeNode<string> two = nodeFactory.CreateNode("Two");
    NTreeNode<string> three = nodeFactory.CreateNode("Three");
    NTreeNode<string> four = nodeFactory.CreateNode("Four");
    NTreeNode<string> five = nodeFactory.CreateNode("Five");
    NTreeNode<string> six = nodeFactory.CreateNode("Six");
    NTreeNode<string> seven = nodeFactory.CreateNode("Seven");
    NTreeNode<string> eight = nodeFactory.CreateNode("Eight");
```

Example 11-12. Using the NTree<T>, NTreeNodeFactory<T>, and NTreeNode<U> classes

```
    NTreeNode<string> nine = nodeFactory.CreateNode("Nine");

    topLevel.AddRoot(one);
    Console.WriteLine("topLevel.GetRoot().CountChildren: " +
            topLevel.GetRoot().CountChildren);

    topLevel.GetRoot().AddNode(two);
    topLevel.GetRoot().AddNode(three);
    topLevel.GetRoot().AddNode(four);

    topLevel.GetRoot().Children[0].AddNode(five);
    topLevel.GetRoot().Children[0].AddNode(eight);
    topLevel.GetRoot().Children[0].AddNode(nine);
    topLevel.GetRoot().Children[1].AddNode(six);
    topLevel.GetRoot().Children[1].Children[0].AddNode(seven);

    Console.WriteLine("Display Entire tree:");
    topLevel.GetRoot().PrintDepthFirst();

    Console.WriteLine("Display tree from node [two]:");
    topLevel.GetRoot().Children[0].PrintDepthFirst();

    Console.WriteLine("Depth First Search:");
    Console.WriteLine("topLevel.DepthFirstSearch(One): " +
            topLevel.GetRoot().DepthFirstSearch("One").Value().ToString());
    Console.WriteLine("topLevel.DepthFirstSearch(Two): " +
            topLevel.GetRoot().DepthFirstSearch("Two").Value().ToString());
    Console.WriteLine("topLevel.DepthFirstSearch(Three): " +
            topLevel.GetRoot().DepthFirstSearch("Three").Value().ToString());
  Console.WriteLine("topLevel.DepthFirstSearch(Four): " +
            topLevel.GetRoot().DepthFirstSearch("Four").Value().ToString());
    Console.WriteLine("topLevel.DepthFirstSearch(Five): " +
            topLevel.GetRoot().DepthFirstSearch("Five").Value().ToString());

    Console.WriteLine("\r\n\r\nBreadth First Search:");
    Console.WriteLine("topLevel.BreadthFirstSearch(One): " +
            topLevel.GetRoot().BreadthFirstSearch("One").Value().ToString());
    Console.WriteLine("topLevel.BreadthFirstSearch(Two): " +
            topLevel.GetRoot().BreadthFirstSearch("Two").Value().ToString());
    Console.WriteLine("topLevel.BreadthFirstSearch(Three): " +
            topLevel.GetRoot().BreadthFirstSearch("Three").Value().ToString());
    Console.WriteLine("topLevel.BreadthFirstSearch(Four): " +
            topLevel.GetRoot().BreadthFirstSearch("Four").Value().ToString());
}
```

The output for this method is shown here:

```
            topLevel.GetRoot().CountChildren: 0
            Display Entire tree:
            this: One
                childNodes[0]: Two
                childNodes[1]: Three
                childNodes[2]: Four
```

```
this: Two
    childNodes[0]: Five
    childNodes[1]: Eight
    childNodes[2]: Nine
this: Five
    childNodes[0]: NULL
    childNodes[1]: NULL
    childNodes[2]: NULL
this: Eight
    childNodes[0]: NULL
    childNodes[1]: NULL
    childNodes[2]: NULL
this: Nine
    childNodes[0]: NULL
    childNodes[1]: NULL
    childNodes[2]: NULL
this: Three
    childNodes[0]: Six
    childNodes[1]: NULL
    childNodes[2]: NULL
this: Six
    childNodes[0]: Seven
    childNodes[1]: NULL
    childNodes[2]: NULL
this: Seven
    childNodes[0]: NULL
    childNodes[1]: NULL
    childNodes[2]: NULL
this: Four
    childNodes[0]: NULL
    childNodes[1]: NULL
    childNodes[2]: NULL
Display tree from node [two]:
this: Two
    childNodes[0]: Five
    childNodes[1]: Eight
    childNodes[2]: Nine
this: Five
    childNodes[0]: NULL
    childNodes[1]: NULL
    childNodes[2]: NULL
this: Eight
    childNodes[0]: NULL
    childNodes[1]: NULL
    childNodes[2]: NULL
this: Nine
    childNodes[0]: NULL
    childNodes[1]: NULL
    childNodes[2]: NULL
Depth First Search:
topLevel.DepthFirstSearch(One): One
topLevel.DepthFirstSearch(Two): Two
topLevel.DepthFirstSearch(Three): Three
topLevel.DepthFirstSearch(Four): Four
topLevel.DepthFirstSearch(Five): Five
```

```
Breadth First Search:
topLevel.BreadthFirstSearch(One): One
topLevel.BreadthFirstSearch(Two): Two
topLevel.BreadthFirstSearch(Three): Three
topLevel.BreadthFirstSearch(Four): Four
```

Discussion

An *n*-ary tree is one that has no limitation on the number of children each parent node may contain. This is in contrast to the binary search tree in Recipe 11.4, in which each parent node may contain only two children nodes.

NTree<T> is a simple class that contains only a constructor and three public methods. Through this object, you can create an *n*-ary tree, set the root node, and obtain the root node in order to navigate and manipulate the tree. An NTree<T> object that can contain at most three children is created in the following manner:

```
NTree<string> topLevel = new NTree<string>(3);
```

An NTree<T> object that can contain at most int.MaxValue children, which allows greater flexibility, is created in the following manner:

```
NTree<string> topLevel = new NTree<string>();
```

The real work is done in the NTreeNodeFactory<T> object and the NTreeNode<U> object, which is nested in the NTreeNodeFactory<T> class. The NTreeNodeFactory<T> class is an object factory that facilitates the construction of all NTreeNode<U> objects. When the factory object is created, the NTree<T> object is passed in to the constructor, as shown here:

```
NTreeNodeFactory<string> nodeFactory = new NTreeNodeFactory<string>
(topLevel);
```

Therefore, when the factory object is created, it knows the maximum number of children that a parent node may have. The factory object provides a public method, CreateNode, that allows for the creation of an NTreeNode<U> object. If an IComparable<T> type object is passed into this method, the IComparable<T> object will be contained within this new node in the nodeValue field. If a null is passed in, the new NTreeNode<U> object will contain the object U with it initialized using the default keyword. The String object can be passed in to this parameter with no modifications. Node creation is performed in the following manner:

```
NTreeNode<string> one = nodeFactory.CreateNode("One");
NTreeNode<string> two = nodeFactory.CreateNode("Two");
NTreeNode<string> three = nodeFactory.CreateNode("Three");
NTreeNode<string> four = nodeFactory.CreateNode("Four");
NTreeNode<string> five = nodeFactory.CreateNode("Five");
NTreeNode<string> six = nodeFactory.CreateNode("Six");

NTreeNode<string> seven = nodeFactory.CreateNode("Seven");
NTreeNode<string> eight = nodeFactory.CreateNode("Eight");
NTreeNode<string> nine = nodeFactory.CreateNode("Nine");
```

The NTreeNode<U> class is nested within the factory class; it is not supposed to be used directly to create a node object. Instead, the factory will create a node object and return it to the caller. NTreeNode<U> has one constructor that accepts two parameters: value, which is an object of type U used to store an object implementing the IComparable<T> interface; and an integer value, maxChildren, which is used to define the total number of child nodes allowed. It is the nodeValue field that you use when you are searching the tree for a particular item.

Adding a root node to the TopLevel NTree<T> object is performed using the AddRoot method of the NTree<T> object:

```
topLevel.AddRoot(one);
```

Each NTreeNode<U> object contains a field called childNodes. This field is an array containing all child nodes attached to this parent node object. The maximum number of children—obtained from the factory class—provides this number, which is used to create the fixed-size array. This array is initialized in the constructor of the NTreeNode<U> object.

The following code shows how to add nodes to this tree:

```
// Add nodes to root.
topLevel.GetRoot().AddNode(two);
topLevel.GetRoot().AddNode(three);
topLevel.GetRoot().AddNode(four);

// Add node to the first node Two of the root.
topLevel.GetRoot().Children[0].AddNode(five);

// Add node to the previous node added, node five.
topLevel.GetRoot().BreadthFirstSearch("Five").AddNode(six);
```

The searching method BreadthFirstSearch is constructed similarly to the way the same method was constructed for the binary search tree in Recipe 11.4. The DepthFirstSearch method is constructed a little differently from the same method in the binary tree. This method uses recursion to search the tree, but it uses a for loop to iterate over the array of child nodes, searching each one in turn. In addition, the current node is checked first to determine whether it matches the targetObj parameter to this method. This is a better-performing design, as opposed to moving this test to the end of the method.

If the RemoveNode method is successful, the array containing all child nodes of the current node is compacted to prevent fragmentation, which allows nodes to be added later in a much simpler manner. The AddNode method only has to add the child node to the end of this array as opposed to searching the array for an open element. The following code shows how to remove a node:

```
// Remove all nodes below node 'Two'.
// Nodes 'Five' and 'Six' are removed.
topLevel.GetRoot().BreadthFirstSearch("Two").RemoveNode(0);
```

```
// Remove node 'Three' from the root node.
topLevel.GetRoot( ).RemoveNode(1);
```

See Also

The "Queue<T> Class" and "IComparable Interface" topics in the MSDN documentation.

11.6   Using a HashSet Object

Problem

You need an object that contains a group of unique unordered objects. This object must be able to be compared to other objects containing unique unordered groups of similar objects. In addition, the two must be able to have the following actions performed on them:

- Union of the items contained by the two container objects
- Intersection of the items contained by the two container objects
- Difference of the items contained by the two container objects

Solution

Use the built in HashSet<T> object.

The methods defined in Table 11-8 are of particular interest to using a HashSet<T> object.

Table 11-8. Members of the HashSet<T> class

Member	Description
Add method	Add a new object to the current HashSet<T> object. Its syntax is: Add(T *obj*) where *obj* is the object of type T to add to this HashSet.
Remove method	Removes an existing object from the current HashSet<T> object. Its syntax is: Remove(T *obj*) where *obj* is the object of type T to remove from this HashSet.
RemoveWhere method	Removes an existing object from the current HashSet<T> object. Its syntax is: RemoveWhere(Predicate<T> *match*) where *match* is the condition in which must be satisfied in order to remove an item or items from this HashSet.

Table 11-8. Members of the HashSet<T> class (continued)

Member	Description
Contains method	Returns a Boolean indicating whether the object passed in exists within this HashSet<T> object. If a true is returned, the object exists; otherwise, it does not. Its syntax is: `Contains(T obj)` where *obj* is the object of type T to be searched for.
UnionWith method	Performs a union operation on the current HashSet<T> object and a second HashSet<T> object. The current HashSet<T> object is modified to contain the union of these two HashSet<T> objects. Its syntax is: `UnionWith(HashSet<T> set)` where *set* is the second HashSet<T> object.
IntersectionWith method	Performs an intersection operation on the current HashSet<T> object and a second HashSet<T> object. The current HashSet<T> object is modified to contain the intersection of these two HashSet<T> objects. Its syntax is: `IntersectionWith(HashSet<T> set)` where *set* is the second HashSet<T> object.
ExceptWith method	Removes all elements in the passed in HashSet<T> object from the HashSet<T> object on which this method was called. The current HashSet<T> object is modified to contain the result of this operation. Its syntax is: `ExceptWith(HashSet<T> set)` where *set* is the second HashSet<T> object.
SymmetricExceptWith method	Performs a difference operation on the current HashSet<T> object and a second HashSet<T> object. The current HashSet<T> object is modified to contain the difference of these two HashSet<T> objects. Its syntax is: `SymmetricExceptWith(HashSet<T> set)` where *set* is the second HashSet<T> object.
SetEquals method	Returns a Boolean indicating whether a second HashSet<T> object is equal to the current HashSet<T> object. Its syntax is: `SetEquals(HashSet<T> set)` where *set* is the second HashSet<T> object.
IsSubsetOf method	Returns a Boolean indicating whether the current HashSet<T> object is a subset of a second HashSet<T> object. Its syntax is: `IsSubsetOf(Set<T> set)` where *set* is the second HashSet<T> object.
IsSupersetOf method	Returns a Boolean indicating whether the current HashSet<T> object is a superset of a second HashSet<T> object. Its syntax is: `IsSupersetOf(HashSet<T> set)` where *set* is the second HashSet<T> object.
IsProperSubsetOf method	Returns a Boolean indicating whether the current HashSet<T> object is a proper subset of a second HashSet<T> object. Its syntax is: `IsProperSubsetOf(Set<T> set)` where *set* is the second HashSet<T> object.

Table 11-8. Members of the HashSet<T> class (continued)

Member	Description
IsProperSupersetOf method	Returns a Boolean indicating whether the current HashSet<T> object is a proper superset of a second HashSet<T> object. Its syntax is: IsProperSupersetOf(HashSet<T> *set*) where *set* is the second HashSet<T> object.
Overlaps method	Returns a Boolean indicating whether the current HashSet<T> object overlaps a second HashSet<T> object. Its syntax is: Overlaps(HashSet<T> *set*) where *set* is the second HashSet<T> object.

Discussion

Sets are containers that hold a group of homogeneous object types. Various mathematical operations can be performed on sets, including the following:

Union

(A ∪ B)

Combines all elements of set A and set B into a resulting HashSet<T> object. If an object exists in both sets, the resulting unioned HashSet<T> object contains only one of those elements, not both.

Intersection

(A ∩ B)

Combines all elements of set A and set B that are common to both A and B into a resulting HashSet<T> object. If an object exists in one set and not the other, the element is not added to the intersectioned HashSet<T> object.

Difference

(A–B)

Combines all elements of set A, except for the elements that are also members of set B, into a resulting HashSet<T> object. If an object exists in both sets A and B, it is not added to the final differenced HashSet<T> object. The difference is equivalent to taking the union of both sets and the intersection of both sets and then removing all elements in the unioned set that exist in the intersectioned set.

Subset

(A ⊂ B)

Returns true if all elements of set A are contained in a second set B; otherwise, it returns false. Set B may contain elements not found in A.

Superset

    (A ⊃ B)

Returns true if all elements of set A are contained in a second set B; otherwise, it returns false. Set A may contain elements not found in B.

Equivalence

    (A == B)

Returns true if both HashSet<T> objects contain the same number of elements and the same value for each element; otherwise, it returns false. This is equivalent to stating that (A ⊂ B) and (B ⊂ A).

The following code creates and populates two HashSet<T> objects:

```
HashSet<int> set1 = new HashSet<int>();
HashSet<int> set2 = new HashSet<int>();

set1.Add(1);
set1.Add(2);
set1.Add(3);
set1.Add(4);
set1.Add(5);
set1.Add(6);

set2.Add(-10);
set2.Add(2);
set2.Add(40);
```

The union operation can be performed by using the UnionWith method and passing in a HashSet<T> with which to union the current HashSet<T>. Essentially, the resulting set contains elements that exist in either of the two HashSet<T> objects or both HashSet<T> objects. The following code demonstrates the union operation:

```
set1.UnionWith(set2);
```

The intersection operation is set up similarly to the union operation. To perform an intersection between two HashSet<T> objects, use the IntersectWith method. Essentially, an element must be in both HashSet<T> A and HashSet<T> B in order for it to be placed in the resulting HashSet<T> object. The following code demonstrates the intersection operation:

```
set1.IntersectionOf(set2);
```

The difference operation is performed through the SymmetricExceptWith method. Essentially, only elements in either set, but not both, are placed in the resulting set. The following code demonstrates the difference operation:

```
set1.SymmetricExceptWith(set2);
```

The subset operation is performed only through a single method called IsSubsetOf. The superset operation is also performed using a single method called IsSupersetOf. The following code demonstrates this operation:

```
bool isSubset = set1.IsSubsetOf(set2);
bool isSuperset = set1.IsSupersetOf(set2);
```

The equivalence operation is performed by using the SetEquals method. The following code demonstrates this operation:

```
bool isEqual = set1.Equals(set2);
```

See Also

The "HashSet and LINQ Set Operations" topics in the MSDN documentation.

CHAPTER 12

Filesystem I/O

12.0 Introduction

This chapter deals with the file system in four distinct ways. The first set of recipes looks at typical file interactions like:

- Creation.
- Reading and writing.
- Deletion.
- Attributes.
- Encoding methods for character data.
- Selecting the correct way (based on usage) to access files via streams.

The second set looks at directory- or folder-based programming tasks such as file creation as well as renaming, deleting, and determining attributes. The third set deals with the parsing of paths and the use of temporary files and paths. The fourth set deals with more advanced topics in filesystem I/O, such as:

- Asynchronous reads and writes.
- Monitoring for certain file system actions.
- Version information in files.
- Using P/Invoke to perform file I/O.

The file-interactions section comes first since it sets the stage for many of the recipes in the temporary file and advanced sections. This is fundamental knowledge that will help you understand the other file I/O recipes and how to modify them for your purposes. The various file and directory I/O techniques are used throughout the more advanced examples to help show a couple of different ways to approach the problems you will encounter working with file system I/O.

Unless otherwise specified, you need the following using statements in any program that uses snippets or methods from this chapter:

```
using System;
using System.IO;
```

12.1   Manipulating File Attributes

Problem

You need to display or manipulate a file's attributes or timestamps.

Solution

To display a file's timestamps, you can use either the static methods of the File class or the instance properties of the FileInfo class. The static methods are GetCreationTime, GetLastAccessTime, and GetLastWriteTime. Each has a single parameter, the path and name of the file for which timestamp information is to be returned, and returns a DateTime value containing the relevant timestamp. For example:

```
public static void DisplayFileTimestamps(string path)
{
    Console.WriteLine(File.GetCreationTime(path));
    Console.WriteLine(File.GetLastAccessTime(path));
    Console.WriteLine(File.GetLastWriteTime(path));
}
```

The instance properties of the FileInfo class are CreationTime, LastAccessTime, and LastWriteTime. Each returns a DateTime value containing the respective timestamp of the file represented by the FileInfo object. The DisplayFileInfoTimestamps extension method allows you to report those values directly from a FileInfo:

```
public static void DisplayFileInfoTimestamps(this FileInfo fileInfo)
{
    Console.WriteLine(fileInfo.CreationTime.ToString( ));
    Console.WriteLine(fileInfo.LastAccessTime.ToString( ));
    Console.WriteLine(fileInfo.LastWriteTime.ToString( ));
}
```

To modify a file's timestamps, you can use either the static methods of the File class or the instance properties of the FileInfo class. The static methods are SetCreationTime, SetLastAccessTime, and SetLastWriteTime. All of them take the path and name of the file for which the timestamp is to be modified as the first parameter and a DateTime value containing the new timestamp as the second, and each returns void. To set them all at once, use the ModifyFileTimestamps method:

```
public static void ModifyFileTimestamps(string path)
{
    File.SetCreationTime(path, DateTime.Parse(@"May 10, 2003"));
    File.SetLastAccessTime(path, DateTime.Parse(@"May 10, 2003"));
    File.SetLastWriteTime(path, DateTime.Parse(@"May 10, 2003"));
}
```

The instance properties are the same as the properties used to display timestamp information: `CreationTime`, `LastAccessTime`, or `LastWriteTime`. To set the timestamp, assign a value of type `DateTime` to the relevant timestamp property. To set all of these properties at once, use the `ModifyTimestamps` extension method for `FileInfo`:

```
public static void ModifyTimestamps(this FileInfo fileInfo, DateTime dt)
{
    fileInfo.CreationTime = dt;
    fileInfo.LastAccessTime = dt;
    fileInfo.LastWriteTime = dt;
}
```

To display or modify a file's attributes, use the instance `Attributes` property. The property's value is a bit mask consisting of one or more members of the `FileAttributes` enumeration. For example, the following two methods (`DisplayFileHiddenAttribute` and `MakeFileHidden`) display or modify if the file has the Hidden attribute:

```
public static void DisplayFileHiddenAttribute(string path)
{
    if (File.Exists(path))
    {
        FileInfo fileInfo = new FileInfo(path);

        // Display whether this file is hidden
        Console.WriteLine("Is file hidden? = " +
            ((fileInfo.Attributes & FileAttributes.Hidden) ==
                FileAttributes.Hidden));
    }
}

public static void MakeFileHidden(this FileInfo fileInfo)
{
    // Modify this file's attributes
    fileInfo.Attributes |= FileAttributes.Hidden;
}
```

Discussion

One of the easier methods of creating a `DateTime` object is to use the static `DateTime.Parse` method. This method accepts a string defining a particular date and is converted to a `DateTime` object.

In addition to timestamp information, a file's attributes may also be obtained and modified. This is accomplished through the use of the public instance `Attributes` property found on a `FileInfo` object. This property returns or modifies a `FileAttributes` enumeration. The `FileAttributes` enumeration is made up of bit flags that can be turned on or off through the use of the bitwise operators &, |, or ^.

Table 12-1 lists each of the flags in the `FileAttributes` enumeration.

Table 12-1. FileAttributes enumeration values

Member name	Description
Archive	Represents the file's archive status that marks the file for backup or removal.
Compressed	Indicates that the file is compressed.
Device	This option is reserved for future use.
Directory	Indicates that this is a directory.
Encrypted	Indicates that a file or directory is encrypted. In the case of a file, its contents are encrypted. In the case of a directory, newly created files will be encrypted by default.
Hidden	Indicates a hidden file.
Normal	Indicates that the file has no other attributes; as such, this attribute cannot be used in combination with others.
NotContentIndexed	Indicates that the file is excluded from the content index service.
Offline	Indicates that the state of the file is offline and its contents will be unavailable.
ReadOnly	Indicates that the file is read-only.
ReparsePoint	Indicates a *reparse point*, a block of data associated with a directory or file.
SparseFile	Indicates a sparse file, which may take up less space on the filesystem than its reported size because zeros in the file are not actually allocated on disk.
System	Indicates that the file is a system file.
Temporary	Indicates a temporary file. It may reside entirely in memory.

In many cases, more than one of these flags can be set at one time. One case in which this is not the case is for the Normal flag, which must be used alone (see description for more details).

See Also

The "File Class," "FileInfo Class," and "FileAttributes Enumeration" topics in the MSDN documentation.

12.2   Renaming a File

Problem

You need to rename a file.

Solution

With all of the bells and whistles that are part of the .NET Framework, you would figure that renaming a file is easy. Unfortunately, there is no specific rename method that can be used to rename a file. Instead, you can use the static Move method of the File class or the instance MoveTo method of the FileInfo class. The static File.Move method can be used to rename a file in the following manner:

```
public static void RenameFile(string originalName, string newName)
{
    File.Move(originalName, newName);
}
```

This code has the effect of renaming the *originalName* file to *newName*.

The `FileInfo.MoveTo` instance method can also be used to rename a file, and this can be exposed directly from the `FileInfo` instance using an extension method. The `Rename` extension method gives easy access to rename functionality right from the `FileInfo` instance:

```
public static class FileExtensions
{
    public static void Rename(this FileInfo originalFile, string newName)
    {
        originalFile.MoveTo(newName);
    }
}
```

Discussion

The `Move` and `MoveTo` methods allow a file to be moved to a different location, but they can also be used to rename files. For example, you could use `RenameFile` to rename a file from *foo.txt* to *bar.dat*:

```
RenameFile("foo.txt","bar.dat");
```

You could also use fully qualified paths to rename them:

```
RenameFile(@"c:\mydir\foo.txt",@"c:\mydir\bar.dat");
```

To use the extension method `Rename`, you simply call it as if it was part of `FileInfo`:

```
FileInfo originalFile = new FileInfo(@"c:\temp\foo.txt");
originalFile.Rename(@"c:\temp\bar.dat");
```

See Also

The "File Class," "Extension Methods," and "FileInfo Class" topics in the MSDN documentation.

12.3   Outputting a Platform-Independent EOL Character

Problem

Your application will run on more than one platform. Different platforms use different end-of-line characters. You want your code to output the correct EOL character without having to write code to handle the EOL character especially for each platform.

Solution

The .NET Framework provides the Environment.NewLine constant, which represents a newline on the given platform. This is the newline string used by all of the framework provided WriteLine methods internally (including Console, Debug, and Trace).

There are a few different scenarios in which this could be useful:

- Formatting a block of text with newlines embedded within it:

```
// Remember to use Environment.NewLine on every block of text
// we format that we want platform-correct newlines at the end of.
string line;
line = String.Format("FirstLine {0} SecondLine {0} ThirdLine {0}",
            Environment.NewLine);
// Get a temp file to work with.
string file = Path.GetTempFileName();
using (FileStream stream = File.Create(file))
{
    byte[] bytes = Encoding.Unicode.GetBytes(line);
    stream.Write(bytes,0,bytes.Length);
}

// Remove the file (good line to set a breakpoint to examine the file
// we created).
File.Delete(file);
```

- You need to use a different newline character than the default one used by StreamWriter (which happens to be Environment.NewLine). You can set the newline that a StreamWriter will use once so that all WriteLines performed by the StreamWriter use that newline instead of having to manually do it each time:

```
// Set up a text writer and tell it to use a certain newline
// string.
// Get a new temp file.
file = Path.GetTempFileName();
line = "Double spaced line";
using (StreamWriter streamWriter = new StreamWriter(file))
{
    // Make this always write out double lines.
    streamWriter.NewLine = Environment.NewLine + Environment.NewLine;
    // WriteLine on this stream will automatically use the newly specified
    // newline sequence (double newline, in our case).
    streamWriter.WriteLine(line);
    streamWriter.WriteLine(line);
    streamWriter.WriteLine(line);
}

// Remove the file (good line to set a breakpoint to check out the file
// we created).
File.Delete(file);
```

- Normal WriteLine calls:

```
// Just use any of the normal WriteLine methods, as they use the
// Environment.NewLine by default.
```

```
line = "Default line";
Console.WriteLine(line);
```

Discussion

`Environment.NewLine` allows you to have peace of mind, whether the platform is using \n or \r\n as the newline or possibly something else. Your code will be doing things the right way for each platform.

One word of caution here: if you are interoperating with a non-Windows operating system via SOAP and Web Services, the `Environment.NewLine` defined here might not be accurate for a stream you send to or receive from that other operating system. Of course, if you are doing Web Services, newlines aren't your biggest concern.

See Also

The "Environment Class" topic in the MSDN documentation.

12.4 Manipulating Directory Attributes

Problem

You need to display or manipulate a directory's attributes or timestamps.

Solution

To display a directory's timestamps, you can use either the set of static methods from the `Directory` object or the set of instance properties from the `DirectoryInfo` object. The static methods are `GetCreationTime`, `GetLastAccessTime`, or `GetLastWriteTime`. For example:

```
public static void DisplayDirectoryTimestamps(string path)
{
    Console.WriteLine(Directory.GetCreationTime(path).ToString( ));
    Console.WriteLine(Directory.GetLastAccessTime(path).ToString( ));
    Console.WriteLine(Directory.GetLastWriteTime(path).ToString( ));
}
```

In each case, *path* is the path to the directory with a timestamp you wish to retrieve, and the method returns a `DateTime` value containing the relevant timestamp. The instance properties are `CreationTime`, `LastAccessTime`, or `LastWriteTime`. The `DisplayTimestamps` extension method for `DirectoryInfo` allows accessing all of these at once:

```
public static void DisplayTimestamps(this DirectoryInfo dirInfo)
{
    Console.WriteLine(dirInfo.CreationTime.ToString( ));
    Console.WriteLine(dirInfo.LastAccessTime.ToString( ));
    Console.WriteLine(dirInfo.LastWriteTime.ToString( ));
}
```

To modify a directory's timestamps, you can use either the static methods of the Directory class or the instance properties of the DirectoryInfo class. The static methods are SetCreationTime, SetLastAccessTime, or SetLastWriteTime. For example:

```
public static void ModifyDirectoryTimestamps(string path, DateTime dt)
{
    Directory.SetCreationTime(path, dt);
    Directory.SetLastAccessTime(path, dt);
    Directory.SetLastWriteTime(path, dt);
}
```

Each method has two parameters: the first is the path to the directory with a timestamp that is to be set, and the second is a DateTime value containing the new timestamp. Each method returns void. The instance properties, all of which are of type DateTime, are CreationTime, LastAccessTime, and LastWriteTime. ModifyTimestamps is an extension method that will modify all three of these timestamps at once:

```
public static void ModifyTimestamps(this DirectoryInfo dirInfo, DateTime dt)
{
  dirInfo.CreationTime = dt;
  dirInfo.LastAccessTime = dt;
  dirInfo.LastWriteTime = dt;
}
```

To display or modify a directory's attributes, use the instance property Attributes as shown in the DisplayDirectoryHiddenAttribute and MakeDirectoryHidden extension method:

```
public static void DisplayDirectoryHiddenAttribute(string path)
{
    DirectoryInfo dirInfo = new DirectoryInfo(path);
    // Display whether this directory is hidden
    Console.WriteLine("Is directory hidden? = " +
        ((dirInfo.Attributes & FileAttributes.Hidden) == FileAttributes.Hidden));
}

public static void MakeDirectoryHidden(this DirectoryInfo dirInfo)
{
  // Modify this directory's attributes
  dirInfo.Attributes |= FileAttributes.Hidden;
}
```

The output of this code is shown here:

```
Directory
Is directory hidden? = False
Is directory hidden? = True
```

Discussion

There are three distinct timestamps associated with any directory. These timestamps are its creation time, its last access time, and its last write time.

In addition to timestamp information, a directory's attributes may also be obtained and modified. This is accomplished through the use of the public instance `Attributes` property found on a `DirectoryInfo` object. This property returns the `FileAttributes` enumeration value (see Table 12-2). The `FileAttributes` enumeration is made up of bit flags that can be turned on or off through the use of the bitwise operators &, |, or ^.

Table 12-2. Definitions of each bit flag in the FileAttributes enumeration

Flag name	Definition
Archive	Typically, backup applications will use this to determine if the file should be backed up again.
Compress	The current directory uses compression.
Directory	The current item is a directory.
Encrypted	The current directory is encrypted.
Hidden	The current directory is hidden.
Normal	The current directory has no other attributes set. When this attribute is set, no others can be set.
NotContentIndexed	The current directory is not being indexed by the indexing service.
Offline	The current directory is offline, and its contents are not accessible unless it is online.
ReadOnly	The current directory is read-only.
ReparsePoint	The current directory contains a reparse point.
SparseFile	The current directory contains large files consisting mostly of zeros.
System	The current directory is used by the system.
Temporary	The current directory is classified as a temporary directory.

In many cases, more than one of these flags may be set at one time. The `Normal` flag is the exception; when this flag is set, no other flag may be set.

See Also

The "Directory Class," "DirectoryInfo Class," and "FileAttributes Enumeration" topics in the MSDN documentation.

12.5   Renaming a Directory

Problem

You need to rename a directory.

Solution

Unfortunately, there is no specific rename method that can be used to rename a directory. However, you can use the instance `MoveTo` method of the `DirectoryInfo` class or the static Move method of the Directory class instead. The static Move method can be used to rename a directory in the following manner:

```
public static void RenameDirectory(string originalName, string newName)
{
    try
    {
        // "rename" it
        Directory.Move(originalName, newName);
    }
    catch(IOException ioe)
    {
        // most likely given the directory exists or isn't empty
        Console.WriteLine(ioe.ToString());
    }
}
```

This code creates a directory using the *originalName* parameter and renames it to the value supplied in the *newName* parameter.

The instance MoveTo method of the DirectoryInfo class can also be used to rename a directory via an extension method named Rename for DirectoryInfo shown here:

```
public static void Rename(this DirectoryInfo dirInfo, string newName)
{
    try
    {
        // "rename" it
        dirInfo.MoveTo(newName);
    }
    catch (IOException ioe)
    {
        // most likely given the directory exists or isn't empty
        Trace.WriteLine(ioe.ToString());
    }
}
```

This code creates a directory using the *originalName* parameter and renames it to the value supplied in the *newName* parameter.

Discussion

The Move and MoveTo methods allow a directory to be moved to a different location. However, when the path remains unchanged up to the directory that will have its name changed, the Move methods act as Rename methods.

See Also

The "Directory Class" and "DirectoryInfo Class" topics in the MSDN documentation.

12.6 Searching for Directories or Files Using Wildcards

Problem

You are attempting to find one or more specific files or directories that might or might not exist within the current file system. The search might need to use wildcard characters in order to widen the search, for example, searching for all usermode dump files in a file system. These files have a *.dmp* extension.

Solution

There are several methods of obtaining this information. The first three methods return a string array containing the full path of each item. The next three methods return an object that encapsulates a directory, a file, or both.

The static `GetFileSystemEntries` method on the `Directory` class returns a string array containing the names of all files and directories within a single directory, for example:

```
public static void DisplayFilesAndSubDirectories(string path)
{
    string[] items = Directory.GetFileSystemEntries(path);
    foreach (string item in items)
    {
        Console.WriteLine(item);
    }
}
```

The static `GetDirectories` method on the `Directory` class returns a string array containing the names of all directories within a single directory. The following method, `DisplayDirs`, shows how you might use it:

```
public static void DisplaySubDirectories(string path)
{
    string[] items = Directory.GetDirectories(path);
    foreach (string item in items)
    {
        Console.WriteLine(item);
    }
}
```

The static `GetFiles` method on the `Directory` class returns a string array containing the names of all files within a single directory. The following method is very similar to `DisplayDirs` but calls `Directory.GetFiles` instead of `Directory.GetDirectories`:

```
public static void DisplayFiles(string path)
{
    string[] items = Directory.GetFiles(path);
    foreach (string item in items)
    {
```

```
            Console.WriteLine(item);
        }
    }
```

These next three methods return an object instead of simply a string. The GetFileSystemInfos method of the DirectoryInfo object returns a strongly typed array of FileSystemInfo objects (that is, of DirectoryInfo and FileInfo objects) representing the directories and files within a single directory. The following example calls the GetFileSystemInfos method to retrieve an array of FileSystemInfo objects representing all the items in a particular directory and then lists a string of display information for FileSystemInfo to the console window. The display information is created by the extension method ToDisplayString on FileSystemInfo:

```
        public static void DisplayDirectoryContents(string path)
        {
            DirectoryInfo mainDir = new DirectoryInfo(path);
            IEnumerable<string> fileSystemDisplayInfos =
                from fsi in mainDir.GetFileSystemInfos()
                where fsi is FileSystemInfo || fsi is DirectoryInfo
                select fsi.ToDisplayString();

            foreach (string s in fileSystemDisplayInfos)
            {
                Console.WriteLine(s);
            }
        }

    public static string ToDisplayInfo(this FileSystemInfo fileSystemInfo)
    {
      string type = "Unknown";
      if (item is DirectoryInfo)
        type = "DIRECTORY";
      else if (item is FileInfo)
        type = "FILE";
      return string.Format(Thread.CurrentThread.CurrentCulture,
        "{0}: {1}", type, this.Name);
    }
```

The output for this code is shown here:

```
    DIRECTORY: MyNestedTempDir
    DIRECTORY: MyNestedTempDirPattern
    FILE: MyTempFile.PDB
    FILE: MyTempFile.TXT
```

The GetDirectories instance method of the DirectoryInfo object returns an array of DirectoryInfo objects representing only subdirectories in a single directory. For example, the following code calls the GetDirectories method to retrieve an array of DirectoryInfo objects and then displays the Name property of each object to the console window:

```
        public static void DisplayDirectories(string path)
        {
```

```
        DirectoryInfo mainDir = new DirectoryInfo(path);
        DirectoryInfo[] items = mainDir.GetDirectories();
        foreach (DirectoryInfo item in items)
        {
            Console.WriteLine("DIRECTORY: " + item.Name);
        }
    }
```

The GetFiles instance method of the DirectoryInfo object returns an array of FileInfo objects representing only the files in a single directory. For example, the following code calls the GetFiles method to retrieve an array of FileInfo objects, and then it displays the Name property of each object to the console window:

```
public static void DisplayFiles(string path)
{
    DirectoryInfo mainDir = new DirectoryInfo(path);
    FileInfo[] items = mainDir.GetFiles();
    foreach (FileInfo item in items)
    {
        Console.WriteLine("FILE: " + item.Name);
    }
}
```

The static GetFileSystemEntries method on the Directory class returns all files and directories in a single directory that match pattern:

```
public static void DisplayFilesDirectories(string path, string pattern)
{
    string[] items = Directory.GetFileSystemEntries(path, pattern);
    foreach (string item in items)
    {
        Console.WriteLine(item);
    }
}
```

The static GetDirectories method on the Directory class returns only those directories in a single directory that match pattern:

```
public static void DisplayDirectories(string path, string pattern)
{
    string[] items = Directory.GetDirectories(path, pattern);
    foreach (string item in items)
    {
        Console.WriteLine(item);
    }
}
```

The static GetFiles method on the Directory class returns only those files in a single directory that match pattern:

```
public static void DisplayFiles(string path, string pattern)
{
    string[] items = Directory.GetFiles(path, pattern);
    foreach (string item in items)
    {
```

```
            Console.WriteLine(item);
        }
    }
```

These next three methods return an object instead of simply a string. The first instance method is GetFileSystemInfos, which returns both directories and files in a single directory that match pattern:

```
    public static void DisplayDirectoryContentsWithPattern(string path,
                                                            string pattern)
    {
        DirectoryInfo mainDir = new DirectoryInfo(path);
        IEnumerable<string> fileSystemDisplayInfos =
            from fsi in mainDir.GetFileSystemInfos(pattern)
            where fsi is FileSystemInfo || fsi is DirectoryInfo
            select fsi.ToDisplayString();

        foreach (string s in fileSystemDisplayInfos)
        {
            Console.WriteLine(s);
        }
    }
```

The GetDirectories instance method returns only directories (contained in the DirectoryInfo object) in a single directory that match pattern:

```
    public static void DisplayDirectories(string path, string pattern)
    {
        DirectoryInfo mainDir = new DirectoryInfo(@"C:\TEMP ");
        DirectoryInfo[] items = mainDir.GetDirectories(pattern);
        foreach (DirectoryInfo item in items)
        {
            Console.WriteLine("DIRECTORY: " + item.Name);          }
    }
```

The GetFiles instance method returns only file information (contained in the FileInfo object) in a single directory that matches pattern:

```
    public static void DisplayFiles(string path, string pattern)
    {
        DirectoryInfo mainDir = new DirectoryInfo(@"C:\TEMP ");
        FileInfo[] items = mainDir.GetFiles(pattern);
        foreach (FileInfo item in items)
        {
            Console.WriteLine("FILE: " + item.Name);
        }
    }
```

Discussion

If you need just an array of strings containing paths to both directories and files, you can use the static method Directory.GetFileSystemEntries. The string array returned does not include any information about whether an individual element is a directory or a file. Each string element contains the entire path to either a directory or file contained within the specified path.

To quickly and easily distinguish between directories and files, use the `Directory.GetDirectories` and `Directory.GetFiles` static methods. These methods return arrays of directory names and filenames. These methods return an array of string objects. Each element contains the full path to the directory or file.

Returning a string is fine if you do not need any other information about the directory or file returned to you or if you are going to need more information for only one of the files returned. It is more efficient to use the static methods to get the list of filenames and just retrieve the `FileInfo` for the ones you need than to have all of the `FileInfo`s constructed for the directory, as the instance methods will do. If you are going to have to access attributes, lengths, or times on every one of the files, you should consider using the instance methods described here.

The instance method `GetFileSystemInfos` returns an array of strongly typed `FileSystemInfo` objects. (The `FileSystemInfo` object is the base class to the `DirectoryInfo` and `FileInfo` objects.) Therefore, you can test whether the returned type is a `DirectoryInfo` or `FileInfo` object using the is or as keywords. Once you know what subclass this object really is, you can cast it to that type and begin using it.

To get only `DirectoryInfo` objects, use the overloaded `GetDirectories` instance method. To get only `FileInfo` objects, use the overloaded `GetFiles` instance method. These methods return an array of `DirectoryInfo` and `FileInfo` objects, respectively; each element of which encapsulates a directory or file.

The patterns that can be provided when filtering the results from `GetFiles` or `GetFileSystemInfos` have certain behaviors to be aware of:

- The pattern cannot contain any of the `InvalidPathChars` and cannot have "..".
- The order in which the items in the array come back is not guaranteed, but you can use `Sort` or order the results in a query.
- When an extension is exactly three characters, the behavior is different in that the pattern will match on any files with those first three characters in the extension.
- "*.htm" returns files having an extension of .htm, .html, .htma, etc.
- When an extension has less than or more than three characters, the pattern will perform exact matching.
- "*.cs" returns only files having an extension of .cs.

See Also

The "DirectoryInfo Class," "FileInfo Class," and "FileSystemInfo Class" topics in the MSDN documentation.

12.7   Obtaining the Directory Tree

Problem

You need to get a directory tree, potentially including filenames, extending from any point in the directory hierarchy. In addition, each directory or file returned must be in the form of an object encapsulating that item. This will allow you to perform operations on the returned objects, such as deleting the file, renaming the file, or examining/changing its attributes. Finally, you potentially need the ability to search for a specific subset of these items based on a pattern, such as finding only files with the *.pdb* extension.

Solution

By calling the GetFileSystemInfos instance method, you can retrieve all of the files and directories down the directory hierarchy from any starting point as an enumerable list:

```
public static IEnumerable<FileSystemInfo> GetAllFilesAndDirectories(string dir)
{
    DirectoryInfo dirInfo = new DirectoryInfo(dir);
    Stack<FileSystemInfo> stack = new Stack<FileSystemInfo>();

    stack.Push(dirInfo);
    while (dirInfo != null || stack.Count > 0)
    {
        FileSystemInfo fileSystemInfo = stack.Pop();
        DirectoryInfo subDirectoryInfo = fileSystemInfo as DirectoryInfo;
        if (subDirectoryInfo != null)
        {
            yield return subDirectoryInfo;
            foreach (FileSystemInfo fsi in subDirectoryInfo.GetFileSystemInfos())
                stack.Push(fsi);
            dirInfo = subDirectoryInfo;
        }
        else
        {
            yield return fileSystemInfo;
            dirInfo = null;
        }
    }
}
```

To display the results of the file and directory retrieval, use the following query:

```
public static void DisplayAllFilesAndDirectories(string dir)
{
    var strings = from fileSystemInfo in GetAllFilesAndDirectories(dir)
                  select fileSystemInfo.ToDisplayString();

    foreach (string s in strings)
        Console.WriteLine(s);
}
```

Since the results are queryable, you don't have to retrieve information about *all* files and directories. The following query uses a case-insensitive comparison to obtain a listing of all files with the extension of *.pdb* that reside in directories that contain Chapter 1:

```
var strings = from fileSystemInfo in GetAllFilesAndDirectories(dir)
              where fileSystemInfo is FileInfo &&
                  fileSystemInfo.FullName.Contains("Chapter 1") &&
                  (string.Compare(fileSystemInfo.Extension, extension,
                          StringComparison.OrdinalIgnoreCase) == 0)
              select fileSystemInfo.ToDisplayString();

foreach (string s in strings)
    Console.WriteLine(s);
```

Discussion

To obtain a tree representation of a directory and the files it contains, you could use recursive iterators in a method like this:

```
public static IEnumerable<FileSystemInfo> GetAllFilesAndDirectories(string dir)
{
    DirectoryInfo dirInfo = new DirectoryInfo(dir);
    FileSystemInfo[] fileSystemInfos = dirInfo.GetFileSystemInfos();
    foreach (FileSystemInfo fileSystemInfo in fileSystemInfos)
    {
        yield return fileSystemInfo;
        if (fileSystemInfo is DirectoryInfo)
        {
            foreach (FileSystemInfo fsi in
                GetAllFilesAndDirectories(fileSystemInfo.FullName))
                yield return fsi;
        }
    }
}

public static void DisplayAllFilesAndDirectories(string dir)
{
    var strings = from fileSystemInfo in GetAllFilesAndDirectories(dir)
                  select fileSystemInfo.ToDisplayString();

    foreach (string s in strings)
        Console.WriteLine(s);
}
```

The main difference between this and the solution code is that this uses recursive iterators and the solution uses iterative iterators and an explicit stack. You would not want to use the recursive iterator method as the performance is in fact O(n * d), where n is the number of FileSystemInfos and d is the depth of the directory hierarchy—which is typically log n.

You can check the performance with the following code if the solution methods are renamed to DisplayAllFilesAndDirectoriesWithoutRecursion and DisplayAllFilesAndDirectoriesWithoutRecursion, respectively:

```
string dir = Environment.GetFolderPath(Environment.SpecialFolder.ProgramFiles);
// list all of the files using recursion
Stopwatch watch1 = Stopwatch.StartNew();
DisplayAllFilesAndDirectories(dir);
watch1.Stop();
Console.WriteLine("*************************");

// list all of the files without recursion
Stopwatch watch2 = Stopwatch.StartNew();
DisplayAllFilesAndDirectoriesWithoutRecursion(dir);
watch2.Stop();
Console.WriteLine("*************************");
Console.WriteLine("Recursive method time elapsed {0}",
                  watch1.Elapsed.ToString());
Console.WriteLine("Non-Recursive method time elapsed {0}",
                  watch2.Elapsed.ToString());
```

See Also

The "DirectoryInfo Class," "FileInfo Class," and "FileSystemInfo Class" topics in the MSDN documentation.

12.8 Parsing a Path

Problem

You need to separate the constituent parts of a path and place them into separate variables.

Solution

Use the static methods of the Path class:

```
public static void ParsePath(string path)
{
    string root = Path.GetPathRoot(path);
    string dirName = Path.GetDirectoryName(path);
    string fullFileName = Path.GetFileName(path);
    string fileExt = Path.GetExtension(path);
    string fileNameWithoutExt = Path.GetFileNameWithoutExtension(path);
    StringBuilder format = new StringBuilder();
    format.Append("ParsePath of {0} breaks up into the following pieces:" +
                  Environment.NewLine + "\tRoot: {1}" +
                  Environment.NewLine + "\t");
    format.Append("Directory Name: {2}" +
                  Environment.NewLine + "\tFull File Name: {3}" +
                  Environment.NewLine + "\t");
```

```
            format.Append("File Extension: {4}" +
                        Environment.NewLine + "\tFile Name Without Extension: {5}" +
                        Environment.NewLine + "");
            Console.WriteLine(format.ToString(),path,root,dirName,
                    fullFileName,fileExt,fileNameWithoutExt);
    }
```

If the string C:\test\tempfile.txt is passed to this method, the output looks like this:

```
ParsePath of C:\test\tempfile.txt breaks up into the following pieces:
        Root: C:\
        Directory Name: C:\test
        Full File Name: tempfile.txt
        File Extension: .txt
        File Name Without Extension: tempfile
```

Discussion

The Path class contains methods that can be used to parse a given path. Using these classes is much easier and less error-prone than writing path- and filename-parsing code. If these classes are not used, you could also introduce security holes into your application if the information gathered from manual parsing routines is used in security decisions for your application. There are five main methods used to parse a path: GetPathRoot, GetDirectoryName, GetFileName, GetExtension, and GetFileNameWithoutExtension. Each has a single parameter, *path*, which represents the path to be parsed:

GetPathRoot

This method returns the root directory of the path. If no root is provided in the path, such as when a relative path is used, this method returns an empty string, not null.

GetDirectoryName

This method returns the complete path for the directory that the file is in.

GetFileName

This method returns the filename, including the file extension. If no filename is provided in the path, this method returns an empty string, not null.

GetExtension

This method returns the file's extension. If no extension is provided for the file or no file exists in the path, this method returns an empty string, not null.

GetFileNameWithoutExtension

This method returns the root filename without the file extension.

Be aware that these methods do not actually determine whether the drives, directories, or even files exist on the system that runs these methods. These methods are string parsers, and if you pass one of them a string in some strange format (such as \\ZY:\foo), it will try to do what it can with it anyway:

```
ParsePath of \\ZY:\foo breaks up into the following pieces:
        Root: \\ZY:\foo
        Directory Name:
        Full File Name: foo
        File Extension:
        File Name Without Extension: foo
```

These methods will, however, throw an exception if illegal characters are found in the path.

To determine whether files or directories exist, use the static `Directory.Exists` or `File.Exists` method.

See Also

The "Path Class" topic in the MSDN documentation.

12.9   Parsing Paths in Environment Variables

Problem

You need to parse multiple paths contained in environment variables, such as PATH or Include.

Solution

You can use the `Path.PathSeparator` field or the ; character to extract individual paths from an environment variable with a value that consists of multiple paths and place them in an array. Then, you can use a `foreach` loop to iterate over each individual path in the PATH environment variable and parse each path. This process is illustrated by the `ParsePathEnvironmentVariable` method:

```
public static void ParsePathEnvironmentVariable( )
{
    string originalPathEnv = Environment.GetEnvironmentVariable("PATH");
    string[] paths = originalPathEnv.Split(Path.PathSeparator);
    foreach (string s in paths)
    {
        string pathEnv = Environment.ExpandEnvironmentVariables(s);
        if(!string.IsNullOrEmpty(pathEnv))
            Console.WriteLine("Individual Path = " + pathEnv);
        Console.WriteLine( );
    }
}
```

If the PATH environment variable contains the following:

```
PATH=Path=C:\WINDOWS\system32;C:\WINDOWS
```

and then the output of the `ParsePathEnvironmentVariable` method is as follows:

```
Individual Path = C:\WINDOWS\system32
Individual Path = C:\WINDOWS
```

Discussion

When working with environment variables in particular, there are a number of cases in which several paths may be concatenated and you need to parse each one individually. To distinguish each individual path from the others, Microsoft Windows uses the semicolon character. (Other operating systems might use a different character; Unix, Linux, and Mac OS X use a colon.) To make sure that we always use the correct path-separation character, the Path class contains a public static field called PathSeparator. This field contains the character used to separate paths in the current platform. This field is marked as read-only, so it cannot be modified.

To obtain each individual path contained in a single string, use the Split instance method from the String class. This method accepts a param array of character values that are used to break apart the string instance. These individual strings containing the paths are returned in a string array. Then, we simply use the foreach loop construct to iterate over each string in this string array and use the static method ExpandEnvironmentVariables of the Environment class to operate on each individual path string. This static method ensures that any environment variables such as %SystemDrive% are converted to their equivalent value, in this case, C:.

See Also

The "Path Class" and "Environment Class" topics in the MSDN documentation.

12.10 Launching and Interacting with Console Utilities

Problem

You have an application that you need to automate and that takes input only from the standard input stream. You need to drive this application via the commands it will take over the standard input stream.

Solution

Say we needed to drive the *cmd.exe* application to display the current time with the TIME /T command (it is possible to just run this command from the command line, but this way we can demonstrate an alternative method to drive an application that responds to standard input). The way to do this is to launch a process that is looking for input on the standard input stream. This is accomplished via the Process class StartInfo property, which is an instance of a ProcessStartInfo class. The Process. Start method will launch a new process, but the StartInfo property controls many of the details of what sort of environment that process executes in.

First, make sure that the StartInfo.RedirectStandardInput property is set to true. This setting notifies the process that it should read from standard input. Then, set the StartInfo.UseShellExecute property to false, because if you were to let the shell launch the process for you, it would prevent you from redirecting standard input.

Once this is done, launch the process and write to its standard input stream as shown in Example 12-1.

Example 12-1. RunProcessToReadStdIn method

```
public static void RunProcessToReadStandardInput( )
{
    Process application = new Process( );
    // Run the command shell.
    application.StartInfo.FileName = @"cmd.exe";

    // Turn on command extensions for cmd.exe.
    application.StartInfo.Arguments = "/E:ON";

    application.StartInfo.RedirectStandardInput = true;

    application.StartInfo.UseShellExecute = false;

    application.Start( );

    StreamWriter input = application.StandardInput;
    // Run the command to display the time.
    input.WriteLine("TIME /T");

    // Stop the application we launched.
    input.WriteLine("exit");
}
```

Discussion

Once the input has been redirected, you can write into the standard input stream of the process by reading the Process.StandardInput property, which returns a StreamWriter. Once you have that, you can send things to the process via WriteLine calls, as shown earlier.

In order to use StandardInput, you have to specify true for the StartInfo property's RedirectStandardInput property. Otherwise, reading the StandardInput property throws an exception.

When UseShellExecute is false, you can use Process only to create executable processes. Normally the Process class can be used to perform operations on the file, such as printing a Microsoft Word document. Another difference when UseShellExecute is set to false is that the working directory is not used to find the executable, so you should be mindful to pass a full path or have the executable on your PATH environment variable.

See Also

The "Process Class," "ProcessStartInfo Class," "RedirectStandardInput Property," and "UseShellExecute Property" topics in the MSDN documentation.

12.11 Locking Subsections of a File

Problem

You need to read or write data from or to a section of a file, and you want to make sure that no other processes or threads can access, modify, or delete the file until you have finished with it.

Solution

Locking out other processes from accessing your file while you are using it is accomplished through the `Lock` method of the `FileStream` class. The following code creates a file from the *fileName* parameter and writes two lines to it. The entire file is then locked using the `Lock` method. While the file is locked, the code goes off and does some other processing; when this code returns, the file is closed, thereby unlocking it:

```
public static void CreateLockedFile(string fileName)
{
    using (FileStream fileStream = new FileStream(fileName,
            FileMode.Create,
            FileAccess.ReadWrite,
            FileShare.ReadWrite))
    {
        using (StreamWriter streamWriter = new StreamWriter(fileStream))
        {
            streamWriter.WriteLine("The First Line");
            streamWriter.WriteLine("The Second Line");
            streamWriter.Flush( );

            try
            {
                // Lock all of the file.
                fileStream.Lock(0, fileStream.Length);

                // Do some lengthy processing here...
                Thread.Sleep(1000);
            }
            finally
            {
                // Make sure we unlock the file.
                // If a process terminates with part of a file locked or closes
                // a file that has outstanding locks, the behavior is undefined,
                // which is MS speak for bad things.
```

```
            fileStream.Unlock(0, fileStream.Length);
        }

        streamWriter.WriteLine("The Third Line");
    }
  }
}
```

Discussion

If a file is opened within your application and the FileShare parameter of the
FileStream.Open call is set to FileShare.ReadWrite or FileShare.Write, other code in
your application can view or alter the contents of the file while you are using it. To
handle file access with more granularity, use the Lock method of the FileStream
object to prevent other code from overwriting all or a portion of your file. Once you
are done with the locked portion of your file, you can call the Unlock method on the
FileStream object to allow other code in your application to write data to that portion of the file.

To lock an entire file, use the following syntax:

```
fileStream.Lock(0, fileStream.Length);
```

To lock a portion of a file, use the following syntax:

```
fileStream.Lock(4, fileStream.Length - 4);
```

This line of code locks the entire file except for the first four characters. Note that
you can lock an entire file and still open it multiple times, as well as write to it.

If another thread is accessing this file, it is possible to see an IOException thrown during the call to either the Write, Flush, or Close methods. For example, the following
code is prone to such an exception:

```
public static void CreateLockedFile(string fileName)
{

    using (FileStream fileStream = new FileStream(fileName,
                            FileMode.Create,
                            FileAccess.ReadWrite,
                            FileShare.ReadWrite))

    {
        using (StreamWriter streamWriter = new StreamWriter(fileStream))
        {
            streamWriter.WriteLine("The First Line");
            streamWriter.WriteLine("The Second Line");
            streamWriter.Flush();

            // Lock all of the file.
            fileStream.Lock(0, fileStream.Length);

            using (StreamWriter streamWriter2 = new StreamWriter(
                    new FileStream(fileName,
```

```
                                        FileMode.Open,
                                        FileAccess.Write,
                                        FileShare.ReadWrite)))
            {
                streamWriter2.Write("foo ");
                try
                {
                    streamWriter2.Close( ); // --> Exception occurs here!
                }
                catch
                {
                    Console.WriteLine(
                "The streamWriter2.Close call generated an exception.");
                }
                streamWriter.WriteLine("The Third Line");
            }
        }
    }
}
```

This code produces the following output:

```
The streamWriter2.Close call generated an exception.
```

Even though streamWriter2, the second StreamWriter object, writes to a locked file, it is when the streamWriter2.Close method is executed that the IOException is thrown.

If the code for this recipe were rewritten as follows:

```
public static void CreateLockedFile(string fileName)
{
    using (FileStream fileStream = new FileStream(fileName,
                                FileMode.Create,

                                FileAccess.ReadWrite,
                                FileShare.ReadWrite))

    {
        using (StreamWriter streamWriter = new StreamWriter(fileStream))
        {
            streamWriter.WriteLine("The First Line");
            streamWriter.WriteLine("The Second Line");
            streamWriter.Flush( );

            // Lock all of the file.
            fileStream.Lock(0, fileStream.Length);

            // Try to access the locked file...
            using (StreamWriter streamWriter2 = new StreamWriter(
                    new FileStream(fileName,
                                FileMode.Open,
                                FileAccess.Write,
                                FileShare.ReadWrite)))
            {
                streamWriter2.Write("foo");
```

```
                        fileStream.Unlock(0, fileStream.Length);
                        streamWriter2.Flush();
                    }
                }
            }
        }
```

no exception is thrown. This is due to the fact that the code closed the `FileStream` object that initially locked the entire file. This action also freed all of the locks on the file that this `FileStream` object was holding onto. Since the `streamWriter2.Write("Foo")` method had written `Foo` to the stream's buffer (but had not flushed it), the string `Foo` was still waiting to be flushed and written to the actual file. Keep this situation in mind when interleaving the opening, locking, and closing of streams. Mistakes in code sometimes manifest themselves a while after they are written. This leads to some bugs that are more difficult to track down, so tread carefully when using file locking.

See Also

The "StreamWriter Class" and "FileStream Class" topics in the MSDN documentation.

12.12 Waiting for an Action to Occur in the Filesystem

Problem

You need to be notified when a particular event occurs in the filesystem, such as the renaming of a file or directory, the increasing or decreasing of the size of a file, the user deleting a file or directory, the creation of a file or directory, or even the changing of a file or directory's attribute(s). However, this notification must occur synchronously. In other words, the application cannot continue unless a specific action occurs to a file or directory.

Solution

The `WaitForChanged` method of the `FileSystemWatcher` class can be called to wait synchronously for an event notification. This is illustrated by the `WaitForZipCreation` method shown in Example 12-2, which waits for an action—more specifically, the action of creating the *Backup.zip* file somewhere on the *C:* drive—to be performed before proceeding on to the next line of code, which is the `WriteLine` statement. Finally, we spin off a thread from the `ThreadPool` to execute the `PauseAndCreateFile` method, which does the actual work of creating the file. By doing this in a background thread, we allow the `FileSystemWatcher` to detect the file creation.

Example 12-2. WaitForZipCreation method

```
public void WaitForZipCreation(string path, string fileName)
{
    FileSystemWatcher fsw = null;
    try
    {
        using (fsw = new FileSystemWatcher())
        {
            string [] data = new string[] {path,fileName};
            fsw.Path = path; fsw.Filter = fileName;
            fsw.NotifyFilter = NotifyFilters.LastAccess | NotifyFilters.LastWrite
                | NotifyFilters.FileName | NotifyFilters.DirectoryName;

            // Run the code to generate the file we are looking for.
            // Normally you wouldn't do this as another source is creating
            // this file.
            if(ThreadPool.QueueUserWorkItem(new WaitCallback(PauseAndCreateFile),
                                                             data))
            {
                // Block waiting for change.
                WaitForChangedResult result =
                            fsw.WaitForChanged(WatcherChangeTypes.Created);
                Console.WriteLine("{0} created at {1}.",result.Name,path);
            }
        }
    }
    catch(Exception e)
    {
        Console.WriteLine(e.ToString());
        throw;
    }
    finally
    {
        File.Delete(fileName);
    }
}
```

The code for `PauseAndCreateFile` is listed here. It is in the form of a `WaitCallback` to be used as an argument to `QueueUserWorkItem` on the `ThreadPool` class. `QueueUserWorkItem` will run `PauseAndCreateFile` on a thread from the .NET thread pool:

```
void PauseAndCreateFile(Object stateInfo)
{
    try
    {
        string[] data = (string[])stateInfo;
        // Wait a sec...
        Thread.Sleep(1000);
        string path = data[0];
        string file = path + data[1];
        Console.WriteLine("Creating {0} in PauseAndCreateFile...",file);
        using (FileStream fileStream = File.Create(file))
```

```
        {
            // Use fileStream var...
        }
    }
    catch(Exception e)
    {
        Console.WriteLine(e.ToString());
        throw;
    }
}
```

Discussion

The WaitForChanged method returns a WaitForChangedResult structure that contains the properties listed in Table 12-3.

Table 12-3. WaitForChangedResult properties

Property	Description
ChangeType	Lists the type of change that occurred. This change is returned as a WatcherChangeTypes enumeration. The values of this enumeration can possibly be ORed together.
Name	Holds the name of the file or directory that was changed. If the file or directory was renamed, this property returns the changed name. Its value is set to null if the operation method call times out.
OldName	The original name of the modified file or directory. If this file or directory was not renamed, this property will return the same value as the Name property. Its value is set to null if the operation method call times out.
TimedOut	Holds a Boolean indicating whether the WaitForChanged method timed out (true) or not (false).

The way we are currently making the WaitForChanged call could possibly block indefinitely. To prevent you from hanging forever on the WaitForChanged call, you can specify a timeout value of 3 seconds as follows:

```
WaitForChangedResult result =
        fsw.WaitForChanged(WatcherChangeTypes.Created, 3000);
```

The NotifyFilters enumeration allows specification of the types of files or folders to watch for as shown in Table 12-4.

Table 12-4. NotifyFilters enumeration

Enumeration Value	Definition
FileName	Name of the file.
DirectoryName	Name of the directory.
Attributes	The file or folder attributes.
Size	The file or folder size.
LastWrite	The date the file or folder last had anything written to it.
LastAccess	The date the file or folder was last opened.
CreationTime	The time the file or folder was created.
Security	The security settings of the file or folder.

See Also

The "FileSystemWatcher Class," "NotifyFilters Enumeration," and "Wait-ForChangedResult Structure" topics in the MSDN documentation.

12.13 Comparing Version Information of Two Executable Modules

Problem

You need to programmatically compare the version information of two executable modules. An executable module is a file that contains executable code, such as an *.exe* or *.dll* file. The ability to compare the version information of two executable modules can be very useful to an application in situations such as:

- Trying to determine if it has all of the "right" pieces present to execute.
- Deciding on an assembly to dynamically load through reflection.
- Looking for the newest version of a file or *.dll* from many files spread out in the local filesystem or on a network.

Solution

Use the `CompareFileVersions` method to compare executable module version information. This method accepts two filenames, including their paths, as parameters. The version information of each module is retrieved and compared. This file returns a `FileComparison` enumeration, defined as follows:

```
public enum FileComparison
{
    Same = 0,
    Newer = 1, // File1 is newer than File2
    Older = 2, // File1 is older than File2
    Error = 3
}
```

The code for the `CompareFileVersions` method is shown in Example 12-3.

Example 12-3. CompareFileVersions method

```
private static FileComparison ComparePart(int p1, int p2)
{
    return p1 > p2 ? FileComparison.Newer :
        (p1 < p2 ? FileComparison.Older : FileComparison.Same );
}

public static FileComparison CompareFileVersions(string file1, string file2)
{
    FileComparison retValue = FileComparison.Error;
    FileVersionInfo file1Version = FileVersionInfo.GetVersionInfo(file1);
```

Example 12-3. CompareFileVersions method (continued)

```
        FileVersionInfo file2Version = FileVersionInfo.GetVersionInfo(file2);

        retValue = ComparePart(file1Version.FileMajorPart,
                               file2Version.FileMajorPart);
        if (retValue != FileComparison.Same)
        {
            retValue = ComparePart(file1Version.FileMinorPart,
                                   file2Version.FileMinorPart);
            if (retValue != FileComparison.Same)
            {
                retValue = ComparePart(file1Version.FileBuildPart,
                                       file2Version.FileBuildPart);
                if (retValue != FileComparison.Same)
                    retValue = ComparePart(file1Version.FilePrivatePart,
                                           file2Version.FilePrivatePart);
            }
        }
        return retValue;
}
```

Discussion

Not all executable modules have version information. If you load a module with no version information using the FileVersionInfo class, you will not provoke an exception, nor will you get null back for the object reference. Instead, you will get a valid FileVersionInfo object with all data members in their initial state (which is null for .NET objects).

Assemblies actually have two sets of version information: the version information available in the assembly manifest and the PE (Portable Executable) file version information. FileVersionInfo reads the assembly manifest version information.

The first action this method takes is to determine whether the two files passed in to the *file1* and *file2* parameters actually exist. If so, the static GetVersionInfo method of the FileVersionInfo class is called to get version information for the two files.

The CompareFileVersions method attempts to compare each portion of the file's version number using the following properties of the FileVersionInfo object returned by GetVersionInfo:

FileMajorPart
   The first 2 bytes of the version number.

FileMinorPart
   The second 2 bytes of the version number.

FileBuildPart
   The third 2 bytes of the version number.

FilePrivatePart
   The final 2 bytes of the version number.

The full version number is comprised of these four parts, making up an 8-byte number representing the file's version number.

The CompareFileVersions method first compares the FileMajorPart version information of the two files. If these are equal, the FileMinorPart version information of the two files is compared. This continues through the FileBuildPart and finally the FilePrivatePart version information values. If all four parts are equal, the files are considered to have the same version number. If either file is found to have a higher number than the other file, it is considered to be the latest version.

See Also

The "FileVersionInfo Class" topic in the MSDN documentation.

12.14 Querying Information for All Drives on a System

Problem

Your application needs to know if a drive (HDD, CD drive, DVD drive, etc.) is available and ready to be written to and/or read from. Additionally, it would be nice to know if you have enough available free space on the drive to write information to.

Solution

Use the various properties in the DriveInfo class as shown here:

```
public static void DisplayAllDriveInfo( )
{
    foreach (DriveInfo drive in DriveInfo.GetDrives( ))
    {
        if (drive.IsReady)
        {
            Console.WriteLine("Drive " + drive.Name + " is ready.");
            Console.WriteLine("AvailableFreeSpace: " + drive.AvailableFreeSpace);
            Console.WriteLine("DriveFormat: " + drive.DriveFormat);
            Console.WriteLine("DriveType: " + drive.DriveType);
            Console.WriteLine("Name: " + drive.Name);
            Console.WriteLine("RootDirectory.FullName: " +
                drive.RootDirectory.FullName);
            Console.WriteLine("TotalFreeSpace: " + drive.TotalFreeSpace);
            Console.WriteLine("TotalSize: " + drive.TotalSize);
            Console.WriteLine("VolumeLabel: " + drive.VolumeLabel);
        }
        else
        {
            Console.WriteLine("Drive " + drive.Name + " is not ready.");
        }
    }
}
```

This code will display something like the following, though of course each system is different and the results will vary:

```
Drive C:\ is ready.
AvailableFreeSpace: 143210795008
DriveFormat: NTFS
DriveType: Fixed
Name: C:\
RootDirectory.FullName: C:\
TotalFreeSpace: 143210795008
TotalSize: 159989886976
VolumeLabel: Vol1

Drive D:\ is ready.
AvailableFreeSpace: 0
DriveFormat: UDF
DriveType: CDRom
Name: D:\
RootDirectory.FullName: D:\
TotalFreeSpace: 0
TotalSize: 3305965568
VolumeLabel: Vol2

Drive E:\ is ready.
AvailableFreeSpace: 4649025536
DriveFormat: UDF
DriveType: CDRom
Name: E:\
RootDirectory.FullName: E:\
TotalFreeSpace: 4649025536
TotalSize: 4691197952
VolumeLabel: Vol3

Drive F:\ is not ready.
```

Of particular interest are the IsReady and AvailableFreeSpace properties. The IsReady property determines if the drive is ready to be queried, written to, or read from but is not terribly reliable as this state could quickly change. If using IsReady, make sure the case where the drive becomes not ready is accounted for. The AvailableFreeSpace property returns the free space on that drive in bytes.

Discussion

Use the DriveInfo class from the .NET Framework to allow you to easily query information on one particular drive or on all drives in the system. To query the information from a single drive, you would use the code in Example 12-4.

Example 12-4. Getting information from a specific drive

```
DriveInfo drive = new DriveInfo("D");
if (drive.IsReady)
    Console.WriteLine("The space available on the D:\\ drive: " +
                        drive.AvailableFreeSpace);
else
    Console.WriteLine("Drive D:\\ is not ready.");
```

Notice that only the drive letter is passed in to the DriveInfo constructor. This drive letter can be either uppercase or lowercase—it does not matter. The next thing you will notice with the code in Example 12-4 and the code in the Solution to this recipe is that the IsReady property is always tested for true before either using the drive or querying its properties. If we did not test this property for true and for some reason the drive was not ready (e.g., a CD was not in the drive at that time), a System.IO. IOException would be returned stating that "The device is not ready." For the Solution to this recipe, the DriveInfo constructor was not used. Instead, the static GetDrives method of the DriveInfo class was used to return an array of DriveInfo objects. Each DriveInfo object in this array corresponds to one drive on the current system.

The DriveType property of the DriveInfo class returns an enumeration value from the DriveType enumeration. This enumeration value identifies what type of drive the current DriveInfo object represents. Table 12-5 identifies the various values of the DriveType enumeration.

Table 12-5. DriveType enumeration values

Enum value	Description
CDRom	This can be a CD-ROM, CD writer, DVD-ROM, or DVD writer drive.
Fixed	This is the fixed drive such as an HDD. Note that USB HDDs fall into this category.
Network	A network drive.
NoRootDirectory	No root directory was found on this drive.
Ram	A RAM disk.
Removable	A removable storage device.
Unknown	Some other type of drive than those listed here.

In the DriveInfo class there are two very similar properties, AvailableFreeSpace and TotalFreeSpace. Each of these properties will return the same value in most cases. However, AvailableFreeSpace also takes into account any disk-quota information for a particular drive. Disk-quota information can be found by right-clicking a drive in Windows Explorer and selecting the Properties pop-up menu item. This displays the Properties page for this drive. On this Properties page, click on the Quota tab to view the quota information for that drive. If the Enable Quota Management checkbox is unchecked, then disk-quota management is disabled, and both the AvailableFreeSpace and TotalFreeSpace properties should be equal.

See Also

The "DriveInfo Class" topic in the MSDN documentation.

12.15 Compressing and Decompressing Your Files

Problem

You need a way to compress a file using one of the stream-based classes without being constrained by the 4 GB limit imposed by the framework classes. In addition, you need a way to decompress the file to allow you to read it back in.

Solution

Use the `System.IO.Compression.DeflateStream` or the `System.IO.Compression.GZipStream` classes to read and write compressed data to a file using a "chunking" routine. The `CompressFile`, `DecompressFile`, and `Decompress` methods shown in Example 12-5 demonstrate how to use these classes to compress and decompress files on the fly.

Example 12-5. The CompressFile and DecompressFile methods

```
/// <summary>
/// Compress the source file to the destination file.
/// This is done in 1MB chunks to not overwhelm the memory usage.
/// </summary>
/// <param name="sourceFile">the uncompressed file</param>
/// <param name="destinationFile">the compressed file</param>
/// <param name="compressionType">the type of compression to use</param>
public static void CompressFile(string sourceFile,
                                string destinationFile,
                                CompressionType compressionType)
{
    if (sourceFile != null)
    {
        FileStream streamSource = null;
        FileStream streamDestination = null;
        Stream streamCompressed = null;

        try
        {
            streamSource = File.OpenRead(sourceFile);
            streamDestination = File.OpenWrite(destinationFile);
            // read 1MB chunks and compress them
            long fileLength = streamSource.Length;

            // write out the fileLength size
            byte[] size = BitConverter.GetBytes(fileLength);
            streamDestination.Write(size, 0, size.Length);
```

Example 12-5. The CompressFile and DecompressFile methods (continued)

```
long chunkSize = 1048576; // 1MB
while (fileLength > 0)
{
    // read the chunk
    byte[] data = new byte[chunkSize];
    streamSource.Read(data, 0, data.Length);

    // compress the chunk
    MemoryStream compressedDataStream =
        new MemoryStream( );

    if (compressionType == CompressionType.Deflate)
        streamCompressed =
            new DeflateStream(compressedDataStream,
                CompressionMode.Compress);
    else
        streamCompressed =
            new GZipStream(compressedDataStream,
                CompressionMode.Compress);

    using (streamCompressed)
    {
        // write the chunk in the compressed stream
        streamCompressed.Write(data, 0, data.Length);
    }
    // get the bytes for the compressed chunk
    byte[] compressedData =
        compressedDataStream.GetBuffer( );

    // write out the chunk size
    size = BitConverter.GetBytes(chunkSize);
    streamDestination.Write(size, 0, size.Length);

    // write out the compressed size
    size = BitConverter.GetBytes(compressedData.Length);
    streamDestination.Write(size, 0, size.Length);

    // write out the compressed chunk
    streamDestination.Write(compressedData, 0,
        compressedData.Length);

    // subtract the chunk size from the file size
    fileLength -= chunkSize;

    // if chunk is less than remaining file use
    // remaining file
    if (fileLength < chunkSize)
        chunkSize = fileLength;
}
}
finally
{
```

Example 12-5. The CompressFile and DecompressFile methods (continued)

```
                streamSource.Close( );
                streamDestination.Close( );
            }
        }
    }


    /// <summary>
    /// This function will decompress the chunked compressed file
    /// created by the CompressFile function.
    /// </summary>
    /// <param name="sourceFile">the compressed file</param>
    /// <param name="destinationFile">the destination file</param>
    /// <param name="compressionType">the type of compression to use</param>
    public static void DecompressFile(string sourceFile,
                                      string destinationFile,
                                      CompressionType compressionType)
    {
        FileStream streamSource = null;
        FileStream streamDestination = null;
        Stream streamUncompressed = null;

        try
        {
            streamSource = File.OpenRead(sourceFile);
            streamDestination = File.OpenWrite(destinationFile);
            // read the fileLength size
            // read the chunk size
            byte[] size = new byte[sizeof(long)];
            streamSource.Read(size, 0, size.Length);
            // convert the size back to a number
            long fileLength = BitConverter.ToInt64(size, 0);
            long chunkSize = 0;
            int storedSize = 0;
            while (fileLength > 0)
            {
                // read the chunk size
                size = new byte[sizeof(long)];
                streamSource.Read(size, 0, size.Length);
                // convert the size back to a number
                chunkSize = BitConverter.ToInt64(size, 0);
                if (chunkSize > fileLength ||
                    chunkSize > workingSet)
                    throw new InvalidDataException( );

                // read the compressed size
                size = new byte[sizeof(int)];
                streamSource.Read(size, 0, size.Length);
                // convert the size back to a number
                storedSize = BitConverter.ToInt32(size, 0);
```

Example 12-5. The CompressFile and DecompressFile methods (continued)

```
            if (storedSize > fileLength ||
                storedSize > workingSet)
                throw new InvalidDataException( );

            if (storedSize > chunkSize)
                throw new InvalidDataException( );

            byte[] uncompressedData = new byte[chunkSize];
            byte[] compressedData = new byte[storedSize];
            streamSource.Read(compressedData, 0,
                compressedData.Length);

            // uncompress the chunk
            MemoryStream uncompressedDataStream =
                new MemoryStream(compressedData);

            if (compressionType == CompressionType.Deflate)
                streamUncompressed =
                    new DeflateStream(uncompressedDataStream,
                        CompressionMode.Decompress);
            else
                streamUncompressed =
                    new GZipStream(uncompressedDataStream,
                        CompressionMode.Decompress);

            using (streamUncompressed)
            {
                // read the chunk in the compressed stream
                streamUncompressed.Read(uncompressedData, 0,
                    uncompressedData.Length);
            }

            // write out the uncompressed chunk
            streamDestination.Write(uncompressedData, 0,
                uncompressedData.Length);

            // subtract the chunk size from the file size
            fileLength -= chunkSize;

            // if chunk is less than remaining file use remaining file
            if (fileLength < chunkSize)
                chunkSize = fileLength;
        }
    }
    finally
    {
        streamSource.Close( );
        streamDestination.Close( );
    }
}
```

The CompressionType enumeration is defined as follows:

```
public enum CompressionType
{
    Deflate,
    GZip
}
```

Discussion

The CompressFile method accepts a path to the source file to compress, a path to the destination of the compressed file, and a CompressionType enumeration value indicating which type of compression algorithm to use (Deflate or GZip). This method produces a file containing the compressed data.

The DecompressFile method accepts a path to the source compressed file to decompress, a path to the destination of the decompressed file, and a CompressionType enumeration value indicating which type of decompression algorithm to use (Deflate or GZip).

The TestCompressNewFile method shown in Example 12-6 exercises the CompressFile and DecompressFile methods defined in the Solution section of this recipe.

Example 12-6. Using the CompressFile and DecompressFile methods

```
public static void TestCompressNewFile()
{
    byte[] data = new byte[10000000];
    for (int i = 0; i < 10000000; i++)
        data[i] = (byte)i;

    FileStream fs =
        new FileStream(@"C:\NewNormalFile.txt",
            FileMode.OpenOrCreate, FileAccess.ReadWrite, FileShare.None);
    using(fs)
    {
        fs.Write(data,0,data.Length);
    }

    CompressFile(@"C:\NewNormalFile.txt", @"C:\NewCompressedFile.txt",
        CompressionType.Deflate);

    DecompressFile(@"C:\NewCompressedFile.txt", @"C:\NewDecompressedFile.txt",
        CompressionType.Deflate);

    CompressFile(@"C:\NewNormalFile.txt", @"C:\NewGZCompressedFile.txt",
        CompressionType.GZip);

    DecompressFile(@"C:\NewGZCompressedFile.txt", @"C:\NewGZDecompressedFile.txt",
        CompressionType.GZip);
```

```
    //Normal file size == 10,000,000 bytes
    //GZipped file size == 155,204
    //Deflated file size == 155,168
    // 36 bytes are related to the GZip CRC
}
```

When this test code is run, we get three files with different sizes. The first file, *NewNormalFile.txt*, is 10,000,000 bytes in size. The *NewCompressedFile.txt* file is 155,168 bytes. The final file, *NewGzCompressedFile.txt* file is 115,204 bytes. As you can see, there is not much difference between the sizes for the files compressed with the DeflateStream class and the GZipStream class. The reason for this is that both compression classes use the same compression/decompression algorithm (i.e., the lossless Deflate algorithm as described in the RFC 1951: Deflate 1.3 specification).

You may be wondering why you would pick one class over the other if they use the same algorithm. There is one good reason: the GZipStream class adds a CRC check to the compressed data to determine if it has been corrupted. If the data has been corrupted, an InvalidDataException is thrown with the statement "The CRC in GZip footer does not match the CRC calculated from the decompressed data." By catching this exception, you can determine if your data is corrupted.

In the Decompress method, there is a possibility for some InvalidDataExceptions to be thrown:

```
            // read the chunk size
            size = new byte[sizeof(long)];
            streamSource.Read(size, 0, size.Length);
            // convert the size back to a number
            chunkSize = BitConverter.ToInt64(size, 0);
    if (chunkSize > fileLength ||
      chunkSize > workingSet)
      throw new InvalidDataException( );

            // read the compressed size
            size = new byte[sizeof(int)];
            streamSource.Read(size, 0, size.Length);
            // convert the size back to a number
            storedSize = BitConverter.ToInt32(size, 0);
    if (storedSize > fileLength ||
      storedSize > workingSet)
      throw new InvalidDataException( );

    if (storedSize > chunkSize)
      throw new InvalidDataException( );

            byte[] uncompressedData = new byte[chunkSize];
            byte[] compressedData = new byte[storedSize];
```

The reason for these checks is that the code is reading in a buffer that may have been tampered with. Since Decompress will actually allocate memory based on the numbers derived from the buffer, it needs to be careful about what those numbers turn out to be. The very basic checks being done here are to check that:

- The size of the chunk is not bigger than the file length.
- The size of the chunk is not bigger than the current program working set.
- The size of the compressed chunk is not bigger than the file length.
- The size of the compressed chunk is not bigger than the current program working set.
- The size of the compressed chunk is not bigger than the actual chunk size.

See Also

The "DeflateStream Class" and "GZipStream" topics in the MSDN documentation.

CHAPTER 13

Reflection

13.0 Introduction

Reflection is the mechanism provided by the .NET Framework to allow you to inspect how a program is constructed. Using reflection, you can obtain information such as the name of an assembly and what other assemblies a given assembly imports. You can even dynamically call methods on an instance of a type in a given assembly. Reflection also allows you to create code dynamically and compile it to an in-memory assembly or to build a symbol table of type entries in an assembly.

Reflection is a very powerful feature of the Framework and, as such, is guarded by the runtime. The ReflectionPermission must be granted to assemblies that are going to access the protected or private members of a type. If you are going to access only the public members of a public type, you will not need to be granted the ReflectionPermission. Code Access Security has only two permission sets that give all reflection access by default: FullTrust and Everything. The LocalIntranet permission set allows for the ReflectionEmit privilege that allows for emitting metadata and creating assemblies or the MemberAccess privilege for performing dynamic invocation of methods on types in assemblies.

In this chapter, you will see how you can use reflection to dynamically invoke members on types, figure out all of the assemblies a given assembly is dependent on, and inspect assemblies for different types of information. Reflection is a great way to understand how things are put together in .NET, and this chapter provides a starting point.

13.1 Listing Referenced Assemblies

Problem

You need to determine each assembly imported by a particular assembly. This information can show you if this assembly is using one or more of your assemblies or if your assembly is using another specific assembly.

Solution

Use the `Assembly.GetReferencedAssemblies` method, as shown in Example 13-1, to obtain the imported assemblies of an assembly.

Example 13-1. Using the Assembly.GetReferencedAssemblies method

```
using System;
using System.Reflection;
using System.Collections.Specialized;

public static void BuildDependentAssemblyList(string path,
                                 StringCollection assemblies)
{
    // maintain a list of assemblies the original one needs
    if(assemblies == null)
        assemblies = new StringCollection( );

    // have we already seen this one?
    if(assemblies.Contains(path)==true)
        return;

    Assembly asm = null;

    // look for common path delimiters in the string
    // to see if it is a name or a path
    if ((path.IndexOf(@"\", 0, path.Length, StringComparison.Ordinal) != -1) ||
        (path.IndexOf("/", 0, path.Length, StringComparison.Ordinal) != -1))
    {
        // load the assembly from a path
        asm = Assembly.LoadFrom(path);
    }
    else
    {
        // try as assembly name
        asm = Assembly.Load(path);
    }

    // add the assembly to the list
    if (asm != null)
    {
        assemblies.Add(path);
    }
```

Example 13-1. Using the Assembly.GetReferencedAssemblies method (continued)

```
    // get the referenced assemblies
    AssemblyName[] imports = asm.GetReferencedAssemblies();

    // iterate
    foreach (AssemblyName asmName in imports)
    {
        // now recursively call this assembly to get the new modules
        //   it references
        BuildDependentAssemblyList(asmName.FullName, assemblies);
    }
}
```

This code returns a `StringCollection` containing the original assembly, all imported assemblies, and the dependent assemblies of the imported assemblies.

If you ran this method against the assembly *C:\CSharpRecipes\bin\Debug\CSharp-Recipes.exe*, you'd get the following dependency tree:

```
        C:\CSharpRecipes\bin\Debug\CSharpRecipes.exe

        mscorlib, Version=2.0.3600.0, Culture=neutral,
PublicKeyToken=b77a5c561934e089

        System, Version=2.0.3600.0, Culture=neutral, PublicKeyToken=b77a5c561934e089

        System.Configuration, Version=2.0.3600.0, Culture=neutral,
            PublicKeyToken=b03f5f7f11d50a3a

        System.Xml, Version=2.0.3600.0, Culture=neutral,
PublicKeyToken=b77a5c561934e089

        System.Security, Version=2.0.3600.0, Culture=neutral,
PublicKeyToken=b03f5f7f11d50a3a

        System.Web.RegularExpressions, Version=2.0.3600.0, Culture=neutral,
            PublicKeyToken=b03f5f7f11d50a3a

        System.Runtime.Serialization.Formatters.Soap, Version=2.0.3600.0,
Culture=neutral,
            PublicKeyToken=b03f5f7f11d50a3a
```

Discussion

Obtaining the imported types in an assembly is useful in determining what assemblies another assembly is using. This knowledge can greatly aid in learning to use a new assembly. This method can also help determine dependencies between assemblies for shipping purposes.

The `GetReferencedAssemblies` method of the `System.Reflection.Assembly` class obtains a list of all the imported assemblies. This method accepts no parameters and returns an array of `AssemblyName` objects instead of an array of `Types`. The

AssemblyName type is made up of members that allow access to the information about an assembly, such as the name, version, culture information, public/private key pairs, and other data.

Note that this method does not account for assemblies loaded using the Assembly. ReflectionOnlyLoad* methods, as it is inspecting for only compile-time references.

 When loading assemblies for inspection using reflection, you should use the ReflectionOnlyLoad* methods. These methods do not allow you to execute code from the loaded assembly. The reasoning is that you may not know if you are loading assemblies containing hostile code or not. These methods prevent any hostile code from executing.

See Also

The "Assembly Class" topic in the MSDN documentation.

13.2 Listing Exported Types

Problem

You need to obtain all the exported types of an assembly. This information allows you to see what types are usable from outside of this assembly.

Solution

Use Assembly.GetExportedTypes to obtain the exported types of an assembly:

```
using System;
using System.Reflection;
using System.Collections.Generic;
using System.IO;

public static void ListExportedTypes(string path)
{
    // Load the assembly.
    Assembly asm = Assembly. ReflectionOnlyLoadFrom(path);
    Console.WriteLine("Assembly: {0} imports:",path);
    // Get the exported types.
    Type[] types = asm.GetExportedTypes( );
    foreach (Type t in types)
    {
        Console.WriteLine ("\tExported Type: {0}",t.FullName);
    }
}
```

The previous example will display all exported, or public, types:

```
Assembly: C:\C#Cookbook\CSharpRecipes.exe imports:
        Exported Type: CSharpRecipes.ClassAndStructs
```

```
Exported Type: CSharpRecipes.Line
Exported Type: CSharpRecipes.Square
Exported Type: CSharpRecipes.CompareHeight
Exported Type: CSharpRecipes.Foo
Exported Type: CSharpRecipes.ObjState
```

Discussion

Obtaining the exported types in an assembly is useful when determining the public interface to that assembly. This ability can greatly aid in learning to use a new assembly or can aid the developer of that assembly in determining all access points to the assembly to verify that they are adequately secure from malicious code. To get these exported types, use the GetExportedTypes method on the System.Reflection.Assembly type. The exported types consist of all of the types that are publicly accessible from outside of the assembly. A type may have public accessibility but not be accessible from outside of the assembly. Take, for example, the following code:

```
public class Outer
{
    public class Inner {}
    private class SecretInner {}
}
```

The exported types are Outer and Outer.Inner; the type SecretInner is not exposed to the world outside of this assembly. If you change the Outer accessibility from public to private, you now have no types accessible to the outside world—the Inner class access level is downgraded because of the private on the Outer class.

See Also

The "Assembly Class" topic in the MSDN documentation.

13.3 Finding Overridden Methods

Problem

You have an inheritance hierarchy that is several levels deep and has many virtual and overridden methods. You need a list of the base class method(s) that are overridden by methods within a derived class.

Solution

Use the MethodInfo.GetBaseDefinition method to determine which method is overridden in what base class. The overloaded FindMethodOverrides method shown in Example 13-2 examines all of the public instance methods in a class and displays which methods override their respective base class methods. This method also determines which base class the overridden method is in. This method accepts an assembly path and name in which to find overriding methods. Note that the *typeName* parameter must be the fully qualified type name (i.e., the complete namespace hierarchy, followed by any containing classes, followed by the type name you are querying).

Example 13-2. The FindMethodOverrides methods

```
public class ReflectionUtils
{
    public static void FindMethodOverrides(string asmPath, string typeName)
    {
        Assembly asm = Assembly.LoadFrom(asmPath);
        Type asmType = asm.GetType(typeName);

        Console.WriteLine("---[" + asmType.FullName + "]---");

        // get the methods that match this type
        MethodInfo[] methods = asmType.GetMethods(BindingFlags.Instance |
            BindingFlags.NonPublic | BindingFlags.Public |
            BindingFlags.Static | BindingFlags.DeclaredOnly);

        var mis = from ms in methods
                    where ms != ms.GetBaseDefinition()
                    select ms.GetBaseDefinition();

        foreach (MethodInfo mi in mis)
        {
            Console.WriteLine();
            Console.WriteLine("Current Method:  " + mi.ToString());

            Console.WriteLine("Base Type FullName:  " + mi.DeclaringType.FullName);
            Console.WriteLine("Base Method:  " + mi.ToString());

            // list the types of this method
            foreach (ParameterInfo pi in mi.GetParameters())
            {
                Console.WriteLine("\tParam {0}: {1}",
                    pi.Name, pi.ParameterType.ToString());
            }
        }
    }
}
```

The second method allows you to determine whether a particular method overrides a method in its base class. It accepts the same two arguments as the first overloaded method, along with the full method name and an array of Type objects representing its parameter types:

```
public class ReflectionUtils
{
    public static void FindMethodOverrides(string asmPath, string typeName,
            string methodName, Type[] paramTypes)
    {
```

```csharp
        Console.WriteLine(Environment.NewLine + "For [Type] Method:  [" +
            typeName + "] " + methodName);

        // We use LoadFrom here to load any dependent DLL's as well
        //   this will prevent a TypeLoadException from occuring
        Assembly asm = Assembly.LoadFrom (asmPath);

        // GetType should throw an exception if the type cannot be found
        //   and it should also ignore the case of the typeName
        Type asmType = asm.GetType(typeName,true,true);
        MethodInfo method = asmType.GetMethod(methodName, paramTypes);

        if (method != null)
        {
            MethodInfo baseDef = method.GetBaseDefinition();
            if (baseDef != method)
            {
                Console.WriteLine("Base Type FullName:  " +
                    baseDef.DeclaringType.FullName);
                Console.WriteLine("Base Method:  " + baseDef.ToString());

                bool foundMatch = false;

                var match = from p in baseDef.GetParameters()
                            join op in paramTypes
                            on p.ParameterType.UnderlyingSystemType
                                equals op.UnderlyingSystemType
                            select p;

                foundMatch = match.Any();

                foreach (ParameterInfo pi in match)
                {
                    // list the params so we can see which one we got
                    Console.WriteLine("\tParam {0}: {1}",
                        pi.Name, pi.ParameterType.ToString());
                }

                // we found the one we were looking for
                if(foundMatch == true)
                {
                    Console.WriteLine("Found Match!");
                }
            }
        }
        Console.WriteLine();
    }
```

The following code shows how to use each of these overloaded methods:

```csharp
public static void FindOverriddenMethods()
{
    Process current = Process.GetCurrentProcess();
```

```
        // Get the path of the current module.
        string path = current.MainModule.FileName;

        // Try the easier one.
        ReflectionUtils.FindMethodOverrides
            (path,"CSharpRecipes.ReflectionUtils+DerivedOverrides");

        // Try the signature FindMethodOverrides.
        ReflectionUtils.FindMethodOverrides(path,
            "CSharpRecipes.ReflectionUtils+DerivedOverrides",
            "Foo",
            new Type[3] {typeof(long), typeof(double), typeof(byte[])});
    }
```

The output of this method, using the BaseOverrides and DerivedOverrides classes defined afterward, is shown here:

```
---[CSharpRecipes.ReflectionUtils+DerivedOverrides]---
Current Method: Void Foo(System.String, Int32)
Base Type FullName: CSharpRecipes.ReflectionUtils+BaseOverrides
Base Method: Void Foo(System.String, Int32)
        Param str: System.String
        Param i: System.Int32

Current Method: Void Foo(Int64, Double, Byte[])
Base Type FullName: CSharpRecipes.ReflectionUtils+BaseOverrides
Base Method: Void Foo(Int64, Double, Byte[])
        Param l: System.Int64
        Param d: System.Double
        Param bytes: System.Byte[]

For [Type] Method: [CSharpRecipes.ReflectionUtils+DerivedOverrides] Foo
Base Type FullName: CSharpRecipes.ReflectionUtils+BaseOverrides
Base Method: Void Foo(Int64, Double, Byte[])
        Param l: System.Int64
        Param d: System.Double
        Param bytes: System.Byte[]
Found Match!
```

In the usage code, you get the path to the test code assembly (*CSharpRecipes.exe*) via the Process class. You then use that to find a class that has been defined in the ReflectionUtils class, called DerivedOverrides.DerivedOverrides derives from BaseOverrides, and they are both shown here:

```
public abstract class BaseOverrides
{
    public abstract void Foo(string str, int i);
    public abstract void Foo(long l, double d, byte[] bytes);
}

public class DerivedOverrides : BaseOverrides
{
    public override void Foo(string str, int i)
    {
```

```
        }

        public override void Foo(long l, double d, byte[] bytes)
        {
        }
    }
```

The first method passes in only the assembly path and the fully qualified type name. This method returns every overridden method for each method that it finds in the Reflection.DerivedOverrides type. If you want to display all overriding methods and their corresponding overridden methods, you can remove the BindingFlags. DeclaredOnly binding enumeration from the GetMethods method call:

```
MethodInfo[] methods = asmType.GetMethods(BindingFlags.Instance |
                   BindingFlags.NonPublic | BindingFlags.Public);
```

This change now produces the following output using the same classes, BaseOverrides and DerivedOverrides:

```
---[CSharpRecipes.ReflectionUtils+DerivedOverrides]---
Current Method: Void Foo(System.String, Int32)
Base Type FullName: CSharpRecipes.ReflectionUtils+BaseOverrides
Base Method: Void Foo(System.String, Int32)
        Param str: System.String
        Param i: System.Int32

Current Method: Void Foo(Int64, Double, Byte[])
Base Type FullName: CSharpRecipes.ReflectionUtils+BaseOverrides
Base Method: Void Foo(Int64, Double, Byte[])
        Param l: System.Int64
        Param d: System.Double
        Param bytes: System.Byte[]

Current Method: System.Type GetType()

Current Method: System.Object MemberwiseClone()

Current Method: System.String ToString()
Base Type FullName: System.Object
Base Method: System.String ToString()

Current Method: Boolean Equals(System.Object)
Base Type FullName: System.Object
Base Method: Boolean Equals(System.Object)
        Param obj: System.Object

Current Method: Int32 GetHashCode()
Base Type FullName: System.Object
Base Method: Int32 GetHashCode()

Current Method: Void Finalize()
Base Type FullName: System.Object
Base Method: Void Finalize()
```

```
For [Type] Method: [CSharpRecipes.ReflectionUtils+DerivedOverrides] Foo
Base Type FullName: CSharpRecipes.ReflectionUtils+BaseOverrides
Base Method: Void Foo(Int64, Double, Byte[])
        Param l: System.Int64
        Param d: System.Double
        Param bytes: System.Byte[]
Found Match!
```

The second method passes in the assembly path, the fully qualified type name, a method name, and the parameters for this method to find the override that specifically matches the signature based on the parameters. In this case, the parameter types of method Foo are long, double, and byte[]. This method displays the method that CSharpRecipes.ReflectionUtils+DerivedOverrides.Foo overrides. The + in the type name represents a nested class.

Discussion

Determining which methods override their base class methods would be a tedious chore if it were not for the GetBaseDefinition method of the System.Reflection. MethodInfo type. This method takes no parameters and returns a MethodInfo object that corresponds to the overridden method in the base class. If this method is used on a MethodInfo object representing a method that is not being overridden—as is the case with a virtual or abstract method—GetBaseDefinition returns the original MethodInfo object.

The code for the FindMethodOverrides methods first loads the assembly using the *asmPath* parameter and then gets the type that is specified by the *typeName* parameter.

Once the type is located, its Type object's GetMethod or GetMethods method is called. GetMethod is used when both the method name and its parameter array are passed in to FindMethodOverrides; otherwise, GetMethods is used. If the method is correctly located and its MethodInfo object obtained, the GetBaseDefinition method is called on that MethodInfo object to get the first overridden method in the nearest base class in the inheritance hierarchy. This MethodInfo type is compared to the MethodInfo type that the GetBaseDefinition method was called on. If these two objects are the same, it means that there were no overridden methods in any base classes; therefore, nothing is displayed. This code will display only the overridden methods; if no methods are overridden, then nothing is displayed.

See Also

Recipe 13.4; see the "Process Class," "Assembly Class," "MethodInfo Class," and "ParameterInfo Class" topics in the MSDN documentation.

13.4 Finding Members in an Assembly

Problem

You need to find one or more members of types in an assembly with a specific name or containing part of a name. This partial name could be, for example, any member starting with the letter *A* or the string "Test."

Solution

Use the `Type.GetMember` method, which returns all members that match a specified criterion:

```
public static void FindMemberInAssembly(string asmPath, string memberName)
{
    var members = from asm in Assembly.LoadFrom(asmPath).GetTypes()
                  from ms in asm.GetMember(memberName, MemberTypes.All,
                      BindingFlags.Public | BindingFlags.NonPublic |
                      BindingFlags.Static | BindingFlags.Instance)
                  select ms;

    foreach (MemberInfo member in members)
    {
        Console.WriteLine("Found " + member.MemberType + ":  " +
            member.ToString() + " IN " +
            member.DeclaringType.FullName);
    }
}
```

The *memberName* argument can contain the wildcard character * to indicate any character or characters. So, to find all methods starting with the string "Test", pass the string "Test*" to the *memberName* parameter. Note that the *memberName* argument is case-sensitive, but the *asmPath* argument is not. If you'd like to do a case-insensitive search for members, add the `BindingFlags.IgnoreCase` flag to the other `BindingFlags` in the call to `Type.GetMember`.

Discussion

The `GetMember` method of the `System.Type` class is useful for finding one or more methods within a type. This method returns an array of `MemberInfo` objects that describe any members that match the given parameters.

> The * character may be used as a wildcard character only at the end of the *name* parameter string. If placed anywhere else in the string, it will not be treated as a wildcard character. In addition, it may be the only character in the *name* parameter; if this is so, all members are returned. No other wildcard characters, such as ?, are supported.

Once you obtain an array of MemberInfo objects, you need to examine what kind of members they are. To do this, the MemberInfo class contains a MemberType property that returns a System.Reflection.MemberTypes enumeration value. This can be any of the values defined in Table 13-1, except for the All value.

Table 13-1. MemberTypes enumeration values

Enumeration value	Definition
All	All member types
Constructor	A constructor member
Custom	A custom member type
Event	An event member
Field	A field member
Method	A method member
NestedType	A nested type
Property	A property member
TypeInfo	A type member that represents a TypeInfo member

See Also

Recipe 13.5; the "Assembly Class," "BindingFlags Enumeration," and "MemberInfo Class" topics in the MSDN documentation.

13.5   Determining and Obtaining Nested Types Within an Assembly

Problem

You need to determine which types have nested types contained within them in your assembly. Determining the nested types allows you to programmatically examine various aspects of some design patterns. Various design patterns may specify that a type will contain another type; for example, the *Decorator* and *State* design patterns make use of object containment.

Solution

Use the DisplayNestedTypes method to iterate through all types in your assembly and list all of their nested types. Its code is:

```
public static void DisplayNestedTypes(string asmPath)
{
var names = from t in Assembly.LoadFrom(asmPath).GetTypes()
            from t2 in t.GetNestedTypes(BindingFlags.Instance |
                BindingFlags.Static |
                BindingFlags.Public |
```

```
                 BindingFlags.NonPublic)
           where !t2.IsEnum && !t2.IsInterface
           select t2.FullName;

    foreach (string name in names)
    {
        Console.WriteLine(name);
    }
}
```

Discussion

The `DisplayNestedTypes` method uses a LINQ query to query all types in the assembly specified by the `asmPath` parameter. The LINQ query also queries for the nested types with the assembly by using the `GetNestedTypes` method of the `Type` class.

Usually the dot operator is used to delimit namespaces and types; however, nested types are somewhat special. Nested types are set apart from other types by the + operator in their fully qualified name when dealing with them in the reflection APIs. By passing this fully qualified name in to the static `GetType` methods, the actual type that it represents can be acquired.

These methods return a `Type` object that represents the type identified by the *typeName* parameter.

 Calling `Type.GetType` to retrieve a type defined in a dynamic assembly (one that is created using the types defined in the `System.Reflection. Emit` namespace) returns a `null` if that assembly has not already been persisted to disk. Typically, you would use the static `Assembly.GetType` method on the dynamic assembly's `Assembly` object.

See Also

Recipe 13.4; see the "Assembly Class" and "BindingFlags Enumeration" topics in the MSDN documentation.

13.6 Displaying the Inheritance Hierarchy for a Type

Problem

You need to determine all of the base types that make up a specific class or struct. Essentially, you need to determine the inheritance hierarchy of a type starting with the base (least derived) type and ending with the specified (most derived) type.

Solution

Use the `DisplayInheritanceChain` method to display the entire inheritance hierarchy for all types existing in an assembly specified by the `asmPath` parameter. Its source code is:

```
public static void DisplayInheritanceChain (string asmPath)
{
    Assembly asm = Assembly.LoadFrom(asmPath);
    var typeInfos = from Type type in asm.GetTypes()
                select new
                {
                    FullName = type.FullName,
                    BaseTypeDisplay = type.GetBaseTypeDisplay()
                };

    foreach(var typeInfo in typeInfos)
    {
        // Recurse over all base types
        Console.WriteLine ("Derived Type: " + typeInfo.FullName);
        Console.WriteLine("Base Type List: " + typeInfo.BaseTypeDisplay);
        Console.WriteLine();
    }
}
```

`DisplayInheritanceChain` takes the path to the assembly and retrieves all of the Types in the assembly using `GetTypes` as part of a query. It then projects the `FullName` of the Type and the `BaseTypeDisplay` for the type. The `BaseTypeDisplay` is a string holding all of the base types and is generated by the extension method `GetBaseTypeDisplay`. `GetBaseTypeDisplay` gets the name of each base type using the `GetBaseTypes` extension method and reverses the order of the types with a call to `Reverse`. The call to `Reverse` is done as the types are most derived to least derived order when discovered by traversing the `BaseType` property of each `Type` encountered, and we want the display to show least derived (`Object`) first. The `<-` string is prepended to each type name to form the base type display string:

```
public static string GetBaseTypeDisplay(this Type type)
{
    IEnumerable<string> baseTypes=
        (from t in type.GetBaseTypes()
        select t.Name).Reverse();
    StringBuilder builder = new StringBuilder();
    foreach(string typeName in baseTypes)
    {
        if (builder.Length == 0)
            builder.Append(typeName);
        else
            builder.AppendFormat("<-{0}",typeName);
    }
    return builder.ToString();
}
```

```
private static IEnumerable<Type> GetBaseTypes(this Type type)
{
    Type current = type;
    while (current != null)
    {
        yield return current;
        current = current.BaseType;
    }
}
```

If you want to obtain only the inheritance hierarchy of a specific type as a string, use the following DisplayInheritanceChain overload:

```
public static void DisplayInheritanceChain(string asmPath,string baseType)
{
    Assembly asm = Assembly.LoadFrom(asmPath);
    string typeDisplay = asm.GetType(baseType).GetBaseTypeDisplay();
    Console.WriteLine(typeDisplay);
}
```

To display the inheritance hierarchy of all types within an assembly, use the first instance of the DisplayInheritanceChain method call. To obtain the inheritance hierarchy of a single type as a string, use the GetBaseTypeDisplay extension method on the Type. In this instance, you are looking for the type hierarchy of the CSharpRecipes.ReflectionUtils+DerivedOverrides nested class:

```
public static void DisplayInheritanceHierarchyType( )
{
    Process current = Process.GetCurrentProcess( );
    // Get the path of the current module.
    string asmPath = current.MainModule.FileName;
    // A specific type
    DisplayInheritanceChain(asmPath,
        "CSharpRecipes.ReflectionUtils+DerivedOverrides");
    // All types in the assembly
    DisplayInheritanceChain(asmPath);
}
```

These methods result in output like the following:

```
Derived Type: CSharpRecipes.Reflection
Base Type List: Object<-Reflection
Derived Type: CSharpRecipes.ReflectionUtils+BaseOverrides
Base Type List: Object<-BaseOverrides

Derived Type: CSharpRecipes.ReflectionUtils+DerivedOverrides
Base Type List: Object<-BaseOverrides <-DerivedOverrides
```

This output shows that when looking at the Reflection class in the CSharpRecipes namespace, its base-type list (or inheritance hierarchy) starts with Object (like all class and struct types in .NET). The nested class BaseOverrides also shows a base-type list starting with Object. The nested class DerivedOverrides shows a more interesting base-type list, where DerivedOverrides derives from BaseOverrides, which derives from Object.

Discussion

Unfortunately, no property of the Type class exists to obtain the inheritance hierarchy of a type. The DisplayInheritanceChain methods in this recipe allow you to obtain the inheritance hierarchy of a type. All that is required is the path to an assembly and the name of the type with the inheritance hierarchy that is to be obtained. The DisplayInheritanceChain method requires only an assembly path since it displays the inheritance hierarchy for all types within that assembly.

The core code of this recipe exists in the GetBaseTypeList method. This is a recursive method that walks each inherited type until it finds the ultimate base class—which is always the object class. Once it arrives at this ultimate base class, it returns to its caller. Each time the method returns to its caller, the next base class in the inheritance hierarchy is added to the string until the final GetBaseTypeList method returns the completed string.

See Also

The "Assembly Class" and "Type.BaseType Method" topics in the MSDN documentation.

13.7   Finding the Subclasses of a Type

Problem

You have a type and you need to find out whether it is subclassed anywhere in an assembly.

Solution

Use the Type.IsSubclassOf method to test all types within a given assembly, which determines whether each type is a subclass of the type specified in the argument to IsSubClassOf:

```
public static IEnumerable<Type> ListSubClassesForType(this Assembly asm,
                                                      Type baseclassType)
{
    return from type in asm.GetTypes()
           where type.IsSubclassOf(baseclassType)
           select type;
}
```

The ListSubClassesForType extension method accepts an assembly path string and a second string containing a fully qualified base class name. This method returns an IEnumerable<Type> representing the subclasses of the type passed to the *baseClass* parameter.

Discussion

The IsSubclassOf method on the Type class allows you to determine whether the current type is a subclass of the type passed in to this method.

The following code shows how to use this method:

```
public static void FindSubclassOfType()
{
    Process current = Process.GetCurrentProcess();
    // get the path of the current module
    string asmPath = current.MainModule.FileName;
    Assembly asm = Assembly.LoadFrom(asmPath);
    Type type = Type.GetType("CSharpRecipes.Reflection+BaseOverrides");
    IEnumerable<Type> subClasses = asm.ListSubClassesForType(type);

    // write out the subclasses for this type
    if(subClasses.Count() > 0)
    {
        Console.WriteLine("{0} is subclassed by:",type.FullName);
        foreach(Type t in subClasses)
        {
            Console.WriteLine("\t{0}",t.FullName);
        }
    }
}
```

First you get the assembly path from the current process, and then you set up use of CSharpRecipes.ReflectionUtils+BaseOverrides as the type to test for subclasses. You call GetSubClasses, and it returns an IEnumerable<Type> that you use to produce the following output:

```
CSharpRecipes.ReflectionUtils+BaseOverrides is subclassed by:
        CSharpRecipes.ReflectionUtils+DerivedOverrides
```

See Also

The "Assembly Class" and "Type Class" topics in the MSDN documentation.

13.8 Finding All Serializable Types Within an Assembly

Problem

You need to find all the serializable types within an assembly.

Solution

Instead of testing the implemented interfaces and attributes on every type, you can query the Type.IsSerialized property to determine whether it is marked as serializable, as the following method does:

```
public static IEnumerable<string> GetSerializableTypeNames(string asmPath)
{
    Assembly asm = Assembly.LoadFrom(asmPath);
    return from type in asm.GetTypes()
           where type.IsSerializable
           select type.FullName;
}
```

The GetSerializableTypeNames method accepts an Assembly through its *asm* parameter. This assembly is searched for any serializable types, and their full names (including namespaces) are returned in an IEnumerable<Type>.

In order to use this method to display the serializable types in an assembly, run the following code:

```
public static void FindSerializable()
{
    Process current = Process.GetCurrentProcess();
    // get the path of the current module
    string asmPath = current.MainModule.FileName;
    IEnumerable<string> typeNames = GetSerializableTypeNames(asmPath);
    // write out the serializable types in the assembly
    if(typeNames.Count() > 0)
    {
        Console.WriteLine("{0} has serializable types:",asmPath);
        foreach(string typeName in typeNames)
        {
            Console.WriteLine("\t{0}",typeName);
        }
    }
}
```

The output of this method is shown here:

```
C:\CSharp Recipes 2nd Edition\Code\CSharpRecipes\bin\Debug\CSharpRecipes.exe
has
serializable types:
        CSharpRecipes.ExceptionHandling+RemoteComponentException
        CSharpRecipes.DelegatesEventsAnonymousMethods+HashtableEventHandler
        CSharpRecipes.Collections+MaxMinSizeDictionary`2
        CSharpRecipes.Collections+MaxMinValueHashtable
        CSharpRecipes.DataStructsAndAlgorithms+DblQueue`1
        CSharpRecipes.ClassAndStructs+DeepClone
        CSharpRecipes.ClassAndStructs+MultiClone
        CSharpRecipes.ClassAndStructs+Serializer`1
```

Discussion

A type may be marked as serializable using the `SerializableAttribute` attribute. Testing for the `SerializableAttribute` attribute on a type can turn into a fair amount of work. This is because the `SerializableAttribute` is a magic attribute that the C# compiler actually strips off your code at compile time. Using ildasm, you will see that this custom attribute just isn't there—normally you see a `.custom` entry for each custom attribute, but not with `SerializableAttribute`. The C# compiler removes it, and instead sets a flag in the metadata of the class. In source code, it looks like a custom attribute, but it compiles into one of a small set of attributes that gets a special representation in metadata. That's why it gets special treatment in the reflection APIs. Fortunately, you do not have to do all of this work. The `IsSerializable` property on the `Type` class returns a `true` if the current type is marked as serializable with the `SerializableAttribute`; otherwise, this property returns `false`.

See Also

The "Assembly Class" and "TypeAttributes Enumeration" in the MSDN documentation.

13.9   Dynamically Invoking Members

Problem

You have a list of method names that you wish to invoke dynamically within your application. As your code executes, it will pull names off this list and attempt to invoke these methods. This technique might be useful to create a test harness for components that reads in the methods to execute from an XML file and executes them with the given arguments.

Solution

The `TestDynamicInvocation` method shown in Example 13-3 calls the `DynamicInvoke` method, which opens the XML configuration file, reads out the test information using LINQ, and executes each test method dynamically.

Example 13-3. Invoking members dynamically

```
public static void TestDynamicInvocation( )
{
    XDocument xdoc = XDocument.Load
        (@"..\..\SampleClassLibrary\SampleClassLibraryTests.xml");
    DynamicInvoke(xdoc, @"SampleClassLibrary.dll");
}
```

The XML document in which the test method information is contained looks like this:

```xml
<?xml version="1.0" encoding="utf-8" ?>
<Tests>
    <Test className='SampleClassLibrary.SampleClass'
methodName='TestMethod1'>
        <Argument>Running TestMethod1</Argument>
    </Test>
    <Test className='SampleClassLibrary.SampleClass'
methodName='TestMethod2'>
        <Parameter>Running TestMethod2</Parameter>
        <Parameter>27</Parameter>
    </Test>
</Tests>
```

DynamicInvoke, as shown in Example 13-4, dynamically invokes the method that is passed to it using the information contained in the XDocument. Each parameter's type is determined by examining the ParameterInfo items on the MethodInfo, and then the values provided are converted to the actual type from a string via the Convert. ChangeType method. Finally, the return value of the invoked method is returned by the MethodBase.Invoke method.

Example 13-4. InvokeMethod method

```csharp
public static void DynamicInvoke(XDocument xdoc, string asmPath)
{
    var test = from t in xdoc.Root.Elements("Test")
                select new
                {
                    typeName = (string)t.Attribute("className").Value,
                    methodName = (string)t.Attribute("methodName").Value,
                    argument = from p in t.Elements("Argument")
                                select new { arg = p.Value }
                };

    // Load the assembly
    Assembly asm = Assembly.LoadFrom(asmPath);

    foreach (var elem in test)
    {
        // create the actual type
        Type dynClassType = asm.GetType(elem.typeName, true, false);

        // Create an instance of this type and verify that it exists
        object dynObj = Activator.CreateInstance(dynClassType);
        if (dynObj != null)
        {
            // Verify that the method exists and get its MethodInfo obj
            MethodInfo invokedMethod = dynClassType.GetMethod(elem.methodName);
            if (invokedMethod != null)
            {
                // Create the argument list for the dynamically invoked methods
```

Example 13-4. InvokeMethod method (continued)

```
        object[] arguments = new object[elem.argument.Count()];
        int index = 0;

        // for each parameter, add it to the list
        foreach (var arg in elem.argument)
        {
            // get the type of the parameter
            Type paramType =
                invokedMethod.GetParameters()[index].ParameterType;

            // change the value to that type and assign it
            arguments[index] =
                Convert.ChangeType(arg.arg, paramType);
            index++;
        }

        // Invoke the method with the parameters
        object retObj = invokedMethod.Invoke(dynObj, arguments);

        Console.WriteLine("\tReturned object: " + retObj);
        Console.WriteLine("\tReturned object: " + retObj.GetType().FullName);
    }
  }
 }
}
```

These are the dynamically invoked methods located on the SampleClass type in the SampleClassLibrary assembly:

```
public bool TestMethod1(string text)
{
    Console.WriteLine(text);
    return (true);
}
public bool TestMethod2(string text, int n)
{
    Console.WriteLine(text + " invoked with {0}",n);
    return (true);
}
```

The output from these methods looks like this:

```
Running TestMethod1
        Returned object: True
        Returned object: System.Boolean
Running TestMethod2 invoked with 27
        Returned object: True
        Returned object: System.Boolean
```

Discussion

Reflection gives you the ability to dynamically invoke both static and instance methods within a type in either the same assembly or in a different one. This can be a very powerful tool to allow your code to determine at runtime which method to call. This determination can be based on an assembly name, a type name, or a method name, though the assembly name is not required if the method exists in the same assembly as the invoking code, if you already have the Assembly object, or if you have a Type object for the class the method is on.

This technique may seem similar to delegates since both can dynamically determine at runtime which method is to be called. Delegates, on the whole, require you to know signatures of methods you might call at runtime, whereas with reflection, you can invoke methods when you have no idea of the signature, providing a much looser binding. However, you will still have to pass in reasonable arguments. More dynamic invocation can be achieved with Delegate.DynamicInvoke, but this is more of a reflection-based method than the traditional delegate invocation.

The DynamicInvoke method shown in the Solution section contains all the code required to dynamically invoke a method. This code first loads the assembly using its assembly name (passed in through the *asmPath* parameter). Next, it gets the Type object for the class containing the method to invoke (the class name is obtained from the Test element's className attribute using LINQ). The method name is then retrieved from the Test element's methodName attribute using LINQ. Once you have all of the information from the Test element, an instance of the Type object is created, and you then invoke the specified method on this created instance:

- First, the static Activator.CreateInstance method is called to actually create an instance of the Type object contained in the local variable dynClassType. The method returns an object reference to the instance of *type* that was created or throws an exception if the object cannot be created.

- Once you have successfully obtained the instance of this class, the MethodInfo object of the method to be invoked is acquired through a call to GetMethod on the Type object.

The instance of the object created with the CreateInstance method is then passed as the first parameter to the MethodInfo.Invoke method. This method returns an object containing the return value of the invoked method. This object is then returned by InvokeMethod. The second parameter to MethodInfo.Invoke is an object array containing any parameters to be passed to this method. This array is constructed based on the number of Parameter elements under each Test element in the XML. You then look at the ParameterInfo of each parameter (obtained from MethodInfo.GetParameters) and use the Convert.ChangeType method to coerce the string value from the XML to the proper type.

The DynamicInvoke method finally displays each returned object value and its type. Note that there is no extra logic required to return different return values from the invoked methods since they are all returned as an object, unlike passing differing arguments to the invoked methods.

See Also

The "Activator Class," "MethodInfo Class," "Convert.ChangeType Method," and "ParameterInfo Class" topics in the MSDN documentation.

13.10 Determining If a Type or Method Is Generic

Problem

You need to test a type and/or a method to determine whether it is generic.

Solution

Use the IsGenericType method of the Type class and the IsGenericMethod method of the MethodInfo class:

```
public static bool IsGenericType(Type type)
{
    return (type.IsGenericType);
}

public static bool IsGenericMethod(MethodInfo mi)
{
    return (mi.IsGenericMethod);
}
```

Discussion

The IsGenericType method examines objects, and the IsGenericMethod method examines methods. These methods will return a true indicating that this object or method accepts type arguments and false indicating that it does not. One or more type arguments indicate that this type is a generic type.

To call these methods, use code like the following:

```
Assembly asm = Assembly.GetExecutingAssembly();
// Get the type.
Type t = typeof(CSharpRecipes.DataStructsAndAlgorithms.PriorityQueue<int>);

bool genericType = IsGenericType(t);

bool genericMethod = false;
foreach (MethodInfo mi in t.GetMethods())
    genericMethod = IsGenericMethod(mi);
```

This code first obtains an Assembly object for the currently executing assembly. Next, the Type object is obtained using the typeof operator. For this method call, you pass in a fully qualified name of an object to this method. In this case, you pass in CSharpRecipes.DataStructsAndAlgorithms.PriorityQueue<int>. Notice at the end is the string <int>. This indicates that this type is a generic type with a single type parameter of type int. In other words, this type is defined as follows:

```
public class PriorityQueue<T> {...}
```

If this type were defined with two type parameters, it would look like this:

```
public class PriorityQueue<T, U> {...}
```

Its fully qualified constructed type would be CSharpRecipes. DataStructsAndAlgorithms.PriorityQueue<int, int>.

This Type object t is then passed into the IsGenericType method, and the return value is true, indicating that this type is indeed generic.

Next, you collect all the MethodInfo objects for this type t using the GetMethods method of the Type t object. Each MethodInfo object is passed into the IsGenericMethod method to determine if it is generic or not.

See Also

The "Type.IsGenericType Method" and "MethodInfo.IsGenericMethod Method" topics in the MSDN documentation.

13.11 Accessing Local Variable Information

Problem

You are building a tool that examines code, and you need to get access to the local variables within a method.

Solution

Use the LocalVariables property on the MethodBody class to return an IList of LocalVariableInfo objects, each of which describes a local variable within the method:

```
public static IList<LocalVariableInfo> GetLocalVars(string asmPath,
                                   string typeName, string methodName)
{
    Assembly asm = Assembly.LoadFrom(asmPath);
    Type asmType = asm.GetType(typeName);
    MethodInfo mi = asmType.GetMethod(methodName);
    MethodBody mb = mi.GetMethodBody();

    IList<LocalVariableInfo> vars = mb.LocalVariables;

    // Display information about each local variable.
    foreach (LocalVariableInfo lvi in vars)
    {
        Console.WriteLine("IsPinned: " + lvi.IsPinned);
        Console.WriteLine("LocalIndex: " + lvi.LocalIndex);
        Console.WriteLine("LocalType.Module: " + lvi.LocalType.Module);
```

```
                    Console.WriteLine("LocalType.FullName: " + lvi.LocalType.FullName);
                    Console.WriteLine("ToString(): " + lvi.ToString());
                }

                return (vars);
            }
```

The GetLocalVars method can be called using the following code:

```
        public static void TestGetLocalVars()
        {
            Process current = Process.GetCurrentProcess();

          // Get the path of the current module.
            string path = current.MainModule.FileName;

          // Get all local var info for the CSharpRecipes.Reflection.GetLocalVars method.
            System.Collections.ObjectModel.ReadOnlyCollection<LocalVariableInfo> vars =
                (System.Collections.ObjectModel.ReadOnlyCollection<LocalVariableInfo>)
                GetLocalVars(path, "CSharpRecipes.Reflection", "GetLocalVars");
        }
```

The output of this method is shown here:

```
IsPinned: False
LocalIndex: 0
LocalType.Module: CommonLanguageRuntimeLibrary
LocalType.FullName: System.Reflection.Assembly
ToString(): System.Reflection.Assembly (0)
IsPinned: False
LocalIndex: 1
LocalType.Module: CommonLanguageRuntimeLibrary
LocalType.FullName: System.Type
ToString(): System.Type (1)
IsPinned: False
LocalIndex: 2
LocalType.Module: CommonLanguageRuntimeLibrary
LocalType.FullName: System.Reflection.MethodInfo
ToString(): System.Reflection.MethodInfo (2)
IsPinned: False
LocalIndex: 3
LocalType.Module: CommonLanguageRuntimeLibrary
LocalType.FullName: System.Reflection.MethodBody
ToString(): System.Reflection.MethodBody (3)
IsPinned: False
LocalIndex: 4
LocalType.Module: CommonLanguageRuntimeLibrary
LocalType.FullName: System.Collections.ObjectModel.ReadOnlyCollection`1[[System.
Reflection.LocalVariableInfo, mscorlib, Version=2.0.0.0, Culture=neutral, Public
KeyToken=b77a5c561934e089]]
ToString(): System.Collections.ObjectModel.ReadOnlyCollection`1[System.Reflectio
n.LocalVariableInfo] (4)
```

The LocalVariableInfo objects for each local variable found in the CSharpRecipes.
Reflection.GetLocalVars method will be returned in the vars IList collection.

Discussion

The LocalVariables property can give you a good amount of information about variables within a method. The LocalVariables property returns an IList<LocalVariableInfo> collection. Each LocalVariableInfo object contains the information described in Table 13-2.

Table 13-2. LocalVariableInfo information

Member	Definition
IsPinned	Returns a bool indicating if the object that this variable refers to is pinned in memory (true) or not (false)
LocalIndex	Returns the index of this variable within this method's body
LocalType	Returns a Type object that describes the type of this variable
ToString	Returns the LocalType.FullName, a space, and then the LocalIndex value surrounded by parentheses

See Also

The "MethodInfo Class," "MethodBody Class," "ReadOnlyCollection<T> Class," and "LocalVariableInfo Class" topics in the MSDN documentation.

13.12 Creating a Generic Type

Problem

You want to create a generic type using only the reflection APIs.

Solution

You create a generic type similarly to how a nongeneric type is created; however, there is an extra step to create the type arguments you want to use in creating this generic type and binding these type arguments to the generic type's type parameters at construction. To do this, you will use a new method added to the Type class called BindGenericParameters:

```
public static void CreateMultiMap(Assembly asm)
{
    // Get the type we want to construct.
    Type typeToConstruct = asm.GetType(
        "CSharpRecipes.DataStructsAndAlgorithms+MultiMap`2");
    // Get the type arguments we want to construct our type with.
Type[] typeArguments = {typeof(int), typeof(string)};
            // Bind these type arguments to our generic type.
    Type newType = typeToConstruct.MakeGenericType(typeArguments);
    // Construct our type.
    DataStructsAndAlgorithms.MultiMap<int, string> mm = (
        DataStructsAndAlgorithms.MultiMap<int,
```

```
                    string>)Activator.CreateInstance(newType);

            // Test our newly constructed type.
            Console.WriteLine("Count == " + mm.Count);
            mm.Add(1, "test1");
            Console.WriteLine("Count == " + mm.Count);
        }
```

The code to test the `CreateMultiMap` method is shown here:

```
        public static void TestCreateMultiMap()
        {
            Assembly asm = Assembly.LoadFrom("C:\\CSharp Recipes 2nd Edition" +
                    "\\Code\\CSharpRecipes\\bin\\Debug\\CSharpRecipes.exe");
            CreateMultiMap(asm);
        }
```

The output of this method is shown here:

```
            Count == 0
            Count == 1
```

Discussion

Type parameters are defined on a class and indicate that any type which is able to be converted to an `Object` is allowed to be substituted for this type parameter (unless, of course, there are constraints placed on this type parameter using the `where` keyword). For example, the following class has two type parameters, `T` and `U`:

```
        public class Foo<T, U> {...}
```

Of course, you do not have to use `T` and `U`; you can instead use another letter or even a full name such as `TypeParam1` and `TypeParam2`.

A type argument is defined as the actual type that will be substituted for the type parameter. In the previously defined class `Foo`, you can replace type parameter `T` with the type argument `int` and type parameter `U` with the type argument `string`.

The `BindGenericParameters` method allows you to substitute type parameters with actual type arguments. This method accepts a single `Type` array parameter. This `Type` array consists of each type argument that will be substituted for each type parameter of the generic type. These type arguments must be added to this `Type` array in the same order as they are defined on the class. For example, the `Foo` class defines type parameters `T` and `U`, in that order. The `Type` array that you define contains an `int` type and a `string` type, in that order. This means that the type parameter `T` will be substituted for the type argument `int`, and `U` will be replaced with a `string` type. The `BindGenericParameters` method returns a `Type` object of the type you specified along with the type arguments.

See Also

The "Type.BindGenericParameters method" topic in the MSDN documentation.

CHAPTER 14
Web

14.0 Introduction

The World Wide Web has worked its way into every nook and cranny of what most
.NET developers encounter when building their solutions today. Web services are
on the rise, and ASP.NET is one of the main players in the web application space.
Because of the general needs to deal with HTML and TCP/IP name resolution and
because uniform resource indicators and uniform resource locators are being used
for more and more purposes, developers need tools to help them concentrate on
building the best web-interactive applications they can. This chapter is dedicated to
taking care of some of the grunge that comes along with programming when the
Web is involved. This is not an ASP.NET tutorial chapter but rather covers some
functionality that developers can use in both ASP.NET and other C#-based applications. For more on ASP.NET, see *ASP.NET Cookbook* and *Programming ASP.NET*,
Second Edition (both from O'Reilly).

14.1 Converting an IP Address to a Hostname

Problem

You have an IP address that you need to resolve into a hostname.

Solution

Use the `Dns.GetHostEntry` method to get the hostname for an IP address. In the following code, an IP address is resolved, and the hostname is accessible from the
`HostName` property of the `IPHostEntry`:

```
using System;
using System.Net;

IPHostEntry iphost = Dns.GetHostEntry("127.0.0.1");
```

```
        string hostName = iphost.HostName;

        // Print out name.
        Console.WriteLine(hostName);
```

Discussion

The `System.Net.Dns` class is provided for simple DNS resolution functionality. The `GetHostEntry` method returns an `IPHostEntry` that can be used to access the hostname via the `HostName` property. If the entry cannot be resolved, the `IPHostEntry` will have a `HostName` that has a string representation of the IP address that was passed in (assuming it is a valid IP address). If the first member of the `AddressList` (`[0]`) is accessed and the `IPAddress.ScopeId` property is checked for these entries, it will throw a `SocketException`.

See Also

The "DNS Class" and "IPHostEntry Class" topics in the MSDN documentation.

14.2   Converting a Hostname to an IP Address

Problem

You have a string representation of a host (such as oreilly.com), and you need to obtain the IP address from this hostname.

Solution

Use the `Dns.GetHostEntry` method to get the IP addresses. In the following code, a hostname is provided to the `GetHostEntry` method, which returns an `IPHostEntry` from which a string of addresses can be constructed. If the hostname does not resolve, a `SocketException` stating "No such host is known" is thrown:

```
using System;
using System.Net;
using System.Text;

public static string HostNameToIP(string hostName)
{
    IPHostEntry iphost = System.Net.Dns.GetHostEntry(hostName);

    IPAddress[] addresses = iphost.AddressList;

    StringBuilder addressList = new StringBuilder();
    foreach(IPAddress address in addresses)
    {
        addressList.AppendFormat("IP Address: {0};", address.ToString());
    }
    return addressList.ToString();
}
```

```
// Writes "IP Address: 208.201.239.37;IP Address: 208.201.239.36;"
Console.WriteLine(HostName2IP("www.oreilly.com"));
```

Discussion

An IPHostEntry can associate multiple IP addresses with a single hostname via the AddressList property. AddressList is an array of IPAddress objects, each of which holds a single IP address. Once the IPHostEntry is resolved, the AddressList can be looped over using foreach to create a string that shows all of the IP addresses for the given hostname. If the entry cannot be resolved, a SocketException is thrown.

See Also

The "DNS Class," "IPHostEntry Class," and "IPAddress" topics in the MSDN documentation.

14.3   Parsing a URI

Problem

You need to split a uniform resource identifier (URI) into its constituent parts.

Solution

Construct a System.Net.Uri object and pass the URI to the constructor. This class constructor parses out the constituent parts of the URI and allows access to them via the Uri properties. You can then display the URI pieces individually, as shown in Example 14-1.

Example 14-1. ParseURI method

```
public static void ParseUri(Uri uri)
{
    try
    {
        // System.Net.Uri class constructor has parsed it for us.
        // new Uri("http://user:password@localhost:8080/www.abc.com/
        //    home%20page.htm?item=1233#stuff")

        StringBuilder uriParts = new StringBuilder();
        uriParts.AppendFormat("AbsoluteURI: {0}{1}",
                        uri.AbsoluteUri,Environment.NewLine);
        uriParts.AppendFormat("AbsolutePath: {0}{1}",
                        uri.AbsolutePath,Environment.NewLine);
        uriParts.AppendFormat("Scheme: {0}{1}",
                        uri.Scheme,Environment.NewLine);
        uriParts.AppendFormat("UserInfo: {0}{1}",
                        uri.UserInfo,Environment.NewLine);
        uriParts.AppendFormat("Authority: {0}{1}",
                        uri.Authority,Environment.NewLine);
```

Example 14-1. ParseURI method (continued)

```
        uriParts.AppendFormat("DnsSafeHost: {0}{1}",
                              uri.DnsSafeHost,Environment.NewLine);
        uriParts.AppendFormat("Host: {0}{1}",
                              uri.Host,Environment.NewLine);
        uriParts.AppendFormat("HostNameType: {0}{1}",
                              uri.HostNameType.ToString( ),Environment.NewLine);
        uriParts.AppendFormat("Port: {0}{1}",uri.Port,Environment.NewLine);
        uriParts.AppendFormat("Path: {0}{1}",uri.LocalPath,Environment.NewLine);
        uriParts.AppendFormat("QueryString: {0}{1}",uri.Query,Environment.NewLine);
        uriParts.AppendFormat("Path and QueryString: {0}{1}",
                              uri.PathAndQuery,Environment.NewLine);
        uriParts.AppendFormat("Fragment: {0}{1}",uri.Fragment,Environment.NewLine);
        uriParts.AppendFormat("Original String: {0}{1}",
                              uri.OriginalString,Environment.NewLine);
        uriParts.AppendFormat("Segments: {0}",Environment.NewLine);
        for (int i = 0; i < uri.Segments.Length; i++)
            uriParts.AppendFormat(" Segment {0}:{1}{2}",
                              i, uri.Segments[i], Environment.NewLine);

        // GetComponents can be used to get commonly used combinations
        // of URI information.
        uriParts.AppendFormat("GetComponents for specialized combinations: {0}",
                              Environment.NewLine);
        uriParts.AppendFormat("Host and Port (unescaped): {0}{1}",
                              uri.GetComponents(UriComponents.HostAndPort,
                              UriFormat.Unescaped),Environment.NewLine);
        UriParts.AppendFormat("HttpRequestUrl (unescaped): {0}{1}",
                              uri.GetComponents(UriComponents.HttpRequestUrl,
                              UriFormat.Unescaped),Environment.NewLine);
        UriParts.AppendFormat("HttpRequestUrl (escaped): {0}{1}",
                              uri.GetComponents(UriComponents.HttpRequestUrl,
                              UriFormat.UriEscaped),Environment.NewLine);
        UriParts.AppendFormat("HttpRequestUrl (safeunescaped): {0}{1}",
                              uri.GetComponents(UriComponents.HttpRequestUrl,
                              UriFormat.SafeUnescaped),Environment.NewLine);
        UriParts.AppendFormat("Scheme And Server (unescaped): {0}{1}",
                              uri.GetComponents(UriComponents.SchemeAndServer,
                              UriFormat.Unescaped),Environment.NewLine);
        UriParts.AppendFormat("SerializationInfo String (unescaped): {0}{1}",
                              uri.GetComponents(UriComponents.SerializationInfoString,
                              UriFormat.Unescaped),Environment.NewLine);
        UriParts.AppendFormat("StrongAuthority (unescaped): {0}{1}",
                              uri.GetComponents(UriComponents.StrongAuthority,
                              UriFormat.Unescaped),Environment.NewLine);
        UriParts.AppendFormat("StrongPort (unescaped): {0}{1}",
                              uri.GetComponents(UriComponents.StrongPort,
                              UriFormat.Unescaped),Environment.NewLine);

        Console.WriteLine(UriParts.ToString( ));
    }
    catch(ArgumentNullException e)
    {
```

Example 14-1. ParseURI method (continued)

```
        Console.WriteLine("Uri string object is a null reference: {0}",e);
    }
    catch(UriFormatException e)
    {
        Console.WriteLine("Uri formatting error: {0}",e); }
    }
}
```

Discussion

The Solution code uses the `Uri` class to do the heavy lifting. URI syntax is well documented but it is easy to get wrong, so lean on the framework `Uri` implementation to handle the rules, as it has been carefully reviewed for correctly handling many cases. You would not want to make a security decision based on a URI you parse yourself. The constructor for the `Uri` class can throw two types of exceptions: an `ArgumentNullException` and a `UriFormatException`. The `ArgumentNullException` is thrown when the uri argument passed is null. The `UriFormatException` is thrown when the uri argument passed is of an incorrect or indeterminate format. Here are the error conditions that can throw a `UriFormatException`:

- An empty Uri was passed in.
- The scheme specified in the `Uri` is not correctly formed. See `CheckSchemeName`.
- The URI passed in contains too many slashes.
- The password specified in the passed-in URI is invalid.
- The hostname specified in the passed-in URI is invalid.
- The filename specified in the passed-in URI is invalid.
- The username specified in the passed-in URI is invalid.
- The host or authority name specified in the passed-in URI cannot be terminated by backslashes.
- The port number specified in the passed-in URI is invalid or cannot be parsed.
- The length of the passed-in URI exceeds 65,534 characters.
- The length of the scheme specified in the passed-in URI exceeds 1023 characters.
- There is an invalid character sequence in the passed-in URI.

 There is no actual validation that occurs for the username, host or authority name, password or port number to insure that they exist or are correct. The validation is simply that they are in the correct format according to the URI specification (RFC 2396).

`System.Net.Uri` provides methods to compare URIs, parse URIs, and combine URIs. It is all you should ever need for URI manipulation and is used by other classes in the Framework when a URI is called for. The syntax for the pieces of a URI is this:

```
[scheme]://[user]:[password]@[host/authority]:[port]/[path];[params]?
[query string]#[fragment]
```

If you pass the following URI to ParseUri:

http://user:password@localhost:8080/www.abc.com/home.htm?item=1233#stuff

it will display the following items:

```
AbsoluteURI: http://user:password@localhost:8080/www.abc.com/home%20page.htm?
item=1233#stuff
AbsolutePath: /www.abc.com/home%20page.htm
Scheme: http
UserInfo: user:password
Authority: localhost:8080
DnsSafeHost: localhost
Host: localhost
HostNameType: Dns
Port: 8080
Path: /www.abc.com/home page.htm
QueryString: ?item=1233
Path and QueryString: /www.abc.com/home%20page.htm?item=1233
Fragment: #stuff
Original String: http://user:password@localhost:8080/www.abc.com/home%20page.htm?
item=1233#stuff
Segments:
    Segment 0: /
    Segment 1: www.abc.com/
    Segment 2: home%20page.htm
GetComponents for specialized combinations:
Host and Port (unescaped): localhost:8080
HttpRequestUrl (unescaped): http://localhost:8080/www.abc.com/home page.htm?
item=1233
HttpRequestUrl (escaped): http://localhost:8080/www.abc.com/home%20page.htm?
item=1233
HttpRequestUrl (safeunescaped): http://localhost:8080/www.abc.com/home page.htm?
item=1233
Scheme And Server (unescaped): http://localhost:8080
SerializationInfo String (unescaped): http://user:password@localhost:8080/
www.abc.com/home page.htm?item=1233#stuff
StrongAuthority (unescaped): user:password@localhost:8080
StrongPort (unescaped): 8080
```

See Also

The "Uri Class," "ArgumentNullException Class," and "UriFormatException Class"
topics in the MSDN documentation.

14.4   Handling Web Server Errors

Problem

You have obtained a response from a web server, and you want to make sure that there were no errors in processing the initial request, such as failing to connect, being redirected, timing out, or failing to validate a certificate. You don't want to have to monitor for all of the different response codes available.

Solution

Check the StatusCode property of the HttpWebResponse class to determine what category of status this StatusCode falls into and return an enumeration value (ResponseCategories) representing the category. This technique will allow you to use a broader approach to dealing with response codes:

```
public static ResponseCategories CategorizeResponse(HttpWebResponse httpResponse)
{
    // Just in case there are more success codes defined in the future
    // by HttpStatusCode, we will check here for the "success" ranges
    // instead of using the HttpStatusCode enum as it overloads some
    // values.
    int statusCode = (int)httpResponse.StatusCode;
    if((statusCode >= 100)&& (statusCode <= 199))
    {
        return ResponseCategories.Informational;
    }
    else if((statusCode >= 200)&& (statusCode <= 299))
    {
        return ResponseCategories.Success;
    }
    else if((statusCode >= 300)&& (statusCode <= 399))
    {
        return ResponseCategories.Redirected;
    }
    else if((statusCode >= 400)&& (statusCode <= 499))
    {
        return ResponseCategories.ClientError;
    }
    else if((statusCode >= 500)&& (statusCode <= 599))
    {
        return ResponseCategories.ServerError;
    }
    return ResponseCategories.Unknown;
}
```

The ResponseCategories enumeration is defined like this:

```
public enum ResponseCategories
{
    Unknown,       // Unknown code ( < 100 or > 599)
    Informational, // Informational codes (100 >= 199)
```

```
    Success,      // Success codes (200 >= 299)
    Redirected,   // Redirection code (300 >= 399)
    ClientError,  // Client error code (400 >= 499)
    ServerError   // Server error code (500 >= 599)
}
```

Discussion

There are five different categories of status codes on an HTTP response, as shown in Table 14-1.

Table 14-1. Categories of HTTP response status codes

Category	Available range	HttpStatusCode defined range
Informational	100–199	100–101
Successful	200–299	200–206
Redirection	300–399	300–307
Client Error	400–499	400–417
Server Error	500–599	500–505

Each of the status codes defined by Microsoft in the .NET Framework is assigned an enumeration value in the HttpStatusCode enumeration. These status codes reflect what can happen when a request is submitted. The web server is free to return a status code in the available range, even if it is not currently defined for most commercial web servers. The defined status codes are listed in RFC 2616—Section 10 for HTTP/1.1.

You are trying to figure out the broad category of the status of the request. You achieve this by inspecting the HttpResponse.StatusCode property, comparing it to the defined status code ranges for HTTP, and returning the appropriate ResponseCategories value.

When dealing with HttpStatusCode, you will notice that there are certain HttpStatusCode flags that map to the same status code value. An example of this is HttpStatusCode.Ambiguous and HttpStatusCode.MultipleChoices, which both map to HTTP status code 300. If you try to use both of these in a switch statement on the HttpStatusCode, you will get the following error because the C# compiler cannot tell the difference:

```
error CS0152: The label 'case 300:' already occurs in this switch statement.
```

See Also

HTTP: The Definitive Guide (O'Reilly); the "HttpStatusCode Enumeration" topic in the MSDN documentation; and HTTP/1.1 RFC 2616—Section 10 Status Codes: *http://www.w3.org/Protocols/rfc2616/rfc2616-sec10.html*.

14.5   Communicating with a Web Server

Problem

You want to send a request to a web server in the form of a GET or POST request. After you send the request to a web server, you want to get the results of that request (the response) from the web server.

Solution

Use the HttpWebRequest class in conjunction with the WebRequest class to create and send a request to a server.

Take the Uri of the resource, the method to use in the request (GET or POST), and the data to send (only for POST requests), and use this information to create an HttpWebRequest, as shown in Example 14-2.

Example 14-2. Communicating with a web server

```
using System.Net;
using System.IO;
using System.Text;

public static HttpWebRequest GenerateHttpWebRequest(Uri uri)
{
    HttpWebRequest httpRequest = (HttpWebRequest)WebRequest.Create(uri);
    return httpRequest;
}

// POST overload
public static HttpWebRequest GenerateHttpWebRequest(Uri uri,
    string postData,
    string contentType)
{
    HttpWebRequest httpRequest = GenerateHttpRequest(uri);

    byte[] bytes = Encoding.UTF8.GetBytes(postData);

    httpRequest.ContentType = contentType;
        //"application/x-www-form-urlencoded"; for forms

    httpRequest.ContentLength = postData.Length;

    using (Stream requestStream = httpRequest.GetRequestStream( ))
    {
        requestStream.Write(bytes, 0, bytes.Length);
    }
    return httpRequest;
}
```

Once you have an HttpWebRequest, you send the request and get the response using the GetResponse method. It takes the newly created HttpWebRequest as input and returns an HttpWebResponse. The following example performs a GET for the *index.aspx* page from the *http://localhost/mysite* web site:

```
HttpWebRequest request =
 GenerateHttpWebRequest(new Uri("http://localhost/mysite/index.aspx"));

using(HttpWebResponse response = (HttpWebResponse) request.GetResponse())
{
    // This next line uses CategorizeResponse from Recipe 14.4.
    if(CategorizeResponse(response)==ResponseCategories.Success)
    {
        Console.WriteLine("Request succeeded");
    }
}
```

You generate the HttpWebRequest, send it and get the HttpWebResponse, then check the success using the CategorizeResponse method from Recipe 14.4.

Discussion

The WebRequest and WebResponse classes encapsulate all of the functionality to perform basic web communications. HttpWebRequest and HttpWebResponse are derived from these classes and provide the HTTP-specific support.

At the most fundamental level, to perform an HTTP-based web transaction, you use the Create method on the WebRequest class to get a WebRequest that can be cast to an HttpWebRequest (so long as the scheme is http:// or https://). This HttpWebRequest is then submitted to the web server in question when the GetResponse method is called, and it returns an HttpWebResponse that can then be inspected for the response data.

See Also

The "WebRequest Class," "WebResponse Class," "HttpWebRequest Class," and "HttpWebResponse Class" topics in the MSDN documentation.

14.6   Going Through a Proxy

Problem

Many companies have a web proxy that allows employees to access the Internet, while at the same time preventing outsiders from accessing the company's internal network. The problem is that to create an application that accesses the Internet from within your company, you must first connect to your proxy and then send information through it, rather than directly out to an Internet web server.

Solution

In order to get an HttpWebRequest successfully through a specific proxy server, you need to set up a WebProxy object with the settings to validate your specific request to a given proxy. Since this function is generic for any request, you can create the AddProxyInfoToRequest method:

```
public static HttpWebRequest AddProxyInfoToRequest(HttpWebRequest httpRequest,
                            Uri proxyUri,
                            string proxyId,
                            string proxyPassword,
                            string proxyDomain)
{
    if(httpRequest != null)
    {
        WebProxy proxyInfo = new WebProxy( );
        proxyInfo.Address = proxyUri;
        proxyInfo.BypassProxyOnLocal = true;
        proxyInfo.Credentials = new NetworkCredential(proxyId,
                                                      proxyPassword,
                                                      proxyDomain);
        httpRequest.Proxy = proxyInfo;
    }
    return httpRequest;
}
```

If all requests are going to go through the same proxy, in the 1.x versions of the Framework, you used the static Select method on the GlobalProxySelection class to set up the proxy settings for all WebRequests. In versions after 1.x, the WebRequest. DefaultWebProxy property should be used:

```
Uri proxyUri = new Uri("http://webproxy:80");
WebRequest.DefaultWebProxy = new WebProxy(proxyURI);

// Old v1.x way of doing this...
//GlobalProxySelection.Select = new WebProxy(proxyURI);
```

Discussion

AddProxyInfoToRequest takes the URI of the proxy and creates a Uri object, which is used to construct the WebProxy object. The WebProxy object is set to bypass the proxy for local addresses and then the credential information is used to create a NetworkCredential object. The NetworkCredential object represents the authentication information necessary for the request to succeed at this proxy and is assigned to the WebProxy.Credentials property. Once the WebProxy object is completed, it is assigned to the Proxy property of the HttpWebRequest, and the request is ready to be submitted.

In order to get the proxy settings for the current user from Internet Explorer, you can use the System.Net.WebRequest.GetSystemWebProxy method and then assign the returned IWebProxy to either the proxy on the HttpWebRequest or the DefaultWebProxy property on the WebRequest:

```
WebRequest.DefaultWebProxy = WebRequest.GetSystemWebProxy();
```

See Also

The "WebProxy Class," "NetworkCredential Class," and "HttpWebRequest Class" topics in the MSDN documentation.

14.7   Obtaining the HTML from a URL

Problem

You need to get the HTML returned from a web server in order to examine it for items of interest. For example, you could examine the returned HTML for links to other pages or for headlines from a news site.

Solution

You can use the methods for web communication that were set up in Recipes 14.4 and 14.5 to make the HTTP request and verify the response; then, you can get at the HTML via the ResponseStream property of the HttpWebResponse object:

```
public static string GetHtmlFromUrl(Uri url)
{
    string html = string.Empty;
    HttpWebRequest request = GenerateHttpWebRequest(url);
    using(HttpWebResponse response = (HttpWebResponse)request.GetResponse())
    {
        if (CategorizeResponse(response) == ResponseCategories.Success)
        {
            Stream responseStream = response.GetResponseStream();
            using(StreamReader reader =
                new StreamReader(responseStream, Encoding.UTF8))
            {
                html = reader.ReadToEnd();
            }
        }
    }
    return html;
}
```

Discussion

The GetHtmlFromUrl method gets a web page using the GenerateHttpWebRequest and GetResponse methods, verifies the response using the CategorizeResponse method, and then, once it has a valid response, starts looking for the HTML that was returned.

The GetResponseStream method on the HttpWebResponse provides access to the body of the message that was returned in a System.IO.Stream object. In order to read the data, instantiate a StreamReader with the response stream and the UTF8 property of the Encoding class to allow for the UTF8-encoded text data to be read correctly from the stream. Then call the StreamReader's ReadToEnd method, which puts all of the content in the string variable called html, and return it.

See Also

The "HttpWebResponse.GetResponseStream Method," "Stream Class," and "String-Builder Class" topics in the MSDN documentation.

14.8   Using the Web Browser Control

Problem

You need to display HTML-based content in a WinForms-based application.

Solution

Use the System.Windows.Forms.WebBrowser class to embed web browser functionality into your application. The Cheapo-Browser seen in Figure 14-1 shows some of the capabilities of this control.

Figure 14-1. The web browser control

While this is not a production quality user interface, it is called Cheapo-Browser for a reason. It can be used to select a web address, display the content, navigate forward and backward, cancel the request, go to the home page, add HTML directly to the control, print the HTML or save it, and finally, enable or disable the context menu inside of the browser window. The WebBrowser control is capable of much more, but this recipe is meant to give you a taste of what is possible. It would be well worth exploring its capabilities further to see what other needs it might fill.

When you add your HTML (`<h1>Hey you added some HTML!</h1>`), it is displayed as shown in Figure 14-2.

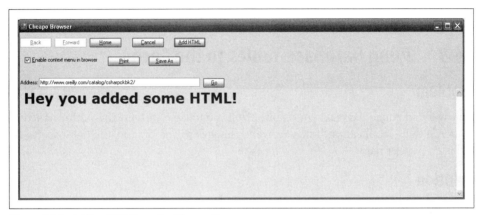

Figure 14-2. Adding HTML to the Cheapo-Browser

The code to accomplish this is rather simple:

```
this._webBrowser.Document.Body.InnerHtml = "<h1>Hey you added some HTML!</h1>";
```

The navigation to a web page is equally trivial:

```
Uri uri = new Uri(this._txtAddress.Text);
this._webBrowser.Navigate(uri);
```

The nice thing about the navigation is the Navigated event that can be subscribed, so you are notified when the navigation has completed. This allows code to spin this off in a thread and then come back to it once it is fully loaded. The event provides a WebBrowserNavigatedEventArgs class that has a Url property to tell the URL of the document that has been navigated to:

```
private void _webBrowser_Navigated(object sender, WebBrowserNavigatedEventArgs e)
{
    // Update with where we ended up in case of redirection
    // from the original Uri.
    this._txtAddress.Text = e.Url.ToString();
    this._btnBack.Enabled = this._webBrowser.CanGoBack;
    this._btnForward.Enabled = this._webBrowser.CanGoForward;
}
```

Discussion

In the 1.x versions of the .NET Framework, embedding a web browser in your Win-Forms application was much more difficult and error-prone. Now there is a .NET-based web browser control. You no longer have to struggle with some of the COM interop issues that could arise while trying to hook up to browser events. This is a good opportunity to make the line between your desktop and web applications blur even further and use the power of a rich client combined with web flexibility.

See Also

The "WebBrowser Class" topic in the MSDN documentation.

14.9   Tying Database Tables to the Cache

Problem

You want to cache datasets you create from a database to help the performance of your ASP.NET application, but you want changes to the data in the database to be reflected in your pages.

Solution

Use the SqlCacheDependency class to expire data in the cache when the underlying database data changes. A SqlCacheDependency sets up a relationship with the database so that, if the data changes, the item in the cache that has this dependency is released from the cache, and the code that established the item can fetch the values from the database again.

To demonstrate this, a SqlCacheDependency object is created for the Authors table in the pubs database in Microsoft SQL Server using the CreateSqlCacheDependency method. The pubs database is a sample database that ships with SQL Server 2000:

```
public SqlCacheDependency CreateSqlCacheDependency(string connStr)
{
    // Make a dependency on the authors database table so that
    // if it changes, the cached data will also be disposed of.

    // Make sure we are enabled for notifications for the db.
    // Note that the parameter has to be the actual connection
    // string, NOT the connection string NAME from web.config.
    SqlCacheDependencyAdmin.EnableNotifications(connStr);

    SqlCacheDependencyAdmin.EnableTableForNotifications(connStr, "Authors");

    // This is case-sensitive, so make sure the first entry
    // matches the entry in the web.config file exactly.
    // The first parameter here must be the connection string
    // NAME, not the connection string itself.
```

```
            return new SqlCacheDependency("pubs", "Authors");
    }
```

The SqlCacheDependencyAdmin class is responsible for talking to SQL Server to set up the necessary infrastructure (triggers and the like for SQL Server 2000, Cache Sync for SQL Server 2005) for the SqlCacheDependency to fire correctly. The SqlCacheDependency has a section in the application's *web.config* file under *configuration/system.web/caching* defining the parameters that the dependency operates under. There are timeout settings for the polling time (for SQL Server 2000, as SQL Server 2005 doesn't poll) and the connection time, as well as a link to the connection string to use via its name. This connection string can be found in the *web.config* file in the *configuration/connectionStrings* section. The two entries are shown here:

```
        <caching>
         <sqlCacheDependency enabled="True" pollTime="60000">
            <databases>
              <add name="pubs" connectionStringName="LocalPubs" pollTime="9000000" />
            </databases>
          </sqlCacheDependency>
         </caching>

     <connectionStrings>
        <add name="LocalPubs" connectionString="Server=(local);Integrated
    Security=True;Database=pubs;Persist Security Info=True"
    providerName="System.Data.SqlClient"/>
        </connectionStrings>
```

Discussion

The main scenario for using SqlDependencyCache is for data that is read frequently but changes very infrequently. The data should be reasonably static, as there is overhead associated with keeping the cache in sync with the database table. While the SqlDependencyCache is for use with Microsoft SQL Server, it is just a derived implementation of a CacheDependency class. CacheDependency-based classes could be written for any other database provider, but surprisingly (or perhaps not so) Microsoft SQL Server is the only database with one provided.

When using the SqlCacheDependency class, the first thing to do is insure that Notifications have been enabled for both the database and the table being monitored for changes. If either of these notifications is not enabled for the database and/or table, a DatabaseNotEnabledForNotificationException will be thrown when constructing the SqlCacheDependency. A SqlCacheDependency can also be created directly from a SqlCommand object.

See Also

Recipe 14.10; the "SqlCacheDependency," "SqlCacheDependencyAdmin," and "CacheDependency" topics in the MSDN documentation.

14.10   Prebuilding an ASP.NET Web Site Programmatically

Problem

You want to prebuild your web site to avoid compilation delays and to avoid the hosting scenario in which source code needs to be on the server.

Solution

Use the `ClientBuildManager` to prebuild your web site into an assembly. In order to prebuild the web site, you must specify:

- The virtual directory for the web application.
- The physical path to the web application directory.
- The location where you want to build the web application.
- Flags that help control the compilation.

To prebuild the web application in the sample code for the book, first retrieve the directory where the web application is located, and then provide a virtual directory name and a location for the web application to build to:

```
string cscbWebPath = GetWebAppPath();

if(cscbWebPath.Length>0)
{
    string appVirtualDir = @"CSCBWeb";
    string appPhysicalSourceDir = cscbWebPath;

    // Make the target an adjacent directory as it cannot be in the same tree
    // or the build manager screams...
    string appPhysicalTargetDir = Path.GetDirectoryName(cscbWebPath) + @"\
BuildCSCB";
```

Next, set up the flags for the compile using the `PrecompilationFlags` enumeration. The `PrecompilationFlags` values are listed in Table 14-2.

Table 14-2. PrecompilationFlags enumeration values

Flag value	Purpose
AllowPartiallyTrustedCallers	Add the APTC attribute to the built assembly.
Clean	Remove any existing compiled image.
CodeAnalysis	Build for code analysis.
Default	Use the default compile options.
DelaySign	DelaySign the assembly.
FixedNames	Assembly generated with fixed names for pages. No batch compilation is performed, just individual compilation.

Table 14-2. PrecompilationFlags enumeration values (continued)

Flag value	Purpose
ForceDebug	Ensure that the assembly is compiled for Debug.
OverwriteTarget	The target assembly should be overwritten if it exists.
Updateable	Insure the assembly is updateable.

To build a debug image and make sure it is created successfully if the compilation is good, the ForceDebug and OverwriteTarget flags are used:

```
PrecompilationFlags flags = PrecompilationFlags.ForceDebug |
                    PrecompilationFlags.OverwriteTarget;
```

The PrecompilationFlags are then stored in a new instance of the ClientBuildManagerParameter class, and the ClientBuildManager is created with the parameters that have been set up for it. To accomplish the prebuild, the PrecompileApplication method is called. Notice that there is an instance of a class called MyClientBuildManagerCallback that is passed to the PrecompileApplication method:

```
ClientBuildManagerParameter cbmp = new ClientBuildManagerParameter();
cbmp.PrecompilationFlags = flags;

ClientBuildManager cbm =
            new ClientBuildManager(appVirtualDir,
                        appPhysicalSourceDir,
                        appPhysicalTargetDir,
                                    cbmp);
MyClientBuildManagerCallback myCallback = new MyClientBuildManagerCallback();
cbm.PrecompileApplication(myCallback);
}
```

The MyClientBuildManagerCallback class is derived from the ClientBuildManagerCallback class and allows the code to receive notifications during the compilation of the web application. The ClientBuildManagerCallback methods have LinkDemands on them, which require that the callback methods also have them. Compiler errors, parsing errors, and progress notifications are all available. In the MyClientBuildManagerCallback class, they are all implemented to write to the debug stream and the console:

```
public class MyClientBuildManagerCallback : ClientBuildManagerCallback
{
    public MyClientBuildManagerCallback()
        : base()
    {
    }

    [PermissionSet(SecurityAction.Demand, Unrestricted = true)]
    public override void ReportCompilerError(CompilerError error)
    {
        string msg = "Report Compiler Error: " + error.ToString();
```

```
        Debug.WriteLine(msg);
        Console.WriteLine(msg);
    }

    [PermissionSet(SecurityAction.Demand, Unrestricted = true)]
    public override void ReportParseError(ParserError error)
    {
        string msg = "Report Parse Error: " + error.ToString( );
        Debug.WriteLine(msg);
        Console.WriteLine(msg);
    }

    [PermissionSet(SecurityAction.Demand, Unrestricted = true)]
    public override void ReportProgress(string message)
    {
        string msg = "Report Progress: " + message;
        Debug.WriteLine(msg);
        Console.WriteLine(msg);
    }
}
```

The output from a successful compilation of the CSCB web site looks like this:

```
Report Progress: Building directory '/CSCBWeb/App_Data'.
Report Progress: Building directory '/CSCBWeb/Role_Database'.
Report Progress: Building directory '/CSCBWeb'.
```

Discussion

ClientBuildManager is actually a thin wrapper around the BuildManager class, which does most of the heavy lifting of the compilation. ClientBuildManager makes it more straightforward to ensure that all the important parts of the web application are addressed, while BuildManager gives a bit more fine-grained control. The ClientBuildManager also allows for subscribing to appdomain notification events such as start, shutdown, and unload, allowing for error handling in the event that the appdomain is going away during a prebuild.

To prebuild applications in ASP.NET without resorting to the ClientBuildManager, an HTTP request can be posted to the web site in the format of *http://server/webapp/ precompile.axd*. The *precompile.axd* "document" triggers an ASP.NET HttpHandler for this that will prebuild the web site for you. This is handled by the *aspnet_compiler.exe* module that essentially wraps the ClientBuildManager functionality.

See Also

The "ClientBuildManager," "ClientBuildManagerParameters," "BuildManager," and "ASP.NET Web Site Precompilation" topics in the MSDN documentation.

14.11 Escaping and Unescaping Data for the Web

Problem

You need to transform data for use in web operations from escaped to unescaped format or vice versa for proper transmission. This escaping and unescaping should follow the format outlined in RFC 2396—Uniform Resource Identifiers (URI): Generic Syntax.

Solution

Use the Uri class static methods for escaping and unescaping data and Uris.

To escape data, use the static Uri.EscapeDataString method, as shown here:

```
string data = "<H1>My html</H1>";
Console.WriteLine("Original Data: {0}",data);
Console.WriteLine();
// public static string EscapeDataString(string stringToEscape);
string escapedData = Uri.EscapeDataString(data);
Console.WriteLine("escaped Data: {0}",escapedData);
Console.WriteLine();

// Output from above code is
//
// Original Data: <H1>My html</H1>
//
// Escaped Data: %3CH1%3EMy%20html%3C%2FH1%3E
```

To unescape the data, use the static Uri.UnescapeDataString method:

```
// public static string UnescapeDataString( string stringToUnescape);
string unescapedData =    Uri.UnescapeDataString(escapedData);
Console.WriteLine("unescaped Data: {0}", unescapedData);
Console.WriteLine();

// Output from above code is
//
// Unescaped Data: <H1>My html</H1>
```

To escape a Uri, use the static Uri.EscapeUriString method:

```
string UriString = "http://user:password@localhost:8080/www.abc.com/" +
    "home page.htm?item=1233;html=<h1>Heading</h1>#stuff";
Console.WriteLine("Original Uri string: {0}",UriString);
Console.WriteLine();

// public static string EscapeUriString(string stringToEscape);
string escapedUriString = Uri.EscapeUriString(UriString);
Console.WriteLine("Escaped Uri string: {0}",escapedUriString);
Console.WriteLine();
// Output from above code is
//
//Original Uri string:
```

```
http://user:password@localhost:8080/www.abc.com/home
//page.htm?item=1233;html=<h1>Heading</h1>#stuff
//
//Escaped Uri string:
//http://user:password@localhost:8080/www.abc.com/home%20page.
//htm?item=1233;
//html=%3Ch1%3EHeading%3C/h1%3E#stuff
```

In case you are wondering why escaping a Uri has its own method (EscapeUriString), take a look at what the escaped Uri looks like if you use Uri. EscapeDataString and Uri.UnescapeDataString on it:

```
// Why not just use EscapeDataString to escape a Uri? It's not picky enough...
string escapedUriData = Uri.EscapeDataString(UriString);
Console.WriteLine("Escaped Uri data: {0}",escapedUriData);
Console.WriteLine();

Console.WriteLine(Uri.UnescapeDataString(escapedUriString));

// Output from above code is
//
//
//Escaped Uri data:
//http%3A%2F%2Fuser%3Apassword%40localhost%3A8080%2Fwww.abc.
//com%2Fhome%20page.htm
//%3Fitem%3D1233%3Bhtml%3D%3Ch1%3EHeading%3C%2Fh1%3E%23stuff
//
//http://user:password@localhost:8080/www.abc.com/home
//page.htm?item=1233;html=<h1>Heading</h1>#stuff
```

Notice that the :, /, :, @, and ? characters get escaped when they shouldn't, which is why you use the EscapeUriString method for Uris.

Discussion

EscapeUriString assumes that there are no escape sequences already present in the string being escaped. The escaping follows the convention set down in RFC 2396 for converting all reserved characters and characters with a value greater than 128 to their hexadecimal format.

In section 2.2 of RFC 2396, it states that the reserved characters are:

;|/| ? |:| @ | & | = | + | $ | ,

The EscapeUriString method is useful when creating a System.Uri object to ensure that the Uri is escaped correctly.

See Also

The "EscapeUriString Method," "EscapeUriData Method," and "Unescape-DataString Method" topics in the MSDN documentation.

14.12 Using the UriBuilder Class

Problem

You want to avoid making URI syntax errors when creating a URI.

Solution

Use the `UriBuilder` class to add each piece without worrying about syntax or placement in the string.

Building a URI programmatically can be challenging to do correctly in all instances. Using the `UriBuilder` can help to simplify it. For instance, if you needed to assemble an HTTP Uri that looked like this:

> *http://user:password@localhost:8080/www.abc.com/*
> *homepagehtm?item=1233;html=<h1>Heading</h1>#stuff*

you would need to understand the layout of the HTTP Uri, which is this:

> *[scheme]://[user]:[password]@[host/authority]:[port]/[path];[params]?*
> *[query string]#[fragment]*

It is very possible that information could come in that has only some of these pieces, or all of the pieces might be present. The `UriBuilder` allows the code to set properties for each of the components of the URI. This is great except for one small glitch. Every time you set the `Query` property, the `UriBuilder` class appends a ? to the front of the query string information. This means if code is written in this manner:

```
UriBuilder ub = new UriBuilder();
ub.Query = "item=1233";
ub.Query += "html-<h1>heading</h1>";
```

the resulting query string looks like this, with two question marks:

```
??item=1233;html=<h1>heading</h1>
```

To correct this sad state of affairs, use the `UriBuilderFix`, which overloads the `Query` property and deals with this in a more reasonable manner. `UriBuilderFix` is a light wrapper for `UriBuilder` that cleans up the `Query` property behavior:

```
public class UriBuilderFix : UriBuilder
{
    public UriBuilderFix() : base()
    {
    }
    public new string Query
    {
        get
        {
            return base.Query;
        }
        set
```

```
        {
          if (!string.IsNullOrEmpty(value))
          {
                if (value[0] == '?')
                    // Trim off the leading ? as the underlying
                    // UriBuilder class will add one to the
                    // query string. Also prepend ; for additional items.
                    base.Query = value.Substring(1);
                else
                    base.Query = value;
          }
          else
                base.Query = string.Empty;
        }
      }
   }
```

The `UriBuilderFix` is used just like the `UriBuilder`, except you now get the expected output from adding to the query string:

```
UriBuilderFix ubf = new
UriBuilderFix();
ubf.Scheme = "http";
ubf.UserName = "user";
ubf.Password = "password";
ubf.Host = "localhost";
ubf.Port = 8080;
ubf.Path = "www.abc.com/home page.htm";

//The Query property contains any query information included in the Uri.
//Query information is separated from the path information by a question mark (?)
//and continues to the end of the Uri. The query information returned includes
//the leading question mark.
//The query information is escaped according to RFC 2396.
//Setting the Query property to null or to System.String.Empty clears the aby
property.
//Note: Do not append a string directly to this property.
//Instead, retrieve the property value as a string, remove the leading question
//mark, append the new query string, and set the property with the combined//
string.

ubf.Query = "item=1233";
ubf.Query += ";html=<h1>heading</h1>";

ubf.Fragment = "stuff";

Console.WriteLine("Absolute Composed Uri: " + ubf.Uri.AbsoluteUri);
Console.WriteLine("Composed Uri: " + ubf.ToString());
```

This example produces the following output:

```
Absolute Composed Uri: http://user:password@localhost:8080/www.abc.com/
home%20page.
  htm?item=1233;html=%3Ch1%3Eheading%3C/h1%3E
```

```
Composed Uri:
http://user:password@localhost:8080/www.abc.com/home%20page.htm?item=1233;html=
%3Ch1%3Eheading%3C/h1%3E
```

Discussion

Even without the addition of the Query behavior in BetterUriBuilder, UriBuilder is a great way to build up Uris without resorting to assembling the whole string yourself. Once the construction of the Uri is complete, get the Uri object from the UriBuilder. Uri property to use it.

See Also

Recipes 14.2 and 14.3; see the "UriBuilder Class" and "Uri Class" topics in the MSDN documentation.

14.13 Inspect and Change Your Web Application Configuration

Problem

You want to be able to modify some settings in your web application configuration file from within a web page.

Solution

Use the System.Configuration.WebConfigurationManager and System.Configuration. Configuration classes to access elements of your web application's configuration settings.

First, get a Configuration object for the configuration settings by calling the OpenWebConfiguration method on the WebConfigurationManager:

```
System.Configuration.Configuration cfg =
    WebConfigurationManager.OpenWebConfiguration(@"/CSCBWeb");
```

Now, use the Configuration object to get a specific section of the settings. The following code retrieves the SqlCacheDependencySection of the configuration:

```
SqlCacheDependencySection sqlCacheDep =
   (SqlCacheDependencySection)cfg.GetSection("system.web/caching/
sqlCacheDependency");
```

The SqlCacheDependencySection allows for creating a new SqlCacheDependencyDatabase and adding it to the configuration, and then saving the new configuration:

```
SqlCacheDependencyDatabase sqlCacheDb = new
        SqlCacheDependencyDatabase("pubs","LocalPubs",9000000);
sqlCacheDep.Databases.Add(sqlCacheDb);
```

```
sqlCacheDep.Enabled = true;
sqlCacheDep.PollTime = 60000;
cfg.Save(ConfigurationSaveMode.Modified);
```

This creates the following section in the *web.config* file for the application:

```
<sqlCacheDependency enabled="True" pollTime="60000">
  <databases>
    <add name="pubs" connectionStringName="LocalPubs" pollTime="9000000" />
  </databases>
</sqlCacheDependency>
```

Now the application is configured to allow a SqlCacheDependency to be created.

Discussion

This may seem like a lot of work at first. It would be pretty easy to rip through the *web.config* file using an XmlTextReader/Writer combination or an XmlDocument. But that would get the settings in only that *web.config* file, not all of the other *web.config* files that merge with the application-level one to make up the true configuration. The WebConfigurationManager allows for accessing the current settings at runtime, not just the static ones on disk in the multiple files.

 One of the results of changing the configuration of a web application programmatically is that it can result in the restart of the application domain for the application. This can cause performance issues on your server. The other major area to consider is security. If the page that executes this code is not secured properly, the application/server hosting the page could be open to attack.

When the configuration is modified during the processing of the web page, the changes are not immediately reflected in the current configuration, as the page needs to finish processing before the configuration can be updated. In the earlier case in which a SqlCacheDependency is configured, the attempt to immediately construct the SqlCacheDependency object will throw an exception stating that the application is not configured to do this. To get around this, you can do the configuration setting work, and then redirect back to the same page with a parameter in the query string that bypasses this setup code and moves right into the code that uses the new configuration (the creation of the SqlCacheDependency, in this case):

```
if (Request.QueryString.Count == 0)
{
    // Add the sqlCache database entry
    // to web.config.
    TestConfig();
    // Now, redirect to ourselves adding a query string.
    // We do this so that the change we made to
    // web.config gets picked up for the code in
    // CreateSqlCacheDependency and SetupCacheDependencies,
    // as it depends on that configuration being present.
```

```
        // If you just create the entry and call the setup
        // code in the same page instance, the internal
        // configuration stuff doesn't refresh and you get
        // an exception when the code can't find the sqlCache
        // section it needs.
        Response.Redirect(Request.RawUrl + "?run=1");
    }
    else
    {
        // Run 14.10.
        CreateSqlCacheDependency();
        // Run 14.11.
        SetupCacheDependencies();
    }
```

See Also

Recipes 14.9 and 14.10; the "WebConfigurationManager Class" and "System.Configuration Namespace" topics in the MSDN documentation.

14.14   Using Cached Results When Working with HTTP for Faster Performance

Problem

You are looking for a way to speed up code that reaches out to the Web via HTTP for content.

Solution

Use the RequestCachePolicy class to determine how your HttpWebRequests react in the presence of a caching entity. RequestCachePolicy has seven levels defined by the RequestCacheLevel enumeration, as shown in Table 14-3.

Table 14-3. RequestCacheLevel enumeration values

Flag value	Purpose
BypassCache	Get content only directly from the server (default setting in .NET).
CacheIfAvailable	Accept the requested item from any cache between the request and the server of the content.
CacheOnly	Accept the request to be fulfilled from only the local cache; throws a WebException if not found in the cache.
Default	Accept content from intermediate caches or from the server directly, subject to the current cache policy and content age (recommended level for most apps, even though it is not the default setting).
NoCacheNoStore	Content will not be accepted from caches nor added to any. Equivalent to the HTTP no-cache directive.
Reload	Get content directly from the server but store response in the cache.
Revalidate	Check the content timestamp on the server against the cache and take the most recent one.

The RequestCachePolicy is set up using the CacheIfAvailable RequestCacheLevel so that the request will always take the "closest" content to enhance retrieval speed. If Default is used, the request is still subject to the underlying cache policy of the system, and that can prevent the use of intermediate caches.

To assign the cache policy, set the CachePolicy property on the HttpWebRequest to the newly created RequestCachePolicy. Once the policy is in place, get the response. The HttpWebResponse object has a property called IsFromCache that tells if the response came from a cache:

```
string html = string.Empty;

// Set up the request (Recipe 14.5 has GenerateHttpWebRequest).
HttpWebRequest request =
    GenerateHttpWebRequest(new Uri("http://www.oreilly.com"));

// Make a cache policy to use cached results if available.
// The default is to bypass the cache in machine.config.
RequestCachePolicy rcpCheckCache =
    new RequestCachePolicy(RequestCacheLevel.CacheIfAvailable);

request.CachePolicy = rcpCheckCache;

HttpWebResponse response = null;
try
{
    response = (HttpWebResponse)request.GetResponse();
}
catch (WebException we)
{
    Console.WriteLine(we.ToString());
}

if(response.IsFromCache==false)
{
    Console.WriteLine("Didn't hit the cache");
}
```

Discussion

The default request cache policy for an appdomain can be set by using the HttpWebRequest.DefaultCachePolicy property. The CachePolicy property shown in the solution sets the policy for a particular request.

The default caching policy is specified in the *machine.config* file in the system.net/ requestCaching element, as shown here:

```
<requestCaching defaultPolicyLevel="BypassCache" isPrivateCache="true"
unspecifiedMaximumAge="1.00:00:00" >
```

See Also

The "RequestCachePolicy Class," "RequestCacheLevel Enumeration," and "Default-CachePolicy Property" topics in the MSDN documentation.

14.15 Checking Out a Web Server's Custom Error Pages

Problem

You have an application that needs to know what custom error pages are set up for the various HTTP error return codes on a given IIS server.

Solution

Use the `System.DirectoryServices.DirectoryEntry` class to talk to the Internet Information Server (IIS) metabase to find out which custom error pages are set up. The metabase holds the configuration information for the web server. `DirectoryEntry` uses the Active Directory IIS service provider to communicate with the metabase by specifying the "IIS" scheme in the constructor for the `DirectoryEntry`:

```
// This is a case-sensitive entry in the metabase.
// You'd think it was misspelled, but you would be mistaken...
const string WebServerSchema = "IIsWebServer";

// Set up to talk to the local IIS server.
string server = "localhost";

// Create a dictionary entry for the IIS server with a fake
// user and password. Credentials would have to be provided
// if you are running as a regular user.
using (DirectoryEntry w3svc =
    new DirectoryEntry(
        string.Format("IIS://{0}/w3svc", server),
            "Domain/UserCode", "Password"))
{
```

Once the connection is established, the web server schema entry is specified to show where the IIS settings are kept (`IIsWebServer`). The `DirectoryEntry` has a property that allows access to its children (`Children`), and the `SchemaClassName` is checked for each entry to see if it is in the web server settings section. Once the web server settings are found, the web root node is located, and from there, the `HttpErrors` property is retrieved. `HttpErrors` is a comma-delimited string that indicates the HTTP error code, the HTTP suberror code, the message type, and the path to the HTML file to serve when this error occurs. To accomplish this, just write a LINQ query to get all of the `HttpErrors`, as shown in Example 14-3. Once the `HttpErrors` are retrieved, use the `Split` method to break this into a string array that allows the code to access the individual values and write them out. The code for carrying out these operations is shown in Example 14-3.

Example 14-3. Finding custom error pages

```
if (w3svc != null)
{
    // Use a regular query expression to
    // select the http errors for all web sites on the machine.
    var httpErrors = from site in
                        w3svc.Children.OfType<DirectoryEntry>()
                      where site.SchemaClassName == WebServerSchema
                      from siteDir in
                        site.Children.OfType<DirectoryEntry>()
                      where siteDir.Name == "ROOT"
                      from httpError in siteDir.Properties["HttpErrors"].OfType<string>
()
                      select httpError;

    // Use eager evaluation to convert this to the array
    // so that we don't requery on each iteration.  We would miss
    // updates to the metabase that occur during execution, but
    // that is a small price to pay versus the requery cost.
    // This will force the evaluation of the query now once.
    string[] errors = httpErrors.ToArray();
    foreach (var httpError in errors)
    {
        //400,*,FILE,C:\WINDOWS\help\iisHelp\common\400.htm
        string[] errorParts = httpError.ToString().Split(',');
        Console.WriteLine("Error Mapping Entry:");
        Console.WriteLine("\tHTTP error code: {0}", errorParts[0]);
        Console.WriteLine("\tHTTP sub-error code: {0}", errorParts[1]);
        Console.WriteLine("\tMessage Type: {0}", errorParts[2]);
        Console.WriteLine("\tPath to error HTML file: {0}", errorParts[3]);
    }
}
```

This could of course have been done without using LINQ to query the metabase and would have looked like Example 14-4.

Example 14-4. Finding custom error pages without LINQ

```
// Can't talk to the metabase for some reason: bail.
if (w3svc != null)
{
    foreach (DirectoryEntry site in w3svc.Children)
    {
        if (site != null)
        {
            using (site)
            {
                // Check all web servers on this box.
                if (site.SchemaClassName == WebServerSchema)
                {
                    // Get the metabase entry for this server.
                    string metabaseDir =
                        string.Format("/w3svc/{0}/ROOT", site.Name);
```

Example 14-4. Finding custom error pages without LINQ (continued)

```csharp
                    if (site.Children != null)
                    {
                        // Find the root directory for each server.
                        foreach (DirectoryEntry root in site.Children)
                        {
                            using (root)
                            {
                                // Did we find the root dir for this site?
                                if (root != null &&
                                    root.Name.Equals("ROOT",
                                        StringComparison.OrdinalIgnoreCase))
                                {
                                    // Get the HttpErrors.
                                    if (root.Properties.Contains("HttpErrors") ==
true)
                                    {
                                        // Write them out.
                                        PropertyValueCollection httpErrors =
root.Properties["HttpErrors"];

                                        if (httpErrors != null)
                                        {
                                            for (int i = 0; i < httpErrors.Count; i++)
                                            {
//400,*,FILE,C:\WINDOWS\help\iisHelp\common\400.htm
                                                string[] errorParts = httpErrors[i].
ToString().Split(',');

                                                Console.WriteLine("Error Mapping
Entry:");

                                                Console.WriteLine("\tHTTP error code:
{0}", errorParts[0]);

                                                Console.WriteLine("\tHTTP sub-error
code: {0}", errorParts[1]);

                                                Console.WriteLine("\tMessage Type:
{0}", errorParts[2]);

                                                Console.WriteLine("\tPath to error
HTML file: {0}", errorParts[3]);
                                            }
                                        }
                                    }
                                }
                            }
                        }
                    }
                }
            }
        }
    }
}
```

At this point, an application could cache these settings for mapping its own error results, or it could dynamically modify the error pages to provide customized content. The important thing to take away is that the settings information for the web server is readily available to all applications with a bit of coding.

Discussion

`System.DirectoryServices.DirectoryEntry` is usually used for Active Directory programming, but it is able to use any of the providers that are available for Active Directory as well. This approach allows code to examine the IIS metabase for both the older style IIS 5.x metabases as well as the newer IIS 6.0 metabase that ships with Windows Server 2003.

In example 14-3, where LINQ was used to query the metabase, a number of interesting things are occurring. The query is walking the metabase hierarchy to retrieve the `HttpErrors`, but it should be noted that the `DirectoryEntry.Children` property is a `DirectoryEntries` collection class. `DirectoryEntries` does support `IEnumerable`, but it does not support `IEnumerable<T>`, which LINQ uses to do its work. The `OfType<DirectoryEntry>` extension method returns the strongly typed `IEnumerable<DirectoryEntry>` from the `IEnumerable` interface supported by `DirectoryEntries`. This is done to find the web site and the root directory and then `OfType<string>` is used to get an enumerable list of strings with the `HttpErrors` in it:

```
// Use a regular query expression to
// select the http errors for all web sites on the machine.
var httpErrors = from site in
                    w3svc.Children.OfType<DirectoryEntry>()
                 where site.SchemaClassName == WebServerSchema
                 from siteDir in
                    site.Children.OfType<DirectoryEntry>()
                 where siteDir.Name == "ROOT"
                 from httpError in siteDir.Properties["HttpErrors"].OfType<string>()
                 select httpError;
```

The query is written using the usual query expression syntax, but it could also be built using what is known as "explicit dot notation" syntax. If we used explicit dot notation syntax for this query, it would look like this:

```
var httpErrors = w3svc.Children.OfType<DirectoryEntry>()
                    .Where(site => site.SchemaClassName == WebServerSchema)
                    .SelectMany(siteDir => siteDir.Children.OfType<DirectoryEntry>())
                    .Where(siteDir => siteDir.Name == "ROOT")
                    .SelectMany<DirectoryEntry, string>(siteDir =>
                    siteDir.Properties["HttpErrors"].OfType<string>());
```

The use of SelectMany is implied in the normal query syntax through the use of multiple from statements. SelectMany allows the query to collapse the results into a single set so that we have IEnumerable<string> as the httpErrors result; if Select was used, it would be IEnumerable<IEnumerable<string>>, which would be a set of string collections instead of one contiguous collection.

In order to build the query in the first place, it can be easier to start out with separate smaller queries and then combine them. When using the explicit dot notation syntax, this is easily recombined as can be seen with the following subqueries:

```
// Break up the query using Explicit dot notation into getting the site, then the
http error
// property values.
var sites = w3svc.Children.OfType<DirectoryEntry>()
            .Where(child => child.SchemaClassName == WebServerSchema)
            .SelectMany(child => child.Children.OfType<DirectoryEntry>());

var httpErrors = sites
                .Where(site => site.Name == "ROOT")
                .SelectMany<DirectoryEntry,string>(site =>
                    site.Properties["HttpErrors"].OfType<string>());

// Combine the query using Explicit dot notation.
var combinedHttpErrors = w3svc.Children.OfType<DirectoryEntry>()
                        .Where(site => site.SchemaClassName == WebServerSchema)
                        .SelectMany(siteDir => siteDir.Children.
OfType<DirectoryEntry>())
                        .Where(siteDir => siteDir.Name == "ROOT")
                        .SelectMany<DirectoryEntry, string>(siteDir =>
                        siteDir.Properties["HttpErrors"].OfType<string>());
```

See Also

The "SelectMany<TSource, TResult> method," "OfType<TResult> method," "HttpErrors [IIS]," "IIS Metabase Properties," and "DirectoryEntry Class" topics in the MSDN documentation.

CHAPTER 15

XML

15.0 Introduction

Extensible Markup Language (XML) is a simple, portable, and flexible way to represent data in a structured format. XML is used in a myriad of ways, from acting as the foundation of web-based messaging protocols such as SOAP, to being one of the more popular ways to store configuration data (such as the *web.config*, *machine.config*, or *security.config* files in the .NET Framework). Microsoft recognized the usefulness of XML to developers and has done a nice job of giving you choices concerning the trade-offs involved. Sometimes you want to simply run through an XML document looking for a value in a read-only cursorlike fashion; other times you need to be able to randomly access various pieces of the document; and sometimes, it is handy to be able to query and work with XML declaratively. Microsoft provides classes such as XmlReader and XmlWriter for lighter access and XmlDocument for full Document Object Model (DOM) processing support. In order to support querying an XML document or constructing XML declaratively, LINQ to XML (also known as XLINQ) is provided in C# 3.0 in the form of the XElement and XDocument classes.

It is likely that you will be dealing with XML in .NET to one degree or another. This chapter explores some of the uses for XML and XML-based technologies such as XPath and XSLT as well as showing how these technologies are used by and sometimes replaced by LINQ to XML. It also explores topics such as XML validation and transformation of XML to HTML.

15.1 Reading and Accessing XML Data in Document Order

Problem

You need to read in all the elements of an XML document and obtain information about each element, such as its name and attributes.

Solution

Create an XmlReader and use its Read method to process the document as shown in Example 15-1.

Example 15-1. Reading an XML document

```
using System;
using System.Xml;
using System.Xml.Linq;

namespace CSharpRecipes
{
    public class AccessXml
    {
        public static void AccessXml()
        {
            // New LINQ to XML syntax for constructing XML
            XDocument xDoc = new XDocument(
                            new XDeclaration("1.0", "UTF-8", "yes"),
                            new XComment("My sample XML"),
                            new XProcessingInstruction("myProcessingInstruction",
                                "value"),
                            new XElement("Root",
                                new XElement("Node1",
                                    new XAttribute("nodeId", "1"), "FirstNode"),
                                new XElement("Node2",
                                    new XAttribute("nodeId", "2"), "SecondNode"),
                                new XElement("Node3",
                                    new XAttribute("nodeId", "1"), "ThirdNode")
                            )
                        );

            // write out the XML to the console
            Console.WriteLine(xDoc.ToString());

            // create an XmlReader from the XDocument
            XmlReader reader = xDoc.CreateReader();
            reader.Settings.CheckCharacters = true;
            int level = 0;
            while (reader.Read())
            {
                switch (reader.NodeType)
                {
                    case XmlNodeType.CDATA:
                        Display(level, "CDATA: {0}", reader.Value);
                        break;
                    case XmlNodeType.Comment:
                        Display(level, "COMMENT: {0}", reader.Value);
                        break;
                    case XmlNodeType.DocumentType:
                        Display(level, "DOCTYPE: {0}={1}",
                                reader.Name, reader.Value);
                        break;
```

Example 15-1. Reading an XML document (continued)

```
                        case XmlNodeType.Element:
                            Display(level, "ELEMENT: {0}", reader.Name);
                            level++;
                            while (reader.MoveToNextAttribute())
                            {
                                Display(level, "ATTRIBUTE: {0}='{1}'",
                                        reader.Name, reader.Value);
                            }
                            break;
                        case XmlNodeType.EndElement:
                            level--;
                            break;
                        case XmlNodeType.EntityReference:
                            Display(level, "ENTITY: {0}", reader.Name);
                            break;
                        case XmlNodeType.ProcessingInstruction:
                            Display(level, "INSTRUCTION: {0}={1}",
                                        reader.Name, reader.Value);
                            break;
                        case XmlNodeType.Text:
                            Display(level, "TEXT: {0}", reader.Value);
                            break;
                        case XmlNodeType.XmlDeclaration:
                            Display(level, "DECLARATION: {0}={1}",
                                        reader.Name, reader.Value);
                            break;
                    }
                }
            }

        private static void Display(int indentLevel, string format,
                                    params object[] args)
        {
            for (int i = 0; i < indentLevel; i++)
                Console.Write(" ");
            Console.WriteLine(format, args);
        }
    }
}
```

This code dumps the XML document in a hierarchical format:

```
<!--My sample XML-->
<?myProcessingInstruction value?>
<Root>
  <Node1 nodeId="1">FirstNode</Node1>
  <Node2 nodeId="2">SecondNode</Node2>
  <Node3 nodeId="1">ThirdNode</Node3>
</Root>
COMMENT: My sample XML
INSTRUCTION: myProcessingInstruction=value
ELEMENT: Root
 ELEMENT: Node1
```

```
ATTRIBUTE: nodeId='1'
TEXT: FirstNode
ELEMENT: Node2
ATTRIBUTE: nodeId='2'
TEXT: SecondNode
ELEMENT: Node3
ATTRIBUTE: nodeId='1'
TEXT: ThirdNode
```

Discussion

Reading existing XML and identifying different node types is one of the fundamental actions that you will need to perform when dealing with XML. The code in the Solution creates an XmlReader from a declaratively constructed XML document and then iterates over the nodes while re-creating the formatted XML for output to the console window.

The Solution shows creating an XML Document by using an XDocument and composing the XML inline using the various XML to LINQ classes such as XElement, XAttribute, XComment and so on:

```
XDocument xDoc = new XDocument(
                new XDeclaration("1.0","UTF-8","yes"),
                new XComment("My sample XML"),
                new
    XProcessingInstruction("myProcessingInstruction","value"),
                new XElement("Root",
                    new XElement("Node1",
                        new XAttribute("nodeId", "1"), "FirstNode"),
                    new XElement("Node2",
                        new XAttribute("nodeId", "2"), "SecondNode"),
                    new XElement("Node3",
                        new XAttribute("nodeId", "1"), "ThirdNode")
                )
            );
```

Once the XDocument has been established, the settings for the XmlReader need to be set up on an XmlReaderSettings object instance via the XmlReader.Settings property. These settings tell the XmlReader to check for any illegal characters in the XML fragment:

```
// create an XmlReader from the XDocument
XmlReader reader = xDoc.CreateReader();
reader.Settings.CheckCharacters = true;
```

The while loop iterates over the XML by reading one node at a time and examining the NodeType property of the current node that the reader is on to determine what type of XML node it is:

```
while (reader.Read())
{
    switch (reader.NodeType)
    {
```

The NodeType property is an XmlNodeType enumeration value that specifies the types of XML nodes that can be present. The XmlNodeType enumeration values are shown in Table 15-1.

Table 15-1. The XmlNodeType enumeration values

Name	Description
Attribute	An attribute node of an element.
CDATA	A marker for sections of text to escape that would usually be treated as markup.
Comment	A comment in the XML: `<!--my comment -->`
Document	The root of the XML document tree.
DocumentFragment	Document fragment node.
DocumentType	The document type declaration.
Element	An element tag: `<myelement>`
EndElement	An end element tag: `</myelement>`
EndEntity	Returned at the end of an entity after calling ResolveEntity.
Entity	Entity declaration.
EntityReference	A reference to an entity.
None	This is the node returned if Read has not yet been called on the XmlReader.
Notation	A notation in the DTD (document type definition).
ProcessingInstruction	The processing instruction: `<?pi myProcessingInstruction?>`
SignificantWhitespace	Whitespace when mixed content model is used or when whitespace is being preserved.
Text	Text content for a node.
Whitespace	The whitespace between markup entries.
XmlDeclaration	The first node in the document that cannot have children: `<?xml version='1.0'?>`

See Also

The "XmlReader Class," "XmlNodeType Enumeration," and "XDocument Class" topics in the MSDN documentation.

15.2   Reading XML on the Web

Problem

Given a URL that points to an XML document, you need to grab the XML.

Solution

Use the XDocument constructor that takes a URL as a parameter:

```
// This requires you set up a virtual directory pointing
// to the sample.xml file included with the sample code
// prior to executing this.
string url = "http://localhost/xml/sample.xml";
XDocument xDoc = XDocument.Load(url);
var query = from e in xDoc.Descendants()
            where e.NodeType == XmlNodeType.Element
            select new
            {
                ElementName = e.Name.ToString(),
                ElementValue = e.Value
            };

foreach(var elementInfo in query)
{
    Console.WriteLine("Element Name: {0}, Value: {1}",
        elementInfo.ElementName,elementInfo.ElementValue);
}
```

Or if you don't want to use LINQ for XML, use the XmlReader constructor that takes a URI as a parameter:

```
string url = "http://localhost/xml/sample.xml";
using (XmlReader reader = XmlReader.Create(url))
{
    while (reader.Read())
    {
        switch (reader.NodeType)
        {
            case XmlNodeType.Element:
                Console.Write("\r\nElement Name: {0}, Value: ",
                    reader.Name);
                break;
            case XmlNodeType.Text:
                Console.Write(reader.Value);
                break;
            case XmlNodeType.CDATA:
                Console.Write(reader.Value);
                break;
        }
    }
}
```

Discussion

By using the Load method on XDocument or XElement, you can quickly load an XML document from the Web and then query it for a set of elements using LINQ. Once the set of elements is returned, a simple foreach loop allows access to the individual elements.

Retrieving XML and examining all of the elements can also be achieved using the `XmlReader.Create` method with a URI. This uses an instance of the `XmlUrlResolver` class to check the URI passed in and then opens a stream to the XML document indicated by the URI. To specify settings on the reader, there is a second overload of `Create` that also takes an `XmlReaderSettings` instance to facilitate this.

The *sample.xml* file being referenced in this code is set up in a virtual directory named *xml* on the local system. The code retrieves the *sample.xml* file from the web server and displays all of the elements in the XML.

sample.xml contains the following XML data:

```
<?xml version='1.0'?>
<!-- My sample XML -->
<?pi myProcessingInstruction?>
<Root>
    <Node1 nodeId='1'>First Node</Node1>
    <Node2 nodeId='2'>Second Node</Node2>
    <Node3 nodeId='3'>Third Node</Node3>
    <Node4><![CDATA[<>\&']]></Node4>
</Root>
```

See Also

The "XDocument Class" and "XmlReader Class" topics in the MSDN documentation.

15.3   Querying the Contents of an XML Document

Problem

You have a large and complex XML document, and you need to find various pieces of information, such as all the information contained within a specific element and having a particular attribute setting. You want to query the XML structure without having to iterate through all the nodes in the XML document and search for a particular item by hand.

Solution

Use the new Language Integrated Query (LINQ) to XML API to query the XML document for the items of interest. LINQ allows you to select elements based on element and attribute values, order the results, and return an `IEnumerable`-based collection of the resulting data, as shown in Example 15-2.

Example 15-2. Querying an XML document with LINQ

```
private static XDocument GetAClue()
{
    return new XDocument(
                new XDeclaration("1.0", "UTF-8", "yes"),
```

Example 15-2. Querying an XML document with LINQ (continued)

```
                new XElement("Clue",
                    new XElement("Participant",
                        new XAttribute("type", "Perpetrator"), "Professor Plum"),
                    new XElement("Participant",
                        new XAttribute("type", "Witness"), "Colonel Mustard"),
                    new XElement("Participant",
                        new XAttribute("type", "Witness"), "Mrs. White"),
                    new XElement("Participant",
                        new XAttribute("type", "Witness"), "Mrs. Peacock"),
                    new XElement("Participant",
                        new XAttribute("type", "Witness"), "Mr. Green"),
                    new XElement("Participant",
                        new XAttribute("type", "Witness"), "Miss Scarlet"),
                    new XElement("Participant",
                        new XAttribute("type", "Victim"), "Mr. Boddy")
                )
            );
}
```

Notice how similar the structure of the XML and the structure of the code is when
using LINQ to construct this XML fragment in the GetAClue method:

```
public static void QueryXml( )
{    XDocument xDoc = GetAClue( );


     // set up the query looking for the married female participants
     // who were witnesses
     var query = from p in xDoc.Root.Elements("Participant")
                 where p.Attribute("type").Value == "Witness" &&
                     p.Value.Contains("Mrs.")
                 orderby (string) p.Value
                 select (string) p.Value;

     // write out the nodes found (Mrs. Peacock and Mrs. White,
     // in this instance) as it is sorted
     foreach (string s in query)
     {
         Console.WriteLine(s);
     }
```

This outputs the following for the LINQ to XML example:

```
Mrs. Peacock
Mrs. White
```

To query an XML document without LINQ, you could also use XPath. In .NET, this
means using the System.Xml.XPath namespace and classes such as XPathDocument,
XPathNavigator, and XPathNodeIterator. LINQ to XML also supports using XPath to
identify items in a query through the XElement.XPathSelectElements method. To see
this method in action, check out Recipe 15.9.

In the following example, you use these classes to select nodes from an XML document that holds members from the board game Clue (or Cluedo, as it is known abroad) and their various roles. You want to be able to select the married female participants who were witnesses to the crime. In order to do this, pass an XPath expression to query the XML dataset, as shown in Example 15-3.

Example 15-3. Querying an XML document with XPath

```
public static void QueryXML( )
{
    XDocument xDoc = GetAClue( );

    using (StringReader reader = new StringReader(xDoc.ToString( )))
    {
        // Instantiate an XPathDocument using the StringReader.
        XPathDocument xpathDoc = new XPathDocument(reader);

        // Get the navigator.
        XPathNavigator xpathNav = xpathDoc.CreateNavigator( );

        // Get up the query looking for the married female participants
        // who were witnesses.
        string xpathQuery =
            "/Clue/Participant[attribute::type='Witness'][contains(text( ),'Mrs.')]";
        XPathExpression xpathExpr = xpathNav.Compile(xpathQuery);

        // Get the nodeset from the compiled expression.
        XPathNodeIterator xpathIter = xpathNav.Select(xpathExpr);

        // Write out the nodes found (Mrs. White and Mrs.Peacock, in this instance).
        while (xpathIter.MoveNext( ))
        {
            Console.WriteLine(xpathIter.Current.Value);
        }
    }
}
```

This outputs the following for the XPath example:

```
Mrs. White
Mrs. Peacock
```

Discussion

Query support is now a first-class citizen in C# with the addition of LINQ. LINQ to XML brings a more intuitive syntax to writing queries for most developers than XPath and, as such, is a welcome addition to the language. XPath is a valuable tool to have in your arsenal if you are dealing with systems that deal with XML extensively, but in many cases, you know what you want to ask for; you just don't know the syntax in XPath. For developers with even minimal SQL experience, querying in C# just got a lot easier:

The XML being worked on in this recipe looks like this:

```
<?xml version='1.0'?>
<Clue>
    <Participant type='Perpetrator'>Professor Plum</Participant>
    <Participant type='Witness'>Colonel Mustard</Participant>
    <Participant type='Witness'>Mrs. White</Participant>
    <Participant type='Witness'>Mrs. Peacock</Participant>
    <Participant type='Witness'>Mr. Green</Participant>
</Clue>;
```

This query says "select all of the Participant elements where the Participant is a witness and their title is "Mrs:"

```
// set up the query looking for the married female participants
// who were witnesses
var query = from p in xDoc.Root.Elements("Participant")
            where p.Attribute("type").Value == "Witness" &&
                p.Value.Contains("Mrs.")
            orderby (string) p.Value
            select (string) p.Value;
```

Contrast this with the same query syntax in XPath:

```
// set up the query looking for the married female participants
// who were witnesses
string xpathQuery =
    "/Clue/Participant[attribute::type='Witness'][contains(text(),'Mrs.')]";
```

Both ways of performing the query have merit, but the issue to consider is how easily will the next developer be able to understand what you have written. It is very easy to break code that is not well understood. Generally, more developers understand SQL than XPath, even with all of the web service work today. This may differ from your experience, but the point is to think of LINQ as not just another syntax, but as a way to make your code more readable by a broader audience of developers. Code is rarely owned by one person, even in the short term, so why not make it easy for those who come after you? After all, you may be on the other side of that coin someday. Let's break down the two queries a bit more. The LINQ query uses some of the new keywords in C# 3.0:

- var indicates to the compiler to expect an inferred type based on the result set.
- from, which is known as the generator, provides a data source for the query to operate on as well as a range variable to allow access to the individual element.
- where allows for a Boolean condition to be applied to each element of the data source to determine if it should be included in the result set.
- orderby determines the sort order of the result set based on the number of elements and indicators of ascending or descending per element. Multiple criteria can be specified for multiple levels of sorting.
- select indicates the sequence of values that will be returned after all evaluation of conditions. This is also referred to as projection of the values.

This means that our syntax can be boiled down as follows:

- from p in xDoc.Root.Elements("Participant") says "Get all of the Participants under the root-level node Clue."
- where p.Attribute("type").Value == "Witness" says "Select only Participants with an attribute called type with a value of Witness."
- && p.Value.Contains("Mrs.") says "Select only Participants with a value that contains 'Mrs.'"
- orderby (string) p.Value says "Order the participants by name in ascending order."
- select (string) p.Value says "Select the value of the Participant elements where all of the previous criteria have been met."

The XPath syntax performs the same function:

- /Clue/Participant says "Get all of the Participants under the root-level node Clue."
- Participant[attribute::type='Witness'] says "Select only Participants with an attribute called type with a value of Witness."
- Participant[contains(text(),'Mrs.')] says "Select only Participants with a value that contains 'Mrs.'"

Put them all together and you get all of the married female participants who were witnesses in both cases with the additional twist for LINQ that it sorted the results as well.

See Also

The "Query Expressions," "XElement Class," and "XPath, reading XML" topics in the MSDN documentation.

15.4 Validating XML

Problem

You are accepting an XML document created by another source, and you want to verify that it conforms to a specific schema. This schema may be in the form of an XML schema (XSD or XML—XDR); alternatively, you want the flexibility to use a document type definition (DTD) to validate the XML.

Solution

Use the XDocument.Validate method and XmlReader.Settings property to validate XML documents against any descriptor document, such as an XSD, a DTD, or an XDR, as shown in Example 15-4.

Example 15-4. Validating XML

```
public static void ValidateXml( )
{
    // open the bookbad.xml file
    XDocument book = XDocument.Load(@"..\..\BookBad.xml");
    // create XSD schema collection with book.xsd
    XmlSchemaSet schemas = new XmlSchemaSet( );
    schemas.Add(null,@"..\..\Book.xsd");
    // wire up handler to get any validation errors
    book.Validate(schemas, settings_ValidationEventHandler);

    // create a reader to roll over the file so validation fires
    XmlReader reader = book.CreateReader( );
    // report warnings as well as errors
    reader.Settings.ValidationFlags =
        XmlSchemaValidationFlags.ReportValidationWarnings;
    // use XML Schema
    reader.Settings.ValidationType = ValidationType.Schema;
    // roll over the XML
    while (reader.Read( ))
    {
        if (reader.NodeType == XmlNodeType.Element)
        {
            Console.Write("<{0}", reader.Name);
            while (reader.MoveToNextAttribute( ))
            {
                Console.Write(" {0}='{1}'", reader.Name,
                    reader.Value);
            }
            Console.Write(">");
        }
        else if (reader.NodeType == XmlNodeType.Text)
        {
            Console.Write(reader.Value);
        }
        else if (reader.NodeType == XmlNodeType.EndElement)
        {
            Console.WriteLine("</{0}>", reader.Name);
        }
    }
}

private static void settings_ValidationEventHandler(object sender,
                                ValidationEventArgs e)
{
        Console.WriteLine("Validation Error Message: {0}", e.Message);
        Console.WriteLine("Validation Error Severity: {0}", e.Severity);
```

Example 15-4. Validating XML (continued)

```
    if (e.Exception != null)
    {
        Console.WriteLine("Validation Error Line Number: {0}",
                e.Exception.LineNumber);
        Console.WriteLine("Validation Error Line Position: {0}",
                e.Exception.LinePosition);
        Console.WriteLine("Validation Error Source: {0}",
                e.Exception.Source);
        Console.WriteLine("Validation Error Source Schema: {0}",
                e.Exception.SourceSchemaObject);
        Console.WriteLine("Validation Error Source Uri: {0}",
                e.Exception.SourceUri);
        Console.WriteLine("Validation Error thrown from: {0}",
                e.Exception.TargetSite);
        Console.WriteLine("Validation Error callstack: {0}",
                e.Exception.StackTrace);
    }
}
```

Discussion

The Solution illustrates how to use the XDocument and XmlReader to validate the *book.xml* document against a *book.xsd* XSD definition file. DTDs were the original way to specify the structure of an XML document, but it has become more common to use XSD since it reached W3C Recommendation status in May 2001. XDR was a predecessor of XSD provided by Microsoft, and, while it might be encountered in existing systems, it should not be used for new development.

The first thing to do is create an XmlSchemaSet to hold your XSD (*book.xsd*) and call the Add method to add the XSD to the XmlSchemaSet. Call the Validate method on the XDocument with the XmlSchemaSet and the handler method for validation events. Now that the validation is mostly set up, a few more items can be set on the XmlReader created from the XDocument. The ValidationFlags property on the XmlReaderSettings allows for signing up for warnings in validation, processing identity constraints during validation, process inline schemas, and allows for attributes that may not be defined in the schema:

```
    // create XSD schema collection with book.xsd
    XmlSchemaSet schemas = new XmlSchemaSet();
    schemas.Add(null,@"..\..\Book.xsd");
    // wire up handler to get any validation errors
    book.Validate(schemas, settings_ValidationEventHandler);
    // create a reader to roll over the file so validation fires
    XmlReader reader = book.CreateReader();
    // report warnings as well as errors
    reader.Settings.ValidationFlags = XmlSchemaValidationFlags.
ReportValidationWarnings;
    // use XML Schema
    reader.Settings.ValidationType = ValidationType.Schema;
```

To perform DTD validation, use a DTD and ValidationType.DTD, and to perform XDR validation, use an XDR schema and ValidationType. XDR.

The settings_ValidationEventHandler function then examines the ValidationEventArgs object passed when a validation error occurs and writes the pertinent information to the console:

```
private static void settings_ValidationEventHandler(object sender,
                                  ValidationEventArgs e)
{
    Console.WriteLine("Validation Error Message: {0}", e.Message);
    Console.WriteLine("Validation Error Severity: {0}", e.Severity);
    if (e.Exception != null)
    {
        Console.WriteLine("Validation Error Line Number: {0}",
                e.Exception.LineNumber);
        Console.WriteLine("Validation Error Line Position: {0}",
                e.Exception.LinePosition);
        Console.WriteLine("Validation Error Source: {0}",
                e.Exception.Source);
        Console.WriteLine("Validation Error Source Schema: {0}",
                e.Exception.SourceSchemaObject);
        Console.WriteLine("Validation Error Source Uri: {0}",
                e.Exception.SourceUri);
        Console.WriteLine("Validation Error thrown from: {0}",
                e.Exception.TargetSite);
        Console.WriteLine("Validation Error callstack: {0}",
                e.Exception.StackTrace);
    }
}
```

You then proceed to roll over the XML document and write out the elements and attributes:

```
// Read all nodes and print out.
while (reader.Read())
{
    if(reader.NodeType == XmlNodeType.Element)
    {
        Console.Write("<{0}", reader.Name);
        while (reader.MoveToNextAttribute())
        {
            Console.Write(" {0}='{1}'", reader.Name,
                    reader.Value);
        }
        Console.Write(">");
    }
    else if (reader.NodeType == XmlNodeType.Text)
    {
        Console.Write(reader.Value);
    }
```

```
            else if (reader.NodeType == XmlNodeType.EndElement)
            {
                Console.WriteLine("</{0}>", reader.Name);
            }
        }
    }
```

The *BookBad.xml* file contains the following:

```
<?xml version="1.0" encoding="utf-8"?>
<Book xmlns="http://tempuri.org/Book.xsd" name="C# Cookbook">
    <Chapter>File System IO</Chapter>
    <Chapter>Security</Chapter>
    <Chapter>Data Structures and Algorithms</Chapter>
    <Chapter>Reflection</Chapter>
    <Chapter>Threading and Synchronization</Chapter>
    <Chapter>Numbers and Enumerations</Chapter>
    <BadElement>I don't belong here</BadElement>
    <Chapter>Strings and Characters</Chapter>
    <Chapter>Classes And Structures</Chapter>
    <Chapter>Collections</Chapter>
    <Chapter>XML</Chapter>
    <Chapter>Delegates, Events, and Anonymous Methods</Chapter>
    <Chapter>Diagnostics</Chapter>
    <Chapter>Toolbox</Chapter>
    <Chapter>Unsafe Code</Chapter>
    <Chapter>Regular Expressions</Chapter>
    <Chapter>Generics</Chapter>
    <Chapter>Iterators and Partial Types</Chapter>
    <Chapter>Exception Handling</Chapter>
    <Chapter>Web</Chapter>
    <Chapter>Networking</Chapter>
</Book>
```

The *book.xsd* file contains the following:

```
<?xml version="1.0" ?>
<xs:schema id="NewDataSet" targetNamespace="http://tempuri.org/Book.xsd"
xmlns:mstns="http://tempuri.org/Book.xsd"
    xmlns="http://tempuri.org/Book.xsd"
    xmlns:xs="http://www.w3.org/2001/XMLSchema"
    xmlns:msdata="urn:schemas-microsoft-com:xml-msdata"
    attributeFormDefault="qualified" elementFormDefault="qualified">
    <xs:element name="Book">
        <xs:complexType>
            <xs:sequence>
                <xs:element name="Chapter" nillable="true"
                    minOccurs="0" maxOccurs="unbounded">
                    <xs:complexType>
                        <xs:simpleContent
                            msdata:ColumnName="Chapter_Text" msdata:Ordinal="0">
                            <xs:extension base="xs:string">
                            </xs:extension>
                        </xs:simpleContent>
                    </xs:complexType>
                </xs:element>
```

```
            </xs:sequence>
            <xs:attribute name="name" form="unqualified" type="xs:string"/>
        </xs:complexType>
    </xs:element>
</xs:schema>
```

When this is run, the following output is generated, showing the validation failure occurring on BadElement:

```
<Book xmlns='http://tempuri.org/Book.xsd' name='C# Cookbook'><Chapter>File System
IO</Chapter>
<Chapter>Security</Chapter>
<Chapter>Data Structures and Algorithms</Chapter>
<Chapter>Reflection</Chapter>
<Chapter>Threading and Synchronization</Chapter>
<Chapter>Numbers and Enumerations</Chapter>
Validation Error Message: The element 'Book' in namespace 'http://tempuri.org/Book.
xsd' has invalid child element 'BadElement' in namespace 'http://tempuri.org/Book.
xsd'. List of possible elements expected: 'Chapter' in namespace 'http://tempuri.org/
Book.xsd'.
Validation Error Severity: Error
Validation Error Line Number: 9
Validation Error Line Position: 6
Validation Error Source:
Validation Error Source Schema:
Validation Error Source Uri: file:///C:/PRJ32/Book_2_0/C%23Cookbook2/Code/
CSharpRecipes/BookBad.xml
Validation Error thrown from:
Validation Error callstack:
<BadElement>I don't belong here</BadElement>
<Chapter>Strings and Characters</Chapter>
<Chapter>Classes And Structures</Chapter>
<Chapter>Collections</Chapter>
<Chapter>XML</Chapter>
<Chapter>Delegates, Events, and Anonymous Methods</Chapter>
<Chapter>Diagnostics</Chapter>
<Chapter>Toolbox</Chapter>
<Chapter>Unsafe Code</Chapter>
<Chapter>Regular Expressions</Chapter>
<Chapter>Generics</Chapter>
<Chapter>Iterators and Partial Types</Chapter>
<Chapter>Exception Handling</Chapter>
<Chapter>Web</Chapter>
<Chapter>Networking</Chapter>
</Book>
```

See Also

The "XmlReader Class," "XmlSchemaSet Class," "ValidationEventHandler Class," "ValidationType Enumeration," and "XDocument Class" topics in the MSDN documentation.

15.5   Creating an XML Document Programmatically

Problem

You have data that you want to put into a more structured form, such as an XML document.

Solution

Suppose you have the information shown in Table 15-2 for an address book that you want to turn into XML.

Table 15-2. Sample address book data

Name	Phone
Tim	999-888-0000
Newman	666-666-6666
Harold	777-555-3333

Use XElement to create the XML for this table:

```
XElement addressBook = new XElement("AddressBook",
                            new XElement("Contact",
                                new XAttribute("name", "Tim"),
                                new XAttribute("phone", "999-888-0000")),
                            new XElement("Contact",
                                new XAttribute("name", "Newman"),
                                new XAttribute("phone", "666-666-6666")),
                            new XElement("Contact",
                                new XAttribute("name", "Harold"),
                                new XAttribute("phone", "777-555-3333")));
// Display XML
Console.WriteLine("Generated XML from XElement:\r\n{0}", addressBook.ToString());
```

This method will give you output like this:

```
<AddressBook>
    <Contact name="Tim" phone="999-888-0000" />
    <Contact name="Newman" phone="666-666-6666" />
    <Contact name="Harold" phone="777-555-3333" />
</AddressBook>
```

Another approach would be to use the XmlWriter to create XML for this table:

```
XmlWriterSettings settings = new XmlWriterSettings();
settings.Indent = true;
using (XmlWriter writer = XmlWriter.Create(Console.Out, settings))
{
    writer.WriteStartElement("AddressBook");
    writer.WriteStartElement("Contact");
    writer.WriteAttributeString("name", "Tim");
    writer.WriteAttributeString("phone", "999-888-0000");
```

```
        writer.WriteEndElement( );
        writer.WriteStartElement("Contact");
        writer.WriteAttributeString("name", "Newman");
        writer.WriteAttributeString("phone", "666-666-6666");
        writer.WriteEndElement( );
        writer.WriteStartElement("Contact");
        writer.WriteAttributeString("name", "Harold");
        writer.WriteAttributeString("phone", "777-555-3333");
        writer.WriteEndElement( );
        writer.WriteEndElement( );
    }
```

This method will give you similar output like this:

```
<AddressBook>
    <Contact name="Tim" phone="999-888-0000" />
    <Contact name="Newman" phone="666-666-6666" />
    <Contact name="Harold" phone="777-555-3333" />
</AddressBook>
```

Or you can use the XmlDocument class to programmatically construct the XML:

```
public static void CreateXml( )
{
    // Start by making an XmlDocument.
    XmlDocument xmlDoc = new XmlDocument( );
    // Create a root node for the document.
    XmlElement addrBook = xmlDoc.CreateElement("AddressBook");
    xmlDoc.AppendChild(addrBook);
    // Create the Tim contact.
    XmlElement contact = xmlDoc.CreateElement("Contact");
    contact.SetAttribute("name","Tim");
    contact.SetAttribute("phone","999-888-0000");
    addrBook.AppendChild(contact);
    // Create the Newman contact.
    contact = xmlDoc.CreateElement("Contact");
    contact.SetAttribute("name","Newman");
    contact.SetAttribute("phone","666-666-6666");
    addrBook.AppendChild(contact);
    // Create the Harold contact.
    contact = xmlDoc.CreateElement("Contact");
    contact.SetAttribute("name","Harold");
    contact.SetAttribute("phone","777-555-3333");
    addrBook.AppendChild(contact);
    // Display XML.
    Console.WriteLine("Generated XML:\r\n{0}",addrBook.OuterXml);
    Console.WriteLine( );
}
```

This method gives the output like this:

```
Generated XML:
<AddressBook><Contact name="Tim" phone="999-888-0000" /><Contact name="Newman"
phone="666-666-6666" /><Contact name="Harold" phone="777-555-3333" /></AddressBook>
```

All methods produce the same XML, but the first and second methods are formatted with indents.

Discussion

Now that you have seen three ways to do this, the question arises: "Which one to use?"

Use XmlDocument when

- Traditional DOM methodology is appropriate.
- The whole document in needed in memory.
- In-memory forward and backward traversal and/or updating is necessary.

Use XmlReader / XmlWriter when

- A streaming methodology is necessary.
- The fastest processing is absolutely required.
- Larger documents are being processed and cannot be loaded all at once.

Use XElement / XDocument when

- Constructing XML declaratively in code (much easier than other methods).
- The querying power of LINQ can assist on top of a streaming methodology.
- A more readable syntax for XML programming for most developers is desired.
- In-memory traversal with query semantics is desired (XDocument).

See Also

The "XElement Class," "XmlDocument Class," "XML Document Object Model (DOM)," "XmlReader Class," and "XmlWriter Class" topics in the MSDN documentation.

15.6 Detecting Changes to an XML Document

Problem

You need to inform one or more classes or components that a node in an XML document has been inserted or removed or had its value changed.

Solution

In order to track changes to an active XML document, subscribe to the events published by the XDocument class. XDocument publishes events for when a node is changing and when it has changed for both the pre- and post-conditions of a node change.

Example 15-5 shows a number of event handlers defined in the same scope as the
DetectXMLChanges method, but they could just as easily be callbacks to functions on
other classes that are interested in the manipulation of the live XML document.

DetectXMLChanges loads an XML fragment you define in the method; wires up the
event handlers for the node events; adds, changes, and removes some nodes to trigger the events; and then writes out the resulting XML.

Example 15-5. Detecting changes to an XML document

```
public static void DetectXmlChanges( )
{
    XDocument xDoc = new XDocument(
                        new XDeclaration("1.0", "UTF-8", "yes"),
                        new XComment("My sample XML"),
                        new XProcessingInstruction("myProcessingInstruction", "value"),
                        new XElement("Root",
                            new XElement("Node1",
                                new XAttribute("nodeId", "1"), "FirstNode"),
                            new XElement("Node2",
                                new XAttribute("nodeId", "2"), "SecondNode"),
                            new XElement("Node3",
                                new XAttribute("nodeId", "1"), "ThirdNode"),
                            new XElement("Node4",
                                new XCData(@"<>\&'"))
                        )
                    );
    //Create the event handlers.
    xDoc.Changing += xDoc_Changing;
    xDoc.Changed += xDoc_Changed;
    // Add a new element node.
    XElement element = new XElement("Node5", "Fifth Element");
    xDoc.Root.Add(element);

    // Change the first node
    //doc.DocumentElement.FirstChild.InnerText = "1st Node";
    if(xDoc.Root.FirstNode.NodeType == XmlNodeType.Element)
        ((XElement)xDoc.Root.FirstNode).Value = "1st Node";

    // Remove the fourth node
    var query = from e in xDoc.Descendants( )
                where (string)(string) e.Name.LocalName == "Node4"
                select (XElement)e;
    XElement[] elements = query.ToArray<XElement>( );
    foreach (XElement xelem in elements)
    {
        xelem.Remove( );
    }
    // Write out the new xml
    Console.WriteLine(xDoc.ToString( ));
    Console.WriteLine( );

}
```

Example 15-6 shows the event handlers from the XDocument, along with one formatting method, WriteElementInfo. This method takes an action string and gets the name and value of the object being manipulated. Both of the event handlers invoke this formatting method, passing the corresponding action string.

Example 15-6. XDocument event handlers and WriteElementInfo method

```
private static void xDoc_Changed(object sender, XObjectChangeEventArgs e)
{
    //Add - An XObject has been or will be added to an XContainer.
    //Name - An XObject has been or will be renamed.
    //Remove - An XObject has been or will be removed from an XContainer.
    //Value - The value of an XObject has been or will be changed.
    //In addition, a change in the serialization of an empty element
    //(either from an empty tag to start/end tag pair or vice versa) raises this event.
    WriteElementInfo("changed", e.ObjectChange, (XObject)sender);
}

private static void xDoc_Changing(object sender, XObjectChangeEventArgs e)
{
    //Add - An XObject has been or will be added to an XContainer.
    //Name - An XObject has been or will be renamed.
    //Remove - An XObject has been or will be removed from an XContainer.
    //Value - The value of an XObject has been or will be changed.
    //In addition, a change in the serialization of an empty element
    //(either from an empty tag to start/end tag pair or vice versa) raises this event.
    WriteElementInfo("changing", e.ObjectChange, (XObject)sender);
}

private static void WriteElementInfo(string action, XObjectChange change, XObject xobj)
{
    if (xobj != null)
        Console.WriteLine("XObject: <{0}> {1} {2} with value {3}",
            xobj.NodeType.ToString(), action, change.ToString(), xobj);
    else
        Console.WriteLine("XObject: {0} {1} with null value",
            action, change.ToString());
}
```

The DetectXmlChanges method results in the following output:

```
XObject: <Element> changing Add with value <Node5>Fifth Element</Node5>
XObject: <Element> changed Add with value <Node5>Fifth Element</Node5>
XObject: <Text> changing Remove with value FirstNode
XObject: <Text> changed Remove with value FirstNode
XObject: <Text> changing Add with value 1st Node
XObject: <Text> changed Add with value 1st Node
XObject: <Element> changing Remove with value <Node4><![CDATA[<>\&']]></Node4>
XObject: <Element> changed Remove with value <Node4><![CDATA[<>\&']]></Node4>

<!--My sample XML-->
<?myProcessingInstruction value?>
<Root>
  <Node1 nodeId="1">1st Node</Node1>
```

```
    <Node2 nodeId="2">SecondNode</Node2>
    <Node3 nodeId="1">ThirdNode</Node3>
    <Node5>Fifth Element</Node5>
</Root>
```

Discussion

The XDocument class is derived from the XElement class. XDocument can also contain a Document Type Declaration (DTD) (XDocumentType), a root element (XDocument.Root), comments (XComment) and processing instructions (XProcessingInstruction). Typically, you would use XElement for constructing most types of XML documents, but if you need to specify any of the above items, use XDocument.

See Also

The "XDocument Class" and "XObjectChangeEventHandler delegate" topics in the MSDN documentation.

15.7   Handling Invalid Characters in an XML String

Problem

You are creating an XML string. Before adding a tag containing a text element, you want to check it to determine whether the string contains any of the following invalid characters:

```
<
>
"
'
&
```

If any of these characters are encountered, you want them to be replaced with their escaped form:

```
&lt;
&gt;
&quot;
&apos;
&amp;
```

Solution

There are different ways to accomplish this, depending on which XML-creation approach you are using. If you are using XElement, the XCData object, or just adding the text directly as the value of the XElement will take care of the proper escaping. If you are using XmlWriter, the WriteCData, WriteString, WriteAttributeString, WriteValue, and WriteElementString methods take care of this for you. If you are using XmlDocument and XmlElements, the XmlElement.InnerText method will handle these characters.

The two ways to handle this using an XElement work like this. The XCData object will wrap the invalid character text in a CDATA section, as shown in the creation of the InvalidChars1 element in the example that follows. The other method, using XElement, is to assign the text as the value of the XElement, and that will automatically escape the text for you, as shown while creating the InvalidChars2 element:

```
// set up a string with our invalid chars
string invalidChars = @"<>\&'";
XElement element = new XElement("Root",
                        new XElement("InvalidChars1",
                            new XCData(invalidChars)),
                        new XElement("InvalidChars2",invalidChars));
Console.WriteLine("Generated XElement with Invalid Chars:\r\n{0}",
                                    element.ToString());
Console.WriteLine();
```

The output from this is:

```
Generated XElement with Invalid Chars:
<Root>
  <InvalidChars1><![CDATA[<>\&']]></InvalidChars1>
  <InvalidChars2>&lt;&gt;\&amp;'</InvalidChars2>
</Root>
```

The two ways to handle this using an XmlWriter work like this. The WriteCData method will wrap the invalid character text in a CDATA section, as shown in the creation of the InvalidChars1 element in the example that follows. The other method, using XmlWriter, is to use the WriteElementString method that will automatically escape the text for you, as shown while creating the InvalidChars2 element:

```
// Set up a string with our invalid chars.
string invalidChars = @"<>\&'";
XmlWriterSettings settings = new XmlWriterSettings();
settings.Indent = true;
using (XmlWriter writer = XmlWriter.Create(Console.Out, settings))
{
    writer.WriteStartElement("Root");
    writer.WriteStartElement("InvalidChars1");
    writer.WriteCData(invalidChars);
    writer.WriteEndElement();
    writer.WriteElementString("InvalidChars2", invalidChars);
    writer.WriteEndElement();
}
```

The output from this is:

```
<?xml version="1.0" encoding="IBM437"?>
<Root>
    <InvalidChars1><![CDATA[<>\&']]></InvalidChars1>
    <InvalidChars2>&lt;&gt;\&amp;'</InvalidChars2>
</Root>
```

There are two ways you can handle this problem with XmlDocument and XmlElement. The first way is to surround the text you are adding to the XML element with a CDATA section and add it to the InnerXML property of the XmlElement:

```
// Set up a string with our invalid chars.
string invalidChars = @"<>\&'";
XmlElement invalidElement1 = xmlDoc.CreateElement("InvalidChars1");
invalidElement1.AppendChild(xmlDoc.CreateCDataSection(invalidChars));
```

The second way is to let the XmlElement class escape the data for you by assigning the text directly to the InnerText property like this:

```
// Set up a string with our invalid chars.
string invalidChars = @"<>\&'";
XmlElement invalidElement2 = xmlDoc.CreateElement("InvalidChars2");
invalidElement2.InnerText = invalidChars;
```

The whole XmlDocument is created with these XmlElements in this code:

```
public static void HandlingInvalidChars()
{
    // Set up a string with our invalid chars.
    string invalidChars = @"<>\&'";

    XmlDocument xmlDoc = new XmlDocument();
    // Create a root node for the document.
    XmlElement root = xmlDoc.CreateElement("Root");
    xmlDoc.AppendChild(root);

    // Create the first invalid character node.
    XmlElement invalidElement1 = xmlDoc.CreateElement("InvalidChars1");
    // Wrap the invalid chars in a CDATA section and use the
    // InnerXML property to assign the value as it doesn't
    // escape the values, just passes in the text provided.
    invalidElement1.InnerXml = "<![CDATA[" + invalidChars + "]]>";
    // Append the element to the root node.
    root.AppendChild(invalidElement1);

    // Create the second invalid character node.
    XmlElement invalidElement2 = xmlDoc.CreateElement("InvalidChars2");
    // Add the invalid chars directly using the InnerText
    // property to assign the value as it will automatically
    // escape the values.
    invalidElement2.InnerText = invalidChars;
    // Append the element to the root node.
    root.AppendChild(invalidElement2);

    Console.WriteLine("Generated XML with Invalid Chars:\r\n{0}",xmlDoc.OuterXml);
    Console.WriteLine();
}
```

The XML created by this procedure (and output to the console) looks like this:

```
Generated XML with Invalid Chars:
<Root><InvalidChars1><![CDATA[<>\&']]></InvalidChars1><InvalidChars2>&lt;&gt;\
&amp;'</InvalidChars2></Root>
```

Discussion

The CDATA node allows you to represent the items in the text section as character data, not as escaped XML, for ease of entry. Normally, these characters would need to be in their escaped format (< for < and so on), but the CDATA section allows you to enter them as regular text.

When the CDATA tag is used in conjunction with the InnerXml property of the XmlElement class, you can submit characters that would normally need to be escaped first. The XmlElement class also has an InnerText property that will automatically escape any markup found in the string assigned. This allows you to add these characters without having to worry about them.

See Also

The "XElement Class," "XCData Class," "XmlDocument Class," "XmlWriter Class," "XmlElement Class," and "CDATA Sections" topics in the MSDN documentation.

15.8   Transforming XML

Problem

You have a raw XML document that you need to convert into a more readable format. For example, you have personnel data that is stored as an XML document, and you need to display it on a web page or place it in a comma-delimited text file for legacy system integration. Unfortunately, not everyone wants to sort through reams of XML all day; they would rather read the data as a formatted list or within a grid with defined columns and rows. You need a method of transforming the XML data into a more readable form as well as into the comma-delimited format.

Solution

The solution for this is to use LINQ to XML to perform a transformation in C#. In the example code, you transform some personnel data from a fictitious business stored in *Personnel.xml*. The data is first transformed into HTML, and then into comma-delimited format:

```
// LINQ way
XElement personnelData = XElement.Load(@"..\..\Personnel.xml");
// Create HTML
XElement personnelHtml =
    new XElement("html",
        new XElement("head"),
        new XElement("body",
            new XAttribute("title","Personnel"),
            new XElement("p",
                new XElement("table",
                    new XAttribute("border","1"),
```

```
                        new XElement("thead",
                            new XElement("tr",
                                new XElement("td","Employee Name"),
                                new XElement("td","Employee Title"),
                                new XElement("td","Years with Company")
                                )
                            ),
                        new XElement("tbody",
                            from p in personnelData.Elements("Employee")
                            select new XElement("tr",
                                new XElement("td",p.Attribute("name").Value),
                                new XElement("td",p.Attribute("title").Value),
                                new XElement("td", p.Attribute("companyYears").Value)
                                )
                            )
                        )
                    )
                )
            );

    personnelHtml.Save(@"..\..\Personnel_LINQ.html");

        // Create CSV output
    var queryCSV = from p in personnelData.Elements("Employee")
                    orderby p.Attribute("name").Value descending
                    select p;
    StringBuilder sb = new StringBuilder();
    foreach(XElement e in queryCSV)
    {
        sb.AppendFormat("{0},{1},{2}{3}",e.Attribute("name").Value,
            e.Attribute("title").Value,e.Attribute("companyYears").Value,
            Environment.NewLine);
    }
    using(StreamWriter writer = File.CreateText(@"..\..\Personnel_LINQ.csv"))
    {
        writer.Write(sb.ToString());
    }
```

The output from the LINQ transformation to CSV is shown here:

```
Rutherford,CEO,27
Chas,Salesman,3
Bob,Customer Service,1
Alice,Manager,12
```

The *Personnel.xml* file contains the following items:

```
<?xml version="1.0" encoding="utf-8"?>
<Personnel>
    <Employee name="Bob" title="Customer Service" companyYears="1"/>
    <Employee name="Alice" title="Manager" companyYears="12"/>
    <Employee name="Chas" title="Salesman" companyYears="3"/>
    <Employee name="Rutherford" title="CEO" companyYears="27"/>
</Personnel>
```

This can also be accomplished using an XSLT stylesheet to transform the XML into another format using the XslCompiledTransform class. First, load the stylesheet for generating HTML output and then perform the transformation to HTML via XSLT using the *PersonnelHTML.xsl* stylesheet. After that, transform the data to comma-delimited format using the *PersonnelCSV.xsl* stylesheet:

```
public static void TransformXML( )
{
    // Create a resolver with default credentials.
    XmlUrlResolver resolver = new XmlUrlResolver( );
    resolver.Credentials = System.Net.CredentialCache.DefaultCredentials;

    // Transform the personnel.xml file to html.
    XslCompiledTransform transform = new XslCompiledTransform( );
    XsltSettings settings = new XsltSettings( );
    // Disable both of these (the default) for security reasons.
    settings.EnableDocumentFunction = false;
    settings.EnableScript = false;
    // Load up the stylesheet.
    transform.Load(@"..\..\PersonnelHTML.xsl",settings,resolver);
    // Perform the transformation.
    transform.Transform(@"..\..\Personnel.xml",@"..\..\Personnel.html");


    // Or transform the Personnel.xml file to comma-delimited format.

    // Load up the stylesheet.
    transform.Load(@"..\..\PersonnelCSV.xsl",settings,resolver);
    // Perform the transformation.
    transform.Transform(@"..\..\Personnel.xml",
        @"..\..\Personnel.csv");
}
```

The *PersonnelHTML.xsl* stylesheet looks like this:

```
<?xml version="1.0" encoding="UTF-8"?>
<xsl:stylesheet version="1.0"
    xmlns:xsl="http://www.w3.org/1999/XSL/Transform"
    xmlns:xs="http://www.w3.org/2001/XMLSchema">
    <xsl:template match="/">
      <html>
        <head />
          <body title="Personnel">
            <xsl:for-each select="Personnel">
              <p>
                <xsl:for-each select="Employee">
                  <xsl:if test="position( )=1">
                      <table border="1">
                          <thead>
                              <tr>
                                <td>Employee Name</td>
                                <td>Employee Title</td>
                                <td>Years with Company</td>
                              </tr>
```

```
                                    </thead>
                                    <tbody>
                                      <xsl:for-each select="../Employee">
                                        <tr>
                                          <td>
                                            <xsl:for-each select="@name">
                                                <xsl:value-of select="." />
                                            </xsl:for-each>
                                          </td>
                                          <td>
                                            <xsl:for-each select="@title">
                                                <xsl:value-of select="." />
                                            </xsl:for-each>
                                          </td>
                                          <td>
                                            <xsl:for-each select="@companyYears">
                                                <xsl:value-of select="." />
                                            </xsl:for-each>
                                          </td>
                                        </tr>
                                            </xsl:for-each>
                                          </tbody>
                                        </table>
                                    </xsl:if>
                                </xsl:for-each>
                            </p>
                        </xsl:for-each>
                    </body>
                </html>
            </xsl:template>
        </xsl:stylesheet>
```

To generate the HTML screen in Figure 15-1, use the *PersonnelHTML.xsl* stylesheet
and the *Personnel.xml* file.

Employee Name	Employee Title	Years with Company
Bob	Customer Service	1
Alice	Manager	12
Chas	Salesman	3
Rutherford	CEO	27

Figure 15-1. Personnel HTML table generated from Personnel.xml

Here is the HTML source for the LINQ transformation:

```
<?xml version="1.0" encoding="utf-8"?>
<html>
  <head />
  <body title="Personnel">
    <p>
      <table border="1">
```

```
      <thead>
        <tr>
          <td>Employee Name</td>
          <td>Employee Title</td>
          <td>Years with Company</td>
        </tr>
      </thead>
      <tbody>
        <tr>
          <td>Bob</td>
          <td>Customer Service</td>
          <td>1</td>
        </tr>
        <tr>
          <td>Alice</td>
          <td>Manager</td>
          <td>12</td>
        </tr>
        <tr>
          <td>Chas</td>
          <td>Salesman</td>
          <td>3</td>
        </tr>
        <tr>
          <td>Rutherford</td>
          <td>CEO</td>
          <td>27</td>
        </tr>
      </tbody>
    </table>
  </p>
 </body>
</html>
```

Here is the HTML source for the XSLT transformation:

```
<html xmlns:xs="http://www.w3.org/2001/XMLSchema">
  <head>
    <META http-equiv="Content-Type" content="text/html; charset=utf-8">
  </head>
  <body title="Personnel">
    <p>
      <table border="1">
        <thead>
          <tr>
            <td>Employee Name</td>
            <td>Employee Title</td>
            <td>Years with Company</td>
          </tr>
        </thead>
        <tbody>
          <tr>
            <td>Bob</td>
            <td>Customer Service</td>
```

```
            <td>1</td>
          </tr>
          <tr>
            <td>Alice</td>
            <td>Manager</td>
            <td>12</td>
          </tr>
          <tr>
            <td>Chas</td>
            <td>Salesman</td>
            <td>3</td>
          </tr>
          <tr>
            <td>Rutherford</td>
            <td>CEO</td>
            <td>27</td>
          </tr>
        </tbody>
      </table>
    </p>
  </body>
</html>
```

To generate comma-delimited output, use *PersonnelCSV.xsl* and *Personnel.xml*; the stylesheet is shown here:

```
<?xml version="1.0" encoding="UTF-8"?>
<xsl:stylesheet version="1.0" xmlns:xsl="http://www.w3.org/1999/XSL/Transform"
xmlns:xs="http://www.w3.org/2001/XMLSchema">
<xsl:output method="text" encoding="UTF-8"/>
    <xsl:template match="/">
                    <xsl:for-each select="Personnel">
                        <xsl:for-each select="Employee">
                            <xsl:for-each select="@name">
                                <xsl:value-of select="." />
                            </xsl:for-each>,<xsl:for-each select="@title">
                                <xsl:value-of select="." />
                             </xsl:for-each>,<xsl:for-each select="@companyYears">
                                 <xsl:value-of select="." />
                            </xsl:for-each>
                    <xsl:text> &#xd;&#xa;</xsl:text>
                        </xsl:for-each>
                    </xsl:for-each>
    </xsl:template>
</xsl:stylesheet>
```

The output from the *PersonnelCSV.xsl* stylesheet is shown here:

```
Bob,Customer Service,1
Alice,Manager,12
Chas,Salesman,3
Rutherford,CEO,27
```

Discussion

XSLT is a very powerful way to transform XML from one format to another. That being said, the capacity that LINQ brings in C# 3.0 to perform XML transformations without having to shell out to another parser or process is very compelling. This means that to perform XML transformations in your applications, you no longer have to understand XSLT syntax or maintain application code in both C# and XSLT. This also means that when reviewing code from other team members, you no longer have to go into separate files to understand what the transformation is doing; it's all C# and all right there.

XSLT is by no means dead or inappropriate as a method for transforming XML; it is simply no longer the only realistic alternative for C# developers. XSLT can still be used with all of the existing XML API in .NET and will continue to be feasible for years to come. Our challenge to you the reader would be to try implementing a transformation in LINQ that you currently have in XSLT and see for yourself the possibilities with LINQ.

When performing transformation using XSLT, there are many overrides for the `XslCompiledTransform.Transform` method. Since `XmlResolver` is an abstract class, you need to use either the `XmlUrlResolver` or the `XmlSecureResolver` or pass null as the `XmlResolver`-typed argument. The `XmlUrlResolver` will resolve URLs to external resources, such as schema files, using the FILE, HTTP, and HTTPS protocols. The `XmlSecureResolver` restricts the resources that you can access by requiring you to pass in evidence, which helps prevent cross-domain redirection in XML.

If you are accepting XML from the Internet, it could easily have a redirection to a site where malicious XML would be waiting to be downloaded and executed if you were not using the `XmlSecureResolver`. If you pass null for the `XmlResolver`, you are saying you do not want to resolve any external resources. Microsoft has declared the null option to be obsolete, and it shouldn't be used anyway because you should always use some type of `XmlResolver`.

XSLT is a very powerful technology that allows you to transform XML into just about any format you can think of, but it can be frustrating at times. The simple need of a carriage return/line feed combination in the XSLT output was such a trial that we were able to find more than 20 different message board requests for help on how to do this! After looking at the W3C spec for XSLT, we found you could do this using the `xsl:text` element like this:

```
<xsl:text> &#xd;&#xa;</xsl:text>
```

The  stands for a hexadecimal 13, or a carriage return, and the
 stands for a hexadecimal 10, or a line feed. This is output at the end of each employee's data from the XML.

See Also

The "XslCompiledTransform Class," "XmlResolver Class," "XmlUrlResolver Class," "XmlSecureResolver Class," and "xsl:text" topics in the MSDN documentation.

15.9 Tearing Apart an XML Document

Problem

You have an XML document that needs to be broken apart into multiple parts. Each part can then be sent to a different destination (possibly a web service) to be processed individually. This solution is useful when you have a large document, such as an invoice, in XML form. For example, with an invoice, you would want to tear off the billing information and send this to Accounting, while sending the shipping information to Shipping, and then send the invoice items to Fulfillment to be processed.

Solution

In order to separate the invoice items, load an XElement with the invoice XML from the *Invoice.xml* file shown in Example 15-7.

Example 15-7. Invoice.xml

```
<?xml version="1.0" encoding="UTF-8"?>
<Invoice invoiceDate='2003-10-05' invoiceNumber='INV-01'>
    <shipInfo>
        <name>Beerly Standing</name>
        <attn>Receiving</attn>
        <street>47 South Street</street>
        <city>Intox</city>
        <state>NH</state>
    </shipInfo>
    <billInfo>
        <name>Beerly Standing</name>
        <attn>Accounting</attn>
        <street>98 North Street</street>
        <city>Intox</city>
        <state>NH</state>
    </billInfo>
    <Items>
        <item partNum="98745">
            <productName>Brown Eyed Stout</productName>
            <quantity>12</quantity>
            <price>23.99</price>
            <shipDate>2003-12-20</shipDate>
        </item>
        <item partNum="34987">
            <productName>Diamond Pearl Lager</productName>
            <quantity>22</quantity>
```

Example 15-7. Invoice.xml (continued)

```
            <price>35.98</price>
            <shipDate>2003-12-20</shipDate>
        </item>
        <item partNum="AK254">
            <productName>Job Site Ale</productName>
            <quantity>50</quantity>
            <price>12.56</price>
            <shipDate>2003-11-12</shipDate>
        </item>
    </Items>
</Invoice>
```

How to tear this invoice apart using an XElement and send the various information pieces to their respective departments is shown in Example 15-8.

Example 15-8. Tearing apart an XML document (XElement)

```
public static void ProcessInvoice( )
{
    XElement invElement = XElement.Load(@"..\..\Invoice.xml");
    // Process the billing information to Accounting
    CreateInvoiceEnvelope(invElement, "BillingEnvelope", "billInfo",
        @"..\..\BillingEnvelope_LINQ.xml");

    // Process the shipping information to Accounting
    CreateInvoiceEnvelope(invElement, "ShippingEnvelope", "shipInfo",
        @"..\..\ShippingEnvelope_LINQ.xml");

    // Process the item information to Fulfillment
    CreateInvoiceEnvelope(invElement, "FulfillmentEnvelope", "Items/item",
        @"..\..\FulfillmentEnvelope_LINQ.xml");
}

private static void CreateInvoiceEnvelope(XElement invElement,
                                string topElementName,
                                string internalElementName,
                                string path)
{
    var query = from i in invElement.DescendantsAndSelf( )
                    where i.NodeType == XmlNodeType.Element &&
                        i.Name == "Invoice"
                    select new XElement(topElementName,
                                new XAttribute(i.Attribute("invoiceDate").Name,
                                        i.Attribute("invoiceDate").Value),
                                new XAttribute(i.Attribute("invoiceNumber").Name,
                                        i.Attribute("invoiceNumber").Value),
                                from e in i.XPathSelectElements(internalElementName)
                                select new XElement(e));
    XElement envelope = query.ElementAt<XElement>(0);
    Console.WriteLine(envelope.ToString( ));
    // save the envelope
    envelope.Save(path);
}
```

The code to tear this invoice apart using an XmlDocument and send the various information pieces to their respective departments is shown in Example 15-9.

Example 15-9. Tearing apart an XML document (XmlDocument)

```
public static void ProcessInvoice( )
{
    XmlDocument xmlDoc = new XmlDocument( );
    // Pick up invoice from deposited directory.
    xmlDoc.Load(@"..\..\Invoice.xml");
    // Get the Invoice element node.
    XmlNode Invoice = xmlDoc.SelectSingleNode("/Invoice");

    // Get the invoice date attribute.
    XmlAttribute invDate =
        (XmlAttribute)Invoice.Attributes.GetNamedItem("invoiceDate");
    // Get the invoice number attribute.
    XmlAttribute invNum =
        (XmlAttribute)Invoice.Attributes.GetNamedItem("invoiceNumber");

    // Process the billing information to Accounting.
    WriteInformation(@"..\..\BillingEnvelope.xml",
                    "BillingEnvelope",
                    invDate, invNum, xmlDoc,
                    "/Invoice/billInfo");

    // Process the shipping information to Shipping.
    WriteInformation(@"..\..\ShippingEnvelope.xml",
                    "ShippingEnvelope",
                    invDate, invNum, xmlDoc,
                    "/Invoice/shipInfo");

    // Process the item information to Fulfillment.
    WriteInformation(@"..\..\FulfillmentEnvelope.xml",
                    "FulfillmentEnvelope",
                    invDate, invNum, xmlDoc,
                    "/Invoice/Items/item");

    // Now send the data to the web services ...
}

private static void WriteInformation(string path,
                            string rootNode,
                            XmlAttribute invDate,
                            XmlAttribute invNum,
                            XmlDocument xmlDoc,
                            string nodePath)
{
    XmlWriterSettings settings = new XmlWriterSettings( );
    settings.Indent = true;
    using (XmlWriter writer =
        XmlWriter.Create(path, settings))
    {
        writer.WriteStartDocument( );
```

Example 15-9. Tearing apart an XML document (XmlDocument) (continued)

```
        writer.WriteStartElement(rootNode);
        writer.WriteAttributeString(invDate.Name, invDate.Value);
        writer.WriteAttributeString(invNum.Name, invNum.Value);
        XmlNodeList nodeList = xmlDoc.SelectNodes(nodePath);
        // Add the billing information to the envelope.
        foreach (XmlNode node in nodeList)
        {
            writer.WriteRaw(node.OuterXml);
        }
        writer.WriteEndElement( );
        writer.WriteEndDocument( );
    }
}
```

The "envelopes" containing the various pieces of XML data for the web services are listed below:

BillingEnvelope XML

```
    <BillingEnvelope invoiceDate="2003-10-05" invoiceNumber="INV-01">
        <billInfo>
            <name>Beerly Standing</name>
            <attn>Accounting</attn>
            <street>98 North Street</street>
            <city>Intox</city>
            <state>NH</state>
        </billInfo>
    </BillingEnvelope>
```

ShippingEnvelope XML

```
    <ShippingEnvelope invoiceDate="2003-10-05" invoiceNumber="INV-01">
        <shipInfo>
            <name>Beerly Standing</name>
            <attn>Receiving</attn>
            <street>47 South Street</street>
            <city>Intox</city>
            <state>NH</statey>
        </shipInfo>
    </ShippingEnvelope>
```

FulfillmentEnvelope XML

```
    <FulfillmentEnvelope invoiceDate="2003-10-05" invoiceNumber="INV-01">
        <item partNum="98745">
            <productName>Brown Eyed Stout</productName>
            <quantity>12</quantity>
            <price>23.99</price>
            <shipDate>2003-12-20</shipDate>
        </item>
        <item partNum="34987">
            <productName>Diamond Pearl Lager</productName>
            <quantity>22</quantity>
            <price>35.98</price>
            <shipDate>2003-12-20</shipDate>
        </item>
```

```
    <item partNum="AK254">
        <productName>Job Site Ale</productName>
        <quantity>50</quantity>
        <price>12.56</price>
        <shipDate>2003-11-12</shipDate>
    </item>
</FulfillmentEnvelope>
```

Discussion

In order to tear apart the invoice, you need to establish what pieces go to which departments. The breakdown of this is that each of the envelopes gets the invoice date and invoice number from the main invoice to give context to the information in the envelope. The billInfo element and children go to the BillingEnvelope, the shipInfo element and children go to the ShippingEnvelope, and the item elements go to the FulfillmentEnvelope. Once these envelopes are constructed, they are sent to the web services for each department to perform its function for this invoice.

In the example program from the Solution, you first load the *Invoice.xml* file and get the attributes you are going to give to each of the envelopes:

```
        // Using XElement
    var query = from i in invElement.DescendantsAndSelf( )
                    where i.NodeType == XmlNodeType.Element &&
                        i.Name == "Invoice"
                    select new XElement(topElementName,
                            new XAttribute(i.Attribute("invoiceDate").Name,
                                    i.Attribute("invoiceDate").Value),
                            new XAttribute(i.Attribute("invoiceNumber").Name,
                                    i.Attribute("invoiceNumber").Value),
                            from e in i.
    XPathSelectElements(internalElementName)
                            select new XElement(e));

        // Using XmlDocument
        XmlDocument xmlDoc = new XmlDocument( );
        // Pick up invoice from deposited directory.
        xmlDoc.Load(@"..\..\Invoice.xml");
        // Get the Invoice element node.
        XmlNode Invoice = xmlDoc.SelectSingleNode("/Invoice");

        // Get the invoice date attribute.
        XmlAttribute invDate =
            (XmlAttribute)Invoice.Attributes.GetNamedItem("invoiceDate");
        // Get the invoice number attribute.
        XmlAttribute invNum =
            (XmlAttribute)Invoice.Attributes.GetNamedItem("invoiceNumber");
```

Then, you establish each envelope with the sections of the invoice that matter to the respective functions (the BillingEnvelope is handled by Accounting, the ShippingEnvelope is handled by Shipping, and the FulfillmentEnvelope is handled by

Fulfillment) by calling the WriteInformation method, starting with the BillingEnvelope:

```
XElement invElement = XElement.Load(@"..\..\Invoice.xml");
// Process the billing information to Accounting
CreateInvoiceEnvelope(invElement, "BillingEnvelope", "billInfo",
    @"..\..\BillingEnvelope_LINQ.xml");

        // Process the billing information to Accounting.
        WriteInformation(@"..\..\BillingEnvelope.xml",
                    "BillingEnvelope",
                    invDate, invNum, xmlDoc,
                    "/Invoice/billInfo");
```

Then the ShippingEnvelope is created:

```
XElement invElement = XElement.Load(@"..\..\Invoice.xml");
// Process the shipping information to Accounting
CreateInvoiceEnvelope(invElement, "ShippingEnvelope", "shipInfo",
    @"..\..\ShippingEnvelope_LINQ.xml");

        // Process the shipping information to Shipping.
        WriteInformation(@"..\..\ShippingEnvelope.xml",
                    "ShippingEnvelope",
                    invDate, invNum, xmlDoc,
                    "/Invoice/shipInfo");
```

Finally, the FulfillmentEnvelope is created:

```
XElement invElement = XElement.Load(@"..\..\Invoice.xml");
// Process the item information to Fulfillment
CreateInvoiceEnvelope(invElement, "FulfillmentEnvelope", "Items/item",
    @"..\..\FulfillmentEnvelope_LINQ.xml");

        // Process the item information to Fulfillment.
        WriteInformation(@"..\..\FulfillmentEnvelope.xml",
                    "FulfillmentEnvelope",
                    invDate, invNum, xmlDoc,
                    "/Invoice/Items/item");
```

At this point, each of the envelopes can be posted to the respective web services interfaces.

 When you append the attributes from the Invoice to the envelopes, you call the XmlNode.Clone method on the XmlAttributes. This is done so that each of the elements has its own separate copy. If you do not do this, then the attribute will appear only on the last element it is assigned to.

See Also

The "XElement Class," "XAttribute Class," "XmlDocument Class," "XmlElement Class," and "XmlAttribute Class" topics in the MSDN documentation.

15.10 Putting Together an XML Document

Problem

You have various pieces of a document in XML form that need to be put together to form a single XML document—the opposite of what was done in Recipe 15.9. In this case, you have received various pieces of an invoice in XML form. For example, one department sent the shipping information as an XML document, one sent the billing information in XML, and another sent invoice line items, also as an XML document. You need a way to put these XML pieces together to form a single XML invoice document.

Solution

In order to reconstitute the original invoice, you need to reverse the process used to create the pieces of the invoice using multiple XElements. There are three parts being sent back to you to help in re-forming the original invoice XML: *BillingEnvelope.xml*, *ShippingEnvelope.xml*, and *Fulfillment.xml*. These are listed below:

BillingEnvelope XML

```
<BillingEnvelope invoiceDate="2003-10-05" invoiceNumber="INV-01">
    <billInfo>
        <name>Beerly Standing</name>
        <attn>Accounting</attn>
        <street>98 North Street</street>
        <city>Intox</city>
        <state>NH</state>
    </billInfo>
</BillingEnvelope>
```

ShippingEnvelope XML

```
<ShippingEnvelope invoiceDate="2003-10-05" invoiceNumber="INV-01">
    <shipInfo>
        <name>Beerly Standing</name>
        <attn>Receiving</attn>
        <street>47 South Street</street>
        <city>Intox</city>
        <state>NH</state>
    </shipInfo>
</ShippingEnvelope>
```

FulfillmentEnvelope XML

```
<FulfillmentEnvelope invoiceDate="2003-10-05" invoiceNumber="INV-01">
    <item partNum="98745">
        <productName>Brown Eyed Stout</productName>
        <quantity>12</quantity>
        <price>23.99</price>
        <shipDate>2003-12-20</shipDate>
    </item>
    <item partNum="34987">
        <productName>Diamond Pearl Lager</productName>
```

```
            <quantity>22</quantity>
            <price>35.98</price>
            <shipDate>2003-12-20</shipDate>
        </item>
        <item partNum="AK254">
            <productName>Job Site Ale</productName>
            <quantity>50</quantity>
            <price>12.56</price>
            <shipDate>2003-11-12</shipDate>
        </item>
    </FulfillmentEnvelope>
```

To put these back together as a single invoice using XElement, reverse the process you went through to break it apart, while inferring the invoice date and invoice number from the BillingEnvelope to help reestablish the invoice, as shown in Example 15-10.

Example 15-10. Rebuilding the invoice

```
public static void ReceiveInvoice()
{
    // LINQ Way

    // load the billing
    XElement billingElement = XElement.Load(@"..\..\BillingEnvelope.xml");
    XElement shippingElement = XElement.Load(@"..\..\ShippingEnvelope.xml");
    XElement fulfillmentElement = XElement.Load(@"..\..\FulfillmentEnvelope.xml");
    XElement invElement = new XElement("Invoice",
                        // get the invoice date attribute
                        billingElement.Attribute("invoiceDate"),
                        // get the invoice number attribute
                        billingElement.Attribute("invoiceNumber"),
                        // add the billInfo back in
                        from b in billingElement.Elements("billInfo")
                        select b,
                        // add the shipInfo back in
                        from s in shippingElement.Elements("shipInfo")
                        select s,
                        // add the items back in under Items
                        new XElement("Items",
                            from f in fulfillmentElement.Elements("item")
                            select f));
    // display Invoice XML
    Console.WriteLine(invElement.ToString());
    Console.WriteLine();

    // save our reconstitued invoice
    invElement.Save(@"..\..\ReceivedInvoice_LINQ.xml");
}
```

The code reconstitutes the invoice and saves it as *ReceivedInvoice_LINQ.xml*, the contents of which are shown here:

```xml
<?xml version="1.0" encoding="utf-8"?>
<Invoice invoiceDate="2003-10-05" invoiceNumber="INV-01">
  <billInfo>
    <name>Beerly Standing</name>
    <attn>Accounting</attn>
    <street>98 North Street</street>
    <city>Intox</city>
    <state>NH</state>
  </billInfo>
  <shipInfo>
    <name>Beerly Standing</name>
    <attn>Receiving</attn>
    <street>47 South Street</street>
    <city>Intox</city>
    <state>NH</state>
  </shipInfo>
  <Items>
    <item partNum="98745">
      <productName>Brown Eyed Stout</productName>
      <quantity>12</quantity>
      <price>23.99</price>
      <shipDate>2003-12-20</shipDate>
    </item>
    <item partNum="34987">
      <productName>Diamond Pearl Lager</productName>
      <quantity>22</quantity>
      <price>35.98</price>
      <shipDate>2003-12-20</shipDate>
    </item>
    <item partNum="AK254">
      <productName>Job Site Ale</productName>
      <quantity>50</quantity>
      <price>12.56</price>
      <shipDate>2003-11-12</shipDate>
    </item>
  </Items>
</Invoice>
```

To put these back together as a single invoice using XmlDocument, see Example 15-11:

Example 15-11. Reconstructing an XML document

```csharp
public static void ReceiveInvoice()
{
    XmlDocument invoice = new XmlDocument();
    XmlDocument billing = new XmlDocument();
    XmlDocument shipping = new XmlDocument();
    XmlDocument fulfillment = new XmlDocument();

    // Get up root invoice node.
    XmlElement invoiceElement = invoice.CreateElement("Invoice");
    invoice.AppendChild(invoiceElement);

    // Load the billing.
    billing.Load(@"..\..\BillingEnvelope.xml");
```

Example 15-11. Reconstructing an XML document (continued)

```
    // Get the invoice date attribute.
    XmlAttribute invDate = (XmlAttribute)
      billing.DocumentElement.Attributes.GetNamedItem("invoiceDate");
    // Get the invoice number attribute.
    XmlAttribute invNum = (XmlAttribute)
      billing.DocumentElement.Attributes.GetNamedItem("invoiceNumber");
    // Set up the invoice with this info.
    invoice.DocumentElement.Attributes.SetNamedItem(invDate.Clone( ));
    invoice.DocumentElement.Attributes.SetNamedItem(invNum.Clone( ));
    // Add the billInfo back in.
    XmlNodeList billList = billing.SelectNodes("/BillingEnvelope/billInfo");
    foreach(XmlNode billInfo in billList)
    {
        invoice.DocumentElement.AppendChild(invoice.ImportNode(billInfo,true));
    }

    // Load the shipping.
    shipping.Load(@"..\..\ShippingEnvelope.xml");
    // Add the shipInfo back in.
    XmlNodeList shipList = shipping.SelectNodes("/ShippingEnvelope/shipInfo");
    foreach(XmlNode shipInfo in shipList)
    {
        invoice.DocumentElement.AppendChild(invoice.ImportNode(shipInfo,true));
    }

    // Load the items.
    fulfillment.Load(@"..\..\FulfillmentEnvelope.xml");

    // Create an Items element in the Invoice to add these under.
    XmlElement items = invoice.CreateElement("Items");

    // Add the items back in under Items.
    XmlNodeList itemList = fulfillment.SelectNodes("/FulfillmentEnvelope/item");
    foreach(XmlNode item in itemList)
    {
        items.AppendChild(invoice.ImportNode(item,true));
    }

    // Add it in.
    invoice.DocumentElement.AppendChild(items.Clone( ));

    // Display Invoice XML.
    Console.WriteLine("Invoice:\r\n{0}",invoice.OuterXml);

    // Save our reconstitued invoice.
    invoice.Save(@"..\..\ReceivedInvoice.xml");
}
```

The code reconstitutes the invoice and saves it as *ReceivedInvoice.xml*, the contents of which are shown here:

```
<Invoice invoiceDate="2003-10-05" invoiceNumber="INV-01"><billInfo><name>Beerly
Standing</name><attn>Accounting</attn><street>98 North Street</street><city>Intox</
city><state>NH</state></billInfo><shipInfo><name>Beerly Standing</name><attn>
Receiving</attn><street>47 South Street</street><city>Intox</city><state>NH</state></
shipInfo><Items><item partNum="98745"><productName>Brown Eyed Stout</productName>
<quantity>12</quantity><price>23.99</price><shipDate>2003-12-20</shipDate></item>
<item partNum="34987"><productName>Diamond Pearl Lager</productName><quantity>22</
quantity><price>35.98</price><shipDate>2003-12-20</shipDate></item><item
partNum="AK254"><productName>Job Site Ale</productName><quantity>50</quantity><price>
12.56</price><shipDate>2003-11-12</shipDate></item></Items></Invoice>
```

Discussion

In the Solution code, the first step is to load the three parts of the invoice:

```
XElement billingElement = XElement.Load(@"..\..\BillingEnvelope.xml");
XElement shippingElement = XElement.Load(@"..\..\ShippingEnvelope.xml");
XElement fulfillmentElement = XElement.Load(@"..\..\FulfillmentEnvelope.xml");
```

Next, you construct the invoice by transforming the three parts into subsections and embedding them in the Invoice like so:

```
XElement invElement = new XElement("Invoice",
                        // get the invoice date attribute
                        billingElement.Attribute("invoiceDate"),
                        // get the invoice number attribute
                        billingElement.Attribute("invoiceNumber"),
                        // add the billInfo back in
                        from b in billingElement.Elements("billInfo")
                        select b,
                        // add the shipInfo back in
                        from s in shippingElement.Elements("shipInfo")
                        select s,
                        // add the items back in under Items
                        new XElement("Items",
                            from f in fulfillmentElement.Elements("item")
                            select f));
```

Note that inside of the XML construction, we select the full set of billInfo, shipInfo, and item elements from the three parts and add them into the Invoice document being constructed. The item parts of the FulfillmentEnvelope are also nested under a new Items containing element.

When implementing the Solution with XmlDocument, the first step is to create a set of XmlDocuments for the Invoice, BillingEnvelope, ShippingEnvelope, and FulfillmentEnvelope. Then, you create the new root Invoice element in the invoice XmlDocument:

```
XmlDocument invoice = new XmlDocument();
XmlDocument billing = new XmlDocument();
XmlDocument shipping = new XmlDocument();
XmlDocument fulfillment = new XmlDocument();
```

```
// Set up root invoice node.
XmlElement invoiceElement = invoice.CreateElement("Invoice");
invoice.AppendChild(invoiceElement);
```

Next, you process the BillingEnvelope, taking the invoice date and number from it and adding it to the Invoice. Then, you add the billing information back in to the invoice:

```
// Load the billing.
billing.Load(@"..\..\BillingEnvelope.xml");
// Get the invoice date attribute.
XmlAttribute invDate = (XmlAttribute)
 billing.DocumentElement.Attributes.GetNamedItem("invoiceDate");
// Get the invoice number attribute.
XmlAttribute invNum = (XmlAttribute)
 billing.DocumentElement.Attributes.GetNamedItem("invoiceNumber");
// Set up the invoice with this info.
invoice.DocumentElement.Attributes.SetNamedItem(invDate.Clone());
invoice.DocumentElement.Attributes.SetNamedItem(invNum.Clone());
// Add the billInfo back in.
XmlNodeList billList = billing.SelectNodes("/BillingEnvelope/billInfo");
foreach(XmlNode billInfo in billList)
{
    invoice.DocumentElement.AppendChild(invoice.ImportNode(billInfo,true));
}
```

The ShippingEnvelope came next:

```
// Load the shipping.
shipping.Load(@"..\..\ShippingEnvelope.xml");
// Add the shipInfo back in.
XmlNodeList shipList = shipping.SelectNodes("/ShippingEnvelope/shipInfo");
foreach(XmlNode shipInfo in shipList)
{
    invoice.DocumentElement.AppendChild(invoice.ImportNode(shipInfo,true));
}
```

And finally, the items from the FulfillmentEnvelope were placed back under an Items element under the main Invoice element:

```
// Load the items.
fulfillment.Load(@"..\..\FulfillmentEnvelope.xml");

// Create an Items element in the Invoice to add these under
XmlElement items = invoice.CreateElement("Items");

// Add the items back in under Items.
XmlNodeList itemList = fulfillment.SelectNodes("/FulfillmentEnvelope/item");
foreach(XmlNode item in itemList)
{
    items.AppendChild(invoice.ImportNode(item,true));
}

// Add it in.
invoice.DocumentElement.AppendChild(items.Clone());
```

One item to be aware of when dealing with multiple XmlDocuments is that when you take a node from one XmlDocument, you cannot just append it as a child to a node in a different XmlDocument because the node has the context of the original XmlDocument. If you try to do this, you will get the following exception message:

```
The node to be inserted is from a different document context.
```

To fix this, use the XmlDocument.ImportNode method, which will make a copy (deep when the second parameter is true, or shallow when the second parameter is false) of the node you are bringing over to the new XmlDocument. For instance, when you add the shipping information like so:

```
invoice.DocumentElement.AppendChild(invoice.ImportNode(shipInfo,true));
```

this line takes the shipInfo node, clones it deeply, then appends it to the main invoice node.

See Also

The "XElement Class," "The Three Parts of a LINQ Query," "XmlDocument Class," "XmlElement Class," and "XmlAttribute Class" topics in the MSDN documentation.

15.11 Validating Modified XML Documents Without Reloading

Problem

You are using the XDocument or the XmlDocument to modify an XML document loaded in memory. Once the document has been modified, the modifications need to be verified, and schema defaults need to be enforced.

Solution

Use the XDocument.Validate method to perform the validation and apply schema defaults and type information.

Create an XmlSchemaSet with the XML Schema document (*book.xsd*) and an XmlReader and then load the *book.xml* file using XDocument.Load:

```
// Create the schema set
XmlSchemaSet xmlSchemaSet = new XmlSchemaSet();
// add the new schema with the target namespace
// (could add all the schema at once here if there are multiple)
xmlSchemaSet.Add("http://tempuri.org/Book.xsd",
    XmlReader.Create(@"..\..\Book.xsd"));
XDocument book = XDocument.Load(@"..\..\Book.xml");
```

Set up a ValidationEventHandler to catch any errors and then call XDocument.
Validate with the schema set and the event handler to validate *book.xml* against the
book.xsd schema:

```
ValidationHandler validationHandler = new ValidationHandler();
ValidationEventHandler validationEventHandler = validationHandler.HandleValidation;
// validate after load
book.Validate(xmlSchemaSet, validationEventHandler);
```

The ValidationHandler class holds the current validation state in a ValidXml property
and the code for the ValidationEventHandler implementation method
HandleValidation:

```
public class ValidationHandler
{
    private object _syncRoot = new object();

    public ValidationHandler()
    {
        lock(_syncRoot)
        {
            // set the initial check for validity to true
            this.ValidXml = true;
        }
    }

    public bool ValidXml { get; private set; }

    public void HandleValidation(object sender, ValidationEventArgs e)
    {
        lock(_syncRoot)
        {
            // we got called, so this isn't valid
            ValidXml = false;
            Console.WriteLine("Validation Error Message: {0}", e.Message);
            Console.WriteLine("Validation Error Severity: {0}", e.Severity);
            if (e.Exception != null)
            {
                Console.WriteLine("Validation Error Line Number: {0}",
                    e.Exception.LineNumber);
                Console.WriteLine("Validation Error Line Position: {0}",
                    e.Exception.LinePosition);
                Console.WriteLine("Validation Error Source: {0}",
                    e.Exception.Source);
                Console.WriteLine("Validation Error Source Schema: {0}",
                    e.Exception.SourceSchemaObject);
                Console.WriteLine("Validation Error Source Uri: {0}",
                    e.Exception.SourceUri);
                Console.WriteLine("Validation Error thrown from: {0}",
                    e.Exception.TargetSite);
                Console.WriteLine("Validation Error callstack: {0}",
                    e.Exception.StackTrace);
            }
        }
```

```
        }
    }
```

Add a new element node that is not in the schema into the XDocument and then call Validate again with the schema set and event handler to revalidate the changed XDocument. If the document triggers any validation events, then the ValidationHandler.ValidXml property is set to false in the ValidationHandler instance:

```
// add in a new node that is not in the schema
// since we have already validated, no callbacks fire during the add...
book.Root.Add(new XElement("BogusElement","Totally"));
// now we will do validation of the new stuff we added
book.Validate(xmlSchemaSet, validationEventHandler);

if (validationHandler.ValidXml)
    Console.WriteLine("Successfully validated modified LINQ XML");
else
    Console.WriteLine("Modified LINQ XML did not validate successfully");
Console.WriteLine();
```

You could also use the XmlDocument.Validate method to perform the validation in a similar fashion to XDocument:

```
string xmlFile = @"..\..\Book.xml";
string xsdFile = @"..\..\Book.xsd";

// Create the schema set.
XmlSchemaSet schemaSet = new XmlSchemaSet();
// Add the new schema with the target namespace
// (could add all the schema at once here if there are multiple).
schemaSet.Add("http://tempuri.org/Book.xsd", XmlReader.Create(xsdFile));

// Load up the XML file.
XmlDocument xmlDoc = new XmlDocument();
// Add the schema.
xmlDoc.Schemas = schemaSet;
```

Load the *book.xml* file into the XmlDocument, set up a ValidationEventHandler to catch any errors, and then call Validate with the event handler to validate *book.xml* against the *book.xsd* schema:

```
// validate after load
xmlDoc.Load(xmlFile);
ValidationHandler handler = new ValidationHandler();
ValidationEventHandler eventHandler = handler.HandleValidation;
xmlDoc.Validate(eventHandler);
```

Add a new element node that is not in the schema into the XmlDocument and then call Validate again with the event handler to revalidate the changed XmlDocument. If the document triggers any validation events, then the ValidationHandler.ValidXml property is set to false:

```
// Add in a new node that is not in the schema.
// Since we have already validated, no callbacks fire during the add...
XmlNode newNode = xmlDoc.CreateElement("BogusElement");
newNode.InnerText = "Totally";
// Add the new element.
xmlDoc.DocumentElement.AppendChild(newNode);
// Now we will do validation of the new stuff we added.
xmlDoc.Validate(eventHandler);

if (handler.ValidXml)
    Console.WriteLine("Successfully validated modified XML");
else
    Console.WriteLine("Modified XML did not validate successfully");
```

Discussion

One advantage to using XmlDocument over XDocument is that there is an override to the XmlDocument.Validate method that allows you to pass a specific XmlNode to validate. This fine grain of control is not present on XDocument. If the XmlDocument is large, this override to Validate should be used:

```
public void Validate(
    ValidationEventHandler validationEventHandler,
    XmlNode nodeToValidate
);
```

One other approach to this problem is to instantiate an instance of the XmlNodeReader with the XmlDocument and then create an XmlReader with validation settings as shown in Recipe 15.4. This would allow for continual validation while the reader navigated through the underlying XML.

The output from running the code is listed here:

```
Validation Error Message: The element 'Book' in namespace 'http://tempuri.org/Book.
xsd' has invalid child element 'BogusElement'. List of possible elements expected:
'Chapter' in namespace 'http://tempuri.org/Book.xsd'.
Validation Error Severity: Error
Validation Error Line Number: 0
Validation Error Line Position: 0
Validation Error Source:
Validation Error Source Schema:
Validation Error Source Uri: file:///C:/PRJ32/Book_2_0/C%23Cookbook2/Code/
CSharpRecipes/Book.xml
Validation Error thrown from:
Validation Error callstack:
Modified XML did not validate successfully
```

Notice that the BogusElement element that you added was not part of the schema for the Book element, so you got a validation error along with the information about where the error occurred. Finally, you got a report that the modified XML did not validate correctly.

See Also

Recipe 15.3; the "XDocument Class," and the "XmlDocument.Validate" topics in the MSDN documentation.

15.12 Extending Transformations

Problem

You want to perform operations that are outside the scope of the transformation technology to include data in the transformed result.

Solution

If you are using LINQ to XML, you can call out to a function directly when transforming the result set, as shown here by the call to `GetErrata`:

```
XElement publications = XElement.Load(@"..\..\publications.xml");
XElement transformedPublications =
    new XElement("PublishedWorks",
        from b in publications.Elements("Book")
        select new XElement(b.Name,
                    new XAttribute(b.Attribute("name")),
                    from c in b.Elements("Chapter")
                    select new XElement("Chapter", GetErrata(c))));
Console.WriteLine(transformedPublications.ToString());
Console.WriteLine();
```

The `GetErrata` method used in the above sample is listed here:

```
private static XElement GetErrata(XElement chapter)
{
    // In here, we could go do other lookup calls (XML, database, web service)
    // to get information to add back in to the transformation result
    string errata = string.Format("{0} has {1} errata",
                            chapter.Value, chapter.Value.Length);
    return new XElement("Errata", errata);
}
```

If you are using XSLT, you can add an extension object to the transformation that can perform the operations necessary based on the node it is passed. This can be accomplished by using the `XsltArgumentList.AddExtensionObject` method. This object you've created (`XslExtensionObject`) can then be accessed in the XSLT and a method called on it to return the data you want included in the final transformed result:

```
string xmlFile = @"..\..\publications.xml";
string xslt = @"..\..\publications.xsl";

//Create the XslTransform and load the stylesheet.
// This is not XslCompiledTransform because it gives a different empty node.
```

```
//Create the XslCompiledTransform and load the stylesheet.
XslCompiledTransform transform = new XslCompiledTransform( );
transform.Load(xslt);

// Load the XML.
XPathDocument xPathDoc = new XPathDocument(xmlFile);

// Make up the args for the stylesheet with the extension object.
XsltArgumentList xslArg = new XsltArgumentList( );
// Create our custom extension object.
XSLExtensionObject xslExt = new XSLExtensionObject( );
xslArg.AddExtensionObject("urn:xslext", xslExt);

// Send output to the console and do the transformation.
using (XmlWriter writer = XmlWriter.Create(Console.Out))
{
    transform.Transform(xPathDoc, xslArg, writer);
}
```

Note that when the extension object is added to the XsltArgumentList, it supplies a
namespace of urn:xslext. This namespace is used in the XSLT stylesheet to reference the object. The XSLExtensionObject is defined here:

```
// Our extension object to help with functionality
public class XslExtensionObject
{
    public XPathNodeIterator GetErrata(XPathNodeIterator nodeChapter)
    {
    // In here, we could go do other lookup calls
    // (XML, database, web service) to get information to
    // add back in to the transformation result.
    string errata =
     string.Format("<Errata>{0} has {1} errata</Errata>",
                    nodeChapter.Current.Value, nodeChapter.Current.Value.Length);
        XmlDocument xDoc = new XmlDocument( );
        xDoc.LoadXml(errata);
        XPathNavigator xPathNav = xDoc.CreateNavigator( );
        xPathNav.MoveToChild(XPathNodeType.Element);
        XPathNodeIterator iter = xPathNav.Select(".");
        return iter;
    }
}
```

The GetErrata method is called during the execution of the XSLT stylesheet to provide data in XPathNodeIterator format to the transformation. The xmlns:xslext
namespace is declared as urn:xslext, which matches the namespace value you
passed as an argument to the transformation. In the processing of the Book template
for each Chapter, an xsl:value-of is called with the select criteria containing a call to
the xslext:GetErrata method. The stylesheet makes the call, as shown here:

```
<xsl:stylesheet version="1.0" xmlns:xsl="http://www.w3.org/1999/XSL/Transform"
    xmlns:xslext="urn:xslext">
    <xsl:template match="/">
```

```
            <xsl:element name="PublishedWorks">
                <xsl:apply-templates/>
            </xsl:element>
        </xsl:template>
        <xsl:template match="Book">
            <Book>
                <xsl:attribute name ="name">
                    <xsl:value-of select="@name"/>
                </xsl:attribute>
                <xsl:for-each select="Chapter">
                    <Chapter>
                        <xsl:value-of select="xslext:GetErrata(/)"/>
                    </Chapter>
                </xsl:for-each>
            </Book>
        </xsl:template>
    </xsl:stylesheet>
```

Discussion

Using LINQ to XML, you can extend your transformation code to include additional logic simply by adding method calls that know how to operate and return XElements. This is simply adding another method call to the query that contributes to the result set, and no additional performance penalty is assessed just by the call. Certainly if the operation is expensive it could slow down the transformation, but this is now easily located when your code is profiled.

The ability to call custom code from inside of an XSLT stylesheet is a very powerful one, but one that should be used cautiously. Adding code like this into stylesheets usually renders them less useful in other environments. If the stylesheet never has to be used to transform XML in another parser, this can be a good way to offload work that is either difficult or impossible to accomplish in regular XSLT syntax.

The sample data used in the Solution is presented here:

```
<?xml version="1.0" encoding="utf-8"?>
<Publications>
    <Book name="Subclassing and Hooking with Visual Basic">
        <Chapter>Introduction</Chapter>
        <Chapter>Windows System-Specific Information</Chapter>
        <Chapter>The Basics of Subclassing and Hooks</Chapter>
        <Chapter>Subclassing and Superclassing</Chapter>
        <Chapter>Subclassing the Windows Common Dialog Boxes</Chapter>
        <Chapter>ActiveX Controls and Subclassing</Chapter>
        <Chapter>Superclassing</Chapter>
        <Chapter>Debugging Techniques for Subclassing</Chapter>
        <Chapter>WH_CALLWNDPROC</Chapter>
        <Chapter>WH_CALLWNDPROCRET</Chapter>
        <Chapter>WH_GETMESSAGE</Chapter>
        <Chapter>WH_KEYBOARD and WH_KEYBOARD_LL</Chapter>
        <Chapter>WH_MOUSE and WH_MOUSE_LL</Chapter>
        <Chapter>WH_FOREGROUNDIDLE</Chapter>
```

```
        <Chapter>WH_MSGFILTER</Chapter>
        <Chapter>WH_SYSMSGFILTER</Chapter>
        <Chapter>WH_SHELL</Chapter>
        <Chapter>WH_CBT</Chapter>
        <Chapter>WH_JOURNALRECORD</Chapter>
        <Chapter>WH_JOURNALPLAYBACK</Chapter>
        <Chapter>WH_DEBUG</Chapter>
        <Chapter>Subclassing .NET WinForms</Chapter>
        <Chapter>Implementing Hooks in VB.NET</Chapter>
    </Book>
    <Book name="C# Cookbook">
        <Chapter>Numbers</Chapter>
        <Chapter>Strings and Characters</Chapter>
        <Chapter>Classes And Structures</Chapter>
        <Chapter>Enums</Chapter>
        <Chapter>Exception Handling</Chapter>
        <Chapter>Diagnostics</Chapter>
        <Chapter>Delegates and Events</Chapter>
        <Chapter>Regular Expressions</Chapter>
        <Chapter>Collections</Chapter>
        <Chapter>Data Structures and Algorithms</Chapter>
        <Chapter>File System IO</Chapter>
        <Chapter>Reflection</Chapter>
        <Chapter>Networking</Chapter>
        <Chapter>Security</Chapter>
        <Chapter>Threading</Chapter>
        <Chapter>Unsafe Code</Chapter>
        <Chapter>XML</Chapter>
    </Book>
    <Book name="C# Cookbook 2.0">
        <Chapter>Numbers and Enumerations</Chapter>
        <Chapter>Strings and Characters</Chapter>
        <Chapter>Classes And Structures</Chapter>
        <Chapter>Generics</Chapter>
        <Chapter>Collections</Chapter>
        <Chapter>Iterators and Partial Types</Chapter>
        <Chapter>Exception Handling</Chapter>
        <Chapter>Diagnostics</Chapter>
        <Chapter>Delegates, Events, and Anonymous Methods</Chapter>
        <Chapter>Regular Expressions</Chapter>
        <Chapter>Data Structures and Algorithms</Chapter>
        <Chapter>File System IO</Chapter>
        <Chapter>Reflection</Chapter>
        <Chapter>Web</Chapter>
        <Chapter>XML</Chapter>
        <Chapter>Networking</Chapter>
        <Chapter>Security</Chapter>
        <Chapter>Threading and Synchronization</Chapter>
        <Chapter>Unsafe Code</Chapter>
        <Chapter>Toolbox</Chapter>
    </Book>
</Publications>
```

See Also

The "LINQ, transforming data" and "XsltArgumentList Class" topics in the MSDN documentation.

15.13 Getting Your Schemas in Bulk from Existing XML Files

Problem

You have come on to a new project in which XML was used for data transmission, but the programmers who came before you didn't use an XSD for one reason or another. You need to generate beginning schema files for each of the XML examples.

Solution

Use the XmlSchemaInference class to infer schema from the XML samples. The GenerateSchemasForDirectory function in Example 15-12 enumerates all of the XML files in a given directory and processes each of them using the GenerateSchemasForFile method. GenerateSchemasForFile uses the XmlSchemaInference.InferSchema method to get the schemas for the given XML file. Once the schemas have been determined, GenerateSchemasForFile rolls over the collection and saves out each schema to an XSD file using a FileStream.

Example 15-12. Generating an XML Schema

```
public static void GenerateSchemasForFile(string file)
{
    // set up a reader for the file
    using (XmlReader reader = XmlReader.Create(file))
    {
        XmlSchemaSet schemaSet = new XmlSchemaSet();
        XmlSchemaInference schemaInference =
                    new XmlSchemaInference();

        // get the schema
        schemaSet = schemaInference.InferSchema(reader);

        string schemaPath = string.Empty;
        foreach (XmlSchema schema in schemaSet.Schemas())
        {
            // make schema file path and write it out
            schemaPath = Path.GetDirectoryName(file) + @"\" +
                        Path.GetFileNameWithoutExtension(file) + ".xsd";
            using (FileStream fs =
                new FileStream(schemaPath, FileMode.OpenOrCreate))
            {
                schema.Write(fs);
```

Example 15-12. Generating an XML Schema (continued)

```
            }
        }
    }
}

public static void GenerateSchemasForDirectory(string dir)
{
    // make sure the directory exists
    if (Directory.Exists(dir))
    {
        // get the files in the directory
        string[] files = Directory.GetFiles(dir, "*.xml");
        foreach (string file in files)
        {
            GenerateSchemasForFile(file);
        }
    }
}
```

The GenerateSchemasForDirectory method can be called like this:

```
// Get the directory two levels up from where we are running.
DirectoryInfo di = new DirectoryInfo(@"..\..");
string dir = di.FullName;
// Generate the schema.
GenerateSchemasForDirectory(dir);
```

Discussion

Having an XSD for the XML files in an application allows for a number of things:

1. Validation of XML presented to the system
2. Documentation of the semantics of the data
3. Programmatic discovery of the data structure through XML reading methods

Using the GenerateSchemasForFile method can jump-start the process of developing schema for your XML, but each schema should be reviewed by the team member responsible for producing the XML. This will help to ensure that the rules as stated in the schema are correct and also to make sure that additional items such as schema default values and other relationships are added. Any relationships that were not present in the example XML files would be missed by the schema generator.

See Also

The "XmlSchemaInference Class" and "XML Schemas (XSD) Reference" topics in the MSDN documentation.

15.14 Passing Parameters to Transformations

Problem

You need to transform some data using a mostly common pattern. For the few data items that could change between transformations, you don't want to have a separate mechanism for each variation.

Solution

If you are using LINQ to XML, simply build a method to encapsulate the transformation code and pass parameters to the method just as you normally would for other code:

```
// transform using LINQ instead of XSLT
string storeTitle = "Hero Comics Inventory";
string pageDate = DateTime.Now.ToString("F");
XElement parameterExample = XElement.Load(@"..\..\ParameterExample.xml");
string htmlPath = @"..\..\ParameterExample_LINQ.htm";
TransformWithParameters(storeTitle, pageDate, parameterExample, htmlPath);

// now change the parameters
storeTitle = "Fabulous Adventures Inventory";
pageDate = DateTime.Now.ToString("D");
htmlPath = @"..\..\ParameterExample2_LINQ.htm";
TransformWithParameters(storeTitle, pageDate, parameterExample, htmlPath);
```

The TransformWithParameters method looks like this:

```
private static void TransformWithParameters(string storeTitle, string pageDate,
    XElement parameterExample, string htmlPath)
{
    XElement transformedParameterExample =
        new XElement("html",
            new XElement("head"),
            new XElement("body",
                new XElement("h3", string.Format("Brought to you by {0} on {1}{2}",
                    storeTitle,pageDate,Environment.NewLine)),
                new XElement("br"),
                new XElement("table",
                    new XAttribute("border","2"),
                    new XElement("thead",
                        new XElement("tr",
                            new XElement("td",
                                new XElement("b","Heroes")),
                            new XElement("td",
                                new XElement("b","Edition")))),
                    new XElement("tbody",
                        from cb in parameterExample.Elements("ComicBook")
                        orderby cb.Attribute("name").Value descending
                        select new XElement("tr",
                                new XElement("td",cb.Attribute("name").Value),
```

```
                    new XElement("td",cb.Attribute("edition").
    Value))))));
        transformedParameterExample.Save(htmlPath);
}
```

If you are using XSLT to perform transformations, use the XsltArgumentList class to pass arguments to the XSLT transformation. This technique allows the program to generate an object for the stylesheet to access (such as a dynamic string) and use while it transforms the given XML file. The storeTitle and pageDate arguments are passed in to the transformation in the following example. The storeTitle is for the title of the comic store, and pageDate is the date the report is run for. These are added using the AddParam method of the XsltArgumentList object instance args:

```
XsltArgumentList args = new XsltArgumentList();
args.AddParam("storeTitle", "", "Hero Comics Inventory");
args.AddParam("pageDate", "", DateTime.Now.ToString("F"));

// Create a resolver with default credentials.
XmlUrlResolver resolver = new XmlUrlResolver();
resolver.Credentials = System.Net.CredentialCache.DefaultCredentials;
```

The XsltSettings class allows changing the behavior of the transformation. If you use the XsltSettings.Default instance, the transformation will be done without allowing scripting or the use of the document( ) XSLT function, as they can be security risks. If the stylesheet is from a trusted source, you can just create an XsltSettings object and use it, but it is better to be safe. Further changes to the code could open it up to use with untrusted XSLT stylesheets:

```
XslCompiledTransform transform = new XslCompiledTransform();
// Load up the stylesheet.
transform.Load(@"..\..\ParameterExample.xslt", XsltSettings.Default, resolver);

// Perform the transformation.
FileStream fs = null;
using (fs = new FileStream(@"..\..\ParameterExample.htm",
        FileMode.OpenOrCreate, FileAccess.Write))
{
    transform.Transform(@"..\..\ParameterExample.xml", args, fs);
}
```

To show the different parameters in action, now you change storeTitle and pageDate again and run the transformation again:

```
// Now change the parameters and reprocess.
args = new XsltArgumentList();
args.AddParam("storeTitle", "", "Fabulous Adventures Inventory");
args.AddParam("pageDate", "", DateTime.Now.ToString("D"));
using (fs = new FileStream(@"..\..\ParameterExample2.htm",
    FileMode.OpenOrCreate, FileAccess.Write))
{
    transform.Transform(@"..\..\ParameterExample.xml", args, fs);
}
```

The *ParameterExample.xml* file contains the following:

```
<?xml version="1.0" encoding="utf-8" ?>
<ParameterExample>
    <ComicBook name="The Amazing Spider-Man" edition="1"/>
    <ComicBook name="The Uncanny X-Men" edition="2"/>
    <ComicBook name="Superman" edition="3"/>
    <ComicBook name="Batman" edition="4"/>
    <ComicBook name="The Fantastic Four" edition="5"/>
</ParameterExample>
```

The *ParameterExample.xslt* file contains the following:

```
<?xml version="1.0" encoding="UTF-8" ?>
<xsl:stylesheet version="1.0" xmlns:xsl="http://www.w3.org/1999/XSL/Transform">
  <xsl:output method="html" indent="yes" />
  <xsl:param name="storeTitle"/>
    <xsl:param name="pageDate"/>

    <xsl:template match="ParameterExample">
    <html>
      <head/>
      <body>
        <h3><xsl:text>Brought to you by </xsl:text>
        <xsl:value-of select="$storeTitle"/><br/>
        <xsl:text> on </xsl:text>
        <xsl:value-of select="$pageDate"/>
        <xsl:text> &#xd;&#xa;</xsl:text>
        </h3>
        <br/>
        <table border="2">
          <thead>
            <tr>
              <td>
                <b>Heroes</b>
              </td>
              <td>
                <b>Edition</b>
              </td>
            </tr>
          </thead>
          <tbody>
            <xsl:apply-templates/>
          </tbody>
        </table>
        </body>
    </html>
</xsl:template>

  <xsl:template match="ComicBook">
  <tr>
    <td>
      <xsl:value-of select="@name"/>
    </td>
    <td>
```

```
      <xsl:value-of select="@edition"/>
    </td>
    </tr>
  </xsl:template>
</xsl:stylesheet>
```

The output from the first transformation using XSLT to *ParameterExample.htm* or using LINQ to ParameterExample_LINQ.htm is shown in Figure 15-2.

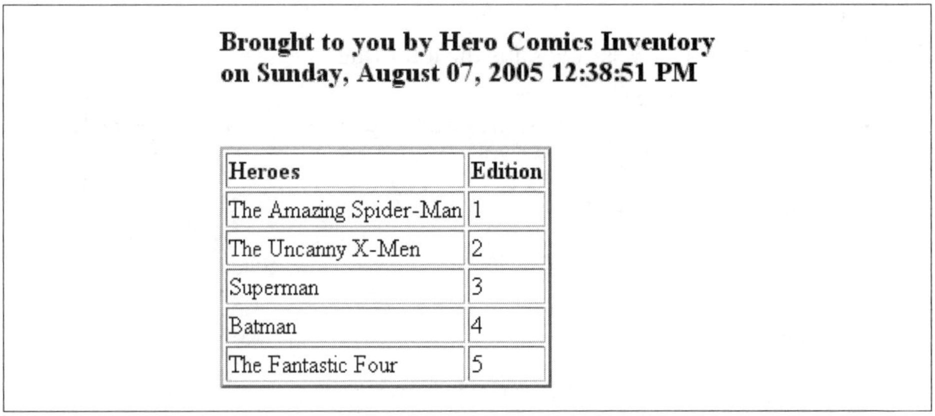

Brought to you by Hero Comics Inventory on Sunday, August 07, 2005 12:38:51 PM

Heroes	Edition
The Amazing Spider-Man	1
The Uncanny X-Men	2
Superman	3
Batman	4
The Fantastic Four	5

Figure 15-2. Output from the first set of parameters

Output from the second transformation using XSLT to *ParameterExample2.htm* or using LINQ to ParameterExample2_LINQ.htm is shown in Figure 15-3.

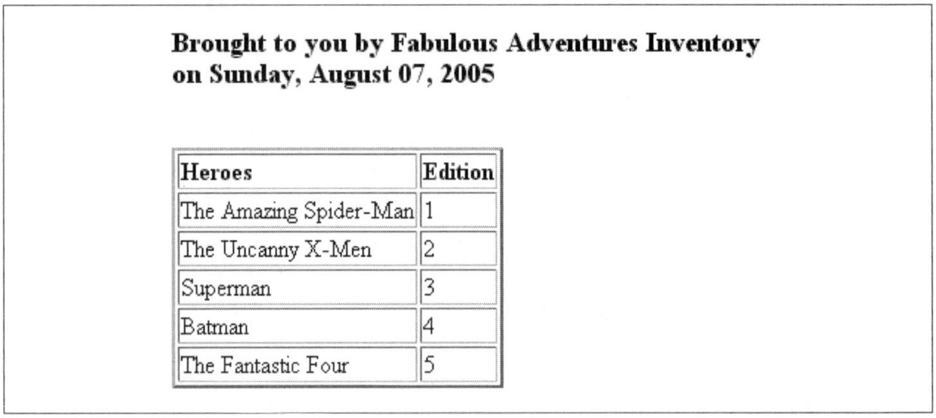

Brought to you by Fabulous Adventures Inventory on Sunday, August 07, 2005

Heroes	Edition
The Amazing Spider-Man	1
The Uncanny X-Men	2
Superman	3
Batman	4
The Fantastic Four	5

Figure 15-3. Output from the second set of parameters

Discussion

Both approaches allow you to templatize your code and provide parameters to modify the output. With the LINQ to XML method, the code is all in .NET, and .NET analysis tools can be used to measure the impact of the transformation. The declarative style of the code conveys the intent more clearly than having to go to the external XSLT file. If you don't know XSLT, you don't have to learn it as you can do it in code now.

If you already know XSLT, you can continue to leverage it. The ability to pass information to the XSLT stylesheet allows a much greater degree of flexibility when designing reports or user interfaces via XSLT transformations. This capability can help customize the output based on just about any criteria you can think of, as the data being passed in is totally controlled by your program. Once you get the hang of using parameters with XSLT, a whole new level of customization becomes possible. As an added bonus, it is portable between environments (.NET, Xalan, etc.).

See Also

The "LINQ, transforming data," "XsltArgumentList Class," and "XsltSettings Class" topics in the MSDN documentation.

CHAPTER 16

Networking

16.0 Introduction

.NET provides many classes to help make network programming easier than many environments that preceded it. There is a great deal of functionality to assist you with tasks such as:

- Building network-aware applications.
- Downloading files via FTP.
- Sending and receiving HTTP requests.
- Getting a higher degree of control using TCP/IP and sockets directly.

In the areas in which Microsoft has not provided managed classes to access networking functionality (such as some of the methods exposed by the WinInet API for Internet connection settings), there is always P/Invoke, so you can code to the Win32 API; you'll explore this in this chapter. With all of the functionality at your disposal in the System.Net namespaces, you can write network utilities very quickly. Let's take a closer look at just a few of the things this section of .NET provides you access to.

16.1 Writing a TCP Server

Problem

You need to create a server that listens on a port for incoming requests from a TCP client. These client requests can then be processed at the server, and any responses can be sent back to the client. Recipe 16.2 shows how to write a TCP client to interact with this server.

Solution

Use the MyTcpServer class created here to listen on a TCP-based endpoint for requests arriving on a given port:

```
class MyTcpServer
{
    #region Private Members
    private TcpListener _listener;
    private IPAddress _address;
    private int _port;
    private bool _listening;
    private object _syncRoot = new object();
    #endregion

    #region CTORs

    public MyTcpServer(IPAddress address, int port)
    {
        _port = port;
        _address = address;
    }
    #endregion // CTORs
```

The TCPServer class has two properties:

- Address, an IPAddress
- Port, an int

These return the current address and port on which the server is listening and the listening state:

```
    #region Properties
    public IPAddress Address
    {
        get { return _address; }
    }

    public int Port
    {
        get { return _port; }
    }

    public bool Listening
    {
        get { return _listening; }
    }
    #endregion
```

The Listen method tells the MyTcpServer class to start listening on the specified address and port combination. You create and start a TcpListener, and then call its AcceptTcpClient method to wait for a client request to arrive. Once the client connects, a request is sent to the thread pool to service the client and that runs the ProcessClient method.

The listener shuts down after serving the client:

```
    #region Public Methods
    public void Listen()
```

```
        {
            try
            {
                lock (_syncRoot)
                {
                    _listener = new TcpListener(_address, _port);

                    // fire up the server
                    _listener.Start();

                    // set listening bit
                    _listening = true;
                }

                // Enter the listening loop.
                do
                {
                    Trace.Write("Looking for someone to talk to... ");

                    // Wait for connection
                    TcpClient newClient = _listener.AcceptTcpClient();
                    Trace.WriteLine("Connected to new client");

                    // queue a request to take care of the client
                    ThreadPool.QueueUserWorkItem(new WaitCallback(ProcessClient),
    newClient);
                }
                while (_listening);
            }
            catch (SocketException se)
            {
                Trace.WriteLine("SocketException: " + se.ToString());
            }
            finally
            {
                // shut it down
                StopListening();
            }
        }
```

The StopListening method is called to stop the TCPServer from listening for requests:

```
        public void StopListening()
        {
            if (_listening)
            {
                lock (_syncRoot)
                {
                    // set listening bit
                    _listening = false;
                    // shut it down
                    _listener.Stop();
                }
            }
        }
        #endregion
```

The ProcessClient method shown in Example 16-1 executes on a thread-pool thread to serve a connected client. It gets the NetworkStream from the client using the TcpClient.GetStream method and then reads the whole request. After sending back a response, it shuts down the client connection.

Example 16-1. ProcessClient method

```
#region Private Methods
private void ProcessClient(object client)
{
    TcpClient newClient = (TcpClient)client;
    try
    {
        // Buffer for reading data
        byte[] bytes = new byte[1024];
        StringBuilder clientData = new StringBuilder( );

        // get the stream to talk to the client over
        using (NetworkStream ns = newClient.GetStream( ))
        {
            // set initial read timeout to 1 minute to allow for connection
            ns.ReadTimeout = 60000;
            // Loop to receive all the data sent by the client.
            int bytesRead = 0;
            do
            {
                // read the data
                try
                {
                    bytesRead = ns.Read(bytes, 0, bytes.Length);
                    if (bytesRead > 0)
                    {
                        // Translate data bytes to an ASCII string and append
                        clientData.Append(
                            Encoding.ASCII.GetString(bytes, 0, bytesRead));
                        // decrease read timeout to 1 second now that data is
                        // coming in
                        ns.ReadTimeout = 1000;
                    }
                }
                catch (IOException ioe)
                {
                    // read timed out, all data has been retrieved
                    Trace.WriteLine("Read timed out: {0}",ioe.ToString( ));
                    bytesRead = 0;
                }
            }
            while (bytesRead > 0);

            Trace.WriteLine("Client says: {0}", clientData.ToString( ));

            // Thank them for their input
            bytes = Encoding.ASCII.GetBytes("Thanks call again!");
```

Example 16-1. ProcessClient method (continued)

```
                // Send back a response.
                ns.Write(bytes, 0, bytes.Length);
            }
        }
        finally
        {
            // stop talking to client
            if(newClient != null)
                newClient.Close();
        }
    }
    #endregion
}
```

A simple server that listens for clients until the Escape key is pressed might look like
the following code:

```
class Program
{
    static MyTcpServer server;
    static void Main()
    {
        // Run the server on a different thread
        ThreadPool.QueueUserWorkItem(RunServer);

        Console.WriteLine("Press Esc to stop the server...");
        ConsoleKeyInfo cki;
        while(true)
        {

            cki = Console.ReadKey();
            if (cki.Key == ConsoleKey.Escape)
                break;
        }
    }

    static void RunServer( object stateInfo )
    {
        // Fire it up
        server = new MyTcpServer(IPAddress.Loopback,55555);
        server.Listen();
    }
}
```

When talking to the MyTcpClient class in Recipe 16.2, the output for the server looks
like this:

```
Press Esc to stop the server...
Looking for someone to talk to... Connected to new client
Looking for someone to talk to... Client says: Just wanted to say hi
Connected to new client
Looking for someone to talk to... Client says: Just wanted to say hi again
Connected to new client
```

```
Looking for someone to talk to... Client says: Are you ignoring me?
Connected to new client
Looking for someone to talk to... Connected to new client
Looking for someone to talk to... Client says: I'll not be ignored! (round 0)
Client says: I'll not be ignored! (round 1)
Connected to new client
Looking for someone to talk to... Connected to new client
Looking for someone to talk to... Client says: I'll not be ignored! (round 2)
Client says: I'll not be ignored! (round 3)
Connected to new client
Looking for someone to talk to... Client says: I'll not be ignored! (round 4)
Connected to new client
Looking for someone to talk to... Client says: I'll not be ignored! (round 5)
Connected to new client
Looking for someone to talk to... Client says: I'll not be ignored! (round 6)
Connected to new client
Looking for someone to talk to... Client says: I'll not be ignored! (round 7)
Connected to new client
Looking for someone to talk to... Client says: I'll not be ignored! (round 8)
[more output follows...]
```

Discussion

The Transmission Control Protocol (TCP) is the protocol used by the majority of traffic on the Internet today. TCP is responsible for the correct delivery of data packets from one endpoint to another. It uses the Internet Protocol (IP) to make the delivery. IP handles getting the packets from node to node; TCP detects when packets are not correct, are missing, or are sent out of order, and it arranges for missing or damaged packets to be resent. The TCPServer class is a basic server mechanism for dealing with requests that come from clients over TCP.

MyTcpServer takes the IP address and port passed in the Listen method and creates a TcpListener on that IPAddress and port. Once created, the TcpListener.Start method is called to start up the server. The blocking AcceptTcpClient method is called to listen for requests from TCP-based clients. Once the client connects, the ProcessClient method is executed. In this method, the server reads request data from the client and returns a brief acknowledgment. The server disconnects from the client by calling NetworkStream.Close and TcpClient.Close. The server stops listening when the StopListening method is called. StopListening takes the server offline by calling TcpListener.Stop.

See Also

The "IPAddress Class," "TcpListener Class," and "TcpClient Class" topics in the MSDN documentation.

16.2 Writing a TCP Client

Problem

You want to interact with a TCP-based server.

Solution

Use the `MyTcpClient` class shown in Example 16-2 to connect to and converse with a TCP-based server by passing the address and port of the server to talk to, using the `System.Net.TcpClient` class. This example will talk to the server from Recipe 16.1.

Example 16-2. MyTcpClient class

```
class MyTcpClient
{

    private TcpClient _client;
    private IPAddress _address;
    private int _port;
    private IPEndPoint _endPoint;
    private bool _disposed;

    public MyTcpClient(IPAddress address, int port)
    {
        _address = address;
        _port = port;
        _endPoint = new IPEndPoint(_address, _port);
    }


    public void ConnectToServer(string msg)
    {
        try
        {
            _client = new TcpClient();
            _client.Connect(_endPoint);

            // Get the bytes to send for the message
            byte[] bytes = Encoding.ASCII.GetBytes(msg);
            // Get the stream to talk to the server on
            using (NetworkStream ns = _client.GetStream())
            {
                // Send message
                Trace.WriteLine("Sending message to server: " + msg);
                ns.Write(bytes, 0, bytes.Length);
                // Get the response
                // Buffer to store the response bytes
                bytes = new byte[1024];

                // Display the response
                int bytesRead = ns.Read(bytes, 0, bytes.Length);
```

Example 16-2. MyTcpClient class (continued)

```
            string serverResponse = Encoding.ASCII.GetString(bytes, 0, bytesRead);
            Trace.WriteLine("Server said: " + serverResponse);
        }
    }
    catch (SocketException se)
    {
        Trace.WriteLine("There was an error talking to the server: " +
            se.ToString( ));
    }
    finally
    {
        Dispose( );
    }
}

#region IDisposable Members

public void Dispose( )
{
    Dispose(true);
    GC.SuppressFinalize(this);
}

private void Dispose(bool disposing)
{
    if (!_disposed)
    {
        if (disposing)
        {
            if (_client != null)
                _client.Close( );
        }
        _disposed = true;
    }
}

#endregion

}
```

To use the MyTcpClient in a program, you can simply create an instance of it and call ConnectToServer to send a request. In this program, you first make three calls to the server to test the basic mechanism. Next, you enter a loop to really pound on it and make sure you force it over the default ThreadPool limit. This verifies that the server's mechanism for handling multiple requests is sound:

```
static void Main( )
{

    MakeClientCallToServer("Just wanted to say hi");
    MakeClientCallToServer("Just wanted to say hi again");
    MakeClientCallToServer("Are you ignoring me?");
```

```
        // Now send a bunch of messages...
        string msg;
        for (int i = 0; i < 100; i++)
        {
            msg = string.Format(Thread.CurrentThread.CurrentCulture,
                        "I'll not be ignored! (round {0})", i);
            ThreadPool.QueueUserWorkItem(new
WaitCallback(MakeClientCallToServer), msg);
        }

        Console.WriteLine("\n Press any key to continue... (if you can find it...
)");
        Console.Read();
    }

    static void MakeClientCallToServer(object objMsg)
    {
        string msg = (string)objMsg;
        MyTcpClient client = new MyTcpClient(IPAddress.Loopback,55555);
        client.ConnectToServer(msg);
    }
```

The output on the client side for this exchange of messages is:

```
Sending message to server: Just wanted to say hi
Server said: Thanks call again!
Sending message to server: Just wanted to say hi again
Server said: Thanks call again!
Sending message to server: Are you ignoring me?
Server said: Thanks call again!
 Press any key to continue... (if you can find it...)
Sending message to server: I'll not be ignored! (round 0)
Sending message to server: I'll not be ignored! (round 1)
Server said: Thanks call again!
Server said: Thanks call again!
Sending message to server: I'll not be ignored! (round 2)
Server said: Thanks call again!
Sending message to server: I'll not be ignored! (round 3)
Sending message to server: I'll not be ignored! (round 4)
Server said: Thanks call again!
Server said: Thanks call again!
Sending message to server: I'll not be ignored! (round 5)
Sending message to server: I'll not be ignored! (round 6)
Server said: Thanks call again!
Server said: Thanks call again!
Sending message to server: I'll not be ignored! (round 7)
Sending message to server: I'll not be ignored! (round 8)
Server said: Thanks call again!
[more output follows...]
```

Discussion

MyTcpClient.ConnectToServer is designed to send one message, get the response, display it as a string, and then close the connection. To accomplish this, it creates a

---

System.Net.TcpClient and connects to the server by calling the `TcpClient.Connect` method. Connect targets the server using an `IPEndPoint` built from the address and port that you passed to the `MyTcpClient` constructor.

`MyTcpClient.ConnectToServer` then gets the bytes for the string using the `Encoding.ASCII.GetBytes` method. Once it has the bytes to send, it gets the `NetworkStream` from the underlying `System.Net.TcpClient` by calling its `GetStream` method and then sends the message using the `TcpClient.Write` method.

In order to receive the response from the server, the blocking `TcpClient.Read` method is called. Once `Read` returns, the bytes are decoded to get the string that contains the response from the server. The connections are then closed and the client ends.

See Also

The "TcpClient Class," "NetworkStream Class," and "Encoding.ASCII Property" topics in the MSDN documentation.

16.3   Simulating Form Execution

Problem

You need to send a collection of name-value pairs to simulate a form being executed on a browser to a location identified by a URL.

Solution

Use the `System.Net.WebClient` class to send a set of name-value pairs to the web server using the `UploadValues` method. This class enables you to masquerade as the browser executing a form by setting up the name-value pairs with the input data. The input field ID is the name, and the value to use in the field is the value:

```
using System;
using System.Net;
using System.Text;
using System.Collections.Specialized;

// In order to use this, you need to run the CSCBWeb project first.
Uri uri = new Uri("http://localhost:7472/CSCBWeb/WebForm1.aspx");
WebClient client = new WebClient();

// Create a series of name/value pairs to send
// Add necessary parameter/value pairs to the name/value container.
NameValueCollection collection = new NameValueCollection()
        { {"Item", "WebParts"},
          {"Identity", "foo@bar.com"},
          {"Quantity", "5"} };
```

```
                Console.WriteLine("Uploading name/value pairs to URI {0} ...",
                    uri.AbsoluteUri);

                // Upload the NameValueCollection.
                byte[] responseArray =
                    client.UploadValues(uri.AbsoluteUri,"POST",collection);
                // Decode and display the response.
                Console.WriteLine("\nResponse received was {0}",
                            Encoding.ASCII.GetString(responseArray));
```

The *WebForm1.aspx* page, which receives and processes this data, looks like this:

```
<%@ Page Language="C#" AutoEventWireup="true" CodeFile="WebForm1.aspx.cs"
    Inherits="WebForm1" %>

<!DOCTYPE html PUBLIC "-//W3C//DTD XHTML 1.0 Transitional//EN" "http://www.w3.org/TR/
xhtml1/DTD/xhtml1-transitional.dtd">

<html xmlns="http://www.w3.org/1999/xhtml">
<head runat="server">
    <title>Untitled Page</title>
</head>
<body>
    <form id="form1" runat="server">
    <div>


                    <asp:Table ID="Table1" runat="server" Height="139px" Width="361px">
                        <asp:TableRow runat="server">
                                <asp:TableCell runat="server"><asp:Label ID="Label1"
                    runat="server" Text="Identity"></asp:Label></asp:TableCell>
                                <asp:TableCell runat="server"><asp:TextBox
ID="Identity"
                    runat="server"/></asp:TableCell>
                         </asp:TableRow>
                         <asp:TableRow runat="server">
                                <asp:TableCell runat="server"><asp:Label ID="Label2"
                    runat="server" Text="Item"></asp:Label></asp:TableCell>
                                <asp:TableCell runat="server"><asp:TextBox ID="Item"
                    runat="server"/></asp:TableCell>
                         </asp:TableRow>
                         <asp:TableRow runat="server">
                                <asp:TableCell runat="server"><asp:Label ID="Label3"
                    runat="server" Text="Quantity"></asp:Label></asp:TableCell>
                                <asp:TableCell runat="server"><asp:TextBox
ID="Quantity"
                    runat="server"/></asp:TableCell>
                         </asp:TableRow>
                         <asp:TableRow runat="server">
                                <asp:TableCell runat="server"></asp:TableCell>
                                <asp:TableCell runat="server"><asp:Button
ID="Button1"
                    runat="server" onclick="Button1_Click" Text="Submit" />
                        </asp:TableCell>
```

```
                    </asp:TableRow>
                </asp:Table>

        </div>
        </form>
    </body>
    </html>
```

The *WebForm1.aspx.cs* code-behind looks like this. The added code is highlighted:

```csharp
using System;
using System.Data;
using System.Configuration;
using System.Collections;
using System.Linq;
using System.Web;
using System.Web.Security;
using System.Web.UI;
using System.Web.UI.WebControls;
using System.Web.UI.WebControls.WebParts;
using System.Web.UI.HtmlControls;

public partial class WebForm1 : System.Web.UI.Page
{
    protected void Page_Load(object sender, EventArgs e)
    {
        if(HttpContext.Current.Request.HttpMethod.ToUpper() == "POST")
            WriteOrderResponse();
    }
    protected void Button1_Click(object sender, EventArgs e)
    {
        WriteOrderResponse();
    }

    private void WriteOrderResponse()
    {
        string response = "Thanks for the order!<br/>";
        response += "Identity: " + Request.Form["Identity"] + "<br/>";
        response += "Item: " + Request.Form["Item"] + "<br/>";
        response += "Quantity: " + Request.Form["Quantity"] + "<br/>";
        Response.Write(response);
    }
}
```

The output from the form execution looks like this:

```
Uploading name/value pairs to URI http://localhost:7472/CSCBWeb/WebForm1.aspx ..


Response received was Thanks for the order!<br/>Identity: foo@bar.com<br/>Item:
WebParts<br/>Quantity: 5<br/>

<!DOCTYPE html PUBLIC "-//W3C//DTD XHTML 1.0 Transitional//EN" "http://www.w3.or
g/TR/xhtml1/DTD/xhtml1-transitional.dtd">
```

```
<html xmlns="http://www.w3.org/1999/xhtml">
<head><title>
        Untitled Page
</title></head>
<body>
    <form name="form1" method="post" action="WebForm1.aspx" id="form1">
<input type="hidden" name="__VIEWSTATE" id="__VIEWSTATE" value="/wEPDwULLTE3NDA4
NzI1OTJkZB2moEknx/mTLCJNLTrBOEGrhM3D" />

    <div>


            <table id="Table1" border="0" height="139" width="361">
        <tr>
                <td><span id="Label1">Identity</span></td><td><input name="Ident
ity" type="text" id="Identity" /></td>
        </tr><tr>
                <td><span id="Label2">Item</span></td><td><input name="Item" typ
e="text" id="Item" /></td>
        </tr><tr>
                <td><span id="Label3">Quantity</span></td><td><input name="Quant
ity" type="text" id="Quantity" /></td>
        </tr><tr>
                <td></td><td><input type="submit" name="Button1" value="Submit"
id="Button1" /></td>
        </tr>
</table>

    </div>

<input type="hidden" name="__EVENTVALIDATION" id="__EVENTVALIDATION" value="/wEW
BQLktuPhBwKM4NreDQL4grehBwKA7JylAQKM54rGBgRICl8TJUTG4pCLohSUmn9Hivnl" /></form>
</body>
</html>
```

Discussion

The WebClient class makes it easy to upload form data to a web server in the common format of a set of name-value pairs. You can see this technique in the call to UploadValues that takes an absolute URI (*http://localhost/FormSim/WebForm1.aspx*), the HTTP method to use (POST), and the NameValueCollection you created (collection). The NameValueCollection is populated with the data for each of the fields on the form by calling its Add method, passing the id of the input field as the name and the value to put in the field as the value. In this example, you fill in the Identity field with *foo@bar.com*, the Item field with Book, and the Quantity field with 5. You then print out the resulting response from the POST to the console window.

See Also

The "WebClient Class" topic in the MSDN documentation.

16.4 Transferring Data via HTTP

Problem

You need to download data from or upload data to a location specified by a URL; this data can be either an array of bytes or a file.

Solution

Use the `WebClient.UploadData` or `WebClient.DownloadData` methods to transfer data using a URL.

To download the data for a web page, do the following:

```
Uri uri = new Uri("http://localhost:4088/CSCBWeb/DownloadData16_4.aspx");

// make a client
using (WebClient client = new WebClient())
{
    // get the contents of the file
    Console.WriteLine("Downloading {0} ",uri.AbsoluteUri);
    // download the page and store the bytes
    byte[] bytes;
    try
    {
        bytes = client.DownloadData(uri);
    }
    catch (WebException we)
    {
        Console.WriteLine(we.ToString());
        return;
    }
    // Write the content out
    string page = Encoding.ASCII.GetString(bytes);
    Console.WriteLine(page);
}
```

This will produce the following output:

```
Downloading http://localhost:4088/CSCBWeb/DownloadData16_4.aspx


<!DOCTYPE html PUBLIC "-//W3C//DTD XHTML 1.0 Transitional//EN" "http://www.w3.or
g/TR/xhtml1/DTD/xhtml1-transitional.dtd">

<html xmlns="http://www.w3.org/1999/xhtml">
<head><title>
        Untitled Page
</title></head>
<body>
    <form name="Form1" method="post" action="DownloadData16_4.aspx" id="Form2">
        <input type="hidden" name="__VIEWSTATE"
value="dDwyMDQwNjUzNDY2Ozs+kS9hguYm9369sybDqmIow0AvxBg=" />
```

```
    <span id="Label1" style="Z-INDEX: 101; LEFT: 142px; POSITION: absolute;
TOP: 164px">This is downloaded html!</span>
    </form>
</body>
</html>
```

You can also download data to a file using DownloadFile:

```
Uri uri = new Uri("http://localhost:4088/CSCBWeb/DownloadData16_4.aspx");
    // Make a client
    using (WebClient client = new WebClient())
    {
    // go get the file
    Console.WriteLine("Retrieving file from {0}...\r\n", uri);
    // get file and put it in a temp file
    string tempFile = Path.GetTempFileName();
    try
    {
        client.DownloadFile(uri, tempFile);
    }
    catch (WebException we)
    {
        Console.WriteLine(we.ToString());
        return;
    }
    Console.WriteLine("Downloaded {0} to {1}", uri, tempFile);
    }
```

This will produce the following output:

```
Retrieving file from http://localhost:4088/CSCBWeb/DownloadData16_4.aspx...

Downloaded http://localhost:4088/CSCBWeb/DownloadData16_4.aspx to C:\Documents a
nd Settings\Jay Hilyard\Local Settings\Temp\tmp6F0.tmp
```

To upload a file to a URL, use UploadFile like so:

```
    // Make a client
    using (WebClient client = new WebClient())
    {
        // Go get the file
        Console.WriteLine("Retrieving file from {0}...\r\n", uri);
        // Get file and put it in a temp file
        string tempFile = Path.GetTempFileName();
        client.DownloadFile(uri,tempFile);
        Console.WriteLine("Downloaded {0} to {1}",uri,tempFile);
    }
```

The code for an ASPX page that could receive this would look like this:

```
using System;
using System.Data;
using System.Configuration;
using System.Collections;
using System.Linq;
using System.Web;
using System.Web.Security;
```

```csharp
using System.Web.UI;
using System.Web.UI.WebControls;
using System.Web.UI.WebControls.WebParts;
using System.Web.UI.HtmlControls;
using System.Diagnostics;

public partial class UploadData16_4 : System.Web.UI.Page
{
    protected void Page_Load(object sender, EventArgs e)
    {
        foreach (string f in Request.Files.AllKeys)
        {
            HttpPostedFile file = Request.Files[f];
            // need to have write permissions for the directory to write to
            try
            {
                string path = Server.MapPath(".") + @"\" + file.FileName;
                file.SaveAs(path);
                Response.Write("Saved " + path);
            }
            catch (HttpException hex)
            {
                // return error information specific to the save
                Response.Write("Failed to save file with error: " +
                    hex.Message);
            }
        }
    }
}
```

This will produce the following output:

```
Uploading to http://localhost:4088/CSCBWeb/UploadData16_4.aspx
Uploaded successfully to http://localhost:4088/CSCBWeb/UploadData16_4.aspx
```

Discussion

WebClient simplifies downloading of files and bytes in files, as these are common tasks when dealing with the Web. The more traditional stream-based method for downloading can also be accessed via the OpenRead method on the WebClient.

See Also

The "WebClient Class" topic in the MSDN documentation.

16.5 Using Named Pipes to Communicate

Problem

You need a way to use named pipes to communicate with another application across the network.

Solution

Use the new `NamedPipeClientStream` and `NamedPipeServerStream` in the System.IO. Pipes namespace. You can then create a client and server to work with named pipes.

In order to use the `NamedPipeClientStream` class, you need some code like that shown in Example 16-3.

Example 16-3. Using the NamedPipeClientStream class

```
using System;
using System.Collections.Generic;
using System.Text;
using System.IO;
using System.Diagnostics;
using System.IO.Pipes;

namespace NamedPipes
{
    class NamedPipeClientConsole
    {
        static void Main( )
        {
            // set up a message to send
            string messageText = "This is my message!";
            int bytesRead;

            // set up the named pipe client and close it when complete
            using (NamedPipeClientStream clientPipe =
                    new NamedPipeClientStream(".","mypipe",
                        PipeDirection.InOut,PipeOptions.None))
            {
                // connect to the server stream
                clientPipe.Connect( );
                // set the read mode to message
                clientPipe.ReadMode = PipeTransmissionMode.Message;

                // write the message ten times
                for (int i = 0; i < 10; i++)
                {
                    Console.WriteLine("Sending message: " + messageText);
                    byte[] messageBytes = Encoding.Unicode.GetBytes(messageText);
                    // check and write the message
                    if (clientPipe.CanWrite)
                    {
                        clientPipe.Write(messageBytes, 0, messageBytes.Length);
                        clientPipe.Flush( );
                        // wait till it is read
                        clientPipe.WaitForPipeDrain( );
                    }

                    // set up a buffer for the message bytes
                    messageBytes = new byte[256];
```

Example 16-3. Using the NamedPipeClientStream class (continued)

```
                do
                {
                    // collect the message bits in the stringbuilder
                    StringBuilder message = new StringBuilder();

                    // read all of the bits until we have the
                    // complete response message
                    do
                    {
                        // read from the pipe
                        bytesRead =
                            clientPipe.Read(messageBytes, 0, messageBytes.Length);
                        // if we got something, add it to the message
                        if (bytesRead > 0)
                        {
                            message.Append(
                                Encoding.Unicode.GetString(messageBytes,
                                                       0, bytesRead));
                            Array.Clear(messageBytes, 0, messageBytes.Length);
                        }
                    }
                    while (!clientPipe.IsMessageComplete);

                    // set to zero as we have read the whole message
                    bytesRead = 0;
                    Console.WriteLine("    Received message: " +
                                        message.ToString());
                }
                while (bytesRead != 0);

            }
        }

        Console.WriteLine("Press Enter to exit...");
        Console.ReadLine();
    }
  }
}
```

Then, to set up a server for the client to talk to, you use the `NamedPipeServerStream` class, as shown in Example 16-4.

Example 16-4. Setting up a server for the client

```
using System;
using System.Collections.Generic;
using System.Text;
using System.IO;
using System.ComponentModel;
using System.IO.Pipes;

namespace NamedPipes
```

Example 16-4. Setting up a server for the client (continued)

```
{
    class NamedPipeServerConsole
    {
        static void Main(string[] args)
        {
            // Start up our named pipe in message mode and close the pipe
            // when done.
            using (NamedPipeServerStream serverPipe = new
                    NamedPipeServerStream("mypipe", PipeDirection.InOut, 1,
                    PipeTransmissionMode.Message, PipeOptions.None))
            {
                // wait for a client...
                serverPipe.WaitForConnection();

                // process messages until the client goes away
                while (serverPipe.IsConnected)
                {
                    int bytesRead = 0;
                    byte[] messageBytes = new byte[256];
                    // read until we have the message, then respond
                    do
                    {
                        // build up the client message
                        StringBuilder message = new StringBuilder();

                        // check that we can read the pipe
                        if (serverPipe.CanRead)
                        {
                            // loop until the entire message is read
                            do
                            {
                                bytesRead =
                                    serverPipe.Read(messageBytes,
                                                0, messageBytes.Length);

                                // got bytes from the stream so add them to the message
                                if (bytesRead > 0)
                                {
                                    message.Append(
                                        Encoding.Unicode.GetString(messageBytes,
                                                                0,bytesRead));
                                    Array.Clear(messageBytes,
                                                0, messageBytes.Length);
                                }
                            }
                            while (!serverPipe.IsMessageComplete);
                        }

                        // if we got a message, write it out and respond
                        if (message.Length > 0)
                        {
                            // set to zero, as we have read the whole message
```

Example 16-4. Setting up a server for the client (continued)

```
                            bytesRead = 0;
                            Console.WriteLine("Received message: " + message.ToString( ));

                            // return the message text we got from the
                            // client in reverse
                            char[] messageChars =
                                message.ToString( ).Trim( ).ToCharArray( );
                            Array.Reverse(messageChars);
                            string reversedMessageText = new string(messageChars);

                            // show the return message
                            Console.WriteLine("    Returning Message: " +
                                reversedMessageText);

                            // write the response
                            messageBytes = Encoding.Unicode.GetBytes(messageChars);
                            if (serverPipe.CanWrite)
                            {
                                // write the message
                                serverPipe.Write(messageBytes, 0, messageBytes.Length);
                                // flush the buffer
                                serverPipe.Flush( );
                                // wait till read by client
                                serverPipe.WaitForPipeDrain( );
                            }
                        }
                    }
                    while (bytesRead != 0);
                }
            }


            // make our server hang around so you can see the messages sent
            Console.WriteLine("Press Enter to exit...");
            Console.ReadLine( );
        }
    }
}
```

Discussion

Named pipes are a mechanism to allow interprocess or intermachine communications in Windows. The .NET Framework has finally provided managed access to named pipes in .NET 3.5, which helps to make it much easier to utilize named pipes in managed applications. In many cases, you could use Windows Communication Foundation (WCF) to set up the server and client code and even provide a named pipe binding to accomplish this as well. It depends on what your application requirements call for as well as what level of the application stack you want to work at. If you have an existing application that sets up a named pipe, why use WCF when you can just connect directly? Using named pipes is like using sockets and keeps your code very close to the pipe. The positive side of this is that there are less code layers to process; the drawback is that you have to do more in terms of message processing.

In the Solution, we created some code to use NamedPipeClientStream and NamedPipeServerStream. The interaction between these two goes like this:

1. The server process is started; it fires up a NamedPipeServerStream and then calls WaitForConnection to wait for a client to connect:

```
// Start up our named pipe in message mode and close the pipe
// when done.
using (NamedPipeServerStream serverPipe = new
        NamedPipeServerStream("mypipe", PipeDirection.InOut, 1,
        PipeTransmissionMode.Message, PipeOptions.None))
{
    // wait for a client...
    serverPipe.WaitForConnection();
```

2. The client process is created; it fires up a NamedPipeClientStream, calls Connect, and connects to the server process:

```
// set up the named pipe client and close it when complete
using (NamedPipeClientStream clientPipe =
        new NamedPipeClientStream(".","mypipe",
                        PipeDirection.InOut,PipeOptions.None))
{
    // connect to the server stream
    clientPipe.Connect();
```

3. The server process sees the connection from the client and then calls IsConnected in a loop looking for messages from the client until the connection is gone:

```
// process messages until the client goes away
while (serverPipe.IsConnected)
{
        // More processing code in here...
}
```

4. The client process then writes a number of messages to the server process using Write, Flush, and WaitForPipeDrain:

```
// set up a message to send
string messageText = "This is my message!";

// write the message ten times
for (int i = 0; i < 10; i++)
{
    Console.WriteLine("Sending message: " + messageText);
    byte[] messageBytes = Encoding.Unicode.GetBytes(messageText);
    // check and write the message
    if (clientPipe.CanWrite)
    {
        clientPipe.Write(messageBytes, 0, messageBytes.Length);
        clientPipe.Flush();
        // wait till it is read
        clientPipe.WaitForPipeDrain();
    }
```

```
        // response processing....
    }
```

5. When the client process receives the response from the server, it reads the message bytes until complete. If the message sending is complete, the NamedPipeClientStream goes out of the scope of the using statement and closes (thereby closing the connection on the client side) and then waits to go away when the user presses Enter:

```
// set up a buffer for the message bytes
messageBytes = new byte[256];
do
{
    // collect the message bits in the stringbuilder
    StringBuilder message = new StringBuilder();

    // read all of the bits until we have the
    // complete response message
    do
    {
        // read from the pipe
        bytesRead =
            clientPipe.Read(messageBytes, 0, messageBytes.
Length);

        // if we got something, add it to the message
        if (bytesRead > 0)
        {
            message.Append(
                Encoding.Unicode.GetString(messageBytes,
                                    0, bytesRead));
            Array.Clear(messageBytes, 0, messageBytes.Length);
        }
    }
    while (!clientPipe.IsMessageComplete);

    // set to zero as we have read the whole message
    bytesRead = 0;
    Console.WriteLine("    Received message: " +
                    message.ToString());
}
while (bytesRead != 0);
```

6. The server process notes that the client has closed the pipe connection via the failed IsConnected call in the while loop. It closes by the NamedPipeServerStream going out of scope of the using statement, which closes the pipe.

The client output looks like this:

```
Sending message: This is my message!
    Received message: !egassem ym si sihT
Sending message: This is my message!
    Received message: !egassem ym si sihT
Sending message: This is my message!
    Received message: !egassem ym si sihT
```

```
Sending message: This is my message!
    Received message: !egassem ym si sihT
Sending message: This is my message!
    Received message: !egassem ym si sihT
Sending message: This is my message!
    Received message: !egassem ym si sihT
Sending message: This is my message!
    Received message: !egassem ym si sihT
Sending message: This is my message!
    Received message: !egassem ym si sihT
Sending message: This is my message!
    Received message: !egassem ym si sihT
Sending message: This is my message!
    Received message: !egassem ym si sihT
Press Enter to exit...
```

The server output looks like this:

```
Received message: This is my message!
    Returning Message: !egassem ym si sihT
Received message: This is my message!
    Returning Message: !egassem ym si sihT
Received message: This is my message!
    Returning Message: !egassem ym si sihT
Received message: This is my message!
    Returning Message: !egassem ym si sihT
Received message: This is my message!
    Returning Message: !egassem ym si sihT
Received message: This is my message!
    Returning Message: !egassem ym si sihT
Received message: This is my message!
    Returning Message: !egassem ym si sihT
Received message: This is my message!
    Returning Message: !egassem ym si sihT
Received message: This is my message!
    Returning Message: !egassem ym si sihT
Received message: This is my message!
    Returning Message: !egassem ym si sihT
Press Enter to exit...
```

The PipeOptions enumeration controls how the pipe operations function. The enumeration values are described in Table 16-1.

Table 16-1. PipeOptions enumeration values

Member name	Description
None	No specific options are specified.
WriteThrough	When writing to the pipe, operations will not return control until the write is accomplished at the server. Without this flag, writes are buffered, and the write returns more quickly.
Asynchronous	Enables Asynchronous pipe usage (calls return immediately and process in the background).

See Also

The "Named Pipes," "NamedPipeClientStream Class," "NamedPipeServerStream Class," and "System.IO.Pipes Namespace" topics in the MSDN documentation.

16.6 Pinging Programmatically

Problem

You want to check a computer's availability on the network.

Solution

Use the `System.Net.NetworkInformation.Ping` class to determine if a machine is available. In the `TestPing` method, an instance of the `Ping` class is created. A ping request is sent using the `Send` method. The `Send` method is synchronous and returns a `PingReply` that can be examined for the result of the ping. You perform the second ping request asynchronously using the `SendAsync` method, after hooking up to the `Ping` class for the `PingCompleted` event. The second parameter of the `SendAsync` method holds a user token value that will be returned to the `pinger_PingCompleted` event handler when the ping is complete. This token can be used to identify requests between the initiation and completion code:

```
public static void TestPing()
{
    System.Net.NetworkInformation.Ping pinger =
        new System.Net.NetworkInformation.Ping();
    PingReply reply = pinger.Send("www.oreilly.com");
    DisplayPingReplyInfo(reply);

    pinger.PingCompleted += pinger_PingCompleted;
    pinger.SendAsync("www.oreilly.com", "oreilly ping");
}
```

The `DisplayPingReplyInfo` method shows some of the more common items you want to know from a ping, such as the `RoundtripTime` and the `Status` of the reply. These can be accessed from those properties on the `PingReply`:

```
private static void DisplayPingReplyInfo(PingReply reply)
{
    Console.WriteLine("Results from pinging " + reply.Address);
    Console.WriteLine("\tFragmentation allowed?: {0}", !reply.Options.
DontFragment);
    Console.WriteLine("\tTime to live: {0}", reply.Options.Ttl);
    Console.WriteLine("\tRoundtrip took: {0}", reply.RoundtripTime);
    Console.WriteLine("\tStatus: {0}", reply.Status.ToString());
}
```

The event handler for the PingCompleted event is the pinger_PingCompleted method. This event handler follows the usual EventHandler convention of the sender object and event arguments. The argument type for this event is PingCompletedEventArgs. The PingReply can be accessed in the Reply property of the event arguments. If the ping was canceled or an exception was thrown, that information can be accessed via the Cancelled and Error properties. The UserState property on the PingCompletedEventArgs class holds the user token value provided in SendAsync:

```
        private static void pinger_PingCompleted(object sender,
    PingCompletedEventArgs e)
        {
            PingReply reply = e.Reply;
            DisplayPingReplyInfo(reply);

            if(e.Cancelled)
            {
                Console.WriteLine("Ping for " + e.UserState.ToString( ) + " was
    cancelled");
            }
            else if (e.Error != null)
            {
                Console.WriteLine("Exception thrown during ping: {0}", e.Error.
    ToString( ));
            }
        }
```

The output from DisplayPingReplyInfo looks like this:

```
    Results from pinging 208.201.239.37
        Fragmentation allowed?: True
        Time to live: 39
        Roundtrip took: 103
        Status: Success
```

Discussion

Ping uses an Internet Control Message Protocol (ICMP) echo request message as defined in RFC 792. If a computer is not reached successfully by the ping request, it does not necessarily mean that the computer is unreachable. Many factors can prevent a ping from succeeding aside from the machine being offline. Network topology, firewalls, packet filters, and proxy servers all can interrupt the normal flow of a ping request. By default, the Windows Firewall installed with Windows XP Service Pack 2 disables ICMP traffic, so if you are having difficulty pinging a machine running XP, check the firewall settings on that machine.

See Also

The "Ping Class," "PingReply Class," and "PingCompleted Event" topics in the MSDN documentation.

16.7   Send SMTP Mail Using the SMTP Service

Problem

You want to be able to send email via SMTP from your program, but you don't want
to learn the SMTP protocol and hand-code a class to implement it.

Solution

Use the System.Net.Mail namespace, which contains classes to take care of the
harder parts of constructing an SMTP-based email message. The System.Net.Mail.
MailMessage class encapsulates constructing an SMTP-based message, and the
System.Net.Mail.SmtpClient class provides the sending mechanism for sending the
message to an SMTP server. SmtpClient does depend on there being an SMTP server
set up somewhere for it to relay messages through. Attachments are added by creating instances of System.Net.Mail.Attachment and providing the path to the file as
well as the media type:

```
// Send a message with attachments
string from = "hilyard@comcast.net";
string to = "hilyard@comcast.net";
MailMessage attachmentMessage = new MailMessage(from, to);
attachmentMessage.Subject = "Hi there!";
attachmentMessage.Body = "Check out this cool code!";
// Many systems filter out HTML mail that is relayed
attachmentMessage.IsBodyHtml = false;
// Set up the attachment
string pathToCode = @"..\..\16_Networking.cs";
Attachment attachment =
    new Attachment(pathToCode,
        MediaTypeNames.Application.Octet);
attachmentMessage.Attachments.Add(attachment);
```

To send a simple email with no attachments, call the System.Net.Mail.MailMessage
constructor with just the to, from, subject, and body information. This version of the
MailMessage constructor simply fills in those items, and then you can pass it to
SmtpClient.Send to send it along:

```
// Bounce this off the local SMTP service. The local SMTP service needs to
// have relaying set up to go through a real email server...
// This could also set up to go against an SMTP server available to
// you on the network
SmtpClient client = new SmtpClient("localhost");
client.Send(attachmentMessage);

// Or just send text
MailMessage textMessage = new MailMessage("hilyard@comcast.net",
                    "hilyard@comcast.net",
                    "Me again",
                    "You need therapy, talking to yourself is one thing but "
+
```

```
                      "writing code to send email is a whole other thing...");
        client.Send(textMessage);
```

Discussion

SMTP stands for the Simple Mail Transfer Protocol, as defined in RFC 821. To take advantage of the support for SMTP mail in the .NET Framework using the System. Net.Mail.SmtpClient class, an SMTP server must be specified to relay the messages through. Since Windows 2000, the operating system has come with an SMTP server that can be installed as part of IIS. In the Solution, the SmtpClient takes advantage of this by specifying "localhost" for the server to connect to, which indicates the local machine is the SMTP relay server. Setting up the SMTP service may not be possible in your network environment, and you may need to use the SmtpClient class to set up credentials to connect to the SMTP server on the network directly.

To set up SMTP relaying after installing the SMTP service via Add/Remove Windows Components in the Control Panel, open the Internet Information Services applet and right-click on the Default SMTP Virtual Server entry. Next, choose Properties. When you select the Delivery tab, you will see the dialog shown in Figure 16-1.

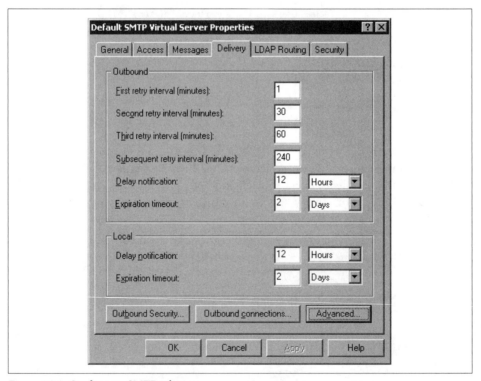

Figure 16-1. Configuring SMTP relaying

Now, click the Advanced button to display the Advanced Delivery dialog that you will use to set the relay parameters, as shown in Figure 16-2.

Figure 16-2. SMTP relaying, Advanced Delivery options

Supply your domain name and the SMTP address for a valid SMTP host, and then email away. Once you have the SMTP service set up, you should configure it to respond to requests from only the local machine, or you could become a target for spammers. To do this, go to the Access tab of the Default SMTP Virtual Server Properties dialog, as shown in Figure 16-3, and select Connection.

Then, once you have selected Connection, select the "Only from the list below" option in the Connection dialog, as shown in Figure 16-4, and click the Add button to add an IP address.

Finally, enter the IP address 127.0.0.1 to give access to only this machine, as shown in Figure 16-5.

Your list will now look like Figure 16-6.

The MediaTypeNames.class used in the solution identifies the Attachment type. The valid attachment types are listed in Table 16-2.

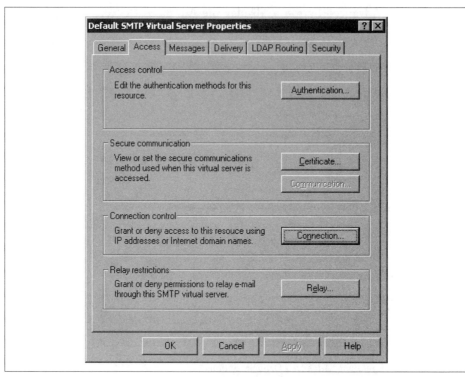

Figure 16-3. Configuring SMTP service

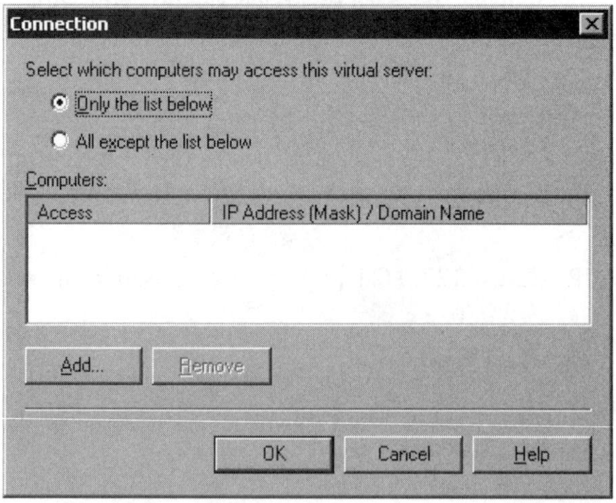

Figure 16-4. Specifying the connections

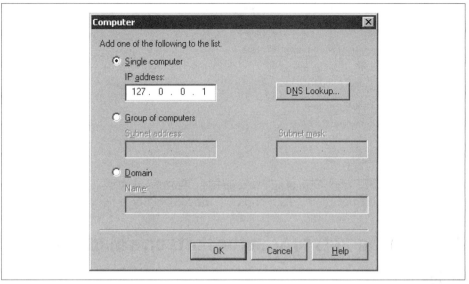

Figure 16-5. Entering the IP address

Figure 16-6. The resulting list

Table 16-2. MediaTypeNames.Attachment values

Name	Description
Octet	The data is not interpreted as any specific type.
Pdf	The data is in Portable Data Format.
Rtf	The data is in Rich Text Format.
Soap	The data is a SOAP document.
Zip	The data is compressed.

See Also

The "Using SMTP for Outgoing Messages," "SmtpMail Class," "MailMessage Class," and "MailAttachment Class" topics in the MSDN documentation.

16.8   Use Sockets to Scan the Ports on a Machine

Problem

You want to determine the open ports on a machine to see where the security risks are.

Solution

Use the CheapoPortScanner class constructed for your use; its code is shown in Example 16-5. CheapoPortScanner uses the Socket class to attempt to open a socket and connect to an address on a given port. The OpenPortFound event is available for a callback when an open port is found in the range supplied to the CheapoPortScanner constructor or in the default range (1 to 65535). By default, CheapoPortScanner will scan the local machine.

Example 16-5. CheapoPortScanner class

```
class CheapoPortScanner
{
    #region Private consts and members
    const int PORT_MIN_VALUE = 1;
    const int PORT_MAX_VALUE = 65535;

    private int _minPort = PORT_MIN_VALUE;
    private int _maxPort = PORT_MAX_VALUE;
    private List<int> _openPorts = null;
    private List<int> _closedPorts = null;
    private string _host = "127.0.0.1"; // localhost
    #endregion

    #region Event
    public class OpenPortEventArgs : EventArgs
    {
```

Example 16-5. CheapoPortScanner class (continued)

```
    int _portNum;
    public OpenPortEventArgs(int portNum) : base()
    {
        _portNum = portNum;
    }

    public int PortNum
    {
    get { return _portNum; }
    }
}

public delegate void OpenPortFoundEventHandler(object sender, OpenPortEventArgs args);
public event OpenPortFoundEventHandler OpenPortFound;
#endregion // Event

#region CTORs & Init code
public CheapoPortScanner()
{
    // Defaults are already set for ports and localhost
    SetupLists();
}

public CheapoPortScanner(string host, int minPort, int maxPort)
{
    if (minPort > maxPort)
        throw new
          ArgumentException("Min port cannot be greater than max port");
    if (minPort < PORT_MIN_VALUE || minPort > PORT_MAX_VALUE)
        throw new ArgumentOutOfRangeException("Min port cannot be less than "+
                    PORT_MIN_VALUE + " or greater than " + PORT_MAX_VALUE);
    if (maxPort < PORT_MIN_VALUE || maxPort > PORT_MAX_VALUE)
        throw new ArgumentOutOfRangeException("Max port cannot be less than "+
                    PORT_MIN_VALUE + " or greater than " + PORT_MAX_VALUE);

    _host = host;
    _minPort = minPort;
    _maxPort = maxPort;
    SetupLists();
}

private void SetupLists()
{
    // Set up lists with capacity to hold half of range
    // Since we can't know how many ports are going to be open,
    // we compromise and allocate enough for half

    // rangeCount is max - min + 1
    int rangeCount = (_maxPort - _minPort) + 1;

    // If there are an odd number, bump by one to get one extra slot.
    if (rangeCount % 2 != 0)
```

Example 16-5. CheapoPortScanner class (continued)

```
            rangeCount += 1;

        // Reserve half the ports in the range for each
        _openPorts = new List<int>(rangeCount / 2);
        _closedPorts = new List<int>(rangeCount / 2);
    }
    #endregion // CTORs & Init code
```

There are two properties on CheapoPortScanner that bear mentioning. The OpenPorts and ClosedPorts properties return a ReadOnlyCollection of type int that is a list of the ports that are open and closed, respectively. Their code is shown in Example 16-6.

Example 16-6. OpenPorts and ClosedPorts properties

```
#region Properties public ReadOnlyCollection<int> OpenPorts
{
    get { return new ReadOnlyCollection<int>(_openPorts); }
}
 public ReadOnlyCollection<int> ClosedPorts
{
    get { return new ReadOnlyCollection<int>(_closedPorts); }
}
#endregion // Properties

#region Private Methods
private void CheckPort(int port)
{
    if (IsPortOpen(port))
    {
        // If we got here, it is open
        _openPorts.Add(port);

        // Notify anyone paying attention
        OpenPortFoundEventHandler openPortFound = OpenPortFound;
        if (openPortFound != null)
         openPortFound(this, new OpenPortEventArgs(port));
    }
    else
    {
        // Server doesn't have that port open
        _closedPorts.Add(port);
    }
}

private bool IsPortOpen(int port)
{
    Socket sock = null;
    try
    {
        // Make a TCP-based socket
        sock = new Socket(AddressFamily.InterNetwork,
```

Example 16-6. OpenPorts and ClosedPorts properties (continued)

```
                        SocketType.Stream,
                        ProtocolType.Tcp);
        // Connect
        sock.Connect(_host, port);
        return true;
    }
    catch (SocketException se)
    {
        if (se.SocketErrorCode == SocketError.ConnectionRefused)
        {
            return false;
        }
        else
        {
            // An error occurred when attempting to access the socket
            Debug.WriteLine(se.ToString());
            Console.WriteLine(se.ToString());
        }
    }
    finally
    {
        if (sock != null)
        {
            if (sock.Connected)
                sock.Disconnect(false);
            sock.Close();
        }
    }
    return false;
}
#endregion
```

The trigger method for the CheapoPortScanner is Scan. Scan will check all of the ports in the range specified in the constructor. The ReportToConsole method will dump the pertinent information about the last scan to the console output stream:

```
#region Public Methods
public void Scan()
{
    for (int port = _minPort; port <= _maxPort; port++)
    {
        CheckPort(port);
    }
}
 public void ReportToConsole()
{
    Console.WriteLine("Port Scan for host at {0}:", _host.ToString());
    Console.WriteLine("\tStarting Port: {0}; Ending Port: {1}",
                        _minPort, _maxPort);
    Console.WriteLine("\tOpen ports:");
    foreach (int port in _openPorts)
    {
```

```
                    Console.WriteLine("\t\tPort {0}", port);
            }
            Console.WriteLine("\tClosed ports:");
            foreach (int port in _closedPorts)
            {
                Console.WriteLine("\t\tPort {0}", port);
            }
        }

        #endregion // Public Methods
    }
```

The PortScan method demonstrates how to use CheapoPortScanner by scanning ports 1–30 on the local machine. It first subscribes to the OpenPortFound event. The handler method for this event, cps_OpenPortFound, writes out the number of any port found open. Next, PortScan calls the Scan method. Finally, it calls ReportToConsole to show the full results of the scan, including the closed ports as well as the open ones:

```
        public static void PortScan ()
        {
            // Do a specific range
            Console.WriteLine("Checking ports 1-30 on localhost...");
            CheapoPortScanner cps = new CheapoPortScanner("127.0.0.1",1,30);
            cps.OpenPortFound +=
                new CheapoPortScanner.OpenPortFoundEventHandler(cps_OpenPortFound);
            cps.Scan();
            Console.WriteLine("Found {0} ports open and {1} ports closed",
                    cps.OpenPorts.Count, cps.ClosedPorts.Count);

            // Do the local machine, whole port range 1-65535
            cps = new CheapoPortScanner();
            cps.Scan();
            cps.ReportToConsole();
        }

        static void cps_OpenPortFound(object sender, CheapoPortScanner.
    OpenPortEventArgs
            args)
        {
            Console.WriteLine("OpenPortFound reported port {0} was open",args.
    PPortNumP);
        }
```

The output for the port scanner as shown appears here:

```
        Checking ports 1-30 on localhost...
        OpenPortFound reported port 22 was open
        OpenPortFound reported port 26 was open
        Found 2 ports open and 28 ports closed
```

Discussion

Open ports on a machine are significant because they indicate the presence of a program listening on those ports. Hackers look for "open" ports as ways to enter your

systems without permission. CheapoPortScanner is an admittedly rudimentary mechanism for checking for open ports, but it demonstrates the principle well enough to
provide a good starting point.

 If you run this on a corporate network, you may quickly get a visit
from your network administrator, as you may set off alarms in some
intrusion-detection systems. Be judicious in your use of this code.

See Also

The "Socket Class" and "Sockets" topics in the MSDN documentation.

16.9   Use the Current Internet Connection Settings

Problem

Your program wants to use the current Internet connection settings without forcing
the user to add them to your application manually.

Solution

Read the current Internet connectivity settings with the InternetSettingsReader class
provided for you in Example 16-7. InternetSettingsReader calls some methods of
the WinINet API via P/Invoke to retrieve current Internet connection information.
The majority of the work is done in setting up the structures that WinINet uses and
then marshaling the structure pointers correctly to retrieve the values.

Example 16-7. InternetSettingsReader class

```
public class InternetSettingsReader
{
    #region WinInet structures
    [StructLayout(LayoutKind.Sequential, CharSet = CharSet.Auto)]
    public struct InternetPerConnOptionList
    {
        public int dwSize; // size of the INTERNET_PER_CONN_OPTION_LIST struct
        public IntPtr szConnection;    // Connection name to set/query options
        public int dwOptionCount;    // Number of options to set/query
        public int dwOptionError;        // On error, which option failed
        public IntPtr options;
    };

    [StructLayout(LayoutKind.Sequential, CharSet = CharSet.Auto)]
    public struct InternetConnectionOption
    {
        static readonly int Size;
        public PerConnOption m_Option;
        public InternetConnectionOptionValue m_Value;
```

Example 16-7. InternetSettingsReader class (continued)

```
    static InternetConnectionOption( )
    {
        InternetConnectionOption.Size =
          Marshal.SizeOf(typeof(InternetConnectionOption));
    }

    // Nested Types
    [StructLayout(LayoutKind.Explicit)]
    public struct InternetConnectionOptionValue
    {
        // Fields
        [FieldOffset(0)]
        public System.Runtime.InteropServices.ComTypes.FILETIME m_FileTime;
        [FieldOffset(0)]
        public int m_Int;
        [FieldOffset(0)]
        public IntPtr m_StringPtr;
    }
}
#endregion

#region WinInet enums
// Options used in INTERNET_PER_CONN_OPTON struct
//
public enum PerConnOption
{
// Sets or retrieves the connection type. The Value member will contain one
// or more of the values from PerConnFlags
        INTERNET_PER_CONN_FLAGS = 1,
// Sets or retrieves a string containing the proxy servers
    INTERNET_PER_CONN_PROXY_SERVER = 2,
// Sets or retrieves a string containing the URLs that do not use the
// proxy server
        INTERNET_PER_CONN_PROXY_BYPASS = 3,
// Sets or retrieves a string containing the URL to the automatic
// configuration script
    INTERNET_PER_CONN_AUTOCONFIG_URL = 4,
}

//
// PER_CONN_FLAGS
//
[Flags]
public enum PerConnFlags
{
    PROXY_TYPE_DIRECT = 0x00000001, // Direct to net
    PROXY_TYPE_PROXY = 0x00000002, // Via named proxy
    PROXY_TYPE_AUTO_PROXY_URL = 0x00000004, // Autoproxy URL
    PROXY_TYPE_AUTO_DETECT = 0x00000008 // Use autoproxy detection
}

    #region P/Invoke defs
```

Example 16-7. InternetSettingsReader class (continued)

```
    [DllImport("WinInet.dll", EntryPoint = "InternetQueryOption",
        SetLastError = true)]

    public static extern bool InternetQueryOption(
        IntPtr hInternet,
        int dwOption,
        ref InternetPerConnOptionList optionsList,
        ref int bufferLength
        );
    #endregion

    #region Private Members
    string _proxyAddr = "";
    int _proxyPort = -1;
    bool _bypassLocal = false;
    string _autoConfigAddr = "";
    string[] _proxyExceptions = null;
    PerConnFlags _flags;
    #endregion

    #region CTOR
    public InternetSettingsReader()
    {
    }
    #endregion
```

Each of the properties of InternetSettingsReader shown in Example 16-8 call into the GetInternetConnectionOption method, which returns an InternetConnectionOption. The InternetConnectionOption structure holds all of the pertinent data for the value being returned, and that value is then retrieved based on what type of value was asked for by the specific properties.

Example 16-8. InternetSettingsReader properties

```
#region Properties
public string ProxyAddr
{
    get
    {
        InternetConnectionOption ico =
            GetInternetConnectionOption(
                PerConnOption.INTERNET_PER_CONN_PROXY_SERVER);
        // Parse out the addr and port
        string proxyInfo = Marshal.PtrToStringUni(
                            ico.m_Value.m_StringPtr);
        ParseProxyInfo(proxyInfo);
        return _proxyAddr;
    }
}
public int ProxyPort
{
```

Example 16-8. InternetSettingsReader properties (continued)

```
    get
    {
        InternetConnectionOption ico =
            GetInternetConnectionOption(
                PerConnOption.INTERNET_PER_CONN_PROXY_SERVER);
        // Parse out the addr and port
        string proxyInfo = Marshal.PtrToStringUni(
                                ico.m_Value.m_StringPtr);
        ParseProxyInfo(proxyInfo);
        return _proxyPort;
    }
}
public bool BypassLocalAddresses
{
    get
    {
        InternetConnectionOption ico =
            GetInternetConnectionOption(
                PerConnOption.INTERNET_PER_CONN_PROXY_BYPASS);
        // Bypass is listed as <local> in the exceptions list
        string exceptions =
            Marshal.PtrToStringUni(ico.m_Value.m_StringPtr);

        if (exceptions.IndexOf("<local>") != -1)
            _bypassLocal = true;
        else
            _bypassLocal = false;
        return _bypassLocal;
    }
}
public string AutoConfigurationAddr
{
    get
    {
        InternetConnectionOption ico =
            GetInternetConnectionOption(
                PerConnOption.INTERNET_PER_CONN_AUTOCONFIG_URL);
        // Get these straight
        _autoConfigAddr =
            Marshal.PtrToStringUni(ico.m_Value.m_StringPtr);
        if (_autoConfigAddr == null)
            _autoConfigAddr = "";
        return _autoConfigAddr;
    }
}
public string[] ProxyExceptions
{
    get
    {
        InternetConnectionOption ico =
            GetInternetConnectionOption(
                PerConnOption.INTERNET_PER_CONN_PROXY_BYPASS);
```

Example 16-8. InternetSettingsReader properties (continued)

```
        // Exceptions are separated by semicolon
        string exceptions =
            Marshal.PtrToStringUni(ico.m_Value.m_StringPtr);
        if (!string.IsNullOrEmpty(exceptions))
        {
            _proxyExceptions = exceptions.Split(';');
        }
        return _proxyExceptions;
    }
}
public PerConnFlags ConnectionType
{
    get
    {
        InternetConnectionOption ico =
            GetInternetConnectionOption(
                PerConnOption.INTERNET_PER_CONN_FLAGS);
        _flags = (PerConnFlags)ico.m_Value.m_Int;

        return _flags;
    }
}

#endregion
private void ParseProxyInfo(string proxyInfo)
{
    if(!string.IsNullOrEmpty(proxyInfo))
    {
        string [] parts = proxyInfo.Split(':');
        if (parts.Length == 2)
        {
            _proxyAddr = parts[0];
            try
            {
                _proxyPort = Convert.ToInt32(parts[1]);
            }
            catch (FormatException)
            {
                // No port
                _proxyPort = -1;
            }
        }
        else
        {
            _proxyAddr = parts[0];
            _proxyPort = -1;
        }
    }
}
```

The GetInternetConnectionOption method shown in Example 16-9 does the heavy lifting as far as communicating with WinINet. First, an InternetPerConnOptionList is created as well as an InternetConnectionOption structure to hold the returned value. The InternetConnectionOption structure is then pinned so that the garbage collector does not move the structure in memory, and the PerConnOption value is assigned to determine what Internet option to retrieve. Marshal.SizeOf is used to determine the size of the two managed structures in unmanaged memory. These values are used to initialize the size values for the structures, which allows the operating system to determine the version of the unmanaged structure being dealt with.

The InternetPerConnOptionList is initialized to hold the option values, and then the WinINet function IntrenetQueryOption is called. The InternetConnectionOption type is filled by using the Marshal.PtrToStructure method, which maps the data from the unmanaged structure containing the InternetConnectionOption data from unmanaged code to the managed object instance, and then the managed version is returned with the value.

Example 16-9. GetInternetConnectionOption method

```
private InternetConnectionOption GetInternetConnectionOption(PerConnOption pco)
{
    // Allocate the list and option
    InternetPerConnOptionList perConnOptList = new InternetPerConnOptionList( );
    InternetConnectionOption ico = new InternetConnectionOption( );
    // Pin the option structure
    GCHandle gch = GCHandle.Alloc(ico, GCHandleType.Pinned);
    // Initialize the option for the data we want
    ico.m_Option = pco;
    // Initialize the option list for the default connection or LAN
    int listSize = Marshal.SizeOf(perConnOptList);
    perConnOptList.dwSize = listSize;
    perConnOptList.szConnection = IntPtr.Zero;
    perConnOptList.dwOptionCount = 1;
    perConnOptList.dwOptionError = 0;
    // Figure out sizes and offsets
    int icoSize = Marshal.SizeOf(ico);
    int optionTotalSize = icoSize;
    // Alloc enough memory for the option
    perConnOptList.options =
        Marshal.AllocCoTaskMem(icoSize);

    long icoOffset = (long)perConnOptList.options + (long)icoSize;
    // Make pointer from the structure
    IntPtr optionListPtr = perConnOptList.options;
    Marshal.StructureToPtr(ico, optionListPtr, false);

    // Make the query
    if (InternetQueryOption(
        IntPtr.Zero,
        75, //(int)InternetOption.INTERNET_OPTION_PER_CONNECTION_OPTION,
        ref perConnOptList,
```

Example 16-9. GetInternetConnectionOption method (continued)

```
         ref listSize) == true)
    {
         // Retrieve the value.
         ico =
(InternetConnectionOption)Marshal.PtrToStructure(perConnOptList.options,
                                    typeof(InternetConnectionOption));
    }
    // Free the COM memory
    Marshal.FreeCoTaskMem(perConnOptList.options);

    // Unpin the structs
    gch.Free();

    return ico;
}
```

Using the `InternetSettingsReader` is demonstrated in the `GetInternetSettings` method shown in Example 16-10. The proxy information is retrieved and displayed to the console here, but could easily be stored in another program for use as proxy information when connecting. See Recipe 14.6 for details on setting up the proxy information for a `WebRequest`.

Example 16-10. Using the InternetSettingsReader

```
public static void GetInternetSettings()
{
    InternetSettingsReader isr = new InternetSettingsReader();
    Console.WriteLine("Current Proxy Address: {0}",isr.ProxyAddr);
    Console.WriteLine("Current Proxy Port: {0}",isr.ProxyPort);
    Console.WriteLine("Current ByPass Local Address setting: {0}",
                        isr.BypassLocalAddresses);
    Console.WriteLine("Exception addresses for proxy (bypass):");
    if(isr.ProxyExceptions != null)
    {
        foreach(string addr in isr.ProxyExceptions)
        {
            Console.WriteLine("\t{0}",addr);
        }
    }
    Console.WriteLine("Proxy connection type: {0}",isr.ConnectionType.ToString());
}
```

Output for the Solution:

```
         Current Proxy Address: CORPORATEPROXY
         Current Proxy Port: 8080
         Current ByPass Local Address setting: True
         Exception addresses for proxy (bypass):
             corporate.com
             <local>
         Proxy connection type: PROXY_TYPE_DIRECT, PROXY_TYPE_PROXY
```

Discussion

The WinInet Windows Internet (WinInet) API is the unmanaged API for interacting with the FTP, HTTP, and Gopher protocols. This API can be used to fill in where managed code leaves off, such as with the Internet configuration settings shown in the Solution. It can also be used for downloading files, working with cookies, and participating in Gopher sessions. You need to understand that WinInet is meant to be a client-side API and is not suited for server-side or service applications; issues could arise in your application from improper usage.

There is a huge amount of information available to the C# programmer directly through the BCL, but at times, you still need to roll up your sleeves and talk to the Win32 API. Even in situations in which restricted privileges are the norm, it is not always out of bounds to create a small assembly that needs enhanced access to do P/Invoke. It can have its access locked down so as not to become a risk to the system.

See Also

The "InternetQueryOption Function [WinInet]" topic in the MSDN documentation.

16.10 Transferring Files Using FTP

Problem

You want to programmatically download and upload files using the File Transfer Protocol (FTP).

Solution

Use the System.Net.FtpWebRequest class to perform these operations. FtpWebRequests are created from the WebRequest class Create method by specifying the URI for the FTP download. In the example that follows, the source code from the first edition of the *C# Cookbook* is the target for the download. A FileStream is opened for the target and then is wrapped by a BinaryWriter. A BinaryReader is created with the response stream from the FtpWebRequest. Then, the stream is read, and the target is written until the entire file has been downloaded. This series of operations is demonstrated in Example 16-11.

Example 16-11. Using the System.Net.FtpWebRequest class

```
// Go get the same code from edition 1
FtpWebRequest request =
    (FtpWebRequest)WebRequest.Create(
    "ftp://ftp.oreilly.com/pub/examples/csharpckbk/CSharpCookbook.zip");

request.Credentials = new NetworkCredential("anonymous", "hilyard@oreilly.com");
using (FtpWebResponse response = (FtpWebResponse)request.GetResponse())
```

Example 16-11. Using the System.Net.FtpWebRequest class (continued)

```
{
    Stream data = response.GetResponseStream( );
    string targetPath = "CSharpCookbook.zip";
    if (File.Exists(targetPath))
        File.Delete(targetPath);

    byte[] byteBuffer = new byte[4096];
    using (FileStream output = new FileStream(targetPath, FileMode.CreateNew))
    {
        int bytesRead = 0;
        do
        {
            bytesRead = data.Read(byteBuffer, 0, byteBuffer.Length);
            if (bytesRead > 0)
            {
                output.Write(byteBuffer, 0, bytesRead);
            }
        }
        while (bytesRead > 0);
    }
}
```

To upload a file, use `FtpWebRequest` to get a stream on the request using `GetRequestStream` and use it to upload the file with. Once the file has been opened and written into the request stream, execute the request by calling `GetResponse` and check the `StatusDescription` property for the result of the operation:

```
string uploadFile = "SampleClassLibrary.dll";
// go get the code from edition 1
Uri ftpSite =
    new Uri("ftp://localhost/Upload/" + uploadFile);
FileInfo fileInfo = new FileInfo(uploadFile);
FtpWebRequest request =
    (FtpWebRequest)WebRequest.Create(
    ftpSite);
request.Method = WebRequestMethods.Ftp.UploadFile;
request.UseBinary = true;
request.ContentLength = fileInfo.Length;
request.Credentials = new NetworkCredential("anonymous", "hilyard@oreilly.com");
byte[] byteBuffer = new byte[4096];
using (Stream requestStream = request.GetRequestStream( ))
{
    using (FileStream fileStream = new FileStream(uploadFile, FileMode.Open))
    {
        int bytesRead = 0;
        do
        {
            bytesRead = fileStream.Read(byteBuffer, 0, byteBuffer.Length);
            if (bytesRead > 0)
            {
                requestStream.Write(byteBuffer, 0, bytesRead);
            }
```

```
        }
        while (bytesRead > 0);
    }
}
using (FtpWebResponse response = (FtpWebResponse)request.GetResponse())
{
    Console.WriteLine(response.StatusDescription);
}
```

Discussion

The File Transfer Protocol (FTP) is defined in RFC 959 and is one of the main ways
files are distributed over the Internet. The port number for FTP is usually 21. Hap-
pily, you don't have to really know much about how FTP works in order to use it.
This could be useful to your applications in automatic download of information
from a dedicated FTP site or in providing automatic update capabilities.

See Also

The "FtpWebRequest Class," "FtpWebResponse Class," "WebRequest Class," and
"WebResponse Class" topics in the MSDN documentation.

CHAPTER 17

Security

17.0 Introduction

There are many ways to secure different parts of your application. The security of running code in .NET revolves around the concept of Code Access Security (CAS). CAS determines the trustworthiness of an assembly based upon its origin and the characteristics of the assembly itself, such as its hash value. For example, code installed locally on the machine is more trusted than code downloaded from the Internet. The runtime will also validate an assembly's metadata and type safety before that code is allowed to run.

There are many ways to write secure code and protect data using the .NET Framework. In this chapter, we explore such things as controlling access to types, encryption and decryption, random numbers, securely storing data, and using programmatic and declarative security.

17.1 Controlling Access to Types in a Local Assembly

Problem

You have an existing class that contains sensitive data, and you do not want clients to have direct access to any objects of this class. Instead, you want an intermediary object to talk to the clients and to allow access to sensitive data based on the client's credentials. What's more, you would also like to have specific queries and modifications to the sensitive data tracked, so that if an attacker manages to access the object, you will have a log of what the attacker was attempting to do.

Solution

Use the *proxy design pattern* to allow clients to talk directly to a proxy object. This proxy object will act as gatekeeper to the class that contains the sensitive data. To keep malicious users from accessing the class itself, make it private, which will at least keep code without the ReflectionPermissionFlag. MemberAccess access (which is currently given only in fully trusted code scenarios such as executing code interactively on a local machine) from getting at it.

The namespaces we will be using are:

```
using System;
using System.IO;
using System.Security;
using System.Security.Permissions;
using System.Security.Principal;
```

Let's start this design by creating an interface, as shown in Example 17-1, that will be common to both the proxy objects and the object that contains sensitive data.

Example 17-1. ICompanyData interface

```
internal interface ICompanyData
{
    string AdminUserName
    {
        get;
        set;
    }

    string AdminPwd
    {
        get;
        set;
    }

    string CEOPhoneNumExt
    {
        get;
        set;
    }

    void RefreshData( );
    void SaveNewData( );
}
```

The CompanyData class shown in Example 17-2 is the underlying object that is "expensive" to create.

Example 17-2. CompanyData class

```
internal class CompanyData : ICompanyData
{
    public CompanyData( )
    {
        Console.WriteLine("[CONCRETE] CompanyData Created");
        // Perform expensive initialization here.
        this.AdminUserName = "admin";
        this.AdminPwd = "password";
```

Example 17-2. CompanyData class (continued)

```
        this.CEOPhoneNumExt = "0000";
    }

    public string AdminUserName
    {
        get;
        set;
    }

    public string AdminPwd
    {
        get;
        set;
    }

    public string CEOPhoneNumExt
    {
        get;
        set;
    }

    public void RefreshData()
    {
        Console.WriteLine("[CONCRETE] Data Refreshed");
    }

    public void SaveNewData()
    {
        Console.WriteLine("[CONCRETE] Data Saved");
    }
}
```

The code shown in Example 17-3 for the security proxy class checks the caller's permissions to determine whether the CompanyData object should be created and its methods or properties called.

Example 17-3. CompanyDataSecProxy security proxy class

```
public class CompanyDataSecProxy : ICompanyData
{
    public CompanyDataSecProxy()
    {
        Console.WriteLine("[SECPROXY] Created");

        // Must set principal policy first.
        appdomain.CurrentDomain.SetPrincipalPolicy(PrincipalPolicy.
            WindowsPrincipal);
    }

    private ICompanyData coData = null;
    private PrincipalPermission admPerm =
        new PrincipalPermission(null, @"BUILTIN\Administrators", true);
```

Example 17-3. CompanyDataSecProxy security proxy class (continued)

```
private PrincipalPermission guestPerm =
    new PrincipalPermission(null, @"BUILTIN\Guest", true);
private PrincipalPermission powerPerm =
    new PrincipalPermission(null, @"BUILTIN\PowerUser", true);
private PrincipalPermission userPerm =
    new PrincipalPermission(null, @"BUILTIN\User", true);

public string AdminUserName
{
    get
    {
        string userName = "";
        try
        {
            admPerm.Demand( );
            Startup( );
            userName = coData.AdminUserName;
        }
        catch(SecurityException e)
        {
            Console.WriteLine("AdminUserName_get failed! {0}",e.ToString( ));
        }
        return (userName);
    }
    set
    {
        try
        {
            admPerm.Demand( );
            Startup( );
            coData.AdminUserName = value;
        }
        catch(SecurityException e)
        {
            Console.WriteLine("AdminUserName_set failed! {0}",e.ToString( ));
        }
    }
}

public string AdminPwd
{
    get
    {
        string pwd = "";
        try
        {
            admPerm.Demand( );
            Startup( );
            pwd = coData.AdminPwd;
        }
        catch(SecurityException e)
        {
```

Example 17-3. CompanyDataSecProxy security proxy class (continued)

```
                    Console.WriteLine("AdminPwd_get Failed! {0}",e.ToString( ));
                }

                return (pwd);
        }
        set
        {
            try
            {
                admPerm.Demand( );
                Startup( );
                coData.AdminPwd = value;
            }
            catch(SecurityException e)
            {
                Console.WriteLine("AdminPwd_set Failed! {0}",e.ToString( ));
            }
        }
    }

    public string CEOPhoneNumExt
    {
        get
        {
            string ceoPhoneNum = "";
            try
            {
                admPerm.Union(powerPerm).Demand( );
                Startup( );
                ceoPhoneNum = coData.CEOPhoneNumExt;
            }
            catch(SecurityException e)
            {
                Console.WriteLine("CEOPhoneNum_set Failed! {0}",e.ToString( ));
            }
            return (ceoPhoneNum);
        }
        set
        {
            try
            {
                admPerm.Demand( );
                Startup( );
                coData.CEOPhoneNumExt = value;
            }
            catch(SecurityException e)
            {
                Console.WriteLine("CEOPhoneNum_set Failed! {0}",e.ToString( ));
            }
        }
    }
    public void RefreshData( )
```

Example 17-3. CompanyDataSecProxy security proxy class (continued)

```
    {
        try
        {
            admPerm.Union(powerPerm.Union(userPerm)).Demand( );
            Startup( );
            Console.WriteLine("[SECPROXY] Data Refreshed");
            coData.RefreshData( );
        }
        catch(SecurityException e)
        {
            Console.WriteLine("RefreshData Failed! {0}",e.ToString( ));
        }
    }

    public void SaveNewData( )
    {
        try
        {
            admPerm.Union(powerPerm).Demand( );
            Startup( );
            Console.WriteLine("[SECPROXY] Data Saved");
            coData.SaveNewData( );
        }
        catch(SecurityException e)
        {
            Console.WriteLine("SaveNewData Failed! {0}",e.ToString( ));
        }
    }

    // DO NOT forget to use [#define DOTRACE] to control the tracing proxy.
    private void Startup( )
    {
        if (coData == null)
        {
#if (DOTRACE)
            coData = new CompanyDataTraceProxy( );
#else
            coData = new CompanyData( );
#endif
            Console.WriteLine("[SECPROXY] Refresh Data");
            coData.RefreshData( );
        }
    }
}
```

When creating the PrincipalPermissions as part of the object construction, you are using string representations of the built-in objects ("BUILTIN\Administrators") to set up the principal role. However, the names of these objects may be different depending on the locale the code runs under. It would be appropriate to use the WindowsAccountType.Administrator enumeration value to ease localization because this value is defined to represent the administrator role as well. We used text here to clarify what was being done and also to access the PowerUsers role, which is not available through the WindowsAccountType enumeration.

If the call to the CompanyData object passes through the CompanyDataSecProxy, then the user has permissions to access the underlying data. Any access to this data may be logged, so the administrator can check for any attempt to hack the CompanyData object. The code shown in Example 17-4 is the tracing proxy used to log access to the various method and property access points in the CompanyData object (note that the CompanyDataSecProxy contains the code to turn this proxy object on or off).

Example 17-4. CompanyDataTraceProxy tracing proxy class

```
public class CompanyDataTraceProxy : ICompanyData
{
    public CompanyDataTraceProxy()
    {
        Console.WriteLine("[TRACEPROXY] Created");
        string path = Path.GetTempPath() + @"\CompanyAccessTraceFile.txt";
        fileStream = new FileStream(path, FileMode.Append,
            FileAccess.Write, FileShare.None);
        traceWriter = new StreamWriter(fileStream);
        coData = new CompanyData();
    }

    private ICompanyData coData = null;
    private FileStream fileStream = null;
    private StreamWriter traceWriter = null;

    public string AdminPwd
    {
        get
        {
            traceWriter.WriteLine("AdminPwd read by user.");
            traceWriter.Flush();
            return (coData.AdminPwd);
        }
        set
        {
            traceWriter.WriteLine("AdminPwd written by user.");
            traceWriter.Flush();
            coData.AdminPwd = value;
        }
    }

    public string AdminUserName
    {
        get
        {
            traceWriter.WriteLine("AdminUserName read by user.");
            traceWriter.Flush();
            return (coData.AdminUserName);
        }
```

Example 17-4. CompanyDataTraceProxy tracing proxy class (continued)

```csharp
        set
        {
            traceWriter.WriteLine("AdminUserName written by user.");
            traceWriter.Flush( );
            coData.AdminUserName = value;
        }
    }

    public string CEOPhoneNumExt
    {
        get
        {
            traceWriter.WriteLine("CEOPhoneNumExt read by user.");
            traceWriter.Flush( );
            return (coData.CEOPhoneNumExt);
        }
        set
        {
            traceWriter.WriteLine("CEOPhoneNumExt written by user.");
            traceWriter.Flush( );
            coData.CEOPhoneNumExt = value;
        }
    }

    public void RefreshData( )
    {
        Console.WriteLine("[TRACEPROXY] Refresh Data");
        coData.RefreshData( );
    }

    public void SaveNewData( )
    {
        Console.WriteLine("[TRACEPROXY] Save Data");
        coData.SaveNewData( );
    }
}
```

The proxy is used in the following manner:

```csharp
// Create the security proxy here.
CompanyDataSecProxy companyDataSecProxy = new CompanyDataSecProxy( );

// Read some data.
Console.WriteLine("CEOPhoneNumExt: " + companyDataSecProxy.CEOPhoneNumExt);

// Write some data.
companyDataSecProxy.AdminPwd = "asdf";
companyDataSecProxy.AdminUserName = "asdf";

// Save and refresh this data.
companyDataSecProxy.SaveNewData( );
companyDataSecProxy.RefreshData( );
```

Note that as long as the CompanyData object was accessible, you could have also written this to access the object directly:

```
// Instantiate the CompanyData object directly without a proxy.
CompanyData companyData = new CompanyData( );

// Read some data.
Console.WriteLine("CEOPhoneNumExt: " + companyData.CEOPhoneNumExt);

// Write some data.
companyData.AdminPwd = "asdf";
companyData.AdminUserName = "asdf";

// Save and refresh this data.
companyData.SaveNewData( );
companyData.RefreshData( );
```

If these two blocks of code are run, the same fundamental actions occur: data is read, data is written, and data is updated/refreshed. This shows you that your proxy objects are set up correctly and function as they should.

Discussion

The *proxy design pattern* is useful for several tasks. The most notable—in COM, COM+, and .NET remoting—is for marshaling data across boundaries such as AppDomains or even across a network. To the client, a proxy looks and acts exactly the same as its underlying object; fundamentally, the proxy object is just a wrapper around the object.

A proxy can test the security and/or identity permissions of the caller before the underlying object is created or accessed. Proxy objects can also be chained together to form several layers around an underlying object. Each proxy can be added or removed depending on the circumstances.

For the proxy object to look and act the same as its underlying object, both should implement the same interface. The implementation in this recipe uses an ICompanyData interface on both the proxies (CompanyDataSecProxy and CompanyDataTraceProxy) and the underlying object (CompanyData). If more proxies are created, they, too, need to implement this interface.

The CompanyData class represents an expensive object to create. In addition, this class contains a mixture of sensitive and nonsensitive data that requires permission checks to be made before the data is accessed. For this recipe, the CompanyData class simply contains a group of properties to access company data and two methods for updating and refreshing this data. You can replace this class with one of your own and create a corresponding interface that both the class and its proxies implement.

The CompanyDataSecProxy object is the object that a client must interact with. This object is responsible for determining whether the client has the correct privileges to access the method or property that it is calling. The get accessor of the `AdminUserName` property shows the structure of the code throughout most of this class:

```csharp
public string AdminUserName
{
    get
    {
        string userName = "";
        try
        {
            admPerm.Demand( );
            Startup( );
            userName = coData.AdminUserName;
        }
        catch(SecurityException e)
        {
            Console.WriteLine("AdminUserName_get Failed!: {0}",e.ToString( ));
        }
        return (userName);
    }
    set
    {
        try
        {
            admPerm.Demand( );
            Startup( );
            coData.AdminUserName = value;
        }
        catch(SecurityException e)
        {
            Console.WriteLine("AdminUserName_set Failed! {0}",e.ToString( ));
        }
    }
}
```

Initially, a single permission (AdmPerm) is demanded. If this demand fails, a SecurityException, which is handled by the catch clause, is thrown. (Other exceptions will be handed back to the caller.) If the Demand succeeds, the Startup method is called. It is in charge of instantiating either the next proxy object in the chain (CompanyDataTraceProxy) or the underlying CompanyData object. The choice depends on whether the DOTRACE preprocessor symbol has been defined. You may use a different technique, such as a registry key to turn tracing on or off, if you wish.

This proxy class uses the private field coData to hold a reference to an ICompanyData type, which can be either a CompanyDataTraceProxy or the CompanyData object. This reference allows you to chain several proxies together.

The CompanyDataTraceProxy simply logs any access to the CompanyData object's information to a text file. Since this proxy will not attempt to prevent a client from accessing the CompanyData object, the CompanyData object is created and explicitly called in each property and method of this object.

See Also

Design Patterns by Gamma et al. (Addison-Wesley).

17.2   Encrypting/Decrypting a String

Problem

You have a string you want to be able to encrypt and decrypt—perhaps a password or software key—which will be stored in some form, such as in a file or the registry. You want to keep this string a secret so that users cannot take this information from you.

Solution

Encrypting the string will help to prevent users from being able to read and decipher the information. The CryptoString class shown in Example 17-5 contains two static methods to encrypt and decrypt a string and two static properties to retrieve the generated key and initialization vector (IV—a random number used as a starting point to encrypt data) after encryption has occurred.

Example 17-5. CryptoString class

```
using System;
using System.Security.Cryptography;

public sealed class CryptoString
{
    private CryptoString( ) {}

    private static byte[] savedKey = null;
    private static byte[] savedIV = null;

     public static byte[] Key
     {
      get { return savedKey; }
      set { savedKey = value; }
     }

     public static byte[] IV
     {
      get { return savedIV; }
      set { savedIV = value; }
     }

    private static void RdGenerateSecretKey(RijndaelManaged rdProvider)
    {
        if (savedKey == null)
        {
            rdProvider.KeySize = 256;
```

Example 17-5. CryptoString class (continued)

```
            rdProvider.GenerateKey( );
            savedKey = rdProvider.Key;
        }
    }

    private static void RdGenerateSecretInitVector(RijndaelManaged rdProvider)
    {
        if (savedIV == null)
        {
            rdProvider.GenerateIV( );
            savedIV = rdProvider.IV;
        }
    }

    public static string Encrypt(string originalStr)
    {
        // Encode data string to be stored in memory.
        byte[] originalStrAsBytes = Encoding.ASCII.GetBytes(originalStr);
        byte[] originalBytes = {};

        // Create MemoryStream to contain output.
        using (MemoryStream memStream = new
                MemoryStream(originalStrAsBytes.Length))
        {
            using (RijndaelManaged rijndael = new RijndaelManaged( ))
            {
                // Generate and save secret key and init vector.
                RdGenerateSecretKey(rijndael);
                RdGenerateSecretInitVector(rijndael);

                if (savedKey == null || savedIV == null)
                {
                    throw (new NullReferenceException(
                        "savedKey and savedIV must be non-null."));
                }

                // Create encryptor and stream objects.
                using (ICryptoTransform rdTransform =
                        rijndael.CreateEncryptor((byte[])savedKey.
                        Clone( ),(byte[])savedIV.Clone( )))
                {
                    using (CryptoStream cryptoStream = new CryptoStream(memStream,
                        rdTransform, CryptoStreamMode.Write))
                    {
                        // Write encrypted data to the MemoryStream.
                        cryptoStream.Write(originalStrAsBytes, 0,
                                originalStrAsBytes.Length);
                        cryptoStream.FlushFinalBlock( );
                        originalBytes = memStream.ToArray( );
                    }
                }
            }
```

Example 17-5. CryptoString class (continued)

```
        }
        // Convert encrypted string.
        string encryptedStr = Convert.ToBase64String(originalBytes);
        return (encryptedStr);
    }

    public static string Decrypt(string encryptedStr)
    {
        // Unconvert encrypted string.
        byte[] encryptedStrAsBytes = Convert.FromBase64String(encryptedStr);
        byte[] initialText = new Byte[encryptedStrAsBytes.Length];

        using (RijndaelManaged rijndael = new RijndaelManaged())
        {
            using (MemoryStream memStream = new MemoryStream(encryptedStrAsBytes))
            {
                if (savedKey == null || savedIV == null)
                {
                    throw (new NullReferenceException(
                            "savedKey and savedIV must be non-null."));
                }

                // Create decryptor and stream objects.
                using (ICryptoTransform rdTransform =
                    rijndael.CreateDecryptor((byte[])savedKey.
                    Clone(),(byte[])savedIV.Clone()))
                {
                    using (CryptoStream cryptoStream = new CryptoStream(memStream,
                    rdTransform, CryptoStreamMode.Read))
                    {
                    // Read in decrypted string as a byte[].
                    cryptoStream.Read(initialText, 0, initialText.Length);
                    }
                }
            }
        }

        // Convert byte[] to string.
        string decryptedStr = Encoding.ASCII.GetString(initialText);
        return (decryptedStr);
    }
}
```

Discussion

The CryptoString class contains only static members, except for the private instance constructor, which prevents anyone from directly creating an object from this class.

This class uses the *Rijndael algorithm* to encrypt and decrypt a string. This algorithm is found in the System.Security.Cryptography.RijndaelManaged class. This algorithm requires a secret key and an initialization vector; both are byte arrays. A random secret key can be generated for you by calling the GenerateKey method on the RijndaelManaged class. This method accepts no parameters and returns void. The generated key is placed in the Key property of the RijndaelManaged class. The GenerateIV method generates a random initialization vector and places this vector in the IV property of the RijndaelManaged class.

The byte array values in the Key and IV properties must be stored for later use and not modified. This is due to the nature of private-key encryption classes, such as RijndaelManaged. The Key and IV values must be used by both the encryption and decryption routines to successfully encrypt and decrypt data.

The SavedKey and SavedIV private static fields contain the secret key and initialization vector, respectively. The secret key is used by both the encryption and decryption methods to encrypt and decrypt data. This is why there are public properties for these values, so they can be stored somewhere secure for later use. This means that any strings encrypted by this object must be decrypted by this object. The initialization vector is there to make deducing the secret key from the encrypted string much more difficult. The initialization vector does this by causing two identical encrypted strings (encrypted with the same key) to look very different in their encrypted form.

Two methods in the CryptoString class, RdGenerateSecretKey and RdGenerateSecretInitVector, are used to generate a secret key and initialization vector when none exists. The RdGenerateSecretKey method generates the secret key, which is placed in the SavedKey field. Likewise, the RdGenerateSecretInitVector generates the initialization vector, which is placed in the SavedIV field. There is only one key and one IV generated for this class. This enables the encryption and decryption routines to have access to the same key and IV information at all times.

The Encrypt and Decrypt methods of the CryptoString class do the actual work of encrypting and decrypting a string. The Encrypt method accepts a string that you want to encrypt and returns an encrypted string. The following code calls this method and passes in a string to be encrypted:

```
string encryptedString = CryptoString.Encrypt("MyPassword");
Console.WriteLine("encryptedString: {0}", encryptedString);
// Get the key and IV used so you can decrypt it later.
byte [] key = CryptoString.Key;
byte [] IV = CryptoString.IV;
```

Once the string is encrypted, the key and IV are stored for later decryption. This method displays:

```
encryptedString: Ah4vkmVKpwMYRT97Q8cVgQ==
```

Note that your output may differ since you will be using a different key and IV value. The following code sets the key and IV used to encrypt the string and then calls the Decrypt method to decrypt the previously encrypted string:

```
CryptoString.Key = key;
CryptoString.IV = IV;
```

```
string decryptedString = CryptoString.Decrypt(encryptedString);
Console.WriteLine("decryptedString: {0}", decryptedString);
```

This method displays:

```
decryptedString: MyPassword
```

There does not seem to be any problem with using escape sequences such as \r, \n, \r\n, or \t in the string to be encrypted. In addition, using a quoted string literal, with or without escaped characters, works without a problem:

```
@"MyPassword"
```

See Also

Recipe 17.3; the "System.Cryptography Namespace," "MemoryStream Class," "ICryptoTransform Interface," and "RijndaelManaged Class" topics in the MSDN documentation.

17.3   Encrypting and Decrypting a File

Problem

You have sensitive information that must be encrypted before it is written to a file that might be in a nonsecure area. This information must also be decrypted before it is read back in to the application.

Solution

Use multiple cryptography providers and write the data to a file in encrypted format. This is accomplished in the following class, which has a constructor that expects an instance of the System.Security.Cryptography.SymmetricAlgorithm class and a path for the file. The SymmetricAlgorithm class is an abstract base class for all cryptographic providers in .NET, so you can be reasonably assured that this class could be extended to cover all of them. This example implements support for TripleDES and Rijndael.

The following namespaces are needed for this solution:

```
using System;
using System.Text;
using System.IO;
using System.Security.Cryptography;
```

The class SecretFile (implemented in this recipe) can be used for TripleDES as shown:

```
// Use TripleDES.
using (TripleDESCryptoServiceProvider tdes = new
    TripleDESCryptoServiceProvider( ))
```

```
    {
        SecretFile secretTDESFile = new SecretFile(tdes,"tdestext.secret");

        string encrypt = "My TDES Secret Data!";
        Console.WriteLine("Writing secret data: {0}",encrypt);
        secretTDESFile.SaveSensitiveData(encrypt);
        // Save for storage to read file.
        byte [] key = secretTDESFile.Key;
        byte [] IV = secretTDESFile.IV;

        string decrypt = secretTDESFile.ReadSensitiveData( );
        Console.WriteLine("Read secret data: {0}",decrypt);
    }
```

To use SecretFile with Rijndael, just substitute the provider in the constructor like this:

```
    // Use Rijndael.
    using (RijndaelManaged rdProvider = new RijndaelManaged( ))
    {
        SecretFile secretRDFile = new SecretFile(rdProvider,"rdtext.secret");

        string encrypt = "My Rijndael Secret Data!";

        Console.WriteLine("Writing secret data: {0}",encrypt);
        secretRDFile.SaveSensitiveData(encrypt);
        // Save for storage to read file.
        byte [] key = secretRDFile.Key;
        byte [] IV = secretRDFile.IV;

        string decrypt = secretRDFile.ReadSensitiveData( );
        Console.WriteLine("Read secret data: {0}",decrypt);
    }
```

Example 17-6 shows the implementation of SecretFile.

Example 17-6. SecretFile class

```
public class SecretFile
{
    private byte[] savedKey = null;
    private byte[] savedIV = null;
    private SymmetricAlgorithm symmetricAlgorithm;
    string path;

    public byte[] Key
    {
        get { return savedKey; }
        set { savedKey = value; }
    }

    public byte[] IV
    {
        get { return savedIV; }
        set { savedIV = value; }
    }
```

Example 17-6. SecretFile class (continued)

```
public SecretFile(SymmetricAlgorithm algorithm, string fileName)
{
    symmetricAlgorithm = algorithm;
    path = fileName;
}

public void SaveSensitiveData(string sensitiveData)
{
    // Encode data string to be stored in encrypted file.
    byte[] encodedData = Encoding.Unicode.GetBytes(sensitiveData);

    // Create FileStream and crypto service provider objects.
    using (FileStream fileStream = new FileStream(path,
                                        FileMode.Create,
                                        FileAccess.Write))
    {
        // Generate and save secret key and init vector.
        GenerateSecretKey();
        GenerateSecretInitVector();

        // Create crypto transform and stream objects.
        using (ICryptoTransform transform =
                    symmetricAlgorithm.CreateEncryptor(savedKey,
                    savedIV))
        {
            using (CryptoStream cryptoStream =
              new CryptoStream(fileStream, transform, CryptoStreamMode.Write))
                {
                    // Write encrypted data to the file.
                    cryptoStream.Write(encodedData, 0, encodedData.Length);
                }
        }
    }
}

public string ReadSensitiveData()
{
    string decrypted = "";

    // Create file stream to read encrypted file back.
    using (FileStream fileStream = new FileStream(path,
                                        FileMode.Open,
                                        FileAccess.Read))
    {
        // Print out the contents of the encrypted file.
        using (BinaryReader binReader = new BinaryReader(fileStream))
        {
            Console.WriteLine("---------- Encrypted Data ---------");
            int count = (Convert.ToInt32(binReader.BaseStream.Length));
            byte [] bytes = binReader.ReadBytes(count);
            char [] array = Encoding.Unicode.GetChars(bytes);
            string encdata = new string(array);
```

Example 17-6. SecretFile class (continued)

```
                Console.WriteLine(encdata);
                Console.WriteLine("---------- Encrypted Data ---------\r\n");

                // Reset the file stream.
                fileStream.Seek(0,SeekOrigin.Begin);

                // Create decryptor.
                using (ICryptoTransform transform =
                    symmetricAlgorithm.CreateDecryptor(savedKey, savedIV))
                {
                    using (CryptoStream cryptoStream = new CryptoStream(fileStream,
                                                    transform,
                                                    CryptoStreamMode.Read))
                    {
                        // Print out the contents of the decrypted file.
                        StreamReader srDecrypted = new StreamReader(cryptoStream,
                                                    new UnicodeEncoding( ));
                        Console.WriteLine("---------- Decrypted Data ---------");
                        decrypted = srDecrypted.ReadToEnd( );
                        Console.WriteLine(decrypted);
                        Console.WriteLine("---------- Decrypted Data ---------");
                    }
                }
            }

        return decrypted;
    }

    private void GenerateSecretKey( )
    {
        if (null != (symmetricAlgorithm as TripleDESCryptoServiceProvider))
        {
            TripleDESCryptoServiceProvider tdes;
            tdes = symmetricAlgorithm as TripleDESCryptoServiceProvider;
            tdes.KeySize = 192; // Maximum key size
            tdes.GenerateKey( );
            savedKey = tdes.Key;
        }
        else if (null != (symmetricAlgorithm as RijndaelManaged))
        {
            RijndaelManaged rdProvider;
            rdProvider = symmetricAlgorithm as RijndaelManaged;
            rdProvider.KeySize = 256; // Maximum key size
            rdProvider.GenerateKey( );
            savedKey = rdProvider.Key;
        }
    }

    private void GenerateSecretInitVector( )
    {
        if (null != (symmetricAlgorithm as TripleDESCryptoServiceProvider))
```

Example 17-6. SecretFile class (continued)

```
        {
            TripleDESCryptoServiceProvider tdes;
            tdes = symmetricAlgorithm as TripleDESCryptoServiceProvider;
            tdes.GenerateIV( );
            savedIV = tdes.IV;
        }
        else if (null != (symmetricAlgorithm as RijndaelManaged))
        {
            RijndaelManaged rdProvider;
            rdProvider = symmetricAlgorithm as RijndaelManaged;
            rdProvider.GenerateIV( );
            savedIV = rdProvider.IV;
        }
    }
}
```

If the SaveSensitiveData method is used to save the following text to a file:

```
This is a test
This is sensitive data!
```

the ReadSensitiveData method will display the following information from this same file:

```
---------- Encrypted Data --------
?????????????????????????????????????????????
---------- Encrypted Data --------

---------- Decrypted Data ---------
This is a test
This is sensitive data!
---------- Decrypted Data ---------
```

Discussion

Encrypting data is essential to many applications, especially ones that store information in easily accessible locations. Once data is encrypted, a decryption scheme is required to restore the data back to an unencrypted form without losing any information. The same underlying algorithms can be used to authenticate the source of a file or message.

The encryption schemes used in this recipe are TripleDES and Rijndael. The reasons for using Triple DES are:

- TripleDES employs symmetric encryption, meaning that a single private key is used to encrypt and decrypt data. This process allows much faster encryption and decryption, especially as the streams of data become larger.

- TripleDES encryption is much harder to crack than the older DES encryption and is widely considered to be of high strength.

- If you wish to use another type of encryption, this recipe can be easily converted using any provider derived from the `SymmetricAlgorithm` class.

- TripleDES is widely deployed in the industry today.

The main drawback to TripleDES is that both the sender and receiver must use the same key and initialization vector (IV) in order to encrypt and decrypt the data successfully. If you wish to have an even more secure encryption scheme, use the Rijndael scheme. This type of encryption scheme is highly regarded as a solid encryption scheme, since it is fast and can use larger key sizes than TripleDES. However, it is still a symmetric cryptosystem, which means that it relies on shared secrets. Use an asymmetric cryptosystem, such as RSA or DSA, for a cryptosystem that uses shared public keys with private keys that are never shared between parties.

See Also

The "SymmetricAlgorithm Class," "TripleDESCryptoServiceProvider Class," and "RijndaelManaged Class" topics in the MSDN documentation.

17.4 Cleaning Up Cryptography Information

Problem

You will be using the cryptography classes in the FCL to encrypt and/or decrypt data. In doing so, you want to make sure that no data (e.g., seed values or keys) is left in memory for longer than you are using the cryptography classes. Hackers can sometimes find this information in memory and use it to break your encryption or, worse, to break your encryption, modify the data, and then reencrypt the data and pass it on to your application.

Solution

In order to clear out the key and initialization vector (or seed), you need to call the `Clear` method on whichever `SymmetricAlgorithm`- or `AsymmetricAlgorithm`-derived class you are using. `Clear` reinitializes the `Key` and `IV` properties, preventing them from being found in memory. This is done after saving the key and IV so that you can decrypt later. Example 17-7 encodes a string and then cleans up immediately afterward to provide the smallest window possible for potential attackers.

Example 17-7. Cleaning up cryptography information

```
using System;
using System.Text;
using System.IO;
using System.Security.Cryptography;

string originalStr = "SuperSecret information";
// Encode data string to be stored in memory.
```

Example 17-7. Cleaning up cryptography information (continued)

```
byte[] originalStrAsBytes = Encoding.ASCII.GetBytes(originalStr);

// Create MemoryStream to contain output.
MemoryStream memStream = new MemoryStream(originalStrAsBytes.Length);
RijndaelManaged rijndael = new RijndaelManaged( );

// Generate secret key and init vector.
rijndael.KeySize = 256;
rijndael.GenerateKey( );
rijndael.GenerateIV( );

// Save the key and IV for later decryption.
byte [] key = rijndael.Key;
byte [] IV = rijndael.IV;

// Create encryptor and stream objects.
ICryptoTransform transform = rijndael.CreateEncryptor(rijndael.Key,
    rijndael.IV);
CryptoStream cryptoStream = new CryptoStream(memStream, transform,
    CryptoStreamMode.Write);

// Write encrypted data to the MemoryStream.
cryptoStream.Write(originalStrAsBytes, 0, originalStrAsBytes.Length);
cryptoStream.FlushFinalBlock( );

// Release all resources as soon as we are done with them
// to prevent retaining any information in memory.
memStream.Close( );
cryptoStream.Close( );
transform.Dispose( );
// This clear statement regens both the key and the init vector so that
// what is left in memory is no longer the values you used to encrypt with.
rijndael.Clear( );
```

You can also make your life a little easier by taking advantage of the using statement, instead of having to remember to manually call each of the Close methods individually. This code block shows how to use the using statement:

```
        public static void CleanUpCryptoWithUsing( )
        {
            string originalStr = "SuperSecret information";
            // Encode data string to be stored in memory.
            byte[] originalStrAsBytes = Encoding.ASCII.GetBytes(originalStr);
            byte[] originalBytes = { };

            // Create MemoryStream to contain output.
            using (MemoryStream memStream = new MemoryStream(originalStrAsBytes.
    Length))
            {
                using (RijndaelManaged rijndael = new RijndaelManaged( ))
                {
                    // Generate secret key and init vector.
```

```
rijndael.KeySize = 256;
rijndael.GenerateKey( );
rijndael.GenerateIV( );
// Save off the key and IV for later decryption.
byte[] key = rijndael.Key;
byte[] IV = rijndael.IV;

// Create encryptor and stream objects.
using (ICryptoTransform transform =
    rijndael.CreateEncryptor(rijndael.Key, rijndael.IV))
{
    using (CryptoStream cryptoStream = new
        CryptoStream(memStream, transform,
        CryptoStreamMode.Write))
    {
        // Write encrypted data to the MemoryStream.
        cryptoStream.Write(originalStrAsBytes, 0,
            originalStrAsBytes.Length);
        cryptoStream.FlushFinalBlock( );
    }
}
}
}
}
```

Discussion

To make sure your data is safe, you need to close the MemoryStream and CryptoStream objects as soon as possible, as well as calling Dispose on the ICryptoTransform implementation to clear out any resources used in this encryption. The using statement makes this process much easier, makes your code easier to read, and leads to fewer programming mistakes.

See Also

The "SymmetricAlgorithm.Clear Method" and "AsymmetricAlgorithm.Clear Method" topics in the MSDN documentation.

17.5 Verifying That a String Remains Uncorrupted Following Transmission

Problem

You have some text that will be sent across a network to another machine for processing. You need to verify that this message has not been modified in transit.

Solution

Calculate a hash value from the string and append it to the string before it is sent to its destination. Once the destination receives the string, it can remove the hash value and determine whether the string is the same one that was initially sent. It is critical that both sides agree on a hash algorithm that will be used. The SHA-256 algorithm is a good choice and an industry standard.

The `CreateStringHash` method takes a `string` as input, adds a hash value to the end of it, and returns the new `string`, as shown in Example 17-8.

Example 17-8. Verifying that a string remains uncorrupted following transmission

```
public class HashOps
{
  // The number 44 is the exact length of the base64 representation
  // of the hash value, which was appended to the string.
  private const int HASH_LENGTH = 44;

    public static string CreateStringHash(string unHashedString)
  {
      byte[] encodedUnHashedString = Encoding.Unicode.GetBytes(unHashedString);
      string stringWithHash = "";

      using (SHA256Managed hashingObj = new SHA256Managed())
      {
        byte[] hashCode = hashingObj.ComputeHash(encodedUnHashedString);

        string hashBase64 = Convert.ToBase64String(hashCode);
        stringWithHash = unHashedString + hashBase64;
      }

      return (stringWithHash);
  }

    public static bool IsStringCorrupted(string stringWithHash,
              out string originalStr)
      {
          // Code to quickly test the handling of a tampered string.
          //stringWithHash = stringWithHash.Replace('a', 'b');

          if (stringWithHash.Length <= HASH_LENGTH)
          {
              originalStr = null;
              return (true);
          }

          string hashCodeString =
              stringWithHash.Substring(stringWithHash.Length - HASH_LENGTH);
          string unHashedString =
              stringWithHash.Substring(0, stringWithHash.Length - HASH_LENGTH);
```

Example 17-8. Verifying that a string remains uncorrupted following transmission (continued)

```
        byte[] hashCode = Convert.FromBase64String(hashCodeString);

        byte[] encodedUnHashedString = Encoding.Unicode.GetBytes(unHashedString);

        bool hasBeenTamperedWith = false;
        using (SHA256Managed hashingObj = new SHA256Managed( ))
        {
          byte[] receivedHashCode = hashingObj.ComputeHash(encodedUnHashedString);
          for (int counter = 0; counter < receivedHashCode.Length; counter++)
          {
            if (receivedHashCode[counter] != hashCode[counter])
            {
                hasBeenTamperedWith = true;
                break;
            }
          }

          if (!hasBeenTamperedWith)
          {
            originalStr = unHashedString;
          }
          else
          {
            originalStr = null;
          }
        }

      return (hasBeenTamperedWith);
    }
}
```

The `IsStringCorrupted` method is called by the code that receives a string with a hash value appended. This method removes the hash value, calculates a new hash value for the string, and checks to see whether both hash values match. If they match, both strings are exactly the same, and the method returns `false`. If they don't match, the string has been tampered with, and the method returns `true`.

Since the `CreateStringHash` and `IsStringCorrepted` methods are static members of a class named `HashOps`, you can call these methods with code like the following:

```
        public static void VerifyNonStringCorruption( )
        {
            string testString = "This is the string that we'll be testing.";
            string unhashedString;
            string hashedString = HashOps.CreateStringHash(testString);

            bool result = HashOps.IsStringCorrupted(hashedString, out
    unhashedString);
            Console.WriteLine(result);
            if (!result)
                Console.WriteLine("The string sent is: " + unhashedString);
            else
```

```
            Console.WriteLine("The string: " + unhashedString +
                " has become corrupted.");
        }
```

The output of this method is shown here when the string is uncorrupted:

```
False
The string sent is: This is the string that we'll be testing.
```

The output of this method is shown here when the string is corrupted:

```
False
The string: This is the string that we'll #$%^(&&*2 be testing.
has become corrupted.
```

Discussion

You can use a hash, checksum, or *cyclic redundancy check* (CRC) to calculate a value based on a message. This value is then used at the destination to determine whether the message has been modified during transmission between the source and destination.

This recipe uses a hash value as a reliable method of determining whether a string has been modified. The hash value for this recipe is calculated using the SHA256Managed class. This hash value is 256 bits in size and produces greatly differing results when calculated from strings that are very similar, but not exactly the same. In fact, if a single letter is removed or even capitalized, the resulting hash value will change considerably.

By appending this value to the string, both the string and hash values can be sent to their destination. The destination then removes the hash value and calculates a hash value of its own based on the received string. These two hash values are then compared. If they are equal, the strings are exactly the same. If they are not equal, you can be sure that somewhere between the source and destination, the string was corrupted. This technique is great for verifying that transmission succeeded without errors, but it does not guarantee against malicious tampering. To protect against malicious tampering, use an asymmetric algorithm: sign the string with a private key and verify the signature with a public key.

The CreateStringHash method first converts the unhashed string into a byte array using the GetBytes method of the UnicodeEncoding class. This byte array is then passed to the ComputeHash method of the SHA256Managed class.

Once the hash value is calculated, the byte array containing the hash code is converted to a string containing base64 digits, using the Convert.ToBase64String method. This method accepts a byte array, converts it to a string of base64 digits, and returns that string. The reason for doing this is to convert all unsigned integers in the byte array to values that can be represented in a string data type. The last thing that this method does is to append the hash value to the end of the string and return the newly hashed string.

The IsStringCorrupted method accepts a hashed string and an out parameter that will return the unhashed string. This method returns a Boolean; as previously mentioned, true indicates that the string has been modified, false indicates that the string is unmodified.

This method first removes the hash value from the end of the StringWithHash variable. Next, a new hash is calculated using the string portion of the StringWithHash variable. These two hash values are compared. If they are the same, the string has been received, unmodified. Note that if you change the hashing algorithm used, you must change it in both this method and the CreateStringHash method. You must also change the HASH_LENGTH constant in the IsStringCorrupted method to an appropriate size for the new hashing algorithm. This number is the exact length of the base64 representation of the hash value, which was appended to the string.

See Also

The "SHA256Managed Class," "Convert.ToBase64String Method," and "Convert.FromBase64String Method" topics in the MSDN documentation.

17.6   Storing Data Securely

Problem

You need to store settings data about individual users for use by your application and keep this data isolated from other instances of your application run by different users.

Solution

You can use isolated storage to establish per-user data stores for your application data and then use hashed values for critical data.

To illustrate how to do this for settings data, you create the following UserSettings class. UserSettings holds only two pieces of information: the user identity (current WindowsIdentity) and the password for your application. The user identity is accessed via the User property, and the password is accessed via the Password property. Note that the password field is created the first time and is stored as a salted hashed value to keep it secure. The combination of the isolated storage and the hashing of the password value helps to strengthen the security of the password by using the *defense in depth* principle. Salting the hash is an extra measure of protection that not only protects the password against dictionary type attacks, but it also prevents an attacker from easily determining if two users have the same password by comparing the hashes.

The settings data is held in XML that is stored in the isolated storage scope and accessed via an XmlDocument instance.

This solution uses the following namespaces:

```
using System;
using System.IO;
using System.IO.IsolatedStorage;
using System.Xml;
using System.Text;
using System.Diagnostics;
using System.Security.Principal;
using System.Security.Cryptography;
```

The UserSettings class is shown in Example 17-9.

Example 17-9. UserSettings class

```
// Class to hold user settings
public class UserSettings
{
    isoFileStream = null;
    XmlDocument settingsDoc = null;
    const string storageName = "SettingsStorage.xml";

    // Constructor
    public UserSettings(string password)
    {
        // Get the isolated storage.
        using (IsolatedStorageFile isoStorageFile =
            IsolatedStorageFile.GetUserStoreForDomain())
        {
            // Create an internal DOM for settings.
            settingsDoc = new XmlDocument();
            // If no settings, create default.
            if(isoStorageFile.GetFileNames(storageName).Length == 0)
            {
                using (IsolatedStorageFileStream isoFileStream =
                    new IsolatedStorageFileStream(storageName,
                                                  FileMode.Create,
                                                  isoStorageFile))
                {
                    using (XmlTextWriter writer = new
                        XmlTextWriter(isoFileStream,Encoding.UTF8))
                    {
                        writer.WriteStartDocument();
                        writer.WriteStartElement("Settings");
                        writer.WriteStartElement("User");
                        // Get current user.
                        WindowsIdentity user = WindowsIdentity.GetCurrent();
                        writer.WriteString(user.Name);
                        writer.WriteEndElement();
                        writer.WriteStartElement("Password");

                        // Pass null to CreateHashedPassword as the salt
                        // to establish one
                        // CreateHashedPassword appears shortly
```

Example 17-9. UserSettings class (continued)

```
                    string hashedPassword =
                            CreateHashedPassword(password,null);
                    writer.WriteString(hashedPassword);
                    writer.WriteEndElement( );
                    writer.WriteEndElement( );
                    writer.WriteEndDocument( );
                    Console.WriteLine("Creating settings for " + user.Name);
                }
            }
        }

        // Set up access to settings store.
        using (IsolatedStorageFileStream isoFileStream =
            new IsolatedStorageFileStream(storageName,
                                    FileMode.Open,
                                    isoStorageFile))
        {
            // Load settings from isolated filestream
            settingsDoc.Load(isoFileStream);
            Console.WriteLine("Loaded settings for " + User);
        }
    }
}
```

The User property provides access to the WindowsIdentity of the user that this set of settings belongs to:

```
// User property
public string User
{
    get
    {
        XmlNode userNode = settingsDoc.SelectSingleNode("Settings/User");
        if(userNode != null)
        {
            return userNode.InnerText;
        }
        return "";
    }
}
```

The Password property gets the salted and hashed password value from the XML store and, when updating the password, takes the plain text of the password and creates the salted and hashed version, which is then stored:

```
// Password property
public string Password
{
    get
    {
        XmlNode pwdNode =
                settingsDoc.SelectSingleNode("Settings/Password");
        if(pwdNode != null)
```

```
        {
            return pwdNode.InnerText;
        }
        return "";
    }
    set
    {
        XmlNode pwdNode =
                settingsDoc.SelectSingleNode("Settings/Password");

        string hashedPassword = CreateHashedPassword(value,null);
        if(pwdNode != null)
        {
            pwdNode.InnerText = hashedPassword;
        }
        else
        {
            XmlNode settingsNode =
                    settingsDoc.SelectSingleNode("Settings");
            XmlElement pwdElem =
                    settingsDoc.CreateElement("Password");
            pwdElem.InnerText=hashedPassword;
            settingsNode.AppendChild(pwdElem);
        }
    }
}
```

The CreateHashedPassword method creates the salted and hashed password. The password parameter is the plain text of the password; the existingSalt parameter is the salt to use when creating the salted and hashed version. If no salt exists, such as the first time a password is stored, existingSalt should be passed as null, and a random salt will be generated.

Once you have the salt, it is combined with the plain text password and hashed using the SHA512Managed class. The salt value is then appended to the end of the hashed value and returned. The salt is appended so that when you attempt to validate the password, you know what salt was used to create the hashed value. The entire value is then base64-encoded and returned:

```
// Make a hashed password.
private string CreateHashedPassword(string password,
                                    byte[] existingSalt)
{
    byte [] salt = null;
    if(existingSalt == null)
    {
        // Make a salt of random size.
        // Create a stronger hash code using RNGCryptoServiceProvider.
        byte[] random = new byte[1];
        RNGCryptoServiceProvider rngSize = new RNGCryptoServiceProvider();
        // Populate with random bytes.
        rngSize.GetBytes(random);
        // Convert random bytes to string.
```

```
            int size = Convert.ToInt32(random);

            // Create salt array.
            salt = new byte[size];

            // Use the better random number generator to get
            // bytes for the salt.
            RNGCryptoServiceProvider rngSalt =
                new RNGCryptoServiceProvider();
            rngSalt.GetNonZeroBytes(salt);
        }
        else
            salt = existingSalt;

            // Turn string into bytes.
            byte[] pwd = Encoding.UTF8.GetBytes(password);

            // Make storage for both password and salt.
            byte[] saltedPwd = new byte[pwd.Length + salt.Length];

            // Add pwd bytes first.
            pwd.CopyTo(saltedPwd,0);
            // now add salt
            salt.CopyTo(saltedPwd,pwd.Length);

            // Use SHA512 as the hashing algorithm.
            byte[] hashWithSalt = null;
            using (SHA512Managed sha512 = new SHA512Managed())
            {
                // Get hash of salted password.
                byte[] hash = sha512.ComputeHash(saltedPwd);

                // Append salt to hash so we have it.
                hashWithSalt = new byte[hash.Length + salt.Length];

                // Copy in bytes.
                hash.CopyTo(hashWithSalt,0);
                salt.CopyTo(hashWithSalt,hash.Length);
            }

            // Return base64-encoded hash with salt.
            return Convert.ToBase64String(hashWithSalt);
        }
```

To check a given password against the stored value (which is salted and hashed), you call IsPasswordValid and pass in the plain text password to check. First, the stored value is retrieved using the Password property and converted from base64. Since you know you used SHA512, there are 512 bits in the hash. But you need the byte size, so you do the math and get that size in bytes. This allows you to figure out where to get the salt from in the value, so you copy it out of the value and call CreateHashedPassword using that salt and the plain text password parameter. This gives you the hashed value for the password that was passed in to verify. Once you have that, you just compare it to the Password property to see whether you have a match and return true or false as appropriate:

```
// Check the password against our storage.
public bool IsPasswordValid(string password)
{
    // Get bytes for password.
    // This is the hash of the salted password and the salt.
    byte[] hashWithSalt = Convert.FromBase64String(Password);

    // We used 512 bits as the hash size (SHA512).
    int hashSizeInBytes = 512 / 8;

    // Make holder for original salt.
    int saltSize = hashWithSalt.Length - hashSizeInBytes;
    byte[] salt = new byte[saltSize];

    // Copy out the salt.
    Array.Copy(hashWithSalt,hashSizeInBytes,salt,0,saltSize);

    // Figure out hash for this password.
    string passwordHash = CreateHashedPassword(password,salt);

    // If the computed hash matches the specified hash,
    // the plain text value must be correct.
    // See if Password (stored) matched password passed in.
    return (Password == passwordHash);
}
}
```

Code that uses the UserSettings class is shown here:

```
class IsoApplication
{
    static void Main(string[] args)
    {
        if(args.Length > 0)
        {
            UserSettings settings = new UserSettings(args[0]);
            if(settings.IsPasswordValid(args[0]))
            {
                Console.WriteLine("Welcome");
                return;
            }
        }
        Console.WriteLine("The system could not validate your credentials");
    }
}
```

The way to use this application is to pass the password on the command line as the first argument. This password is then checked against the UserSettings, which is stored in the isolated storage for this particular user. If the password is correct, the user is welcomed; if not, the user is shown the door.

Discussion

Isolated storage allows an application to store data that is unique to the application and the user running it. This storage allows the application to write out state information that is not visible to other applications or even other users of the same application. Isolated storage is based on the code identity as determined by the CLR, and it stores the information either directly on the client machine or in isolated stores that can be opened and roam with the user. The storage space available to the application is directly controllable by the administrator of the machine on which the application operates.

The Solution uses isolation by User, AppDomain, and Assembly by calling IsolatedStorageFile.GetUserStoreForDomain. This creates an isolated store that is accessible by only this user in the current assembly in the current AppDomain:

```
// Get the isolated storage.
isoStorageFile = IsolatedStorageFile.GetUserStoreForDomain( );
```

The *Storeadm.exe* utility will allow you to see which isolated-storage stores have been set up on the machine by running the utility with the /LIST command-line switch. *Storeadm.exe* is part of the .NET Framework SDK and can be located in your Visual Studio installation directory under the *\SDK\v2.0\Bin* subdirectory.

The output after using the UserSettings class would look like this:

```
C:\>storeadm /LIST
Microsoft (R) .NET Framework Store Admin 1.1.4322.573
Copyright (C) Microsoft Corporation 1998-2002. All rights reserved.

Record #1
[Domain]
<System.Security.Policy.Url version="1">
    <Url>file://D:/PRJ32/Book/IsolatedStorage/bin/Debug/IsolatedStorage.exe</
Url>

</System.Security.Policy.Url>

[Assembly]
<System.Security.Policy.Url version="1">
    <Url>file://D:/PRJ32/Book/IsolatedStorage/bin/Debug/IsolatedStorage.exe</
Url>

</System.Security.Policy.Url>

        Size : 1024
```

Passwords should never be stored in plain text, period. It is a bad habit to get into, so in the UserSettings class, you have added the salting and hashing of the password value via the CreateHashedPassword method and verification through the IsPasswordValid method. Adding a salt to the hash helps to strengthen the protection on the value being hashed so that the isolated storage, the hash, and the salt now protect the password you are storing.

See Also

The "IsolatedStorageFile Class," "IsolatedStorageStream Class," "About Isolated Storage," and "ComputeHash Method" topics in the MSDN documentation.

17.7   Making a Security Assert Safe

Problem

You want to assert that at a particular point in the call stack, a given permission is available for all subsequent calls. However, doing this can easily open a security hole to allow other malicious code to spoof your code or to create a back door into your component. You want to assert a given security permission, but you want to do so in a secure and efficient manner.

Solution

In order to make this approach secure, you need to call Demand on the permissions that the subsequent calls need. This makes sure that code that doesn't have these permissions can't slip by due to the Assert. The Demand is done to ensure that you have indeed been granted this permission before using the Assert to short-circuit the stackwalk. This is demonstrated by the function CallSecureFunctionSafelyAndEfficiently, which performs a Demand and an Assert before calling SecureFunction, which in turn does a Demand for a ReflectionPermission.

The code listing for CallSecureFunctionSafelyAndEfficiently is shown in Example 17-10.

Example 17-10. CallSecureFunctionSafelyAndEfficiently function

```
public static void CallSecureFunctionSafelyAndEfficiently( )
{

    // Set up a permission to be able to access nonpublic members
    // via reflection.
    ReflectionPermission perm =
        new ReflectionPermission(ReflectionPermissionFlag.MemberAccess);

    // Demand the permission set we have compiled before using Assert
    // to make sure we have the right before we Assert it. We do
    // the Demand to ensure that we have checked for this permission
    // before using Assert to short-circuit stackwalking for it, which
    // helps us stay secure, while performing better.
    perm.Demand( );

    // Assert this right before calling into the function that
    // would also perform the Demand to short-circuit the stack walk
    // each call would generate. The Assert helps us to optimize
    // our use of SecureFunction.
```

Example 17-10. CallSecureFunctionSafelyAndEfficiently function (continued)

```
    perm.Assert();
    // We call the secure function 100 times but only generate
    // the stackwalk from the function to this calling function
    // instead of walking the whole stack 100 times.
    for(int i=0;i<100;i++)
    {
        SecureFunction();
    }
}
```

The code listing for SecureFunction is shown here:

```
        public static void SecureFunction()
        {
            // Set up a permission to be able to access nonpublic members
            // via reflection.
            ReflectionPermission perm =
                new ReflectionPermission(ReflectionPermissionFlag.MemberAccess);

            // Demand the right to do this and cause a stackwalk.
            perm.Demand();

            // Perform the action here...
        }
```

Discussion

In the demonstration function CallSecureFunctionSafelyAndEfficiently, the function you are calling (SecureFunction) performs a Demand on a ReflectionPermission to ensure that the code can access nonpublic members of classes via reflection. Normally, this would result in a stackwalk for every call to SecureFunction. The Demand in CallSecureFunctionSafelyAndEfficiently is there only to protect against the usage of the Assert in the first place. To make this more efficient, you can use Assert to state that all functions issuing Demands that are called from this one do not have to stackwalk any further. The Assert says stop checking for this permission in the call stack. In order to do this, you need the permission to call Assert.

The problem comes in with this Assert, as it opens up a potential luring attack where SecureFunction is called via CallSecureFunctionSafelyAndEfficiently, which calls Assert to stop the Demand stackwalks from SecureFunction. If unauthorized code without ReflectionPermission were able to call CallSecureFunctionSafelyAndEfficiently, the Assert would prevent the SecureFunction Demand call from determining that there is some code in the call stack without the proper rights. This is the power of the call stack checking in the CLR when a Demand occurs.

In order to protect against this, you issue a Demand for the ReflectionPermission needed by SecureFunction in CallSecureFunctionSafelyAndEfficiently to close this hole before issuing the Assert. The combination of this Demand and the Assert causes you to do one stackwalk instead of the original 100 that would have been caused by the Demand in SecureFunction.

Security optimization techniques, such as using Assert in this case (even though it isn't the primary reason to use Assert), can help class library as well as control developers who are trusted to perform Asserts in order to speed the interaction of their code with the CLR; but if used improperly, these techniques can also open up holes in the security picture. This example shows that you can have both performance and security where secure access is concerned.

If you are using Assert, be mindful that stackwalk overrides should never be made in a class constructor. Constructors are not guaranteed to have any particular security context, nor are they guaranteed to execute at a specific point in time. This lack leads to the call stack not being well defined, and Assert used here can produce unexpected results.

One other thing to remember with Assert is that you can have only one active Assert in a function at a given time. If you Assert the same permission twice, a SecurityException is thrown by the CLR. You must revert the original Assert first using RevertAssert. Then, you can declare the second Assert.

See Also

The "CodeAccessSecurity.Assert Method," "CodeAccessSecurity.Demand Method," "CodeAccessSecurity.RevertAssert Method," and "Overriding Security Checks" topics in the MSDN documentation.

17.8   Verifying That an Assembly Has Been Granted Specific Permissions

Problem

When your assembly requests optional permissions (such as asking for disk access to enable users to export data to disk as a product feature) using the SecurityAction. RequestOptional flag, it might or might not get those permissions. Regardless, your assembly will still load and execute. You need a way to verify whether your assembly actually obtained those permissions. This can help prevent many security exceptions from being thrown. For example, if you optionally requested read/write permissions on the registry but did not receive them, you could disable the user interface controls that are used to read and store application settings in the registry.

Solution

Check to see if your assembly received the optional permissions using the `SecurityManager.IsGranted` method like this:

```
using System;
using System.Text.RegularExpressions;
using System.Web;
using System.Net;
using System.Security;

Regex regex = new Regex(@"http://www\.oreilly\.com/.*");
WebPermission webConnectPerm = new WebPermission(NetworkAccess.
Connect,regex);
if(SecurityManager.IsGranted(webConnectPerm))
{
    // Connect to the O'Reilly site.
}
```

This code sets up a `Regex` for the O'Reilly web site and then uses it to create a `WebPermission` for connecting to that site and all sites containing the string. You then check the `WebPermission` by calling `SecurityManager.IsGranted` to see whether you have permission to do this.

Discussion

The `IsGranted` method is a lightweight way of determining whether permission is granted for an assembly without first incurring the full stackwalk that a `Demand` gives you. Note, however, that once you exercise the code that performs the `Demand`, the full stackwalk will then take place. The drawback to this approach is that the code is still subject to a luring attack if `Assert` is misused, so you need to consider where the call to `IsGranted` is being made in the overall scheme of your security.

Some of the reasons you might design an assembly to have optional permissions is for deployment in different customer scenarios. In some scenarios (such as desktop applications), it might be acceptable to have an assembly that can perform more robust actions (talk to a database, create network traffic via HTTP, etc.). In other scenarios, you can defer these actions if the customer does not wish to grant enough permissions for these extra services to function.

See Also

The "WebPermission Class," "SecurityManager Class," and "IsGranted Method" topics in the MSDN documentation.

17.9 Minimizing the Attack Surface of an Assembly

Problem

Someone attacking your assembly will first attempt to find out as many things as possible about your assembly and then use this information in constructing the attack(s). The more surface area you give to attackers, the more they have to work with. You need to minimize what your assembly is allowed to do so that, if an attacker is successful in taking it over, the attacker will not have the necessary privileges to do any damage to the system.

Solution

Use the `SecurityAction.RequestRefuse` enumeration member to indicate, at an assembly level, the permissions that you do not wish this assembly to have. This will force the CLR to refuse these permissions to your code and will ensure that, even if another part of the system is compromised, your code cannot be used to perform functions that it does not need the rights to do.

The following example allows the assembly to perform file I/O as part of its minimal permission set but explicitly refuses to allow this assembly to have permissions to skip verification:

```
[assembly: FileIOPermission(SecurityAction.RequestMinimum,Unrestricted=true)]
[assembly: SecurityPermission(SecurityAction.RequestRefuse,
            SkipVerification=false)]
```

Discussion

Once you have determined what permissions your assembly needs as part of your normal security testing, you can use `RequestRefuse` to lock down your code. If this seems extreme, think of scenarios in which your code could be accessing a data store containing sensitive information, such as social security numbers or salary information. This proactive step can help you show your customers that you take security seriously and can help defend your interests in case a break-in occurs on a system that your code is part of.

One serious consideration with this approach is that the use of `RequestRefuse` marks your assembly as partially trusted. This in turn prevents it from calling any strong-named assembly that hasn't been marked with the `AllowPartiallyTrustedCallers` attribute.

See Also

Chapter 8 of Microsoft Patterns & Practices Group: *http://msdn.microsoft.com/library/default.asp?url=/library/en-us/dnnetsec/html/THCMCh08.asp*; see the "SecurityAction Enumeration" and "Global Attributes" topics in the MSDN documentation.

17.10   Obtaining Security/Audit Information

Problem

You need to obtain the security rights and/or audit information for a file or registry key.

Solution

When obtaining security/audit information for a file, use the static GetAccessControl method of the File class to obtain a System.Security.AccessControl.FileSecurity object. Use the FileSecurity object to access the security and audit information for the file. These steps are demonstrated in Example 17-11.

Example 17-11. Obtaining security audit information

```
public static void ViewFileRights()
{
    // Get security information from a file.
    string file = @"c:\FOO.TXT";
    FileSecurity fileSec = File.GetAccessControl(file);
    DisplayFileSecurityInfo(fileSec);
}

public static void DisplayFileSecurityInfo(FileSecurity fileSec)
{
    Console.WriteLine("GetSecurityDescriptorSddlForm: {0}",
        fileSec.GetSecurityDescriptorSddlForm(AccessControlSections.All));

    foreach (FileSystemAccessRule ace in
            fileSec.GetAccessRules(true, true, typeof(NTAccount)))
    {
        Console.WriteLine("\tIdentityReference.Value: {0}",
                        ace.IdentityReference.Value);
        Console.WriteLine("\tAccessControlType: {0}", ace.AccessControlType);
        Console.WriteLine("\tFileSystemRights: {0}", ace.FileSystemRights);
        Console.WriteLine("\tInheritanceFlags: {0}", ace.InheritanceFlags);
        Console.WriteLine("\tIsInherited: {0}", ace.IsInherited);
        Console.WriteLine("\tPropagationFlags: {0}", ace.PropagationFlags);

        Console.WriteLine("-----------------\r\n\r\n");
    }

    foreach (FileSystemAuditRule ace in
            fileSec.GetAuditRules(true, true, typeof(NTAccount)))
    {
        Console.WriteLine("\tIdentityReference.Value: {0}",
                        ace.IdentityReference.Value);
        Console.WriteLine("\tAuditFlags: {0}", ace.AuditFlags);
        Console.WriteLine("\tFileSystemRights: {0}", ace.FileSystemRights);
        Console.WriteLine("\tInheritanceFlags: {0}", ace.InheritanceFlags);
        Console.WriteLine("\tIsInherited: {0}", ace.IsInherited);
```

Example 17-11. Obtaining security audit information (continued)

```
        Console.WriteLine("\tPropagationFlags: {0}", ace.PropagationFlags);

        Console.WriteLine("-----------------\r\n\r\n");
    }

    Console.WriteLine("GetGroup(typeof(NTAccount)).Value: {0}",
                    fileSec.GetGroup(typeof(NTAccount)).Value);
    Console.WriteLine("GetOwner(typeof(NTAccount)).Value: {0}",
                    fileSec.GetOwner(typeof(NTAccount)).Value);

    Console.WriteLine("-------------------------------------\r\n\r\n\r\n");
}
```

These methods produce the following output:

```
        GetSecurityDescriptorSddlForm: O:BAG:SYD:PAI(A;;FA;;;SY)(A;;FA;;;BA)
            IdentityReference.Value: NT AUTHORITY\SYSTEM
            AccessControlType: Allow
            FileSystemRights: FullControl
            InheritanceFlags: None
            IsInherited: False
            PropagationFlags: None
            -----------------

            IdentityReference.Value: BUILTIN\Administrators
            AccessControlType: Allow
            FileSystemRights: FullControl
            InheritanceFlags: None
            IsInherited: False
            PropagationFlags: None
            -----------------

        GetGroup(typeof(NTAccount)).Value: NT AUTHORITY\SYSTEM
        GetOwner(typeof(NTAccount)).Value: BUILTIN\Administrators
```

When obtaining security/audit information for a registry key, use the `GetAccess-Control` instance method of the `Microsoft.Win32.RegistryKey` class to obtain a `System.Security.AccessControl.RegistrySecurity` object. Use the `RegistrySecurity` object to access the security and audit information for the registry key. These steps are demonstrated in Example 17-12.

Example 17-12. Getting security or audit information for a registry key

```
public static void ViewRegKeyRights()
{
    // Get security information from a registry key.
    using (RegistryKey regKey =
        Registry.LocalMachine.OpenSubKey(@"SOFTWARE\MyCompany\MyApp"))
    {
        RegistrySecurity regSecurity = regKey.GetAccessControl();
        DisplayRegKeySecurityInfo(regSecurity);
    }
```

Example 17-12. Getting security or audit information for a registry key (continued)

```
}

public static void DisplayRegKeySecurityInfo(RegistrySecurity regSec)
{
    Console.WriteLine("GetSecurityDescriptorSddlForm: {0}",
        regSec.GetSecurityDescriptorSddlForm(AccessControlSections.All));

    foreach (RegistryAccessRule ace in
            regSec.GetAccessRules(true, true, typeof(NTAccount)))
    {
        Console.WriteLine("\tIdentityReference.Value: {0}",
                        ace.IdentityReference.Value);
        Console.WriteLine("\tAccessControlType: {0}", ace.AccessControlType);
        Console.WriteLine("\tRegistryRights: {0}", ace.RegistryRights.ToString( ));
        Console.WriteLine("\tInheritanceFlags: {0}", ace.InheritanceFlags);
        Console.WriteLine("\tIsInherited: {0}", ace.IsInherited);
        Console.WriteLine("\tPropagationFlags: {0}", ace.PropagationFlags);

        Console.WriteLine("----------------\r\n\r\n");
    }

    foreach (RegistryAuditRule ace in
            regSec.GetAuditRules(true, true, typeof(NTAccount)))
    {
        Console.WriteLine("\tIdentityReference.Value: {0}",
                        ace.IdentityReference.Value);
        Console.WriteLine("\tAuditFlags: {0}", ace.AuditFlags);
        Console.WriteLine("\tRegistryRights: {0}", ace.RegistryRights.ToString( ));
        Console.WriteLine("\tInheritanceFlags: {0}", ace.InheritanceFlags);
        Console.WriteLine("\tIsInherited: {0}", ace.IsInherited);
        Console.WriteLine("\tPropagationFlags: {0}", ace.PropagationFlags);

        Console.WriteLine("----------------\r\n\r\n");
    }
    Console.WriteLine("GetGroup(typeof(NTAccount)).Value: {0}",
                    regSec.GetGroup(typeof(NTAccount)).Value);
    Console.WriteLine("GetOwner(typeof(NTAccount)).Value: {0}",
                    regSec.GetOwner(typeof(NTAccount)).Value);

    Console.WriteLine("---------------------------------------\r\n\r\n\r\n");
}
```

These methods produce the following output:

```
GetSecurityDescriptorSddlForm: O:S-1-5-21-329068152-1383384898-682003330-1004G:S-1-
5-21-329068152-1383384898-682003330-513D:

AI(A;ID;KR;;;BU)(A;CIIOID;GR;;;BU)(A;ID;KA;;;BA)(A;CIIOID;GA;;;BA)(A;ID;KA;;;SY)(A;CI
        IOID;GA;;;SY)(A;ID;KA;;;S-1-5-21-329068152-1383384898-682003330-
        1004)(A;CIIOID;GA;;;CO)
            IdentityReference.Value: BUILTIN\Users
            AccessControlType: Allow
            RegistryRights: ReadKey
```

```
    InheritanceFlags: None
    IsInherited: True
    PropagationFlags: None
-----------------

    IdentityReference.Value: BUILTIN\Users
    AccessControlType: Allow
    RegistryRights: -2147483648
    InheritanceFlags: ContainerInherit
    IsInherited: True
    PropagationFlags: InheritOnly
-----------------

    IdentityReference.Value: BUILTIN\Administrators
    AccessControlType: Allow
    RegistryRights: FullControl
    InheritanceFlags: None
    IsInherited: True
    PropagationFlags: None
-----------------

    IdentityReference.Value: BUILTIN\Administrators
    AccessControlType: Allow
    RegistryRights: 268435456
    InheritanceFlags: ContainerInherit
    IsInherited: True
    PropagationFlags: InheritOnly
-----------------

    IdentityReference.Value: NT AUTHORITY\SYSTEM
    AccessControlType: Allow
    RegistryRights: FullControl
    InheritanceFlags: None
    IsInherited: True
    PropagationFlags: None
-----------------

    IdentityReference.Value: NT AUTHORITY\SYSTEM
    AccessControlType: Allow
    RegistryRights: 268435456
    InheritanceFlags: ContainerInherit
    IsInherited: True
    PropagationFlags: InheritOnly
-----------------

    IdentityReference.Value: OPERATOR-C1EFE0\Admin
    AccessControlType: Allow
    RegistryRights: FullControl
    InheritanceFlags: None
    IsInherited: True
    PropagationFlags: None
-----------------
```

```
IdentityReference.Value: CREATOR OWNER
AccessControlType: Allow
RegistryRights: 268435456
InheritanceFlags: ContainerInherit
IsInherited: True
PropagationFlags: InheritOnly
-----------------

GetGroup(typeof(NTAccount)).Value: OPERATOR-C1EFE0\None
GetOwner(typeof(NTAccount)).Value: OPERATOR-C1EFE0\Admin
--------------------------------------
```

Discussion

The essential method that is used to obtain the security information for a file or registry key is the GetAccessControl method. When this method is called on the RegistryKey object, a RegistrySecurity object is returned. However, when this method is called on a File class, a FileSecurity object is returned. The RegistrySecurity and FileSecurity objects essentially represent a Discretionary Access Control List (DACL), which is what developers writing code in unmanaged languages such as C++ are used to working with.

The RegistrySecurity and FileSecurity objects each contain a list of security rules that has been applied to the system object that it represents. The RegistrySecurity object contains a list of RegistryAccessRule objects, and the FileSecurity object contains a list of FileSystemAccessRule objects. These rule objects are the equivalent of the Access Control Entries (ACE) that make up the list of security rules within a DACL.

System objects other than just the File class and RegistryKey object allow security privileges to be queried. Table 17-1 lists all the .NET Framework classes that return a security object type and what that type is. In addition, the rule-object type that is contained in the security object is also listed.

Table 17-1. List of all *Security and *AccessRule objects and the types to which they apply

Class	Object returned by the GetAccessControl method	Rule-object type contained within the security object
Directory	DirectorySecurity	FileSystemAccessRule
DirectoryInfo	DirectorySecurity	FileSystemAccessRule
EventWaitHandle	EventWaitHandleSecurity	EventWaitHandleAccessRule
File	FileSecurity	FileSystemAccessRule
FileInfo	FileSecurity	FileSystemAccessRule
FileStream	FileSecurity	FileSystemAccessRule
Mutex	MutexSecurity	MutexAccessRule
RegistryKey	RegistrySecurity	RegistryAccessRule
Semaphore	SemaphoreSecurity	SemaphoreAccessRule

The abstraction of a system object's DACL through the *Security objects and the abstraction of a DACL's ACE through the *AccessRule objects allows easy access to the security privileges of that system object. In previous versions of the .NET Framework, these DACLs and their ACEs would have been accessible only in unmanaged code. With the .NET 2.0 Framework and later, you now have access to view and program these objects.

See Also

Recipe 17.11; the "System.IO.File.GetAccessControl Method," "System.Security.AccessControl.FileSecurity Class," "Microsoft.Win32.RegistryKey.GetAccessControl Method," and "System.Security.AccessControl.RegistrySecurity Class" topics in the MSDN documentation.

17.11 Granting/Revoking Access to a File or Registry Key

Problem

You need to change the security privileges of either a file or registry key programmatically.

Solution

The code shown in Example 17-13 grants and then revokes the ability to perform write actions on a registry key.

Example 17-13. Granting and revoking the right to perform write actions on a registry key

```
public static void GrantRevokeRegKeyRights()
{
    NTAccount user = new NTAccount(@"WRKSTN\ST");

    using (RegistryKey regKey = Registry.LocalMachine.OpenSubKey(
                        @"SOFTWARE\MyCompany\MyApp"))
    {
        GrantRegKeyRights(regKey, user, RegistryRights.WriteKey,
            InheritanceFlags.None, PropagationFlags.None, AccessControlType.Allow);
        RevokeRegKeyRights(regKey, user, RegistryRights.WriteKey,
                    InheritanceFlags.None, PropagationFlags.None,
                    AccessControlType.Allow)
    }
}

public static void GrantRegKeyRights(RegistryKey regKey,
                                NTAccount user,
                                RegistryRights rightsFlags,
                                InheritanceFlags inherFlags,
```

Example 17-13. Granting and revoking the right to perform write actions on a registry key

```
                                    PropagationFlags propFlags,
                                    AccessControlType actFlags)
{
    RegistrySecurity regSecurity = regKey.GetAccessControl();

    RegistryAccessRule rule = new RegistryAccessRule(user, rightsFlags, inherFlags,
                                            propFlags, actFlags);
    regSecurity.AddAccessRule(rule);
    regKey.SetAccessControl(regSecurity);
}

public static void RevokeRegKeyRights(RegistryKey regKey,
                                    NTAccount user,
                                    RegistryRights rightsFlags,
                                    InheritanceFlags inherFlags,
                                    PropagationFlags propFlags,
                                    AccessControlType actFlags)
{
    RegistrySecurity regSecurity = regKey.GetAccessControl();

    RegistryAccessRule rule = new RegistryAccessRule(user, rightsFlags, inherFlags,
                                            propFlags, actFlags);
    regSecurity.RemoveAccessRuleSpecific(rule);

    regKey.SetAccessControl(regSecurity);
}
```

The code shown in Example 17-14 grants and then revokes the ability to delete a file.

Example 17-14. Granting and revoking the right to delete a file

```
public static void GrantRevokeFileRights()
{
    NTAccount user = new NTAccount(@"WRKSTN\ST");

    string file = @"c:\FOO.TXT";
    GrantFileRights(file, user, FileSystemRights.Delete, InheritanceFlags.None,
                PropagationFlags.None, AccessControlType.Allow);
    RevokeFileRights(file, user, FileSystemRights.Delete, InheritanceFlags.None,
                PropagationFlags.None, AccessControlType.Allow);
}

public static void GrantFileRights(string file,
                                    NTAccount user,
                                    FileSystemRights rightsFlags,
                                    InheritanceFlags inherFlags,
                                    PropagationFlags propFlags,
                                    AccessControlType actFlags)
{
    FileSecurity fileSecurity = File.GetAccessControl(file);
```

```
    FileSystemAccessRule rule = new FileSystemAccessRule(user, rightsFlags,
                                                inherFlags, propFlags,
                                                actFlags);
    fileSecurity.AddAccessRule(rule);
    File.SetAccessControl(file, fileSecurity);
}

public static void RevokeFileRights(string file,
                                NTAccount user,
                                FileSystemRights rightsFlags,
                                InheritanceFlags inherFlags,
                                PropagationFlags propFlags,
                                AccessControlType actFlags)
{
    FileSecurity fileSecurity = File.GetAccessControl(file);

    FileSystemAccessRule rule = new FileSystemAccessRule(user, rightsFlags,
                                                inherFlags, propFlags,
                                                actFlags);
    fileSecurity.RemoveAccessRuleSpecific(rule);
    File.SetAccessControl(file, fileSecurity);
}
```

Discussion

When granting or revoking access rights on a file or registry key, you need two things. The first is a valid NTAccount object. This object essentially encapsulates a user or group account. A valid NTAccount object is required in order to create either a new RegistryAccessRule or a new FileSystemAccessRule. The NTAccount identifies the user or group this access rule will apply to. Note that the string passed in to the NTAccount constructor must be changed to a valid user or group name that exists on your machine. If you pass in the name of an existing user or group account that has been disabled, an IdentityNotMappedException will be thrown with the message "Some or all identity references could not be translated."

The second item that is needed is either a valid RegistryKey object, if you are modifying security access to a registry key, or a string containing a valid path and filename to an existing file. These objects will have security permissions either granted to them or revoked from them.

Once these two items have been obtained, you can use the second item to obtain a security object, which contains the list of access-rule objects. For example, the following code obtains the security object for the registry key HKEY-LOCAL_MACHINE\SOFTWARE\MyCompany\MyApp:

```
        RegistryKey regKey = Registry.LocalMachine.OpenSubKey(
                            @"SOFTWARE\MyCompany\MyApp");
        RegistrySecurity regSecurity = regKey.GetAccessControl();
```

The following code obtains the security object for the *FOO.TXT* file:

```
string file = @"c:\FOO.TXT";
FileSecurity fileSecurity = File.GetAccessControl(file);
```

Now that you have your particular security object, you can create an access-rule object that will be added to this security object. To do this, you need to create a new access rule. For a registry key, you have to create a new `RegistryAccessRule` object, and for a file, you have to create a new `FileSystemAccessRule` object. To add this access rule to the correct security object, you call the `SetAccessControl` method on the security object. Note that `RegistryAccessRule` objects can be added only to `RegistrySecurity` objects, and `FileSystemAccessRule` objects can be added only to `FileSecurity` objects.

To remove an access-rule object from a system object, you follow the same set of steps, except that you call the `RemoveAccessRuleSpecific` method instead of `AddAccessRule`. `RemoveAccessRuleSpecific` accepts an access-rule object and attempts to remove the rule that exactly matches this rule object from the security object. As always, you must remember to call the `SetAccessControl` method to apply any changes to the actual system object.

For a list of other classes that allow security permissions to be modified programmatically, see Recipe 17.12.

See Also

Recipe 17.10; the "System.IO.File.GetAccessControl Method," "System.Security.AccessControl.FileSecurity Class," "System.Security.AccessControl.FileSystemAccessRule Class," "Microsoft.Win32.RegistryKey.GetAccessControl Method," "System.Security.AccessControl.RegistrySecurity Class," and "System.Security.AccessControl.RegistryAccessRule Class" topics in the MSDN documentation.

17.12   Protecting String Data with Secure Strings

Problem

You need to store sensitive information, such as a social security number, in a string. However, you do not want prying eyes to be able to view this data in memory.

Solution

Use the `SecureString` object. To place text from a stream object within a `SecureString` object, use the following method:

```
public static SecureString CreateSecureString(StreamReader secretStream)
{
    SecureString secretStr = new SecureString( );
    char buf;
```

```
        while (secretStream.Peek( ) >= 0)
        {
            buf = (char)secretStream.Read( );
            secretStr.AppendChar(buf);
        }

        // Make the secretStr object read-only.
        secretStr.MakeReadOnly( );

        return (secretStr);
    }
```

To pull the text out of a SecureString object, use the following method:

```
    public static void ReadSecureString(SecureString secretStr)
    {
        // In order to read back the string, you need to use some special
methods.
        IntPtr secretStrPtr = Marshal.SecureStringToBSTR(secretStr);
        string nonSecureStr = Marshal.PtrToStringBSTR(secretStrPtr);

        // Use the unprotected string.
        Console.WriteLine("nonSecureStr = {0}", nonSecureStr);

        Marshal.ZeroFreeBSTR(secretStrPtr);

        if (!secretStr.IsReadOnly( ))
        {
            secretStr.Clear( );
        }
    }
```

Discussion

A SecureString object is designed specifically to contain string data that you want to keep secret. Some of the data you may want to store in a SecureString object would be a social security number, a credit card number, a PIN number, a password, an employee ID, or any other type of sensitive information.

This string data is automatically encrypted immediately upon being added to the SecureString object, and it is automatically decrypted when the string data is extracted from the SecureString object. The encryption is one of the highlights of using this object.

Another feature of a SecureString object is that when the MakeReadOnly method is called, the SecureString becomes immutable. Any attempt to modify the string data within the read-only SecureString object causes an InvalidOperationException to be thrown. Once a SecureString object is made read-only, it cannot go back to a read/write state. However, you need to be careful when calling the Copy method on an existing SecureString object. This method will create a new instance of the SecureString object on which it was called, with a copy of its data. However, this new SecureString object is now readable and writable. You should review your code to determine if this new SecureString object should be made read-only similarly to its original SecureString object.

 The SecureString object can be used only on Windows 2000 (with Service Pack 3 or greater) or later operating system.

In this recipe, you create a SecureString object from data read in from a stream. This data could also come from a char* using unsafe code. The SecureString object contains a constructor that accepts a parameter of this type in addition to an integer parameter that takes a length value, which determines the number of characters to pull from the char*.

Getting data out of a SecureString object is not obvious at first glance. There are no methods to return the data contained within a SecureString object. In order to accomplish this, you must use two static methods on the Marshal class. The first is the SecureStringToBSTR, which accepts your SecureString object and returns an IntPtr. This IntPtr is then passed into the PtrToStringBSTR method, also on the Marshal class. The PtrToStringBSTR method then returns an unsecure String object containing your decrypted string data.

Once you are done using the SecureString object, you should call the static ZeroFreeBSTR method on the Marshal class to zero out any memory allocated when extracting the data from the SecureString. As an added safeguard, you should call the Clear method of the SecureString object to zero out the encrypted string from memory. If you have made your SecureString object read-only, you will not be able to call the Clear method to wipe out its data. In this situation, you must either call the Dispose method on the SecureString object (the use of a using block would be preferable here) or rely on the garbage collector to remove the SecureString object and its data from memory.

Notice that when you pull a SecureString object into an unsecure String, its data becomes viewable by a malicious hacker. So it may seem pointless to go through the trouble of using a SecureString when you are just going to convert it into an insecure String. However, by using a SecureString, you narrow the window of opportunity for a malicious hacker to view this data in memory. In addition, some APIs accept a SecureString as a parameter so that you don't have to convert it to an unsecure String. The ProcessStartInfo, for example, accepts a password in its Password property as a SecureString object.

 The SecureString object is not a silver bullet for securing your data. It is, however, another layer of defense you can add to your application.

See Also

The "SecureString Class" topic in the MSDN documentation.

17.13 Securing Stream Data

Problem

You want to use the TCP server in Recipe 17.1 to communicate with the TCP client in Recipe 17.2. However, you need to encrypt the communication and verify that it has not been tampered with in transit.

Solution

Replace the NetworkStream class with the more secure SslStream class on both the client and the server. The code for the more secure TCP client, TCPClient_SSL, is shown in Example 17-15 (changes are in boldface).

Example 17-15. TCPClient_SSL class

```
class TCPClient_SSL
{
    private TcpClient _client = null;
    private IPAddress _address = IPAddress.Parse("127.0.0.1");
    private int _port = 5;
    private IPEndPoint _endPoint = null;

    public TCPClient_SSL(string address, string port)
    {
        _address = IPAddress.Parse(address);
        _port = Convert.ToInt32(port);
        _endPoint = new IPEndPoint(_address, _port);
    }

    public void ConnectToServer(string msg)
    {
        try
        {
            using (client = new TcpClient())
            {
                client.Connect(_endPoint);

                using (SslStream sslStream = new SslStream(_client.GetStream(),
                    false, new RemoteCertificateValidationCallback(
                        CertificateValidationCallback)))
                {
                    sslStream.AuthenticateAsClient("MyTestCert2");

                    // Get the bytes to send for the message.
                    byte[] bytes = Encoding.ASCII.GetBytes(msg);
```

Example 17-15. TCPClient_SSL class (continued)

```
                    // Send message.
                    Console.WriteLine("Sending message to server: " + msg);
                            sslStream.Write(bytes, 0, bytes.Length);

                    // Get the response.
                    // Buffer to store the response bytes.
                    bytes = new byte[1024];

                    // Display the response.
                    int bytesRead = sslStream.Read(bytes, 0, bytes.Length);
                    string serverResponse = Encoding.ASCII.GetString(bytes, 0,
                        bytesRead);
                    Console.WriteLine("Server said: " + serverResponse);
                }
            }
        }
        catch (SocketException e)
        {
            Console.WriteLine("There was an error talking to the server: {0}",
            e.ToString( ));
        }
    }

    private bool CertificateValidationCallback(object sender,
                X509Certificate certificate, X509Chain chain,
                SslPolicyErrors sslPolicyErrors)
    {
        if (sslPolicyErrors == SslPolicyErrors.None)
        {
            return true;
        }
        else
        {
            if (sslPolicyErrors == SslPolicyErrors.RemoteCertificateChainErrors)
            {
                Console.WriteLine("The X509Chain.ChainStatus returned an array " +
                    "of X509ChainStatus objects containing error information.");
            }
            else if (sslPolicyErrors ==
                    SslPolicyErrors.RemoteCertificateNameMismatch)
            {
                Console.WriteLine("There was a mismatch of the name " +
                    "on a certificate.");
            }
            else if (sslPolicyErrors ==
                    SslPolicyErrors.RemoteCertificateNotAvailable)
            {
                Console.WriteLine("No certificate was available.");
            }
            else
            {
                Console.WriteLine("SSL Certificate Validation Error!");
```

Example 17-15. TCPClient_SSL class (continued)

```
            }
        }
        Console.WriteLine(Environment.NewLine +
                        "SSL Certificate Validation Error!");
        Console.WriteLine(sslPolicyErrors.ToString());
        return false;
    }
}
```

The new code for the more secure TCP server, TCPServer_SSL, is shown in Example 17-16 (changes are in boldface).

Example 17-16. TCPServer_SSL class

```
class TCPServer_SSL
{
    private TcpListener _listener = null;
    private IPAddress _address = IPAddress.Parse("127.0.0.1");
    private int _port = 55555;

    #region CTORs
    public TCPServer_SSL()
    {
    }

    public TCPServer_SSL(string address, string port)
    {
        _port = Convert.ToInt32(port);
        _address = IPAddress.Parse(address);
    }
    #endregion // CTORs

    #region Properties
    public IPAddress Address
    {
        get { return _address; }
        set { _address = value; }
    }

    public int Port
    {
        get { return _port; }
        set { _port = value; }
    }
    #endregion

    public void Listen()
    {
        try
        {
            _using_(listener = new TcpListener(_address, _port))
            {
```

Example 17-16. TCPServer_SSL class (continued)

```
                // Fire up the server.
                listener.Start( );

                // Enter the listening loop.
                while (true)
                {
                    Console.Write("Looking for someone to talk to... ");

                    // Wait for connection.
                    TcpClient newClient = _listener.AcceptTcpClient( );
                    Console.WriteLine("Connected to new client");

                    // Spin a thread to take care of the client.
                    ThreadPool.QueueUserWorkItem(new WaitCallback(ProcessClient),
                                        newClient);
                }
            }
        }
        catch (SocketException e)
        {
            Console.WriteLine("SocketException: {0}", e);
        }
        finally
        {
            // Shut it down.
            _listener.Stop( );
        }

        Console.WriteLine("\nHit any key (where is ANYKEY?) to continue...");
        Console.Read( );
    }

    private void ProcessClient(object client)
    {
        using (TcpClient newClient = (TcpClient)client)
        {
            // Buffer for reading data.
            byte[] bytes = new byte[1024];
            string clientData = null;

            using (SslStream sslStream = new SslStream(newClient.GetStream( )))
             {
                 sslStream.AuthenticateAsServer(GetServerCert("MyTestCert2"), false,
                                    SslProtocols.Default, true);

                // Loop to receive all the data sent by the client.
                int bytesRead = 0;
                while ((bytesRead = sslStream.Read(bytes, 0, bytes.Length)) != 0)
                {
                    // Translate data bytes to an ASCII string.
                    clientData = Encoding.ASCII.GetString(bytes, 0, bytesRead);
                    Console.WriteLine("Client says: {0}", clientData);
```

Example 17-16. TCPServer_SSL class (continued)

```
                // Thank them for their input.
                bytes = Encoding.ASCII.GetBytes("Thanks call again!");

                // Send back a response.
                sslStream.Write(bytes, 0, bytes.Length);
            }
        }
    }
}

    private static X509Certificate GetServerCert(string subjectName)
    {
        X509Store store = new X509Store(StoreName.My, StoreLocation.LocalMachine);
        store.Open(OpenFlags.ReadOnly);
        X509CertificateCollection certificate =
            store.Certificates.Find(X509FindType.FindBySubjectName,
                                    subjectName, true);
        if (certificate.Count > 0)
            return (certificate[0]);
        else
            return (null);
    }
}
```

Discussion

For more information about the inner workings of the TCP server and client and
how to run these applications, see Recipes 17.1 and 17.2. In this recipe, you will
cover only the changes needed to convert the TCP server and client to use the
SslStream object for secure communication.

The SslStream object uses the SSL protocol to provide a secure encrypted channel on
which to send data. However, encryption is just one of the security features built into
the SslStream object. Another feature of SslStream is that it detects malicious or even
accidental modification to the data. Even though the data is encrypted, it may
become modified during transit. To determine if this has occurred, the data is signed
with a hash before it is sent. When it is received, the data is rehashed and the two
hashes are compared. If both hashes are equivalent, the message arrived intact; if the
hashes are not equivalent, then something modified the data during transit.

The SslStream object also has the ability to use client and/or server certificates to
authenticate the client and/or the server as well as allowing the client to pass a certificate to the server if the client also needs to prove identity to the server. These certificates are used to prove the identity of the issuer. For example, if a client attaches to a
server using SSL, the server must provide a certificate to the client that is used to
prove that the server is who it says it is. In order to do this, the certificate must be

issued by a trusted authority. All trusted certificates are stored on the client in its root certificate store.

To allow the TCP server and client to communicate successfully, you need to set up an X.509 certificate that will be used to authenticate the TCP server. To do this, you set up a test certificate using the *makecert.exe* utility. This utility can be found in the *<drive>:\Program Files\Microsoft Visual Studio 9.0\Common7\Tools\Bin* directory. The syntax for creating a simple certificate is as follows:

```
makecert -r -pe -n "CN=MyTestCert2" -e 01/01/2036
         -sr localMachine c:\MyAppTestCert.cer
```

The options are defined as follows:

`-r`

The certificate will be self-signed. Self-signed certificates are often created and signed by the developer of a web site in order to facilitate testing of that site before it is moved into production. Self-signed certificates offer no evidence that the site is legitimate.

`-pe`

The certificate's private key will be exportable so that it can be included in the certificate.

`-n "CN=MyTestCert2"`

The publisher's certificate name. The name follows the "CN=" text.

`-e 01/01/2036`

The date at which this certificate expires.

`-sr localMachine`

The store where this certificate will be located. In this case, it is `localMachine`. However, you can also specify `currentUser` (which is the default if this switch is omitted).

The final argument to the *makecert.exe* utility is the output filename, in this case *c:\MyAppTestCert.cer*. This will create the certificate in the *c:\MyAppTestCert.cer* file on the hard drive.

The next step involves opening Windows Explorer and right-clicking on the *c:\MyAppTestCert.cer* file. This will display a pop-up menu with the Install Certificate menu item. Click this menu item and a wizard will be started to allow you to import this *.cer* file into the certificate store. The first dialog box of the wizard is shown in Figure 17-1. Click the Next button to go to the next step in the wizard.

The next step in the wizard allows you to choose the certificate store in which you want to install your certificate. This dialog is shown in Figure 17-2. Keep the defaults and click the Next button.

The final step in the wizard is shown in Figure 17-3. On this dialog, click the Finish button.

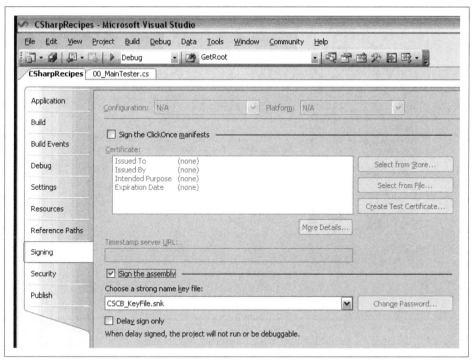

Figure 17-1. The first step of the Certificate Import Wizard

After you click the Finish button, the message box shown in Figure 17-4 is displayed, warning you to verify the certificate that you wish to install. Click the Yes button to install the certificate.

Finally, the message box in Figure 17-5 is displayed, indicating that the import was successful.

At this point, you can run the TCP server and client, and they should communicate successfully.

To use the SslStream in the TCP server project, you need to create a new SslStream object to wrap the TcpClient object:

```
SslStream sslStream = new SslStream(newClient.GetStream( ));
```

Before you can use this new stream object, you must authenticate the server using the following line of code:

```
sslStream.AuthenticateAsServer(GetServerCert("MyTestCert2"),
                    false, SslProtocols.Default, true);
```

The GetServerCert method finds the server certificate used to authenticate the server. Notice the name passed in to this method; it is the same as the publisher's certificate name switch used with the *makecert.exe* utility (see the *–n* switch). This certificate is returned from the GetServerCert method as an X509Certificate object. The next

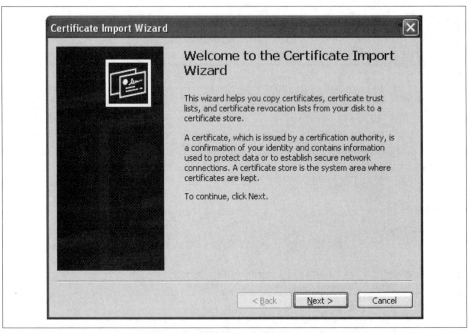

Figure 17-2. Specifying a certificate store in the Certificate Import Wizard

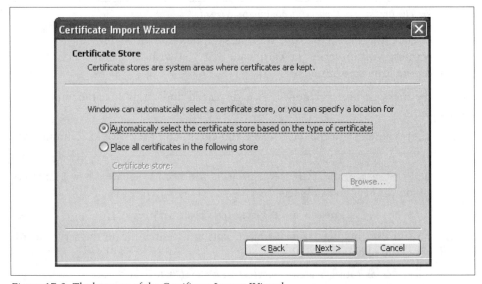

Figure 17-3. The last step of the Certificate Import Wizard

argument to the AuthenticateAsServer method is false, indicating that a client certificate is not required. The SslProtocols.Default argument indicates that the authentication mechanism (SSL 2.0, SSL 3.0, TLS 1.0, or PCT 1.0) is chosen based on what is

Figure 17-4. *The security warning*

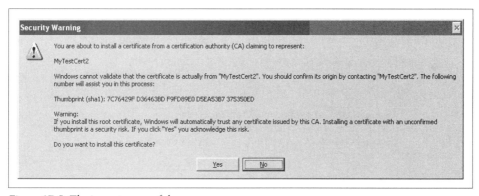

Figure 17-5. *The import successful message*

available to the client and server. The final argument indicates that the certificate will be checked to see whether it has been revoked.

To use the SslStream in the TCP client project, you create a new SslStream object, a bit differently from how it was created in the TCP server project:

```
SslStream sslStream = new SslStream(_client.GetStream(), false,
        new
    RemoteCertificateValidationCallback(CertificateValidationCallback));
```

This constructor accepts a stream from the _client field, a false indicating that the stream associated with the _client field will be closed when the Close method of the SslStream object is called, and a delegate that validates the server certificate. The CertificateValidationCallback method is called whenever a server certificate needs to be validated. The server certificate is checked, and any errors are passed into this delegate method to allow you to handle them as you wish.

The AuthenticateAsClient method is called next to authenticate the server:

```
sslStream.AuthenticateAsClient("MyTestCert2");
```

As you can see, with a little extra work, you can replace the current stream type you are using with the SslStream to gain the benefits of the SSL protocol.

See Also

The "SslStream Class" topic in the MSDN documentation.

17.14 Encrypting web.config Information

Problem

You need to encrypt data within a *web.config* file programmatically.

Solution

To encrypt data within a *web.config* file section, use the following method:

```
public static void EncryptWebConfigData(string appPath,
                                        string protectedSection,
                                        string dataProtectionProvider)
{
    System.Configuration.Configuration webConfig =
                WebConfigurationManager.OpenWebConfiguration(appPath);
    ConfigurationSection webConfigSection = webConfig.
GetSection(protectedSection);

    if (!webConfigSection.SectionInformation.IsProtected)
    {
        webConfigSection.SectionInformation.
ProtectSection(dataProtectionProvider);
        webConfig.Save();
    }
}
```

To decrypt data within a *web.config* file section, use the following method:

```
public static void DecryptWebConfigData(string appPath, string
protectedSection)
{
    System.Configuration.Configuration webConfig =
                WebConfigurationManager.OpenWebConfiguration(appPath);
```

```
                ConfigurationSection webConfigSection = webConfig.
    GetSection(protectedSection);

            if (webConfigSection.SectionInformation.IsProtected)
            {
                webConfigSection.SectionInformation.UnprotectSection( );
                webConfig.Save( );
            }
        }
    }
```

You will need to add the `System.Web` and `System.Configuration` DLLs to your project before this code will compile.

Discussion

To encrypt data, you can call the `EncryptWebConfigData` method with the following arguments:

```
EncryptWebConfigData("/WebApplication1", "appSettings",
                     "DataProtectionConfigurationProvider");
```

The first argument is the virtual path to the web application, the second argument is the section that you want to encrypt, and the last argument is the data protection provider that you want to use to encrypt the data.

The `EncryptWebConfigData` method uses the virtual path passed into it to open the *web.config* file. This is done using the `OpenWebConfiguration` static method of the `WebConfigurationManager` class:

```
System.Configuration.Configuration webConfig =
    WebConfigurationManager.OpenWebConfiguration(appPath);
```

This method returns a `System.Configuration.Configuration` object, which you use to get the section of the *web.config* file that you wish to encrypt. This is accomplished through the `GetSection` method:

```
ConfigurationSection webConfigSection = webConfig.
    GetSection(protectedSection);
```

This method returns a `ConfigurationSection` object that you can use to encrypt the section. This is done through a call to the `ProtectSection` method:

```
webConfigSection.SectionInformation.ProtectSection(dataProtectionProvider);
```

The `dataProtectionProvider` argument is a string identifying which data protection provider you want to use to encrypt the section information. The two available providers are `DpapiProtectedConfigurationProvider` and `RsaProtectedConfigurationProvider`. The `DpapiProtectedConfigurationProvider` class makes use of the Data Protection API (DPAPI) to encrypt and decrypt data. The `RsaProtectedConfigurationProvider` class makes use of the `RsaCryptoServiceProvider` class in the .NET Framework to encrypt and decrypt data.

The final step to encrypting the section information is to call the Save method of the System.Configuration.Configuration object. This saves the changes to the *web.config* file. If this method is not called, the encrypted data will not be saved.

To decrypt data within a *web.config* file, you can call the DecryptWebConfigData method with the following parameters:

```
DecryptWebConfigData("/WebApplication1", "appSettings");
```

The first argument is the virtual path to the web application; the second argument is the section that you want to encrypt.

The DecryptWebConfigData method operates very similarly to the EncryptWebConfigData method, except that it calls the UnprotectSection method to decrypt the encrypted data in the *web.config* file:

```
webConfigSection.SectionInformation.UnprotectSection();
```

If you encrypt data in the *web.config* file using this technique, the data will automatically be decrypted when the web application accesses the encrypted data in the *web.config* file.

See Also

The "System.Configuration.Configuration Class" topic in the MSDN documentation.

17.15 Obtaining the Full Reason a SecurityException Was Thrown

Problem

You need more information as to why a SecurityException was thrown.

Solution

Use the new properties available on the SecurityException object, as shown in Table 17-2.

Table 17-2. SecurityException Properties

Property	Description
Action	This property returns a SecurityAction enumeration value indicating the cause of the security check failure. Possible values can be any of the following:
	Assert
	Demand
	DemandChoice
	Deny

Table 17-2. SecurityException Properties (continued)

Property	Description
	InheritanceDemand
	InheritanceDemandChoice
	LinkDemand
	LinkDemandChoice
	PermitOnly
	RequestMinimum
	RequestOptional
	RequestRefuseusing
Data	An IDictionary of user-defined key-value pairs.
Demanded	Returns the permission(s) that caused the Demand to fail. The returned object needs to be cast to a Permission, PermissionSet, or PermissionSetCollection type in order to access its information. You can use the is keyword to determine which one of these types this property returned.
DenySetInstance	Returns the denied permission(s) that caused the Demand to fail. This property contains a value whenever a Deny higher up in the stack causes a Demand to fail. The returned object needs to be cast to a Permission, PermissionSet, or PermissionSetCollection type in order to access its information. You can use the is keyword to determine which one of these types this property returned.
FailedAssemblyInfo	Returns an AssemblyName object for the assembly where this exception occurred (i.e., the assembly where the Demand that failed was called).
FirstPermissionThatFailed	Returns an IPermission object of the first permission that failed. This is useful when several permissions in a permission set were demanded at one time. This property identifies which permission caused the exception to occur.
Method	Returns a MethodInfo object for the method where this exception originated. If the cause of the exception was due to a Deny or PermitOnly, the method containing the Deny or PermitOnly will be returned by this property. From this object you can also obtain information on the type and assembly that contain this method.
PermitOnlySetInstance	Returns the permission(s) that were set by a PermitOnly at the point where the security exception was thrown. The returned object needs to be cast to a Permission, PermissionSet, or PermissionSetCollection type in order to access its information. You can use the is keyword to determine which one of these types this property returned.
URL	Returns a string representing the URL of the assembly where this exception originated.
Zone	Returns a SecurityZone enumeration value indicating the zone of the assembly where this exception originated. Possible values can be any of the following:
	Internet
	Intranet
	MyComputer
	NoZone
	Trusted
	Untrusted

Discussion

These new properties on the SecurityException class provide much more insight into what caused the exception to be thrown. For example, if you think a Demand has failed, you can examine the Action property to determine that it was in fact the Demand. Next, you can use the Demanded property to find out exactly what permission(s) the Demand attempted to demand. You can compare this to the GrantedSet property, which contains the permission(s) that were granted to the assembly. Now that you know what caused the Demand to fail, you can use the Method, FailedAssemblyInfo, and URL properties to determine where the failure occurred.

The Data property can be a very useful property to a developer. This property contains key-value pairs that the developer creates and fills with information concerning why this exception occurred. In this property, you can place variable names and the data they contained at the time of the exception. This can give you even more clues as to why this exception was thrown. Be very careful that you do not leak this information out to the user. An attacker can use this information to gain more understanding of your application and overcome its defenses. See Recipe 17.11 for more information on the Exception.Data property.

See Also

The "SecurityException" topic in the MSDN documentation.

17.16   Achieving Secure Unicode Encoding

Problem

You want to make sure that your UnicodeEncoding or UTF8Encoding class detects any errors, such as an invalid sequence of bytes.

Solution

Use the constructor for the UnicodeEncoding class that accepts three parameters:

```
UnicodeEncoding encoding = new UnicodeEncoding(false, true, true);
```

Or use the constructor for the UTF8Encoding class that accepts two parameters:

```
UTF8Encoding encoding = new UTF8Encoding(true, true);
```

Discussion

The final argument to both these constructors should be true. This turns on error detection for this class. Error detection will help when an attacker somehow is able to access and modify a Unicode- or a UTF8-encoded stream of characters. If the attacker is not careful, she can invalidate the encoded stream. If error detection is turned on, it will be a first defense in catching these invalid encoded streams.

When error detection is turned on, errors such as the following are dealt with by throwing an ArgumentException:

- Leftover bytes that do not make up a complete encoded character sequence exist.
- An invalid encoded start character was detected. For example, a UTF8 character does not fit into one of the following classes: Single-Byte, Double-Byte, Three-Byte, Four-Byte, Five-Byte, or Six-Byte.
- Extra bits are found after processing an extra byte in a multibyte sequence.
- The leftover bytes in a sequence could not be used to create a complete character.
- A high surrogate value is not followed by a low surrogate value.
- In the case of the GetBytes method, the byte[] that is used to hold the resulting bytes is not large enough.
- In the case of the GetChars method, the char[] that is used to hold the resulting characters is not large enough.

If you use a constructor other than the one shown in this recipe or if you set the last parameter in this constructor to false, any errors in the encoding sequence are ignored, and no exception is thrown.

See Also

The "UnicodeEncoding Class" and "UTF8Encoding Class" topic in the MSDN documentation.

17.17   Obtaining a Safer File Handle

Problem

You want more security when manipulating an unmanaged file handle than a simple IntPtr can provide.

Solution

Use the Microsoft.Win32.SafeHandles.SafeFileHandle object to wrap an existing unmanaged file handle:

```
public static void WriteToFileHandle(IntPtr hFile)
{
    // Wrap our file handle in a safe handle wrapper object.
    using (Microsoft.Win32.SafeHandles.SafeFileHandle safeHFile =
        new Microsoft.Win32.SafeHandles.SafeFileHandle(hFile, true))
    {
        // Open a FileStream object using the passed-in safe file handle.
        using (FileStream fileStream = new FileStream(safeHFile,
                FileAccess.ReadWrite))
```

```
        {
            // Flush before we start to clear any pending unmanaged actions.
            fileStream.Flush();

            // Operate on file here.
            string line = "Using a safe file handle object";

            // Write to the file.
            byte[] bytes = Encoding.ASCII.GetBytes(line);
            fileStream.Write(bytes,0,bytes.Length);
        }
    }
    // Note that the hFile handle is invalid at this point.
}
```

The SafeFileHandle constructor takes two arguments. The first is an IntPtr that contains a handle to an unmanaged resource. The second argument is a Boolean value, where true indicates that the handle will always be released during finalization, and false indicates that the safeguards that force the handle to be released during finalization are turned off. Unless you have an extremely good reason to turn off these safeguards, it is recommended that you always set this Boolean value to true.

Discussion

A SafeFileHandle object contains a single handle to an unmanaged file resource. This class has two major benefits over using an IntPtr to store a handle—critical finalization and prevention of handle recycling attacks. The SafeFileHandle is seen by the garbage collector as a critical finalizer, due to the fact that one of the SafeFileHandle's base classes is CriticalFinalizerObject. The garbage collector separates finalizers into two categories: critical and noncritical. The noncritical finalizers are run first, followed by the critical finalizers. If a FileStream's finalizer flushes any data, it can assume that the SafeFileHandle object is still valid, because the SafeFileHandle finalizer is guaranteed to run after the FileStream's.

The Close method on the FileStream object will also close its underlying SafeFileHandle object.

Since the SafeFileHandle falls under critical finalization, it means that the underlying unmanaged handle is always released (i.e., the SafeFileHandle.ReleaseHandle method is always called), even in situations in which the AppDomain is corrupted and/or shutting down or the thread is being aborted. This will prevent resource handle leaks.

The SafeFileHandle object also helps to prevent handle recycling attacks. The operating system aggressively tries to recycle handles, so it is possible to close one handle and open another soon afterward and get the same value for the new handle. One way an attacker will take advantage of this is by forcing an accessible handle to close on one thread while it is possibly still being used on another in the hope that the handle will be recycled quickly and used as a handle to a new resource, possibly one that the attacker does not have permission to access. If the application still has this original handle and is actively using it, data corruption could be an issue.

Since this class inherits from the SafeHandleZeroOrMinusOneIsInvalid class, a handle value of zero or minus one is considered an invalid handle.

See Also

The "Microsoft.Win32.SafeHandles.SafeFileHandle Class" topic in the MSDN documentation.

CHAPTER 18

Threading and Synchronization

18.0 Introduction

A *thread* represents a single flow of execution logic in a program. Some programs never need more than a single thread to execute efficiently, but many do, and that is what this chapter is about. Threading in .NET allows you to build responsive and efficient applications. Many applications have a need to perform multiple actions at the same time (such as user interface interaction and processing data), and threading provides the capability to achieve this. Being able to have your application perform multiple tasks is a very liberating and yet complicating factor in your application design. Once you have multiple threads of execution in your application, you need to start thinking about what data in your application needs to be protected from multiple accesses, what data could cause threads to develop an interdependency that could lead to deadlocking (Thread A has a resource that Thread B is waiting for, and Thread B has a resource that Thread A is waiting for), and how to store data you want to associate with the individual threads. You will explore some of these issues to help you take advantage of this wonderful capability of the .NET Framework. You will also see the areas where you need to be careful and items to keep in mind while designing and creating your multithreaded application.

18.1 Creating Per-Thread Static Fields

Problem

Static fields, by default, are shared between threads within an application domain. You need to allow each thread to have its own nonshared copy of a static field, so that this static field can be updated on a per-thread basis.

Solution

Use ThreadStaticAttribute to mark any static fields as not shareable between threads:

```
using System;
using System.Threading;

public class Foo
{
    [ThreadStaticAttribute()]
    public static string bar = "Initialized string";
}
```

Discussion

By default, static fields are shared between all threads that access these fields in the same application domain. To see this, you'll create a class with a static field called bar and a static method to access and display the value contained in this field:

```
using System;
using System.Threading;

public class ThreadStaticField
{
    public static string bar = "Initialized string";

    public static void DisplayStaticFieldValue()
    {
        string msg =
            string.Format("{0} contains static field value of: {1}",
                Thread.CurrentThread.GetHashCode(),
                ThreadStaticField.bar);
        Console.WriteLine(msg);
    }
}
```

Next, create a test method that accesses this static field both on the current thread and on a newly spawned thread:

```
public static void TestStaticField()
{
    ThreadStaticField.DisplayStaticFieldValue();

    Thread newStaticFieldThread =
        new Thread(ThreadStaticField.DisplayStaticFieldValue);

    newStaticFieldThread.Start();

    ThreadStaticField.DisplayStaticFieldValue();
}
```

This code displays output that resembles the following:

```
9 contains static field value of: Initialized string
10 contains static field value of: Initialized string
9 contains static field value of: Initialized string
```

In the preceding example, the current thread's hash value is 9, and the new thread's hash value is 10. These values will vary from system to system. Notice that both threads are accessing the same static bar field. Next, add the ThreadStaticAttribute to the static field:

```
public class ThreadStaticField
{
        [ThreadStaticAttribute()]
    public static string bar = "Initialized string";

    public static void DisplayStaticFieldValue()
    {
        string msg =
            string.Format("{0} contains static field value of: {1}",
                Thread.CurrentThread.GetHashCode(),
                ThreadStaticField.bar);
        Console.WriteLine(msg);
    }
}
```

Now, output resembling the following is displayed:

```
9 contains static field value of: Initialized string
10 contains static field value of:
9 contains static field value of: Initialized string
```

Notice that the new thread returns a null for the value of the static bar field. This is the expected behavior. The bar field is initialized only in the first thread that accesses it. In all other threads, this field is initialized to null. Therefore, it is imperative that you initialize the bar field in all threads before it is used.

Remember to initialize any static field that is marked with ThreadStaticAttribute before it is used in any thread. That is, this field should be initialized in the method passed in to the ThreadStart delegate. You should make sure to not initialize the static field using a field initializer as shown in the prior code, since only one thread gets to see that initial value.

The bar field is initialized to the "Initialized string" string literal before it is used in the first thread that accesses this field. In the previous test code, the bar field was accessed first, and, therefore, it was initialized in the current thread. Suppose you were to remove the first line of the TestStaticField method, as shown here:

```
public static void TestStaticField()
{
    // ThreadStaticField.DisplayStaticFieldValue();
```

```
    Thread newStaticFieldThread =
        new Thread(ThreadStaticField.DisplayStaticFieldValue);
    newStaticFieldThread.Start( );

    ThreadStaticField.DisplayStaticFieldValue( );
}
```

This code now displays similar output to the following:

```
10 contains static field value of: Initialized string
9 contains static field value of:
```

The current thread does not access the bar field first and therefore does not initialize it. However, when the new thread accesses it first, it does initialize it.

Note that adding a static constructor to initialize the static field marked with this attribute will still follow the same behavior. Static constructors are executed only one time per application domain.

See Also

The "ThreadStaticAttribute Attribute" and "Static Modifier (C#)" topics in the MSDN documentation.

18.2   Providing Thread-Safe Access to Class Members

Problem

You need to provide thread-safe access through accessor functions to an internal member variable.

The following NoSafeMemberAccess class shows three methods: ReadNumericField, IncrementNumericField, and ModifyNumericField. While all of these methods access the internal numericField member, the access is currently not safe for multithreaded access:

```
public static class NoSafeMemberAccess
{
    private static int numericField = 1;

    public static void IncrementNumericField( )
    {
        ++numericField;
    }

    public static void ModifyNumericField(int newValue)
    {
        numericField = newValue;
    }

    public static int ReadNumericField( )
    {
```

```
            return (numericField);
        }
    }
```

Solution

NoSafeMemberAccess could be used in a multithreaded application, and therefore it must be made thread-safe. Consider what would occur if multiple threads were calling the IncrementNumericField method at the same time. It is possible that two calls could occur to IncrementNumericField while the numericField is updated only once. In order to protect against this, you will modify this class by creating an object that you can lock against in critical sections of the code:

```csharp
public static class SaferMemberAccess
{

    private static int numericField = 1;
        private static object syncObj = new object();

    public static void IncrementNumericField( )
    {

            lock(syncObj)              {
            ++numericField;
            }
    }

    public static void ModifyNumericField(int newValue)
    {

            lock(syncObj)              {
            numericField = newValue;
        }
    }

    public static int ReadNumericField( )
    {

            lock (syncObj)              {
            return (numericField);
            }
    }
}
```

Using the lock statement on the syncObj object lets you synchronize access to the numericField member. This now makes all three methods safe for multithreaded access.

Discussion

Marking a block of code as a critical section is done using the lock keyword. The lock keyword should not be used on a public type or on an instance out of the control of the program, as this can contribute to deadlocks. Examples of this are using the "this" pointer, the type object for a class (typeof(MyClass)), or a string literal

---

("MyLock"). If you are attempting to protect code in only public static methods, the System.Runtime.CompilerServices.MethodImpl attribute could also be used for this purpose with the MethodImplOption.Synchronized value:

```
[MethodImpl (MethodImplOptions.Synchronized)]
public static void MySynchronizedMethod( )
{
}
```

There is a problem with synchronization using an object such as syncObj in the SaferMemberAccess example. If you lock an object or type that can be accessed by other objects within the application, other objects may also attempt to lock this same object. This will manifest itself in poorly written code that locks itself, such as the following code:

```
public class DeadLock
{
    public void Method1( )
    {
        lock(this)
        {
            // Do something.
        }
    }
}
```

When Method1 is called, it locks the current DeadLock object. Unfortunately, any object that has access to the DeadLock class may also lock it. This is shown here:

```
using System;
using System.Threading;

public class AnotherCls
{
    public void DoSomething( )
    {
        DeadLock deadLock = new DeadLock( );
        lock(deadLock)
        {
            Thread thread = new Thread(deadLock.Method1);
            thread.Start( );

            // Do some time-consuming task here.
        }
    }
}
```

The DoSomething method obtains a lock on the deadLock object and then attempts to call the Method1 method of the deadLock object on another thread, after which a very long task is executed. While the long task is executing, the lock on the deadLock object prevents Method1 from being called on the other thread. Only when this long task ends, and execution exits the critical section of the DoSomething method, will the

Method1 method be able to acquire a lock on the this object. As you can see, this can become a major headache to track down in a much larger application.

Jeffrey Richter has come up with a relatively simple method to remedy this situation, which he details quite clearly in the article "Safe Thread Synchronization" in the January 2003 issue of *MSDN Magazine*. His solution is to create a private field within the class on which to synchronize. Only the object itself can acquire this private field; no outside object or type may acquire it. This solution is also now the recommended practice in the MSDN documentation for the lock keyword. The DeadLock class can be rewritten, as follows to fix this problem:

```
public class DeadLock
{
    private object syncObj = new object();

    public void Method1()
    {
        lock(syncObj)
        {
            // Do something.
        }
    }
}
```

Now in the DeadLock class, you are locking on the internal syncObj, while the DoSomething method locks on the DeadLock class instance. This resolves the deadlock condition, but the DoSomething method still should not lock on a public type. Therefore, change the AnotherCls class like so:

```
public class AnotherCls
{
    private object deadLockSyncObj = new object();

    public void DoSomething()
    {
        DeadLock deadLock = new DeadLock();
        lock(deadLockSyncObj)
        {
            Thread thread = new Thread(deadLock.Method1);
            thread.Start();

            // Do some time-consuming task here.
        }
    }
}
```

Now the AnotherCls class has an object of its own to protect access to the DeadLock class instance in DoSomething instead of locking on the public type.

To clean up your code, you should stop locking any objects or types except for the synchronization objects that are private to your type or object, such as the syncObj in the fixed DeadLock class. This recipe makes use of this pattern by creating a static syncObj object within the SaferMemberAccess class. The IncrementNumericField, ModifyNumericField, and ReadNumericField methods use this syncObj to synchronize access to the numericField field. Note that if you do not need a lock while the numericField is being read in the ReadNumericField method, you can remove this lock block and simply return the value contained in the numericField field.

 Minimizing the number of critical sections within your code can significantly improve performance. Use what you need to secure resource access, but no more.

If you require more control over locking and unlocking of critical sections, you might want to try using the overloaded static Monitor.TryEnter methods. These methods allow more flexibility by introducing a timeout value. The lock keyword will attempt to acquire a lock on a critical section indefinitely. However, with the TryEnter method, you can specify a timeout value in milliseconds (as an integer) or as a TimeSpan structure. The TryEnter methods return true if a lock was acquired and false if it was not. Note that the overload of the TryEnter method that accepts only a single parameter does not block for any amount of time. This method returns immediately, regardless of whether the lock was acquired.

The updated class using the Monitor methods is shown in Example 18-1.

Example 18-1. Using Monitor methods

```csharp
using System;
using System.Threading;

public static class MonitorMethodAccess
{
    private static int numericField = 1;
    private static object syncObj = new object();

    public static object SyncRoot
    {
        get { return syncObj; }
    }

    public static void IncrementNumericField()
    {
        if (Monitor.TryEnter(syncObj, 250))
        {
            try
            {
                ++numericField;
            }
            finally
            {
                Monitor.Exit(syncObj);
            }
        }
    }
```

Example 18-1. Using Monitor methods (continued)

```
        }
    }

    public static void ModifyNumericField(int newValue)
    {
        if (Monitor.TryEnter(syncObj, 250))
        {
            try
            {
                numericField = newValue;
            }
            finally
            {
                Monitor.Exit(syncObj);
            }
        }
    }

    public static int ReadNumericField()
    {
        if (Monitor.TryEnter(syncObj, 250))
        {
            try
            {
                return (numericField);
            }
            finally
            {
                Monitor.Exit(syncObj);
            }
        }

        return (-1);
    }
}
```

Note that with the TryEnter methods, you should always check to see whether the lock was in fact acquired. If not, your code should wait and try again or return to the caller.

You might think at this point that all of the methods are thread-safe. Individually, they are, but what if you are trying to call them and you expect synchronized access between two of the methods? If ModifyNumericField and ReadNumericField are used one after the other by Class 1 on Thread 1 at the same time Class 2 is using these methods on Thread 2, locking or Monitor calls will not prevent Class 2 from modifying the value before Thread 1 reads it. Here is a series of actions that demonstrates this:

Class 1 Thread 1

Calls ModifyNumericField with 10.

Class 2 Thread 2

Calls `ModifyNumericField` with 15.

Class 1 Thread 1

Calls `ReadNumericField` and gets 15, not 10.

Class 2 Thread 2

Calls `ReadNumericField` and gets 15, which it expected.

In order to solve this problem of synchronizing reads and writes, the calling class needs to manage the interaction. The external class can accomplish this by using the `Monitor` class to establish a lock on the exposed synchronization object `SyncRoot` from `MonitorMethodAccess`, as shown here:

```
int num = 0;
if(Monitor.TryEnter(MonitorMethodAccess.SyncRoot,250))
{
    MonitorMethodAccess.ModifyNumericField(10);
    num = MonitorMethodAccess.ReadNumericField( );
    Monitor.Exit(MonitorMethodAccess.SyncRoot);
}
Console.WriteLine(num);
```

See Also

The "Lock Statement," "Thread Class," and "Monitor Class" topics in the MSDN documentation; see the "Safe Thread Synchronization" article in the January 2003 issue of *MSDN Magazine*.

18.3   Preventing Silent Thread Termination

Problem

An exception thrown in a spawned worker thread will cause this thread to be silently terminated if the exception is unhandled. You need to make sure all exceptions are handled in all threads. If an exception happens in this new thread, you want to handle it and be notified of its occurrence.

Solution

You must add exception handling to the method that you pass to the `ThreadStart` delegate with a try-catch, try-finally, or try-catch-finally block. The code to do this is shown in Example 18-2 in bold.

Example 18-2. Preventing silent thread termination

```
using System;
using System.Threading;

public class MainThread
```

Example 18-2. Preventing silent thread termination (continued)

```
{
    public void CreateNewThread()
    {
        // Spawn new thread to do concurrent work.
        Thread newWorkerThread = new Thread(Worker.DoWork);
        newWorkerThread.Start();
    }
}

public class Worker
{
    // Method called by ThreadStart delegate to do concurrent work
    public static void DoWork ()
    {
        try         {
            // Do thread work here.
        }         catch       {
            // Handle thread exception here.
            // Do not re-throw exception.
        }           finally        {
            // Do thread cleanup here.
        }
    }
}
```

Discussion

If an unhandled exception occurs in the main thread of an application, the main thread terminates, along with your entire application. An unhandled exception in a spawned worker thread, however, will terminate only that thread. This will happen without any visible warnings, and your application will continue to run as if nothing happened.

Simply wrapping an exception handler around the Start method of the Thread class will not catch the exception on the newly created thread. The Start method is called within the context of the current thread, not the newly created thread. It also returns immediately once the thread is launched, so it isn't going to wait around for the thread to finish. Therefore, the exception thrown in the new thread will not be caught since it is not visible to any other threads.

If the exception is rethrown from the catch block, the finally block of this structured exception handler will still execute. However, after the finally block is finished, the rethrown exception is, at that point, rethrown. The rethrown exception cannot be handled and the thread terminates. If there is any code after the finally block, it will not be executed, since an unhandled exception occurred.

Never rethrow an exception at the highest point in the exception-handling hierarchy within a thread. Since no exception handlers can catch this rethrown exception, it will be considered unhandled, and the thread will terminate after all `finally` blocks have been executed.

What if you use the `ThreadPool` and `QueueUserWorkItem`? This method will still help you because you added the handling code that will execute inside the thread. Just make sure you have the `finally` block set up so that you can notify yourself of exceptions in other threads as shown earlier.

In order to provide a last-chance exception handler for your WinForms application, you need to hook up to two separate events. The first event is the `System.AppDomain.CurrentDomain.UnhandledException` event, which will catch all unhandled exceptions in the current AppDomain on worker threads; it will not catch exceptions that occur on the main UI thread of a WinForms application. See Recipe 7.13 for more information on the `System.AppDomain.UnhandledException` event. In order to catch those, you also need to hook up to the `System.Windows.Forms.Application.ThreadException`, which will catch unhandled exceptions in the main UI thread. See Recipe 7.13 for more information about the `ThreadException` event.

See Also

The "Thread Class" and "Exception Class" topics in the MSDN documentation.

18.4 Being Notified of the Completion of an Asynchronous Delegate

Problem

You need a way of receiving notification from an asynchronously invoked delegate that it has finished. This scheme must allow your code to continue processing without having to constantly call `IsCompleted` in a loop or to rely on the `WaitOne` method. Since the asynchronous delegate will return a value, you must be able to pass this return value back to the invoking thread.

Solution

Use the `BeginInvoke` method to start the asynchronous delegate, but use the first parameter to pass a callback delegate to the asynchronous delegate, as shown in Example 18-3.

Example 18-3. Getting notification on completion of an anonymous delegate

```
using System;
using System.Threading;

public class AsyncAction2
{
    public void CallbackAsyncDelegate()
    {
        AsyncCallback callBack = DelegateCallback;

        AsyncInvoke method1 = TestAsyncInvoke.Method1;
        Console.WriteLine("Calling BeginInvoke on Thread {0}",
            Thread.CurrentThread.ManagedThreadId);
        IAsyncResult asyncResult = method1.BeginInvoke(callBack, method1);

        // No need to poll or use the WaitOne method here, so return to the calling
// method.
        return;
    }

    private static void DelegateCallback(IAsyncResult iresult)
    {
        Console.WriteLine("Getting callback on Thread {0}",
            Thread.CurrentThread.ManagedThreadId);
        AsyncResult asyncResult = (AsyncResult)iresult;
        AsyncInvoke method1 = (AsyncInvoke)asyncResult.AsyncDelegate;

        int retVal = method1.EndInvoke(asyncResult);
        Console.WriteLine("retVal (Callback): " + retVal);
    }
}
```

This callback delegate will call the DelegateCallback method on the thread the method was invoked on when the asynchronous delegate is finished processing.

The following code defines the AsyncInvoke delegate and the asynchronously invoked static method TestAsyncInvoke.Method1:

```
public delegate int AsyncInvoke();

public class TestAsyncInvoke
{
    public static int Method1()
    {
        Console.WriteLine("Invoked Method1 on Thread {0}",
            Thread.CurrentThread.ManagedThreadId );
        return (1);
    }
}
```

To run the asynchronous invocation, create an instance of the AsyncAction class and call the CallbackAsyncDelegate method like so:

```
AsyncAction aa2 = new AsyncAction();
aa2.CallbackAsyncDelegate();
```

The output for this code is shown next. Note that the thread ID for Method1 is different:

```
Calling BeginInvoke on Thread 9
Invoked Method1 on Thread 10
Getting callback on Thread 10
retVal (Callback): 1
```

Discussion

The asynchronous delegates in this recipe are created and invoked in the same fashion as the asynchronous delegate in Recipe 18.3. Instead of using the IsCompleted property to determine when the asynchronous delegate is finished processing (or the WaitOne method to block for a specified time while the asynchronous delegate continues processing), This recipe uses a callback to indicate to the calling thread that the asynchronous delegate has finished processing and that its return value, ref parameter values, and out parameter values are available.

Invoking a delegate in this manner is much more flexible and efficient than simply polling the IsCompleted property to determine when a delegate finishes processing. When polling this property in a loop, the polling method cannot return and allow the application to continue processing. A callback is also better than using a WaitOne method, since the WaitOne method will block the calling thread and allow no processing to occur.

The CallbackAsyncDelegate method in this recipe makes use of the first parameter to the BeginInvoke method of the asynchronous delegate to pass in another delegate. This contains a callback method to be called when the asynchronous delegate finishes processing. After calling BeginInvoke, this method can now return, and the application can continue processing; it does not have to wait in a polling loop or be blocked while the asynchronous delegate is running.

The AsyncInvoke delegate that is passed into the first parameter of the BeginInvoke method is defined as follows:

```
public delegate void AsyncCallback(IAsyncResult ar)
```

When this delegate is created, as shown here, the callback method passed in, DelegateCallback, will be called as soon as the asynchronous delegate completes:

```
AsyncCallback callBack = new AsyncCallback(DelegateCallback);
```

DelegateCallback will not run on the same thread as BeginInvoke but rather on a Thread from the ThreadPool. This callback method accepts a parameter of type IAsyncResult. You can cast this parameter to an AsyncResult object within the method and use it to obtain information about the completed asynchronous delegate, such as its return value, any ref parameter values, and any out parameter values. If the delegate instance that was used to call BeginInvoke is still in scope, you can just pass the IAsyncResult to the EndInvoke method. In addition, this object can obtain any state information passed into the second parameter of the BeginInvoke method. This state information can be any object type.

The DelegateCallback method casts the IAsyncResult parameter to an AsyncResult object and obtains the asynchronous delegate that was originally called. The EndInvoke method of this asynchronous delegate is called to process any return value, ref parameters, or out parameters. If any state object was passed in to the BeginInvoke method's second parameter, it can be obtained here through the following line of code:

```
object state = asyncResult.AsyncState;
```

See Also

The "AsyncCallback Delegate" topic in the MSDN documentation.

18.5   Storing Thread-Specific Data Privately

Problem

You want to store thread-specific data discovered at runtime. This data should be accessible only to code running within that thread.

Solution

Use the AllocateDataSlot, AllocateNamedDataSlot, or GetNamedDataSlot method on the Thread class to reserve a *thread local storage* (TLS) slot. Using TLS, a large object can be stored in a data slot on a thread and used in many different methods. This can be done without having to pass the structure as a parameter.

For this example, a class called ApplicationData here represents a set of data that can grow to be very large in size:

```
public class ApplicationData
{
    // Application data is stored here.
}
```

Before using this structure, a data slot has to be created in TLS to store the class. GetNamedDataSlot is called to get the appDataSlot. Since that doesn't exist, the default behavior for GetNamedDataSlot is to just create it. The following code creates an instance of the ApplicationData class and stores it in the data slot named appDataSlot:

```
ApplicationData appData = new ApplicationData();
Thread.SetData(Thread.GetNamedDataSlot("appDataSlot"), appData);
```

Whenever this class is needed, it can be retrieved with a call to Thread.GetData. The following line of code gets the appData structure from the data slot named appDataSlot:

```
ApplicationData storedAppData =
        (ApplicationData)Thread.GetData(Thread.GetNamedDataSlot("appDataSlot"));
```

At this point, the storedAppData structure can be read or modified. After the action has been performed on storedAppData, then storedAppdata must be placed back into the data slot named appDataSlot:

```
Thread.SetData(Thread.GetNamedDataSlot("appDataSlot"), storedAppData);
```

Once the application is finished using this data, the data slot can be released from memory using the following method call:

```
Thread.FreeNamedDataSlot("appDataSlot");
```

The HandleClass class in Example 18-4 shows how TLS can be used to store a structure.

Example 18-4. Using TLS to store a structure

```
using System;
using System.Threading;

public class HandleClass
{
    public static void Main( )
    {
        // Create structure instance and store it in the named data slot.
        ApplicationData appData = new ApplicationData( );
        Thread.SetData(Thread.GetNamedDataSlot("appDataSlot"), appData);

        // Call another method that will use this structure.
        HandleClass.MethodB( );

        // When done, free this data slot.
        Thread.FreeNamedDataSlot("appDataSlot");
    }

    public static void MethodB( )
    {
        // Get the structure instance from the named data slot.
        ApplicationData storedAppData =
            (ApplicationData)Thread.GetData(Thread.GetNamedDataSlot("appDataSlot"));

        // Modify the ApplicationData.

        // When finished modifying this data, store the changes back
        // into the named data slot.
        Thread.SetData(Thread.GetNamedDataSlot("appDataSlot"),
                       storedAppData);
```

Example 18-4. Using TLS to store a structure (continued)

```
        // Call another method that will use this data.
        HandleClass.MethodC( );
    }

    public static void MethodC( )
    {
        // Get the instance from the named data slot.
        ApplicationData storedAppData =
            (ApplicationData)Thread.GetData(Thread.GetNamedDataSlot("appDataSlot"));

        // Modify the data.

        // When finished modifying this data, store the changes back into
        // the named data slot.
        Thread.SetData(Thread.GetNamedDataSlot("appDataSlot"), storedAppData);
    }
}
```

Discussion

Thread local storage is a convenient way to store data that is usable across method calls without having to pass the structure to the method or even without knowledge about where the structure was actually created.

Data stored in a named TLS data slot is available only to that thread; no other thread can access a named data slot of another thread. The data stored in this data slot is accessible from anywhere within the thread. This setup essentially makes this data global to the thread.

To create a named data slot, use the static Thread.GetNamedDataSlot method. This method accepts a single parameter, *name*, that defines the name of the data slot. This name should be unique; if a data slot with the same name exists, then the contents of that data slot will be returned, and a new data slot will not be created. This action occurs silently; there is no exception thrown or error code available to inform you that you are using a data slot someone else created. To be sure that you are using a unique data slot, use the Thread.AllocateNamedDataSlot method. This method throws a System.ArgumentException if a data slot already exists with the same name. Otherwise, it operates similarly to the GetNamedDataSlot method.

It is interesting to note that this named data slot is created on every thread in the process, not just the thread that called this method. This fact should not be much more than an inconvenience to you, though, since the data in each data slot can be accessed only by the thread that contains it. In addition, if a data slot with the same name was created on a separate thread and you call GetNamedDataSlot on the current thread with this name, none of the data in any data slot on any thread will be destroyed.

GetNamedDataSlot returns a LocalDataStoreSlot object that is used to access the data slot. Note that this class is not creatable through the use of the new keyword. It must be created through one of the AllocateDataSlot or AllocateNamedDataSlot methods on the Thread class.

To store data in this data slot, use the static Thread.SetData method. This method takes the object passed in to the *data* parameter and stores it in the data slot defined by the *dataSlot* parameter.

The static Thread.GetData method retrieves the object stored in a data slot. This method retrieves a LocalDataStoreSlot object that is created through the Thread. GetNamedDataSlot method. The GetData method then returns the object that was stored in that particular data slot. Note that the object returned might have to be cast to its original type before it can be used.

The static method Thread.FreeNamedDataSlot will free the memory associated with a named data slot. This method accepts the name of the data slot as a string and, in turn, frees the memory associated with that data slot. Remember that when a data slot is created with GetNamedDataSlot, a named data slot is also created on all of the other threads running in that process. This is not really a problem when creating data slots with the GetNamedDataSlot method because, if a data slot exists with this name, a LocalDataStoreSlot object that refers to that data slot is returned, a new data slot is not created, and the original data in that data slot is not destroyed.

This situation becomes more of a problem when using the FreeNamedDataSlot method. This method will free the memory associated with the data slot name passed in to it for all threads, not just the thread that it was called on. Freeing a data slot before all threads have finished using the data within that data slot can be disastrous to your application.

A way to work around this problem is to not call the FreeNamedDataSlot method at all. When a thread terminates, all of its data slots in TLS are freed automatically. The side effect of not calling FreeNamedDataSlot is that the slot is taken up until the garbage collector determines that the thread the slot was created on has finished and the slot can be freed.

If you know the number of TLS slots you need for your code at compile time, consider using the ThreadStaticAttribute on a static field of your class to set up TLS-like storage.

See Also

The "Thread Local Storage and Thread Relative Static Fields," "ThreadStaticAttribute Attribute," and "Thread Class" topics in the MSDN documentation.

18.6 Granting Multiple Access to Resources with a Semaphore

Problem

You have a resource you want only a certain number of clients to access at a given time.

Solution

Use a semaphore to enable resource-counted access to the resource. For example, if you have an Xbox 360 and a copy of Halo3 (the resource) and a development staff eager to blow off some steam (the clients), you have to synchronize access to the Xbox 360. Since the Xbox 360 has four controllers, up to four clients can be playing at any given time. The rules of the house are that when you die, you give up your controller.

To accomplish this, create a class called Halo3Session with a Semaphore called _Xbox360 like this:

```
public class Halo3Session
{
    // A semaphore that simulates a limited resource pool.
    private static Semaphore _Xbox360;
```

In order to get things rolling, you need to call the Play method, as shown in Example 18-5, on the Halo3Session class.

Example 18-5. Play method

```
public static void Play( )
{
    // An Xbox360 has 4 controller ports so 4 people can play at a time
    // We use 4 as the max and zero to start with, as we want Players
    // to queue up at first until the Xbox360 boots and loads the game
    //
    using (_Xbox360 = new Semaphore(0, 4, "Xbox360"))
    {
        using (ManualResetEvent GameOver =
            new ManualResetEvent(false))
        {
            //
            // 9 Players log in to play
            //
            List<Xbox360Player.PlayerInfo> players =
                new List<Xbox360Player.PlayerInfo>() {
                    new Xbox360Player.PlayerInfo { Name="Igor", Dead=GameOver},
                    new Xbox360Player.PlayerInfo { Name="AxeMan", Dead=GameOver},
                    new Xbox360Player.PlayerInfo { Name="Dr. Death",Dead=GameOver},
                    new Xbox360Player.PlayerInfo { Name="HaPpyCaMpEr",Dead=GameOver},
                    new Xbox360Player.PlayerInfo { Name="Executioner",Dead=GameOver},
```

Example 18-5. Play method (continued)

```
                new Xbox360Player.PlayerInfo { Name="FragMan",Dead=GameOver},
                new Xbox360Player.PlayerInfo { Name="Beatdown",Dead=GameOver},
                new Xbox360Player.PlayerInfo { Name="Stoney",Dead=GameOver},
                new Xbox360Player.PlayerInfo { Name="Pwned",Dead=GameOver}
                };

        foreach (Xbox360Player.PlayerInfo player in players)
        {
            Thread t = new Thread(Xbox360Player.JoinIn);

            // put a name on the thread
            t.Name = player.Name;
            // fire up the player
            t.Start(player);
        }

        // Wait for the Xbox360 to spin up and load Halo3 (3 seconds)
        Console.WriteLine("Xbox360 initializing...");
        Thread.Sleep(3000);
        Console.WriteLine(
            "Halo3 loaded & ready, allowing 4 players in now...");

        // The Xbox360 has the whole semaphore count.  We call
        // Release(4) to open up 4 slots and
        // allow the waiting players to enter the Xbox360(semaphore)
        // up to four at a time.
        //
        _Xbox360.Release(4);

        // wait for the game to end...
        GameOver.WaitOne( );
    }
  }
}
```

The first thing the Play method does is to create a new semaphore that has a maximum resource count of 4 and a name of _Xbox360. This is the semaphore that will be used by all of the player threads to gain access to the game. A ManualResetEvent called GameOver is created to track when the game has ended:

```
public class Xbox360Player
{
    public class PlayerInfo
    {
        public ManualResetEvent Dead {get; set;}
        public string Name {get; set;}
    }

    //... more class
}
```

To simulate the developers, you create a thread for each with its own Xbox360Player. PlayerInfo class instance to contain the player name and a reference to the original GameOver ManualResetEvent held in the Dead event on the PlayerInfo, which indicates the player has died. The thread creation is using the ParameterizedThreadStart delegate, which takes the method to execute on the new thread in the constructor, but also allows you to pass the data object directly to a new overload of the Thread.Start method.

Once the players are in motion, the Xbox 360 "initializes" and then calls Release on the semaphore to open four slots for player threads to grab onto, and then waits until it detects that the game is over from the firing of the Dead event for the player.

The players initialize on separate threads and run the JoinIn method, as shown in Example 18-6. First they open the Xbox 360 semaphore by name and get the data that was passed to the thread. Once they have the semaphore, they call WaitOne to queue up to play. Once the initial four slots are opened or another player "dies," then the call to WaitOne unblocks and the player "plays" for a random amount of time, and then dies. Once the players are dead, they call Release on the semaphore to indicate their slot is now open. If the semaphore reaches its maximum resource count, the GameOver event is set.

Example 18-6. JoinIn method

```
public static void JoinIn(object info)
{
    // open up the semaphore by name so we can act on it
    using (Semaphore Xbox360 = Semaphore.OpenExisting("Xbox360"))
    {
        // get the data object
        PlayerInfo player = (PlayerInfo)info;

        // Each player notifies the Xbox360 they want to play
        Console.WriteLine("{0} is waiting to play!", player.Name);

        // they wait on the Xbox360 (semaphore) until it lets them
        // have a controller
        Xbox360.WaitOne();

        // The Xbox360 has chosen the player! (or the semaphore has
        // allowed access to the resource...)
        Console.WriteLine("{0} has been chosen to play. " +
            "Welcome to your doom {0}. >:)", player.Name);

        // figure out a random value for how long the player lasts
        System.Random rand = new Random(500);
        int timeTillDeath = rand.Next(100, 1000);

        // simulate the player is busy playing till they die
        Thread.Sleep(timeTillDeath);
```

Example 18-6. JoinIn method (continued)

```
        // figure out how they died
        rand = new Random( );
        int deathIndex = rand.Next(6);

        // notify of the player's passing
        Console.WriteLine("{0} has {1} and gives way to another player",
            player.Name, _deaths[deathIndex]);

        // if all ports are open, everyone has played and the game is over
        int semaphoreCount = Xbox360.Release( );
        if (semaphoreCount == 3)
        {
            Console.WriteLine("Thank you for playing, the game has ended.");
            // set the Dead event for the player
            player.Dead.Set( );
            // close out the semaphore
            Xbox360.Close( );
        }
    }
}
```

When the Play method is run, output similar to the following is generated:

```
Igor is waiting to play!
AxeMan is waiting to play!
Dr. Death is waiting to play!
HaPpyCaMpEr is waiting to play!
Executioner is waiting to play!
FragMan is waiting to play!
Beatdown is waiting to play!
Xbox360 initializing...
Stoney is waiting to play!
Pwned is waiting to play!
Halo3 loaded & ready, allowing 4 players in now...
Igor has been chosen to play. Welcome to your doom Igor. >:)
Dr. Death has been chosen to play. Welcome to your doom Dr. Death. >:)
AxeMan has been chosen to play. Welcome to your doom AxeMan. >:)
Executioner has been chosen to play. Welcome to your doom Executioner. >:)
Dr. Death has was captured and gives way to another player
AxeMan has was captured and gives way to another player
Executioner has was captured and gives way to another player
Pwned has been chosen to play. Welcome to your doom Pwned. >:)
HaPpyCaMpEr has been chosen to play. Welcome to your doom HaPpyCaMpEr. >:)
Beatdown has been chosen to play. Welcome to your doom Beatdown. >:)
Igor has was captured and gives way to another player
FragMan has been chosen to play. Welcome to your doom FragMan. >:)
Beatdown has shot their own foot and gives way to another player
Stoney has been chosen to play. Welcome to your doom Stoney. >:)
HaPpyCaMpEr has shot their own foot and gives way to another player
Pwned has shot their own foot and gives way to another player
FragMan has shot their own foot and gives way to another player
Stoney has choked on a rocket and gives way to another player
Thank you for playing, the game has ended.
```

Discussion

Semaphores are primarily used for resource counting and are available cross-process when named (as they are based on the underlying kernel semaphore object). *Cross-process* may not sound too exciting to many .NET developers until they realize that cross-process also means *cross-AppDomain*. Say you are creating additional AppDomains to hold assemblies you are loading dynamically that you don't want to stick around for the whole life of your main AppDomain; the semaphore can help you keep track of how many are loaded at a time. Being able to control access up to a certain number of users can be useful in many scenarios (socket programming, custom thread pools, etc.).

See Also

The "Semaphore," "ManualResetEvent," and "ParameterizedThreadStart" topics in the MSDN documentation.

18.7   Synchronizing Multiple Processes with the Mutex

Problem

You have two processes or AppDomains that are running code with actions that you need to coordinate.

Solution

Use a named `Mutex` as a common signaling mechanism to do the coordination. A named `Mutex` can be accessed from both pieces of code even when running in different processes or AppDomains.

One situation in which this can be useful is when you are using shared memory to communicate between processes. The `SharedMemoryManager` class presented in this recipe will show the named `Mutex` in action by setting up a section of shared memory that can be used to pass serializable objects between processes. The "server" process creates a `SharedMemoryManager` instance, which sets up the shared memory and then creates the `Mutex` as the initial owner. The "client" process then also creates a `SharedMemoryManager` instance that finds the shared memory and hooks up to it. Once this connection is established, the "client" process then sets up to receive the serialized objects and waits until one is sent by waiting on the `Mutex` the "server" process created. The "server" process then takes a serializable object, serializes it into the shared memory, and releases the `Mutex`. It then waits on it again so that when the "client" is done receiving the object, it can release the `Mutex` and give control back to the "server." The "client" process that was waiting on the `Mutex` then deserializes the object from the shared memory and releases the `Mutex`.

In the example, you will send the Contact structure, which looks like this:

```
[StructLayout(LayoutKind.Sequential)]
[Serializable()]
public struct Contact
{
    public string _name;
    public int _age;
}
```

The "server" process code to send the Contact looks like this:

```
// Create the initial shared memory manager to get things set up.
using(SharedMemoryManager<Contact> sm =
    new SharedMemoryManager<Contact>("Contacts",8092))
{
    // This is the sender process.

    // Launch the second process to get going.
    string processName = Process.GetCurrentProcess().MainModule.FileName;
    int index = processName.IndexOf("vshost");
    if (index != -1)
    {

        string first = processName.Substring(0, index);
        int numChars = processName.Length - (index + 7);
        string second = processName.Substring(index + 7, numChars);

        processName = first + second;
    }
    Process receiver = Process.Start(
        new ProcessStartInfo(
            processName,
            "Receiver"));

    // Give it 5 seconds to spin up.
    Thread.Sleep(5000);

    // Make up a contact.
    Contact man;
    man._age = 23;
    man._name = "Dirk Daring";

    // Send it to the other process via shared memory.
    sm.SendObject(man);
}
```

The "client" process code to receive the Contact looks like this:

```
// Create the initial shared memory manager to get things set up.
using(SharedMemoryManager<Contact> sm =
    new SharedMemoryManager<Contact>("Contacts",8092))
{

    // Get the contact once it has been sent.
    Contact c = (Contact)sm.ReceiveObject();
```

```
            // Write it out (or to a database...)
            Console.WriteLine("Contact {0} is {1} years old.",
                              c._name, c._age);
            // Show for 5 seconds.
            Thread.Sleep(5000);
        }
```

The way this usually works is that one process creates a section of shared memory backed by the paging file using the unmanaged Win32 APIs CreateFileMapping and MapViewOfFile. Currently there is no purely managed way to do this, so you have to use P/Invoke, as you can see in Example 18-7 in the constructor code for the SharedMemoryManager and the private SetupSharedMemory method. The constructor takes a name to use as part of the name of the shared memory and the base size of the shared memory block to allocate. It is the base size because the SharedMemoryManager has to allocate a bit extra for keeping track of the data moving through the buffer.

Example 18-7. Constructor and SetupSharedMemory private method

```
public SharedMemoryManager(string name,int sharedMemoryBaseSize)
{
    if (string.IsNullOrEmpty(name))
        throw new ArgumentNullException("name");

    if (sharedMemoryBaseSize <= 0)
        throw new ArgumentOutOfRangeException("sharedMemoryBaseSize",
            "Shared Memory Base Size must be a value greater than zero");

    // Set name of the region.
    _memoryRegionName = name;
    // Save base size.
    _sharedMemoryBaseSize = sharedMemoryBaseSize;
    // Set up the memory region size.
    _memRegionSize = (uint)(_sharedMemoryBaseSize + sizeof(int));
    // Set up the shared memory section.
    SetupSharedMemory();
}

private void SetupSharedMemory()
{
    // Grab some storage from the page file.
    _handleFileMapping =
        PInvoke.CreateFileMapping((IntPtr)INVALID_HANDLE_VALUE,
                        IntPtr.Zero,
                        PInvoke.PageProtection.ReadWrite,
                        0,
                        _memRegionSize,
                        _memoryRegionName);
    if (_handleFileMapping == IntPtr.Zero)
    {
        throw new Win32Exception(
            "Could not create file mapping");
```

```
    }

    // Check the error status.
    int retVal = Marshal.GetLastWin32Error( );
    if (retVal == ERROR_ALREADY_EXISTS)
    {

        // We opened one that already existed.
        // Make the mutex not the initial owner
        // of the mutex since we are connecting
        // to an existing one.
        _mtxSharedMem = new Mutex(false,
            string.Format("{0}mtx{1}",
                typeof(TransferItemType), _memoryRegionName));
    }
    else if (retVal == 0)
    {
        // We opened a new one.
        // Make the mutex the initial owner.
        _mtxSharedMem = new Mutex(true,
            string.Format("{0}mtx{1}",
                typeof(TransferItemType), _memoryRegionName));
    }
    else
    {
        // Something else went wrong.
        throw new Win32Exception(retVal, "Error creating file mapping");
    }

    // Map the shared memory.
    _ptrToMemory = PInvoke.MapViewOfFile(_handleFileMapping,
                                FILE_MAP_WRITE,
                                0, 0, IntPtr.Zero);
    if (_ptrToMemory == IntPtr.Zero)
    {
        retVal = Marshal.GetLastWin32Error( );
        throw new Win32Exception(retVal, "Could not map file view");
    }

    retVal = Marshal.GetLastWin32Error( );
    if (retVal != 0 && retVal != ERROR_ALREADY_EXISTS)
    {
        // Something else went wrong.
        throw new Win32Exception(retVal, "Error mapping file view");
    }
}
```

The code to send an object through the shared memory is contained in the SendObject method, as shown in Example 18-8. First, it checks to see if the object being sent is indeed serializable by checking the IsSerializable property on the type of the object. If the object is serializable, an integer with the size of the serialized object and the serialized object content are written out to the shared memory section. Then, the Mutex is released to indicate that there is an object in the shared memory. It then waits on the Mutex again to wait until the "client" has received the object.

Example 18-8. SendObject method

```
public void SendObject(TransferItemType transferObject)
{
    // Can send only Seralizable objects.
    if (!transferObject.GetType().IsSerializable)
        throw new ArgumentException(
            string.Format("Object {0} is not serializeable.",
                transferObject));
    // Create a memory stream, initialize size.
    using (MemoryStream ms = new MemoryStream())
    {
        // Get a formatter to serialize with.
        BinaryFormatter formatter = new BinaryFormatter();
        try
        {
            // Serialize the object to the stream.
            formatter.Serialize(ms, transferObject);

            // Get the bytes for the serialized object.
            byte[] bytes = ms.GetBuffer();

            // Check that this object will fit.
            if(bytes.Length + sizeof(int) > _memRegionSize)
            {
                string fmt =
                    "{0} object instance serialized to {1} bytes " +
                    "which is too large for the shared memory region";

                string msg =
                    string.Format(fmt,
                        typeof(TransferItemType),bytes.Length);

                throw new ArgumentException(msg, "transferObject");
            }

            // Write out how long this object is.
            Marshal.WriteInt32(this._ptrToMemory, bytes.Length);

            // Write out the bytes.
            Marshal.Copy(bytes, 0, this._ptrToMemory, bytes.Length);
        }
        finally
        {
            // Signal the other process using the mutex to tell it
            // to do receive processing.
            _mtxSharedMem.ReleaseMutex();

            // Wait for the other process to signal it has received
            // and we can move on.
```

Example 18-8. SendObject method (continued)

```
            _mtxSharedMem.WaitOne( );
        }
    }
}
```

The `ReceiveObject` method shown in Example 18-9 allows the client to wait until there is an object in the shared memory section and then reads the size of the serialized object and deserializes it to a managed object. It then releases the `Mutex` to let the sender know to continue.

Example 18-9. ReceiveObject method

```
public TransferItemType ReceiveObject( )
{
    // Wait on the mutex for an object to be queued by the sender.
    _mtxSharedMem.WaitOne( );

    // Get the count of what is in the shared memory.
    int count = Marshal.ReadInt32(_ptrToMemory);
    if (count <= 0)
    {
        throw new InvalidDataException("No object to read");
    }

    // Make an array to hold the bytes.
    byte[] bytes = new byte[count];

    // Read out the bytes for the object.
    Marshal.Copy(_ptrToMemory, bytes, 0, count);

    // Set up the memory stream with the object bytes.
    using (MemoryStream ms = new MemoryStream(bytes))
    {

        // Set up a binary formatter.
        BinaryFormatter formatter = new BinaryFormatter( );

        // Get the object to return.
        TransferItemType item;
        try
        {
            item = (TransferItemType)formatter.Deserialize(ms);
        }
        finally
        {
            // Signal that we received the object using the mutex.
            _mtxSharedMem.ReleaseMutex( );
        }
        // Give them the object.
        return item;
    }
}
```

Discussion

A Mutex is designed to give mutually exclusive (thus the name) access to a single resource. A Mutex can be thought of as a cross-process named Monitor, where the Mutex is "entered" by waiting on it and becoming the owner, then "exited" by releasing the Mutex for the next thread that is waiting on it. If a thread that owns a Mutex ends, the Mutex is released automatically.

Using a Mutex is slower than using a Monitor as a Monitor is a purely managed construct, whereas a Mutex is based on the Mutex kernel object. A Mutex cannot be "pulsed" as can a Monitor, but it can be used across processes which a Monitor cannot. Finally, the Mutex is based on WaitHandle, so it can be waited on with other objects derived from WaitHandle, like Semaphore and the event classes.

The SharedMemoryManager and PInvoke classes are listed in their entirety in Example 18-10.

Example 18-10. SharedMemoryManager and PInvoke classes

```
/// <summary>
/// Class for sending objects through shared memory using a mutex
/// to synchronize access to the shared memory
/// </summary>
public class SharedMemoryManager<TransferItemType> : IDisposable
{
    #region Consts
    const int INVALID_HANDLE_VALUE = -1;
    const int FILE_MAP_WRITE = 0x0002;
    /// <summary>
    /// Define from Win32 API.
    /// </summary>
    const int ERROR_ALREADY_EXISTS = 183;
    #endregion

    #region Private members
    IntPtr _handleFileMapping = IntPtr.Zero;
    IntPtr _ptrToMemory = IntPtr.Zero;
    uint _memRegionSize = 0;
    string _memoryRegionName;
    bool disposed = false;
    int _sharedMemoryBaseSize = 0;
    Mutex _mtxSharedMem = null;
    #endregion

    #region Construction / Cleanup
    public SharedMemoryManager(string name,int sharedMemoryBaseSize)
    {
        // Can be built for only Seralizable objects
        if (!typeof(TransferItemType).IsSerializable)
            throw new ArgumentException(
                string.Format("Object {0} is not serializeable.",
                    typeof(TransferItemType)));
```

Example 18-10. SharedMemoryManager and PInvoke classes (continued)

```
        if (string.IsNullOrEmpty(name))
            throw new ArgumentNullException("name");

        if (sharedMemoryBaseSize <= 0)
            throw new ArgumentOutOfRangeException("sharedMemoryBaseSize",
                "Shared Memory Base Size must be a value greater than zero")

        // Set name of the region.
        _memoryRegionName = name;
        // Save base size.
        _sharedMemoryBaseSize = sharedMemoryBaseSize;
        // Set up the memory region size.
        _memRegionSize = (uint)(_sharedMemoryBaseSize + sizeof(int));
        // Set up the shared memory section.
        SetupSharedMemory();
    }

    private void SetupSharedMemory()
    {
        // Grab some storage from the page file.
        _handleFileMapping =
            PInvoke.CreateFileMapping((IntPtr)INVALID_HANDLE_VALUE,
                            IntPtr.Zero,
                            PInvoke.PageProtection.ReadWrite,
                            0,
                            _memRegionSize,
                            _memoryRegionName);

        if (_handleFileMapping == IntPtr.Zero)
        {
            throw new Win32Exception(
                "Could not create file mapping");
        }

        // Check the error status.
        int retVal = Marshal.GetLastWin32Error();
        if (retVal == ERROR_ALREADY_EXISTS)
        {
            // We opened one that already existed.
            // Make the mutex not the initial owner
            // of the mutex since we are connecting
            // to an existing one.
            _mtxSharedMem = new Mutex(false,
                string.Format("{0}mtx{1}",
                    typeof(TransferItemType), _memoryRegionName));
        }
        else if (retVal == 0)
        {
            // We opened a new one.
            // Make the mutex the initial owner.
            _mtxSharedMem = new Mutex(true,
                string.Format("{0}mtx{1}",
```

Example 18-10. SharedMemoryManager and PInvoke classes (continued)

```
                        typeof(TransferItemType), _memoryRegionName));
    }
    else
    {
        // Something else went wrong.
        throw new Win32Exception(retVal, "Error creating file mapping");
    }

    // Map the shared memory.
    _ptrToMemory = PInvoke.MapViewOfFile(_handleFileMapping,
                              FILE_MAP_WRITE,
                              0, 0, IntPtr.Zero);

    if (_ptrToMemory == IntPtr.Zero)
    {
        retVal = Marshal.GetLastWin32Error();
        throw new Win32Exception(retVal, "Could not map file view");
    }

    retVal = Marshal.GetLastWin32Error();
    if (retVal != 0 && retVal != ERROR_ALREADY_EXISTS)
    {
        // Something else went wrong.
        throw new Win32Exception(retVal, "Error mapping file view");
    }
}

~SharedMemoryManager()
{
    // Make sure we close.
    Dispose(false);
}

public void Dispose()
{
    Dispose(true);
    GC.SuppressFinalize(this);
}

private void Dispose(bool disposing)
{
    // Check to see if Dispose has already been called.
    if (!this.disposed)
    {
        CloseSharedMemory();
    }
    disposed = true;
}

private void CloseSharedMemory()
{
    if ( ptrToMemory != IntPtr.Zero)
```

Example 18-10. SharedMemoryManager and PInvoke classes (continued)

```csharp
        {
            // Close map for shared memory.
            PInvoke.UnmapViewOfFile(_ptrToMemory);
            _ptrToMemory = IntPtr.Zero;
        }
        if (_handleFileMapping != IntPtr.Zero)
        {
            // Close handle.
            PInvoke.CloseHandle(_handleFileMapping);
            _handleFileMapping = IntPtr.Zero;
        }
    }
    public void Close()
    {
        CloseSharedMemory();
    }
    #endregion

    #region Properties
    public int SharedMemoryBaseSize
    {
        get { return _sharedMemoryBaseSize; }
    }
    #endregion

    #region Public Methods
    /// <summary>
    /// Send a serializable object through the shared memory
    /// and wait for it to be picked up.
    /// </summary>
    /// <param name="transferObject"></param>
    public void SendObject(TransferItemType transferObject)
    {
        // Create a memory stream, initialize size.
        using (MemoryStream ms = new MemoryStream())
        {
            // Get a formatter to serialize with.
            BinaryFormatter formatter = new BinaryFormatter();
            try
            {
                // Serialize the object to the stream.
                formatter.Serialize(ms, transferObject);

                // Get the bytes for the serialized object.
                byte[] bytes = ms.ToArray();

                // Check that this object will fit.
                if(bytes.Length + sizeof(int) > _memRegionSize)
                {
                    string fmt = "
                        "{0} object instance serialized to {1} bytes " +
```

Example 18-10. SharedMemoryManager and PInvoke classes (continued)

```
                        "which is too large for the shared memory region";

                    string msg =
                        string.Format(fmt,
                            typeof(TransferItemType),bytes.Length);

                    throw new ArgumentException(msg, "transferObject");
                }

                // Write out how long this object is.
                Marshal.WriteInt32(this._ptrToMemory, bytes.Length);

                // Write out the bytes.
                Marshal.Copy(bytes, 0, this._ptrToMemory, bytes.Length);
            }
            finally
            {
                // Signal the other process using the mutex to tell it
                // to do receive processing.
                _mtxSharedMem.ReleaseMutex();

                // Wait for the other process to signal it has received
                // and we can move on.
                _mtxSharedMem.WaitOne();
            }
        }
    }

    /// <summary>
    /// Wait for an object to hit the shared memory and then deserialize it.
    /// </summary>
    /// <returns>object passed</returns>
    public TransferItemType ReceiveObject()
    {

        // Wait on the mutex for an object to be queued by the sender.
        _mtxSharedMem.WaitOne();

        // Get the count of what is in the shared memory.
        int count = Marshal.ReadInt32(_ptrToMemory);
        if (count <= 0)
        {
            throw new InvalidDataException("No object to read");
        }

        // Make an array to hold the bytes.
        byte[] bytes = new byte[count];

        // Read out the bytes for the object.
        Marshal.Copy(_ptrToMemory, bytes, 0, count);

        // Set up the memory stream with the object bytes.
```

Example 18-10. SharedMemoryManager and PInvoke classes (continued)

```
        using (MemoryStream ms = new MemoryStream(bytes))
        {

            // Set up a binary formatter.
            BinaryFormatter formatter = new BinaryFormatter( );

            // Get the object to return.
            TransferItemType item;
            try
            {
                item = (TransferItemType)formatter.Deserialize(ms);
            }
            finally
            {
                // Signal that we received the object using the mutex.
                _mtxSharedMem.ReleaseMutex( );
            }
            // Give them the object.
            return item;
        }
    }
    #endregion
}

public class PInvoke
{
    #region PInvoke defines
    [Flags]
    public enum PageProtection : uint
    {

        NoAccess = 0x01,
        Readonly = 0x02,
        ReadWrite = 0x04,
        WriteCopy = 0x08,
        Execute = 0x10,
        ExecuteRead = 0x20,
        ExecuteReadWrite = 0x40,
        ExecuteWriteCopy = 0x80,
        Guard = 0x100,
        NoCache = 0x200,
        WriteCombine = 0x400,
    }
    [DllImport("kernel32.dll", SetLastError = true)]
    public static extern IntPtr CreateFileMapping(IntPtr hFile,
        IntPtr lpFileMappingAttributes, PageProtection flProtect,
        uint dwMaximumSizeHigh,
        uint dwMaximumSizeLow, string lpName);

    [DllImport("kernel32.dll", SetLastError = true)]
    public static extern IntPtr MapViewOfFile(IntPtr hFileMappingObject, uint
        dwDesiredAccess, uint dwFileOffsetHigh, uint dwFileOffsetLow,
```

Example 18-10. SharedMemoryManager and PInvoke classes (continued)

```
        IntPtr dwNumberOfBytesToMap);

    [DllImport("kernel32.dll", SetLastError = true)]
    public static extern bool UnmapViewOfFile(IntPtr lpBaseAddress);

    [DllImport("kernel32.dll", SetLastError = true)]
    public static extern bool CloseHandle(IntPtr hObject);
    #endregion
}
```

See Also

The "Mutex" and "Mutex Class" topics in the MSDN documentation and *Programming Applications for Microsoft Windows*, Fourth Edition, by Jeffrey Richter (Microsoft Press).

18.8   Using Events to Make Threads Cooperate

Problem

You have multiple threads that need to be served by a server, but only one can be served at a time.

Solution

Use an `AutoResetEvent` to notify each thread when it is going to be served. For example, a diner has a cook and multiple waitresses. The waitresses can keep bringing in orders, but the cook can serve up only one at a time. You can simulate this with the Cook class shown in Example 18-11.

Example 18-11. Using events to make threads cooperate

```
public class Cook
{
    public static AutoResetEvent OrderReady = new AutoResetEvent(false);

    public void CallWaitress()
    {
        // We call Set on the AutoResetEvent and don't have to
        // call Reset like we would with ManualResetEvent to fire it
        // off again. This sets the event that the waitress is waiting for
        // in PlaceOrder.
        OrderReady.Set();
    }
}
```

The Cook class has an AutoResetEvent called OrderReady that the cook will use to tell the waiting waitresses that an order is ready. Since there is only one order ready at a time, and this is an equal-opportunity diner, the waitress who has been waiting longest gets her order first. The AutoResetEvent allows for just signaling the single thread when you call Set on the OrderReady event.

The Waitress class has the PlaceOrder method that is executed by the thread. PlaceOrder takes an object parameter, which is passed in from the call to t.Start in the next code block. The Start method uses a ParameterizedThreadStart delegate, which takes an object parameter. PlaceOrder has been set up to be compatible with it. It takes the AutoResetEvent passed in and calls WaitOne to wait until the order is ready. Once the Cook fires the event enough times that this waitress is at the head of the line, the code finishes:

```
public class Waitress
{
    public static void PlaceOrder(object signal)
    {
        // Cast the AutoResetEvent so the waitress can wait for the
        // order to be ready.
        AutoResetEvent OrderReady = (AutoResetEvent)signal;
        // Wait for the order...
        OrderReady.WaitOne();
        // Order is ready....
        Console.WriteLine("Waitress got order!");
    }
}
```

The code to run the "diner" creates a Cook and spins off the Waitress threads, and then calls all waitresses when their orders are ready by calling Set on the AutoResetEvent:

```
// We have a diner with a cook who can serve up only one meal at a time.
Cook Mel = new Cook();

// Make up five waitresses and tell them to get orders.
for (int i = 0; i < 5; i++)
{
    Thread t = new Thread(Waitress.PlaceOrder);
    // The Waitress places the order and then waits for the order.
    t.Start(Cook.OrderReady);
}

// Now we can go through and let people in.
for (int i = 0; i < 5; i++)
{
    // Make the waitresses wait...
    Thread.Sleep(2000);
    // OK, next waitress, pickup!
    Mel.CallWaitress();
}
```

Discussion

There are two types of events, `AutoResetEvent` and `ManualResetEvent`. There are two main differences between the events. The first is that `AutoResetEvents` release only one of the threads that are waiting on the event while a `ManualResetEvent` will release all of them when `Set` is called. The second difference is that when `Set` is called on an `AutoResetEvent`, it is automatically reset to a nonsignaled state, while the `ManualResetEvent` is left in a signaled state until the `Reset` method is called.

See Also

The "AutoResetEvent" and "ManualResetEvent" topics in the MSDN documentation and *Programming Applications for Microsoft Windows*, (Fourth Edition) by Microsoft Press.

18.9 Get the Naming Rights for Your Events

Problem

You want to have code running in worker threads, or in other processes or AppDomains, to be able to wait on an event.

Solution

Use the `EventWaitHandle` class. With it, you can create a named event that will allow any code running on the local machine to find and wait on the event. `AutoResetEvent` and `ManualResetEvent` are excellent for signaling events in threaded code and even between AppDomains if you are willing to go through the hassle of passing the event reference around. Why bother? Both of them derive from `EventWaitHandle`, but neither exposes the naming facility. `EventWaitHandle` can not only take the name of the event, but also can take an `EventResetMode` parameter to indicate if it should act like a `ManualResetEvent` (`EventResetMode.ManualReset`) or an `AutoResetEvent` (`EventResetMode.AutoReset`). Named events have been available to Windows developers for a long time, and the `EventWaitHandle` class can serve as a named version of either an `AutoResetEvent` or a `ManualResetEvent`.

To set up a named `EventWaitHandle` that operates as a `ManualResetEvent`, do this:

```
// Make a named manual reset event.
EventWaitHandle ewhSuperBowl =
    new EventWaitHandle(false, // Not initially signaled
                        EventResetMode.ManualReset,
                        @"Champs");
// Spin up three threads to listen for the event.
for (int i = 0; i < 3; i++)
{
    Thread t = new Thread(ManualFan);
```

```
        // The fans wait anxiously...
        t.Name = "Fan " + i;
        t.Start( );
    }
    // Play the game.
    Thread.Sleep(10000);
    // Notify people.
    Console.WriteLine("Patriots win the SuperBowl!");
    // Signal all fans.
    ewhSuperBowl.Set( );
    // Close the event.
    ewhSuperBowl.Close( );
```

The `ManualFan` method is listed here:

```
public static void ManualFan( )
{
    // Open the event by name.
    EventWaitHandle ewhSuperBowl =
        new EventWaitHandle(false,
                            EventResetMode.ManualReset,
                            @"Champs");

    // Wait for the signal.
    ewhSuperBowl.WaitOne( );
    // Shout out.
    Console.WriteLine("\"They're great!\" says {0}",Thread.CurrentThread.Name);
    // Close the event.
    ewhSuperBowl.Close( );
}
```

The output from the manual event code will resemble the listing here (the `ManualFan` threads might be in a different order):

```
Patriots win the SuperBowl!
"They're great!" says Fan 2
"They're great!" says Fan 1
"They're great!" says Fan 0
```

To set up a named `EventWaitHandle` to operate as an `AutoResetEvent`, do this:

```
    // Make a named auto reset event.
    EventWaitHandle ewhSuperBowl =
        new EventWaitHandle(false, // Not initially signalled
                            EventResetMode.AutoReset,
                            @"Champs");
    // Spin up three threads to listen for the event.
    for (int i = 0; i < 3; i++)
    {
        Thread t = new Thread(AutoFan, i);
        // The fans wait anxiously...
        t.Name = "Fan " + i;
        t.Start( );
    }
    // Play the game.
    Thread.Sleep(10000);
```

```
// Notify people.
Console.WriteLine("Patriots win the SuperBowl!");
// Signal one fan at a time.
for (int i = 0; i < 3; i++)
{
    Console.WriteLine("Notify fans");
    ewhSuperBowl.Set();
}
// Close the event.
ewhSuperBowl.Close();
```

The AutoFan method is listed here:

```
public static void AutoFan()
{
    // Open the event by name.
    EventWaitHandle ewhSuperBowl =
        new EventWaitHandle(false,
                            EventResetMode.AutoReset,
                            @"Champs");
    // Wait for the signal.
    ewhSuperBowl.WaitOne();
    // Shout out.
    Console.WriteLine("\"Yahoo!\" says {0}", Thread.CurrentThread.Name);
    // Close the event.
    ewhSuperBowl.Close();
}
```

The output from the automatic event code will resemble the listing here (the AutoFan threads might be in a different order):

```
Patriots win the SuperBowl!
Notify fans
"Yahoo!" says Fan 0
Notify fans
"Yahoo!" says Fan 2
Notify fans
"Yahoo!" says Fan 1
```

Discussion

EventWaitHandle is defined as deriving from WaitHandle, which in turn derives from MarshalByRefObject. EventWaitHandle implements the IDisposable interface:

```
public class EventWaitHandle : WaitHandle

public abstract class WaitHandle : MarshalByRefObject, IDisposable
```

WaitHandle derives from MarshalByRefObject so you can use it across AppDomains, and it implements IDisposable to make sure the event handle gets released properly.

The EventWaitHandle class can also open an existing named event by calling the OpenExisting method and get the event's access-control security from GetAccessControl.

When naming events, one consideration is how it will react in the presence of terminal sessions. *Terminal sessions* are the underlying technology behind Fast User switching and Remote Desktop, as well as Terminal Services. The consideration is due to how kernel objects (such as events) are created with respect to the terminal sessions. If a kernel object is created with a name and no prefix, it belongs to the Global namespace for named objects and is visible across terminal sessions. By default, EventWaitHandle creates the event in the Global namespace. A kernel object can also be created in the Local namespace for a given terminal session, in which case the named object belongs to the specific terminal session namespace. If you pass the *Local* namespace prefix (*Local\[EventName]*), then the event will be created in the local session for events that should be visible from only one terminal session:

```
// Open the event by local name.
EventWaitHandle ewhSuperBowl =
    new EventWaitHandle(false,
                        EventResetMode.ManualReset,
                        @"Local\Champs");
```

Named events can be quite useful not only when communicating between processes, AppDomains, or threads, but also when debugging code that uses events, as the name will help you identify which event you are looking at if you have a number of them.

See Also

The "EventWaitHandle," "AutoResetEvent," "ManualResetEvent," and "Kernel Object Namespaces (Platform SDK Help)" topics in the MSDN documentation.

18.10 Performing Atomic Operations Among Threads

Problem

You are operating on data from multiple threads and want to insure that each operation is carried out fully before performing the next operation from a different thread.

Solution

Use the Interlocked family of functions to insure atomic access. Interlocked has methods to increment and decrement values, add a specific amount to a given value, exchange an original value for a new value, compare the current value to the original value, and exchange the original value for a new value if it is equal to the current value.

To increment or decrement an integer value, use the Increment or Decrement methods, respectively:

```
int i = 0;
long l = 0;
```

```
Interlocked.Increment(ref i); // i = 1
Interlocked.Decrement(ref i); // i = 0
Interlocked.Increment(ref l); // l = 1
Interlocked.Decrement(ref i); // l = 0
```

To add a specific amount to a given integer value, use the Add method:

```
Interlocked.Add(ref i, 10); // i = 10;
Interlocked.Add(ref l, 100); // l = 100;
```

To replace an existing value, use the Exchange method:

```
string name = "Mr. Ed";
Interlocked.Exchange(ref name, "Barney");
```

To check if another thread has changed a value out from under the existing code before replacing the existing value, use the CompareExchange method:

```
int i = 0;
double runningTotal = 0.0;
double startingTotal = 0.0;
double calc = 0.0;
for (i = 0; i < 10; i++)
{
    do
    {
        // Store of the original total
        startingTotal = runningTotal;

        // Do an intense calculation.
        calc = runningTotal + i * Math.PI * 2 / Math.PI;
    }
    // Check to make sure runningTotal wasn't modified
    // and replace it with calc if not. If it was,
    // run through the loop until we get it current.
    while (startingTotal !=
        Interlocked.CompareExchange(
            ref runningTotal, calc, startingTotal));
}
```

Discussion

In an operating system like Microsoft Windows, with its ability to perform preemptive multitasking, certain considerations must be given to data integrity when working with multiple threads. There are many synchronization primitives to help secure sections of code, as well as signal when data is available to be modified. To this list is added the capability to perform operations that are guaranteed to be atomic in nature.

If there has not been much threading or assembly language in your past, you might wonder what the big deal is and why you need these atomic functions at all. The basic reason is that the line of code written in C# ultimately has to be translated down to a machine instruction, and along the way, the one line of code written in C# can turn into multiple instructions for the machine to execute. If the machine has to execute multiple instructions to perform a task and the operating system allows for preemption, it is possible that these instructions may not be executed as a block. They could be interrupted by other code that modifies the value being changed by the original line of C# code in the middle of the C# code being executed. As you can imagine, this could lead to some pretty spectacular errors, or it might just round off the lottery number that keeps a certain C# programmer from winning the big one.

Threading is a powerful tool, but like most "power" tools, you have to understand its operation to use it effectively and safely. Threading bugs are notorious for being some of the most difficult to debug, as the runtime behavior is not constant. Trying to reproduce them can be a nightmare. Recognizing that working in a multithreaded environment imposes a certain amount of forethought about protecting data access, and understanding when to use the Interlocked class will go a long way toward preventing long, frustrating evenings with the debugger.

See Also

The "Interlocked" and "Interlocked Class" topics in the MSDN documentation.

18.11 Optimizing Read-Mostly Access

Problem

You are operating on data that is mostly read with occasional updates and want to perform these actions in a thread-safe but efficient manner.

Solution

Use the ReaderWriterLockSlim to give multiple read/single write access with the capacity to upgrade the lock from read to write. The example we use to show this is that of a Developer starting a new project. Unfortunately, the project is under-staffed, so the Developer has to respond to tasks from many other individuals on the team by themselves. Each of the other team members will also ask for status updates on their tasks, and some can even change the priority of the tasks the Developer is assigned.

The act of adding a task to the Developer using the AddTask method is protected with a write lock using the ReaderWriterLockSlim by calling EnterWriteLock and ExitWriteLock when complete:

```
public void AddTask(Task newTask)
{
    try
    {
        _rwlSlim.EnterWriteLock();
        // if we already have this task (unique by name)
        // then just accept the add as sometimes people
        // give you the same task more than once :)
```

```
                var taskQuery = from t in _tasks
                                where t == newTask
                                select t;
                if (taskQuery.Count<Task>() == 0)
                {
                    Console.WriteLine("Task " + newTask.Name + " was added to
    developer");
                    _tasks.Add(newTask);
                }
            }
            finally
            {
                _rwlSlim.ExitWriteLock();
            }
        }
```

When a project team member needs to know about the status of a task, they call the IsTaskDone method, which uses a read lock on the ReaderWriterLockSlim by calling EnterReadLock and ExitReadLock:

```
        public bool IsTaskDone(string taskName)
        {
            try
            {
                _rwlSlim.EnterReadLock();
                var taskQuery = from t in _tasks
                                where t.Name == taskName
                                select t;
                if (taskQuery.Count<Task>() > 0)
                {
                    Task task = taskQuery.First<Task>();
                    Console.WriteLine("Task " + task.Name + " status was reported.");
                    return task.Status;
                }
            }
            finally
            {
                _rwlSlim.ExitReadLock();
            }
            return false;
        }
```

There are certain managerial members of the team that have the right to increase the priority of the tasks they assigned to the Developer. This is accomplished by calling the IncreasePriority method on the Developer. IncreasePriority uses an upgradable lock on the ReaderWriterLockSlim by first calling the EnterUpgradeableLock method to acquire a read lock, and then, if the task is in the queue, it upgrades to a write lock in order to adjust the priority of the task. Once the priority is adjusted, the write lock is released, which degrades the lock back to a read lock, and that lock is released by calling ExitUpgradeableReadLock:

```
public void IncreasePriority(string taskName)
{
    try
    {
        _rwlSlim.EnterUpgradeableReadLock();
        var taskQuery = from t in _tasks
                        where t.Name == taskName
                        select t;
        if(taskQuery.Count<Task>()>0)
        {
            Task task = taskQuery.First<Task>();
            _rwlSlim.EnterWriteLock();
            task.Priority++;
            Console.WriteLine("Task " + task.Name +
                " priority was increased to " + task.Priority +
                " for developer");
            _rwlSlim.ExitWriteLock();
        }
    }
    finally
    {
        _rwlSlim.ExitUpgradeableReadLock();
    }
}
```

Discussion

The ReaderWriterLockSlim was created to replace the existing ReaderWriterLock for a number of reasons:

- Performance: ReaderWriterLock was more than 5 times slower than using a Monitor.
- Recursion semantics of ReaderWriterLock were not standard and were broken in some thread reentrancy cases.
- The upgrade lock method is nonatomic in ReaderWriterLock.

While the ReaderWriterLockSlim is only about two times slower than the Monitor, it is more flexible and prioritizes writes, so in few write, many read scenarios, it is more scalable than the Monitor. There are also methods to determine what type of lock is held as well as how many threads are waiting to acquire it.

By default, lock acquisition recursion is disallowed. If you call EnterReadLock twice, you get a LockRecursionException. Lock Recursion can be enabled by passing a LockRecusionPolicy.SupportsRecursion enumeration value to the constructor overload of ReaderWriterLockSlim that accepts it. Even though it is possible to enable lock recursion, it is generally discouraged, as it complicates things to no small degree, and these are not fun issues to debug.

There are some scenarios where the ReaderWriterLockSlim is not appropriate for use, although most of these are not applicable to everyday development:

- SQLCLR: Due to the incompatible HostProtection attributes, ReaderWriter-LockSlim is precluded from use in SQL Server CLR scenarios.

- Host using Thread aborts: Because it doesn't mark critical regions, hosts that use this won't know that it will be harmed by thread aborts, so if the host uses them, it will cause issues in the hosted AppDomains.

- It cannot handle asynchronous exceptions (thread aborts, out of memory, etc.) and could end up with corrupt lock state, which could cause deadlocks or other issues.

The entire code base for the example is listed here:

```csharp
static Developer _dev = new Developer(15);
static bool _end = false;

/// <summary>
/// </summary>
public static void TestReaderWriterLockSlim()
{
    LaunchTeam(_dev);
    Thread.Sleep(10000);
}

private static void LaunchTeam(Developer dev)
{
    LaunchManager("CTO", dev);
    LaunchManager("Director", dev);
    LaunchManager("Project Manager", dev);
    LaunchDependent("Product Manager", dev);
    LaunchDependent("Test Engineer", dev);
    LaunchDependent("Technical Communications Professional", dev);
    LaunchDependent("Operations Staff", dev);
    LaunchDependent("Support Staff", dev);
}

public class TaskInfo
{
    private Developer _dev;
    public string Name { get; set; }
    public Developer Developer
    {
        get { return _dev; }
        set { _dev = value; }
    }
}

private static void LaunchManager(string name, Developer dev)
{
    ThreadPool.QueueUserWorkItem(
        new WaitCallback(CreateManagerOnThread),
```

```
            new TaskInfo() { Name = name, Developer = dev });
    }

    private static void LaunchDependent(string name, Developer dev)
    {
        ThreadPool.QueueUserWorkItem(
            new WaitCallback(CreateDependentOnThread),
            new TaskInfo() { Name = name, Developer = dev });
    }

    private static void CreateManagerOnThread(object objInfo)
    {
        TaskInfo taskInfo = (TaskInfo)objInfo;
        Console.WriteLine("Added " + taskInfo.Name + " to the project...");
        TaskManager mgr = new TaskManager(taskInfo.Name, taskInfo.Developer);
    }

    private static void CreateDependentOnThread(object objInfo)
    {
        TaskInfo taskInfo = (TaskInfo)objInfo;
        Console.WriteLine("Added " + taskInfo.Name + " to the project...");
        TaskDependent dep = new TaskDependent(taskInfo.Name, taskInfo.Developer);
    }

    public class Task
    {
        public Task(string name)
        {
            Name = name;
        }

        public string Name { get; set; }
        public int Priority { get; set; }
        public bool Status { get; set; }

        public override string ToString()
        {
            return this.Name;
        }

        public override bool Equals(object obj)
        {
            Task task = obj as Task;
            if(task != null)
                return this.Name == task.Name;
            return false;
        }

        public override int GetHashCode()
        {
            return this.Name.GetHashCode();
        }
    }
```

```csharp
public class Developer
{
    /// <summary>
    /// Dictionary for the tasks
    /// </summary>
    private List<Task> _tasks = new List<Task>();
    private ReaderWriterLockSlim _rwlSlim = new ReaderWriterLockSlim();
    private System.Threading.Timer _timer;
    private int _maxTasks;

    public Developer(int maxTasks)
    {
        // the maximum number of tasks before the developer quits
        _maxTasks = maxTasks;
        // do some work every 1/4 second
        _timer = new Timer(new TimerCallback(DoWork), null, 1000, 250);
    }

    // Execute a task
    protected void DoWork(Object stateInfo)
    {
        ExecuteTask();
        try
        {
            _rwlSlim.EnterWriteLock();
            // if we finished all tasks, go on vacation!
            if (_tasks.Count == 0)
            {
                _end = true;
                Console.WriteLine("Developer finished all tasks, go on vacation!");
                return;
            }

            if (!_end)
            {
                // if we have too many tasks quit
                if (_tasks.Count > _maxTasks)
                {
                    // get the number of unfinished tasks
                    var query = from t in _tasks
                                where t.Status == false
                                select t;
                    int unfinishedTaskCount = query.Count<Task>();

                    _end = true;
                    Console.WriteLine("Developer has too many tasks, quitting! " +
                        unfinishedTaskCount + " tasks left unfinished.");
                }
            }
            else
                _timer.Dispose();
        }
        finally
        {
```

```
                _rwlSlim.ExitWriteLock( );
            }
        }

    public void AddTask(Task newTask)
    {
        try
        {
            _rwlSlim.EnterWriteLock( );
            // if we already have this task (unique by name)
            // then just accept the add as sometimes people
            // give you the same task more than once :)
            var taskQuery = from t in _tasks
                            where t == newTask
                            select t;
            if (taskQuery.Count<Task>( ) == 0)
            {
                Console.WriteLine("Task " + newTask.Name + " was added to
developer");
                _tasks.Add(newTask);
            }
        }
        finally
        {
            _rwlSlim.ExitWriteLock( );
        }
    }

    /// <summary>
    /// Increase the priority of the task
    /// </summary>
    /// <param name="taskName">name of the task</param>
    public void IncreasePriority(string taskName)
    {
        try
        {
            _rwlSlim.EnterUpgradeableReadLock( );
            var taskQuery = from t in _tasks
                            where t.Name == taskName
                            select t;
            if(taskQuery.Count<Task>( )>0)
            {
                Task task = taskQuery.First<Task>( );
                _rwlSlim.EnterWriteLock( );
                task.Priority++;
                Console.WriteLine("Task " + task.Name +
                    " priority was increased to " + task.Priority +
                    " for developer");
                _rwlSlim.ExitWriteLock( );
            }
        }
        finally
        {
            _rwlSlim.ExitUpgradeableReadLock( );
```

```
        }
    }

    /// <summary>
    /// Allows people to check if the task is done
    /// </summary>
    /// <param name="taskName">name of the task</param>
    /// <returns>False if the taks is undone or not in the list, true if done</returns>
    public bool IsTaskDone(string taskName)
    {
        try
        {
            _rwlSlim.EnterReadLock();
            var taskQuery = from t in _tasks
                            where t.Name == taskName
                            select t;
            if (taskQuery.Count<Task>() > 0)
            {
                Task task = taskQuery.First<Task>();
                Console.WriteLine("Task " + task.Name + " status was reported.");
                return task.Status;
            }
        }
        finally
        {
            _rwlSlim.ExitReadLock();
        }
        return false;
    }

    private void ExecuteTask()
    {
        // look over the tasks and do the highest priority
        var queryResult =   from t in _tasks
                            where t.Status == false
                            orderby t.Priority
                            select t;
        if (queryResult.Count<Task>() > 0)
        {
            // do the task
            Task task = queryResult.First<Task>();
            task.Status = true;
            task.Priority = -1;
            Console.WriteLine("Task " + task.Name + " executed by developer.");
        }
    }
}

public class TaskManager : TaskDependent
{
    private System.Threading.Timer _mgrTimer;

    public TaskManager(string name, Developer taskExecutor) :
```

```
        base(name, taskExecutor)
    {
        // intervene every 2 seconds
        _mgrTimer = new Timer(new TimerCallback(Intervene), null, 0, 2000);
    }

    // Intervene in the plan
    protected void Intervene(Object stateInfo)
    {
        ChangePriority();
        // developer ended, kill timer
        if (_end)
        {
            _mgrTimer.Dispose();
            _developer = null;
        }
    }

    public void ChangePriority()
    {
        if (_tasks.Count > 0)
        {
            int taskIndex = _rnd.Next(0, _tasks.Count - 1);
            Task checkTask = _tasks[taskIndex];
            // make those developers work faster on some random task!
            if (_developer != null)
            {
                _developer.IncreasePriority(checkTask.Name);
                Console.WriteLine(Name + " intervened and changed priority for task "
+
                                    checkTask.Name);
            }
        }
    }
}

public class TaskDependent
{
    protected List<Task> _tasks = new List<Task>();
    protected Developer _developer;
    protected Random _rnd = new Random();
    private Timer _taskTimer;
    private Timer _statusTimer;

    public TaskDependent(string name, Developer taskExecutor)
    {
        Name = name;
        _developer = taskExecutor;
        // add work every 1 second
        _taskTimer = new Timer(new TimerCallback(AddWork), null, 0, 1000);
        // check status every 3 seconds
        _statusTimer = new Timer(new TimerCallback(CheckStatus), null, 0, 3000);
    }
```

```
// Add more work to the developer
protected void AddWork(Object stateInfo)
{
    SubmitTask();
    // developer ended, kill timer
    if (_end)
    {
        _taskTimer.Dispose();
        _developer = null;
    }
}

// Check Status of work with the developer
protected void CheckStatus(Object stateInfo)
{
    CheckTaskStatus();
    // developer ended, kill timer
    if (_end)
    {
        _statusTimer.Dispose();
        _developer = null;
    }
}

public string Name { get; set; }

public void SubmitTask()
{
    int taskId = _rnd.Next(10000);
    string taskName = "(" + taskId + " for " + Name + ")";
    Task newTask = new Task(taskName);
    if (_developer != null)
    {
        _developer.AddTask(newTask);
        _tasks.Add(newTask);
    }
}

public void CheckTaskStatus()
{
    if (_tasks.Count > 0)
    {
        int taskIndex = _rnd.Next(0, _tasks.Count - 1);
        Task checkTask = _tasks[taskIndex];
        if (_developer != null &&
            _developer.IsTaskDone(checkTask.Name))
        {
            Console.WriteLine("Task " + checkTask.Name + " is done for " + Name);
            // remove it from the todo list
            _tasks.Remove(checkTask);
        }
    }
}
```

You can see the series of events in the project in the output. The point at which the Developer has had enough is highlighted:

```
Added CTO to the project...
Added Director to the project...
Added Project Manager to the project...
Added Product Manager to the project...
Added Test Engineer to the project...
Added Technical Communications Professional to the project...
Added Operations Staff to the project...
Added Support Staff to the project...
Task (6267 for CTO) was added to developer
Task (6267 for CTO) status was reported.
Task (6267 for CTO) priority was increased to 1 for developer
CTO intervened and changed priority for task (6267 for CTO)
Task (6267 for Director) was added to developer
Task (6267 for Director) status was reported.
Task (6267 for Director) priority was increased to 1 for developer
Director intervened and changed priority for task (6267 for Director)
Task (6267 for Project Manager) was added to developer
Task (6267 for Project Manager) status was reported.
Task (6267 for Project Manager) priority was increased to 1 for developer
Project Manager intervened and changed priority for task (6267 for Project
Manager)
Task (6267 for Product Manager) was added to developer
Task (6267 for Product Manager) status was reported.
Task (6267 for Technical Communications Professional) was added to developer
Task (6267 for Technical Communications Professional) status was reported.
Task (6267 for Operations Staff) was added to developer
Task (6267 for Operations Staff) status was reported.
Task (6267 for Support Staff) was added to developer
Task (6267 for Support Staff) status was reported.
Task (6267 for Test Engineer) was added to developer
Task (5368 for CTO) was added to developer
Task (5368 for Director) was added to developer
Task (5368 for Project Manager) was added to developer
Task (6153 for Product Manager) was added to developer
Task (913 for Test Engineer) was added to developer
Task (6153 for Technical Communications Professional) was added to developer
Task (6153 for Operations Staff) was added to developer
Task (6153 for Support Staff) was added to developer
Task (6267 for Product Manager) executed by developer.
Task (6267 for Technical Communications Professional) executed by developer.
Task (6267 for Operations Staff) executed by developer.
Task (6267 for Support Staff) executed by developer.
Task (6267 for CTO) priority was increased to 2 for developer
CTO intervened and changed priority for task (6267 for CTO)
Task (6267 for Director) priority was increased to 2 for developer
Director intervened and changed priority for task (6267 for Director)
Task (6267 for Project Manager) priority was increased to 2 for developer
Project Manager intervened and changed priority for task (6267 for Project
Manager)
Task (6267 for Test Engineer) executed by developer.
Task (7167 for CTO) was added to developer
```

Task (7167 for Director) was added to developer
Task (7167 for Project Manager) was added to developer
Task (5368 for Product Manager) was added to developer
Task (6153 for Test Engineer) was added to developer
Task (5368 for Technical Communications Professional) was added to developer
Task (5368 for Operations Staff) was added to developer
Task (5368 for Support Staff) was added to developer
Task (5368 for CTO) executed by developer.
Task (5368 for Director) executed by developer.
Task (5368 for Project Manager) executed by developer.
Task (6267 for CTO) status was reported.
Task (6267 for Director) status was reported.
Task (6267 for Project Manager) status was reported.
Task (913 for Test Engineer) status was reported.
Task (6267 for Technical Communications Professional) status was reported.
Task (6267 for Technical Communications Professional) is done for Technical
Communications Professional
Task (6267 for Product Manager) status was reported.
Task (6267 for Product Manager) is done for Product Manager
Task (6267 for Operations Staff) status was reported.
Task (6267 for Operations Staff) is done for Operations Staff
Task (6267 for Support Staff) status was reported.
Task (6267 for Support Staff) is done for Support Staff
Task (6153 for Product Manager) executed by developer.
Task (2987 for CTO) was added to developer
Task (2987 for Director) was added to developer
Task (2987 for Project Manager) was added to developer
Task (7167 for Product Manager) was added to developer
Task (4126 for Test Engineer) was added to developer
Task (7167 for Technical Communications Professional) was added to developer
Task (7167 for Support Staff) was added to developer
Task (7167 for Operations Staff) was added to developer
Task (913 for Test Engineer) executed by developer.
Task (6153 for Technical Communications Professional) executed by developer.
Developer has too many tasks, quitting! 21 tasks left unfinished.
Task (6153 for Operations Staff) executed by developer.
Task (5368 for CTO) priority was increased to 0 for developer
CTO intervened and changed priority for task (5368 for CTO)
Task (5368 for Director) priority was increased to 0 for developer
Director intervened and changed priority for task (5368 for Director)
Task (5368 for Project Manager) priority was increased to 0 for developer
Project Manager intervened and changed priority for task (5368 for Project
Manager)
Task (6153 for Support Staff) executed by developer.
Task (4906 for Product Manager) was added to developer
Task (7167 for Test Engineer) was added to developer
Task (4906 for Technical Communications Professional) was added to developer
Task (4906 for Operations Staff) was added to developer
Task (4906 for Support Staff) was added to developer
Task (7167 for CTO) executed by developer.
Task (7167 for Director) executed by developer.

```
Task (7167 for Project Manager) executed by developer.
Task (5368 for Product Manager) executed by developer.
Task (6153 for Test Engineer) executed by developer.
Task (5368 for Technical Communications Professional) executed by developer.
Task (5368 for Operations Staff) executed by developer.
Task (5368 for Support Staff) executed by developer.
Task (2987 for CTO) executed by developer.
Task (2987 for Director) executed by developer.
Task (2987 for Project Manager) executed by developer.
Task (7167 for Product Manager) executed by developer.
Task (4126 for Test Engineer) executed by developer.
```

See Also

The "ReaderWriterLockSlim" and "SQL Server Programming and Host Attributes"
topics in the MSDN documentation.

CHAPTER 19
Toolbox

19.0 Introduction

Every programmer has a certain set of routines that he refers back to and uses over and over again. These utility functions are usually bits of code that are not provided by any particular language or framework. This chapter is a compilation of utility routines that we have gathered during our time with C# and the .NET Framework. The type of things we share in this chapter are:

- Determining the path for various locations in the operating system.
- Interacting with services.
- Inspecting the Global Assembly Cache.
- Message queuing.

It is a grab bag of code that can help to solve a specific need while you are working on a larger set of functionality in your application.

19.1   Dealing with Operating System Shutdown, Power Management, or User Session Changes

Problem

You want to be notified whenever the operating system or a user has initiated an action that requires your application to shut down or be inactive (user logoff, remote session disconnect, system shutdown, hibernate/restore, etc.). This notification will allow you have your application respond gracefully to the changes.

Solution

Use the `Microsoft.Win32.SystemEvents` class to get notification of operating system, user session change, and power management events. The `RegisterForSystemEvents` method shown next hooks up the five event handlers necessary to capture these events and would be placed in the initialization section for your code:

```
public static void RegisterForSystemEvents()
{
    // Always get the final notification when the event thread is shutting down
    // so we can unregister.
    SystemEvents.EventsThreadShutdown +=
        new EventHandler(OnEventsThreadShutdown);
    SystemEvents.PowerModeChanged +=
        new PowerModeChangedEventHandler(OnPowerModeChanged);
    SystemEvents.SessionSwitch +=
        new SessionSwitchEventHandler(OnSessionSwitch);
    SystemEvents.SessionEnding +=
        new SessionEndingEventHandler(OnSessionEnding);
    SystemEvents.SessionEnded +=
        new SessionEndedEventHandler(OnSessionEnded);
}
```

The `EventsThreadShutdown` event notifies you of when the thread that is distributing the events from the `SystemEvents` class is shutting down so that you can unregister the events on the `SystemEvents` class if you have not already done so. The `PowerModeChanged` event triggers when the user suspends or resumes the system from a suspended state. The `SessionSwitch` event is triggered by a change in the logged-on user. The `SessionEnding` event is triggered when the user is trying to log off or shut down the system, and the `SessionEnded` event is triggered when the user is actually logging off or shutting down the system.

The events can be unregistered using the `UnregisterFromSystemEvents` method. `UnregisterFromSystemEvents` should be called from the termination code of your Windows Form, user control, or any other class that may come and go, as well as from one other area shown later in the recipe:

```
private static void UnregisterFromSystemEvents()
{
    SystemEvents.EventsThreadShutdown -=
        new EventHandler(OnEventsThreadShutdown);
    SystemEvents.PowerModeChanged -=
        new PowerModeChangedEventHandler(OnPowerModeChanged);
    SystemEvents.SessionSwitch -=
        new SessionSwitchEventHandler(OnSessionSwitch);
    SystemEvents.SessionEnding -=
        new SessionEndingEventHandler(OnSessionEnding);
    SystemEvents.SessionEnded -=
        new SessionEndedEventHandler(OnSessionEnded);
}
```

Since the events exposed by SystemEvents are static, if you are using them in a section of code that could be invoked multiple times (secondary Windows Form, user control, monitoring class, etc.), you *must* unregister your handlers, or you will cause memory leaks in the application.

The SystemEvents handler methods are the individual event handlers for each of the events that have been subscribed to in RegisterForSystemEvents. The first handler to cover is the OnEventsThreadShutdown handler. It is essential that your handlers are unregistered if this event fires, as the notification thread for the SystemEvents class is going away, and the class may be gone before your application is. If you haven't unregistered before that point, you will cause memory leaks, so add a call to UnregisterFromSystemEvents into this handler as shown here:

```
private static void OnEventsThreadShutdown(object sender, EventArgs e)
{
    Debug.WriteLine("System event thread is shutting down, no more notifications.
");

    // Unregister all our events as the notification thread is going away.
    UnregisterFromSystemEvents();
}
```

The next handler to explore is the OnPowerModeChanged method. This handler can report the type of power management event through the Mode property of the PowerModeEventChangedArgs parameter. The Mode property has the PowerMode enumeration type and specifies the event type through the enumeration value contained therein:

```
private static void OnPowerModeChanged(object sender, PowerModeChangedEventArgs
e)
{
    // Power mode is changing.
    switch (e.Mode)
    {
        case PowerModes.Resume:
            Debug.WriteLine("PowerMode: OS is resuming from suspended state");
            break;
        case PowerModes.StatusChange:
            Debug.WriteLine("PowerMode: There was a change relating to the power"
+
                " supply (weak battery, unplug, etc..)");
            break;
        case PowerModes.Suspend:
            Debug.WriteLine("PowerMode: OS is about to be suspended");
            break;
    }
}
```

The next three handlers all deal with operating system session states. They are OnSessionSwitch, OnSessionEnding, and OnSessionEnded. Handling all three of these events covers all of the operating system session state transitions that your application may need to worry about. In OnSessionEnding, there is a SessionEndingEventArgs parameter, which has a Cancel member. This Cancel member allows you to request that the session not end if set to false. Code for the three handlers is shown in Example 19-1.

Example 19-1. OnSessionSwitch, OnSessionEnding, and OnSessionEnded handlers

```
private static void OnSessionSwitch(object sender, SessionSwitchEventArgs e)
{
    // Check reason.
    switch (e.Reason)
    {
        case SessionSwitchReason.ConsoleConnect:
            Debug.WriteLine("Session connected from the console");
            break;
        case SessionSwitchReason.ConsoleDisconnect:
            Debug.WriteLine("Session disconnected from the console");
            break;
        case SessionSwitchReason.RemoteConnect:
            Debug.WriteLine("Remote session connected");
            break;
        case SessionSwitchReason.RemoteDisconnect:
            Debug.WriteLine("Remote session disconnected");
            break;
        case SessionSwitchReason.SessionLock:
            Debug.WriteLine("Session has been locked");
            break;
        case SessionSwitchReason.SessionLogoff:
            Debug.WriteLine("User was logged off from a session");
            break;
        case SessionSwitchReason.SessionLogon:
            Debug.WriteLine("User has logged on to a session");
            break;
        case SessionSwitchReason.SessionRemoteControl:
            Debug.WriteLine("Session changed to or from remote status");
            break;
        case SessionSwitchReason.SessionUnlock:
            Debug.WriteLine("Session has been unlocked");
            break;
    }
}

private static void OnSessionEnding(object sender, SessionEndingEventArgs e)
{
    // True to cancel the user request to end the session, false otherwise
    e.Cancel = false;
    // Check reason.
    switch(e.Reason)
    {
        case SessionEndReasons.Logoff:
            Debug.WriteLine("Session ending as the user is logging off");
            break;
        case SessionEndReasons.SystemShutdown:
```

```
            Debug.WriteLine("Session ending as the OS is shutting down");
            break;
    }
}

private static void OnSessionEnded(object sender, SessionEndedEventArgs e)
{
    switch (e.Reason)
    {
        case SessionEndReasons.Logoff:
            Debug.WriteLine("Session ended as the user is logging off");
            break;
        case SessionEndReasons.SystemShutdown:
            Debug.WriteLine("Session ended as the OS is shutting down");
            break;
    }
}
```

Discussion

The .NET Framework provides many opportunities to get feedback from the system when there are changes due to either user or system interactions. The SystemEvents class exposes more events than just the ones used in this recipe. For a full listing, see Table 19-1.

Table 19-1. The SystemEvents events

Value	Description
DisplaySettingsChanged	User changed display settings.
DisplaySettingsChanging	Display settings are changing.
EventsThreadShutdown	Thread listening for system events is terminating.
InstalledFontsChanged	User added or removed fonts.
PaletteChanged	User switched to an application with a different palette.
PowerModeChanged	User suspended or resumed the system.
SessionEnded	User shut down the system or logged off.
SessionEnding	User is attempting to shut down the system or log off.
SessionSwitch	The currently logged-in user changed.
TimeChanged	User changed system time.
TimerElapsed	A Windows timer interval expired.
UserPreferenceChanged	User changed a preference in the system.
UserPreferenceChanging	User is trying to change a preference in the system.

Keep in mind that these are system events. Therefore, the amount of work done in the handlers should be kept to a minimum, so the system can move on to the next task.

The notifications from `SystemEvents` come on a dedicated thread for raising these events. In a Windows Forms application, you will need to get back on to the correct user interface thread before updating a UI with any of this information, using one of the various methods for doing so (`Control.BeginInvoke`, `Control.Invoke`, `BackgroundWorker`).

See Also

The "SystemEvents Class," "PowerModeChangedEventArgs Class," "SessionEndedEventArgs Class," "SessionEndingEventArgs Class," "SessionSwitchEventArgs Class," "TimerElapsedEventArgs Class," "UserPreferenceChangingEventArgs Class," and "UserPreferenceChangedEventArgs Class" topics in the MSDN documentation.

19.2 Controlling a Service

Problem

You need to programmatically manipulate a service that your application interacts with.

Solution

Use the `System.ServiceProcess.ServiceController` class to control the service. `ServiceController` allows you to interact with an existing service and to read and change its properties. In the example, it will be used to manipulate the ASP.NET State Service. The name, the service type, and the display name are easily available from the `ServiceName`, `ServiceType`, and `DisplayName` properties:

```
ServiceController scStateService = new ServiceController("COM+ Event System");
Console.WriteLine("Service Name: " + scStateService.ServiceName);
Console.WriteLine("Service Type: " + scStateService.ServiceType.ToString());
Console.WriteLine("Display Name: " + scStateService.DisplayName);
```

The ServiceType enumeration has a number of values, as shown in Table 19-2.

Table 19-2. The ServiceType enumeration values

Value	Description
Adapter	Service that serves a hardware device
FileSystemDriver	Driver for the filesystem (kernel level)
InteractiveProcess	Service that communicates with the desktop
KernelDriver	Low-level hardware device driver

Table 19-2. The ServiceType enumeration values (continued)

Value	Description
RecognizerDriver	Driver for identifying filesystems on startup
Win32OwnProcess	Win32 program that runs as a service in its own process
Win32ShareProcess	Win32 program that runs as a service in a shared process such as SvcHost

One useful task is to determine a service's dependents. The services that depend on the current service are accessed through the DependentServices property, an array of ServiceController instances (one for each dependent service):

```
foreach (ServiceController sc in scStateService.DependentServices)
{
    Console.WriteLine(scStateService.DisplayName + " is depended on by: " +
            sc.DisplayName);
}
```

To see the services that the current service does depend on, the ServicesDependedOn array contains ServiceController instances for each of those:

```
foreach (ServiceController sc in scStateService.ServicesDependedOn)
{
    Console.WriteLine(scStateService.DisplayName + " depends on: " +
            sc.DisplayName);
}
```

One of the most important things about services is what state they are in. A service doesn't do much good if it is supposed to be running and it isn't—or worse yet, it is supposed to be disabled (perhaps as a security risk) and isn't. To find out the current status of the service, check the Status property. For this example, the original state of the service will be saved, so it can be restored later in the originalState variable:

```
Console.WriteLine("Status: " + scStateService.Status);
// Save original state.
ServiceControllerStatus originalState = scStateService.Status;
```

If a service is stopped, it can be started with the Start method. First, check if the service is stopped, and then, once Start has been called on the ServiceController instance, the WaitForStatus method should be called to make sure that the service started. WaitForStatus can take a timeout value so that the application is not waiting forever for the service to start in the case of a problem:

```
// If it is stopped, start it.
TimeSpan serviceTimeout = TimeSpan.FromSeconds(60);
if (scStateService.Status == ServiceControllerStatus.Stopped)
{
    scStateService.Start();
    // Wait up to 60 seconds for start.
    scStateService.WaitForStatus(ServiceControllerStatus.Running,
serviceTimeout);
}
    Console.WriteLine("Status: " + scStateService.Status);
```

Services can also be paused. If the service is paused, the application needs to check if it can be continued by looking at the CanPauseAndContinue property. If so, the Continue method will get the service going again, and the WaitForStatus method should be called to wait until it does:

```
// If it is paused, continue.
if (scStateService.Status == ServiceControllerStatus.Paused)
{
    if(scStateService.CanPauseAndContinue)
    {
        scStateService.Continue();
        // Wait up to 60 seconds for running.
        scStateService.WaitForStatus(ServiceControllerStatus.Running,
                    serviceTimeout);
    }
}
Console.WriteLine("Status: " + scStateService.Status);

// Should be running at this point.
```

Determining if a service can be stopped is done through the CanStop property. If it can be stopped, then stopping it is a matter of calling the Stop method followed by WaitForStatus:

```
// Can we stop it?
if (scStateService.CanStop)
{
    scStateService.Stop();
    // Wait up to 60 seconds for stop.
    scStateService.WaitForStatus(ServiceControllerStatus.Stopped,
serviceTimeout);
}
Console.WriteLine("Status: " + scStateService.Status);
```

Now it is time to set the service back to how you found it. The originalState variable has the original state, and the switch statement holds actions for taking the service from the current stopped state to its original state:

```
// Set it back to the original state.
switch (originalState)
{
    case ServiceControllerStatus.Stopped:
        if (scStateService.CanStop)
        {
            scStateService.Stop();
        }
        break;
    case ServiceControllerStatus.Running:
        scStateService.Start();
        // Wait up to 60 seconds for stop.
        scStateService.WaitForStatus(ServiceControllerStatus.Running,
                    serviceTimeout);
        break;
    case ServiceControllerStatus.Paused:
```

```
            // If it was paused and is stopped, need to restart so we can pause.
            if (scStateService.Status == ServiceControllerStatus.Stopped)
            {
                scStateService.Start();
                // Wait up to 60 seconds for start.
                scStateService.WaitForStatus(ServiceControllerStatus.Running,
                            serviceTimeout);
            }
            // Now pause.
            if (scStateService.CanPauseAndContinue)
            {
                scStateService.Pause();
                // Wait up to 60 seconds for stop.
                scStateService.WaitForStatus(ServiceControllerStatus.Paused,
                            serviceTimeout);
        }
        break;
    }
```

In order to be sure that the Status property is correct on the service, the application should call Refresh to update it before testing the value of the Status property. Once the application is done with the service, call the Close method:

```
scStateService.Refresh();
Console.WriteLine("Status: " + scStateService.Status.ToString());

// Close it.
scStateService.Close();
```

Discussion

Services run many of the operating system functions today. They usually run under a system account (LocalSystem, NetworkService, LocalService) or a specific user account that has been granted specific permissions and rights. If your application uses a service, then this is a good way to determine if everything for the service to run is set up and configured properly before your application attempts to use it. Not all applications depend on services directly. But if your application does, or you have written a service as part of your application, it can be handy to have an easy way to check the status of your service and possibly correct the situation.

See Also

The "ServiceController Class" and "ServiceControllerStatus Enumeration" topics in the MSDN documentation.

19.3   List What Processes an Assembly Is Loaded In

Problem

You want to know what current processes have a given assembly loaded.

Solution

Use the `GetProcessesAssemblyIsLoadedIn` method that we've created for this purpose to return a list of processes that a given assembly is loaded in. `GetProcessesAssemblyIsLoadedIn` takes the filename of the assembly to look for (such as *System.Data.dll*), and then gets a list of the currently running processes on the machine by calling `Process.GetProcesses`. It then searches the processes to see if the assembly is loaded into any of them. When found in a process, that `Process` object is projected into an enumerable set of `Process` objects. The iterator for the set of processes found is returned from the query:

```
public static IEnumerable<Process> GetProcessesAssemblyIsLoadedIn(
                                              string assemblyFileName)
{
    var processes = from process in Process.GetProcesses( )
                    where process.ProcessName != "System" &&
                          process.ProcessName != "Idle"
                    from ProcessModule processModule in process.Modules
                    where processModule.ModuleName.Equals(assemblyFileName,
                                       StringComparison.OrdinalIgnoreCase)
                    select process;
    return processes;
}
```

Discussion

In some circumstances, such as when uninstalling software or debugging version conflicts, it is beneficial to know if an assembly is loaded into more than one process. By quickly getting a list of the `Process` objects that the assembly is loaded in, you can narrow the scope of your investigation.

The following code uses this routine:

```
string searchAssm = "System.Data.dll";
var processes = Toolbox.GetProcessesAssemblyIsLoadedIn(searchAssm);
foreach (Process p in processes)
{
    Console.WriteLine("Found {0} in {1}",searchAssm, p.MainModule.ModuleName);
}
```

The preceding code might produce output like this (you may see more if you have other applications running):

```
Found System.Data.dll in WebDev.WebServer.EXE
Found System.Data.dll in devenv.exe
Found System.Data.dll in CSharpRecipes.vshost.exe
```

Since this is a diagnostic function, you will need `FullTrust` security access to use this method.

Note that in the query, the `System` and `Idle` processes are avoided for inspection by the query:

```
var processes = from process in Process.GetProcesses()
                where process.ProcessName != "System" &&
                      process.ProcessName != "Idle"
                from ProcessModule processModule in process.Modules
```

This is due to the `Modules` collection throwing a `Win32Exception` as those processes are not able to be examined using the `Modules` collection on the process.

See Also

The "Process Class," "ProcessModule Class," and "GetProcesses Method" topics in the MSDN documentation.

19.4   Using Message Queues on a Local Workstation

Problem

You need a way to disconnect two components of your application (such as a web service endpoint and processing logic) so that the first component has to worry about only formatting the instructions, and the bulk of the processing occurs in the second component.

Solution

Use the `MQWorker` class shown here in both the first and second components to write and read messages to and from a message queue. `MQWorker` uses the local message-queuing services to do this. The queue pathname is supplied in the constructor, and the existence of the queue is checked in the `SetUpQueue` method:

```
class MQWorker : IDisposable
{
    private bool _disposed;
    private string _mqPathName;
    MessageQueue _queue;

    public MQWorker(string queuePathName)
    {
        if (string.IsNullOrEmpty(queuePathName)
            throw new ArgumentNullException("queuePathName");

        _mqPathName = queuePathName;

        SetUpQueue();
    }
```

SetUpQueue creates a message queue of the supplied name using the MessageQueue class if none exists. It accounts for the scenario in which the message-queuing services are running on a workstation computer. In that situation, it makes the queue private, as that is the only type of queue allowed on a workstation:

```
private void SetUpQueue()
{
    // See if the queue exists; create it if not.
    if (!MessageQueue.Exists(_mqPathName))
    {
        try
        {
            _queue = MessageQueue.Create(_mqPathName);
        }
        catch (MessageQueueException mqex)
        {
            // See if we are running on a workgroup computer.
            if (mqex.MessageQueueErrorCode ==
                MessageQueueErrorCode.UnsupportedOperation)
            {
                string origPath = _mqPathName;
                // Must be a private queue in workstation mode.
                int index = _mqPathName.ToLower().IndexOf("private$");
                if (index == -1)
                {
                    // Get the first \.
                    index = _mqPathName.IndexOf(@"\");
                    // Insert private$\ after server entry.
                    _mqPathName = _mqPathName.Insert(index + 1, @"private$\");

                    if (!MessageQueue.Exists(_mqPathName))
                        _queue = MessageQueue.Create(_mqPathName);
                    else
                        _queue = new MessageQueue(_mqPathName);
                }
            }
        }
    }
    else
    {
        _queue = new MessageQueue(_mqPathName);
    }
}
```

The SendMessage method sends a message to the queue to set up in the constructor. The body of the message is supplied in the body parameter, and then an instance of System.Messaging.Message is created and populated. The BinaryMessageFormatter is used to format the message, as it enables larger volumes of messages to be sent with fewer resources than does the default XmlMessageFormatter. Messages are set to be persistent by setting the Recoverable property to true. Finally, the Body is set, and the message is sent:

```
public void SendMessage(string label, string body)
{
    if (_queue != null)
    {
        Message msg = new Message();
        // Label our message.
        msg.Label = label;

        // Override the default XML formatting with binary
        // as it is faster (at the expense of legibility while debugging).
        msg.Formatter = new BinaryMessageFormatter();
        // Make this message persist (causes message to be written
        // to disk).
        msg.Recoverable = true;
        msg.Body = body;
        _queue.Send(msg);
    }
}
```

The ReadMessage method reads messages from the queue set up in the constructor by creating a Message object and calling its Receive method. The message formatter is set to the BinaryMessageFormatter for the Message, since that is how we write to the queue. Finally, the body of the message is returned from the method:

```
public string ReadMessage()
{
    Message msg = null;
    msg = _queue.Receive();
    msg.Formatter = new BinaryMessageFormatter();
    return (string)msg.Body;
}

public void Dispose()
{
    Dispose(true);
    GC.SuppressFinalize(this);
}

private void Dispose(bool disposing)
{
    if (!this._disposed)
    {
        if (disposing)
            _queue.Dispose();

        _disposed = true;
    }
}
```

To show how the MQWorker class is used, the following example creates an MQWorker. It then sends a message (a small blob of XML) using SendMessage and then retrieves it using ReadMessage:

```
// NOTE: Message Queue services must be set up for this to work.
// This can be added in Add/Remove Windows Components.

// This is the right syntax for workstation queues.
//MQWorker mqw = new MQWorker(@".\private$\MQWorkerQ");
using (MQWorker mqw = new MQWorker(@".\MQWorkerQ"))
{
    string xml = "<MyXml><InnerXml location=\"inside\"/></MyXml>";
    Console.WriteLine("Sending message to message queue: " + xml);
    mqw.SendMessage("Label for message", xml);
    string retXml = mqw.ReadMessage();
    Console.WriteLine("Read message from message queue: " + retXml);
}
```

Discussion

Message queues are very useful when you are attempting to distribute the processing load for scalability purposes. Without question, using a message queue adds overhead to the processing; as the messages must travel through the infrastructure of MSMQ, overhead would not incur without it. One benefit is that MSMQ allows your application to spread out across multiple machines, so there can be a net gain in production. Another advantage is that this supports reliable asynchronous handling of the messages so that the sending side can be confident that the receiving side will get the message without the sender having to wait for confirmation. The Message Queue services are not installed by default but can be installed through the Add/Remove Windows Components applet in Control Panel. Using a message queue to buffer your processing logic from high volumes of requests (such as in the web service scenario presented earlier) can lead to more stability and ultimately can produce more throughput for your application through using multiple reader processes on multiple machines.

See Also

The "Message Class" and "MessageQueue Class" topics in the MSDN documentation.

19.5 Finding the Path to the Current Framework Version

Problem

You need the path to where the version of the .NET Framework you are running on is located.

Solution

Use the `GetRuntimeDirectoryRuntimeDirectory` method (implemented in `System.Runtime.InteropServices.RuntimeEnvironment`) to return the full path to the folder that the current version of .NET is installed in:

```
public static string GetCurrentFrameworkPath()
{

    return
System.Runtime.InteropServices.RuntimeEnvironment.GetRuntimeDirectory();
}
```

Discussion

There are many reasons why you might want to know the current framework path, including:

- Manually loading the configuration files in the *config* directory to check settings.
- Dynamically adding references for system components in a code generator.

The list could go on and on. Since the method to get to the path is pretty far down a namespace chain (`System.Runtime.InteropServices.RuntimeEnvironment`), it is provided for your programming convenience.

See Also

The "Version Class" and "Version.ToString Method" topics in the MSDN documentation.

19.6   Determining the Versions of an Assembly That Are Registered in the Global Assembly Cache (GAC)

Problem

You need to determine all of the versions of an assembly that are currently installed in the GAC.

Solution

Use the `PrintGacRegisteredVersions` method (implemented here) to display all of the versions (both native and managed) of an assembly in the GAC. In order to be complete, the code looks for *.dll*, *.exe*, and the native versions of *.dll* and // *.exe* files in the Global Assembly Cache:

```
    public static void PrintGacRegisteredVersions(string assemblyFileName)
    {

        Console.WriteLine("Searching for GAC Entries for {0}\r\n", assemblyFileName);
        // Get the filename without the extension as that is the subdirectory
        // name in the GAC where it would be registered.
        string assemblyFileNameNoExt = Path.
GetFileNameWithoutExtension(assemblyFileName);

        // Need to look for both the native images as well as "regular" .dlls and .
exes.
        string searchDLL = assemblyFileNameNoExt + ".dll";
        string searchEXE = assemblyFileNameNoExt + ".exe";
        string searchNIDLL = assemblyFileNameNoExt + ".ni.dll";
        string searchNIEXE = assemblyFileNameNoExt + ".ni.exe";
```

The Directory.GetFiles method is used in a LINQ query to determine if any of those versions are present in the GAC, which is located in the *[Windows]\ASSEMBLY* folder.

 The *ASSEMBLY* folder is not visible through Windows Explorer, as the GAC shell extension gets in the way. But if you run a Command Prompt window, you can maneuver to the *[Windows]\ASSEMBLY* folder and see how things are stored in the GAC.

```
// Query the GAC
var files = from file in Directory.GetFiles(gacPath, "*", SearchOption.
AllDirectories)
            let fileInfo = new FileInfo(file)
            where fileInfo.Name == searchDLL    ||
                  fileInfo.Name == searchEXE    ||
                  fileInfo.Name == searchNIDLL ||
                  fileInfo.Name == searchNIEXE
            select fileInfo.FullName;
```

Now that you have a master list of the versions of this file in the GAC, you display the information for each individual item by examining the FileVersionInfo and writing it out to the console:

```
    foreach (string file in files)
    {
        // Grab the version info and print.
        FileVersionInfo fileVersion = FileVersionInfo.GetVersionInfo(file);
        if (file.IndexOf("NativeImage",StringComparison.OrdinalIgnoreCase) != -1)
        {
            Console.WriteLine("Found {0} in the GAC under {1} as a native image",
                assemblyFileNameNoExt, Path.GetDirectoryName(file));
        }
        else
        {
            Console.WriteLine("Found {0} in the GAC under {1} with version " +
                    "information:\r\n{2}",
```

```
                    assemblyFileNameNoExt, Path.GetDirectoryName(file),
                fileVersion.ToString( ));
        }
    }
}
```

The output from this when looking for *mscorlib* looks like this:

```
Searching for GAC Entries for mscorlib

Found mscorlib in the GAC under C:\WINDOWS\ASSEMBLY\NativeImages_v2.0.50727_32\m
scorlib\9a485a2c7533b6601064c8e660bb8a5d as a native image
Found mscorlib in the GAC under C:\WINDOWS\ASSEMBLY\NativeImages1_v1.1.4322\msco
rlib\1.0.5000.0__b77a5c561934e089_c6f4d3b7 as a native image
Found mscorlib in the GAC under C:\WINDOWS\ASSEMBLY\NativeImages1_v1.1.4322\msco
rlib\1.0.5000.0__b77a5c561934e089_65ce95c7 as a native image
Found mscorlib in the GAC under C:\WINDOWS\ASSEMBLY\GAC_32\mscorlib\2.0.0.0__b77
a5c561934e089 with version information:
File:            C:\WINDOWS\ASSEMBLY\GAC_32\mscorlib\2.0.0.0__b77a5c561934e089\
mscorlib.dll
InternalName:    mscorlib.dll
OriginalFilename: mscorlib.dll
FileVersion:     2.0.50727.1378 (REDBITSB2.050727-1300)
FileDescription: Microsoft Common Language Runtime Class Library
Product:         Microsoftr .NET Framework
ProductVersion:  2.0.50727.1378
Debug:           False
Patched:         False
PreRelease:      False
PrivateBuild:    False
SpecialBuild:    False
Language:        English (United States)

Searching for GAC Entries for System.Web.dll

Found System.Web in the GAC under C:\WINDOWS\ASSEMBLY\NativeImages_v2.0.50727_32
\System.Web\48209ad55221a8f04c621153965925e4 as a native image
Found System.Web in the GAC under C:\WINDOWS\ASSEMBLY\GAC_32\System.Web\2.0.0.0_
_b03f5f7f11d50a3a with version information:
File:            C:\WINDOWS\ASSEMBLY\GAC_32\System.Web\2.0.0.0__b03f5f7f11d50a3
a\System.Web.dll
InternalName:    System.Web.dll
OriginalFilename: System.Web.dll
FileVersion:     2.0.50727.1378 (REDBITSB2.050727-1300)
FileDescription: System.Web.dll
Product:         Microsoftr .NET Framework
ProductVersion:  2.0.50727.1378
Debug:           False
Patched:         False
PreRelease:      False
PrivateBuild:    False
SpecialBuild:    False
Language:        English (United States)
```

```
Found System.Web in the GAC under C:\WINDOWS\ASSEMBLY\GAC\System.Web\1.0.5000.0_
_b03f5f7f11d50a3a with version information:
File:             C:\WINDOWS\ASSEMBLY\GAC\System.Web\1.0.5000.0__b03f5f7f11d50a3
a\System.Web.dll
InternalName:     System.Web.dll
OriginalFilename: System.Web.dll
FileVersion:      1.1.4322.2037
FileDescription:  System.Web.dll
Product:          Microsoft (R) .NET Framework
ProductVersion:   1.1.4322.2037
Debug:            False
Patched:          False
PreRelease:       False
PrivateBuild:     False
SpecialBuild:     False
Language:         English (United States)
```

Discussion

The ability to have multiple versions of assemblies on a machine and having absolute binding mechanisms to the specific version of an assembly, were proclaimed as the cure to *.dll hell*. *.dll hell* was the case in which two applications linked to a *.dll* of the same name in a common folder (such as *System32*), but each application needed a different version of the *.dll*. Problems occurred when you attempted to run one application or the other, depending upon which version was present. With assemblies and the GAC, this scenario occurs only when the application is improperly configured by allowing it to use newer versions of an assembly automatically or via publisher policy issues. Perhaps things are better now. In any case, they are different, and the starting point for debugging assembly loads is to figure out what is on the system. This can be helped by looking at the Assembly Binding Log Viewer (*FUSLOGVW.exe*). But having a way to just see what is on the system with a particular filename and what versions are included can be a very useful thing.

See Also

The "Directory Class," "ArrayList Class," and "FileVersionInfo Class" topics in the MSDN documentation.

19.7   Capturing Output from the Standard Output Stream

Problem

You want to capture output that is going to the standard output stream from within your C# program.

Solution

Use the `Console.SetOut` method to capture and release the standard output stream. `SetOut` sets the standard output stream to whatever `System.IO.TextWriter`-based stream it is handed. To capture the output to a file, create a `StreamWriter` to write to it, and set that writer using `SetOut`. Now when `Console.WriteLine` is called, the output goes to the `StreamWriter`, not to stdout, as shown here:

```
try
{
    Console.WriteLine("Stealing standard output!");
    using (StreamWriter writer = new StreamWriter(@"c:\log.txt"))
    {
        // Steal stdout for our own purposes...
        Console.SetOut(writer);

        Console.WriteLine("Writing to the console... NOT!");

        for (int i = 0; i < 10; i++)
            Console.WriteLine(i);

    }
}
catch(IOException e)
{
    Debug.WriteLine(e.ToString());
    return ;
}
```

To restore writing to the standard output stream, create another `StreamWriter`. This time, call the `Console.OpenStandardOutput` method to acquire the standard output stream and use `SetOut` to set it once again. Now calls to `Console.WriteLine` appear on the console again:

```
// Recover the standard output stream so that a
// completion message can be displayed.
using (StreamWriter standardOutput =
        new StreamWriter(Console.OpenStandardOutput()))
{
        standardOutput.AutoFlush = true;
        Console.SetOut(standardOutput);
        Console.WriteLine("Back to standard output!");
}
```

The console output from this code looks like this:

```
Stealing standard output!
Back to standard output!
```

log.txt contains the following after the code is executed:

```
Writing to the console... NOT!
0
1
```

```
2
3
4
5
6
7
8
9
```

Discussion

Redirecting the standard output stream inside of the program may seem a bit anti-quated. But consider the situation when you're using another class that writes information to this stream. You don't want the output to appear in your application, but you have to use the class. This could also be useful if you create a small launcher application to capture output from a console application.

See Also

The "Console.SetOut Method," "Console.OpenStandardOutput Method," and "StreamWriter Class" topics in the MSDN documentation.

19.8 Running Code in Its Own AppDomain

Problem

You want to run code isolated from the main part of your application.

Solution

Create a separate AppDomain to run the code using the AppDomain.CreateDomain method. CreateDomain allows the application to control many aspects of the AppDomain being created like the security environment, the AppDomain settings, and base paths for the AppDomain. To demonstrate this, the code creates an instance of the RunMe class (shown in full later in this recipe) and calls the PrintCurrentAppDomainName method. This prints the name of the AppDomain where the code is running:

```
public static void RunCodeInNewAppDomain( )
{
    AppDomain myOwnAppDomain = AppDomain.CreateDomain("MyOwnAppDomain");
    // Print out our current AppDomain name.
    RunMe rm = new RunMe( );
    rm.PrintCurrentAppDomainName( );
```

Now, you create an instance of the RunMe class in the "MyOwnAppDomain" AppDomain by calling CreateInstance on the AppDomain. We pass CreateInstance the module and type information necessary for constructing the type, and it returns an ObjectHandle.

We can then retrieve a proxy to the instance running in the AppDomain by taking the returned ObjectHandle and casting it to a RunMe reference using the Unwrap method:

```
// Create our RunMe class in the new AppDomain.
Type adType = typeof(RunMe);
ObjectHandle objHdl =
    myOwnAppDomain.CreateInstance(adType.Module.Assembly.FullName,
                        adType.FullName);

// Unwrap the reference.
RunMe adRunMe = (RunMe)objHdl.Unwrap();
```

The PrintCurrentAppDomainName method is called on the RunMe instance in the "MyOwnAppDomain" AppDomain, and it prints out "Hello from MyOwnAppDomain!". The AppDomain is unloaded using AppDomain.Unload and the program terminates:

```
    // Make a call on the toolbox.
    adRunMe.PrintCurrentAppDomainName();

    // Now unload the AppDomain.
    AppDomain.Unload(myOwnAppDomain);
}
```

The RunMe class is defined here. It inherits from MarshalByRefObject, as that allows you to retrieve the proxy reference when you call Unwrap on the ObjectHandle and have the calls on the class remoted into the new AppDomain. The PrintCurrentApp-DomainName method simply accesses the FriendlyName property on the current AppDomain and prints out the "Hello from {AppDomain}!" message:

```
public class RunMe : MarshalByRefObject
{
    public RunMe()
    {
        PrintCurrentAppDomainName();
    }

    public void PrintCurrentAppDomainName()
    {
        string name = AppDomain.CurrentDomain.FriendlyName;
        Console.WriteLine("Hello from {0}!", name);
    }
}
```

The output from this example is shown here:

```
Hello from CSharpRecipes.vshost.exe!
Hello from CSharpRecipes.vshost.exe!
Hello from MyOwnAppDomain!
Hello from MyOwnAppDomain!
```

Discussion

Isolating code in a separate AppDomain is overkill for something as trivial as this example, but it demonstrates that code can be executed remotely in an AppDomain created by your application. There are six overloads for the CreateDomain method, and each adds a bit more complexity to the AppDomain creation. In situations in which the isolation or configuration benefits outweigh the complexities of not only setting up a separate AppDomain but debugging code in it as well, it is a useful tool. A good real-world example is hosting a separate AppDomain to run ASP.NET pages outside of the normal ASP.NET environment, though this is truly a nontrivial usage.

See Also

The "AppDomain Class," "AppDomain.CreateDomain Method," and "ObjectHandle Class" topics in the MSDN documentation.

19.9 Determining the Operating System and Service Pack Version of the Current Operating System

Problem

You want to know the current operating system and service pack.

Solution

Use the GetOSAndServicePack method shown in Example 19-2 to get a string representing the current operating system and service pack. GetOSAndServicePack uses the Environment.OSVersion property to get the version information for the operating system and then determines the "official" name of the OS from that. The OperatingSystem class retrieved from Environment.OSVersion has a property for the service pack called ServicePack. The two strings are then merged together and returned as the OS and service pack string.

Example 19-2. GetOSAndServicePack method

```
public static string GetOSAndServicePack( )
{
    // Get the current OS info
    OperatingSystem os = Environment.OSVersion;
    string osText = string.Empty;
    // if version is 5, then it is Win2K, XP, or 2003
    switch (os.Version.Major)
    {
        case 5:
            switch (os.Version.Minor)
            {
                case 0: osText = "Windows 2000";
                    break;
                case 1: osText = "Windows XP";
                    break;
                case 2: osText = "Windows Server 2003";
                    break;
```

Example 19-2. GetOSAndServicePack method (continued)

```
                default: osText = os.ToString( );
                    break;
            }
            break;
        case 6:
            switch (os.Version.Minor)
            {
                case 0: osText = "Windows Vista";
                    break;
                case 1: osText = "Windows Server 2008";
                    break;
                default: osText = os.ToString( );
                    break;
            }
            break;
    }
    if (!string.IsNullOrEmpty(osText))
    {
        // get the text for the service pack
        string spText = os.ServicePack;
        // build the whole string
        return string.Format("{0} {1}", osText, spText);
    }
    // Unknown OS so return version
    return os.VersionString;
}
```

Discussion

Enabling your application to know the current operating system and service pack allows you to include that information in debugging reports and in the about box (if you have one) for your application. The simple knowledge of the correct operating system and service pack transmitted through your support department can save you hours in debugging time. It is well worth making available, so your support department can easily direct your clients to it in case they cannot otherwise locate it.

See Also

The "Environment.OSVersion Property" and "OperatingSystem Class" topics in the MSDN documentation.

CHAPTER 20

Numbers and Enumerations

20.0 Introduction

Simple types are value types that are a subset of the built-in types in C#, although, in fact, the types are defined as part of the .NET Framework Class Library (.NET FCL). Simple types are made up of several numeric types and a `bool` type. These numeric types consist of a decimal type (`decimal`), nine integral types (`byte`, `char`, `int`, `long`, `sbyte`, `short`, `uint`, `ulong`, `ushort`), and two floating-point types (`float`, `double`). Table 20-1 lists the simple types and their fully qualified names in the .NET Framework.

Table 20-1. The simple data types

Fully qualified name	Alias	Value range
System.Boolean	bool	true or false
System.Byte	byte	0 to 255
System.SByte	sbyte	-128 to 127
System.Char	char	0 to 65535
System.Decimal	decimal	-79,228,162,514,264,337,593,543,950,335 to 79,228,162,514,264,337,593,543,950,335
System.Double	double	-1.79769313486232e308 to 1.79769313486232e308
System.Single	float	-3.40282347E+38 to 3.40282347E+38
System.Int16	short	-32768 to 32767
System.Uint16	ushort	0 to 65535
System.Int32	int	-2,147,483,648 to 2,147,483,647
System.UInt32	uint	0 to 4,294,967,295
System.Int64	long	-9,223,372,036,854,775,808 to 9,223,372,036,854,775,807
System.UInt64	ulong	0 to 18,446,744,073,709,551,615

When dealing with floating point data types, precision can be can be more important than the range of the data values. The precision of the floating point data types is listed in Table 20-2.

Table 20-2. Floating point precision

Floating point type	Precision
System.Single (float)	7 digits
System.Double (double)	15–16 digits
System.Decimal (decimal)	28–29 digits

When trying to decide between using floats and decimals, think of the following:

- Floats were designed for scientists to represent inexact quantities over the entire range of precisions and magnitudes used in physics.
- Decimals were designed for use by ordinary humans who do math in base ten and do not require more than a handful of digits past the decimal point.

The C#-reserved words for the various data types are simply aliases for the fully qualified type name. Therefore, it does not matter whether you use the type name or the reserved word: the C# compiler will generate identical code.

It should be noted that the following types are not Common Language Specification-compliant (CLS-compliant): sbyte, ushort, uint, and ulong. They might not be supported by other .NET languages as a result of this. Enumerations implicitly inherit from System.Enum, which in turn inherits from System.ValueType. Enumerations have a single use: to describe items of a specific group. For example, the colors red, blue, and yellow could be defined by the enumeration ShapeColor; likewise, square, circle, and triangle could be defined by the enumeration Shape. These enumerations would look like the following:

```
enum ShapeColor
{
    Red, Blue, Yellow
}

enum Shape
{
    Square = 2, Circle = 4, Triangle = 6
}
```

Each item in the enumeration receives a numeric value regardless of whether you assign one or not. Since the compiler automatically adds the numbers starting with zero and incrementing by one, for each item in the enumeration, the ShapeColor enumeration previously defined would be exactly the same if it were defined in the following manner:

```
enum ShapeColor
{
```

```
    Red = 0, Blue = 1, Yellow = 2
}
```

Enumerations are good code-documenting tools. For example, it is more intuitive to write the following:

```
ShapeColor currentColor = ShapeColor.Red;
```

instead of this:

```
int currentColor = 0;
```

Either mechanism will work, but the first method is easy to read and understand, especially for a new developer taking over someone else's code. It also has the benefit of being type-safe in C#, which the use of raw ints does not provide. The CLR sees enumerations as members of their underlying types, so it is not type-safe for all languages.

20.1 Converting Between Degrees and Radians

Problem

When using the trigonometric functions of the Math class, all units are in radians. You have some angles measured in degrees and want to convert these to radians in order to use them with the members of the Math class, and some angles measured in radians that need to be in degrees.

Solution

To convert a value in degrees to radians, multiply it by math.PI/180:

```
using System;

public static double ConvertDegreesToRadians (double degrees)
{
    return  ((Math.PI / 180) * degrees);
}
```

To convert a value in radians to degrees, multiply it by 180/mathPI:

```
using System;

public static double ConvertRadiansToDegrees(double radians)
{
    return ((180 / Math.PI) * radians);
}
```

Discussion

All of the static trigonometric methods in the Math class use radians as their unit of measure for angles. It is very handy to have conversion routines to convert between radians and degrees, especially when a user is required to enter data in degrees rather than radians. After all, humans understand degrees better than radians.

The static field `Math.PI` contains the constant 3.14151265358979323846.

20.2 Using the Bitwise Complement Operator with Various Data Types

Problem

The bitwise complement operator (~) is overloaded to work directly with `int`, `uint`, `long`, `ulong`, and enumeration data types consisting of the underlying types `int`, `uint`, `long`, and `ulong`. However, you need to perform a bitwise complement operation on a different numeric data type.

Solution

To use the bitwise complement operator with any data type, you must cast the resultant value of the bitwise operation to the type you wish to work with. The following code demonstrates this technique with the byte data type:

```
byte y = 1;
byte result = (byte)~y;
```

The value assigned to `result` is 254.

Discussion

The following code shows incorrect use of the bitwise complement operator on the byte data type:

```
byte y = 1;
Console.WriteLine("~y = " + ~y);
```

This code outputs the following surprising value:

```
-2
```

Clearly, the result from performing the bitwise complement of the byte variable is incorrect; it should be 254. In fact, byte is an unsigned data type, so it cannot be equal to a negative number. If you rewrite the code as follows:

```
byte y = 1;
byte result = ~y;
```

you get a compile-time error: "Cannot implicitly convert type 'int' to 'byte.'" This error message gives some insight into why this operation does not work as expected. To fix this problem, you must explicitly cast this value to a byte before you assign it to the result variable, as shown here:

```
byte y = 1;
byte result = (byte)~y;
```

This cast is required because the bitwise operators are overloaded to operate only on int, uint, long, ulong, bool, and enumeration data types. When one of the bitwise operators is used on another data type, that data type is converted to the supported data type that is the best conversion based on overload resolution. Therefore, a byte data type is converted to an int before the bitwise complement operator is evaluated:

```
       0x01 // byte y = 1;
OxFFFFFFFE // The value 01h is converted to an int and its
           // bitwise complement is taken.
           // This bit pattern equals -2 as an int.
       OxFE // The resultant int value is cast to its original byte data type.
```

Notice that the int data type is a signed data type, unlike the byte data type. This is why you receive -2 for a result instead of the expected value 254. This conversion of the byte data type to its nearest equivalent is called *numeric promotion*. Numeric promotion also comes into play when you use differing data types with binary operators, including the bitwise binary operators.

 Numeric promotion is discussed in detail in the C# Language Specification document in section 7.2.6 (this document is available at *http://msdn2.microsoft.com/en-us/vcsharp/Aa336809.aspx*). Understanding how numeric promotion works is essential when using operators on differing data types and when using operators with a data type that is not overloaded to handle them. Knowing this can save you hours of debugging time.

20.3   Converting a Number in Another Base to Base10

Problem

You have a string containing a number in base2 (binary), base8 (octal), base10 (decimal), or base16 (hexadecimal). You need to convert this string to its equivalent integer value and display it in base10.

Solution

To convert a number in another base to base10, use the overloaded static Convert. ToInt32 method on the Convert class:

```
string base2 = "11";
string base8 = "17";
string base10 = "110";
string base16 = "11FF";

Console.WriteLine("Convert.ToInt32(base2, 2) = " +
                  Convert.ToInt32(base2, 2));

Console.WriteLine("Convert.ToInt32(base8, 8) = " +
                  Convert.ToInt32(base8, 8));
```

```
Console.WriteLine("Convert.ToInt32(base10, 10) = " +
                  Convert.ToInt32(base10, 10));

Console.WriteLine("Convert.ToInt32(base16, 16) = " +
                  Convert.ToInt32(base16, 16));
```

This code produces the following output:

```
Convert.ToInt32(base2, 2) = 3
Convert.ToInt32(base8, 8) = 15
Convert.ToInt32(base10, 10) = 110
Convert.ToInt32(base16, 16) = 4607
```

Discussion

The static `Convert.ToInt32` method has an overload that takes a string containing a number and an integer defining the base of this number. This method then converts the numeric string into an `integer`, `Console.WriteLine`, and then converts the number to base10 and displays it.

The other static methods of the `Convert` class, such as `ToByte`, `ToInt64`, and `ToInt16`, also have this same overload, which accepts a number as a string and the base in which this number is expressed. Unfortunately, these methods convert from a string value expressed in base2, base8, base10, and base16 only. They do not allow for converting a value to a string expressed in any other base types than base10. However, the `ToString` methods on the various numeric types do allow for this conversion.

See Also

The "Convert Class" and "Converting with System.Convert" topics in the MSDN documentation.

20.4 Determining Whether a String Is a Valid Number

Problem

You have a string that possibly contains a numeric value. You need to know whether this string contains a valid number.

Solution

Use the static `TryParse` method of any of the numeric types. For example, to determine whether a string contains a double, use the following method:

```
string str = "12.5";
double result = 0;
if(double.TryParse(str,
        System.Globalization.NumberStyles.Float,
        System.Globalization.NumberFormatInfo.CurrentInfo,
        out result))
```

```
        {
            // Is a double!
        }
```

Discussion

This recipe shows how to determine whether a string contains only a numeric value. The TryParse method returns true if the string contains a valid number without the exception that you will get if you use the Parse method.

See Also

The "Parse" and "TryParse" topics in the MSDN documentation.

20.5   Rounding a Floating-Point Value

Problem

You need to round a number to a whole number or to a specific number of decimal places.

Solution

To round any number to its nearest whole number, use the overloaded static Math. Round method, which takes only a single argument:

```
int x = (int)Math.Round(2.5555); // x == 3
```

If you need to round a floating-point value to a specific number of decimal places, use the overloaded static Math.Round method, which takes two arguments:

```
decimal x = Math.Round(2.5555, 2); // x == 2.56
```

Discussion

The Round method is easy to use; however, you need to be aware of how the rounding operation works. The Round method follows the IEEE Standard 754, section 4 standard. This means that if the number being rounded is halfway between two numbers, the Round operation will always round to the even number. An example will show what this means to you:

```
decimal x = Math.Round(1.5); // x == 2
decimal y = Math.Round(2.5); // y == 2
```

Notice that 1.5 is rounded up to the nearest even whole number and 2.5 is rounded down to the nearest even whole number. Keep this in mind when using the Round method.

This method is known as Banker's Rounding; it was invented because it introduces less bias when rounding large sets of numbers which often have halves in them—as sets containing currencies often do.

See Also

The "Math Class" topic in the MSDN documentation.

20.6 Choosing a Rounding Algorithm

Problem

The Math.Round method will round the value 1.5 to 2; however, the value 2.5 will also be rounded to 2 using this method. You may always want to round to the greater number in this type of situation (e.g., round 2.5 to 3 instead of 2). Conversely, you might want to always round to the lesser number (e.g., round 1.5 to 1).

Solution

Use the static Math.Floor method to always round up when a value is halfway between two whole numbers:

```
public static double RoundUp(double valueToRound)
{
    return Math.Floor(valueToRound + 0.5);
}
```

Use the following technique to always round down when a value is halfway between two whole numbers:

```
public static double RoundDown(double valueToRound)
{
    double floorValue = Math.Floor(valueToRound);
    if ((valueToRound - floorValue) > .5)
    {
        return floorValue + 1;
    }
    else
    {
        return floorValue;
    }
}
```

Discussion

The static Math.Round method rounds to the nearest even number (see Recipe 1.8 for more information). However, there are some times that you do not want to round a number in this manner. The static Math.Floor method can be used to allow for different manners of rounding.

The methods used to round numbers in this recipe do not round to a specific number of decimal points; rather, they round to the nearest whole number.

See Also

The "Math Class" topic in the MSDN documentation.

20.7   Converting Between Temperature Scales

Problem

You have a temperature reading measured in one temperature scale and need to convert it to another scale.

Solution

To convert between Celsius, Fahrenheit, and Kelvin, use the following methods:

```
public static double CelsiusToFahrenheit(double celsius)
{
    return (1.8 * celsius) + 32;
}

public static double FahrenheitToCelsius(double fahrenheit)
{
    return 1.8 * (fahrenheit - 32);
}

public static double CelsiusToKelvin(double celsius)
{
    return celsius + 273;
}

public static double KelvinToCelsius(double kelvin)
{
    return kelvin - 273;
}

public static double FahrenheitToKelvin(double fahrenheit)
{
    return CelsiusToKelvin(FahrenheitToCelsius(fahrenheit));
}

public static double KelvinToFahrenheit(double kelvin)
{
    return CelsiusToFahrenheit(KelvinToCelsius(kelvin));
}
```

Discussion

There are three main temperature scales that are in use today: Celsius, Fahrenheit, and Kelvin. The *Celsius* scale (°C) is used in most of the world to measure air temperatures. In the United States, the *Fahrenheit* scale (°F) is used to measure temperatures at or near the surface, while the Celsius scale is used to measure upper air temperatures. The *Kelvin* (K) scale is used by scientists and for astronomical temperatures.

 All three temperature scales are related to each other through the "triple point of water." The triple point of water is the temperature at which water vapor, liquid water, and ice can coexist simultaneously. The triple point occurs at 0.01 °C (273.16 K or 32.02 °F).

20.8   Safely Performing a Narrowing Numeric Cast

Problem

You need to cast a value from a larger value to a smaller one, while gracefully handling conditions that result in a loss of information. For example, casting a long to an int results in a loss of information only if the long data type is greater than int. MaxSize.

Solution

The simplest way to do this check is to use the checked keyword. The following extension method accepts two long data types and attempts to add them together. The result is stuffed into an int data type. If an overflow condition exists, the OverflowException is thrown:

```
using System;

public static class NumbersEnums
{
    public static void AddChecked(this long lhs, long rhs)
    {
        int result = checked((int)(lhs + rhs));
    }
}
```

This is the simplest method. However, if you do not want the overhead of throwing an exception and having to wrap a lot of code in try/catch blocks to handle the overflow condition, you can use the MaxValue and MinValue fields of each type. A check using these fields can be done prior to the conversion to insure that no loss of information occurs. If this does occur, the code can inform the application that this cast will cause a loss of information. You can use the following conditional statement to determine whether sourceValue can be cast to a short without losing any information:

```
// Our two variables are declared and initialized.
int sourceValue = 34000;
short destinationValue = 0;

// Determine if sourceValue will lose information in a cast to a short.
if (sourceValue <= short.MaxValue && sourceValue >= short.MinValue)
{
    destinationValue = (short)sourceValue;
}
else
{
    // Inform the application that a loss of information will occur.
}
```

Discussion

A *narrowing conversion* occurs when a larger type is cast down to a smaller type. For instance, consider casting a value of type Int32 to a value of type Int16. If the Int32 value is smaller than or equal to the Int16.MaxValue field and the Int32 value is higher than or equal to the Int16.MinValue field, the cast will occur without error or loss of information. Loss of information occurs when the Int32 value is larger than the Int16.MaxValue field or the Int32 value is lower than the Int16.MinValue field. In either of these cases, the most significant bits of the Int32 value are truncated and discarded, changing the value after the cast.

If a loss of information occurs in an unchecked context, it will occur silently without the application noticing. This problem can cause some very insidious bugs that are hard to track down. To prevent this, check the value to be converted to determine whether it is within the lower and upper bounds of the type that it will be cast to. If the value is outside these bounds, then code can be written to handle this situation. This code could force the cast not to occur and/or possibly inform the application of the casting problem. This solution can aid in the prevention of hard-to-find arithmetic bugs creeping into your applications.

You should understand that both techniques shown in the Solution section are valid. However, the technique you use will depend on whether you expect to hit the overflow case on a regular basis or only occasionally. If you expect to hit the overflow case quite often, you might want to choose the second technique of manually testing the numeric value. Otherwise, it might be easier to use the checked keyword, as in the first technique.

In C#, code can run in either a *checked* or *unchecked* context; by default, the code runs in an unchecked context. In a checked context, any arithmetic and conversions involving integral types are examined to determine whether an overflow condition exists. If so, an `OverflowException` is thrown. In an unchecked context, no `OverflowException` will be thrown when an overflow condition exists.

A checked context can be set up by using the `/checked{+}` compiler switch by setting the Check for Arithmetic Overflow/Underflow project property to `true`, or by using the `checked` keyword. An unchecked context can be set up using the `/checked-` compiler switch by setting the Check for Arithmetic Overflow/Underflow project property to `false` or by using the `unchecked` keyword.

You should be aware of the following when performing a conversion:

- Casting from a `float`, `double`, or `decimal` type to an integral type results in the truncation of the fractional portion of this number. Furthermore, if the integral portion of the number exceeds `MaxValue` for the target type, the result will be undefined unless the conversion is done in a `checked` context, in which case it will trigger an `OverflowException`.

- Casting from a `float` or `double` to a `decimal` results in the `float` or `double` being rounded to 28 decimal places.

- Casting from a `double` to a `float` results in the `double` being rounded to the nearest `float` value.

- Casting from a `decimal` to a `float` or `double` results in the `decimal` being rounded to the resulting type (`float` or `double`).

- Casting from an `int`, `uint`, or `long` to a `float` could result in the loss of precision, but never magnitude.

- Casting from a `long` to a `double` could result in the loss of precision, but never magnitude.

See Also

The "Checked Keyword" and "Checked and Unchecked" topics in the MSDN documentation.

20.9   Displaying an Enumeration Value as a String

Problem

You need to display the textual or numeric value of an enumeration member.

Solution

To display an enumeration value as a string, use the ToString method that each enumeration member inherits from System.Enum.

Using the following ValidShape enumeration type as an example, you can obtain the textual and numeric values so that you can display them:

```
enum ValidShape
{
    Square, Circle, Cylinder, Octagon
}
```

Using the ToString method of the ValidShape enumeration type, you can derive the value of a specific ValidShape enumeration value directly:

```
Console.WriteLine(ValidShape.Circle.ToString());
Console.WriteLine(ValidShape.Circle.ToString("G"));
Console.WriteLine(ValidShape.Circle.ToString("D"));
Console.WriteLine(ValidShape.Circle.ToString("F"));
Console.WriteLine(ValidShape.Circle.ToString("X"));
```

This generates the following output:

```
Circle
Circle
1
Circle
00000001
```

If you are working with a variable of type ValidShape, the enumeration values can be derived in the same manner:

```
ValidShape shapeStyle = ValidShape.Cylinder;

Console.WriteLine(shapeStyle.ToString());
Console.WriteLine(shapeStyle.ToString("G"));
Console.WriteLine(shapeStyle.ToString("D"));
Console.WriteLine(shapeStyle.ToString("F"));
Console.WriteLine(shapeStyle.ToString("X"));
```

The following is displayed:

```
Cylinder
Cylinder
2
Cylinder
00000002
```

Discussion

Deriving the textual or numeric representation of an enumeration value is a simple matter of using the ToString instance method on the Enum type. This method can accept a character indicating the type of formatting to place on the enumeration value. The character can be one of the following: G, g, D, d, X, x, F, or f. See Table 20-3 for a description of these formatting types.

Table 20-3. Formatting types

Formatting type	Name	Description
G or g	(General)	Displays the string representation of the enumeration value.
F or f	(Flag)	Displays the string representation of the enumeration value. The enumeration is treated as if it were a bit field.
D or d	(Decimal)	Displays decimal equivalent of the enumeration.
X or x	(Hexadecimal)	Displays hexadecimal equivalent of the enumeration.

When printing out the values of an enumeration with the Flags attribute, the information displayed takes into account that more than one of the enumeration values may have been ORed together. The output will be all of the enumerations printed out as strings separated by commas or as the ORed numeric value, depending on the formatting chosen. For example, consider if the Flags attribute was placed on the IceCreamToppings enumeration as follows:

```
[Flags]
public enum IceCreamToppings
{
    HotFudge = 1,
    Cherry = 2,
    WhippedCream = 4
}
```

Now if you use the same pattern with this enumeration as the previous ones for displaying the output using the different formatting types like this:

```
IceCreamToppings toppings =
    IceCreamToppings.HotFudge | IceCreamToppings.WhippedCream;

Console.WriteLine(toppings.ToString());
Console.WriteLine(toppings.ToString("G"));
Console.WriteLine(toppings.ToString("D"));
Console.WriteLine(toppings.ToString("F"));
Console.WriteLine(toppings.ToString("X"));
```

you will see the following output:

```
HotFudge, WhippedCream
HotFudge, WhippedCream
5
HotFudge, WhippedCream
00000005
```

This provides a flexible way of extracting the flags that you are currently using on an enumeration type.

See Also

The "Enum.ToString Method" and the "Enumeration Format Strings" topics in the MSDN documentation.

20.10 Converting Plain Text to an Equivalent Enumeration Value

Problem

You have the textual value of an enumeration element, possibly from a database or text file. This textual value needs to be converted to a usable enumeration type.

Solution

The static Parse method on the Enum class allows the textual value of an enumeration element to be converted to a usable enumeration value. For example:

```
try
{
    Language proj1Language = (Language)Enum.Parse(typeof(Language),
                             "VBNET");
    Language proj2Language = (Language)Enum.Parse(typeof(Language),
                             "UnDefined");
}
catch (ArgumentException e)
{
    // Handle an invalid text value here
    //(such as the "UnDefined" string)
}
```

where the Language enumeration is defined as:

```
enum Language
{
    Other = 0, CSharp = 1, VBNET = 2, VB6 = 3
}
```

Discussion

The static Enum.Parse method converts text to a specific enumeration value. This technique is useful when a user is presented a list of values, with each value defined in an enumeration. When the user selects an item from this list, the text chosen can be easily converted from its string representation to its equivalent enumeration value using Enum.Parse. This method returns an object, which must then be cast to the target enum type in order to use it.

In addition to passing `Enum.Parse` a single enumeration value as a string, you can also pass the enumeration value as its corresponding numeric value. For example, consider the following line:

```
Language proj1Language = (Language)Enum.Parse(typeof(Language),
                            "VBNET");
```

You can rewrite this as follows to perform the exact same action:

```
Language proj1Language = (Language)Enum.Parse(typeof(Language), "2");
```

This is assuming that the `Language.VBNET` enumeration value is equal to 2.

Another interesting feature of the `Parse` method is that it can accept a comma-delimited list of enumeration names or values and then logically OR them together. The following example creates an enumeration with the languages `VBNET` and `CSharp` ORed together:

```
Language proj1Language = (Language)Enum.Parse(typeof(Language),
                        "CSharp, VBNET");
```

Each individual element of the comma-delimited list is trimmed of any whitespace, so it does not matter if you add any whitespace between each item in this list.

See Also

The "Enum.Parse Method" topic in the MSDN documentation.

20.11 Testing for a Valid Enumeration Value

Problem

When you pass a numeric value to a method that accepts an enumeration type, it is possible to pass a value that does not exist in the enumeration. You want to perform a test before using this numeric value to determine if it is indeed one of the ones defined in this enumeration type.

Solution

To prevent this problem, test for the specific enumeration values that you allow for the enumeration-type parameter using a `switch` statement to list the values.

Using the following `Language` enumeration:

```
enum Language
{
    Other = 0, CSharp = 1, VBNET = 2, VB6 = 3
}
```

Suppose you have a method that accepts the `Language` enumeration, such as the following method:

```csharp
public void HandleEnum(Language language)
{
    // Use language here...
}
```

You need a method to define the enumeration values you can accept in HandleEnum. The CheckLanguageEnumValue method shown here does that:

```csharp
public static bool CheckLanguageEnumValue(Language language)
{
    switch (language)
    {
        // All valid types for the enum listed here
        // This means only the ones we specify are valid.
        // Not any enum value for this enum
        case Language.CSharp:
        case Language.Other:
        case Language.VB6:
        case Language.VBNET:
            break;
        default:
        Debug.Assert(false, language +
            " is not a valid enumeration value to pass.");
        return false;
    }
    return true;
}
```

Discussion

Although the Enum class contains the static IsDefined method, it should not be used. IsDefined uses reflection internally, which incurs a performance penalty. Also, versioning of the enumeration is not handled well. Consider the scenario in which you add the value ManagedCPlusPlus to the Languages enum in the next version of your software. If IsDefined is used to check the argument here, it will allow MgdCpp as a valid value, since it is defined in the enumeration, even though the code for which you are validating the parameter is not designed to handle it. By being specific with the switch statement shown in CheckLanguageEnumValue, you reject the MgdCpp value, and the code does not try to run in an invalid context. This, after all, is what you were after in the first place.

The enumeration check should always be used whenever the method is visible to external objects. An external object can invoke methods with public visibility, so any enumerated value passed in to this method should be screened before it is actually used.

Methods with private visibility may not need this extra level of protection. Use your own judgment on whether to use the CheckLanguageEnumValue method to evaluate enumeration values passed in to private methods.

The `HandleEnum` method can be called in several different ways. Three of these are shown here:

```
HandleEnum(Language.CSharp)
HandleEnum((Language)1)
HandleEnum((Language)someVar) // Where someVar is an int type
```

Any of these method calls is valid. Unfortunately, the following method calls are also valid:

```
HandleEnum((Language)100)

int someVar = 100;
HandleEnum((Language)someVar)
```

These method calls will also compile without errors, but odd behavior will result if the code in `HandleEnum` tries to use the value passed in to it (in this case, the value 100). In many cases, an exception will not even be thrown; `HandleEnum` just receives the value 100 as an argument, as if it were a legitimate value of the `Language` enumeration.

The `CheckLanguageEnumValue` method prevents this from happening by screening the argument for valid `Language` enumeration values. The following code shows the modified body of the `HandleEnum` method:

```
public void HandleEnum(Language language)
{
    if (CheckLanguageEnumValue(language))
    {
        // Use language here...
    }
    else
    {
        // Deal with the invalid language value here...
    }
}
```

See Also

To test for a valid enumeration within an enumeration marked with the `Flags` attribute, see Recipe 20.12.

20.12 Testing for a Valid Enumeration of Flags

Problem

You need to determine if a given value is a valid enumeration value or a valid combination of enumeration values (i.e., bit flags ORed together in an enumeration marked with the `Flags` attribute).

Solution

To make it possible to test whether a value is a valid enumeration value or some combination of valid enumeration values, add an `All` member to the existing enumeration equal to all the members of the enumeration ORed together. Then, use the `HandleFlagsEnum` method to do the test.

There is a problem with using `Enum.IsDefined` with an enumeration marked with the `Flags` attribute. Consider if the `IceCreamToppings` enumeration was written as follows:

```
[Flags]
public enum IceCreamToppings
{
    HotFudge = 1,
    Cherry = 2,
    WhippedCream = 4
}
```

Valid values for `IceCreamToppings` are the set of numbers {1, 2, 3, 4, 5, 6, 7}. However, the values 3, 5, 6, and 7 are not explicitly represented in this enumeration. The value 3 is equal to the `HotFudge` and `Cherry` enumeration members ORed together, and the value 7 is equal to all of the enumeration members ORed together. For the values 3, 5, 6, and 7, the `Enum.IsDefined` method will return `false`, indicating that these are not valid values, when in fact they are. You need a way to determine if a correct set of flags has been passed into a method.

To fix this problem, you can add a new member to the `Language` enumeration to define all values for which the `Language` enumeration is valid. In this case, the `Language` enumeration would be rewritten as:

```
[Flags]
public enum IceCreamToppings
{
    HotFudge = 1,
    Cherry = 2,
    WhippedCream = 4,
    All = (HotFudge | Cherry | WhippedCream)
}
```

The new `All` enumeration member is equal to all other `IceCreamToppings` members ORed together. Now, when you want to validate a `IceCreamToppings` flag, all you have to do is the following:

```
public static bool ValidateFlagsEnum(IceCreamToppings topping)
{
    return ((topping>0) && ((topping & IceCreamToppings.All) == topping));
}
```

Discussion

If you want to use the ValidateFlagsEnum method with existing code, all that is required is to add an All member to the existing enumeration. The All member should be equal to all the members of the enumeration ORed together.

The ValidateFlagsEnum method then uses this All member to determine if an enumeration value is valid. This is accomplished by ANDing the topping value with IceCreamToppings.All and then verifying that the result equals the original topping parameter.

This method can also be overloaded to handle the underlying type of the enumeration as well (in this case, the underlying type of the IceCreamToppings enumeration is an integer). The following code determines if an integer variable contains a valid IceCreamToppings enumeration value:

```
public static bool ValidateFlagsEnum(int topping)
{
    return ((topping>0) && ((topping & (int)IceCreamToppings.All) == topping));
}
```

The overloaded ValidateFlagsEnum methods return true if the topping parameter is valid and false otherwise.

See Also

To test for a valid enumeration within an enumeration not marked with the Flags attribute, see Recipe 20.11.

20.13 Using Enumerated Members in a Bit Mask

Problem

An enumeration of values is needed to act as bit flags that can be ORed together to create a combination of values (flags) in the enumeration.

Solution

Mark the enumeration with the Flags attribute:

```
[Flags]
public enum RecycleItems
{
    None          = 0x00,
    Glass         = 0x01,
    AluminumCans  = 0x02,
    MixedPaper    = 0x04,
    Newspaper     = 0x08
}
```

Combining elements of this enumeration is a simple matter of using the bitwise OR operator (|). For example:

```
RecycleItems items = RecycleItems.Glass | RecycleItems.Newspaper;
```

Discussion

Adding the Flags attribute to an enumeration marks this enumeration as individual bit flags that can be ORed together. Using an enumeration of flags is no different than using a regular enumeration type. It should be noted that failing to mark an enumeration with the Flags attribute will not generate an exception or a compile-time error, even if the enumeration values are used as bit flags.

The addition of the Flags attribute provides you with two benefits. First, if the Flags attribute is placed on an enumeration, the ToString and ToString("G") methods return a string consisting of the name of the constant(s) separated by commas. Otherwise, these two methods return the numeric representation of the enumeration value. Note that the ToString("F") method returns a string consisting of the name of the constant(s) separated by commas, regardless of whether this enumeration is marked with the Flags attribute. For an indication of why this works in this manner, see the "F" formatting type in Table 20-3 in Recipe 20.9.

The second benefit is that when you examine the code and encounter an enumeration, you can better determine the developer's intention for this enumeration. If the developer explicitly defined this as containing bit flags (with the Flags attribute), you can use it as such.

An enumeration tagged with the Flags attribute can be viewed as a single value or as one or more values combined into a single enumeration value. If you need to accept multiple languages at a single time, you can write the following code:

```
RecycleItems items = RecycleItems.Glass | RecycleItems.Newspaper;
```

The variable items is now equal to the bit values of the two enumeration values ORed together. These values ORed together will equal 3, as shown here:

```
RecycleItems.Glass          0001
RecycleItems.AluminumCans   0010
ORed bit values             0011
```

The enumeration values were converted to binary and ORed together to get the binary value 0011 or 3 in base10. The compiler views this value both as two individual enumeration values (RecycleItems.Glass and RecycleItems.AluminumCans) ORed together or as a single value (3).

To determine if a single flag has been turned on in an enumeration variable, use the bitwise AND (&) operator, as follows:

```
RecycleItems items = RecycleItems.Glass | RecycleItems.Newspaper;
if((items & RecycleItems.Glass) == RecycleItems.Glass)
    Console.WriteLine("The enum contains the C# enumeration value");
```

```
        else
            Console.WriteLine("The enum does NOT contain the C# value");
```

This code will display the text "The enum contains the C# enumeration value." The ANDing of these two values either will produce zero if the variable items does not contain the value RecycleItems.Glass, or it will produce the value RecycleItems. Glass if items contains this enumeration value. Basically, ANDing these two values looks like this in binary:

```
RecycleItems.Glass | RecycleItems.AluminumCans 0011
RecycleItems.Glass                              0001
ANDed bit values                                0001
```

This is dealt with in more detail in Recipe 20.14.

In some cases, the enumeration can grow quite large. You can add many other recyclable items to this enumeration, as shown here:

```
[Flags]
public enum RecycleItems
{
    None            = 0x00,
    Glass           = 0x01,
    AluminumCans    = 0x02,
    MixedPaper      = 0x04,
    Newspaper       = 0x08,
    TinCans         = 0x10,
    Cardboard       = 0x20,
    ClearPlastic    = 0x40,
}
```

When a RecycleItems enumeration value is needed to represent all recyclable items, you would have to OR together each value of this enumeration:

```
RecycleItems items = RecycleItems.Glass | RecycleItems.AluminumCans |
                     RecycleItems.MixedPaper;
```

Instead of doing this, you can simply add a new value to this enumeration that includes all recyclable items as follows:

```
[Flags]
public enum RecycleItems
{
    None            = 0x00,
    Glass           = 0x01,
    AluminumCans    = 0x02,
    MixedPaper      = 0x04,
    Newspaper       = 0x08,
    TinCans         = 0x10,
    Cardboard       = 0x20,
    ClearPlastic    = 0x40,
    All = (None | Glass | AluminumCans | MixedPaper | Newspaper | TinCans |
          Cardboard | ClearPlastic)
}
```

Now there is a single enumeration value, All, that encompasses every value of this enumeration. Notice that there are two methods of creating the All enumeration value. The second method is much easier to read. Regardless of which method you use, if individual language elements of the enumeration are added or deleted, you will have to modify the All value accordingly.

 A None value should be provided for all enums even where "none of the above" does not make sense, because it is always legal to assign literal zero to an enum, and because enum variables, which begin their lives as assigned to their default values, start as zero.

Similarly, you can also add values to capture specific subsets of enumeration values as follows:

```
[Flags]
enum Language
{
    CSharp = 0x0001, VBNET = 0x0002, VB6 = 0x0004, Cpp = 0x0008,
    CobolNET = 0x000F, FortranNET = 0x0010, JSharp = 0x0020,
    MSIL = 0x0080,
    All = (CSharp | VBNET | VB6 | Cpp | FortranNET | Jsharp | MSIL),
    VBOnly = (VBNET | VB6),
    NonVB = (CSharp | Cpp | FortranNET | Jsharp | MSIL)
}
```

Now you have two extra members in the enumerations, one that encompasses VB-only languages (Languages.VBNET and Languages.VB6) and one that encompasses non-VB languages.

20.14 Determining Whether One or More Enumeration Flags Are Set

Problem

You need to determine if a variable of an enumeration type, consisting of bit flags, contains one or more specific flags. For example, given the following enumeration Language:

```
[Flags]
enum Language
{
    CSharp = 0x0001, VBNET = 0x0002, VB6 = 0x0004, Cpp = 0x0008
}
```

determine, using Boolean logic, if the variable lang in the following line of code contains a language such as Language.CSharp and/or Language.Cpp:

```
Language lang = Language.CSharp | Language.VBNET;
```

Solution

To determine if a variable contains a single bit flag that is set, use the following conditional:

```
if((lang & Language.CSharp) == Language.CSharp)
{
    // Lang contains at least Language.CSharp.
}
```

To determine if a variable exclusively contains a single bit flag that is set, use the following conditional:

```
if(lang == Language.CSharp)
{
    // lang contains only the Language.CSharp.
}
```

To determine if a variable contains a set of bit flags that are all set, use the following conditional:

```
if((lang & (Language.CSharp | Language.VBNET)) ==
   (Language.CSharp | Language.VBNET))
{
    // lang contains at least Language.CSharp and Language.VBNET.
}
```

To determine if a variable exclusively contains a set of bit flags that are all set, use the following conditional:

```
if((lang | (Language.CSharp | Language.VBNET)) ==
   (Language.CSharp | Language.VBNET))
{
    // lang contains only the Language.CSharp and Language.VBNET.
}
```

Discussion

When enumerations are used as bit flags and are marked with the Flags attribute, they usually will require some kind of conditional testing to be performed. This testing necessitates the use of the bitwise AND (&) and OR (|) operators.

Testing for a variable having a specific bit flag set is done with the following conditional statement:

```
if((lang & Language.CSharp) == Language.CSharp)
```

where lang is of the Language enumeration type.

The & operator is used with a bit mask to determine if a bit is set to 1. The result of ANDing two bits is 1 only when both bits are 1; otherwise, the result is 0. You can use this operation to determine if a specific bit flag is set to a 1 in the number containing the individual bit flags. If you AND the variable lang with the specific bit flag you are testing for (in this case, Language.CSharp), you can extract that single specific bit flag. The expression (lang & Language.CSharp) is solved in the following manner if lang is equal to Language.CSharp:

```
Language.CSharp   0001
lang              0001
ANDed bit values  0001
```

If lang is equal to another value, such as Language.VBNET, the expression is solved in the following manner:

```
Language.CSharp   0001
lang              0010
ANDed bit values  0000
```

Notice that ANDing the bits together returns the value Language.CSharp in the first expression and 0x0000 in the second expression. Comparing this result to the value you are looking for (Language.CSharp) tells you whether that specific bit was turned on.

This method is great for checking specific bits, but what if you want to know whether only one specific bit is turned on (and all other bits turned off) or off (and all other bits turned on)? To test if only the Language.CSharp bit is turned on in the variable lang, you can use the following conditional statement:

```
if(lang == Language.CSharp)
```

Consider if the variable lang contained only the value Language.CSharp. The expression using the OR operator would look like this:

```
lang = Language.CSharp;
if ((lang != 0) &&(Language.CSharp == (lang | Language.CSharp)))
{
    // CSharp is found using OR logic.
}

Language.CSharp 0001
lang 0001
ORed bit values 0001
```

Now, add a language value or two to the variable lang and perform the same operation on lang:

```
lang = Language.CSharp | Language.VB6 | Language.Cpp;
if ((lang != 0) &&(Language.CSharp == (lang | Language.CSharp)))
{
    // CSharp is found using OR logic.
}

Language.CSharp 0001
lang 1101
ORed bit values 1101
```

The first expression results in the same value as you are testing against. The second expression results in a much larger value than Language.CSharp. This indicates that the variable lang in the first expression contains only the value Language.CSharp, whereas the second expression contains other languages besides Language.CSharp (and may not contain Language.CSharp at all).

Using the OR version of this formula, you can test multiple bits to determine if they are both on and all other bits are off. This is done in the following conditional statement:

```
if((lang != 0) && ((lang | (Language.CSharp | Language.VBNET)) ==
    (Language.CSharp | Language.VBNET)))
```

Notice that to test for more than one language you simply OR the language values together. By switching the first | operator to an & operator, you can determine if at least these bits are turned on. This is done in the following conditional statement:

```
if((lang != 0) && ((lang & (Language.CSharp | Language.VBNET)) ==
    (Language.CSharp | Language.VBNET)))
```

When testing for multiple enumeration values, it may be beneficial to add a value to your enumeration, which ORs together all the values you want to test for. If you wanted to test for all languages except Language.CSharp, your conditional statement(s) would grow quite large and unwieldy. To fix this, you add a value to the Language enumeration that ORs together all languages except Language.CSharp. The new enumeration looks like this:

```
[Flags]
enum Language
{
    CSharp = 0x0001, VBNET = 0x0002, VB6 = 0x0004, Cpp = 0x0008,
    AllLanguagesExceptCSharp = VBNET | VB6 | Cpp
}
```

and your conditional statement might look similar to the following:

```
if((lang != 0) && (lang | Language.AllLanguagesExceptCSharp) ==
    Language. AllLanguagesExceptCSharp)
```

This is quite a bit smaller, easier to manage, and easier to read.

Use the AND operator when testing if one or more bits are set to 1.
Use the OR operator when testing if one or more bits are set to 0.

20.15 Determining the Integral Part of a Decimal or Double

Problem

You need to find the integer portion of a decimal or double number.

Solution

You can find the integer portion of a decimal or double by truncating it to the whole number closest to zero. To do so, use the overloaded static System.Math.Truncate method, which takes either a decimal or a double as an argument and returns the same type:

```
decimal pi = (decimal)System.Math.PI;
decimal decRet = System.Math.Truncate(pi); // decRet = 3

double trouble = 5.555;
double dblRet = System.Math.Truncate(trouble);
```

Discussion

The Truncate method helps to "round" out the mathematical capabilities of the Framework. The Truncate method has the net effect of simply dropping the fractional portion of the number and returning the integral part. Once floating-point numbers get over a certain size, they do not actually have a fractional part, but have only an approximate representation of their integer portion.

See Also

The "System.Math.Truncate Method" topic in the MSDN documentation.

Index

Symbols

- character, 80–82, 112, 390
$ character, 391, 392
& bitwise AND operator, 82–85, 813,
    816–818
&& operator, 82–85
* operator, 80–82
*= operator, 80–82
+ character, 80–82, 390, 501
+= operator, 80–82
, (comma), 63, 572
/ character, 80–82, 112
/= operator, 80–82
: (colon), 63
; character, 468, 469
-= operator, 80–82
== operator, 87
=> operator, 345
? type modifier, 158
?: operator, 82–85
\ character, 113
^ character, 113, 392
{ } (curly braces), 348
| bitwise OR operator, 82–85, 813, 816–818
|| operator, 82–85
~ bitwise complement operator, 193, 796,
    797

A

Abrams, Brad, 124
access control
    across data repositories, 16–19
    changing privileges, 693–696

    local variable information, 512–514
    order of XML data, 548–552
    read-mostly, 757–769
    runtime settings, 540
    semaphores and, 734–738
    tables and, 18
    thread-safe, 719–725
    types in assemblies, 651–661
Access Control Entries (ACE), 692, 693
accessor functions, 719–725
ACE (Access Control Entries), 692, 693
Action<T> delegate, 203, 364
actions (see events)
Activator class, 510
addition operator, 80–82
AddNode method, 429
AddProxyInfoToRequest method, 526
AddUniqueNode method, 429
ADO.NET
    Command object, 18, 24
    Connection object, 18, 24
    LINQ to ADO.NET, 1, 24
    LINQ to Entities, 1, 2, 24
algorithms
    calculated hash, 398
    contained object cache, 396
    CryptoHash method, 396, 397
    DES, 669
    DSA, 670
    folding hash, 395
    Rijndael, 663, 665–670
    rounding, 800
    RSA, 670
    SHA-256, 672–676

We'd like to hear your suggestions for improving our indexes. Send email to *index@oreilly.com*.

binary data
    decoding base64, 54–55, 675
    encoding as base64, 53–54
    encoding base64, 679
binary functions, 364
binary predicates, 364
binary trees, 418–432
BinaryFormatter class, 4
BinaryMessageFormatter class, 781, 782
BinaryPredicate<T> delegate, 364
BinaryReader class, 648
BinarySearchCountAll method, 183, 185
BinarySearchGetall method, 185–188
BinaryTree<T> class
    AddNode method, 424
    constructors and, 424
    creating binary trees, 418–432
    overview, 429
    Print method, 424
    Root property, 424
    SearchDepthFirst method, 424
    solution code example, 425–428
    TreeSize property, 424
BinaryTreeNode<T> class
    AddNode method, 425
    AddUniqueNode method, 425
    Children property, 425
    constructors, 425
    DepthFirstSearch method, 425
    GetValue method, 425
    Left property, 425
    nodeValue property, 429
    overview, 429
    PrintDepthFirst method, 425
    RemoveLeftNode method, 425
    RemoveRightNode method, 425
    Right property, 425
    solution code example, 425–428
BinaryWriter class, 648
bit masks, enumerations in, 812–815
bitmap files, 53–55
bitwise operators
    AND operator, 82–85, 813, 816–818
    complement operator, 193, 796, 797
    OR operator, 82–85, 813, 816–818
bmpAsString string, 54
Boolean (bool) data type
    bitwise complement operator, 797
    calculated hash, 398
    converting, 91, 93, 95
    converting strings to, 59
    FalseString property, 61

listed, 793
Parse method support, 60
structures and, 69
TrueString property, 61
Boolean logic
    Boolean theorems, 88–91
    error-free, 85–88
    overloading operators and, 82–85
    setting bit flags, 815–818
BooleanSwitch class
    configuration files and, 287
    Enabled property, 287, 289
    tracing and, 289
box command, 134
boxing operations
    as operator and, 98
    casting operator and, 98
    defined, 70
    determining occurrences, 133–136
    generics and, 138, 144
    structures and, 69
break statement, 222
browsers (see web browsers)
BuildManager class, 534
business entities, adding hooks, 237–239
Byte (byte) data type
    bitwise complement operator, 796, 797
    converting, 91, 93, 95, 96
    listed, 793
    Parse method support, 60
byte[]
    converting to strings, 56–57
    decoding strings, 54–55
    encoding binary data, 53–54
    passing strings to methods, 57–59
    Unicode encoding and, 713

C

C# language
    automatic properties, 142, 156
    closures, 356–361
    command-line format, 112
    functionality, xvii
    web site resources, xvii
cache
    performance and, 541–543
    tying database tables to, 530–531
CacheDependency class, 531
calculated hash, 398
CallSecureFunctionSafelyAndEfficiently
        function, 683, 684
carriage-return character, 383, 578

P

About the Authors

Jay Hilyard has been developing Windows applications for more than 15 years and for .NET for more than 7 of those. He has published numerous articles in *MSDN Magazine*, and he currently works on the New Product Team at Newmarket International in Portsmouth, New Hampshire.

Stephen Teilhet has been working with the .NET platform since the pre-alpha version of the .NET 1.0 Framework was being developed by Microsoft. Currently, he works for Ounce Labs, enhancing their static security code analysis tool to find vulnerabilities in several languages, including C# and Visual Basic.

Colophon

The animal on the cover of *C# 3.0 Cookbook*, Third Edition, is a garter snake (*Thamnophis sirtalis*). Named because their longitudinal stripes resemble those on garters once used to hold up men's socks, garter snakes are easily identified by their distinctive stripes: a narrow stripe down the middle of the back with a broad stripe on each side of it. Color and pattern variations enable them to blend into their native environments, helping them evade predators. They are the most common snake in North America and the only species of snake found in Alaska.

Garter snakes have keeled scales—one or more ridges down the central axis of the scales—giving them a rough texture and lackluster appearance. Adult garter snakes generally range in length between 46 and 130 centimeters (one and a half feet to over four feet). Females are usually larger than males, with shorter tails and a bulge where the body and tail meet.

Female garters are ovoviviparous, meaning they deliver "live" young that have gestated in soft eggs. Upon delivery, most of the eggs and mucous membranes have broken, which makes their births appear live. Occasionally, a baby will be born still inside its soft shell. A female will usually deliver 10 to 40 babies: the largest recorded number of live babies birthed by a garter snake is 98. Once emerging from their mothers, baby garters are completely independent and must begin fending for themselves. During this time they are most susceptible to predation, and over half of all baby garters die before they are one year old.

Garter snakes are one of the few animals able to eat toads, newts, and other amphibians with strong chemical defenses. Although diets vary depending on their environments, garter snakes mostly eat earthworms and amphibians; however, they occasionally dine on baby birds, fish, and small rodents. Garter snakes have toxic saliva (harmless to humans), which they use to stun or kill their prey before swallowing them whole.

The cover image is from a 19th-century engraving from the Dover Pictorial Archive. The cover font is Adobe ITC Garamond. The text font is Linotype Birka; the heading font is Adobe Myriad Condensed; and the code font is LucasFont's TheSans Mono Condensed.

Try the online edition
free for 45 days

Get the information you need when you need it, with Safari Books Online. Safari Books Online contains the complete version of the print book in your hands plus thousands of titles from the best technical publishers, with sample code ready to cut and paste into your applications.

Safari is designed for people in a hurry to get the answers they need so they can get the job done. You can find what you need in the morning, and put it to work in the afternoon. As simple as cut, paste, and program.

To try out Safari and the online edition of the above title FREE for 45 days, go to www.oreilly.com/go/safarienabled and enter the coupon code GDKLRFA.

To see the complete Safari Library visit:
safari.oreilly.com

70502

Related Titles from O'Reilly

.NET and C#

ADO.NET Cookbook

ADO.NET 3.5 Cookbook, *2nd Edition*

ASP.NET 2.0 Cookbook, *2nd Edition*

ASP.NET 2.0: A Developer's Notebook

Building an ASP.NET Web 2.0 Portal

C# 3.0 in a Nutshell, *3rd Edition*

C# Cookbook, *2nd Edition*

C# Design Patterns

C# in a Nutshell, *2nd Edition*

C# Language Pocket Reference

Exchange Server 2007 Administration: The Definitive Guide

Head First C#

Learning ASP.NET 2.0 with AJAX

Learning C# 2005, *2nd Edition*

Learning WCF

MCSE Core Elective Exams in a Nutshell

.NET and XML

.NET Gotchas

Programming Atlas

Programming ASP.NET, *3rd Edition*

Programming ASP.NET AJAX

Programming C#, *4th Edition*

Programming MapPoint in .NET

Programming .NET 3.5

Programming .NET Components, *2nd Edition*

Programming .NET Security

Programming .NET Web Services

Programming Visual Basic 2005

Programming WCF Services

Programming WPF, *2nd Edition*

Programming Windows Presentation Foundation

Programming the .NET Compact Framework

Visual Basic 2005: A Developer's Notebook

Visual Basic 2005 Cookbook

Visual Basic 2005 in a Nutshell, *3rd Edition*

Visual Basic 2005 Jumpstart

Visual C# 2005: A Developer's Notebook

Visual Studio Hacks

Windows Developer Power Tools

XAML in a Nutshell

Our books are available at most retail and online bookstores.

To order direct: 1-800-998-9938 • *order@oreilly.com* • *www.oreilly.com*

Online editions of most O'Reilly titles are available by subscription at *safari.oreilly.com*

The O'Reilly Advantage

Stay Current and Save Money

Order books online:
www.oreilly.com/order_new

Questions about our
products or your order:
order@oreilly.com

Join our email lists: Sign up
to get topic specific email
announcements or new
books, conferences, special
offers and technology news
elists@oreilly.com

For book content
technical questions:
booktech@oreilly.com

To submit new book
proposals to our editors:
proposals@oreilly.com

Contact us:
O'Reilly Media, Inc.
1005 Gravenstein Highway N.
Sebastopol, CA U.S.A. 95472
707-827-7000 or
800-998-9938
www.oreilly.com

Did you know that if you register
your O'Reilly books, you'll get
automatic notification and upgrade
discounts on new editions?

**And that's not all! Once you've registered
your books you can:**

» Win free books, T-shirts and O'Reilly Gear

» Get special offers available only to registered
O'Reilly customers

» Get free catalogs announcing all our new
titles (US and UK Only)

**Registering is easy! Just go to
www.oreilly.com/go/register**